Hesketh Pearson's highly praised biography, first published in 1942 and here reissued in paperback, has been accepted as the standard work on Bernard Shaw. It was written with the close co-operation of Shaw, who not only supplied what he called 'unique private history' but also checked and corrected all the facts, contributed many passages and authenticated or rejected anecdotes provided by others. His own words are used frequently both to explain his thoughts and to show the lucid way in which he expressed them, and the recorded conversations with Pearson bring alive Shaw's gaiety, magnetism and greatness.

From Shaw's harsh musical criticism and fascinating writings to Ellen Terry, to his revolutionary contribution to English theatre and long preoccupation with death, Hesketh Pearson leaves no aspect of his subject unexplored. In telling the story of Shaw's remarkable career, he provides a brilliant portrait both of the man himself and of the intellectual life of 1880 to 1940, peopled by a multitude of celebrities.

Born in Worcestershire in 1887, Hesketh Pearson took up acting and achieved some measure of fame before leaving the stage in 1931 to write. He was the author of many full-length biographies, all of them much acclaimed and widely appreciated for their wit, accuracy and unorthodox approach; they include *Conan Doyle, Gilbert and Sullivan* and *The Life of Oscar Wilde*. He died in London in 1964.

·BERNARD·
SHAW

A Biography by

Hesketh Pearson

Introduction by Richard Ingrams

UNWIN PAPERBACKS
London   Sydney

First published in Great Britain by Collins Publishers Ltd 1942
Reissued by Macdonald and Jane's, Macdonald and Company (Publishers)
Ltd 1975
First published in paperback by Unwin ® Paperbacks, an imprint of
Unwin Hyman Limited, in 1987

UNWIN HYMAN LIMITED
Denmark House, 37–39 Queen Elizabeth Street,
London SE1 2QB
and
40 Museum Street, London WC1A 1LU

Allen & Unwin Australia Pty Ltd
8 Napier Street, North Sydney, NSW 2060, Australia

Unwin Paperbacks with Port Nicholson Press
60 Cambridge Terrace, Wellington, New Zealand

British Library Cataloguing in Publication Data

Pearson, Hesketh
    Bernard Shaw : a biography.
1. Shaw, Bernard——Biography 2. Dramatists
English——20th century——Biography
I. Title
822'.912   PR5366
ISBN 0–04–928072–4

Printed in Great Britain by Guernsey Press, Guernsey, Channel Islands.

To
GLADYS
(who helped)

CONTENTS

LIST OF ILLUSTRATIONS

INTRODUCTION

'The qualities I admire above all in others,' Hesketh Pearson wrote, 'are good nature, good sense and good nonsense.' Bernard Shaw had them all in abundance. In many respects he was unattractive; his dislike of the poor, his denigration of Shakespeare, his distaste for normal things like children, drink, sex and earth burial – all these were regrettable, as was his sometimes grovelling admiration for strong men and dictators. But even his most odious opinions were rendered excusable by his never-failing cheerfulness, his good humour and his wit.

Pearson was the ideal biographer for him. He was not an antiquarian who burrowed into the past in order to get away from the present. Nor was he one of those who wish to promote themselves at the expense of their subjects. He never obtrudes his own views without good reason and is not at pains to impress the reader with the extent of his researches even when these are considerable. He wrote so unassumingly that some critics thought him superficial. Edmund Wilson and George Orwell, for example, used the expressions 'journalism' and 'hack' in relation to his *Oscar Wilde*. Such views are quite wide of the mark, and it is interesting to find a fellow story-teller, Graham Greene, a man with a greater appreciation of the skills required, giving a different verdict. Reviewing *Conan Doyle*, Greene praised the 'admirable forthrightness' of Pearson who had, he said, 'some of the qualities of Dr. Johnson – a plainness, an honesty, a sense of ordinary life going on all the time.'

He also had what his friend Hugh Kingsmill commended in Boswell – 'the rare quality of a disinterested delight in the spectacle of human nature'.

In writing of 'great men' there is a tendency either to debunk or to idolise. Pearson did neither. Though capable in his youth of schoolboyish hero-worship, he was never by temperament envious or subservient. He knew his own mind and brimmed with self-respect. He wrote: 'My attitude of indifference to the opinions of others is partly due to a lack of vanity. A man is vain when he accepts the world's estimation of himself, conceited when content with his own. I have more conceit than vanity, as I am quite satisfied with my own opinion on any subject and think little of the world's.'

His attitude, which made a strong appeal to Bernard Shaw, was also due to the fact that, like Shaw, he was virtually a self-educated man. Born in 1887 at Hawford near Worcester he was the son of rich, respectable, conservative, church-going parents. His two grandfathers, his godfather and three of his uncles were in holy orders. When Pearson failed to distinguish himself at Bedford School in any way, he was earmarked by his father for the church. This move was implacably resisted and it was decided that the next best thing was a life of commerce; and so a job was acquired for him in a shipping office. In the meantime he developed a consuming love of Shakespeare who now took the place of God in his affections. He learned whole plays by heart and went without meals in order to be able to afford tickets for Beerbohm Tree's productions at His Majesty's Theatre. At the age of twenty-one he inherited £1000 which he spent on travel in North and South America. Returning to England he joined his brother who was running a car business in Brighton and, when this went into a decline, he applied in 1911 for work as an actor in Beerbohm Tree's company. It was typical of Pearson that he should go direct to Tree, the greatest actor-manager of the day, and typical of Tree that he should warm to Pearson and take him on.

During the years before the Great War, Pearson came under the spell of Frank Harris, the swashbuckling ruffian with a dash of genius who stormed through the Nineties and the Edwardian period leaving a trail of havoc and deflowered virgins in his wake. Pearson wrote: 'One thing about him greatly attracted youngsters fresh from school or varsity; his declaration that life was more important than literature, copulation than scholarship.' It was as a disciple, and almost agent, of Harris that Pearson first came to meet Shaw, and an account of that meeting is given in this book.

Pearson's early heroes, as he went through the process of rebelling against his bourgeois inheritance, were Frank Harris and Oscar Wilde whose *Soul of Man under Socialism* made a deep impression. He did not read Shaw until he joined the army in 1914 when like many other young soldiers he was bowled over by *Common Sense about the War* (see p. 341) which appeared as a shining light amid the fog of chauvinistic humbug being generated at that time by other writers who should have known better. Pearson then read all of Shaw's plays and installed their author in his private pantheon alongside Wilde and Harris.

He included enthusiastic profiles of Shaw and Harris in his

first book *Modern Men and Mummers* (1921) and it was as a result of this that he first met the critic and biographer Hugh Kingsmill who had also in his younger days been a follower of Frank Harris. Their meeting led to a lifelong friendship and an interchange of letters, ideas and jokes which were crucial to Pearson's development. Kingsmill's philosophy was, briefly, that there exists a conflict in man between the will and the imagination, the personal and the collective. The will is expressed in the world of action, power and politics; the imagination in poetry, art, religion and mysticism. Many artists abandon work of imagination for prophecy and propaganda, because it offers an escape from their personal dissatisfaction.

It was as a direct result of Kingsmill's influence that Pearson came to see Shaw in a proper perspective. Kingsmill explained how Shaw in 'looking for the kingdom of God outside himself' became a Utopian, or what Kingsmill termed a Dawnist, that is someone in search of a New Dawn. The end of the road for the revolutionary or the Dawnist was in fact Fascism, the worship of the strong man, he being the only person sufficiently ruthless to hurry the new world into existence. The worship of Napoleon by the intellectuals of the Romantic period, like Hazlitt, was exactly parallelled by Shaw's idolisation of Stalin.

All this was clarified by Kingsmill's insight which enabled Pearson to see what was wrong with Shaw. At the same time, being a better balanced, though not more profound critic than Kingsmill, Pearson had a healthier appreciation of what was right with him, above all his humour, or what Chesterton called his 'intellectual geniality'.

It was Pearson's belief based on his own experience, that the age of forty is a turning point. 'The truth is,' he said, 'that until one finishes the painful process of mental growth and character-formation somewhere in the region of forty, nearly every year shifts the angle of one's outlook.' He himself was forty-two when he gave up the stage and wrote his first biography, a life of Erasmus Darwin. (Indirectly he was enabled to do this by Shaw. There was at the time, 1929, a craze among collectors for Shaw manuscripts and first editions of which Pearson had a good hoard. He sold it for £200, enough for him and his family to live off while he wrote his book.) In the next decade he wrote lives of Sydney Smith, William Hazlitt, Gilbert and Sullivan, Henry Labouchere, Tom Paine, and General John Nicholson. These books were on the whole favourably received by the critics but none of them sold particularly well. It was in 1938 that Pearson

7

first discussed with Kingsmill the idea of doing a life of Shaw. When Pearson suggested it to Shaw he replied on a postcard 'Don't', adding that the books by Frank Harris and Archibald Henderson had contained all the relevant material. Knowing that this was not the case, Pearson went to see Shaw on 21 October, 1938. Shaw was then eighty-two. 'If you want to be debunked with a loving hand,' Pearson said, 'I'm your man.' At length Shaw gave his blessing to the biography and thereafter provided Pearson with every assistance. He had admired Pearson's *The Smith of Smiths* and was no doubt influenced by the fact that G. K. Chesterton, whom he loved, had written an enthusiastic introduction to that book. He was additionally attracted to Pearson as a man, finding in him many of the attributes he had admired in Frank Harris. Harris had been a cowboy in his youth, and Pearson first came to sit at Shaw's feet not as a university student but as a young soldier on his way to the wars. Pearson had a wide knowledge of the world, not being remotely intellectual, and like Shaw he was an instinctive rebel, opposed to all political and literary establishments. Pearson always spoke his mind. He refused to read a word of Karl Marx, though prepared to acknowledge that he was a profound influence on Shaw. 'It is far better to know nothing like me,' he told Shaw, 'than to know everything and get it all wrong like you.' Shaw liked this approach. 'I find your company both restful and invigorating,' he told him.

Bernard Shaw is unique among Pearson's books. It was written not only with Shaw's help but actually re-worded and amended by him before it was published. Shaw persuaded Pearson that no one would know the difference between the original text and his own interpolations. In fact it is not difficult to detect Shaw's hand at work, as in the musical description of Frank Harris – ' . . . an artistically metrical voice that would have made his reputation as the statue in Don Giovanni . . . he tromboned his way through the world . . .' – phrases that are typical Shaw. One can also compare Pearson's account of Shaw rehearsing the original production of *Androcles and the Lion* given in his memoirs *Thinking It Over* (1938) and the same story as it appears in this book:

' . . . he danced about the stage, spouting bits from all the parts with folded arms, turned our serious remarks into amusing quips . . .'

Thinking It Over

' . . . he danced about the stage, spouting bits from all the parts

8

with folded arms, turned our serious remarks into amusing quips and our funniments into tragedies . . .'

Bernard Shaw

That 'and our funniments into tragedies' is an obvious Shavian embellishment. Elsewhere, as in the passages on politics, Shaw's hand is more marked. It would be wrong however to think that such interference compromised Pearson's objectivity or that the additions and alterations were made against his will. Pearson always believed in allowing his subjects to speak for themselves through direct quotation, and in this, his only book on a living person, he carried the idea further and let Shaw tell the story in his own words whenever he felt like it. As Shaw was so utterly candid, nothing was lost in the process, though one could argue that in the interests of style Pearson's simple narrative would have been better left without those Shavian 'funniments'.

'It remains to be seen', Pearson wrote in his obituary of Shaw, 'whether the reputation of the man who survived five reigns will survive fifty.' He prefaced his book with Max Beerbohm's verdict on Shaw: 'As a personality he is immortal', the implication being that whatever happened to Shaw's plays and propaganda, people would continue to be interested in Shaw. This possibility must have occurred to Shaw himself when Pearson's book became a best-seller. At any rate, after its success, his attitude towards it changed. Pearson wrote: 'Having cautioned me before publication that if a word were said to connect him to the book he would take the most desperate steps to disclaim it, he now spoke openly of the help he had given me; and on seeing my copy of it during a visit, he opened it to write on the flyleaf underneath my signature: "Also his humble collaborator – G. Bernard Shaw".'

Richard Ingrams
February 1975

NOTE

Up to the end of the section entitled 'Grand Old Boy' I was greatly helped in the writing of this book by Bernard Shaw, who not only gave me a deal of what he called 'unique private history', but corrected and checked all the facts, supplied many passages either by word of mouth or in typescript, authenticated or rejected the anecdotes that had been told of him by other people, and enabled me, while maintaining my impartiality as a biographer, to make the story of his life and the development of his personality as much like an autobiography as a work written in the third person can be. A few episodes which for one reason or another were omitted from the original edition have now been added.

The remaining sections, from 'Shaw Criticizes his Biographer' to 'The Modern Methuselah', were published as a Postscript, and continue the chronicle up to the end of his life. The passages between us during this last decade, some spoken, some written, were set down as they appear here at the time of their occurrence, and are therefore as authentic as the rest of the biography.

THE RESPONSIBLE PARTIES

'I AM SUPPOSED to be descended from Macduff,' said Shaw to me, 'and although I am not subject to feudal feelings it pleases me that an ancestor of mine is a character in one of Shakespeare's plays.'

It occurred to me that he might not have been equally pleased if his ancestor had been, say, the Drunken Porter in the same play, but I said nothing; and here we are only concerned with his less remote forebears.

Seldom do human beings inherit their main characteristics directly from their parents, and Shaw is probably the only famous man in history whose outstanding mental traits were clearly apparent in his father and mother. From the first he derived his humour, from the second his imagination.

His father, George Carr Shaw, came of a family that had first set foot in Ireland towards the close of the seventeenth century. It was a respectable family, which produced bankers, clergymen, stockbrokers, civil servants and even baronets, all of whom had a strong pedigree-sense and talked of 'the Shaws' as a race apart. George Carr was unlucky; he was brought up along with thirteen brothers and sisters by a widowed mother whose poverty kept the household on short rations. But the knowledge that they were 'Shaws' enabled them to face the future with equanimity and in due time their gentility was rewarded, George Carr obtaining a sinecure in the Four Courts (the Dublin Courts of Justice). The office was abolished in 1850, but as no member of his family could be allowed to suffer merely because there was no longer an excuse to pay him a salary he was given a pension of £60 a year. This he sold, bought a wholesale corn business—the Shaws being too respectable for retail trade—and confidently hoped that he would spend the rest of his life in comfort on the profits. He knew nothing whatever about flour, his partner was equally

11

ignorant, and as they acted on the assumption that the business would make money while they looked on, it did not prosper.

George Carr was born with a kind heart, a sense of humour and a total lack of professional aptitude or commercial ability. His humour took the form of a sense of comedic anti-climax so keen that disasters that would have reduced another man to tears reduced him to helpless laughter. Not long after he had invested in the corn business one of its chief customers went bankrupt owing it a lot of money. The blow prostrated his partner, but although George Carr was well-nigh ruined his son declares that 'he found the magnitude of the catastrophe so irresistibly amusing that he had to retreat hastily from the office to an empty corner of the warehouse and laugh until he was exhausted'. This sense of anti-climax, plenteously bequeathed to his son, was so much a part of his nature that though a Protestant he could not suppress it when discussing the Bible. 'The more sacred an idea or a situation was by convention,' wrote his son, 'the more irresistible was it to him as the jumping-off place for a plunge into laughter. Thus, when I scoffed at the Bible he would instantly and quite sincerely rebuke me, telling me, with what little sternness was in his nature, that I should not speak so ; that no educated man would make such a display of ignorance ; that the Bible was universally recognized as a literary and historical masterpiece ; and as much more to the same effect as he could muster. But when he had reached the point of feeling really impressive, a convulsion of internal chuckling would wrinkle up his eyes ; and (I knowng all the time quite well what was coming) he would cap his eulogy by assuring me, with an air of perfect fairness, that even the worst enemy of religion could say no worse of the Bible than that it was the damndest parcel of lies ever written. He would then rub his eyes and chuckle for quite a long time. It became an unacknowledged game between us that I should provoke him to exhibitions of this kind.'

But he did not require much provocation. When he took his small son for a first dip in the sea, he gave the lad a serious talk on the vital necessity of learning to swim. 'When I was a boy of only fourteen,' he ended impressively, 'my knowledge of swimming enabled me to save your Uncle Robert's life.' After a pause to let this sink in, he added confidentially, 'And to tell you the truth I never was so sorry for anything in my life afterwards.' He then plunged into the sea, had a good swim and chuckled all the way home.

He was in fact a thoroughly amiable fellow with an agreeable appearance in spite of a squint. Sir William Wilde had tried to correct this squint by an operation, but 'overdid the correction so much that my father squinted the other way all the rest of his life.' Having bought the flour business that was going to keep the wolf from the door, George Carr Shaw fell in love with Elizabeth Gurly and asked her to marry him. He was past forty, about twice her age.

It is doubtful whether she loved him. It is doubtful whether she ever loved any one. But George Carr provided a means of escape from an intolerable position. After her mother's death she had been reared by a little humpbacked angel-faced tyrannical aunt, who scolded, punished and bullied her in order to make her a paragon of good-breeding, to marry her to someone of distinction, and to keep her in complete ignorance of everything that could be left to the doctor, the solicitor and the servants. In return for this Spartan training Elizabeth Gurly was to inherit the fortune of the sweet-visaged old witch. George Carr Shaw was not on the list of distinguished men eligible for marriage with Miss Lucinda Elizabeth (Bessie) Gurly. He was amusing, but he was middle-aged; he was a gentleman, but he had no money. His own view was that all objections against the match were invalidated by the simple fact that he was a Shaw and that in any case his flour business, coupled with the witch's fortune, could make life genteel enough. But Bessie Gurly's relatives thought they held a trump card and the moment she announced the engagement they played it. 'He's a drunkard,' they said. She promptly tackled her fiancé on the subject. He was shocked by the accusation and eloquently assured her that he was a fanatical teetotaller, though he omitted to add that his hatred of alcohol was due to the agonies of remorse he always suffered after his frequent bouts of intoxication.

They were married, and to celebrate their wedding the humpbacked aunt cut her disobedient niece out of her will. During the honeymoon the youthful Mrs Shaw had an unpleasant surprise. While staying at Liverpool she found a number of empty bottles in a cupboard. Putting two and two together she concluded that her husband had emptied them. She rushed from the house and made for the docks, where it occurred to her that she might become a stewardess on some liner and place the ocean between herself and the thirsty teetotaller. But the drunken and eloquent dock-hands frightened

13

her far more than the harmless gentleman she had left behind, so she fled back to make the best of him. By temperament she was well equipped for such a situation. She was able to withdraw into herself and exist in a world of her own imagination which was incomparably better than the world of reality that had treated her so harshly. Her mental independence, imaginative self-sufficiency, and ability to live in the domain of the spirit, were inherited by her son, George Bernard Shaw, who was born on July 26th, 1865, at 3 Upper Synge Street (afterwards changed to 33 Synge Street), Dublin.

He had two sisters older than himself. None of them received much attention from their parents, spending their earliest days almost exclusively in the company of nurses and servants, except when playing with their father on his return from his office every evening. When they grew out of this childish phase there were no displays of affection in the family; no one seemed to care for or to be dependent upon any one else; it was a perfect atmosphere for the development of anarchic self-determination, and the boy became 'a Freethinker before I knew how to think'; which accounted for the lack of ordinary emotion in the later Shaw, for his intense individualism and his longing for communism. 'Though I was not ill-treated—my parents being quite incapable of any sort of inhumanity—the fact that nobody cared for me particularly gave me a frightful self-sufficiency, or rather a power of starving in imaginary feasts, that may have delayed my development a good deal, and leaves me to this hour a treacherous brute in matters of pure affection.'

Another influence that helped to form the future socialist was not appreciated at the time: 'I had my meals in the kitchen, mostly of stewed beef, which I loathed, badly cooked potatoes, sound or diseased as the case might be, and much too much tea out of brown delft teapots left to "draw" on the hob until it was pure tannin. Sugar I stole. I was never hungry, because my father, often insufficiently fed in his childhood, had such a horror of child hunger that he insisted on unlimited bread and butter being always within our reach. When I was troublesome a servant thumped me on the head until one day, greatly daring, I rebelled, and, on finding her collapse abjectly, became thenceforth uncontrollable. I hated the servants and liked my mother because, on the one or two rare and delightful occasions when she buttered my bread for me, she buttered it thickly instead of merely wiping a knife on it. Her almost complete neglect of me had the advantage that I could idolize her to the utmost pitch of my imagination and had no sordid or disillusioning contacts with her. It was a privilege to be taken for a walk or a visit with her, or on an excursion.

'My ordinary exercise whilst I was still too young to be allowed out by myself was to be taken out by a servant, who was supposed to air me on the banks of the canal or round the fashionable squares where the atmosphere was esteemed salubrious and the surroundings gentlemanly. Actually she took me into the slums to visit her private friends, who dwelt in squalid tenements. When she met a generous male acquaintance who insisted on treating her she took me into the public house bars, where I was regaled with lemonade and ginger-beer; but I did not enjoy these treats, because my father's eloquence on the evil of drink had given me an impression that a public house was a wicked place into which I should not have been taken. Thus were laid the foundations of my life-long hatred of poverty, and the devotion of all my public life to the task of exterminating the poor and rendering their resurrection for ever impossible.'

He received his first moral lesson from his father, who expressed such a horror of alcohol that the boy made up his mind never to touch it and became a convinced teetotaller. 'One night, when I was still about as tall as his boots, he took me out for a walk. In the course of it I conceived a monstrous, incredible suspicion. When I got home I stole to my mother and in an awestruck whisper said to her, "Mamma, I think Papa's drunk." She turned away with impatient disgust and said, "When is he ever anything else?" I have never believed in anything since: then the scoffer began.' The father's habits had two considerable effects on his family: they were cut off from the social life of the numerous Shaw clan; and in self-defence they had to develop a sense of humour. 'If you asked him to dinner or to a party, he was not always quite sober when he arrived; and he was invariably scandalously drunk when he left. Now a convivial drunkard may be exhilarating in convivial company. Even a quarrelsome or boastful drunkard may be found entertaining by people who are not particular. But a miserable drunkard—and my father, in theory, a teetotaller, was racked with shame and remorse even in his cups—is unbearable. We were finally dropped socially. After my early childhood I cannot remember ever paying a visit to a relative's house. If my mother and father had dined out, or gone to a party, their children would have been much more astonished than if the house had caught fire.' Luckily the intoxication of Shaw senior did not turn him into a fiend: 'He was a *lonely* drinker at the grocer-publican's. He was never "carried out blind"; drink did not affect him that way, nor did he drink enough to take him quite off his legs. But he was quite unmistakeably drunk, stupefied, apparently sleep-walking, and if remonstrated with, apt to fly into sudden momentary rages in which he would snatch something up and dash it on the floor.' Drunk or sober he was usually amiable; but 'the drunkenness was so humiliating that it would have been unendurable if we had not taken refuge in laughter. It had to be either a family tragedy or a family joke; and it was on the whole a healthy instinct that decided us to get what ribald fun was possible out of it, which, however, was very little indeed. ... A boy who has seen "the governor", with an imperfectly wrapped-up goose under one arm and a ham in the same condition under the other (both purchased under heaven knows what delusion of festivity), butting at the garden wall of our Dalkey cottage in the belief that he was pushing open the gate, and transforming his tall hat to a concertina in the process, and who, instead of being overwhelmed with shame and anxiety at the spectacle, has been so disabled by merriment (uproariously shared by the maternal uncle) that he has hardly been able to rush to the rescue of the hat and pilot its wearer to safety, is clearly not a boy who will make tragedies of trifles instead of making trifles of tragedies. If you cannot get rid of the family skeleton, you may as well make it dance.'

The only member of the family who did not extract an ounce of fun out of all this was Mrs Shaw. She was born without 'comedic impulses'; and when we remember that she had been brought up with country lady strictness to occupy a leading position in social life with the necessary money to keep it up, and that before she was thirty she had found herself a social outcast tied to a drunkard with three children and a dwindling income, we are bound to admit that only a female Falstaff could have revelled in her position and prospects. Under the circumstances it was almost inevitable that she should have ignored her husband and neglected her children. Believing that correct behaviour was inborn, 'too humane to inflict what she had suffered on any child', not realizing that they needed guidance and not caring what they ate or

16

drank, she abandoned her offspring to the promptings of nature, regarding them as phenomena which 'occurred', like the milkman. She was incapable of unkindness, capable of solitude to any extent, long-suffering but conclusively unforgiving if an offender overstepped a certain line, profound and reserved, humane but not quite human, and in later years her son would sometimes wonder how she had ever managed to become the mother of three children.

The world into which she retreated from the responsibilities she would not shoulder was the world of music. She possessed a mezzo-soprano voice of exceptional purity of tone and she began to take singing-lessons from a strange person named George John Vandaleur Lee, who lived in the next street. Lee was 'a man of mesmeric vitality and force', whose sole interest in life was vocal music. After many years of experiment and observation he had discovered a method of teaching singing which was entirely unlike any other method then in vogue. This 'method' became his religion and he devoted his life to it. Naturally he was hated by all the orthodox teachers, who voted him a quack and a charlatan, and as his method was entirely successful they had every reason for running him down. He was a tireless organizer of concerts and operas, and as a conductor he could hypnotize amateur orchestras into giving passable performances of overtures, 'selections' and scores of operas and oratorio. He imparted his 'method' to Mrs Shaw, who was soon converted to the new faith ; and he trained her voice so well that she became his leading singer. She also became his 'general musical factotum' and when his brother died he shared a house with the Shaws at No. 1 Hatch Street. 'The arrangement was economical ; for we could not afford to live in a fashionable house, and Lee could not afford to give lessons in an unfashionable one, though, being a bachelor, he needed only a music room and a bedroom.' Lee also bought a cottage in Dalkey and presented it to Mrs Shaw. It was situated 'high up on Torca Hill, with all Dublin Bay from Dalkey Island to Howth visible from the garden, and all Killiney Bay with the Wicklow mountains in the background from the hall door.'

Thus Lee's advent in the household of his chief pupil had a great influence on the life of the youthful Shaw. Nature and music were to play the chief parts in his education. In health and hygiene, too, Lee's views left their mark on the mind of the boy: 'He said that people should sleep with their windows open. The daring of this appealed to me; and I have done so ever since. He ate brown bread instead of white: a startling eccentricity. He had no faith in doctors, and when my mother had a serious illness took her case in hand unhesitatingly and at the end of a week or so gave my trembling father leave to call in a leading Dublin doctor, who simply said, "My work is done," and took his hat.' On the other hand the youngsters did not care for him personally: 'When my mother introduced him to me, he played with me for the first and last time; but as his notion of play was to decorate my face with moustaches and whiskers in burnt cork in spite of the most furious resistance I could put up, our encounter was not a success; and the defensive attitude in which it left me lasted, though without the least bitterness, until the decay of his energies and the growth of mine put us on more than equal terms.'

'A DEVIL OF A CHILDHOOD!'

BABY SHAW was christened by a clerical uncle; his godfather was too drunk to turn up at the ceremony, so the sexton was ordered to renounce the devil and all his works on the child's behalf. Going bail for the future G.B.S. might be regarded as about the riskiest undertaking in the history of the Established Church, but one baby looks very much like another and the sexton never wavered. The infant's godmother shouldered her responsibility in the same spirit. After giving him a Bible with a gilt clasp and edges, larger than those given to his sisters because his sex entitled him to a heavier book just as it necessitated heavier boots, she practically dropped his acquaintance, only saw him about four times in the next twenty years, and never once alluded to the affair at the font.

He first became conscious of events in the outside world when in 1861 he noticed the black borders of the newspaper columns announcing the death of the Prince Consort. Later he was impressed by the headlines dealing with the American Civil War, the Yelverton divorce case and the court-martial

18

on Captain Robertson. He had the usual childish conception of the universe: 'I thought of the earth as being an immense ground floor with a star studded ceiling which was the floor of heaven, and a basement which was hell.' But scepticism was quickly stirred in him. Having been told that a particularly nasty medicine was delicious, he never thereafter allowed himself to be persuaded that he was enjoying himself when the evidence of his senses proved the contrary. And he objected to nursery language: 'Certain persons used to adapt themselves to my childishness by patting me on the head and talking in what they thought a childish way to me; and I remember how I resented the personal liberty and despised the unbecoming and offensive imposture. They all made the same mistake. Instead of being natural, in which condition they would have been quite childish enough to put me at my ease, they affected imbecility—a very different thing to childishness, and open to instant detection by any sane infant.'

Young Shaw's religious training was either uncomfortable or sketchy. In the pre-Lee days his father read family prayers; and for a few years the three children attended a Sunday school in order to learn texts, and went to church in order to fidget. At a later date he thought of that church as the house of Satan: 'In my small boyhood I was a victim of the inhuman and absurd custom of compelling young children to sit out morning service every Sunday. To sit motionless and speechless in your best suit in a dark stuffy church on a morning that is fine outside the building, with your young limbs aching with unnatural quiet, your restless imagination tired of speculating about the same grown-up people in the same pews every Sunday, your conscience heavy with the illusion that you are the only reprobate present sufficiently wicked to long for the benediction, and to wish that they would sing something out of an opera instead of Jackson in F, not to mention hating the clergyman as a sanctimonious bore, and dreading the sexton as a man likely to turn bad boys out and possibly to know them at sight by official inspiration: all this is enough to lead any sensitive youth to resolve that when he grows up and can do as he likes, the first use he will make of his liberty will be to stay away from church.'

This weekly penance preyed upon his mind and one night he dreamt that he was dead and about to meet his Maker: 'The picture of Heaven which the efforts of the then Established Church of Ireland had conveyed to my childish imagina-

19

tion, was a waiting-room with walls of pale sky-coloured tabbinet, and a pew-like bench running all round, except at one corner, where there was a door. I was, somehow, aware that God was in the next room, accessible through the door. I was seated on the bench with my ankles tightly interlaced to prevent my legs dangling, behaving myself with all my might before the grown-up people, who all belonged to the Sunday congregation, and were either sitting on the bench as if at church or else moving solemnly in and out as if there were a dead person in the house. A grimly-handsome lady, who usually sat in a corner seat near me in church, and whom I believed to be thoroughly conversant with the arrangements of the Almighty, was to introduce me presently into the next room—a moment which I was supposed to await with joy and enthusiasm. Really, of course, my heart sank like lead within me at the thought ; for I felt that my feeble affection of piety could not impose on Omniescence, and that one glance of that all-searching eye would discover that I had been allowed to come to Heaven by mistake. Unfortunately for the interest of this narrative, I awoke, or wandered off into another dream, before the critical moment arrived.'

The boredom he had endured in church was never forgotten and twenty years after he had been forced to sit through a service he made a suggestion for relieving the tedium of religious observances: 'If some enterprising clergyman with a cure of souls in the slums were to hoist a board over his church door with the inscription, "Here men and women after working hours may dance without getting drunk on Fridays ; hear good music on Saturdays ; pray on Sundays ; discuss public affairs without molestation from the police on Mondays ; have the building for any honest purpose they please —theatricals, if desired—on Tuesdays ; bring the children for games, amusing drill, and romps on Wednesdays ; and volunteer for a thorough scrubbing down of the place on Thursdays" —well, it would be all very shocking, no doubt ; but after all, it would not interfere with the Bishop of London's salary.' He did not extend this licence to cathedrals, which he valued as places where, for most of the time, persons of all religions or of no religion could 'make their souls' in silence, undisturbed by any sectarian performance.

Both in church and at Sunday school he was taught to believe that God was a Protestant and a gentleman and that all Roman Catholics went to hell when they died, neither of

20

which beliefs placed the Almighty in a very favourable light. At home his religious instruction was left to the nurse, 'who used to tell me that if I were not good, by which she meant that if I did not behave with a single eye to her personal convenience, the cock would come down the chimney. . . . This event seemed to me so apocalyptic that I never dared to provoke it nor even to ask myself in what way I should be the worse for it.' Certain doctrines aroused his immediate antagonism. For example he was told that the dog and the parrot were not creatures like himself but were brutal while he was reasonable. Being on intimate terms with both of them he rejected the distinction. His father was not seriously concerned over such matters and allowed him to be present at religious discussions when incidents in the New Testament were subjected to what might be called the Lower Criticism. On one occasion the raising of Lazarus was described by the boy's maternal uncle as a clever ruse on the part of Jesus, who had arranged with Lazarus to sham death and then come to life at the right moment. This view of the incident appealed to the youngster's sense of humour. Religion could be treated lightly by the elder Shaw, but not respectability, for when he found his son playing in the street with a schoolfellow whose father sold nails in a shop, he gravely warned him that it was undignified and indeed dishonourable 'to associate with persons engaged in retail trade'.

In view of the father's comparative indifference to religion, of the mother's steadfast determination to spare her children the pious horrors of her own upbringing, and of the boredom inflicted on a sensitive youth by the services in a Protestant church, it is remarkable that the boy Shaw should have voluntarily embraced the religious formality of private prayer. But it was the only outlet for his budding literary genius: 'I cannot recall the words of the final form I adopted; but I remember that it was in three movements, like a sonata, and in the best Church of Ireland style. It ended with the Lord's Prayer; and I repeated it every night in bed. I had been warned by my nurse that warm prayers were no use, and that only by kneeling by my bedside in the cold could I hope for a hearing; but I criticized this admonition unfavourably on various grounds, the real one being my preference for warmth and comfort. I did not disparage my nurse's authority in these matters because she was a Roman Catholic: I even tolerated her practice of sprinkling me with holy water occasionally. But her asceti-

21

cism did not fit the essentially artistic and luxurious character of my devotional exploits. Besides, the penalty did not apply to my prayer; for it was not a petition. I had too much sense to risk my faith by begging for things I knew very well I should not get; so I did not care whether my prayers were answered or not: they were a literary performance for the entertainment and propitiation of the Almighty; and though I should not have dreamt of daring to say that if He did not like them He might lump them (perhaps I was too confident of their quality to apprehend such a rebuff), I certainly behaved as if my comfort were an indispensable condition of the performance taking place at all. The Lord's Prayer I used once or twice as a protective spell. Thunderstorms are much less common in Ireland than in England; and the first two I remember frightened me horribly. During the second I bethought me of the Lord's Prayer, and steadied myself by repeating it.'

His secular education was equally senseless and quite as useless. It began with a governess. 'She puzzled me with her attempts to teach me to read; for I can remember no time at which a page of print was not intelligible to me, and can only suppose that I was born literate. She tried to give me and my two sisters a taste for poetry by reciting "Stop; for thy tread is on an empire's dust" at us, and only succeeded, poor lady, in awakening our sense of derisive humor. She punished me by little strokes with her fingers that would not have discomposed a fly, and even persuaded me that I ought to cry and feel disgraced on such occasions. She gave us judgment books and taught us to feel jubilant when after her departure we could rush to the kitchen crying "No marks to-day" and to hang back ashamed when this claim could not be substantiated. She taught me to add, subtract, and multiply, but could not teach me division, because she kept saying two into four, three into six, and so forth without ever explaining what the word "into" meant in this connection. This was explained to me on my first day at school; and I solemnly declare that it was the only thing I ever learnt at school.' After the governess he was taught for a while by his clerical uncle and 'to such purpose that when his lessons were ended by my being sent to school, I knew more Latin grammar than any other boy in the First Latin Junior, to which I was relegated. After a few years in that establishment I had forgotten most of it.'

'That establishment' was the Wesleyan Connexional School (now Wesley College) in Dublin, which he entered at the age of ten and where he remained for a while, a complete failure as a schoolboy. 'Our places in class were alphabetical and therefore immovable,' he told me. 'The master of the First Latin Junior practised what we called "going up" in my first days at school, with the result that, thanks to my clerical uncle, I shot at once to the top; but this was my only experience of it. The advantage of the alphabetical arrangement was that if I could snatch a look at the book before the class began I could guess the part of the lesson at which the questions would arrive at the letter S and prepare accordingly at the cost of reading a dozen lines. I never did any "prep" at home for the Wesleyan, being an incorrigibly lazy shirk at that age, and a shameless liar in making "excuses".' Most of the boys belonged to the Church of Ireland, but as the Wesleyan teaching was not Roman Catholic (the only distinction that counts in Ireland) no parent worried about the different doctrinal tint. Shaw's utterly undistinguished record in his classes, except for first places in 'Composition' (childish essay-writing apparently), was explained by him at a later date: 'I cannot learn anything that does not interest me. My memory is not indiscriminate: it rejects and selects; and its selections are not academic. I have no competitive instinct; nor do I crave for prizes and distinctions: consequently I have no interest in competitive examinations: if I won, the disappointment of my competitors would distress me instead of gratifying me: if I lost, my self-esteem would suffer. Besides, I have far too great a sense of my own importance to feel that it could be influenced by a degree or a gold medal or what not. There is only one sort of school that could have qualified me for academic success; and that is the sort in which the teachers take care that the pupils shall be either memorising their lessons continuously, with all the desperate strenuousness that terror can inspire, or else crying with severe physical pain. I was never in a school where the teachers cared enough about me, or about their ostensible profession, or had time enough to take any such trouble; so I learnt nothing at school, not even what I could and would have learned if any attempt had been made to interest me. I congratulate myself on this; for I am firmly persuaded that every unnatural activity of the brain is as mischievous as any unnatural activity of the body, and that pressing people to learn things they do not want to know is as unwholesome and disastrous as feeding them on sawdust.' He further asserted that even 'experience fails to teach where there is no desire to learn'.

In after years he declared: 'I am very sorry; but I cannot learn languages. I have tried hard, only to find that men of ordinary capacity can learn Sanscrit in less time than it takes me to buy a German dictionary.' Yet he was willing to admit that he would probably have picked up as much Latin as French 'if Latin had not been made the excuse for my school imprisonment and degradation', the memory of which provoked an explosion from him when he was asked to allow a scene from *Saint Joan* to be published in a schoolbook: 'NO. I lay my eternal curse on whomsoever shall now or at any time hereafter make schoolbooks of my works and make me hated as Shakespear is hated. My plays were not designed as instruments of torture. All the schools that lust after them get this answer, and will never get any other from G. Bernard Shaw.'

Mathematics also failed to allure him and remained for him a mere concept: 'I never used a logarithm in my life, and could not undertake to extract the square root of four without misgiving.' 'When I have to make an arithmetical calculation, I have to do it step by step with pencil and paper, slowly, reluctantly, and with so little confidence in the result that I dare not act on it without "proving" the sum by a further calculation involving more ciphering.' 'You propound a complicated arithmetical problem: say the cubing of a number containing four digits. Give me a slate and half an hour's time, and I can produce a wrong answer.' 'My own incapacity for numerical calculation is so marked that I reached my fourteenth year before I solved the problem of how many herrings one could buy for elevenpence in a market where a herring and a half fetched three halfpence.'

Even if he had wished to learn Latin and mathematics, a school was the last place in which to acquire knowledge because it was worse than a prison: 'In a prison, for instance, you are not forced to read books written by the warders and the governor (who of course would not be warders and governors if they could write readable books), and beaten or otherwise tormented if you cannot remember their utterly unmemorable contents. In the prison you are not forced to sit listening to turnkeys discoursing without charm or interest on subjects that they don't understand and don't care about, and are therefore incapable of making you understand or care about. In a prison they may torture your body; but they do not torture your brains; and they protect you against violence and outrage from your fellow-prisoners. In a school you have none of these advantages.'

The futility of treating boys as criminals and expecting them to behave as Christians was shown when they were left to themselves: 'I remember once, at school, the resident head master was brought down to earth by the sudden illness of his wife. In the confusion that ensued it became necessary to leave one of the schoolrooms without a master. I was in the class that occupied that schoolroom. To have sent us home would have been to break the fundamental bargain with our parents by which the school was bound to keep us out of their way for half the day at all hazards. Therefore an appeal had to be made to our better feelings: that is, to common humanity, not to make a noise. But the head master had never admitted any common humanity with us. We had been carefully broken in to regard him as a being quite aloof from and above us: one not subject to error or suffering or death or illness or mortality. Consequently sympathy was impossible; and if the unfortunate lady did not perish, it was because, as I now comfort myself with guessing, she was too much preoccupied with her own pains, and possibly making too much noise herself, to be conscious of the pandemonium downstairs.' Such scenes made him sceptical as to the value of school discipline, and when in after years he was asked to do something for the school in the village where he lived he hardly knew what to reply: 'As the school kept the children quiet during my working hours, I did not for the sake of my own personal convenience want to blow it up with dynamite as I should like to blow up most schools. So I asked for guidance. "You ought to give a prize," said the lady. I asked if there was a prize for good conduct. As I expected, there was: one for the best-behaved boy and another for the best-behaved girl. On reflection I offered a handsome prize for the worst-behaved boy and girl on condition that a record should be kept of their subsequent careers and compared with the records of the best-behaved, in order to ascertain whether the school criterion of good conduct was valid out of school. My offer was refused because it would not have had the effect of encouraging the children to give as little trouble as possible, which is of course the real object of all conduct prizes in schools.'

He came to the conclusion that schools existed for the sake of the parents, who did not wish to be plagued with their children's society yet were anxious to keep them out of mischief ; for the sake of the masters, who had to earn their livings ; and for the sake of the institutions themselves, because they made money out of the pupils.

Shaw went to two or three more schools after the Wesleyan Connexional, but saw no reason to change his opinion that 'those who have been taught most know least', largely on account of the general assumption 'that any way of doing things that is unnatural, laborious and painful is virtuous, and particularly good for children'. He had however received considerable instruction in 'lying, dishonourable submission to tyranny, dirty stories, a blasphemous habit of treating love and maternity as obscene jokes, hopelessness, evasion, derision, cowardice, and all the blackguard's shifts by which the coward intimidates other cowards'. And he summed up his days of pupilage in a pregnant phrase: 'Oh, a devil of a childhood!'

Late in life he made one recantation. The Governess's Benevolent Institution sent him the usual appeal for a subscription. He suddenly realized the folly of his boast that he had been born literate. He was still quite positive that he had learned absolutely nothing at school, that school had only interrupted his real education and imprisoned him. But who, then, had taught him all that a child was capable of learning before he went to school? Clearly his governess, Miss Caroline Hill, whom he had stupidly ridiculed. Stung with remorse and shame he straightway gave his bankers an order to pay an annual subscription—not too generous considering the magnitude of his crime—to the G.B.I.

COMPENSATIONS

BUT THERE were compensations for the misery of school. There were, for example, his relations, who provided him with enough 'comic relief' to serialize in the class-room behind the

26

master's back and gain him the reputation of a first-class liar. From these relations we may select two uncles and read his descriptions of them.

Uncle Walter, his mother's brother, was a surgeon on board an Atlantic liner, and often stayed with the Shaws in the periods between his sea-trips. He 'had an extraordinary command of picturesque language, partly derived by memory from the Bible and Prayer Book, and partly natural. The conversation of the navigating staffs and pursers of our ocean services was at that time (whatever it may be to-day) extremely Rabelaisian and profane. Falstaff himself could not have held his own with my uncle in obscene anecdotes, unprintable limericks and fantastic profanity; and it mattered nothing to him whether his audience consisted of his messmates on board ship or his schoolboy nephew: he performed before each with equal gusto. To do him justice, he was always an artist in his obscenity and blasphemy, and therefore never sank to the level of illiterate blackguardism. His efforts were controlled, deliberate, fastidiously chosen and worded. But they were all the more effective in destroying all my incalculated childish reverence for the verbiage of religion, for its legends and personifications and parables. In view of my subsequent work in the world it seems providential that I was driven to the essentials of religion by the reduction of every factitious or fictitious element in it to the most irreverent absurdity.'

Uncle William, his father's brother, was not intentionally funny, but the bald facts of his life were sufficiently curious to make his nephew admit: 'Though I can always make my extravaganzas appear credible, I cannot make the truth appear so.' Uncle William was a dignified and amiable person: 'In early manhood he was not only an inveterate smoker, but so insistent a toper that a man who made a bet that he would produce Barney Shaw sober, and knocked him up at six in the morning with that object, lost his bet. But this might have happened to any common drunkard. What gave the peculiar Shaw finish and humor to the case was that my uncle suddenly and instantly gave up smoking and drinking at one blow, and devoted himself to his accomplishment of playing the ophicleide. In this harmless and gentle pursuit he continued, a blameless old bachelor, for many years, and then, to the amazement of Dublin, renounced the ophicleide and all its works, and married a lady of distinguished social position and great piety. She declined, naturally, to have anything to do with us ; and, as far as I know, treated the rest of the family in the same way. Anyhow, I never saw her, and only saw my uncle furtively by the roadside after his marriage, when he would make hopeless attempts to save me, in the pious sense of the word, not perhaps without some secret Shavian enjoyment of the irreverent pleasantries with which I scattered my path to perdition. He was reputed to sit with a Bible on his knees, and an opera glass to his eyes, watching the ladies' bathing place in Dalkey ; and my sister, who was a swimmer, confirmed this gossip as far as the opera glass was concerned.

'But this was only the prelude to a very singular conclusion, or rather catastrophe. The fantastic imagery of the Bible so gained on my uncle that he took off his boots, explaining that he expected to be taken up to heaven at any moment like Elijah, and that he felt that his boots would impede his celestial flight. He then went a step further, and hung his room with all the white fabrics he could lay hands on, alleging that he was the Holy Ghost. At last he became silent, and remained so to the end. His wife, warned that his harmless fancies might change into dangerous ones, had him removed to a private asylum in the north of Dublin. My father thought that a musical appeal might prevail with him, and went in search of the ophicleide. But it was nowhere to be found. He took a flute to the asylum instead ; for every Shaw of that generation seemed able to play any wind instrument at sight. My uncle, still obstinately mute, contemplated the flute for a while, and then played "Home, Sweet Home" on it. My father had to be content with this small success, as nothing more could be got out of his brother. A day or two later my uncle, impatient for heaven, resolved to expedite his arrival there. Every possible weapon had been carefully removed from his reach ; but his custodians reckoned without the Shavian originality. They had left him somehow within reach of a carpet bag. He put his head into it, and in a strenuous effort to decapitate or strangle himself by closing it on his neck, perished of heart failure. I should be glad to believe that, like Elijah, he got the heavenly reward he sought ; for he was a fine upstanding man and a gentle creature, nobody's enemy but his own, as the saying is.'

Comedy in one form or another seemed to be inseparable from the Shaw clan, the most famous member of which has explained how he came to write a unique interpretation of

28

the funeral march in Beethoven's 'Eroica' Symphony: 'I was born with an unreasonably large stock of relations, who have increased and multiplied ever since. My aunts and uncles were legion, and my cousins as the sands of the sea without number. Consequently, even a low death-rate meant, in the course of mere natural decay, a tolerably steady supply of funerals for a by no means affectionate but exceedingly clannish family to go to. Add to this that the town we lived in, being divided in religious opinion, buried its dead in two great cemeteries, each of which was held by the opposite faction to be the ante-chamber of perdition, and by its own patrons to be the gate of paradise. These two cemeteries lay a mile or two outside the town ; and this circumstance, insignificant as it appears, had a marked effect on the funerals, because a considerable portion of the journey to the tomb was made along country roads. Now the sorest bereavement does not cause men to forget wholly that time is money. Hence, though we used to proceed slowly and sadly enough through the streets or terraces at the early stages of our progress, when we got into the open a change came over the spirit in which the coachmen drove. Encouraging words were addressed to the horses ; whips were flicked ; a jerk all along the line warned us to slip our arms through the broad elbow-straps of the mourning-coaches, which were balanced on longitudinal poles by enormous and totally inelastic springs ; and then the funeral began in earnest. Many a clinking run have I had through that bit of country at the heels of some deceased uncle who had himself many a time enjoyed the same sport. But in the immediate neighbourhood of the cemetery the houses recommenced ; and at that point our grief returned upon us with overwhelming force: we were able barely to crawl along to the great iron gates where a demoniacal black pony was waiting with a sort of primitive gun-carriage and a pall to convey our burden up the avenue to the mortuary chapel, looking as if he might be expected at every step to snort fire, spread a pair of gigantic bat's wings, and vanish, coffin and all, in thunder and brimstone. Such were the scenes which have disqualified me for life from feeling the march of the "Eroica" symphony as others do. It is that fatal episode where the oboe carries the march into the major key and the whole composition brightens and steps out, so to speak, that ruins me. The moment it begins, I instinctively look beside me for an elbow-strap ; and the voices of the orchestra are lost in those of three men, all

29

holding on tight as we jolt and swing madly to and fro, the youngest, a cousin, telling me a romantic tale of an encounter with the Lord Lieutenant's beautiful consort in the hunting-field (an entirely imaginary incident); the eldest, an uncle, giving my father an interminable account of an old verge watch which cost five shillings and kept perfect time for forty years subsequently; and my father speculating as to how far the deceased was cut short by his wife's temper, how far by alcohol, and how far by what might be called natural causes. When the sudden and somewhat unprepared relapse of the movement into the minor key takes place, then I imagine that we have come to the houses again. Finally I wake up completely, and realize that for the last page or two of the score I have not been listening critically to a note of the performance. I do not defend my conduct, present or past: I merely describe it so that my infirmities may be duly taken into account in weighing my critical verdicts. Boyhood takes its fun where it finds it, without looking beneath the surface; and, since society chose to dispose of its dead with a grotesque pageant out of which farcical incidents sprang naturally and inevitably at every turn, it is not to be wondered at that funerals made me laugh when I was a boy nearly as much as they disgust me now that I am older . . .'

EX PROPRIO MOTU

AT HOME Shaw's growth was unimpeded by discipline: 'We as children had to find our way in a household where there was neither hate nor love, fear nor reverence, but always personality.' Unlike most boys he disliked games. For him 'cricket, save in its humorous, brief, and only tolerable form of tip and run, was a grosser bore than anything else' except football. And he was adult enough not to gorge himself sick when he got the chance: 'I remember stealing about four dozen apples from the orchard of a relative . . . and retiring to a loft with a confederate to eat them. But when I had eaten eighteen I found, though I was still in robust health, that it was better fun to pelt the hens with the remaining apples than to continue the banquet.' But he possessed the normal boy's curiosity. On being told that a cat always fell on its legs when dropped from a height, he tried the experiment from a window on the first floor with complete success. Though humane, he was mischievous when anything in the nature of a harlequinade was feasible. One day, perceiving an inhabited but unattended perambulator outside a house, he and another youth rushed it as fast as they could to the end of the street, where they turned it at right angles so suddenly that the baby was shot into the middle of the street, when they fled in panic from the scene. They never heard what became of the baby, and they made no enquiries. There were many more outbreaks of animal spirits, for when I asked him, 'Were you often in hot water as a youngster?' he replied, 'I was *always* in hot water.'

Among his schoolmates he was chiefly notable as a romancer, for which his early love of literature was to some extent responsible. 'I have no recollection of being taught to read or write,' he once declared. 'The whole vocabulary of English literature, from Shakespear to the latest edition of the *Encyclopædia Britannica*, but excluding the articles in *Nature*, of which I often do not understand a single sentence, is so completely and instantaneously at my call that I have never had to consult a thesaurus except once or twice when for some reason I wanted a third or fourth synonym.' This extraordinary gift, which in Shakespeare has led to the quaint assumption that his plays must have been written by someone with a classical education, might have been divined by anyone who had taken the trouble to notice what Shaw as a boy of five or six was reading. He disliked all 'children's books', such as *Swiss Family Robinson*, which he thought dull and dishonest. He liked *Robinson Crusoe*. He loved *Pilgrim's Progress*, which he read aloud to his father, who told him that 'grievous' was not pronounced 'griev-i-ous.'. He was momentarily pleased with a book containing coloured plates of gorgeous and fantastic beetles, but found that the pictures quickly palled 'for the mind soon thirsted for a new idea'. He discovered *The Arabian Nights* in the country house of his mother's aunt, and was so enthralled by the stories that when he awoke each morning and saw the strips of sunshine between the window-

31

shutters he jumped out of bed, threw them open and read in bed until he was called. When he mentioned his treasure to his aunt, who thought nothing of equipping him with spurs and mounting him on a frisky pony of which he was mortally afraid, and which ran away with him finally, she 'hid it away from me lest it should break my soul as the pony might have broken my neck. This way of producing hardy bodies and timid souls is so common in country-houses that you may spend hours in them listening to stories of broken collar-bones, broken backs, and broken necks, without coming upon a single spiritual adventure or daring thought.' But the aunt reckoned without her nephew, who was intent on spiritual adventures. He found the volume, which she had hidden perfunctorily in the clothes-press, and kept it henceforth safe beneath the mattress of his bed.

At an age when most children are just mastering their alphabet, this one was deep in bound volumes of *All the Year Round*, in which he discovered *A Day's Ride* by Charles Lever, finding in the hero's 'unsuccessful encounters with the facts of life a poignant quality that romantic fiction lacked'. He grappled with Dickens's *Great Expectations* at about the same period and gained his first knowledge of the French Revolution from *A Tale of Two Cities*. 'I also struggled with *Little Dorrit* at this time. I say "struggled"; for the books oppressed my imagination most fearfully, so real were they to me. It was not until I became a cynical *blasé* person of twelve or thirteen that I read *Pickwick, Bleak House,* and the intervening works.'

He first came across Shakespeare in Cassell's monthly parts illustrated by Selous, under whose plates were printed scraps of the text. Later he read 'the longer bits left out' and gained his knowledge of English history from Shakespeare as he had learned French history from Dumas: 'I was saturated with the Bible and with Shakespear before I was ten years old. . . . Stung by the airs of a schoolfellow who alleged that he had read Locke *On The Human Understanding*, I attempted to read the Bible straight through, and actually got to the Pauline Epistles before I broke down in disgust at what seemed to me their inveterate crookedness of mind.' Incidentally his altogether unsuspected knowledge of the Bible thus acquired enabled him to make such a promising beginning at a Scripture examination in school that the master told him that he could win second place if he would work for it.

His reply was that second place would let everyone know that there was one boy who knew more than himself. He came out as an Also Ran.

The depth and diversity of his reading quickened his imagination. He began to create a world of his own which was full of fantastic and burlesque happenings. He was the hero of every incident, fighting duels, conducting battles against kings and conquering them, making love to their queens and winning them. He was all-powerful and always victorious, supreme in war, irresistible in love. There were no relations, no friends in his dreams; he stood alone, a foundling, a superman. In the world of reality he was excessively sensitive, diffident and shy, quickly reduced to tears and wretchedly timid, but extraordinarily impudent. 'The impudence was quite genuine and unconscious,' he said to me. 'I suppose I was born free from many of the venerations and inhibitions which restrain the tongues of most small boys.' The contrast between his imagined existence and his actual lot was painful, and he tried to hide his want of courage with braggadocio. Sometimes his attempts were successful, at other times he failed miserably. 'I will strike you dead at my feet!' he threatened a boy who had called his bluff. The boy remained calm, and the boaster fled in dismay. Such mortifications were dreadful and the victim remembered them nearly forty years later when he spoke through the mouth of one of his characters, John Tanner: 'A sensitive boy's humiliations may be very good fun for ordinary thick-skinned grown-ups; but to the boy himself they are so acute, so ignominious, that he cannot confess them—cannot but deny them passionately.'

Once his show of bravery cost him as dearly as the vexation of defeat: 'When I was a very small boy, my romantic imagination, stimulated by early doses of fiction, led me to brag to a still smaller boy so outrageously that he, being a simple soul, really believed me to be an invincible hero. I cannot remember whether this pleased me much; but I do remember very distinctly that one day this admirer of mine, who had a pet goat, found the animal in the hands of a larger boy than either of us, who mocked him and refused to restore the animal to his rightful owner. Whereupon, naturally, he came weeping to me, and demanded that I should rescue the goat and annihilate the aggressor. My terror was beyond description: fortunately for me, it imparted such a ghastliness to my voice and aspect as I, under the eyes of my poor little dupe,

33

advanced on the enemy with that hideous extremity of cowardice which is called the courage of despair, and said, "You let go that goat," that he abandoned his prey and fled, to my unforgettable, unspeakable relief. I have never since exaggerated my prowess in bodily combat.'

His usual method of exercising his imagination was less exhausting. He lied frequently to get himself out of scrapes and told fabulous stories. Always playing a part, in order to mask his sensitiveness, he frequently cast himself for the villain of the piece, partly because villains were much more interesting than heroes, partly because his villainy did not provoke the antagonism of his hearers as tales of his heroism did, and partly because he was greatly attracted by the sardonic vein of Mephistopheles in Gounod's *Faust,* to say nothing of his scarlet costume and his habit of coming up through traps. He used to paint frescoes in water-colour of Mephisto on the white-washed walls of his Dalkey bedroom, thus supplying another proof that nature copies art, 'for when Nature completed my countenance in 1880 or thereabouts . . . I found myself equipped with the upgrowing moustaches and eyebrows, and the sarcastic nostrils of the operatic fiend whose airs I had sung as a child, and whose attitudes I had affected in my boyhood.'

But stories of his evil exploits did not wholly satisfy his nature, which was already taking a derisive and comedic turn. He entertained his friends at school with incidents in the home life of the Shaws, gave them humorous versions of episodes in the *Iliad* and the *Odyssey,* and invented an extraordinary character named Lobjoit (a sort of 'Mrs 'Arris') whose adventures kept them in fits of laughter and probably lowered the standard of education at the Wesleyan Connexional throughout the period of his fancied being.

THE TESTAMENT OF ART

'IT IS SURELY a better education for a boy to know Beethoven's sonatas well enough to whistle them than to know the Odes of Horace well enough to recite them,' remarked Shaw. I agreed, adding quietly, 'Or the works of Karl Marx well enough to quote them.'

The musical activities of his family were the most important part of Shaw's education. His mother's partnership with Lee had a tremendous effect on his life. Operas, concerts and oratorios were constantly being rehearsed at home and before he was fifteen he knew by heart many works by the great masters, from Handel and Beethoven to Verdi and Gounod, and could whistle them from beginning to end or sing them in a language that would have been mistaken for Italian by an Irishman, for Irish by an Italian. Above all he loved Mozart, whose opera *Don Giovanni* taught him how to write seriously without being dull: 'In my small-boyhood I by good luck had an opportunity of learning the Don thoroughly, and if it were only for the sense of the value of fine workmanship which I gained from it, I should still esteem that lesson the most important part of my education. Indeed, it educated me artistically in all sorts of ways, and disqualified me only in one— that of criticizing Mozart fairly.'

It was through music that he became sceptical concerning the teachings of the Established Church and the religion of gentility inculcated by his father: 'My first childish doubt as to whether God could really be a good Protestant was suggested by my observation of the deplorable fact that the best voices available for combination with my mother's in the works of the great composers had been unaccountably vouch-

35

safed to Roman Catholics. Even the divine gentility was presently called in question, for some of these vocalists were undeniably connected with retail trade. . . . If religion is that which binds men to one another, and irreligion that which sunders, then must I testify that I found the religion of my country in its musical genius and its irreligion in its churches and drawing-rooms.'

Though Shaw's musical culture was derived entirely from the serious activities of his mother and Lee, his father's family, though comparatively illiterate musically, had a strong turn that way. Every sort of instrument was played by uncles, aunts and cousins. 'My father destroyed his domestic peace by immoderate indulgence in the trombone,' though it is reasonable to infer that his good health was due to it: 'The chief objection to playing wind-instruments is that it prolongs the life of the player beyond all reasonable limits. If you want to become phthisis-proof, drink-proof, cholera-proof, and, in short, immortal, play the trombone well and play it constantly.' Apparently Shaw senior, not content with destroying his domestic peace, carried the matter further, for when his son became a critic of music he treated his readers to a reminiscence: 'My own father, armed with a trombone, and in company with some two dozen others of ascertained gentility, used to assemble on summer evenings on a riverside promenade on the outskirts of my native town, and entertain their fellow-citizens with public-spirited minstrelsy. In fact, my father not only played his trombone part, but actually composed it as he went along, being an indifferent reader-at-sight, but an expert at what used to be known as "vamping". What my father's son might have said had he been compelled to criticize these performances in his present capacity is a point upon which I shall pursue no unfilial speculation: suffice it that such music must have been infinitely better and more hopeful than no music at all.'

The member of a household where music was all-important and nothing else of any importance, young Shaw was naturally taken to the opera at an age when most boys go to their first pantomime: 'I did not know then what an opera was, though I could whistle a good deal of opera music. I had seen in my mother's album photographs of all the great opera singers, mostly in evening dress. In the theatre I found myself before a gilded balcony filled with persons in evening dress whom I took to be the opera singers. I picked out one massive dark lady as Alboni, and wondered how soon she would stand up and sing. I was puzzled by the fact that I was made to sit with my back to the singers instead of facing them. When the curtain went up, my astonishment and delight were unbounded.'

After that he went opera-mad; not even the pirates and highwaymen in fiction were so fascinating as the leading tenors and sopranos on the stage; and he explored a new and more wonderful world of fable and adventure. Some years later, after he had bought a vocal score of *Lohengrin*, compared with which the operas of Donizetti seemed commonplace, his romantic illusion was shattered by a peep behind the scenes: 'My earliest reminiscence of an eminent operatic artist off the stage dates from a certain performance of Lucrezia Borgia, at which I, then in my teens, managed to get behind the scenes. The tenor was a fine young man from the sunny South, who was going to be the successor of Mario. At that time everybody was going to succeed Mario. The particular child of Nature in question made a deep impression on me as he went on to sing the interpolated aria Deserto sulla terra between the last two acts. As he passed me he cleared his throat demonstratively, and in the most natural and spontaneous way imaginable spat right into the midst of a group of women who were seated chattering just behind the proscenium. Immediately the question presented itself, Can a man look like Lohengrin, sing like Lohengrin, feel like Lohengrin, raise the Donizetti-ridden stage to the level of Lohengrin, before he has himself reached the phase of having misgivings as to the considerateness of promiscuous expectoration? . . . Anyhow I made up my mind that no demand for a more serious view of the lyric stage would come from the Italian tenors.'

Before that disillusion he had also been captivated by the theatre, where he saw on his first visit a couple of farces, a three-act play by Tom Taylor, and a complete Christmas pantomime, then an ordinary evening's programme which must have trained the playgoers of that day to sit through anything, from a Wagner opera to a revivalist meeting, with cheerful complacence; though we must remember that long waits in pit queues were not in fashion, the audience obtaining entrance to the theatre in a scrimmage: 'In my barbarous youth, when one of the pleasures of theatre-going was the fierce struggle at the pit-door, I learnt a lesson which I have never forgotten: namely, that the secret of getting in was to wedge myself into the worst of the crush. When ribs and breastbone were on the verge of collapse, and the stout lady in front, after passionately calling on her escort to take her out of it if he considered himself a man, had resigned herself to death, my hopes of a place in the front row ran high. If the pressure slackened I knew I was being extruded into the side eddies where the feeble and half-hearted were throwing away their chance of a good seat for such paltry indulgences as freedom to breathe and a fully expanded skeleton.'

The greatest actor of those days was Barry Sullivan, whose fascination, grace and force made a deep impression on Shaw: 'His stage fights in Richard II and Macbeth appealed irresistibly to a boy spectator like myself: I remember one delightful evening when two inches of Macbeth's sword, a special fighting sword carried in that scene only, broke off and whizzed over the heads of the cowering pit (there were no stalls then) to bury itself deep in the front of the dress circle after giving those who sat near its trajectory more of a thrill than they had bargained for. Barry Sullivan was a tall powerful man with a cultivated resonant voice: his stage walk was the perfection of grace and dignity; and his lightning swiftness of action, as when in the last scene of Hamlet he shot up the stage and stabbed the king four times before you could wink, all provided a physical exhibition which attracted audiences quite independently of the play.' He was a touring 'star' but as a rule he only toured himself and had to make the best of the local stock company for all the other parts in the plays. Shaw's critical faculties must have been highly developed even as a boy because a local Ophelia reduced him to such paroxysms of laughter that he 'narrowly escaped ejection from the theatre', and he was able to tell when Sullivan's acting was below par.

Sullivan was the last of a famous school of superhuman actors, and Shaw became conscious of a new histrionic epoch when the London production of Albery's *Two Roses* visited Dublin. The success of this play was due to an actor whose performance was totally unlike anything seen before. He had a tall thin figure; his walk was peculiar, his gestures strange, his voice nasal, his personality sinister; yet there was a weird dignity about him, and he was different from the others: he was 'modern'. Shaw felt instinctively 'that a new drama inhered in this man, though I had then no conscious notion that I was destined to write it'; and the fact that 'this man' never saw himself in the new drama was responsible for Shaw's later attacks on him. His name was Henry Irving.

The bare suggestion that he was going to be a writer, still less a playwright, would have been laughed at by the youthful Shaw. It never dawned on one who had not even been conscious of learning the alphabet that writing was an attainment, or that the gift of dramatizing life was in any way exceptional. Writing and telling stories were as natural to him as breathing. He no more wished to write than a duck to swim, for 'you cannot want a thing and have it too'. Following the normal desire of a boy to be a pirate, a highwayman and an engine-driver, he longed to play wicked baritones in operas ; which phase was followed by his highest ambition : to be another Michael Angelo. He never missed an opportunity of looking at the pictures in the National Gallery of Ireland, where he often found himself alone with the officials. 'It was by prowling in this gallery that I learnt to recognize the work of the old masters at sight.' He occasionally bought but mostly borrowed books about painting and spent hours studying reproductions of the great Italian and Flemish painters, more profitable hours than those spent in Dublin's two cathedrals, restored out of the profits of the drink trade. He went through the routine of free-hand drawing, practical geometry, and perspective at the official School of Design subsidized by South Kensington ; but the instruction there failed to do more than convince him that he was a hopeless failure 'on no better grounds than that I found I could not draw like Michael Angelo or paint like Titian at the first attempt without knowing how'.

Although Shaw, unlike most people, was more impressed by the fine eighteenth century buildings than by the dirt and drabness of Dublin, he did not care for the city, and the happiest day of his life was that on which his mother told him that they were going to live at Dalkey. He had been there already on an excursion, had clambered 'all over Killiney hill looking at the endless pictures nature painted for me', but from his tenth to his fifteenth year the family spent the summer months there. He was keenly susceptible to natural beauty and the Dalkey scenery was a revelation to him. 'There is not two penn'orth of Alpine mountain or tree in that landscape ; but I have never seen more beautiful skies, even in Venice ; and I always look at the sky.' He felt that the glories unfolded to him in every direction were his personal posses-

sion for ever, like the books he had read, the music he had
heard, the pictures he had seen ; and thus was his voluntary
education completed.

GROWTH

THE CONTRAST between the freedom of Dalkey and the restriction of Dublin, between the airy commons and the fetid slums, provided the later Shaw with one of his picturesque proposals for the improvement of the human race: 'Of the many wild absurdities of our existing social order perhaps the most grotesque is the costly and strictly enforced reservation of large tracts of country as deer forests and breeding grounds for pheasants whilst there is so little provision of the kind made for children. I have more than once thought of trying to introduce the shooting of children as a sport, as the children would then be preserved very carefully for ten months in the year, thereby reducing their death rate far more than the fusillades of the sportsmen during the other two would raise it. At present the killing of a fox except by a pack of foxhounds is regarded with horror but you may and do kill children in a hundred and fifty ways provided you do not shoot them or set a pack of dogs on them. It must be admitted that the foxes have the best of it ; and indeed a glance at our pheasants, our deer, and our children will convince the most sceptical that the children have decidedly the worst of it.'

It happened that the man who wrote that passage first became conscious of his nature when wandering through the furze bushes near his Dalkey home. Before that moment of self-realization he had been a healthily destructive lad, playing 'the boy buccaneer with no more conscience than a fox in a poultry farm'. In *Man and Superman* there is a scene in which Ann accuses Tanner of having done a lot of damage in his youth: 'You ruined all the young fir trees by chopping off their leaders with a wooden sword. You broke all the cucumber frames with your catapult. You set fire to the common: the police arrested Tavy for it because he ran away when he

41

couldn't stop you.' Tanner answers: 'These were battles, bombardments, stratagems to save our scalps from the red Indians.' The episode of setting fire to the common struck me as probably autobiographical, so I asked Shaw for details. He replied:

'At the age of 12 or thereabouts I was with two other boys on the seaside slope of Torca Hill, Dalkey, when the question arose whether it would not be a lark to set the gorse on fire. Boy number 3 remonstrated strongly, but, being unable to prevail, bolted down the hill to the road, where he was arrested by the police, who saw a terrific conflagration raging and a boy running away. It is the innocent who suffer. I and boy number 2, appalled by the burst of flame which sprang from our match, bolted up the hill (we both lived higher up), where I learnt presently that number 3 was in custody.

'It was outside my code of honor to let another bear the burden of my guilt; so I put on my best jacket and called on the landlord of the hill, Mr Hercules Macdonell, who received me on the terrace of his villa with a gravity equal to my own. I orated on the thoughtlessness of youth with an eloquence beyond my years, and finally received a letter to the police inspector to say that the matter could be let drop. I duly delivered this, and found that number 3 had been released. The fire had meanwhile been extinguished by sense of humor.'

'I have no doubt that my fondness for long words and my budding literary gift stood me in good stead with Hercules' the neighbours' gardeners.

This was Shaw's first speech. Had he explained to Hercules that the blazing hillside was due to the curiosity of G.B.S. rather than the thoughtlessness of youth he would have been nearer the mark. Not a few of his letters and articles in the press were written partly with a desire to make the sparks fly, and nothing could quench his thirst for knowledge: 'I have always despised Adam because he had to be tempted by the woman, as she was by the serpent, before he could be induced to pluck the apple from the tree of knowledge I should have swallowed every apple on the tree the moment the owner's back was turned.'

Self-knowledge came to him suddenly, out of the dark, not long after his interview with Hercules Macdonell: 'One evening, as I was wandering through the furze bushes on Torca Hill in the dusk, I suddenly asked myself why I went on repeating my prayer every night when, as I put it, I did not believe in it. Being thus brought to book by my intellectual conscience I felt obliged in common honesty to refrain from superstitious practices ; and that night, for the first time since I could speak, I did not say my prayers. I missed them so much that I asked myself another question. Why am I so uncomfortable about it? Can this be conscience? But next night the discomfort wore off so much that I hardly noticed it ; and the night after I had forgotten all about my prayers as completely as if I had been born a heathen.' Having no longer his prayers to fall back on, having to stand on his own feet, he started thinking things out for himself: 'I began to have scruples, to feel obligations, to find that veracity and honor were no longer goody-goody expressions in the mouths of grown-up people, but compelling principles in myself. . . . The change that came to me was the birth in me of moral passion ; and I declare that according to my experience moral passion is the only real passion. . . . All the other passions were in me before ; but they were idle and aimless—mere childish greediness and cruelties, curiosities and fancies, habits and superstitions, grotesque and ridiculous to the mature intelligence. When they suddenly began to shine like newly lit flames it was by no light of their own, but by the radiance of the dawning moral passion. That passion dignified them, gave them conscience and meaning, found them a mob of appetites and organized them into an army of purposes and principles. My soul was born of that passion.'

Reformation seemed to be in the air just then because Shaw's father 'reduced his teetotalism from theory to practice when a mild fit, which felled him on our doorstep one Sunday afternoon, convinced him that he must stop drinking or perish'. He stopped drinking and remained sober for the rest of his life. But drunk or sober he could not evoke the sympathy of his wife, who broke up the home in 1872 and went to London, whither Lee had already repaired in the belief that his musical gifts would gain him a reputation and a fortune. Mrs Shaw, anxious to earn a living as a teacher of singing, took her daughters with her. One of them died of consumption at Ventnor shortly after leaving Ireland: she 'had hair of a flaming red seen only in the Scottish Highlands'. The other, a brunette, was a promising singer, and the family hoped that

43

with Lee's assistance she would become a prima donna. G.B.S.
and his father settled in lodgings at 61 Harcourt Street,
Dublin.

'LIFE IS REAL'

THE FAMILY had been getting poorer and poorer while the
head of it had been fighting a losing battle in a decaying
business, and when G.B.S. was about thirteen an effort was
made to turn him into a source of income. A friend of the
family got him an introduction to Messrs Scott, Spain &
Rooney, a firm of cloth merchants. The lad would have preferred to interview Spain, whose name was more romantic,
but he was ushered into the presence of Scott, who looked
him over briefly and would have engaged him but for the
arrival of Rooney, a much older man, who catechized him
and decided that he was too young for the job. He never
ceased to be grateful to Rooney.

But the family did not appreciate Rooney's sympathy with
youth and a year or two later, through the influence of an
uncle, the boy became a clerk in a first-class and intensely
snobbish firm of land agents at 18*s*. a month, thus committing
what he afterwards described as 'that sin against my nature',
the attempt 'to earn an honest living'. It was an excellent start
for anyone who wished to become a land agent, which in
those days was a remunerative profession in Ireland, but it was
a poor start for one who wished to become a wicked baritone,
and whenever the principals were absent from the office Shaw
taught operatic selections to the young gentlemen who had
paid premiums for learning something else. One day an
apprentice was doing full justice to his tuition when Uniacke
Townshend, the senior partner of the firm, walked in. Instantly
all the juniors became absorbed in their books except the
vocalist, who was carried too far away by his song to notice
the sudden abstraction of his audience. Townshend nearly

44

had a seizure, hastily sought refuge in his office, and remained there for some time panting. Even after his recovery he could not bring himself to comment on the scene, which he probably thought he had imagined.

Young Shaw was still more troublesome on a less celestial plane, and Townshend, getting wind of his atheistical opinions, ordered him not to discuss religion during office hours. Townshend cannot be blamed for refusing to convert his land agency into a debating society, but the effect of his order on a naturally communicative youngster was repressive: Shaw simmered inwardly for a considerable period and at length spouted *coram populo*. The immediate cause of his first appearance in print was the visit to Dublin of the evangelical revivalist firm of Moody and Sankey, the first of whom preached, driving people to God with threats of hell, the second sang, drawing people to God with the notes of a dove. Shaw went to their performance, was neither driven nor drawn, and wrote a letter printed in *Public Opinion* on April 3rd, 1875, in which he attributed the success of the undertaking, not to a revival of religion, but to publicity, curiosity, novelty and excitement. The effect of the revival on individuals, he asserted, had 'a tendency to make them highly objectionable members of society'.

This was not by any means Shaw's first literary composition: before he was ten he had written a short story about a man with a gun attacking another man, presumably without a gun, in the Glen of the Downs; on several occasions he had sent reams of manuscript, expository or imaginative, to various journals; and throughout his business career he kept up a brisk correspondence of a highly romantic order with an old friend named Edward McNulty. But Moody and Sankey were responsible for his first public appearance as a writer; and because he was born with the gift of literary self-expression and so took it for granted, he experienced no thrill in seeing his printed words. 'It was no more exciting than the taste of water in my mouth,' he said. Music was still his chief interest in life, although he was passing through a phase of Shelley-worship.

When his mother sold the household furniture and departed for London she left the family piano behind. 'I suddenly found myself in a house where there was no music and could be none unless I made it myself.' So he began to teach himself how to play the piano, not with five-finger exercises but with

45

the overture to *Don Giovanni*, 'thinking rightly that I had better start with something I knew well enough to hear whether my fingers were on the right notes or not. There were plenty of vocal scores of operas and oratorios in our lodging; and although I never acquired any technical skill as a pianist, and cannot to this day play a scale with any certainty of not foozling it, I acquired what I wanted: the power to take a vocal score and learn its contents as if I had heard it rehearsed by my mother and her colleagues. . . . I bought more scores, among them one of *Lohengrin*, through which I made the revolutionary discovery of Wagner. I bought arrangements of Beethoven's symphonies, and discovered the musical regions that lie outside opera and oratorio. . . . When I look back on all the banging, whistling, roaring, and growling inflicted on nervous neighbours doing this process of education, I am consumed with useless remorse. But what else could I have done?'

While the residents in Harcourt Street were suffering acutely from the sounds that came from No. 61, Shaw was finding relief from the misery he endured as a land agent's junior clerk, one of whose most unpleasant jobs it was to collect weekly rents from impoverished tenants, compared with which a voluntary visit to Mountjoy prison was a jolly experience. His social conscience was also awakened by the discovery, in going through the papers of an Irish crown solicitor, that many offences committed by drunken soldiers in a certain camp were overlooked because the law would have treated them as grave crimes and punished them with barbarous ferocity: 'The effect produced by these revelations on my raw youth was a sense of heavy responsibility for conniving at their concealment. I felt that if camp and barrack life involved these things, they ought to be known. I had been caught by the great wave of scientific enthusiasm which was then passing over Europe as a result of the discovery of Natural Selection by Darwin, and of the blow it dealt to the vulgar Bible-worship and redemption mongering which had hitherto passed among us for religion. I wanted to get at the facts. I was prepared for the facts being unflattering: had I not already faced the fact that instead of being a fallen angel I was first cousin to a monkey?'

That he was distantly related to a monkey was further suggested by the fact that he was climbing in his profession: 'By the time I had attained to thirty shillings a month, the most active and responsible official in the office, the cashier, vanished; and as we were private bankers to some extent, our clients drawing cheques on us, and so forth, someone had to take his place without an hour's delay. An elder substitute grumbled at the strange job, and, though an able man in his way, could not make his cash balance. It became necessary, after a day or two of confusion, to try the office-boy as a stop-gap whilst the advertisements for a new cashier of appropriate age and responsibility were going forward. Immediately the machine worked again quite smoothly. I, who never knew how much money I had of my own (except when the figure was zero), proved a model of accuracy as to the money of others. I acquired my predecessor's very neat handwriting, my own being too sloped and straggly for the cash book. The efforts to fill my important place more worthily slackened. I bought a tailed coat, and was chaffed about it by the apprentices. My salary was raised to £48 a year, which was as much as I expected at sixteen and much less than the firm would have had to pay to a competent adult; in short, I made good in spite of myself, and found, to my dismay, that Business, instead of expelling me as the worthless impostor I was, was fastening upon me with no intention of letting me go.'

For four years he remained a model cashier, detesting the job 'as cordially as any sane person lets himself detest anything he cannot escape from'. By his twentieth year his salary was £84, and his employers had such a high opinion of his honesty and diligence that they could not have guessed the measure of his discontent. At first his objection to a business career had been due to his boredom with it, his interest in music, painting and literature. Then a rather curious thing happened: 'I never thought of myself as destined to become what is called a great man: indeed I was diffident to the most distressing degree; and I was ridiculously credulous as to the claims of others to superior knowledge and authority. But one day in the office I had a shock. One of the apprentices, by name C. J. Smyth, older than I and more a man of the world, remarked that every young chap thought he was going to be a great man. On a really modest youth this commonplace would have had no effect. It gave me so perceptible a jar that I suddenly became aware that I had never thought I was to be a great man simply because I had always taken it as a matter of course. The incident passed without leaving

47

any preoccupation with it to hamper me; and I remained as diffident as ever because I was still as incompetent as ever. But I doubt whether I ever recovered my former complete innocence of subconscious intention to devote myself to the class of work that only a few men excel in, and to accept the responsibilities that attach to its dignity.' It followed as a matter of course that he had to leave Dublin: 'My business in life could not be transacted in Dublin out of an experience confined to Ireland. I had to go to London just as my father had to go to the Corn Exchange. London was the literary centre for the English language, and for such artistic culture as the realm of the English language (in which I proposed to be king) could afford. There was no Gaelic League in those days, nor any sense that Ireland had in herself the seed of culture. Every Irishman who felt that his business in life was on the higher planes of the cultural professions felt that he must have a metropolitan domicile and an international culture: that is, he felt that his first business was to get out of Ireland. I had the same feeling.'

Apart from this practical reason for going, Shaw had come to dislike Dublin: 'A certain flippant futile derision and be-littlement that confuses the noble and serious with the base and ludicrous seems to me peculiar to Dublin.' Further: 'I am not enamoured of failure, of poverty, of obscurity, and of the ostracism and contempt which these imply; and these were all that Dublin offered to the enormity of my unconscious ambition.' The inhabitants of Dublin, whether collectively or individually, were not to his taste. 'Like all Irishmen, I dislike the Irish,' he once told me. 'On principle?' I asked. 'No, on instinct,' he promptly replied, adding that William Morris had been quite right in saying that the Irish had all the virtues but he hated them, the Scotch all the vices but he loved them. Shaw did not see his home country again for nearly thirty years and made no secret of his desire to keep away from it, writing in 1896: 'I shewed my own appreciation of my native land in the usual Irish way by getting out of it as soon as I possibly could; and I cannot say that I have the smallest intention of settling there again as long as the superior attractions of St Helena (not to mention London) are equally available.'

His method of leaving was abrupt. In March 1876 he gave his employers a month's notice. They thought he was dissatisfied with his salary and declared their intention of making his position more eligible. 'My only fear was that they should make it so eligible that all excuse for throwing it up would be taken from me. I thanked them and said I was resolved to go; and I had, of course, no reason in the world to give them for my resolution. They were a little hurt, and explained to my uncle that they had done their best, but that I seemed to have made up my mind. I had.' His father, with an eye to his future employment, got the firm to write a testimonial to his efficiency as a cashier, and failed to understand why this kindly action should have thrown G.B.S. into a transport of rage.

After enjoying the luxury of not having to go to the office for a few days, he packed a carpet bag and took the boat for England with no regrets, no sentimental farewells. Up to that time he had only fallen in love with dream-women. Music, books and paintings had spoiled him for 'anything so prosaic as a real woman', and such love-making as he had indulged in may be inferred from a memory put into the mouth of one of his characters: 'Do you remember a dark-eyed girl named Rachel Rosetree? I got up a love-affair with her; and we met one night in the garden and walked about very uncomfortably with our arms round one another, and kissed at parting, and were most conscientiously romantic. If that love-affair had gone on, it would have bored me to death . . .'

MECCA

ON A MORNING in early spring G.B.S. stepped from the train on to the platform at Euston and was addressed by a porter in a strange tongue: 'Ensm' faw weel?' Not having read Dickens for nothing, he mentally restored an aitch or two, and, fearing he would not know how to enter or leave so peculiar-looking an object as a hansom cab, asked for a four-wheeler. Dickens had been dead for six years; but to Shaw London was the novelist's creation and the names of the streets through which he drove seemed to come straight from the pages of Dickens. London was at its best and the young Irishman could not help feeling elated as he surveyed the city he proposed to conquer. He had no notion of how to start the campaign; he had no programme, no plan, no method, no definite goal. 'In the ordinary connotation of the word I am the least ambitious of men. I have said, and I confirm it here, that I am so poor a hand at pushing and struggling, and so little interested in their rewards, that I have risen by sheer gravitation, too industrious by acquired habit to stop working (I work as my father drank), and too lazy and timid by nature to lay hold of half the opportunities or a tenth of the money that a conventionally ambitious man would have grasped strenuously.' Without faith or hope he doggedly wrote books—five full-sized novels—as a beaver builds dams, and hated them and was ashamed of them when he had written them. They were the taskwork of his apprenticeship: he wrote because he knew he must keep on doing something, and could do nothing else. But those dreadful penniless years of task work left him thoroughly professionalized. Writing gave him no trouble henceforth. And he learnt the startling consolation he later on put into the mouth of Cæsar: 'He who has never hoped can never despair.'

He found his mother and sister in a *cul de sac* off the Brompton Road called Victoria Grove, which in those days had a countrified air, being surrounded by orchards and market-gardens. Here, at Number 13, a semi-detached villa, his mother was trying to earn a livelihood by teaching, his sister by singing. 'My father, left in Dublin, spared us a pound a week from his slender resources; and by getting into debt and occasionally extracting ourselves by drawing on a maternal inheritance of £4000 over which my mother had a power of appointment, and which therefore could be realized bit by bit as her three children came of age, we managed to keep going somehow.' But it was not easy and Shaw's arrival did not make it easier. One of the first things he did was to ask his mother to teach him how to sing. This added nothing to the family income. Then he learned 'to play the classical symphonies and overtures in strict time by hammering the bass in piano duets' with his sister. This did not relieve the situation. Then he drove his mother nearly crazy by playing his favourite selections from Wagner's Ring. This provided nothing but a painful memory: 'She never complained at the time, but confessed it after we separated, and said that she had sometimes gone away to cry. If I had committed a murder I do not think it would trouble my conscience very much ; but this I cannot bear to think of. If I had to live my life over again I should devote it to the establishment of some arrangement of headphones and microphones or the like whereby the noises made by musical maniacs should be audible to themselves only. In Germany it is against the law to play the piano with the window open. But of what use is that to the people in the house? It should be made felony to play a musical instrument in any other than a completely sound-proof room. The same should apply to loud speakers on pain of confiscation.'

Shaw had not the smallest real intention of helping to balance the family budget, but other people drove him to work in spite of his subconscious resolution to do nothing of the kind. The first to force his hand was G. J. Lee, who had disgusted Mrs Shaw by abandoning his 'method', shaving his whiskers, waxing his moustache, and as Vandaleur Lee, setting up as a quack teacher at 13 Park Lane, charging large fees for turning out prima donnas in twelve lessons. While Mrs Shaw was gently dropping the man who had given her a religion only to become its Judas, Shaw was playing the piano at Lee's musical parties and getting his first peep at the musical half-bohemian side of English 'society'. In return for his assistance as an accompanist, Lee became music critic to *The Hornet,* letting Shaw write the criticisms and take the cash. The job soon came to an end because the concert agents objected to the criticisms, withdrew their advertisements and killed the paper. Shaw was relieved, because the editor had tried to brighten up his serious reviews with musical chit-chat ; but it meant that he was again 'open to offers' ; and though, being painfully shy, he resolutely refused all invitations to meet people who might have been able to help him, he felt sure his well-meaning acquaintances would not rest until he was safely installed in some quite detestable job. 'I dodged every opening instinctively . . . I was an incorrigible Unemployable. I kept up pretences (to myself as much as others) for sometime. I answered advertisements, not too offensively . . . I can remember an interview with a bank manager in Onslow Gardens (procured for me, to my dismay, by an officious friend with whom I *had* dined) with a view to employment in the bank. I entertained him so brilliantly (if I may use an adverb with which in later years I was much plagued by friendly critics) that we parted on the best of terms, he declaring that, though I certainly ought to get something to do without the least difficulty, he did not feel that a bank clerkship was the right job for me.'

The next person to drive him into uncongenial employment was his authoress cousin, Mrs Cashel Hoey, who in 1879 introduced him to the secretary of the Edison Telephone Company, which occupied the basement of a block of offices in Queen Victoria Street. He was given a berth in the Way-Leave Department and spent his days in trying to persuade dwellers in the East End of London 'to allow the Company to put insulators and poles and derricks and the like on their roofs to carry the telephone lines'. He enjoyed the exploration but hated the interviewing: 'My sensitiveness, which was extreme, in spite of the brazen fortitude which I simulated, made the impatient rebuffs I had to endure occasionally, especially from much worried women who mistook me for an advertisement canvasser, ridiculously painful to me.' Edison's telephone was not a success. The British stockbroker did not like it because 'it bellowed your most private communications all over the house instead of whispering them with some sort of discretion', and the business was soon merged in the National Telephone Company; but Edison's invention was not entirely wasted, for it provided Shaw with a job for several months and enabled him, when he became head of the Department, to rub shoulders with American workers, who 'sang obsolete sentimental songs with genuine emotion', used frightful language, 'worked with ferocious energy which was out of all proportion to the actual result achieved', refused to be slave-driven by anyone but an American, thought Edison the greatest genius of all time, and had an utter contempt for the British workmen who refused to hustle or be hustled.

When the Company was swallowed up by the larger concern Shaw managed to get out of it, and except for an odd job two years later, when he made a pound or two by counting the votes at an election in Leyton, he never again sinned against his nature by attempting to earn an honest living. But throughout the first years of his life in London he expressed various aspects of his nature in articles which he sent to all the leading papers and which were regularly returned by them with pleasure, or, as they expressed it, with regret. All but one, which dealt with 'Christian Names'

and was published by G. R. Sims in his paper *One and All*.
In this, the first of his innumerable bits of journalism to
see the light, Shaw advised parents not to give their children
pompous or stupid christian names: 'Never confer an uncommon name . . . which has been borne by any personage
known to history. A person so christened resembles a jackdaw
with a peacock's tail, which he has not himself assumed, and
which he has, therefore, the grace to be ashamed of. Constantly and consciously in a false position, the unhappy man,
registered in comparison to a standard which he can never
hope to reach, is soon looked on as a failure, and falls into
contempt beneath the weight of his own name.' Equally:
'Except in a few cases, where genius exists so strongly that
it cannot be stifled (though even then it can be modified), he
who bears a fool's name will be held in a fool's estimation,
which he will end by justifying.'

Shaw was so grateful for the 15s. which he received for
this article that he sat down and wrote something much
better. It was apparently much too much better, because
its return was followed by the paper's demise, perhaps from
the effect of his 'brilliant contribution' on the editorial staff.
Altogether he earned £6 with his pen during the nine years
1876-85, the balance being made up of £5 for writing a
patent-medicine advertisement and 5s. for turning out some
verses intended as a parody but taken seriously, commissioned
by a fellow-lodger.

Except for a Passion Play in blank verse, which he abandoned too near the beginning to rank it as Opus I, having
got no farther than a character sketch of Our Lady as a
shrew, the years 1879-83 were occupied by novel-writing.
He wrote five, and the exercise of writing them did him a
lot of good. It may be said of them (to adapt a remark
of Oscar Wilde's) that there are two ways of disliking the
works of Bernard Shaw: one way is to dislike them, the other
is to like his novels. When he was forced to re-read them,
long after he had become famous as a dramatist, he thought
them 'just readable enough to be intolerable' and hated them.
They are written in the classical style which now seems
ridiculously stilted and self-conscious (it still survived almost
vernacularly in Ireland) and they lack his natural exuber-
ance, though there are occasional touches of his peculiar
humour. For example, in his first novel *Immaturity* he pictures the youthful hero Smith, obviously himself, walking

in the cloisters of Westminster Abbey with an air of deep appreciation, and he explains why the young man is so deeply appreciative: 'A discerning observer might have marked him by his hushed step, impressed bearing, and reflective calm, as a confirmed freethinker.'

As a matter of fact Shaw was then passing through a phase of bellicose atheism. He was present at a bachelor party in Kensington when someone declared that a man who had scoffed at the mission of Moody and Sankey had been slain by a righteously wrathful deity and carried home on a shutter. This started an argument, in the course of which 'it was alleged by the most evangelical of the disputants that Charles Bradlaugh, the most formidable atheist on the Secularist platform, had taken out his watch publicly and challenged the Almighty to strike him dead in five minutes if he really existed and disapproved of atheism'. A member of the party instantly asserted that Bradlaugh had never done anything of the kind and had publicly repudiated the story. Upon which Shaw retorted that if Bradlaugh had not done so, he ought to have done so: 'The omission, I added, was one which could easily be remedied there and then, as I happened to share Mr Bradlaugh's views as to the absurdity of the belief in these violent interferences with the order of nature by a short-tempered and thin-skinned supernatural deity. Therefore—and at that point I took out my watch. The effect was electrical. Neither sceptics nor devotees were prepared to abide the result of the experiment. In vain did I urge the pious to trust in the accuracy of their deity's aim with a thunderbolt, and the justice of his discrimination between the innocent and the guilty. In vain did I appeal to the sceptics to accept the logical outcome of their scepticism: it soon appeared that when thunderbolts were in question there were no sceptics. Our host, seeing that his guests would vanish precipitately if the impious challenge were uttered, leaving him alone with a solitary infidel under sentence of extermination in five minutes, interposed and forbade the experiment, pleading at the same time for a change of subject. I of course complied, but could not refrain from remarking that though the dreadful words had not been uttered, yet, as the thought had been formulated in my mind, it was very doubtful whether the consequences could be averted by sealing my lips. However, the rest appeared to feel that the game would be played according to the rules, and that it mattered very little what I thought so long as I said nothing. Only the leader of the evangelical party, I thought, was a little preoccupied until five minutes had elapsed and the weather was still calm.'

A thoughtful friend, anxious to save Shaw from hell-fire, begged Father Addis of the Brompton Oratory to attempt his conversion to Roman Catholicism. Quite willing to argue the matter out, and curious to explore the mind of Father Addis, Shaw repaired to a cell in the Oratory: 'The universe exists, said the father: somebody must have made it. If that somebody exists, said I, somebody must have made him. I grant that for the sake of argument, said the Oratorian. I grant you a maker of God. I grant you a maker of the maker of God. I grant you as long a line of makers as you please; but an infinity of makers is unthinkable and extravagant: it is no harder to believe in number one than in number fifty thousand or fifty million; so why not accept number one and stop there, since no attempt to get behind him will remove your logical difficulty? By your leave, said I, it is as easy for me to believe that the universe made itself as that a maker of the universe made himself: in fact much easier; for the universe visibly exists and makes itself as it goes along, whereas a maker for it is a hypothesis. Of course we could get no further on these lines. He rose and said that we were like two men working a saw, he pushing it forward and I pushing it back, and cutting nothing; but when we had dropped the subject and were walking through the refectory, he returned to it for a moment to say that he should go mad if he lost his belief. I, glorying in the robust callousness of youth and the comedic spirit, felt quite comfortable and said so: though I was touched, too, by his evident sincerity.'

This is clearly the hero of *Immaturity,* which closes on the following note: 'As Smith recrossed the bridge, he stopped and stood in one of the recesses to meditate on his immaturity, and to look upon the beauty of the still expanses of white moonlight and black shadows which lay before him. At last he shook his head negatively, and went home.'

Immaturity was written in 1879 and refused by every publisher in London. Chapman and Hall's reader, George Meredith, just said 'No'. Macmillan's reader, John Morley, was sufficiently impressed by the book to consider Shaw as a possible contributor to *The Pall Mall Gazette* which he edited. Shaw called and Morley asked him what he thought he could do. Shaw thought he could write about art. 'Pooh! Anybody can write about art,' replied Morley contemptuously. 'Oh, *can* they!?' was Shaw's withering retort, upon which Morley decided that he would be an impossible contributor. Half a century later Shaw published *Immaturity* himself, explaining that the character of the artist in the novel had been suggested by the landscape painter Cecil Lawson. Having been introduced to the Lawson family by his mother, he sometimes went to their house in Cheyne Walk on Sunday evenings, the only house except Lee's he ever visited in those early days. An abnormal shyness, which is the form vanity takes in youth, tormented him on these occasions and made him unmannerly and arrogant in social intercourse: 'I suffered such agonies of shyness that I sometimes walked up and down the Embankment for twenty minutes or more before venturing to knock at the door: indeed I should have funked it altogether, and hurried home asking myself what was the use of torturing myself when it was so easy to run away, if I had not been instinctively aware that I must never let myself off in this manner if I meant ever to do anything in the world. Few men can have suffered more than I did in my youth from simple cowardice or been more horribly ashamed of it. I shirked and hid when the peril, real or imaginary, was of the sort that I had no vital interest in facing; but when such an interest was at stake, I went ahead and suffered accordingly. The worst of it was that when I appeared in the Lawsons' drawing-room I did not appeal to the good nature of the company as a pardonably and even becomingly bashful novice. I had not then tuned the Shavian note to any sort of harmony; and I have no doubt the Lawsons found me discordant, crudely self-assertive, and insufferable.'

His second novel was *The Irrational Knot*, which like its predecessor contains several good touches, such as 'I have been waiting ever since I knew him for an excuse to hate him', and went the round of the publishers without evoking the least sign of interest. 'I had no means of knowing, and was too young and inexperienced to guess, that what was the matter was not any lack of literary competence on my part, but the antagonism raised by my hostility to respectable Victorian thought and society. I was left without a ray of hope; yet I did not stop writing novels. . . .'

His determination to fill five quarto pages of cheap white paper a day, wet or fine, whether he felt like it or not, was made easier by his office training: 'I had so much of the schoolboy and the clerk still in me th   if my five pages ended in the middle of a sentence I did not ɪinish it until next day. On the other hand, if I missed a day, I made up for it by doing a double task on the morrow.' While writing *The Irrational Knot* it happened that Bizet's opera *Carmen* was fresh to London and Shaw used it as a safety-valve for his romantic impulses. When tired of the atmosphere he was trying to create, he threw down his pen, went to the piano and forgot the sordid realism of his book 'in the glamorous society of Carmen and her crimson toreador and yellow dragoon'.

Opus 3, *Love Among the Artists,* was his most carefully considered and individual novel. For the first time he worked the old Shakespearean trick of making the woman go all-out for the man, while the hero, modelled on Beethoven, was the first of a line of historical characters whose imputed share in Shaw's powers of entertainment makes them a good deal more pleasant than their originals could have been. The book marks a cardinal turning point in Shaw's development. The first two novels are confidently rationalistic, especially *The Irrational Knot,* which was written without hesitation, almost impetuously, from beginning to end. The hero, a cultivated artisan, who in argument and force of character walks over the futile ladies and gentlemen to whose society his musical accomplishments give him the entry, is a novelty which is not yet relished except by cultivated artisans, a growing but not numerous class. It shows that Shaw, still innocent of professed socialism, was ripe for conversion. But it finished his jejune career as a rationalist material freethinker. He found he could get no farther on this line, and quite definitely and consciously abandoned it and took for his theme the degrees and contrasts of that entirely mystical (or super-rational) thing called genius, the conflicts of which with Philistine common-sense were to be henceforth the material for his comedy. Accordingly, *Love Among the Artists,* unlike *The Knot,* has no catastrophe and no ending. It just stops. Writing it was a slower business, interrupted by a first illness (a humiliating exposure of his mortality) and even by having to read over what he had already written to pick up the dropped thread of his narrative. 'A fully vaccinated person, guaranteed immune from smallpox for the whole of my natural life,' Shaw nevertheless fell a victim to the epidemic of 1881, surviving it with a considerable beard and a disbelief in medical orthodoxy that was to last his life, much to the annoyance of many eminent doctors.

His next piece of fiction, *Cashel Byron's Profession,* might almost be described as a thriller. He had been witnessing a number of boxing-matches and his interest in them, which made him study the subject in the British Museum reading room and eventually produced this book, was felt by him to be a streak of original sin. No one certainly was ever less of 'a sportsman' than G.B.S., whose general attitude to games was expressed in a remark to me: 'After profound reflection I have come to the conclusion that mankind is fit for nothing better at present than the chasing of a ball about a field. Perhaps in another thousand years it may prove equal to the moral and intellectual effort of finally kicking the ball out of the field.' Once, after seeing a game of baseball, he was asked to go to another. His comment was: 'When a man asks you to come and see baseball played twice it sets you asking yourself why you went to see it played once. That is a totally un-answerable question. It is a mad world.' His own share in the universal lunacy very nearly made him a best-seller: 'I never think of *Cashel Byron's Profession* without a shudder at the narrowness of my escape from becoming a successful novelist at the age of twenty-six. At that moment an adventurous publisher might have ruined me.' Even without an adventurous publisher the book was serialized in the socialist magazine called *To-day,* then put on the market in a shilling edition and duly pirated in America, making a lot of money for everyone concerned except the author, who wrote it for his own amusement but soon regretted that he had given way to such a boyish frolic: 'The glove fight and the conventional lived-happy-ever-afterwards ending, to which I had never previously condescended, exposed me for the first time to the humiliation of favourable reviewing and of numbering my readers in some thousands. But long before this my self-respect took alarm at the contemplation of the things I had made. I resolved to give up mere character sketching . . . and at once to produce a novel which should be a gigantic grapple with the whole social problem.'

His attempt to grapple with the whole social problem proved exhausting. Having written two chapters of phenomenal length, which merely cleared the ground before the serious business commenced, he gave it up, and eventually this prefatory matter was serialized and published as a book entitled *An Unsocial Socialist,* concerning which we have an interesting autobiographical note on the author's creative method: 'One day, as I was sitting in the reading room of the British Museum, beginning my fifth and last novel, *An Unsocial Socialist,* I saw a young lady with an attractive and arresting expression, bold, vivid, and very clever, working at one of the desks. On that glimpse of a face I instantly conceived the character and wrote the description of Agatha Wylie. I have never exchanged a word with that lady; never made her acquaintance; saw her again under the same circumstances but very few times; yet if I mention her name, which became well known in literature (she too was writing a novel then, and perhaps had the hero suggested to her by my profile), she will be set down as Agatha Wylie to her dying day, with heaven knows how much more scandalous invention added to account for my supposed intimate knowledge of her character. Before and since, I have used living models as freely as a painter does, and in much the same way: that is, I have sometimes made a fairly faithful portrait founded on intimate personal intercourse, and sometimes, as in Agatha's case, developed what a passing glance suggested to my imagination. In the latter case it has happened sometimes that the incidents I have invented on the spur of such a glance have hit the facts so nearly that I have found myself accused of unpardonable violations of personal privacy. I hardly expect to be believed when I say that I once invented a servant for one of my models and found afterwards that he actually had just such a servant. Between the two extremes of actual portraiture and pure fancy work suggested by a glance or an anecdote, I have copied nature with many degrees of fidelity, combining studies from life in the same book or play with those types and composites and traditional figures of the novel and the stage which are called pure fictions.'

Shaw had no success with his novels. He sent them to publishers in England and America and collected about sixty refusals. The five heavy brown-paper parcels came and went, each of them raising with its reappearance the grave financial question of how to get a sixpence to post it on to another publisher. His persistent failure to obtain a word of encouragement hardened him, made him self-sufficient, bred in him an insensitiveness to praise or blame. Eventually all but the first were serialized in long-forgotten magazines and pirated by American publishers, so actively in one case that Shaw, convinced that the firm thoroughly appreciated his work, gave them the publishing rights of his later books. Another firm, Harper & Brothers, sent him a complimentary £10 for an edition they brought out in 1887, thus acquiring a moral copyright, no legal one being then possible. Years afterwards a rival publisher violated this moral copyright by bringing out a competing edition. Shaw immediately returned the £10 on the ground that the moral copyright had proved ineffective: 'Harper nearly dropped dead with astonishment on receiving his £10 back. The firm has never been the same since.' As for his own earnings, Shaw was able to announce in 1892 that the royalties on the sale of his novels had increased 170 per cent in the years 1889-91, a generous hint to any publisher in search of a fiction-writer whose popularity was advancing by leaps and bounds: 'I doubt if any other living novelist can show such a record,' he said. 'In fact 170 is an understatement; for the exact figures were two and tenpence for 1889 and seven and tenpence for the year 1891.'

For the first nine years of his life in London Shaw's mother, by working as a music teacher, managed to supplement her husband's contribution, the remnant of her £4000, and the interest on an Irish mortgage (say another pound a week) sufficiently to keep her son alive with a roof over his head but not too presentably dressed. 'The true artist,' says Tanner in *Man and Superman*, 'will let his wife starve, his children go barefoot, his mother drudge for his living at seventy, sooner than work at anything but his art.' Shaw acted up to that principle and made no secret of it: 'I was an able-bodied and able-minded young man in the strength of my youth; and my family, then heavily embarrassed, needed my help urgently. That I should have chosen to be a burden to them instead was, according to all the conventions of peasant lad fiction, monstrous. Well, without a blush I embraced the monstrosity. I did not throw myself into the struggle for life: I threw my mother into it. I was not a staff to my father's old age: I hung on to his coat tails. His reward was to live just long enough to read a review of one of these silly novels written in an obscure journal by a personal friend of my own . . . prefiguring me to some extent as a considerable author. I think, myself, that this was a handsome reward, far better worth having than a nice pension from a dutiful son struggling slav-ishly for his parent's bread in some sordid trade. Handsome or not, it was the only return he ever had for the little pension he contrived to export from Ireland for his family. My mother reinforced it by drudging her elder years at the art of music which she had followed in her prime freely for love. I only helped to spend it. People wondered at my heartlessness: one young and romantic lady had the courage to remonstrate openly and indignantly with me, "for the which," as Pepys said of the shipwright's wife who refused his advances, "I did respect her." Callous as Comus to moral babble, I steadily wrote my five pages a day and made a man of myself (at my mother's expense) instead of a slave.'

POVERTY, POTATOES AND POLITICS

FROM 1876 TO 1885 Shaw scarcely put his nose outside London and very nearly had to wear the same suit of clothes through-out that time. He was poor, 'as timid as a mouse', and fre-quently unpresentable in the daytime. 'I remember once buy-ing a book entitled *How to Live on Sixpence a Day,* a point on which at that time circumstances compelled me to be press-ingly curious. I carried out its instructions faithfully for a whole afternoon; and if ever I had an official biography issued, I shall certainly have it stated therein, in illustration of my fortitude and self-denial, that I lived for some time on sixpence a day.' There was an element of truth in a personal confession that appeared in one of his dramatic criticisms, written in 1896: 'My main reason for adopting literature as a profession was, that as the author is never seen by his clients, he need not dress respectably. As a stockbroker, a doctor, or a man of business, I should have had to wear starched linen and a tall hat, and to give up the use of my knees and elbows. Literature is the only genteel profession that has no livery— for even your painter meets his sitters face to face—and so I

61

chose literature. You, friendly reader, though you buy my articles, have no idea of what I look like in the street. If you did, you would probably take in some other paper.'

His impecuniosity during those nine years was such that 'for two acute moments' he walked the streets in broken boots, and a pair of trousers with holes worn in the seat, hidden by a tailed coat whose colour had gradually turned from black to green with 'cuffs whose edges were trimmed by the scissors, and a tall hat so limp with age that I had to wear it back-to-front to enable me to take it off without doubling up the brim'. With his pale eyes, white face, straggly ginger beard, tall bony upright figure and striding resolute manner, he may have seemed formidable to street-urchins ; but he certainly did not conciliate the snobbery of publishers. Except when he could raise an occasional shilling for the theatre, he perambulated the streets, becoming shabbier and shabbier in appearance as the years passed by, and at length achieving a condition of 'indescribable seediness'. His chief recreations were visits to the National Gallery (on free days) and Hampton Court. Like Samuel Butler he made a second home of the reading room in the British Museum, where he began by studying all the books on etiquette•he could discover in the catalogue, being especially grateful to the author of *The Manners and Tone of Good Society*. Until then his one remembered lesson in good manners had been administered by an aunt. In his boyhood he had demurred to the description of a certain girl as 'the pretty Miss So and So'. Whereupon his aunt had reproved him : 'Remember always that the least plain girl in a house is the family beauty.' The books on polite behaviour which he devoured in the British Museum explained among other grave matters the use of the finger-bowl ; and they freed him from the fear of behaving incorrectly which haunts the socially untrained. On more serious points he was less well advised : 'As it never occurred to me to conceal my opinions any more than my nationality, and as I had, besides, an unpleasant trick of contradicting everyone from whom I thought I could learn anything in order to draw him out and enable me to pick his brains, I think I must have impressed many amiable persons as an extremely disagreeable and undesirable young man.'

Contrary to the legends that grew up round him later on he defended evening dress as the most democratic of all attires, as he could look exactly like a duke in it. It carried him through his after-dinner appearances until one evening at the

Opera it caught on some projection and came to pieces. But by that time he could afford a new one. Meanwhile he had two experiences that could not have happened to him in the light of day: 'I remember one evening during the novel-writing period when nobody would pay a farthing for a stroke of my pen, walking along Sloane Street in that blessed shield of literary shabbiness, evening dress. A man accosted me with an eloquent appeal for help, ending with the assurance that he had not a penny in the world. I replied, with exact truth, "Neither have I." He thanked me civilly, and went away, apparently not in the least surprised, leaving me to ask myself why I did not turn beggar too, since I felt sure that a man who did it as well as he must be in comfortable circumstances.

'Another reminiscence. A little past midnight, in the same costume, I was turning from Piccadilly into Bond Street, when a lady of the pavement, out of luck that evening so far, confided to me that the last bus for Brompton had passed, and that she should be grateful to any gentleman who would give her a lift in a hansom. My old-fashioned Irish gallantry had not then been worn off by age and England: besides, as a novelist who could find no publisher, I was touched by the similarity of our trades and predicaments. I excused myself very politely on the ground that my wife (invented for the occasion) was waiting for me at home, and that I felt sure so attractive a lady would have no difficulty in finding another escort. Unfortunately this speech made so favourable an impression on her that she immediately took my arm and declared her willingness to go anywhere with me, on the flattering ground that I was a perfect gentleman. In vain did I try to persuade her that in coming up Bond Street and deserting Piccadilly she was throwing away her last chance of a hansom: she attached herself so devotedly to me that I could not without actual violence shake her off. At last I made a stand at the end of Old Bond Street. I took out my purse; opened it; and held it upside down. Her countenance fell, poor girl! She turned on her heel with a melancholy flirt of her skirt, and vanished.'

After the deaths of Lee and Cecil Lawson he made no further raids on society, cutting himself off completely from the artistic and social life of London and deciding after lunching at the Savile Club that he would never be a literary man or consort with such: 'I might have spent my life sitting watching these fellows taking in each other's washing and learning no more of the world than a tic in a typewriter if I had been fool enough.' Apparently it did not strike him that consorting with politicians, actors, economists, musicians, plumbers, or any other class, was just as narrowing and certainly more nauseating. Just before taking this decision he met the most remarkable personality in the literary world of his time. Possibly because of his sister, who sang beautifully, he got to know Lady Wilde, at one of whose receptions Oscar Wilde went and spoke to him with the evident intention of being specially kind: 'We put each other out frightfully; and this odd difficulty persisted between us to the very last, even when we were no longer boyish novices and had become men of the world with plenty of skill in social intercourse. I saw him very seldom, as I avoided literary and artistic coteries like the plague, and refused the few invitations I received to go into society with burlesque ferocity, so as to keep out of it without offending people past their willingness to indulge me as a privileged lunatic.'

There is no doubt that nearly everybody he met thought him, if not mad, at least eccentric. In 1881, following a long course of Shelley, he became a vegetarian, and spoke of meat-eating as a 'cannibalism with its heroic dish omitted'. He had three main objections to a carnivorous diet. Firstly, it was abominable: animals were our fellow-creatures, and he had a strong sense of kinship with them. 'It amuses me to talk to animals in a sort of jargon I have invented for them; and it seems to me that it amuses them to be talked to, and that they respond to the tone of the conversation, though its intellectual content may to some extent escape them. I am quite sure, having made the experiment several times on dogs left in my care as part of the furniture of hired houses, that an animal who has been treated as a brute, and is consequently undeveloped socially (as human beings remain socially undeveloped under the same circumstances) will, on being talked to as a fellow-creature, become friendly and companionable in a very short time. . . . I find it impossible to associate with animals on any other terms. Further, it gives me extraordinary gratification to find a wild bird treating me with confidence, as robins sometimes do. It pleases me to conciliate an animal who is hostile to me. What is more, an animal who will not be conciliated offends me. There is at the Zoo a morose maned lion who will tear you to pieces if he gets half a chance. There is also a very handsome maneless lion with whom you may play more safely than with most St Bernard dogs, as he seems to need nothing but plenty of attention and admiration to put him into the best of humours. I do not feel towards these two lions as a carpenter does towards two pieces of wood, one hard and knotty, and the other easy to work ; nor as I do towards two motor bicycles, one troublesome and dangerous, and the other in perfect order. I feel towards the two lions as I should towards two men similarly diverse. I like one and dislike the other. If they got loose and were shot, I should be distressed in the one case whilst in the other I should say "Serve the brute right!" This is clearly fellow-feeling. And it seems to me that the plea of the humanitarian is a plea for widening the range of fellow-feeling.' This did not mean that the killing of animals or insects or even men was wrong. In mere self-defence human beings frequently had to destroy mice, rats, rabbits, wolves, deer, and snakes, just as they had to destroy habitual criminals: 'We see the Buddhist having his path swept before him lest he should tread on an insect and kill it ; but we do not see what the Buddhist does when he catches a flea that has kept him awake for an hour.' In fact there was all the difference in the world between exterminating a pest and eating it.

Secondly, flesh-eating was socially harmful: 'It involves a prodigious slavery of men to animals. Cows and sheep, with their *valetaille* of accoucheurs, graziers, shepherds, slaughtermen, butchers, milkmaids, and so forth, absorb a mass of human labour that should be devoted to the breeding and care of human beings. Some day, I hope, we shall live on air, and get rid of all the sanitary preoccupations which are so unpleasantly aggravated by meat-eating.'

Thirdly, there was the question of health and strength. 'I hate to see dead people walking about: it's unnatural,' he once wrote, and though he never pretended to enjoy perfect health he was 'seldom less than ten times as well as an ordinary carcass eater'. The strongest of animals, the bull, was a vegetarian ; even the lion, when it tore open its prey, fed on the undigested vegetables in the stomach, not on the flesh ; whilst the finest athletes in the world never touched scorched corpses. Indeed the penalty of being a vegetarian was an accumulation of energy that could not normally be dissipated. Shaw required 'about an hour and a half of navvying every day to work off all my steam. . . . What I want is a job of work. Thinning a jungle for preference. But whitewashing will serve.'

Vegetarianism however was not solely responsible for his store of energy: 'I am a teetotaller because my family has already paid the Shaw debt to the distilling industry so munificently as to leave me no further obligations, and because my mind requires no artificial stimulant. . . . I flatly declare that a man fed on whisky and dead bodies cannot do the finest work of which he is capable.' Nevertheless he was willing to grant, when discussing the subject with me, 'that as most people are quite incapable of five minutes consecutive and constructive thought, very little real harm is done by the total eclipse of such mental faculties as they possess'. His vitality was further increased by a dislike of tobacco. His father had objected 'to that startling innovation, bank holiday, as calculated to lead to excessive smoking and idleness', and G.B.S. could not help feeling that his parent's views on alcohol and nicotine were sound, if a trifle shaky in their personal application. 'As a boy,' he told me, 'I may have been idiot enough to think that the blackening of one's lungs was a necessary part of manliness. But before I was out of my teens I had begun to realize that it was silly to pay the sweep to clean our chimneys when we filled our rooms with the filthy fumes of a noxious weed. There is quite enough dirt and stuffiness in the world without adding to it.'

It was suggested during the war of 1914-18 that a vegetable diet had been responsible for the opinions, writings and personality of G.B.S., and as there was a strong probability just then that the nation would have to feed on vegetables or starve, the suggestion might have caused a general panic if Shaw had not restored national confidence with: 'There are millions of vegetarians in the world, but only one Bernard Shaw. . . . You do not obtain eminence quite so cheaply as by eating macaroni instead of mutton chops.' All the same he had confessed on a previous occasion that vegetarians, like pharisees, were not as other men were: 'The odd thing about being a vegetarian is, not that the things that happen to other people don't happen to me—they all do—but that they happen differently: pain is different, pleasure different, fever different, cold different, even love different.' In other words, Shaw was different. Vegetables suited his nature. 'A man of my spiritual intensity does not eat corpses,' he said; the point being that John was not a baptist because he ate locusts and wild honey: he ate locusts and wild honey because he was a baptist. In effect a vegetarian diet, by increasing a man's energy, emphasizes his leading characteristics. A criminal does not become a christian by eating potatoes and cabbages ; he becomes more criminal, just as Shaw became more Shavian ; and as there are far more criminals than christians in the world, there is a strong argument in favour of carnivorous feeding.

Shaw had plenty of energy before he became a vegetarian, and novel-writing did not absorb it. With the object of using it up and of steadying his nerves he joined a debating club in 1879 with a friend, James Lecky, who had aroused his interest in Phonetics. This club was known as The Zetetical Society, and the members discussed evolution, atheism, and so on, their gods being John Stuart Mill, Charles Darwin, Herbert Spencer, Huxley, Malthus and Ingersoll. During one of the debates, which were held at the Woman's Protective and Provident League in Great Queen Street, Shaw made his first plunge into controversy : he rose to his feet, shaking with nerves, and heard himself speaking. He was pitifully self-conscious and felt certain when he sat down that he had made a fool of himself. There and then he resolved that he would never miss a meeting and never miss an opportunity to speak, however much he might suffer in the process. He kept this resolution, suffering agonies before his turn came, and wondering whether anyone could hear the painful hammering of his heart. He was so nervous that he could not read his notes, so apprehensive that he could not remember them. He assumed that everyone realized his condition, was amazed when asked to take the chair at his third appearance, guessed that he had been able to cover his fright with an outward semblance of calm, but gave the imposture away to the secretary when his hand shook so much that he could scarcely sign the minutes of the last meeting.

Having loosened his tongue, he made more use of it than those who had never been tongue-tied. He joined every debating group, every argumentative circle, to which he could obtain an introduction. He attended public meetings and lectures, of which there were then dozens every Sunday, and always spoke in the debate. He likened himself to 'an officer afflicted with cowardice, who takes every opportunity of going under fire to get over it and learn his business.' For a year or two he did this without any further object than to increase his personal capacity by acquiring a new and very necessary public accomplishment. Not until his haunting of public meetings brought him under the spell of Henry George's eloquence did he rise from the benches as a casual debater to the platform as a desperately earnest propagandist of socialism.

It was in September 1882 that Shaw, aged 26, wandered into the Memorial Hall, Farringdon Street, and found Henry George preaching Land Nationalization and the Single Tax. The eloquent American meant to set England on fire with his proposals. He certainly set Shaw on fire. 'Until I heard George that night I had been chiefly interested, as an atheist, in the conflict between science and religion. George switched me over to economics. I became very excited over his *Progress and Poverty,* which I got for sixpence, so excited that I brought the subject up at a meeting of Hyndman's Democratic Federation, where I was told that no one was qualified to discuss the question until he had read Karl Marx. Off I went to the British Museum, where I read *Das Kapital* in Deville's French translation—it had not then been done into English. That was the turning-point in my career. Marx was a revelation. His abstract economics, I discovered later, were wrong, but he rent the veil. He opened my eyes to the facts of history and civilization, gave me an entirely fresh conception of the universe, provided me with a purpose and a mission in life. I went back to the Democratic Federation, burning with the new zeal, full of the new gospel, only to find that not a soul there except Hyndman and myself had read a word of Marx.'

As one who has not read Karl Marx, who has no intention of reading Karl Marx, and who would far rather die than read Karl Marx, it is a little difficult for me to trace the precise nature of his influence on Shaw ; but that *Das Kapital* had a tremendous effect on him there is not the smallest doubt ; it converted him to socialism, turned him into a revolutionary writer, made him a political agitator, changed his outlook, directed his energy, influenced his art, gave him a religion, and, as he claimed, made a man of him. I asked him once whether he had admired any big figure in the political world of his time. 'No one, after reading Karl Marx, can be imposed on by Gladstones and such,' he answered. So we had better leave it at that.

From the moment that Shaw imbibed the gospel according to Saint Marx he began to preach it on every possible occasion, under every sort of condition, though as time went on he corrected the errors in Marx's economic creed and worked out the distinctively British brand of socialism known as Fabianism. For twelve years he spoke on the average three times a week at the street corner, in the market squares, in the parks, in the great provincial and metropolitan town halls, in the City Temple, at the British Association, in the humblest political hole-and-corner assemblies—in short wherever he could get his foot in—and soon found himself in such demand as a principal speaker that he was never at a loss for a platform. It was first come first served with the applicants, however distinguished, however obscure. Not until a long illness disabled him when he was just over forty, and led to his marriage, was this weekly routine of public oratory broken and ended ; but he remained in demand as a public speaker and could finally fill the largest halls and two streets with the overflow. He enjoyed the work as the average man enjoys golf or tennis. In fact it was his exercise and recreation as well as his business in life ; and so he was much happier than the man who spends half his life in searching for means to be happy. 'I first caught the ear of the British public on a cart in Hyde Park to the blaring of brass bands,' he wrote ; which was true in both senses of the phrase, for one of his first open-air attempts was delivered in Hyde Park to three loafers lying on their backs in the grass, one of whom without getting up called out ' 'ear, 'ear,' whenever Shaw paused for breath. Another time in Hyde Park he spoke his best for an hour and a half in the pelting rain to an audience of six policemen, who had been sent to keep an eye on him. The water poured steadily down their capes all the time. He tried to convert them, though he held that the only people who could not be made to listen were those who were paid to do it.

Twice Shaw was nearly landed in prison. Any policeman can charge a speaker at a street meeting with 'obstruction' by deposing that if any pedestrian or vehicle had wished to exercise his right to pass over the particular spot on which the speaker or his audience happened to be standing, their presence would have obstructed him. William Morris's comment on this when his Socialist League fell a victim to it was that such obstruction was a crime which we were all committing from the cradle to the grave. Experienced and sensible policemen take care not to make trouble by interfering with meetings held at customary pitches where they do no harm. But from time to time a fanatically pious constable, to whom secularist street corner propaganda is intolerable blasphemy, or a zealously conservative one, to whom socialist denunciations of capitalism are rank sedition, will bring a charge of obstruction. Then the fat is in the fire. The law is on the constable's side; and when he has rashly set it in motion it cannot be stopped, however heartily the authorities may execrate the excessive zeal of their agent. The Society holding the meeting raises the banner of Free Speech and continues to meet in defiance of the law. The speakers are arrested week after week. Crowds assemble to see the fun, and create a very real obstruction. The magistrates have to sentence the speakers to pay fines or go to prison. To keep the agitation going volunteer speakers willing to go to prison for Free Speech have to be found. When the agitation becomes formidable, the religious bodies, whose gospel meetings and collections in the open air keep them in existence, wake up to the danger. The Government, quite willing to suppress atheists and socialists, suddenly finds itself up against the might of the Free Churches and the Church Army. The Home Secretary hastily orders the police to capitulate. The street corner triumphs; and everything goes on as before for some years, when some raw police recruit starts the process all over again with the same result. Shaw volunteered for prison martyrdom in two Free Speech conflicts with the police: 'As my luck would have it, on the first occasion the police capitulated on the eve of the day on which I had undertaken to address a prohibited meeting and refuse to pay a fine; and on the second a rival organization put up a rival martyr, and, on a division, carried his election over my head, to my great relief.'

Having conquered the nervousness which agonized his first efforts as a public speaker, Shaw became a thoroughly efficient mob orator, knowing all the objections and courting the interruptions for which he had replies ready, crushing or conciliatory as the circumstances might demand. He never gave the expected answer if he could help it, as he soon learnt Robert Owen's lesson 'Never argue: repeat your assertion.' But he took good care to make the repetition sound like a good argument.

Hecklers were an easy prey for him because, as they always used the same arguments and asked the same questions, all he had to do was to draw on his stock of effective replies, and deliver them with an air of impromptu spontaneity, having already made use of them about a hundred times. He was an adept at stealing his opponent's thunder

70

instead of contradicting him. When the capitalists tried to raise a scare by declaring that socialism would drive capital out of the country, he made the most of the danger by citing the enormous foreign investments of the capitalists and challenging them to name a single socialist proposal that would not have the effect of keeping capital at home. The scare was dropped like a hot potato. When an opponent brought off an effective stroke of eloquence, he promptly tacked a bit of his own on to it. A good example of this trick occurred in the course of a public debate with the leader of the Freethinkers, G. W. Foote. 'Let truth and falsehood grapple, whichever be truth and whichever be false-hood,' perorated Foote: 'for, as grand old John Milton said, "Whoever knew truth put to the worse in a free and open encounter?"' Following the applause, Shaw rose and said: 'I do not know, gentlemen, what a free and open encounter might bring about; but if John Milton asks me whoever saw truth put to shame in such an encounter with falsehood as it has a chance of having in the present state of society, then I reply to John Milton that George Bernard Shaw has seen it put to shame very often!'

Once, on Barmouth sands, where the orators of the Fabian Summer School were competing with the Pierrots, a lady put a question to Shaw which completely floored him. It was 'If I had £50 under socialism what would become of it?' He was about to own that this apparently simple and prac-tical question was unanswerable when a man shouted another question. Shaw answered it at sufficient length to make the audience forget the lady. He apologized to her privately after-wards. He treasured the question as one equally applicable to all the 'isms'.

It was all done for The Cause: he never took a penny for a speech in his life, though he often handed round the hat for his party. He challenged questioning on any subject. At an election meeting in Dover a local journalist took up the challenge. 'How much do they pay you for this job?' he shouted. Instantly Shaw offered to sell him his emoluments for £5. The man hesitated. Shaw reduced his offer to £4. Still the man said nothing, and the dutch-auction went on: One pound? No bid. Five shillings? No? Half-a-crown? A shilling? Sixpence? But the man would not even give a penny for the speaker's fees, and Shaw remained master of the situation.

The provincial Sunday Societies offered the usual ten guineas on condition that he kept off religion and politics. He thanked them, regretted that he never lectured on any other subjects, and always dealt with them in the most controversial manner, but added that his fee was his third class return fare if the ticket cost more than he could afford. The reply was always the same. On those terms he might lecture to them every Sunday in the year, as they felt sure that his good taste would make all subjects innocuous in his hands. This was not mere disinterestedness on Shaw's part: quite the contrary. It was for The Cause. He knew that those who pay the piper call the tune; and as he meant to call the tune himself he took care to be both paymaster and piper.

What troubled Shaw was not opposition, but the lack of it. The stormy meetings at which he had to keep up a running fight of repartee with a noisy and hostile audience were very exceptional. The rule was a full house, warm applause, unanimous consent. But nothing else happened. 'This,' said Shaw, 'is a little too like Christianity. They listen piously: they agree: they follow me about from place to place to hear me say it again and again. But nothing comes of it.' Such applause did not elate him: he hardly noticed it. Once he felt ashamed when, returning from a successful meeting in Battersea, he found himself walking behind a respectable middle-aged man and wife. They had heard the lecture and were discussing it. 'When I hear a man able to talk like that,' said the man, 'I feel like a worm.' Shaw felt like the meanest of impostors. It was at this meeting that someone rose and said, 'I don't agree (on such and such a point) with Bernard Shaw. Of course I know that he can argue me down and smash me to pieces; but does that matter to me? I have my principles still.' Shaw praised this view; warned the audience not to be taken in by clever speechifying; and confessed that he could put up just as good a platform case for the most reactionary toryism as for socialism.

Shaw learnt some useful lessons as an agitator. It is not easy now to imagine the atmosphere and circumstances in which he began. In the early eighties one of the periodic slumps produced by competitive over-production had thrown masses of workers out of employment. In those days there was no dole, no unemployment insurance. Unemployment meant starvation; and the Registrar-General's returns always contained a column in which deaths were frankly registered under that head. It was easy to organize meetings and processions of angry and hungry men, for whom no revolutionary gospel was too strong. Even the *agents provocateurs*—the 'coppers' narks' with their stock proposals to set fire to London in five places (one of them was always the Tower)—seemed reasonable to their audiences When Morris said that as far as he could see the only hope for the workers was in revolution, nobody thought that revolution was impossible. Even the churches were invaded by 'church parades' of the unemployed, organized by Hyndman's Democratic Federation. Shaw attended one at St John's Church in the Waterloo Road, where the Bishop of London, astounded at having his sermon interrupted by the cries of questioning and dissent proper to noisy election meetings, stopped, and said, "This is a Church." It was an exciting time for young socialists; and Shaw felt himself being carried along by a fierce popular movement full of the promise of change. The London west end clubs had their windows broken. Matters seemed to be at boiling point when suddenly trade revived, and once more there was thirty shillings a week for everybody who wanted a job.

The effect was magical. The incipient revolution vanished in a night. The hot gospellers, who had had crowds of many hundreds listening eagerly to their insurrectionary eloquence, found themselves with audiences of ten, mostly 'comrades'. The dreaded revolutionary Democratic Federation became as negligible as the three tailors of Tooley Street; and the respectable constitutional wire-pulling Fabian Society stole the front of the stage from it. The lesson was not lost on Shaw. 'You can buy any revolution off for thirty bob a week,' he concluded. The capitalists took the hint. Hence the dole.

Meanwhile, another change was taking place which led to his dropping his regular weekly activity as a platform and street corner preacher. The little societies calling themselves Leagues and Federations, with their local branches, mostly in debt over rent, subsisted on precarious penny-a-week subscriptions and coppers collected in their hats at their meetings, with scraps of profit from the sale of *Justice* (Hyndman's paper), *The Commonweal* (Morris's paper), and sundry tracts. For some years they provided Shaw with the audiences he wanted: weekly wage-earning working-class folk in the open air or in cheap little halls where the seats

73

were all free. But they sooner or later made the discovery that when Shaw was the attraction not only were the little halls too small for the audience, but that most of these were not heroes of the horny hand and the fustian coat (an obsolete description formerly current among the Chartists) but people who were quite well able to pay half-crowns and even five shillings for reserved seats. Shaw, to his disgust, found himself speaking in fashionable concert halls to rows of ladies in cart-wheel hats, escorted by very obvious young city men and professionals, with shopkeepers in the shilling seats and the proletariat uncomfortable and shy in the free seats (if any) at the back. Some of the local societies lived for years on a single Shaw lecture. He had to drop the poorer workers, and put forward a new set of arguments for socialism in the middle classes. But he had no fancy for being used in this fashion as a money-maker. He threw his whole budget of applications for lectures into the waste paper basket; and from that time (about 1898) abandoned his weekly pulpiteering, thenceforth speaking only on special occasions like any other politician.

THE FABIAN SOCIETY

For some time Shaw was at a loss for an organization to work with for his new faith. There was a Georgite Society called the England Land Restoration League. He joined it, but resigned on finding that it regarded capital as sacred and was definitely anti-Marx. The Guild of St Matthew, a Christian Socialist body formed and dominated by Stewart Headlam, a 'silenced' Church of England clergyman, made much of Shaw as a lecturer, but was not open to him as a member because, to put it mildly, he did not accept the Thirty-Nine Articles, and told the Christian Socialist parsons that they were chaplains of a pirate ship. There seemed nothing for it but the Democratic Federation, formed and dominated by Henry Mayers Hyndman, a Victorian cosmopolitan gentleman (the type, never numerous, is now extinct) who had been converted by Karl Marx in person, but had been disowned by him because he had published a Marxist pamphlet entitled *England For All* in which he had used Marx's arguments without mentioning his name. Marx was then known as a very wicked man who in 1861 had organized a subversive and dreaded conspiracy called 'The International', and in 1871 had actually defended the Commune of Paris, which, as every English politician thought he knew, was an organization of female incendiaries called *petroleuses*. In 1881 Hyndman had taken up the Marxist running with his Democratic Federation, which subsequently committed itself up to the hilt by changing its name to the Social-Democratic Federation, and professed to be a revived International. Hyndman's culture, imposing presence,[1] eloquence, literary skill, and sincere conviction, backed by the insurgent unemployed, made such an impression that the members of the Federation were estimated in the capitalist press at 4000, when 40 would have been much nearer the mark, just as the 1861 Red International was credited with fabulous revenues when its annual income amounted in fact to eighteen shillings.

Shaw was on the point of joining *faute de mieux* when a tract entitled 'Why are the Many Poor?' fell into his hands. It was published by the Fabian Society, the name of which appealed to him, for it suggested an educated group. He got the Society's address from the tract and turned up at their next meeting.

The Fabian Society, like so many organizations devoted to human welfare, began with a higher conception of man than was warranted by the facts. A Scottish Rosminian philosopher named Thomas Davidson, having spent many years of travel in Europe and America, presumably with his eyes shut, came to London and founded a Fellowship of the New Life. An original member was Havelock Ellis, and in view of the fact that it included a future British Prime Minister, J. Ramsay MacDonald, there is little need to add that its object was to reconstruct society 'in accordance with the highest moral possibilities'. Its method was to found a colony of superior persons somewhere in South Amer-

[1] Shaw told me that 'the description of Tanner in *Man and Superman* is a pen portrait of the external Hyndman'.

75

ica and realize those possibilities as an example to the rest of mankind. Certain members, notably Hubert Bland, were not convinced that Brazil was a more eligible field than England for the highest moral possibilities; and some of them knew that dozens of such colonies had been founded in America and had either been absorbed by capitalism like the Mormons and the Oneida Perfectionists or else been failures. With a less elevated view of human nature, they split the David-sonian circle and seceded from the Fellowship as a new body calling itself the Fabian Society, which explained its name on the title-page of its first tract: 'For the right moment you must wait, as Fabius did most patiently, when warring against Hannibal, though many censured his delays; but when the time comes you must strike hard, as Fabius did, or your waiting will be in vain and fruitless.' There is no historical authority for this quotation. It was invented *ad hoc* by Frank Podmore, an eminent member of the Society for Psychical Research; and it was followed by the uncom-promising statement that 'the Fabian Society consists of Socialists'.

In 1884 the Fabians were meeting in the house of E. R. Pease, also a Psychical Researcher. He later became the Society's secretary and historian; and his address was 17 Osnaburgh Street, N.W. Shaw lived just opposite. His first appearance at No. 17 was on May 16th of that year ('This meeting was made memorable by the first appearance of Bernard Shaw,' he wrote in pencil beneath the minutes at a later date); and he joined the Society, then about eight months old, on September 5th, being elected to its Executive Committee the following January. The Fabians, thoughtful, clever, full of social compunction, well read, critical, deadly serious but able to laugh at themselves on occasion, and all converted and avowed socialists, were exactly the people whom he could work with and lead. Their second tract, unmis-takably written by Shaw, could have come from no other socialist society. The language and humour of it are not those of 'the many poor'. They are 'educated' and bourgeois to the last degree. Witness the following extracts:

'Under existing circumstances, wealth cannot be enjoyed without dishonour, or foregone without misery.'

'The most striking result of our present system of farming out the national land and capital to private individuals has been the division of society into hostile classes, with large appetites and no dinners at one extreme, and large dinners and no appetites at the other.'

'The practice of entrusting the land of the nation to private persons in the hope that they will make the best of it has been discredited by the consistency with which they have made the worst of it.'

'The established Government has no more right to call itself the State than the smoke of London has to call itself the weather.'

But Shaw knew that the Fabian Society, to follow up Marx, must drop literary fireworks, and engage in a fact and figure war; and for that he had already picked his man.

Among the debaters at the Zetetical Society's meetings in 1879 was a broad-browed fellow of 21, short, with small hands and feet, whose features reminded people of Napoleon III. He was a Millite in politics, an upper division civil servant by profession, and his name was Sidney Webb. 'The most fortunate thing that ever happened to me was finding Sidney Webb at a debating society and forcing my acquaintance on him,' Shaw told me recently. 'Each of us was the other's complement. He knew everything that I didn't know; and I knew everything he didn't know, which was precious little. He was competent: I was incompetent. He was English: I was Irish. He was politically and administratively experienced: I was a novice. He was extraordinarily able and quite respectable: I was a futile Bohemian. He was an indefatigable investigator: I was an intuitive guesser. I was an artist and a metaphysician: to him I was in both capacities a freak, but a clever, amusing and curable one. Above all he was simple, single and solid, always true to himself: I was dramatic and as selflessly able to adopt five hundred different characters as Shakespear or Molière, Dumas or Dickens. He was at all points the very collaborator I needed; and I just grabbed him.'

This Macaulayish string of contrasts might be continued to show that the advantage was not all on one side. Shaw's theatrical qualities made for publicity. They advertised themselves so effectively that he has been described too often as an inveterate self-advertiser. Webb's qualities had no limelight on them. He could not or would not get into the papers: Shaw could not keep out of them. Webb could not dramatize himself and act the part; but Shaw could dramatize him even for himself. It was impossible to be close to Shaw without getting into his spotlight. Nobody could say of Webb what Shaw said of himself in those early days when he had done nothing but perpetrate novels which no publisher would touch: that his reputation grew with every failure. Later on he boasted of having fifteen reputations. Webb had none until he had one and one only, founded on a prodigious output of unique achievement. But Shaw foresaw the achievement and anticipated it by inventing the great Sidney Webb before the great Sidney actually existed. He had panache enough for two; and panache was something to which Webb could not stoop, it being unnatural to him, whilst it was part of Shaw's nature, just as buffoonery was part of his nature. Webb had sufficient sense of humour; but he was not a bit of a buffoon; and when comic relief was needed to ease a situation Shaw was useful to him.

On the whole they made an ideal couple. And there was the bond between them that united all the Fabians: social compunction, and the craze which Tolstoy's children called *Weltverbesserungswahn*: the desire to make a better job of human society than capitalism was making of it.

Shaw told Webb about his discovery of the Fabian Society. They perambulated Whitehall together for hours on several successive days, their discussions ranging over—whatever such discussions range over. Webb was easily persuaded to attend a meeting of the new Society. Like Shaw he felt at home there, and joined.

The new recruit was a human encyclopaedia. His career as a young man had been dotted with prizes, exhibitions and scholarships. With an ability to take in the entire contents of a printed page at a glance and to photograph it indelibly on his mind, with a memory that retained every single thing that interested him, and a mental orderliness so precise that no addition to his vast stores of knowledge could produce congestion, it was hardly surprising that he should have been first in every examination for which he had entered. As he was never bored, had a passion for knowledge and an ardour for service, the Fabian Society was as glad to receive him as he was glad to be received. The fact that he could not use his hands, being unable to deal with a tyre puncture or drive in a nail, was quite unimportant. The fact that he could use his head, deal with an argument and drive in a fact, was all-important.

He and Sydney Olivier were resident clerks in the Colonial Office, and Olivier, a handsome revolutionary aristocrat, was also roped in. The Society, run so far by Bland and his talented and attractive wife Edith Nesbit, was soon dominated by four men: Shaw, Webb, Olivier, and the latter's college friend, Graham Wallas. These four became members of the Hampstead Historic Club, which had grown out of a Marxist reading circle, wherein 'a young Russian lady used to read out "Capital" in French to us until we began to quarrel'. Shaw, Webb and Olivier always walked together to Hampstead and back to attend the meetings of the Club which were held fortnightly, at first in private houses and later at the Hampstead Private Subscription Library.[1] There they discussed the economic evolution of Europe and analysed all the gospels of social reform from More to Marx and Proudhon: there too they worked out what came to be known as Fabian Socialism. All the members were on 'quite ruthless terms' with one another, though it took them some time to get used to Shaw, whose method of settling any friction that arose was to betray the confidences of all the parties to it openly in a wildly exaggerated form, the effect of which was that the grievance was forgotten in the general reprobation and denial of Shaw's revelations. Probably his peculiar appearance helped him as a humorist: his complexion was dead white, his cheek and chin were decorated with orange patches of whisker, and someone likened his face to 'an unskilfully poached egg'.

The original Fabians were all over the shop as philosophical anarchists, barricade insurrectionists, atheists, currency cranks, Christian Socialists, single taxers, converts made by reading various books, including the second part of Goethe's *Faust*, and the Utopians; but Bland, a typical suburban Tory Democrat, had led the Fabian secession as a parliamentarian; and when he was reinforced by the Shaw-Webb contingent the flood tide of constitutionalism became irresistible, and all compromises with the anarchists were abandoned. Shaw, when he was asked how long it would take to get socialism into working order, no longer replied that 'a fortnight would be ample for the purpose'. He hammered in the warning that

[1] In Stanley House, High Street, Hampstead.

the insurrectionist notion that capitalism in full swing on Monday could be changed into socialism in full swing on Wednesday by storming the Bastille on Tuesday was a delusion and a snare. Against the catastrophic and apocalyptic hot gospellers he appealed to the Fabian sense of humour, which effectively prevented them from taking themselves too seriously. In fact the Shavian levity, irreverence, and occasional outbreaks of sheer nonsense, alienated many passionate reformers, who thought 'the drawing-room socialists' callous and cynical; but the new leaders were glad to be rid of them, and they went.

Shaw's first reported public speech was made in January 1885 before the Industrial Remuneration Conference, at which the Fabian Society, represented by two delegates, emerged from its drawing-room obscurity. Shaw opened his address in the following manner: 'It is the desire of the President that nothing shall be said that might give pain to particular classes. I am about to refer to a modern class, burglars, and if there is a burglar present I beg him to believe that I cast no reflection upon his profession. I am not unmindful of his great skill and enterprise; his risks, so much greater than those of the most speculative capitalist, extending as they do to risk of liberty and life, or of his abstinence; nor do I overlook his value to the community as an employer on a large scale, in view of the criminal lawyers, policemen, turnkeys, gaol-builders and sometimes hangmen that owe their livelihoods to his daring undertakings. . . . I hope any shareholders and landlords who may be present will accept my assurance that I have no more desire to hurt their feelings than to give pain to burglars: I merely wish to point out that all three inflict on the community an injury of precisely the same nature.'

BLOODY SUNDAY IN TRAFALGAR
SQUARE

TRADE DEPRESSION culminated in the years 1886-7. The unemployed got out of hand. The Democratic Federation made the most of their opportunity and on a February day in '86 marched with the workless from Trafalgar Square to Hyde Park, passing through Pall Mall whilst the police, through a mistake which cost their chief his place, were waiting for them elsewhere. The rich men gathered in their club windows to see the fun. The unemployed, fancying that they were being mocked, broke the club windows, and went on to the Park, where they held their meeting. Some of the stragglers looted a shop or two and held up the carriage of a lady by the Achilles Statue. Hyndman, John Burns and two others were arrested and tried as ringleaders; but by good luck the foreman of the jury was an imposing Christian Socialist in whose hands the rest were sheep; and the four were acquitted. This beginning of insurrection grew until it centred on a supposed right to hold meetings in Trafalgar Square. The cry of Free Speech rallied all the workers to the socialists. A grand mass meeting in the Square was announced for the 13th November, 1887, thereafter to be known as Bloody Sunday. The police prohibited it under an Act which empowered them to 'regulate' processions. Shaw read the Act (nobody else gave tuppence for it), and contended that a power to regulate was not only not a power to prohibit, but was a statutory recognition of the right to process. On this he held that the prohibition should be ignored and the right asserted. It was characteristic of the legal streak in him that he should put himself technically in order in this way. He accordingly took part in the procession and was one of the speakers on Clerkenwell Green, where the northern contingents assembled for the march.

With him were William Morris and Annie Besant, whom he had persuaded to join the Fabians. She was easily the greatest public speaker in London, and possibly in Europe. No audience could resist her eloquence. Shaw spoke on the Green, exhorting the people to be orderly but resolute as they marched in their irresistible numbers to the Square. Shelley's 'Ye are many; they are few' was still able to delude him.

It never did again. Morris went to a place at the head of the procession. Shaw took a more modest place just where he stood. Mrs Besant asked Shaw, to whom she was deeply attached, whether she might march with him. He objected strongly to her running the risk of a conflict with the police, and said that if she insisted she must look after herself; but her aggressive courage and determination were not to be denied; and the two marched together.

All went well until they reached Bloomsbury. There, in the open space at the west end of High Holborn, they were astonished to meet the forward section of the procession in frantic flight, pursued and bludgeoned by a handful of police.

It is possible that Mrs Besant may have expected Shaw to do something heroic. But there was nothing heroic to be done, except not to run away. All he said to her was, 'You must keep out of this,' whereupon she immediately vanished and made for the Square. He saw no more of her that day. A man rushed up to him crying, 'Shaw: give us a lead. What are we to do?' 'Nothing,' said Shaw. 'Let every man get to the Square as best he can.'

The mêlée was surrounded by a fringe of sightseers. Shaw joined them and saw the last incident of the rout: an elderly middle-class Jew putting up his fists and tackling a young policeman who knocked him out with his baton. That was the end of the battle on the north; and Shaw made his way to the Square unmolested.

The southern procession made a tougher fight of it. It made its way across Westminster Bridge and into Whitehall, where the old soldiers in it heard the barrack bugles sounding the Boot and Saddle. When Shaw reached the Square the cavalry had just arrived and were riding round it in threes with a grey-suited civilian on the middle horse in the first three. He was the magistrate, and was there to read the Riot Act before the troops charged.

He did not read it. The police had finished the job; and for the rest of the afternoon the soldiers rode slowly round and the civilians walked round, shepherded by groups of police walking four abreast. Shaw was walking in this manner with Stuart Glennie; a Scottish philosophic historian known to the irreverent young Fabians as The Majestic Ruin, and having as his mission the propagation of the news that the world had gone definitely wrong in the direction of Christianity in 6000 B.C. and must be led back to the path of reason before any political reform could be of use. Shaw was pushed against the nearest file of four policemen: he apologized and they were civil. Then something like the beginning of a panic occurred: a few started to run; but Stuart Glennie, suddenly becoming a militant Highlander, cried 'Stand, stand', which so astonished everyone that the incident came to nothing.

Before Shaw's arrival another Scotsman had become the hero of the day. Cunninghame Graham and John Burns, then known as 'the man with the red flag', they two alone, had not only marched into the Square, but when they were opposed by the multitudinous forces of the Crown, proceeded to force their way and actually put up a fight before they were overwhelmed. Graham, tall and picturesque, was 'knocked about sufficiently to enable him to spend his six weeks' imprisonment in the comparative luxury of the prison infirmary. Burns, a shorter man, was not hurt. Shaw asked him afterwards how he had managed. 'I started fibbing about with my fists over my head,' said John, 'and it kept their sticks off me.' Probably the police discriminated. Burns as an orator was a spellbinder, and very popular.

The anger of the people with the police was extreme: they would not even be knocked up in the morning by them for some time. Even the thoughtful middle-class Edward Carpenter, the poet of *Towards Democracy*, forgot himself so far as to write of 'that crawling thing, a policeman'. He had been manhandled in the affray. Working-class London thirsted for vengeance; and Mrs Besant, indomitable, would not hear of defeat. They must return to the Square next Sunday and show that they too could use the big stick. Meanwhile she performed prodigies that put the men to shame. She organized the defence of the prisoners, collected funds, enlisted the support of the *Pall Mall Gazette* under the editorship of W. T. Stead, dashed into the police courts and stormed the witness stands, haranguing the astonished magistrates and overawing the police, and ran a paper called *The Link* to make pennies and publicity.

Shaw failed her completely. His first step was to write to Morris urging him to use all his influence to prevent any more hopeless street fighting. But Morris had already learnt his lesson. He had seen the first onslaught of the police and the utter rout that followed, and never thereafter cherished any Shelleyan illusions about the invincibility of the unarmed, unorganized, undisciplined millions. The issue between returning to the Square or not was decided at a meeting opened by Mrs Besant, who moved a resolution to return to the Square and continue the fight to the bitter end in a speech of such magnificence that the applause shook the building. A stranger would have said that any one opposing her would have found himself in a perilous and despised minority of one.

G. W. Foote, between whom and Annie there was no love lost, rose and moved the amendment. 'What are you asked to do?' he said. 'You are to go back to the Square, where you are to contemplate the police. And the police are to contemplate you.' He was listened to in dead silence, the audience hating him. Shaw rose and seconded the amendment. He had not studied the history of the Paris Commune in vain. He explained in detail what a fight with the authorities meant. It meant, as they had just found to their cost, barricades. Barricades did not build themselves. They had to be made from overthrown buses and drays, and piles of furniture taken from the neighbouring houses and shops. Were they seriously prepared for all that? And the fire they had to face was not that of old-fashioned muzzle-loading muskets but of the new machine guns that sprayed bullets at the rate of 250 per minute. He, too, was listened to in uneasy silence. The audience loathed him. But they knew that the two cowardly defeatists were right. When the division was counted it was Mrs Besant who was in a minority of one, deserted even by her seconder.

Shaw had the satisfaction, such as it was, of carrying his legal point against the Government. In the prosecution of Graham and Burns the Crown dropped the Act under which the procession had been prohibited and proceeded under another statute. Finally it turned out that there was no right of meeting in Trafalgar Square, as it was legally the property of the Commissioner of Woods and Forests. By that time every one was sick of the subject, and glad to have this excuse to be rid of it.

The last incident in the affair delighted Shaw. Leaving a

Fabian meeting in the hall which is now the New Gallery, at which he had delivered a lecture, he found himself close behind Cunninghame Graham. A man said to Graham 'Who is this Bernard Shaw anyhow? What has he done?' 'He was the first man to run away from Trafalgar Square on Bloody Sunday,' replied Graham with perfect gravity.

Shaw told the story to everyone except Graham. His comment was: 'He flattered me. I had not even that much sense.'

He was sometimes reminded by the more pugnacious comrades that mobs do not always run away: history records their victories. How about the French Revolution for instance? On such occasions Shaw would reply by asserting that the French monarchy could have crushed the revolution if it had not been foolish enough to believe that Marie Antoinette's gambling debts were more important than the wages of its soldiers, who did not fraternize with the mob until their pay was four years in arrear. The pay of a London police constable in 1887 was only twenty-four shillings a week; but it was never in arrear, and the pension was certain. Consequently, though the constables were all proletarians, not one of them ever fraternized with the people or hesitated to knock them about or do their worst against them in the magistrates' courts. It was true, he admitted, that though insurgent mobs always began by running away, the defeat and humiliation started in them a sullen rage which, if the provocation continued long enough, made them murderous, destructive, even fearless. He had felt the beginnings of it in himself. But what good would their destructiveness do them? If they murdered the police they destroyed their own security. If they burnt houses they would burn palaces and mansions instead of burning their own wretched slums. If they demolished Buckingham Palace and the Houses of Parliament, and massacred the royal family and all the M.P.s, they would only be at the mercy of the first competent and ambitious adventurer who, in the character of a saviour of society, should collect enough money to hire, train and equip an army and pay it regularly, like Cromwell, Napoleon, and the rest. No: God save the people from themselves!

There was an important moral for Shaw in the whole affair, insignificant as it now seems. A day or two after it occurred a man who had listened to Shaw's speech on Clerkenwell Green stopped him in the street and reproached him bitterly for leading poor men into a defeat from which he could do nothing to rescue them. He had no defence against this accusation. He had never thought of himself as a leader nor felt the responsibilities of one. Like all the nineteenth century democrats he had assumed that 'the people' had leadership, initiative and political wisdom in themselves, and that he was a person of no importance except as a mouthpiece of socialism. He now recalled how in the middle of the rout the other man had come to him with his 'Shaw: give us a lead. Tell us what to do,' only to unmask his utter futility, and the helplessness of the crowd. It was not a pleasant awakening; but it was a salutary one. He broke away at once from Lincoln's formula of government of the people by the people for the people. Government of the people for the people by all means: that was democracy; and he was still a democrat. But government *by* the people, no. 'Let them try writing their own plays first,' he said. 'Government is not everybody's job. It is a highly skilled vocation.' He might have called himself a Tory Democrat had not that title been just taken by Lord Randolph Churchill, who was not a socialist. Shaw was convinced that democracy without socialism is nonsense. He would not even have the people choose their leaders. 'They always choose the second best,' he said. Later on he was to propose a scheme for allowing the people to choose, but restricting their choice to the competent.

This hardening of his realism was the work of the police batons in Trafalgar Square.

THE UPSHOT AND END OF
FABIANISM

THE FABIANS were not in their element in the street fighting. It was not their job. As orators many of them eschewed the street pitches, though Shaw liked the open air because the ventilation was good and 'you cannot have an unwilling audience'. They were, said Shaw, 'overlooked in the excitements of the unemployed agitation'. Besides, it called for martyrdom, which he described as 'the only way in which a man can become famous without ability'. They knew 'that property does not hesitate to shoot, and that now, as always, the unsuccessful revolutionist may expect calúmny, perjury, cruelty, judicial and military massacre without mercy'; and they fully intended to be at the State end of the gun if there was going to be any shooting. Their philosophy expressed their personal feelings. 'I am a thinker, not a fighter,' said Shaw. 'When the shooting begins I shall get under the bed, and not emerge until we come to real constructive business'; a remark which shows that he was also an optimist, because his revolutionary friends would have begun constructive business by taking out their revolvers and if necessary looking for him under every bed in the kingdom.

At any rate, by 1887 the Fabians had got rid of their anarchists and other irreconcilables, if indeed any such had ever existed. Henceforth their methods were to be constitutional: they aimed at making socialism genteel. Thus Shaw would carefully explain that the principles of communism had already been accepted in England: 'Most people will tell you that communism is known only in this country as a visionary project advocated by a handful of amiable cranks. Then they will stroll off across the common bridge, along the common embankment, by the light of the common gas lamp shining alike on the just and the unjust, up the common street, and into the common Trafalgar Square, where, on the smallest hint on their part that communism is to be tolerated for an instant in a civilized country, they will be handily bludgeoned by the common policeman, and haled off to the common gaol. When you suggest to these people that the application of communism to the bread supply is only an extension, involving no new 'principle, of its application to street lighting, they are bewildered.'

The Fabian method of permeating every kind of organization with socialist principles was certainly more successful than the intransigent policy of the Democratic Federation, which wanted to enlist the proletariat under its banner, start a revolt and then run the show itself. 'I could not carry on,' said Hyndman, 'unless I expected the revolution at ten o'clock next Monday morning.' Though Shaw himself embraced the Fabian method, recognizing that England was not ripe for revolution, he was sceptical as to its ultimate sufficiency and rather despised the slow and cowardly alternative. Addressing the Economic Section of the British Association at Bath in September '88, he said what he felt: 'I venture to claim your respect for those enthusiasts who still refuse to believe that millions of their fellow creatures must be left to sweat and suffer in hopeless toil and degradation whilst parliaments and vestries grudgingly muddle and grope towards paltry instalments of betterment. The right is so clear, the wrong so intolerable, the gospel so convincing, that it seems to them that it *must* be possible to enlist the whole body of workers— soldiers, policemen, and all—under the banner of brotherhood and equality ; and at one great stroke to set Justice on her rightful throne. Unfortunately, such an army of light is no more to be gathered from the human product of nineteenth century civilization than grapes are to be gathered from thistles. But if we feel glad of that impossibility ; if we feel relieved that the change is to be slow enough to avert personal risk to ourselves ; if we feel anything less than acute disappointment and bitter humiliation at the discovery that there is yet between us and the promised land a wilderness in which many must perish miserably of want and despair: then I submit to you that our institutions have corrupted us to the most dastardly degree of selfishness.'

Although the Fabian was the only socialist group to achieve

any sort of success, its membership was always small, starting with about forty and never greatly exceeding two thousand. And although it became as respectable as the Church of England, its early life was nomadic ; for it was kicked out of Anderton's Hotel, Fleet Street, after a tumultuous debate with the anti-state communists of the Socialist League, and expelled from the Dr Williams Library in Gordon Square, where a Christian Socialist clergyman, who held that the first of the Thirty-Nine Articles of the Church of England is in fact a declaration of Atheism, alluded to Queen Victoria as 'a vulgar old German lady'.

The Society was at a loss for a meeting place until Olivier, who had a vein of sardonic humour, bethought him of Willis's Rooms, at that time a superselect chamber used for conferences by Cabinet Ministers, scientific bigwigs and bishops, where the chairman's table was draped in crimson and furnished with silver candlesticks and two footmen in liveries of Spanish splendour were at his service. And all this for one guinea! Olivier's unmistakably aristocratic appearance, and the learned title 'Fabian Society', opened Willis's doors without question ; and the Society met there until Willis's discovered that the eighteenth century had long expired, and made a final bid for existence as a very expensive restaurant.

A printed report of one of the meetings in Willis's Rooms has come down to us. It is headed 'Butchered to make a Fabian holiday'. The liberal politicians of that day included three hybrids called liberal-imperialists: Herbert Asquith, Edward Grey and Richard Haldane. Haldane was by way of being a bit of a philosopher, as he had a fancy for collecting odd religions and utopian sects, and was tolerant and very good-natured. He was easily induced to accept an invitation from this queer Fabian Society to lecture to them across the crimson table-cloth and the silver candlesticks, and perhaps knock a little common sense into them. To his amazement he found himself in the hands of a group, not of utopian faddists, but of practised debaters and economists who knew the liberal creed inside and out, and had been tearing it to pieces for years. Shaw went for him ; Webb went for him ; Graham Wallas finally murdered him in the best speech of the debate. Haldane took it in perfect good-humour. His physical build was much broader and stouter than any of the Fabians ; and when he said, 'If I am attacked by Mr Webb I shall shelter myself behind the burly form of Mr Bernard Shaw,' the evening passed off with a laugh. Haldane lived not only to be Lord Chancellor but the first to join the new Labour Party.

If Asquith could have been persuaded to come to Willis's Rooms the history of England might have been different. But he would stoop no lower than the Working Men's College, which he patronized to the extent of delivering there a most lucid exposition of university *laisser-faire* economics. The Fabians were in the audience, waiting for him, licking their lips. At the end of his lecture he turned to leave the platform when Shaw rose and asked whether he was not going to discuss the question. Asquith, annoyed at what he regarded as a piece of impudence, said 'Certainly not,' and went out. It was the mistake of his life, as the Fabians were the only socialists who could have opened his eyes as they opened Haldane's. At least that was the Fabian view; and the fact that Asquith, in spite of his perfect lucidity, finally passed out of date, gives weight to it.

By that time the governing class, expert in taking up labour advocates, republican municipal socialists, and others who showed enough serious ability or popularity to be dangerous, and petting them until they were thoroughly tamed, was turning its attention to the Fabians. At Beatrice Webb's dinners in Grosvenor Road, where the food was wholesome but the drink wineless, the only question being 'Beer or whisky, sir?' Cabinet Ministers, backed by peeresses, were to be met. Shaw was actually heard of at dinners of the great, at which he amused himself by telling the great ladies allotted to be taken in by him and shepherded through the mazes of precedence, to go in when they pleased as 'nobody goes in before me'.

But at last the politicians found out that instead of making use of the Webbs the Webbs were making use of them and landing them in all sorts of measures which were part of the drive towards socialism which they abhorred and meant to resist with all their might. The Fabians were definitely and decisively dropped by fashionable society.

Shaw's independent vogue as a playwright and a literary celebrity grew to such an extent that every theatrical success of his produced its group of invitations from lion-hunting hostesses; but he was less polite in this department than in politics and would not be a diner-out nor a society clown. Some of his lady friends had titles but he happened to like them personally. His formula was 'I am not proud. Let them all come if they have any business with me.' An ambassador and a royal prince who ventured into Adelphi Terrace on these terms were as well received as commoners; and the viscountesses, if not exactly six a penny there, contributed some fast friends to his list.

I shall make no attempt to sum up the achievements of the Fabian Society, or even to judge whether Shaw's share in it was worth while. Enough to say that the plutocrats were grateful. Noting the Webb-shavian demonstration of what could be done by state organization, they changed Fabian Socialism into State Capitalism, while retaining their property rights in the sources of production. Thus the work done by the Fabians effectually reinforced capitalistic commerce and finance in the west. What was called socialism did however become the state policy and religion in Russia, and Webb (then Baron Passfield) tried to induce his countrymen to learn from the U.S.S.R. instead of vituperating her leaders. It was uphill work.

But in one respect Shaw's share in Fabian propaganda was certainly worth while. He was singular among his fellow-workers in his aestheticism; and if it had not been for him *Fabian Essays,* published in December 1889, would have looked as unattractive as a Government blue book. It might have been called 'Socialism Without Tears'. It was certainly Socialism Without Marx, as it discarded his value theory and made neither mention nor use of his dialectic. Shaw spared no pains over the editing and artistic appearance of the volume. He got Walter Crane to design the cover, and when the printer did not come up to scratch he wrote a letter to the reader of the Newcastle-on-Tyne publisher who had brought out *Cashel Byron's Profession:*

'Personally I have lost faith in you, because I believe the artistic sense to be the true basis of moral rectitude: and a more horrible offence against Art than what you have put above Crane's design on the cover of the Essays, has never been perpetrated even in Newcastle. I reject your handbill with disdain, with rage, with contumelious epithets. You must re-set the authors' names in the same type as "price one shilling", and the words "Essays by" must on no account be in a different type. To aim at having as many different founts as possible on the same sheet is worthy of a jobbing printer at work on a bookmaker's handbill; but that you who turn out your Camelot title-pages so well should condescend to such barbarism simply destroys my faith in human nature. . . .

Of the hellish ugliness of the block of letterpress headed "What the Press says," I cannot trust myself to write, lest I be betrayed into intemperance of language. . . . Some time ago you mentioned something about changing the cover of *Cashel Byron*, and introducing a design of some pugilistic kind. This is to give you formal notice that if you do anything of the sort without first submitting the cover to me, I will have your heart's blood.

> 'Yours respectfully,
>
> 'G. BERNARD SHAW.'

A ROMANCE

BY SOME CURIOUS MISCHANCE professional reformers nearly always dislike one another and quarrel. This may be due to the fact that only violently self-assertive men try to meddle with the universe, or that reformers have a higher opinion of themselves than other men, or that they are too much alike and hate to see their defects in another. Whatever the cause, the idealists who fight for the under-dog always end by fighting one another for the place of upper-dog. Hyndman quarrelled with everyone in the Democratic Federation who attempted to behave like Hyndman and at last he was left with a crowd of humble disciples but only one Hyndman.

An early member of the Democratic Federation was a very famous man, William Morris, who before he became a socialist had made a public reputation as the poet of *The Earthly Paradise,* and a more esoteric one as an artist-craftsman, his furniture, designs and wallpapers having revolutionized many domestic interiors. Kelmscott House in Hammersmith, and the unaltered medieval manor house in Gloucestershire, with the famous Merton factory, made a Mecca to which artists resorted from all parts of Great Britain, from France and America. Nothing in the two houses was 'interesting'; everything was either handsome or useful, and mostly both; but there were no mirrors, which perhaps explains why the owner was so like a Viking, his hair and beard, though right and proper to him, suggesting that combs, brushes and razors were equally outside his scheme. His suit and shirt were blue; and Andrew Lang wrote of the shock of meeting his favourite poet and mistaking him for a ship's purser. When he read his own verses he shifted his weight rhythmically from one foot to the other like an elephant. He was subject to attacks of gout and to a form of epilepsy which exploded in bursts of temper that left him shattered and apologetic. At public meetings, whenever a speaker irritated him, he would tug single hairs from his moustache, growling very audibly 'Damfool! damfool!'

At first he was humbly ready to accept the leadership of Hyndman or any other leader who could lead, having no conceit of himself in that capacity. Hyndman, a brilliantly clever and self-assured man who always took his own leadership as a matter of course, accepted this position without a doubt as to its propriety. Morris was not in the least self-assured, and nobody would ever have dreamt of calling him brilliantly clever. He was simply what is known as a great man ; but as he was entirely and incorruptibly aesthetic, his greatness was appreciated only by cultivated people who knew him intimately. He sought Shaw's acquaintance because he was amused by the opening chapters of *An Unsocial Socialist,* Shaw's fifth and last novel. Rejected by all the publishers it appeared in a monthly magazine called *To-Day* which Henry Hyde Champion, Hyndman's lieutenant, had just purchased.

Shaw, himself a born aesthete, saw at a glance that Hyndman, in assuming the leadership of Morris, was biting off more than he could chew. He rapidly found favour with Morris, was invited to Kelmscott House, and became a frequent and favourite Fabian lecturer in the little meeting hall, a converted coach house attached to it, and still (1940) apparently unchanged. He was not at all surprised when Hyndman and Morris presently quarrelled, not only because he held that Englishmen always quarrel, but because the two were both the sons of rich parents and, having had no personal experience of poverty to tame them, had all the petulance which this exceptional condition produces in strong personalities.

The occasion of the quarrel was of no consequence ; but there was a terrific flare-up in the committee of the Federation ; and Morris, though commanding a majority, marched his men away to form the Socialist League, which for some years spent his money and wore out his patience by its continual quarrelling, its hopeless ignorance and incompetence, and its pretence on democratic principles to equality with him. When he left it, the League died instantly ; and Morris, admitting that he supposed socialism must come in Sidney Webb's way, reformed his few sensible disciples as the quiet little Hammersmith Socialist Society, which eschewed parliamentary politics and delivered the pure milk of the communist gospel on Sundays until his death in 1896. He did not live to see the Russian question and the Irish question, after years of talk in parliaments and dumas, settled at last by blood and iron as if Sidney Webb had never been born.

As to Hyndman, he changed his Democratic Federation into a Social-Democratic Federation; and though it never federated anything or anybody he kept it together as a little band of Marxists (really devoted Hyndmanists) until Marxist Russia backed out of the Four Years War at Brest Litovsk, when his British patriotism blazed forth in a furious denunciation of Lenin as the arch-scoundrel of the universe, whilst Shaw and Webb stood fast and said, 'Lenin's side is our side.' Shaw was wrong, however, in saying of Hyndman 'He will never die: he will survive us all.' He did die, but not until, at the age of 80, he married a young woman who, after his death, committed suicide because she could not bear to live without him.

Thus, in the last years of the nineteenth century, avowed self-conscious English socialism was represented by four bodies: Hyndman's Federation, Morris's League, Headlam's Guild of St Matthew, and the Fabian Society. The first three did not survive their founders, and never had any effect in Downing Street. The Fabian Society, when its old leaders practically retired from its counsels, was swamped in the Labour Party it had itself created. Webb had outgrown its resources and had side-tracked it by founding the London School of Economics and *The New Statesman*. However, its annual series of public lectures, at which Shaw was the star speaker until his retirement from the platform 'through advancing years' in 1933, kept it to the fore as a propagandist centre; and though Shaw's retirement led to some financial difficulties which obliged it for the first time to modify its subscription terms, which had before been entirely voluntary (with no rule except Pay What You Can Afford, and, if you stopped paying anything for too long, being struck off the membership roll), the Society began to show signs of renewed life in younger hands. By then Shaw was too old to take any part in the revival.

These lectures taught Shaw another lesson. They were of his best; and his platform colleagues were highly selected, able, and masters of their subjects. They attempted to solve all the current problems, to give all the relevant facts, and to suggest all the feasible remedies. They were sufficiently well known to have every claim on public attention; and the country enjoyed what it called a Free Press. Yet not one of their lectures was reported; and as they all spoke extempore from a few notes that went into the waste paper basket at the end of the evening, the lectures got no farther than the audience, whilst in next day's newspapers the platitudes and worn-out party slogans of every parliamentary careerist were quoted as if they were oracles. Shaw's lectures covered a whole scheme of modern religion, psychology, and philosophy. Not a word of them would now remain were it not that the substance of them is recorded in the prefaces which appeared in his volumes of plays. It is true that syllabuses of the lectures were printed in the prospectuses; but Shaw never in his lectures made the smallest reference to the syllabus (Why say things twice over? he said when remonstrated with) just as his prefaces made no reference to the plays and were entirely independent of them. Freedom of the Press, he said, means freedom to Suppress. At last the Society fell back on written lectures and had them published; but this was after Shaw's retirement.

So much for the socialist societies with whom Shaw's public destiny was concerned. Let us return to his private relations with Morris. He was surprised, not disagreeably, to learn that Morris had found one of his novels readable. (Morris could read anything except Wordsworth.) When they met they got on very well together; for the Federation had not yet split, nor had the Fabian Society yet developed the policy which later on threw it into conflict with the Socialist League. Shaw's economic lucidity and fertility in illustration were exactly what Morris needed to complement his art doctrine, and to dispose of the Philistine opponents to whom art meant nothing that was not eccentric and disreputable. In their private inter-course socialism was never mentioned. Men who could talk to one another about the stained glass and twelfth-century statues in Chartres, and the churches of San Zeno in Verona and San Ambrogio in Milan, were not likely to squabble about Marx's theory of value. Shaw knew the value, not only of the twelfth-century statues, but of William Morris, and readily understood his medieval and Chaucerian side, which seemed merely affected and ridiculous to the Philistines.

His conquest of Morris was completed by the Nordau incident. Nordau was being accepted as a great authority on art by the presses of America and Europe, mainly because he denounced all the leaders in modern art, including Morris, as morbid degenerates ; and Shaw knew as well as Morris that, as he put it, Nordau did not know enough about art to know that he knew nothing about it. When Shaw, in a review of Nordau's *Entartung* (Degeneration) which is now entitled *The Sanity of Art,* cut Nordau into bits, a job over which Morris would have simply lost his temper, Morris was boundlessly delighted. His rule that it is waste of time to talk to a man who does not know what he is talking about now operated fully in Shaw's favour ; and thenceforth Shaw was admitted as an adept and given access to the stores of knowledge which Morris, apparently a petulant and violently prejudiced veteran who would tolerate nothing later than Chaucer and Van Eyck except the pictures of his friend Burne-Jones, had up his sleeve all the time.

These good relations were not disturbed when the Fabian Society, setting out to capture parliament, had to fight pitched battles with the anti-state communists of the Socialist League. I asked Shaw fifty years later how he had managed to get round this clash. Shaw replied that between the two there was no clash. 'The truth is,' he wrote, 'that though Morris died long before the foundation of the Labour Party in Parliament, and its acceptance as the official Opposition and finally as the Government under a socialist Prime Minister, had brought the Fabian policy to the test of experience and smashed it, Morris knew by instinct that the Westminster Parliament would sterilize the socialists, corrupt or seduce them, and change them from intransigent revolutionists into intriguers for Cabinet rank as Yesmen and bunk merchants in the service of the governing class, claiming all the time that they represented the interests of the proletariat. I was twenty-two years younger than Morris, and had not then gone into the history and nature of the Westminster Party system. Besides, democracy as an ideal with a big D still influenced Parliament very strongly. Its realization by adult suffrage was nearly thirty years off ; the Irish question was still apparently making its way to constitutional settlement through Parliament under Parnell ; the question of communism in Russia did not yet exist ; and the dictatorships which now fill the European landscape were undreamt of. As to Ramsay MacDonald, he was known then only as a very intransigent socialist whose chances of getting into parliament were infinitesimal. Yet I had my share of Morris's instinct. I knew and preached that the

Marxian Class War was not really a class war, as half the proletariat was parasitic on property and was keeping the whole south of England as conservative as Bond Street or Oxford University; but I knew that it was none the less a war; and I very much doubted whether capitalism would give in without bloodshed. However, I also saw that the parliamentary path had to be explored to its utmost limits—to breaking point in fact—before any one would listen to more revolutionary proposals; and anyhow the Leaguers were impossible in committee as compared to the Fabians; so when they attacked us I fought them for all I was worth. But all the time I was much more Morrisian than they were or ever could be; and so our private relations were never spoilt. And then, you see, I am not an easy man to quarrel with even when my opponents hate me, which Morris certainly didn't. Not to mention, by the way, that I was much less trying to Mrs Morris as a socialist intruder in her beautiful house, than some of the comrades who occasionally pushed in and did not know when to go away.'

And so the Morris family enjoyed Shaw's wit and common sense and did not limit him to the Sunday evenings in the coach house. Morris even found a name for his idiosyncrasy. 'The word Shavian,' Shaw told me, 'began when William Morris found in a medieval MS. by one Shaw the marginal comment "Sic Shavius, sed inepte". It provided a much needed adjective; for Shawian is obviously impossible and unbearable.'

They made a curious pair when debating at the Kelmscott House meetings, which all the thoughtful young men of the day attended. One particularly thoughtful young man named H. G. Wells described Shaw as 'a raw, aggressive Dubliner', lean, 'with a thin flame-coloured beard beneath his white illuminated face'. Another referred to Morris's odd way of thrusting his hands behind his back as if afraid he might be tempted to assault Shaw. Someone said that Shaw was a mixture of Mephistopheles and Jesus Christ. Certainly his christian charity could be absolutely diabolic, for when Morris was growling savagely Shaw was smiling sweetly.

Mrs Morris took no part in Morris's socialist activities, and never appeared at the suppers which followed the Sunday evening lectures. Jenny Morris, the elder of two daughters, also remained aloof and invisible; and Shaw did not meet her until she became a lifelong invalid through the inherited epilepsy which in Morris himself produced nothing worse than explosions of temper. But May Morris, the younger daughter, took up her father's socialism and appeared as hostess at the suppers. Her beauty, and her wonderful Rossettian dressing, made a grave and mystical impression on Shaw, quite unlike the ordinary sexual entanglements in which he was involved elsewhere. When they were both old people she asked him for a chapter on Morris for the last volume of her edition of his collected works. He complied ; and into this chapter he interpolated, for her private perusal, the story of their early love affair. Her first comment was 'Really, Shaw!' but on further consideration and consultation with her friends she resolved to publish it on the very sensible ground that, as it would be told some day, it had better be done by a master pen from first-hand knowledge than dug up by some literary ghoul as a titbit of biographical scandal. From this extraordinary document I quote his account of the affair :

'One Sunday evening after lecturing and supping, I was on the threshold of the Hammersmith house when I turned to make my farewell, and at this moment she came from the dining-room into the hall. I looked at her, rejoicing in her lovely dress and lovely self ; and she looked at me very carefully and quite deliberately made a gesture of assent with her eyes. I was immediately conscious that a Mystic Betrothal was registered in heaven, to be fulfilled when all the material obstacles should melt away, and my own position rescued from the squalors of my poverty and unsuccess ; for subconsciously I had no doubt of my rank as a man of genius. Less reasonably I had no doubt that she, too, knew her own value, a knowledge that involved a knowledge of everyone else's. I did not think it necessary to say anything. To engage her in any way—to go to Morris and announce that I was taking advantage of the access granted to me as comrade-Communist to commit his beautiful daughter to a desperately insolvent marriage, did not occur to me as a socially possible proceeding. It did not occur to me even that fidelity to the Mystic Betrothal need interfere with the ordinary course of my relations with other women. I made no sign at all: I had no doubt that the thing was written on the skies for both of us. So nothing happened except that the round of Socialist agitation went on and brought us together from time to time as before.'

Shaw's reference to his poverty is misleading. He was no longer seedy and impecunious. He was earning at least £400 a year as a journalist-critic; and some of his experiments with the new Jaeger clothing were dazzling. But he knew that to anyone brought up in Morris's House Beautiful life on £400 a year would have seemed squalid. So he goes on to say, 'If I could not immediately marry the beautiful daughter, I could all the more light-heartedly indulge my sense of her beauty.' His light-heartedness soon met its deserts:

'Suddenly, to my utter stupefaction, and I suspect to that of Morris also, the beautiful daughter married one of the comrades.'

The happy man was Henry Halliday Sparling, a socialist *litterateur* for whom Morris had found some employment on the Kelmscott Press.

'This was perfectly natural, and entirely my own fault for taking the Mystical Betrothal for granted; but I regarded it, and still regard it in spite of all reason, as the most monstrous breach of faith in the history of romance. The comrade was even less eligible than I; for he was no better off financially; and, though he could not be expected to know this, his possibilities of future eminence were more limited. But he was a convinced Socialist and regular speaker for the Cause, and his character was blameless; so there was nothing to be done but accept the situation. Apparently my limitless imagination had deceived me in the matter of the Mystical Betrothal.

'But it had not deceived me in the least. For it presently happened that the overwork and irregular habits of the combination of continual propaganda with professional artistic activities, which killed Morris ten years before his time, reduced me to a condition in which I needed rest and change very pressingly. The young couple thereupon invited me to stay with them for awhile. I accepted, and so found myself most blessedly resting and content in their house, which had the Morris charm; for she had inherited her father's sense of beauty and also his literary faculty in a form curiously Miltonic as well as Morrisian. Everything went well for a time in that *ménage à trois*. She was glad to have me in the house; and he was glad to have me because I kept her in good humor and produced a cuisine that no mere husband could elicit. It was probably the happiest passage in our three lives.

'But the violated Betrothal was avenging itself. It made me from the first centre of the household; and when I had quite recovered and there was no longer any excuse for staying unless I proposed to do so permanently and parasitically, her legal marriage dissolved as all illusions do; and the mystic marriage asserted itself irresistibly. I had to consummate it or vanish.'

Sparling's account of the *ménage à trois* virtually confirmed Shaw's though, knowing nothing of the mystical betrothal, he thought Shaw had betrayed him. He told Holbrook Jackson (from whom I had it) that after completely captivating his wife Shaw suddenly disappeared, leaving behind him a desolated female who might have been an iceberg so far as her future relations with her husband went.

Shaw goes further into the pros and cons of the situation:

'When it became evident that the Betrothal would not suffer this to be an innocent arrangement the case became complicated. To begin with, the legal husband was a friend whose conduct towards me had always been irreproachable. To be welcomed in his house and then steal his wife was revolting to my sense of honor and socially inexcusable; for though I was as extreme a freethinker on sexual and religious questions as any sane human being could be, I was not the dupe of the Bohemian Anarchism that is very common in socialist and literary circles. I knew that a scandal would damage both of us and damage The Cause as well. It seems easy in view of my later position to have sat down together as three friends and arranged a divorce; but at that time I could not afford to marry and I was by no means sure that he could afford to be divorced. Besides, I hated the idea of a prosaic and even mercenary marriage: that, somehow or other, was not on the plane of the Mystic Betrothal. The more I reasoned about the situation the worse it was doomed to appear. So I did not argue about it. I vanished.

'Then the vengeance of the violated Betrothal consummated itself in a transport of tragedy and comedy. For the husband vanished too! The *ménage* which had prospered so pleasantly as a *ménage à trois* proved intolerable as a *ménage à deux*. This marriage, which all the mystic powers had forbidden from the first, went to pieces when the unlucky pair no longer had me between them. Of the particulars of the rupture I know nothing; but in the upshot he fled to the Continent and eventually submitted chivalrously to being divorced as the guilty party, though the alternative was technically arranged for him. If I recollect aright he married again, this time I hope more suitably, and lived as happily as he might until his death, which came sooner than an actuary would have predicted.

'The beautiful one abolished him root and branch, resuming her famous maiden name, and, for all I could prove, abolished me too. But I know better.

'Forty years or so later I was motoring one day through Gloster when the spell of Kelmscott Manor came upon me. I turned off the high road from Lechlade to Oxford and soon found myself in the church with the tempting candlesticks that nobody ever stole, and at the grave of William and Jane Morris, which I had never seen before. I was soon on the garden flagway to the ancient door of the Manor House. It was opened by a young lady whose aspect terrified me. She was obviously strong enough to take me by the scruff of the neck, and pitch me neck and crop out of the curtilage; and she looked as if for two pins she would do it as she demanded sternly who I was. I named myself apologetically. The Mystical Betrothal, strong as ever, operated at once, though the athletic lady (Miss Lobb) could have known nothing about it. She threw the door wide open as if I belonged to the place and had been away for ten minutes or so; and presently the beautiful daughter and I, now harmless old folks, met again as if nothing had happened.'

Though the romance is thus permitted to close with an episode more appropriate to a play by Barrie than a polemic by Shaw, the reality, as always, had a Shakespearean quality.

Sparling's second marriage, to a Scotswoman, was an extremely happy one; yet, such is the nature of man, he never forgave Shaw for making it possible, believing, in spite of the sequel, that Shaw had been deliberately disloyal to him. Few romantic readers will forgive Shaw for being so loyal. The lady can hardly have done so.

May Morris died at Kelmscott on October 16th, 1938. After reading the account of their relationship, I asked Shaw whether at their last meeting she had referred to the Mystic Betrothal. 'No, no,' said Shaw; 'besides, my wife was present.'

By that time May had lost the beauty that had made Burne-Jones paint her as the lovely girl on his *Golden Stairs*. It may have disappeared with her happiness; for someone who knew her well when she was about forty described her to me as tall and masculine, with a moustache. Shaw, prompted by me, remembered the moustache, but maintained that it made a pair of lines so decorative that they would have enchanted the finest Maori tattoo-artist. 'Otherwise,' he said, 'do you suppose she would have kept them when the faintest touch of a razor would have removed them? Hang it all, man, it was neither a Victor Emmanuel nor a Chaplin-Hitler!'

THE READING ROOM

THE SHAWS remained at 13 Victoria Grove for about four years after the arrival of G.B.S. in London ; then, realizing at last that they could not afford a whole house, they went to a first floor in Fitzroy Street, No. 37, where they lodged in the last house on the left before reaching Fitzroy Square, going north ; after that they moved to a second floor in 36 Osnaburgh Street, now St Catherine's Home, but for a brief space, as Shaw said, St Bernard's Home. Finally Mrs Shaw and her son occupied the two top floors of No. 29 Fitzroy Square, her daughter being then on the stage and frequently touring the provinces in the light operas which preceded the musical comedies. Shaw has left a grossly exaggerated picture of Fitzroy Square in the early nineties :

'I live, when I am at home, in a London square which is in a state of transition from the Russell Square private house stage to the Soho or Golden Square stage of letting for all sorts of purposes. There are a couple of clubs, with "bars" and social musical evenings, not unrelieved by occasional clog dances audible a quarter of a mile off. There is a residence for the staff of a monster emporium which employs several talented tenors behind its counters. There is a volunteer headquarters in which the band practises on the first floors whilst the combatants train themselves for the thousand yards range by shooting through Morris tubes in the area. Yet I have sat at work on a summer evening, with every window in the square open and all these resources in full blast, and found myself less disturbed than I have been by a single private pianoforte, of the sort that the British householder thinks "brilliant", played by a female with no music in her whole composition, simply getting up an "accomplishment" either to satisfy her own vanity or to obey the orders of her misguided mother. Now if such females had spinets to play on instead of pianos, I should probably not hear them. Again, take the fiddle. It is a good sign, no doubt, that it is so much more generally practised than it used to be. But it is a terribly powerful instrument in neighbourhoods where only millionaires can afford to live in detached houses.'

A great deal of Shaw's time during the first nine years of his life in London was spent in the reading room of the British Museum, which was his study and library as the Fabian Executive was his university. He worked there daily, to the moral and intellectual benefit of 'not less than a million people'—his own cautious estimate of those who had seen his plays and read his articles.

No place in the world holds such an assortment of oddities as may be seen at any hour of the day in the reading room of the British Museum, where the revolutionist who would reform the world with dynamite sits next to the scholar who would faint at the sight of a split infinitive, where the man who would murder anyone for love jostles the man who could not commit adultery for money, where the priest who is compiling the life of a saint raises a pyramid of books between himself and the fellow who is enjoying a treatise on pornography. It is an extraordinary gathering, composed chiefly of budding Lenins and broken Samuel Butlers, but containing every sort of curiosity, from earnest seekers to heavy sleepers Though not a fruitful mart for money-makers, racketeers may graduate there with advantage, as an experience of Shaw's proved:

'I remember once, at a time when I made daily use of the reading room of the British Museum—a magnificent communistic institution— I gave a £2 copying job to a man whose respectable poverty would have moved a heart of stone: an ex-schoolmaster, whose qualifications were out of date, and who, through no particular fault of his own, had drifted at last into the reading room as less literate men drift into Salvation Army Shelters. He was a sober, well-spoken, well-conducted, altogether unobjectionable man, really fond of reading, and eminently eligible for a good turn of the kind I did him. His first step in the matter was to obtain from me an advance of five shillings; his next, to sublet the commission to another person in similar circumstances for one pound fifteen, and so get it entirely off his mind and return to his favorite books. This second, or rather third party, however, required an advance from my acquaintance of one-and-sixpence, nominally to buy paper, really to go out for a drink, having obtained which, he handed over the contract to a fourth party, who was willing to do it for one pound thirteen and sixpence. Speculation raged for a day or two as the job was passed on ; and it reached bottom at last in the hands of the least sober copyist in the room, who actually did the work for five shillings, and borrowed endless sixpences from me from that time to the day of her death, which each sixpence probably accelerated to the extent of fourpence, and staved off to the extent of twopence.'

Shaw learnt a lot about human nature as well as from books in the reading room, and people who think some of his more fantastic creations far-fetched would revise their opinions after spending a few months in the Shavian library. Three of the curious characters who frequented the reading room in his day appealed to some of his main interests and deserve a place in his biography. The first was Thomas Tyler:

'Throughout the eighties at least, and probably for some years before, the British Museum reading room was used daily by a gentleman of such astonishing and crushing ugliness that no one who had once seen him could ever thereafter forget him. He was of fair complexion, rather golden red than sandy ; aged between forty-five and sixty ; and dressed in frock coat and tall hat of presentable but never new appearance. His figure was rectangular, waistless, neckless, ankleless, of middle height, looking shortish because, though he was not particularly stout, there was nothing slender about him. His ugliness was not unamiable: it was accidental, external, excrescential. Attached to his face from the left ear to the point of his chin was a monstrous goitre, which hung down to his collar bone, and was very inadequately balanced by a smaller one on his right eyelid. Nature's malice was so overdone in his case that it somehow failed to produce the effect of repulsion it seemed to have aimed at. When you first met Thomas Tyler you could think of nothing else but whether surgery could really do nothing for him. But after a very brief acquaintance you never thought of his disfigurements at all, and talked to him as you might to Romeo or Lovelace ; only, so many people, especially women, would not risk the preliminary ordeal, that he remained a man apart and a bachelor all his days. I am not to be frightened or prejudiced by a tumor; and I struck up a cordial acquaintance with him, in the course of which he kept me pretty closely on the track of his work at the Museum, in which I was then, like himself, a daily reader.'

Tyler was a specialist in pessimism, translated Ecclesiastes, and wrote a book on Shakespeare's Sonnets, in which he wrongly identified 'Mr W. H.' with the Earl of Pembroke and guessed the 'black mistress' to be Mary Fitton. Shaw reviewed this book, thereby making the world conscious of Tyler's theories.

Another strange character with whom Shaw must have rubbed shoulders in the reading room was Samuel Butler, whose views on evolution put Shaw on the track which led to his own religion; but they did not become acquainted till later. Shaw told me this story of Butler:

'In my early days I was a member of the West Central Branch of the Fabian Society. The Branch consisted of four members: myself, the secretary, the treasurer, and a gentleman who was crazy on the subject of bimetallism. The secretary spent the whole of his spare time in writing to famous men asking them to lecture to the Branch. Some of them, Mr Gladstone for one, were courteous enough to decline the honor; the rest didn't reply. No one ever turned up at the meetings. I myself never turned up. The bimetallist had a clear run for his money.

'Then one day my eye lit on the announcement that Samuel Butler was going to lecture to the Branch on the *Odyssey*, the feminine authorship of which he was then bent on proving. I felt sure he hadn't the smallest idea of what he had let himself in for. His audience would consist at the outside of six persons, one of whom would almost certainly embroil him in a discussion on bimetallism. So I wrote to everyone I could think of, begging them to come and if possible gag the bimetallist. I extracted promises from about forty, quite twenty of whom turned up; so Butler addressed the largest gathering the Branch had ever been able to muster.

'Half way through the lecture there was a pause while Butler consulted his notes. The opportunity was too good to be missed. Up got the bimetallist. But as I had prepared for this, he sat down again under the persuasion of two strong men posted on either side of him. Butler's lecture was so interesting and his manner so engaging that after one more abortive attempt the bimetallist forgot the currency question and borrowed my copy of the *Odyssey*, which he returned at a later date with a number of marginal notes on bimetallism. At the meeting I opened the debate by agreeing enthusiastically that Nausicaa wrote the *Odyssey*. Nobody dissented: and Butler went home satisfied and rather gratified.'

As an influence on his career, apart from his soul, the third character was of infinitely greater consequence to Shaw. This was William Archer, who was to become famous as a dramatic critic and as the English translator of Ibsen's plays. Archer was a tall good-looking Scot, whose expression of austere reserve quite concealed his emotions. People thought he had no sentiment and no humour, and his friendship with Shaw was founded on the latter's quick realization that he had a large allotment of both. Some dozen years after they had formed a friendship in the reading room Shaw wrote of Archer: 'He has the reputation of being inflexible, impartial, rather cold but scrupulously just, and entirely incorruptible. I believe this impression is produced by his high cheek-bones, the ascetic outline of his chin and jaw, and his habit of wearing a collar which gives his head the appearance of being wedged by the neck into a jampot.' Towards the close of his career as a dramatic critic Archer was able to boast that he had 'slept through the greater part of the world's drama' from Sophocles to Shaw, which partly explains why he was always so happy in the theatre and why he and Shaw, though temperamentally poles apart, remained such good friends.

Archer made the first move. He frequently found himself sitting next to a fellow of about his own age whose appearance was as peculiar as his tastes. A man with a pallid skin and bright red hair and beard, who read Marx's *Das Kapital* in the intervals of studying an orchestral score of Wagner's *Tristan und Isolde*, was strange enough to provoke the interest of a less inquisitive man than Archer. At any rate Shaw's face, combined with his taste, was his fortune, because Archer made his acquaintance and started him on his career as a critic by getting him books to review at two guineas a thousand words for *The Pall Mall Gazette*, then edited by W. T. Stead. This was a godsend to Shaw, who had just been turned down as a book-reviewer for *The St James's Gazette* because the editor, Frederick Greenwood, to whom Hyndman had recommended

Shaw as 'another Heine', was horrified by the indifference to the death of his wife displayed by a character in one of Shaw's novels.

A little later the picture critic of *The World* died and the editor Edmund Yates asked his dramatic critic Archer to double the jobs. Archer was on the point of refusing, for the absurd reason that he knew nothing about painting, when Shaw told him that he would soon learn all that was necessary about pictures by looking at them. So Archer accepted, stipulating that Shaw should go the round of the galleries with him to prevent him from falling asleep. As a result of Shaw's company Archer was able to write 'informed' criticisms of the exhibitions and sent Shaw half the sum he had received for the first batch. Shaw promptly returned the cheque; Archer sent it back; Shaw again refused it, saying: 'No man has a right of property in the ideas of which he is the mouthpiece. . . . If I am to be paid for what I suggested to you, the painters must clearly be paid for what they suggested to me. . . . The devil has presented you with a depraved conception disguised as conscientiousness.' On this Archer threw in his hand and told Yates that the work was really being done by Shaw. Yates saw that the work was what he wanted, and made Shaw art critic to *The World* at fivepence a line, which brought him in rather less than £40 a year; but as at the same time he was being paid for picture criticisms in Annie Besant's magazine *Our Corner,* he was able in his first year's journalism (1885) to earn as much as £112, which was fortunate because in that year his father died and the family ceased to receive £1 a week from Dublin.

It is clear from all this that he lacked ordinary ambition, for he was pushed into all his early jobs by friends, especially Archer; and though he was from the beginning a steady worker, he cared so little for the rewards of hard work that he missed countless opportunities another man would have seized. Moreover, from the outset of his critical career he refused to compromise: 'I have twice had to resign very desirable positions on the critical staff of London papers of first-rate pretension—in one case because I was called upon as a recognized part of my duties to write corrupt puffs of the editor's personal friends, with full liberty, in return, to corruptly puff my own; and in the other, because my sense of style revolted against the interpolation in my articles of sentences written by the proprietor's wife to express her rapturous opinion of artists, unknown to fame and me, who had won her heart by their hospitality.'

He was far from being as good a critic of books and pictures as he afterwards became of music and plays; but he could not help being enlivening and he would have been readable if his subject had been trigonometry. 'If you do not say a thing in an irritating way, you may just as well not say it at all,' he asserted, 'since nobody will trouble themselves about anything that does not trouble them.' His method was 'to find the right thing to say, and then say it with the utmost levity', the real joke being that he was always in earnest. Thus one of his criticisms opened with the phrase: 'During the past month Art has suffered an unusually severe blow at the hands of the Royal Academy by the opening of the annual exhibition at Burlington House.' And another closed with: 'No man has ever seen anything that Millais could not paint, although many men have painted things that he cannot see.' But all we need to know of Shaw as a critic of painting is that he encouraged the movement called Impressionism, championed Whistler, praised Burne-Jones and Madox Brown, drew the line at Goodall, R.A., and declared before cinematography was dreamt of that nearly everything then being done by brush and pencil would one day be done much better by the camera.

Shaw's relations with his early editors were not always harmonious. He started well with W. T. Stead, whose exposure of the White Slave Traffic aroused his enthusiasm to such an extent that he offered to sell copies of *The Pall Mall Gazette* in the streets because the bookstalls had boycotted the paper. But Stead was a puritan who had brooded so intensely on sex that his brain had gone maggoty, sex and sin being in his view synonymous terms. Shaw soon realized that he was a crude stunt journalist, quite incapable of learning anything from experience. He once asked Shaw to support him at a public meeting in Queen's Hall: 'I attended accordingly, only to find that he did not know what a public meeting was (he thought it was just like a prayer meeting), or what public procedure was, or what a chairman was. Treating the assembly as his congregation and nothing else, he rose and said, "Let us utter one great Damn!" Then he burst into hysterical prayer; and I left. He had no suspicion that to invite Catholics, Jews, Agnostics, Hindoos, and so forth to support him at a public meeting, and then treat them to a revivalist orgy, was in any way indelicate or improper.'

110

Never happy unless he was regenerating somebody or something, Stead suddenly decided to regenerate the stage. As actresses were often pretty, he felt sure they must be immoral; so he started going to theatres to see what was what. When Shaw got to hear of Stead's self-imposed task, he exploded: 'What do you mean, you foolish William Stead, by an immoral actress? I will take you into any church you like, and show you gross women who are visibly gorged by every kind of excess, with coarse voices and bloated features, to whom money means unrestrained gluttony and marriage unrestrained sensuality; but against whose characters—whose "purity" as you call it—neither you nor their pastors dare level a rebuke. And I will take you to the theatre and show you women whose work requires a constant physical training, an unblunted nervous sensibility, and a fastidious refinement and self-control which one week of ordinary plutocratic fat-feeding and self-indulgence would wreck, and who anxiously fulfil these requirements; and yet, when you learn that they do not allow their personal relations to be regulated by your gratuitously unnatural and vicious English marriage laws, you will not hesitate to call them "immoral" . . . When you sit in the stalls, think of this, and as the curtain rises and your eyes turn from the stifling grove of fat naked shoulders round you to the decent and refined lady on the stage, humble your bumptious spirit with a new sense of the extreme perversity and wickedness of that uncharitable Philistine bringing-up of yours. Hoping that your mission will end in your own speedy and happy conversion, I am, as ever, your patient mentor, G.B.S.'

Another of Stead's ingenious schemes was to establish world-concord by taking a crowd of geniuses with him on a round of visits to the monarchs of Europe. Shaw, asked by Stead to be one of the geniuses, said that the arrangement should be reversed: the kings, with nothing to do but pay state visits, ought to call on the geniuses, who were already overworked. If such a plan were carried out, Shaw said he would be delighted to receive any monarch Stead cared to bring along and give him all the hints he needed.

Shaw also contributed to *The Scots Observer*, but regarded its editor, W. E. Henley, as 'a tragic example of the combination of imposing powers of expression with nothing important to express'. He had however an uncritical enthusiasm for literature; and in reviewing one of his books Shaw wrote, 'He delights in puerile novels about prize-fighting like *Cashel Byron's Profession.*' Because they shared a liking for the work of Mozart and Berlioz, Henley asked Shaw to write on music for his paper. Shaw admired Wagner, but Henley hated him and wrote passages abusing his music into Shaw's articles. This, added to Henley's constant attacks on the socialists, annoyed Shaw, who stopped reviewing for *The Scots Observer ;* and when Henley wrote to complain, Shaw hurled a thunderbolt at him, denouncing him as the master of his fate, the captain of his soul, whose head was bloody but unbowed, yet whose hat was always being doffed to the police and the upper classes. After which Henley did not ask him for any more articles on music, and was surprised when at the next press day at the Royal Academy Shaw, instead of scowling aloof, hailed him as if they were on the most cordial terms.

Shaw had one more slight disagreement with an editor. H. W. Nevinson was conducting a literary page in *The Daily Chronicle* and asked Shaw to do a column and a half's review of five books on music at the usual terms, which were some pence and an odd halfpenny 'per stick': a superstition from the Chronicle's origin as an obscure local paper dealing with old-world reporters. Now Shaw was a most conscientious trade-unionist. He never underbid a competitor and never lost a chance of raising literary wages. His very indifference to money made him play at being rapacious where needier men dared not risk giving offence to editors and newspaper proprietors. He promptly declared that the word 'stick' (a compositor's measure) meant nothing to him and that his terms were three guineas a column with a minimum of five pounds, incidentally calling *The Daily Chronicle* the Islington Eagle, the City Road Serpent, the Hoxton Harbinger, or anything else he could invent, the *Chronicle* having in fact begun as the *Clerkenwell Times.*

The reply was:

'Dear Sir, I am directed by the editor to inform you that he will see you damned before he gives you more than five pounds for the article in question.'

Shaw continued the correspondence in the same key:

'Dear Sir, Please inform the editor that I will see him and you and the whole *Chronicle* staff boiled in Hell before I will do it for that money.'

Shaw won, as he always did. Again and again the order was

112

given that he was to be struck off the list of contributors and never mentioned in the paper. Again and again Massingham, Henry Norman or Nevinson, who ran the editorial staff, ceased cursing his insolence and came back to him for more.

It must however be remarked that the correspondence just quoted, though apparently reckless, was really carefully tactful in the Shavian manner on both sides. Shaw's maxim was 'Never spare the feelings of touchy people. Hit them bang on the nose, and let them hit back. Then they can't quarrel with you.' This was so successful that his clever friends soon picked it up. Shaw, when he seemed most irresponsible, was generally following out a considered policy. Otherwise his audacities would be—for so apprehensive a man—quite unaccountable.

The first use Shaw made of the income he began to earn in 1885 was to buy a presentable and even startling wardrobe, which included an attire of brown knitted wool, combining jacket, waistcoat and trousers all in one piece. It was the creation of a German doctor named Jaeger, who believed that the world would be a better place and its inhabitants much healthier if all-woollen clothes were universally worn. Shaw felt that there was something to be said for the doctor's belief and made the experiment. He did more. As there was no rush of martyrs for the new faith, he ran the gauntlet of the west end in this remarkable raiment, walking down the length of Tottenham Court Road and then along Oxford Street as far as Marble Arch and back. Men have been lynched for less, but he survived the excursion unscarred. He even went to Hammersmith and let May Morris see him in it. But he took care to provide smart clothes for ordinary non-experimental use, and was thenceforth never again shabby.

WOMEN

'A MAN'S SOCIALISTIC acquisitiveness must be keen enough to make him actually prefer spending two or three nights a week in speaking and debating, or in picking up social information even in the most dingy and scrappy way, to going to the theatre, or dancing or drinking, or even sweethearting, if he is to become a really competent propagandist.'

This remark of Shaw's will explain a good deal in the story of his relationship with women. The fact that they were not of primary importance in his life is balanced by the fact that he often made them of primary importance in his art, the explanation of which is that they always appealed far more to his imagination than to his bodily needs. From boyhood onwards he dreamed of fair women, but there was a strain of feminine fastidiousness in him that frequently prevented him from realizing in the flesh what was ideal in the spirit. Even in the domain of carnal desire, there was an impersonality, an anonymity, about his requirements that showed his longing to lift the physical experience on to a more imaginative plane. He once told Cecil Chesterton, who had asked whether he was a puritan in practice, that the sexual act was to him monstrous and indecent and that he could not understand how any self-respecting man and woman could face each other in the daylight after spending the night together. When St John Ervine, reading *Back to Methuselah,* objected to the wry face made by Eve when the serpent whispers the secret of reproduction to her, Shaw said that what made the God of the Eden legend incredible was His deliberate combination of the reproductive with the excretory organs and consequently of love with shame. Shaw doubted whether children should know who were their parents or the parents be able to identify one another. The most satisfactory method, thought Shaw, would be for a crowd of healthy men and women to meet in the dark, to couple, and then to separate without having seen one another's faces. He pointed out that what actually happens is the maintenance of two distinct classes of women, the one polyandrous and disreputable and the other monogamous and reputable. Men have their fill of polygamy among the polyandrous ones with the certainty that they can hand them over to the police if they become importunate later on. Finally they marry one of the monogamous ones and live happily ever afterwards.

Love, in the sense of a close relationship based on sexual need, played no part in Shaw's life. 'What people call love is impossible except as a joke (and even then one of the two is sure to turn serious) between two strangers meeting accidentally at an inn or in a forest path.' It was the picturesque aspect of the affair that attracted him; the inn and the forest path were the stock settings of the romantic novelist; and there were few moments in his early life when he did not exercise his powers of invention in telling himself stories about women. Thus he came to believe from his own experience that imagined love played a more important part in life than real love, for the imagination beggared reality and personal contact was a poor substitute for the dreams women could so easily evoke. 'The ideal love-affair is one conducted by post,' he assured me: 'My correspondence with Ellen Terry was a wholly satisfactory love-affair. I could have met her at any time; but I did not wish to complicate such a delightful intercourse. She got tired of five husbands; but she never got tired of me. My relations with Mrs Patrick Campbell were as innocent as those of King Magnus with Orinthia in *The Apple Cart*. She had worn out two husbands; but her last letter to me, written immediately before her death, began "Dear, dear Joey." '

Being highly imaginative he was extremely susceptible to feminine beauty and charm, especially when they were conveyed to him through the medium of art. He fell in love with Ellen Terry as an actress, not as a woman; and he first caught sight of May Morris against a very effective background. He was not altogether aware of this, because in a letter about a dancer named Aurelia Pertoldi he wrote: 'I fell head over ears in love with her on the stage, but off it I found I had no use for her, thus reversing my usual practice, which is to be proof against all seductions of the footlights, but susceptible to the unpainted private woman.' This illusion was due to the indifference he had felt, as a professional critic, to the allure

115

of pretty but commonplace actresses. That it was an illusion is proved by his letter to Alma Murray (Mrs Alfred Forman) who played in the first production of *Arms and The Man*: 'I shall not now accept your invitation to call and talk the part over, because whenever any woman gives me the pleasure your playing to-night did, I cannot help falling violently in love with her; and I can no longer support the spectacle of Forman's domestic happiness.' The last sentence was merely Shaw's blarney, which he exercised quite irresponsibly on every woman with whom he flirted, and he flirted with nearly every woman. It was both his safeguard and the expression of his romanticism. But it sometimes had a devastating effect on the women, who were differently constituted and not so easily satisfied.

His conquests were numerous. One notable victim was Annie Besant, the finest platform orator of her generation, whose enthusiastic humourless nature was utterly unlike his. She had as many gods as she had enthusiasms, and each god was immediately and totally eclipsed when the next one came along. People who knew her when she was propagating atheism under the influence of Bradlaugh and evolution under Edward Aveling's were amazed a little later to find her propagating socialism under the influence of Shaw and staggered not long after to find her propagating theosophy under the influence of Madame Blavatsky. Each god and each cause were completely forgotten when superseded by another deity and another belief.

When first they met Annie Besant took a strong dislike to Shaw, largely on account of his levity. Then, in the spring of '85, he became an object of Besant hagiolatry. When it was announced that he was to lecture on socialism to the Dialectical Society he was warned that she would make mincemeat of him. 'Such was her power as an orator,' Shaw told me, 'that if she asserted that "aye violet is not aye rose" and then thrillingly challenged the world in her contralto voice to contradict that profundity if they dared, all her listeners believed that they had been converted from thinking the opposite.' At the Dialectical Society Shaw resigned himself to the inevitable, and fired off his speech as best he could. But when he sat down, she did not get up; and the opposition was led by someone else, who was promptly cut to bits by Annie Besant. Everyone gasped; Shaw gasped; and when at the conclusion of the meeting she asked him to nominate her for election to the Fabian Society, he gasped again.

She invited him to spend an evening at her house in Avenue Road, now demolished, where they played piano-duets. To please him with her playing in the duets she practised alone like a schoolgirl, and always played the right notes coldly and accurately at a moderate speed while he played wrong ones with a fire that she continually frustrated. She serialized his novels in her magazine *Our Corner,* appointed him art critic, and when she offended its secularist subscribers (Bradlaugh's old Guard) by embracing socialism and it ceased to pay its way, she paid for his contributions out of her private account until he found her out and removed himself from the pay list, padding the paper with his unpublished novels as he had before padded *To-Day.* They were constantly on the platform together ; and he walked home with her, carrying the handbag that never quitted her, always complaining of its weight and defeating her indignant attempts to capture it from him until she at last guessed that his unmanly conduct was part of a puzzling side of him of which she had no comprehension.

That side was his incorrigible comedy. Of that she had absolutely none. It puzzled and provoked her. She could not give it an audience and what is comedy without an audience? Like Peel, she had no small talk. Like Bradlaugh, she was a wonder on the platform and in private life nothing. Bradlaugh in private life was a bore when his monologue lost its novelty (Shaw declares that the only men he ever met who were totally incapable of conversation were Bradlaugh and Charles Dilke) ; but Mrs Besant was not even a bore: she was either a great priestess or nothing.

Nothing was just what happened between the piano duets ; and these were terrible. At last she found herself waiting for him in the evenings, and waiting in vain. But Annie was not a woman to be neglected or trifled with. Shaw insisted on their relations being put on a serious footing. As her husband was alive and she could not marry, she drew up a contract setting forth the terms on which they were to live together as man and wife, and presented it to him for signature. He read it. 'Good God!' he exclaimed, 'this is worse than all the vows of all the Churches on earth. I had rather be legally married to you ten times over.'

She would have nothing less than her contract, which she had expected him to sign with his heart's blood ; and when he not only laughed at it, but was evidently quite serious in refusing to be bound by it, she demanded her letters back. He collected what he could of them, and at a further and final interview gave them to her. She produced a casket in which she had kept all his letters, and, convulsed with suppressed tears, handed them to him. 'What! You won't even keep my letters!' he said. 'I don't want them.' The correspondence went into the fire. And that was the end of their private relations.

There can be no doubt that the parting was something worse for the lady than a *mauvaise quart d'heure*. Her hair turned grey: she even thought of suicide. But nothing private could hold her down for long. The Trafalgar Square business coming just then took her quite out of her private self. The straitening of her means through the loss of the Bradlaugh connexion became serious; and she asked Shaw to make Stead give her some reviewing work on the *Pall Mall Gazette*. Shaw did for her what Archer had done for him. He had been sent for review a very long book entitled *The Secret Doctrine*, by Helena Petrova Blavatsky; and this he handed to Annie telling her to write the review and leave him to settle with the *Gazette*.

It cured her completely. Theosophy was exactly what she needed: a religion in which she could be an archpriestess. She left the Fabian Society, in which, except on the platform, she had been merely a fifth wheel to the coach driven so efficiently by the Old Gang, and in which she left no trace except the only essay in the Fabian book which is in comparison with the others infantile, and which she would not allow Shaw to edit by a single word or comma.

One day Shaw, in the editor's sanctum of *The Star*, picked up a proof headed 'Why I Became a Theosophist'. He turned to the signature: it was Annie Besant. He instantly rushed round to her office in Fleet Street and asked her whether she knew that Blavatsky had been exposed at a meeting of the Psychical Society at which he (Shaw) had been present, as having worked a miracle at her shrine at Adyar by a conjuring trick? She knew all about it, and, rightly, did not consider that it made any difference to theosophy even if she believed in the exposure, which she didn't. Shaw played his last card. 'Why need you go to Thibet for a Mahatma? Here and now is your Mahatma. I am your Mahatma.' But the charm was broken. They remained good friends; but the rest of her career was Shawless.

Many years later he met in Bombay her adopted son Krishnamurti, whom he describes as the most beautiful human being he ever saw. He approved strongly of him because he had shown both high character and common sense in refusing to be put forward as the Star of the East, a new Messiah. 'Do you ever see Mrs Besant now?' he asked. 'Every day,' was the reply. 'How is she?' 'Very well ; but at her great age she cannot think consecutively.' 'She never could,' whispered Shaw. Krishnamurti smiled.

Meanwhile the wife of another leading Fabian was openly surrendering to Shaw's charm. Hubert Bland was an original member of the Davidson circle, and the leader of the secession which became the Fabian Society. He and his wife, a poetess who became famous by her fairy stories under her maiden name of Edith Nesbit, had the infant Society completely in their hands when it was invaded and captured by the big four—Shaw, Webb, Olivier, Wallas. Bland was sensible enough to accept the new situation on condition of sharing the high command as treasurer. But they did not mix well. The Four were liberals, Londoners, and positivists. Bland was military, conservative and suburban by birth and temperament. He was a Coleridgean metaphysician, and ended as a Roman Catholic. On the Fabian Committee he formed a party of one, and had a sufficiently formidable personality to save the Society from becoming one-sided in the Webbian direction. He and Webb were incompatible ; and there would have been constant rows if Shaw had not always chipped in and kept the peace. Shaw understood Bland, used occasionally to box with him, and got him a job on a paper, which led to his making a journalistic reputation.

'You and I,' Shaw wrote to Bland, 'according to the most sacred second-hand principles, should be prosperous men of business : I for the sake of my poor dear mother, who in her old age has to live on a second floor and eke out the domestic purse by teaching schoolgirls to sing, you for the sake of your clever and interesting wife and pretty children. In bygone days, when I had nothing to show for myself except rejected MSS. and was reproached over and over again, more or less directly, with being an idle, heartless, selfish scoundrel, and I myself was too young to have my eyes quite open, I would absolutely go now and then to look after some opening which I had no real intention of taking, but which I still thought it necessary to find some external reason for not taking. No doubt you have done the same thing in some form or other. Now I have no faintest hesitation left. The second-hand system on which "I ought" to have been a stockbroker has absolutely no validity for me. My one line of progress is from writing stories, reviews and articles, more and more towards writing fully and exhaustively what I like. And of course my mother, the victim of my selfishness, is a hearty, independent and jolly person, instead of a miserable old woman dragged at the chariot wheels of her miserable son, who had dutifully sacrificed himself for her comfort. Imagine Mrs Bland as the wife of a horrible city snob with a huge villa, a carriage, and several thousand a year, which is exactly what on moral principles it was your duty to have made her. You and I have followed our original impulse and our reward is that we have been conscious of its existence and can rejoice therein. The coming into clearer light of this consciousness has not occurred to me as a crisis. It has been gradual. I do not proceed by crises. My tendency is rather to overlook changes in myself and proceed on absolute assumptions until the consequences pull me up with a short turn.'

There were moments when Mrs Bland might have exchanged her impulsive husband for the villa, the carriage and several thousand a year, because his enormous physical strength and virility not only taxed her severely but involved the services of two supplementary wives whom she had to see through their maternal difficulties. He could hardly claim a strictly monogamous fidelity on her part; and she had no scruples about falling in love with Shaw, whom she described as plain but 'one of the most fascinating men I ever met'. His handsome figure, rich voice and Irish accent, made an immediate effect on her; and she expressed her emotions fully in her poems. She noticed all his defects, thought him untrustworthy because he repeated everything he heard and embroidered the truth, saw how grossly he flattered women and how men tried to belittle him, saying with assumed contempt 'Oh, it's only Shaw!' but could not help admiring him. To comfort herself she emphasized his displeasing qualities; but it was no good; her passion crept into her poems, in one of which she spoke of his 'maddening white face'. Shaw altered 'white' to 'dark', and steered her through her infatuation as best he could, finally keeping her just off the rocks. 'It is only natural that a man should establish friendly relationships with the wives of his friends,' he remarked to me; 'but if he is wise he

120

puts all idea of sex out of the question.' Bland never made Sparling's mistake about Shaw. He understood him and appreciated his loyal friendship. Though they never met after the retirement of the Fabian Old Gang in 1911, and the parties at Well Hall in the days of Bland's vogue as a feuilletonist were Shawless, yet when Bland was troubled on his deathbed by doubts as to whether his provision for the education of his favourite son would see him through Cambridge, his last word to his daughter was, 'If it is not enough, ask Shaw.' Shaw's relations with Mrs Bland ended in an enduring friendship, she observing with interest the old familiar symptoms in her female acquaintances: 'Miss —— pretends to hate him,' she wrote, 'but my own impression is that she is head over ears in love with him.'

That indeed was the impression of several women concerning other members of their sex. Mrs Sidney Webb was quite convinced that no woman except herself could withstand the Shavian charm, and she was equally convinced that Shaw philandered with his worshippers in order to get material for his plays. Shaw admitted this, more or less: 'It is not the small things that women miss in me, but the big things. My pockets are always full of the small change of love-making; but it is magic money, not real money. . . . I am fond of women (or one in a thousand, say); but I am in earnest about quite other things. To most women one man and one lifetime make a world. I require whole populations and historical epochs to engage my interests seriously and make the writing machine (for that is what G.B.S. is) work at full speed and pressure: love is only diversion and recreation to me.' The women who fell in love with him, he complained, worried and tormented him and suffered misery and destroyed their peace of mind and made scenes which they could not act; while he—could act and did. Mrs Webb admired his performance and realized that no one who did not 'live' the part could have played it so well. 'You cannot fall in love with a sprite,' she declared; 'and Shaw is a sprite in such matters, not a real person.'

His physical reactions were certainly not those of the average man. 'Only twice in my life have I been sexually infatuated,' he told me; 'once as a young man and once in middle life.' Up to the age of twenty-nine he was 'perfectly continent except for the involuntary incontinences of dreamland, which were very infrequent'. His chastity was not in the least dictated by moral scruples. He attributed it to a fastidiousness which could not endure the streets, and to the shabbiness of his attire; for the moment he could afford to dress presentably one of his mother's singing pupils, a widow named Mrs Jenny Patterson, invited him to tea and virtually raped him. 'I permitted her,' he explained, 'being intensely curious on the subject. Never having regarded myself as an attractive man, I was surprised; but I kept up appearances successfully. Since that time, whenever I have been left alone in a room with a susceptible female, she has invariably thrown her arms round me and declared she adored me.' Believing that sexual experience was 'a necessary completion of human growth', he preferred to gain his knowledge from someone who knew how to impart it, and allowed himself to be seduced, recording the occurrence in a short story written two years after he met Mrs Patterson. Though the speaker in the story is Don Giovanni, who has to refer to duelling, some of its passages are more or less autobiographical:

'At last a widow lady at whose house I sometimes visited, and of whose sentiments towards me I had not the least suspicion, grew desperate at my stupidity, and one evening threw herself into my arms. The surprise, the flattery, and my inexperience, overwhelmed me. I was incapable of the brutality of repulsing her; and indeed for nearly a month I enjoyed without scruple the pleasure she gave me, and sought her company whenever I could find nothing better to do. It was my first consummated love affair; and though for nearly two years the lady had no reason to complain of my fidelity, I found the romantic side of our intercourse, which seemed never to pall on her, tedious, unreasonable, and even forced and insincere except at rare moments, when the power of love made her beautiful, body and soul. Unfortunately, I had no sooner lost my illusions, my timidity, and my boyish curiosity about women, than I began to attract them irresistibly. My amusement at this soon changed to dismay. I became the subject of fierce jealousies: in spite of my utmost tact there was not a married friend of mine with whom I did not find myself sooner or later within an ace of a groundless duel.'

Jenny Patterson was not only 'sexually insatiable' but insanely jealous; and as Shaw continued to flirt with other women she provided him with enough material to make his fortune as a writer of emotional 'scenes'. Actually all she did was to give him a character for his least successful play. 'Mrs Patterson was my model for Julia,' he wrote to me; 'and the first act of *The Philanderer* is founded on a very horrible scene between her and Florence Farr.[1] I did not lose my temper on that occasion: I kept it for several hours; but the strain was unforgettable, and I never saw Mrs Patterson again nor answered one of the storm of letters and telegrams that lasted for months afterwards. And she never forgave me. This was not vindictiveness on my part: I left her £100 in my will, which she never inherited as she died long ago, in memory of her kindness to me during our intimacy; but it was clear that I could not go through life pursued by an ungovernable jealous woman making violent scenes whenever I spoke to any other woman. She was amazingly jealous, not merely in love but in every other relation in life, regardless of sex. I can keep my temper under ordinary injuries, though woe betide those who, like Jenny, push the strain too far.'

Convinced that, in the years to come, critics and biographers will deduce all sorts of things from Shaw's works without an ounce of evidence to go on, I asked him whether any other scene in his plays was autobiographical or founded on fact. He replied: 'The first half of the first act of *The Philanderer* is the only scene in my plays founded not too disagreeably on something that actually occurred; but to make it bearable (which in its reality it was not) it had to be reproduced as a work of art, not as a chronicle. The characters, for instance, are not portraits. In several of my plays they are, though the incidents are fictitious. Therefore I should not class *The Philanderer* as nearer to life than the others, or as near as some of them. It is true to nature only as a study of jealousy, and a sketch of the Ibsen fashion of that moment.' He forgot that the hero of the play is unmistakably himself in his Irish flirtations.

Jenny Patterson disappeared from Shaw's life after a few

---

[1] Shaw refers to an earlier 'scene' with Jenny in a letter to Florence Farr dated May 1st, 1891: 'Not for forty thousand such relations will I forego one forty-thousandth part of my relation with you. Every grain of cement she shakes from it falls like a block of granite on her own flimsy castle in the air, the work of my own imagination. The silly triumph with which she takes, with the air of a conqueror, that which I have torn out of my own entrails for her, almost brings the lightning down upon her. Imagine being told—but I cannot write it. Damnation! triple damnation! You must give me back my peace.'

years of 'stormy intercourse'. Though she never forgave him she left her property to a relative of his instead of to her own nephew when she died in 1924. Florence Farr, the cause of the disruption, acted leading parts in two of Shaw's early plays and was on terms of sexual intimacy with him. He described her as 'a young independent professional woman, who enjoyed, as such, an exceptional freedom of social intercourse in artistic circles in London. As she was clever, good-natured, and very good-looking, all her men friends fell in love with her. This had occurred so often that she had lost all patience with the hesitating preliminaries of her less practised adorers. Accordingly, when they clearly longed to kiss her, and she did not dislike them sufficiently to make their gratification too great a strain on her excessive good-nature, she would seize the stammering suitor firmly by the wrists, bring him into her arms by a smart pull, and saying "Let's get it over," allow the startled gentleman to have his kiss, and then proceed to converse with him at her ease on subjects of more general interest.'

Shaw found this 'amiable woman with semi-circular eyebrows' a pleasant change from Jenny Patterson; for she felt about sex exactly as every man likes the woman he is not in love with to feel about it. She was incapable of jealousy and never gave him the least trouble. Having been told that she had received a number of letters from him, I broached the subject and got this reply: 'I did not write any letters to Florence Farr.[1] I saw her too often. She attached no more importance to what you call love affairs than Casanova or Frank Harris; and she was too good-natured to refuse anything to anyone she really liked. I think she was rather proud of her Leporello list, which contained 14 names in 1894. I met her at one of the annual soirées of the Hammersmith Socialist Society. She was then trying her hand at embroidery with May Morris. I knew her quite well before the *Arms and The Man* episode. *Arms* was preceded by Yeats's *Land of Heart's Desire*; and she, having a very good speaking voice,

[1] Shaw's memory is shaky. The few letters he wrote to Florence Farr have recently been published. They tell us nothing fresh about him. Carbon copies of the following might have been sent to Ellen Terry and Mrs. Patrick Campbell without perplexing them: 'This is to certify that you are my best and dearest love, the regenerator of my heart, the holiest joy of my soul, my treasure, my salvation, my rest, my reward, my darling youngest child, my secret glimpse of heaven, my angel of the Annunciation. . . .'

presently drifted into a circle where she declaimed Yeats's verses to a sort of lyre which Dolmetsch made for her. I never joined that circle. Finally she went to the east as a rhapsodist and died there.'

Shaw's intimacy with Florence Farr had as little effect on him as on her. 'In permanence and seriousness,' he confessed, 'my consummated love affairs count for nothing beside the ones that were either unconsummated or ended by discarding that relation.' He found sex hopeless as a basis for permanent relations, never dreamt of marriage in connexion with it, and once wrote to Frank Harris: 'You may count the women who have left me nothing to desire on less than the fingers of one hand. To these occasions I attach comparatively no importance ; it is the others which endure.'

Nevertheless he extracted some pleasure out of these unimportant occasions: 'I liked sexual intercourse because of its amazing power of producing a celestial flood of emotion and exaltation of existence which, however momentary, gave me a sample of what may one day be the normal state of being for mankind in intellectual ecstasy. I always gave the wildest expression to this in a torrent of words, partly because I felt it due to the woman to know what I felt in her arms, and partly because I wanted her to share it. But except, perhaps, on one occasion I never felt quite convinced that I had carried the lady more than half as far as she had carried me.' Perhaps, if he had talked less, he would have been able to carry a woman all the way with him: for later on he denounced Shelley's *Epipsychidion* as the worst love poem in the world because no woman could possibly believe that she was a bit like its obviously imaginary subject. But we get his final confession in *Man and Superman,* where Don Juan says: 'I also had my moments of infatuation in which I gushed nonsense and believed it. Sometimes the desire to give pleasure by saying beautiful things so rose in me on the flood of emotion that I said them recklessly. At other times I argued against myself with a devilish coldness that drew tears. But I found it just as hard to escape when I was cruel as when I was kind. When the lady's instinct was set on me, there was nothing for it but lifelong servitude or flight.'

We must repeat that Shaw put his work as a socialist first, his recreation as a philanderer second ; and he did not find it difficult to do so. People were so enslaved by sex, he once argued, that a celibate appeared to them a sort of monster:

'They forgot that not only whole priesthoods, official and unofficial, from Paul to Carlyle and Ruskin, have defied the tyranny of sex, but immense numbers of ordinary citizens of both sexes have, either voluntarily or under pressure of circumstances easily surmountable, saved their energies for less primitive activities.' His own public activities were never neglected for the sake of a woman, because no woman could absorb his interests and energies: 'It is only when I am being used that I can feel my own existence, enjoy my own life. All my love affairs end tragically because the woman *cant* use me. They lie low and let me imagine things about them; but in the end a frightful unhappiness, an unspeakable weariness comes; and the Wandering Jew must go on in search of someone who can use him to the utmost of his capacity. Everything real in life is based on *need*.'

Thus even his closest friends were unaware of the extent of his love affairs; for in a talk I had with Lord Passfield and Mrs Sidney Webb, the former credited Shaw with but 'one divagation', which the latter at once qualified with—'And that one forced on him.' But this testimonial must have referred to his married life only; for Webb had once said to him, 'You certainly do warm both hands at the fire of life,' and they knew all about Mrs Patterson and Florence Farr. Shaw himself said that one of the blessings of marriage is that a married man is no longer fair game for every woman who takes a fancy to him. He forgot to add that it is a game seldom played according to the rules.

There were other adventures; but it is unnecessary and perhaps not very edifying to record them. One, however, must be mentioned; for it explains why Shaw was never flattered by the attraction he found himself exercising on women. While still in his twenties he was himself attracted by Eleanor, the youngest daughter of Karl Marx. She was one of his Dark Ladies, very striking in appearance and very clever. He saw her constantly in the British Museum reading room, where she was working as a literary hack for eighteenpence an hour. When Shaw became a Marxist and took the platform for The Cause, they became acquainted as socialist comrades, and a fairly cordial friendship ensued. But before their relations had warmed into anything more intimate on her side, a rival snatched the prize from him. She announced to her friends that she was about to burn her boats and live with another comrade: Doctor (of Science) Edward Aveling.

Aveling was a man for whom it is impossible to find an epithet. He had, according to Shaw, an incorruptible integrity as a militant atheist, a Shelleyan, a Darwinian and a Marxist, and would, Shaw believes, have gone to the stake rather than deny or surrender a jot of his convictions. But as a borrower of money and a swindler and seducer of women his record was unapproachable. On the same day he would borrow sixpence from the poorest man within his reach on pretence of having forgotten his purse, and three hundred pounds from the richest to free himself from debts that he never paid. He had the art of coaching for science examinations, and girl students would scrape money together to pay him in advance his fee for twelve lessons. The more fortunate ones got nothing worse for their money than letters of apology for breaking the lesson engagements. The others were seducd and had their microscopes appropriated. When he and Eleanor agreed to live together (he was married and had deserted his wife) Bradlaugh and Mrs Besant had cast him off, and neither Hyndman nor the Fabians would have anything to do with him. He and Eleanor joined the Socialist League; but Morris soon took his measure and dropped him. He tried the Independent Labour Party when Keir Hardie founded it; but Keir had no use for middle-class scamps. For some years Eleanor, through her close relations with Friederich Engels in his complete retirement, managed to persuade the German Social-Democrats that his house was still the centre of British socialism, and that she and Aveling were the only genuinely representative members of The Cause in London. Meanwhile Eleanor was in front at all the international socialist congresses as official translator, mercilessly guying all the speeches she disagreed with, and giving a fiery eloquence to the ones of which she approved. And she worked like a Trojan at home for the new Gasworkers' Union led by Mr Will Thorne.

At last Aveling's wife died; and the Germans took it for granted that the highly idealized Marx-Aveling union would now be legalized. But they reckoned without their Edward. When it came to the point Eleanor discovered that he had already taken advantage of his legal freedom to marry somebody else. She said she had better commit suicide; and he took no steps to prevent this convenient solution of his domestic difficulties, rather allowing her every facility for it. Accordingly she killed herself. Her sister had done so before, simply to avoid growing old.

Now one of Aveling's virtues was a complete freedom from hypocrisy. Whatever he did, he did without concealment, without shame, with a *désinvolture* that almost forbade disapprobation. The tragedy of the death of Marx's unhappy daughter might have been the gayest of comedies for all the trouble he took to excuse his part in it or to deplore its catastrophe. When Engels denounced him to the German Party, and he became the most execrated villain in socialist Europe, he went on his way undisturbed. He was, the doctors told him, suffering from a mortal internal disease ; and he waited for his death apparently without a tremor or a regret. He died at last like an atheist saint, spouting Shelley in the glory of the setting sun to the unspeakable edification of the beholders.

Where in all this was the lesson for Shaw? It lay in the fact that no woman seemed able to resist Aveling. Now Aveling was not a handsome man. He was undersized, had the eyes of a basilisk, and it was said of him that he would have been interesting in a zoological museum as a reptile but impossible as a man. Short of actual deformation he had every aesthetic disadvantage except a voice like a euphonium of extraordinary resonance and beauty of tone. Shaw knew that squint-eyed Wilkes, who boasted of being only a quarter of an hour behind the handsomest man in Europe, and Mirabeau, who was likened to a tiger pitted with smallpox, had been 'successful' with women ; and he had before him the example of Aveling. He could hardly with such evidence regard his involuntary conquests as flattering. He was positively relieved and reassured when he heard a clever lady novelist, whom he had been entertaining with his conversation, say in another room, not knowing that he had followed her, 'That man Shaw is an intolerable bore.' He found too that he had to face instinctive hatreds as well as instinctive attractions, and to learn how to disarm those whom he could not conciliate.

Shaw, by the way, was on quite pleasant terms with Aveling, who was an agreeable fellow enough, and much loved by his old dog, which he could hardly have been if he had been personally cruel. In *The Doctor's Dilemma* the part of Lois Dubedat is made up from the exploits of Aveling, from Richard Wagner's *End of a Musician in Paris,* and from a correspondence with a lady who deified her dead husband as Jennifer does in the play. I asked Shaw whether Aveling's case was unique in his experience. He said no : he had been on equally pleasant terms with three others, two clergymen and

128

a retired colonel, all of whom combined a pleasing absence of aggressive vices with a total lack of conscience in money matters and sexual relations.

On the latter point Shaw himself can hardly be classed as scrupulous. Our marriage laws were then, as they still are, unreasonable. The reaction against Victorian ideals, to which Ibsen had given a gigantic impulse, and against crude fundamentalist religion, which had become quite incredible, made it impossible for the intelligentsia to accept either convention or official religion as a guide to conduct. Shaw was a leading exponent of Ibsenism; and Oscar Wilde was reducing conventional morals to absurdity in the irresistible conversational performances wherein his greatness lay. The fact that civilization depends on people behaving as they are expected to behave, on the observance of conventions and constitutions, was forgotten in the pressing need for criticizing the conventions and constitutions and creeds and bringing them up to date. The stress which Shaw later on came more and more to lay on this was latent in his mind even when he wrote *The Quintessence of Ibsenism ;* for whenever his friends consulted him about entering into illicit unions of the Marx-Aveling type, he invariably urged the woman on no account to burn her boats without the protection and status of a legal marriage.

Unavowed relations, though he detested their clandestinity, were negligible; and women who were economically independent had to consider their cases as exceptional; but these apart, Shaw warned all his young revolutionary disciples that disregard of the conventions brought so much friction into private life that it was quite troublesome enough to be a socialist or an agnostic without professing Free Love as well. His version of 'Do not throw out dirty water until you get in fresh' was 'Do not break an old convention until you have established a new one.' Surrounded as he was with men who had married their deceased wives' sisters, and with wives and husbands of criminals and lunatics who could escape from their chains only by breaking them, he could not pretend that his rule was always practicable; but he kept people in mind of it as far as he could.

We may remark that although he persuaded Florence Farr to divorce the husband who had deserted her lest he should turn up again and assert his legal claims, and although Jenny Patterson was a widow, the idea of marrying Shaw, which they were quite free to do, seems never to have occurred to them or to him. But he did not live with them: appearances were always kept up. To allow a woman to compromise herself without giving her the legal status of a wife was outside his otherwise very liberal view of sexual relations.

In his opinion, however, the part played by sex in life was grossly exaggerated by his contemporaries. Nobody can read the final scenes in *Man and Superman*, or witness a performance of them, without guessing that Shaw never for a moment thought of himself as a paterfamilias, or contemplated any other mode of life than that of those two confirmed old bachelors, Kant and Schopenhauer. He always drew a sharp distinction between legalized joint households without children, like his own and that of the Webbs, and the marriages of Bland and Olivier, who were parents as well as husbands. He was fond of saying that all love affairs are different; but he did not forget that the same may be said of marriages, and that the differences are not only between children and no children but also between one child (Graham Wallas's case) and a houseful of them, like that of his friend, Sir Oliver Lodge, who entertained him after one of his lectures in Birmingham at a supper party crowded with young men. This went on until Shaw, wanting to go to bed, whispered to Sir Oliver, 'When are these chaps going to get a move on?' meaning 'When will they get up and go home?' 'But they are my sons,' said Sir Oliver. Shaw collapsed.

Of the many women who wrote love-letters to G.B.S. it is only necessary to speak of one, because of possible misunderstandings should her diary or his correspondence be published. Her name was Erica Cotterill, and she began a prolonged series of communications while his plays were being performed at the Court Theatre. 'Erica opened fire with an impassioned plea that we should meet,' he told me. 'I warned her that nothing could come of it. But her correspondence became longer and warmer; so I started giving her a little advice. Instead of putting her off, this incited her to more eloquent appeals, and at length I met her, hoping that a rational interview would abate her enthusiasm. It had precisely the opposite effect, and she did a monstrous thing: she arrived at a cottage in this village in order to see me and be near me. I at once explained the whole position to my wife, so as to prepare her for possible incidents and intrusions. Though I had strongly advised Erica to remain invisible, she stupidly called at our house. My wife of course was furious and showed by her manner that the girl's behaviour was highly improper. Then, as you are aware, Charlotte wrote forbidding her to call again. This did not prevent Erica from maintaining a barrage of letters to me, several of which would have led an ignorant reader to believe that we had been sexually intimate. One phrase I recall ran something like this: "At night, when I have you alone to myself." Now that can only bear one interpretation except the true one, which was that Erica lived in a fanciful world of her own. However, as the whole affair was extremely distasteful to Charlotte, who accused me of encouraging the girl, you must keep this to yourself until no one's feelings can be hurt by reference to it.'

Charlotte's letter, which had been shown me by a friend of Erica's, was firmly expressed. It informed Erica that when a woman made a declaration of her feelings to a married man they were bound in honour to see no more of one another. The present case was a specially dangerous one, said Charlotte, because her husband was not a common man, and if Erica and he became at all intimate he would be a necessity of life to her and their ultimate unavoidable parting would cause unnecessary pain. 'I could not trust him to keep you at a distance,' Charlotte confessed: 'he is quite friendly and sympathetic with everybody, from dogs and cats to dukes and duchesses, and none of them can imagine that his universal friendliness is not a special regard for them. He has already allowed you to become far more attached to him than he should, and I do not intend to let you drift any further into an impossible position.' Charlotte ended by saying that her letter admitted of no argument or reply, that she would enter into no correspondence on the subject, and that her decision was quite inevitable and irrevocable.

MUSIC

DINING ONE DAY at a vegetarian restaurant, when still in his twenties, Shaw got into conversation with an illiterate phrenologist, who accused him of being 'a septic'. 'Why? Have I no bump of veneration?' asked Shaw. 'Bump!' exclaimed the phrenologist: 'It's a hole!' Out of that cavity came Shaw's fame; his lack of veneration was his most conspicuous quality as a writer; it made his reputation as a critic.

T. P. O'Connor, an Irish journalist and M.P., raised enough cash in 1888 to start a new London evening newspaper. He called it *The Star*; and its policy was the liberalism of Gladstone in 1860, plus Home Rule for Ireland. Except for Home Rule 'Tay Pay' was completely out of date. Not so his assistant editor, H. W. Massingham, who made him give Shaw a job as leader writer. But Shaw's leaderettes not only bewildered T.P., who protested that not for five hundred years would it be possible to publish them, but got him into hot water with John Morley, the liberal leader whose countenance seemed all the world to him. Between Morley and Massingham he could not make up his good-natured mind to sack Shaw. From his perplexity he was rescued by Shaw, who suggested 'Let me write two columns every week about music, an unpolitical subject.' T.P. jumped at it, and gave Shaw *carte blanche* to say what he liked about music, stipulating only, 'For Christ's sake don't tell us anything about Bach in B minor!' Shaw promised; but as it happened the opening sentence of his very first criticism began, 'The number of empty seats at the performance of Bach's Mass in B minor . . .'

From May 1888 to May 1890, for the sum of two guineas a week, Shaw discoursed on many matters, including music, under the pseudonym of Corno di Bassetto, the name of an instrument that gave forth melancholy sounds suitable for a funeral; and as Shaw was out to kill the technical jargon which passed for musical criticism, he could not have hit upon a more appropriate title. 'Seriousness', he wrote, 'is only a small man's affectation of bigness'; and the crushing boredom with which the average person reads programme-notes, books and newspaper columns on music was completely absent while Shaw was diverting himself on the subject. He wrote in order to be read by people who did not know a crotchet from a quaver; and for the first and only time in the history of British criticism, the man in the street could enjoy a column of journalism devoted to music. In a country where solemnity passes for profundity and irreverence for superficiality, it was naturally assumed that he did not know what he was writing about. Actually he knew quite as much about it as any of the academic folk who were scandalized because the layman had been made to laugh; and it is pleasant to record that while the Parrys, Stanfords, Mackenzies and other musical bigwigs of that time were holding up their hands in shocked amazement, the greatest of English composers, Edward Elgar, then a young and struggling teacher of music, was enjoying Shaw's quips so heartily that when they met one another in late life the composer was able to quote many passages which the critic had long forgotten.

His two years on *The Star* was followed by four years on *The World* at a salary of £5 a week. His new editor was Edmund Yates, who offered him the post of music critic at the suggestion of William Archer. Shaw jumped at it, and many other people jumped on account of it. Dismissing his book and picture criticisms as the struggles of one who was finding his feet, we may therefore say that Shaw's career as a critic was in three stages: taking a preliminary canter in *The Star,* getting into his proper stride in *The World,* and finishing up with a terrific sprint as dramatic critic to *The Saturday Review.* He had the four chief virtues of a great journalistic critic: readability, irreverence, individuality and courage. He did not pose as an oracle: 'Never in my life have I penned an impartial criticism; and I hope I never may. As long as I have a want, I am necessarily partial to the fulfilment of that want, with a view to which I must strive with all my wit to infect everyone else with it.' 'Criticism cannot give an absolutely true and just account of any artist; it can at best explain its point of view and then describe the artist from that point of view.' His own freedom and honesty as a critic were partly due to his isolation, and when it was proposed that a critics' club should be formed he explained his principle while rejecting the proposal: 'Now clearly a critic should not belong to a club at all. He should not know anybody: his hand should be against every man, and every man's hand against his. . . . People have pointed out evidence of personal feeling in my notices as if they were accusing me of a misdemeanour, not knowing that a criticism written without personal feeling is not worth reading. It is the capacity for making good or bad art a personal matter that makes a man a critic. The artist who accounts for my disparagement by alleging personal animosity on my part is quite right: when people do less than their best, and do that less at once badly and self-complacently, I hate them, loathe them, detest them, long to tear them limb from limb and strew them in gobbets about

133

the stage or platform. . . . In the same way, really fine artists inspire me with the warmest personal regard, which I gratify in writing my notices without the smallest reference to such monstrous conceits as justice, impartiality, and the rest of the ideals. When my critical mood is at its height, personal feeling is not the word : it is passion : the passion for artistic perfection—for the noblest beauty of sound, sight and action—that rages in me. Let all young artists look to it, and pay no heed to the idiots who declare that criticism should be free from personal feeling. The true critic, I repeat, is the man who becomes your personal enemy on the sole provocation of a bad performance, and will only be appeased by good performances. Now this, though well for art and for the people, means that the critics are, from the social or clubable point of view, veritable fiends. They can only fit themselves for other people's clubs by allowing themselves to be corrupted by kindly feelings foreign to the purpose of art.'

Throughout the six years that Shaw devoted to music he never once troubled to make his views agreeable to the authorities. He championed Wagner, who was then considered mad by the critics and professors. He ridiculed the absurd traditions of the operatic stage, and was refused complimentary seats at Covent Garden as a consequence. He exposed the pretentiousness of writers on music with an 'analysis' of Hamlet's soliloquy on suicide in the same scientific style: 'Shakespear, dispensing with the customary exordium, announces his subject at once in the infinitive, in which mood it is presently repeated after a short connecting passage in which, brief as it is, we recognize the alternative and negative forms on which so much of the significance of repetition depends. Here we reach a colon ; and a pointed pository phrase, in which the accent falls decisively on the relative pronoun, brings us to the first full stop.' He asked whether it was just that a literary critic should be forbidden to make his living in that way on pain of being interviewed by two doctors and a magistrate, and haled off to Bedlam forthwith, whilst the more a musical critic did it the deeper the veneration he inspired.

The musical entertainments provided for royal visitors to London excited his derision, and he described the programme given before the Shah of Persia at Covent Garden as 'the most extravagantly Bedlamite hotch-potch on record, even in the annals of State concerts. It was evidently the work of a committee on which conflicting views had to be reconciled. Thus, view No. 1 was that the Shah is a gentleman of ordinary and somewhat vulgar European musical taste ; therefore let him hear the overture to *William Tell*. View No. 2 ; The Shah is an idiot ; therefore ply him with the mad scene from *Lucia*. View No. 3 : The Shah's artistic culture is deep, earnest, severe, and German ; therefore strike up the great Leonora overture by Beethoven. View No. 4 : It does not matter what the Shah is ; we are going to let him see what Covent Garden can do ; therefore let us put on the fourth act of *Faust*, which is one of our big things. View No. 5 : The Shah is a savage and a voluptuary ; therefore treat him to the Brocken corroboree from Boito's *Mefistofele*, as the most unseemly thing we can very well do under the circumstances.'

The presentation of wreaths and baskets of flowers to popular singers at the conclusion of their pieces was then a common custom. Shaw noted that an Australian prima donna, Madame Melba, 'received flowers across the footlights in those large baskets which English ladies and gentlemen invariably carry with them in the theatre, and which they present to singers in moments of uncontrollable admiration' ; but he also observed that the recipients of such favours always seemed astonished when the gifts appeared, and he begged them to 'consider for a moment how insanely impossible it is that a wreath as big as a cart-wheel could be the spontaneous offering of an admiring stranger'.

Conductors, singers, executants of all sorts, impresarios, stage-managers and brother-critics were not spared by G.B.S., who claimed to possess 'that power of accurate observation, which is commonly called cynicism by those who have not got it'. He even told his readers what was wrong with them : 'It is all work and no play in the brain department that makes John Bull such an uncommonly dull boy.' The English brain was so dense, he declared, that it was only by a strenuous and most desperately serious effort that the Englishman could set his intellect in action. The average Londoner was as void of feeling for the fine arts as a man could be without collapsing bodily.

He criticized the programmes of the Philharmonic Society, advising 'the compulsory retirement of all directors at the age of ninety-five, into a lethal chamber if possible' ; and he wrote of the leading professors of music, Frederic Cowen, Alexander Mackenzie, Hubert Parry and Villiers Stanford, in a manner

135

that explains why they were all knighted. 'I am sure literary composition is infinitely more difficult than musical composition, yet I never thought of going to a professor to learn it,' said G.B.S., who dealt with Stanford's oratorio *Eden* thus: 'Who am I that I should be believed, to the disparagement of eminent musicians? If you doubt that *Eden* is a masterpiece, ask Dr Parry and Dr Mackenzie, and they will applaud it to the skies. Surely Dr Mackenzie's opinion is conclusive; for is he not the composor of *Veni Creator,* guaranteed as excellent music by Professor Stanford and Dr Parry? You want to know who Dr Parry is? Why, the composer of *Blest Pair of Sirens,* as to the merits of which you have only to consult Dr Mackenzie and Professor Stanford.' Parry, by the way, never composed another oratorio after Shaw had advised him to burn the scores of two he had already written.

Nor was Shaw imposed upon by the ponderous works of men with international reputations: 'Dvorak's *Requiem* bored Birmingham so desperately that it was unanimously voted a work of extraordinary depth and impressiveness, which verdict I record with a hollow laugh, and allow the subject to drop by its own portentous weight. Besides, I do not wish to belie that steward who introduced me to his colleague on Thursday morning (when I was looking for a seat) as "one of these complimentary people".' Of Gounod's *Redemption* he wrote: 'I have no more to say generally than that if you will only take the precaution to go in long enough after it commences and to come out long enough before it is over you will not find it wearisome.' He described Brahms' *Requiem* as so execrably dull that the very flattest of funerals would seem like a ballet after it: 'There are some sacrifices which should not be demanded twice from any man; and one of them is listening to Brahms' *Requiem.*' His later apologies to Brahms went no further than to say that now that he really knew the *Requiem* he found it very good fun.

Like all the greatest essayists Shaw revealed himself in his criticisms, their chief attraction being the personal digressions, their unique quality the conscious self-portraiture. He struck the note almost at once: 'I know that this metaphor is mixed, and I don't care: it is as well to come to an early understanding on these points.' His seemingly irresponsible gaiety of spirit is apparent on almost every page. One may open any volume at random and come upon phrases that have the oddly honest Shavian ring:

'I am proof against all illusions except illusions which flatter me; I am middle-aged in years and patriarchal in wisdom.'

'I do not mind confessing that I do not know half as much as you would suppose from my articles; but in the kingdom of the deaf the one-eared is king.'

'Some day I must write a supplement to Schumann's *Advice to Young Musicians*. The title will be Advice to Old Musicians; and the first precept will run, "Dont be in a hurry to contradict G.B.S., as he never commits himself on a musical subject until he knows at least six times as much about it as you do."'

'I do not smoke, do not drink, and feel like a pickpocket whenever circumstances compel me to lounge.'

'I am unfortunately so constituted that if I were actually in heaven itself I should have to earn my enjoyment of it by turning out and doing a stroke of work of some sort, at any rate of at least a fortnight's hard labor for one celestial evening hour. There is nothing so insufferable as happiness, except perhaps unhappiness; and this is at the bottom of the inferiority of Gounod and Mendelssohn to Handel as oratorio writers.'

'It has taken me nearly twenty years of studied self-restraint, aided by the natural decay of my faculties, to make myself dull enough to be accepted as a serious person by the British public; and I am not sure that I am not still regarded as a suspicious character in some quarters.'

'I yield to no man in the ingenuity and persistence with which I seize every opportunity of puffing myself and my affairs; but I never nauseate the public by getting myself praised. . . . Any sort of notoriety will serve my turn equally.'

'As a rule I do not hazard guesses about artists until I have privately ascertained that my guesses are correct.'

'There is nothing that soothes me more after a long and maddening course of pianoforte recitals than to sit and have my teeth drilled by a finely skilled hand.'

'By simply assassinating less than a dozen men, I could leave London without a single orchestral wind instrument player of the first rank.'

'In literature the ambition of the novice is to acquire the literary language: the struggle of the adept is to get rid of it.'

(On a cornet soloist outside a public house.) 'The man played with great taste and pathos; but, to my surprise, he had no knowledge of musical etiquette, for when, on his

137

holding his hat to me for a donation, I explained that I was a member of the Press, he still seemed to expect me to pay for my entertainment.'

'The other evening, feeling rather in want of a headache, I bethought me that I had not been to a music-hall for a long time.'

'We put up even with the nightingale only by giving it credit for poetic fancies that never came into its head.'

(On the editor of *The Star*.) 'At last our relations became so strained that we came to the very grave point of having to exchange assurances that we esteemed one another beyond all created mortals.'

In June 1891 an influenza epidemic gave Shaw another excuse to discuss something more interesting than a concert: 'The most important event in the musical world since my last article, from my point of view, has been the influenza catching me, or, as my friends preposterously insist on putting it, my catching the influenza. Fortunately for me, many cases of critics and singers disabled by it had occurred under my eyes within a few weeks; so that by scrupulously doing the very reverse of what they did in the way of treatment, I managed to come through without missing a single engagement. I abstained from medical advice and ammoniated quinine; I treated the fever by enjoying the morning air at an open window in an entirely unprotected condition for a prolonged period before finishing up with a cold bath; I stimulated myself by transitions from the overwhelming heat of the crowded St James's Hall to the chill coolness of Regent Street at night; I wore my lightest attire; I kept out of bed as much as possible, and held on to railings and lamp-posts when the temptation to seek a brief repose at full length in the streets became almost irresistible, as it did once or twice on the day when the fever was at its height; I fed myself resolutely (though not on the corpses of slain animals), and took no alcohol in any form. The result was that I routed the enemy in a series of pitched battles, in which I was assailed successively with delirium, with weakness and fever, with pains in various portions of my person, including a specially ingenious one in the eyeballs, and, finally, with a vulgar and abominable cold in the head, which pursued me with unabated rage for forty-eight hours before it lost heart. Had I drugged the fiend, coddled him, inebriated him, and lavished doctors' fees on him, no doubt I should have left *The World* musicless for three weeks at least. As it was, I did more work in the five days during which the combat lasted than in the five days before that. Singers will now know how to deal with their foe. It is always worth while to fly in the face of that unvenerable survival of witchcraft which calls itself medical science. To recover triumphantly under such circumstances becomes a point of honor.'

Shaw resigned his post as music critic to *The World* when Edmund Yates died in May '94. Yates's successor begged him to continue until the end of the season, which he did. His place was then taken by Robert Hichens, who had trained himself as a musician. The professors and entrepreneurs breathed again.

OFF DUTY

'THE SECRET of being miserable is to have leisure to bother about whether you are happy or not,' wrote Shaw. 'The cure for it is occupation, because occupation means preoccupation; and the preoccupied person is neither happy nor unhappy, but simply active and alive, which is pleasanter than any happiness until you are tired of it. That is why it is necessary to happiness that one should be tired. Music after dinner is pleasant: music before breakfast is so unpleasant as to be clearly unnatural. To people who are not overworked holidays are a nuisance. To people who are, and who can afford them, they are a troublesome necessity. A perpetual holiday is a good working definition of hell.'

Shakespeare had a few words to say on the subject of holidays:

If all the year were playing holidays,
To sport would be as tedious as to work ;
But when they seldom come, they wish'd for come,
And nothing pleaseth but rare accidents.

139

Yet Shakespeare would not have agreed with Shaw's notion of a holiday, which was simply a change of work. When worn out by socialistic activities, he wrote a play; and the occasional holidays he took when a critic were occupied in using up his superfluous energy, in picking up information, and in exercising his powers of criticism. In fact one might describe his writings as a holiday for himself and his readers. A friend of his once said that he would not care to have Shaw as a companion on a long tour. The remark was repeated to Shaw, who admitted that he would always be 'trying to say smart things and this after a time might tend to become boresome'. But his smart things would not have been anything like so tiring as his insatiable curiosity. He scarcely ever relaxed, his mind and legs being equally active. Apparently only one companion was ever able to 'steep his senses in forgetfulness'. He had taken an afternoon off and had strolled into some naval exhibition in Chelsea, where he met Oscar Wilde and spent a few delightful hours with him. They saw a replica of Nelson's *Victory* and 'a set of P. & O. cabins which made one seasick by mere association of ideas. I dont know why I went or why Wilde went; but we did; and the question what the devil we were doing in that galley tickled us both. It was my sole experience of Oscar's wonderful gift as a raconteur. I remember particularly an amazingly elaborate story . . . an example of the cumulation of a single effect, as in Mark Twain's story of the man who was persuaded to put lightning conductor after lightning conductor at every possible point on his roof until a thunder-storm came and all the lightning in the heavens went for his house and wiped it out.

'Oscar's much more carefully and elegantly worked out story was of a young man who invented a theatre stall which economized space by ingenious contrivances which were all described. A friend of his invited twenty millionaires to meet him at dinner so that he might interest them in the invention. The young man demonstrated that by his invention a theatre holding six hundred people could be made to accommodate a thousand; at which point the millionaires were eager and ready to make his fortune. Unfortunately he went on to calculate the annual gain in all the theatres and concert halls in the world; then in all the church offertories, and so on, piling up the pecuniary, moral and religious effects of the invention until at the end of an hour he had estimated a profit of several thousand millions plus the millennium: the climax of course being that the millionaires folded their tents and silently stole away, leaving the ruined inventor a marked man for life.

'Wilde and I got on extraordinarily well on this occasion. I had not to talk myself, but listen to a man telling me stories better than I could have told them. . . . He was in a tweed suit and low hat like myself, and had been detected and had detected me in the act of clandestinely spending a happy day at Rosherville Gardens instead of pontificating in his frock-coat and so forth. And he had an audience on whom not one of his subtlest effects was lost. And so for once our meeting was a success; and I understood why Morris, when he was dying slowly, enjoyed a visit from Wilde more than from anybody else.'

And so for once, it may be added, Shaw could not help relaxing. The difference between the two men was illustrated by a story Robert Ross told me: 'I once met Shaw in Chartres Cathedral. He asked me to take him round and tell him everything I knew about the stained-glass windows. By dint of relentless examination he pumped me dry of every scrap of information I possessed, and at the end of an hour I was fit only for a Turkish bath and alcoholic stimulants. Now Oscar would have told me wonderful stories about those windows— all made up on the spur of the moment, of course—and at the end of an hour I should still have been begging for more.'

Shaw's hunger for knowledge was unappeasable. For more restful souls his trips abroad would have been tasks. In September '91 he accompanied a party of The Art-Workers Guild to Venice. The expedition was organized by a Cambridge don named Thomas Okey, who experienced some difficulty in arranging for Shaw's diet. The vegeterian did not seem to mind; he starved cheerfully until Okey hit on the expedient of telling the head waiters that one of their party was under a religious vow to abstain from meat, after which Shaw travelled in comfort as a holy man, well provided with dishes to his taste. But his taste in architecture would have horrified most holy men. He compared the cathedral at Milan to a very expensive wedding cake. 'It disgusted me: it struck me as representing the result of giving a *carte blanche* order for the biggest thing of the kind that could be done. . . . I greatly prefer San Ambrogio.' The exterior of St Mark's at Venice he pronounced ideal for a railway station. Generally speaking, the Venetians 'did nothing architecturally that gives me the sensation I remember getting many years ago when I saw St John's Chapel in the Tower of London. . . . So, somehow, Italy seems to me a humbug. . . . The first day we were here was a very fine day; and it convinced me completely that the only painter who had the least notion of what he had to paint was Turner.' Shaw wrote a long letter to William Morris, 'because I must work off my growing irritation and escape for a moment from the fearful solitude created by these twenty-seven men, about twenty of whom seem to me to be capable of admiring everything except beauty'. Fortunately Venice provided other things to occupy the attention besides churches and sightseers: 'You should see Walker and Cockerell. Their faces and necks are mere mosquito pastures —all red spots. I have protected myself by burning pastilles which make a fume so noxious that I have all but succumbed to it myself. I have also been fortunate in discouraging fleas, which soon abandon the settlements they find on me. The fact is, I perspire freely. My keys, for instance, get quite dulled with rust in a short time. I am convinced that the damp gives the fleas rheumatism, which must be a hideously unpleasant complaint for an insect which has to jump for its life every few seconds. Hence they soon quit me.' Even the gondoliers did not come up to the mark. He had heard that they usually chanted the verses of Tasso—'a practice which was suspended for some reason during my stay in Venice: at least no gondolier ever did it in my hearing'. In '94 he again joined The Art-Workers Guild on a journey to Italy, where in Genoa he was pleased to find a theatre on the third floor of a Renaissance skyscraper, admired the great staircases of the palaces, and was with difficulty persuaded not to smash a famous artist's marble representation of Jenner vaccinating a child's arm.

Shaw had scarcely been inside a church since childhood, but for reasons not wholly concerned with prayer in the orthodox sense he became a churchgoer in Italy. He took exception to 'the innumerable daily services which disturb the truly religious visitor. If these were decently and intelligently conducted by genuine mystics to whom the Mass was no mere rite or miracle, but a real communion, the celebrants might reasonably claim a place in the church as their share of the common human right to its use. But the average Italian priest, personally unclean, and with chronic catarrh of the nose and throat, produced and maintained by sleeping and living in

142

frowsty, ill-ventilated rooms, punctuating his gabbled Latin only by expectorative hawking, and making the decent guest sicken and shiver every time the horrible splash of· spitten mucus echoes along the vaulting from the marble steps of the altar: this unseemly wretch should be seized and put out, bell, book, candle and all, until he learns to behave himself. The English tourist is often lectured for his inconsiderate behaviour in Italian churches, for walking about during service, talking loudly, thrusting himself rudely between a worshipper and an altar to examine a painting, even for stealing chips of stone and scrawling his name on statues. But as far as the mere disturbance of the services is concerned, the often very evident disposition of the tourist—especially the experienced tourist—to regard the priest and his congregation as troublesome intruders, a week spent in Italy will convince any unprejudiced person that this is a perfectly reasonable attitude. I have seen inconsiderate British behaviour often enough both in church and out of it. The slow-witted Englishman who refuses to get out of the way of the Host, and looks at the bellringer going before it with "Where the devil are you shoving to?" written in every pucker of his free-born British brow, is a familiar figure to me; but I have never seen any stranger behave so insufferably as the officials of the church habitually do. It is the sacristan who teaches you, when once you are committed to tipping him, not to waste your good manners on the kneeling worshippers who are snatching a moment from their daily round of drudgery and starvation to be comforted by the Blessed Virgin or one of the saints: it is the officiating priest who makes you understand that the congregation are past shocking by any indecency that you would dream of committing, and that the black looks of the congregation are directed at the foreigner and the heretic only, and imply a denial of your right as a human being to your share of the use of the church. That right should be unflinchingly asserted on all proper occasions. I know no contrary right by which the great Catholic churches made for the world by the great church-builders should be monopolized by any sect as against any man who desires to use them.'

A more deeply religious atmosphere prevailed in the Bayreuth Festival Playhouse than in the Catholic Churches. In spite of having to cross 'that unquiet North Sea, the very thought of which sets my entrails aquake', Shaw often went to Bayreuth, spending many pleasant hours in the scented pine-woods on the surrounding hills. The journey had its drawbacks, but there were compensatory moments: 'I write under difficulties this week. I am not a good sailor. After being rocked in the cradle of the deep all night, I am at present being rocked in a Dutch railway carriage. I have been in it for five hours, and I assure you that if an express were to come in the opposite direction on the same line of rails and smash the whole affair, Bassetto included, into pulp, I should make no unmanly complaints. After all, there is something grand in being able to look death in the face with a smile of welcome ; but I should enjoy it more if I could look life in the face without feeling so poorly.

'It is later in the day ; and I think life is, perhaps, worth living after all. To drive up the Rhine from Bonn to Coblenz, whilst the hours advance from afternoon to night, is better than a dozen Press views of different schools of landscape. Cologne Cathedral, too, has affected me. I am extremely susceptible to stained glass, and the old glass there transports me, whilst the new glass makes me long to transport it—with bricks. Yes, I confess I am enjoying the evening. I wish that when that terrific shower caught me in Cologne my mackintosh had not split up the back like a trick coat in a farce, throwing the younger posterity of the Three Kings into derisive convulsions. I wish I knew whether that very genial market woman really gave me, as she implied, an enormous bargain for the sake of my *beaux yeux* (one and elevenpence for half a pound of grapes and six little hard pears), or whether she swindled me ; and I wish I could go back by Channel Tunnel. But still, for the moment, I do not regret having been born.'

In those days everyone visited Bayreuth in order to hear *Parsifal*, which could be heard nowhere else, and most pilgrims were feeling too devout to notice what the eye of Shaw picked out in the landscape: 'Glancing through Baedeker as I bowl along Bayreuthward I perceive that the chief feature of the Wagner district is a great lunatic asylum. At Neumarkt an official railway colporteur thrusts into my hand a great red placard inscribed with a Warnung! (German spelling is worse than indifferent) against pickpockets at Bayreuth. This is a nice outcome of *Parsifal*. In the town an enterprising tradesman offers "the *Parsifal* slippers" at 2m.50 the pair as "the height of novelty". It is a desperately stupid little town, this Bayreuth. . . . However, there are hills with fine woods to wander through, and blackberries, raspberries, and other sorts of edible berries, about the names of which no two persons agree, to be had for the picking.' Some twenty years after his first visit Shaw wrote from Bayreuth to William Archer: 'This place, as far as the theatre is concerned, is incredibly unchanged: it is exactly as if you and I and Dibdin (Dibdin's dead, by the way, isn't he?) were there yesterday. . . . The lunatic asylum has the same air of being deserted for the theatre.'

Although impressed by *Parsifal* and *Tristan* he freely criticized the obsolete stage-management. 'Now if you, my Wagnerian friends, wonder how I can scoff thus at so impressive a celebration, I reply that Wagner is dead, and that the evil of deliberately making the Bayreuth Festival Playhouse a temple of dead traditions, instead of an arena for live impulses, has begun already. It is because I, too, am an enthusiastic Wagnerite that the Bayreuth management cannot deceive me by dressing itself in the skin of the dead lion.' The singing was earnest but horribly contrary to the method of Vandaleur Lee. 'Perhaps the reason why these Bayreuth artists interest me so much less than they ought to, is that they make no mistakes, and I am consequently deprived of an irritant to which I have become accustomed in London.' Once he complained to Levi, the conductor of *Parsifal,* about the bass singer who had howled the music of Gurnemanz like a wolf: 'Levi appeared surprised, and, contemptuous of "glatt" *bel canto,* declared that the singer had the best bass voice in Germany, and challenged me to find him anyone who could sing the part better, to which I could only respond with sufficient emphasis by offering to sing it better myself, upon which he gave me up as a lunatic.'

The effect of his Bayreuth criticisms on pious Wagnerians was, he said, as if he had brawled in church. He praised Richter's conducting of *The Mastersingers,* but his career as a critic was over when Siegfried Wagner commenced to dominate the Festivals. Siegfried came to London in the nineties and Shaw reminisced about his father and encouraged him as a conductor ; but a later experience was disappointing: 'His conducting was too depressing to be describable as maddening ; but it made us all feel as if we were at a garden party in a cathedral town being welcomed by a highly connected curate who failed to find any tea for us.'

Perhaps it is not quite accurate to describe Shaw as 'off

duty' when he was at Bayreuth: 'It is desperately hard work, this daily scrutiny of the details of an elaborate performance from four to past ten,' he wrote. 'Yet there are people who imagine I am taking a holiday.' He was at any rate fond of taking a busman's holiday, and one Saturday evening in September '89, feeling in need of change and country air, he went down the river to Greenwich with William Archer. They struggled into the gallery of Morton's Theatre and witnessed the principal touring company's 789th performance of *Dorothy*, a musical comedy that had been a greater success in London than the most popular of the Gilbert and Sullivan operas. Readers of *The Star* were entertained by his account of the piece, but they would have enjoyed it still more if they had known that the prima donna was the critic's sister, Lucy, the tenor his brother-in-law.

'The tenor, originally, I have no doubt, a fine young man, but now cherubically adipose, was evidently counting the days until death should release him from the part of Wilder. He had a pleasant speaking voice; and his affability and forbearance were highly creditable to him under the circumstances; but Nature rebelled in him against the loathed strains of a seven hundred-times repeated role. He omitted the song in the first act, and sang "Though Born a Man of High Degree" as if with the last rally on an energy decayed and a willing spirit crushed. The G at the end was a vocal earthquake. And yet methought he was not displeased when the inhabitants of Greenwich, coming fresh to the slaughter, encored him. . . .

'The comic part, being simply that of a circus clown transferred to the lyric stage, is better suited for infinite repetition; and the gentleman who undertook it addressed a comic lady called Priscilla as Sarsaparilla during his interludes between the *haute-école* acts of the prima donna and tenor, with a delight in the rare aroma of the joke, and in the roars of laughter it elicited, which will probably never pall. But anything that he himself escaped in the way of tedium was added tenfold to his unlucky colleagues, who sat out his buffooneries with an expression of deadly malignity. I trust the gentleman may die in his bed; but he would be unwise to build too much on doing so. There is a point at which tedium becomes homicidal mania.

'The ladies fared best. The female of the human species has not yet developed a conscience: she will apparently spend her

life in artistic self-murder by induced Dorothitis without a
pang of remorse, provided she be praised and paid regularly.
Dorothy herself, a beauteous young lady of distinguished
mien, with an immense variety of accents ranging from the
finest Tunbridge Wells English (for genteel comedy) to the
broadest Irish (for repartee and low comedy), sang without
the slightest effort and without the slightest point, and was
all the more desperately vapid because she suggested artistic
gifts wasting in complaçent abeyance. . . .

'The pack of hounds darted in at the end of the second
act evidently full of the mad hope of finding something new
going on; and their depression, when they discovered it was
Dorothy again, was pitiable. The S.P.C.A. should interfere.
If there is no law to protect men and women from Dorothy,
there is at least one that can be strained to protect dogs.

'I did not wait for the third act. My companion had several
times all but fallen into the pit from sleep and heaviness of
spirit combined; and I felt as if I were playing Geoffrey
Wilder for the millionth night.'

Shaw's visit to *Dorothy* proves that nine years of London
life had not made him pine for fresh air. He was a product
of civilization and did not care for the primitive horrors of
the countryside, which were praised as rustic delights by his
friend Henry Salt, a fellow-vegetarian. Salt lived at Tilford
in the Surrey hills and asked Shaw to stay with him and his
wife for a couple of days. 'As he is a sensible companion for
a walk and a talk—if only he would, like a sensible man, con-
fine himself to the Thames Embankment—I at last consented
to the experiment,' wrote Shaw, 'and even agreed to be
marched to the summit of a scenic imposture called Hindhead,
and there shown the downs of the South Coast, the Ports-
mouth Road (the Knightsbridge end of which I prefer), and,
above all, the place where three men were hanged for murder-
ing someone who had induced them to take a country walk
with him.

'London was clean, fresh, and dry as I made my way to
Waterloo after rising at the unnatural hour of seven on Sunday morning. . . . Between Farnham and Tilford there are
nearly half a dozen hills and not one viaduct. Over these I
trudged uphill on my toes and downhill on my heels, making
at each step an oozy quagmire full of liquid gamboge. As the
landscape grew less human, the rain came down faster, reducing my book to a pulp and transferring the red of the cover

147

to my saturated grey jacket. Some waterproof variety of bird screaming with laughter at me from a plantation, made me understand better than before why birds are habitually shot. ... My sleeves by this time struck cold to my wrists. Hanging my arms disconsolately so as to minimize the unpleasant repercussion, I looked down at my clinging knees, and instantly discharged a pint of rain water and black dye over them from my hat brim.'

He got to Salt's place at last; his clothes were dried; he had a fit of sneezing, was dosed by Mrs Salt with spirits of camphor, which nearly killed him, and was then marched out to see the countryside.

'Frensham Pond, like a waterworks denuded of machinery, lay to leeward of us, with a shudder passing over it from head to foot at every squall. I sympathized with it, and looked furtively at Salt, to see whether the ineffable dreariness of the scene had not dashed him. But he was used to it, and, when we got home, began to plan an excursion to Hindhead for the morrow. The mere suggestion brought on a fresh fit of sneezing.

'Next morning I got up at eight to see the sun and hear the birds. I found, however, that I was up before them; and I neither saw nor heard them until I got back to the metropolis. Salt was jubilant because the wind was north-east, which made rain impossible. So after breakfast we started across the hills to Hindhead, through a mist that made the cows look like mammoths and the ridges like Alpine chains. When we were well out of reach of shelter the rain began. Salt declared that it would be nothing; that it could never hold out against the north-east wind. Nevertheless it did. ... Salt was in the highest spirits. The discovery of a wet day in a north-east wind elated him as the discovery of a comet elates an astronomer. As to Mrs Salt, the conclusion she drew from it all was that I must come down another day. The rain gave her no more concern than if she had been a duck; and I could not help wondering whether her walking costume was not in reality a skilfully contrived bathing dress. She seemed perfectly happy, though the very sheep were bawling plaintively at the sky, and a cow to which I gave a friendly slap in passing was so saturated that the water squirted up my sleeve to the very armpit. ... Before we got home, my clothes contained three times as much water as they had gathered the day before. When I

148

again resumed them they seemed to have been borrowed in an emergency from a very young brother.

'I need not describe my walk back to Farnham after dinner. It rained all the way; but at least I was getting nearer to London. I have had change of air and a holiday; and I have no doubt I shall be able to throw off their effect in a fortnight or so.'

After that experience it may seem strange that Shaw frequently spent holidays with the Salts, discussing humanitarianism and vegetarianism with Henry and playing piano-duets with his wife. The Salts found him useful about the house, making his bed with methodical precision and helping to wash-up after meals in a conscientious and exemplary fashion. On the other hand his habitual scepticism gave them anxious moments whenever tramps turned up with stories of hardship. One such visitor told of a terrible wound, the scar of which he would probably carry with him to the grave. Shaw felt unable to accept his assurance and asked one or two pointed questions. Gravely put out by this reflection on his honesty, the tramp began to take off his clothes. Faced with suffering as an alternative to faith, Shaw instantly capitulated and proclaimed his unqualified belief in the man's story.

Some of the people with whom he stayed found him so useful about the house that they witnessed his departure with a sigh of relief. 'You invite him down to your place because you think he will entertain your guests with his brilliant conversation,' complained one of his hostesses; 'and before you know where you are he has chosen a school for your son, made your will for you, regulated your diet, and assumed all the privileges of your family solicitor, your housekeeper, your clergyman, your doctor, your dressmaker, your hairdresser, and your estate agent. When he has finished with everybody else, he incites the children to rebellion. And when he can find nothing more to do, he goes away and forgets all about you.'

In fact he was an incurably restless busybody. Except when his health was shattered and he was bedridden he could scarcely remain inert for twenty consecutive minutes. Yet he made desperate attempts to take things easy. At Christmas, 1889, for example, he nearly drove himelf mad in a vain effort to achieve repose. The carol-singers started him off: 'The only music I had heard this week is Waits. To sit up working until two or three in the morning, and then, just as I am losing myself in my first sleep, to hear *Venite adoremus*, more generally known as Ow, cam let Haz adore Im, welling forth from a cornet (English pitch), a saxhorn (Society of Arts pitch, or thereabouts), and a trombone (French pitch), is the sort of thing that breaks my peace and destroys my good will towards men. Coming on top of a very arduous month, it reduced me last Saturday to a condition of such complete addledness, that it became evident that my overwrought brain would work itself soft in another fortnight unless an interval of complete mental vacuity could be induced.

'Obviously the thing to do was to escape from the magnetic atmosphere of London, and slow down in some empty-headed place where I should be thoroughly bored. Somebody suggested Broadstairs. I had always supposed Broadstairs to be a show place at Wapping; but I found that it was half-way between Margate and Ramsgate, in neither of which famous watering-places had I ever set foot.'

So to Broadstairs he went. 'Let no man henceforth ever trifle with Fate so far as actually to seek boredom. Before I was ten minutes here, I was bored beyond description. The air of the place is infernal. In it I hurry about like a mouse suffocating in oxygen. The people here call it "ozone" and consider it splendid; but there is a visible crust over them, a sort of dull terra-cotta surface which they pretend to regard as a sign of robust health. As I consume in the ozone, this terrible limekiln crust is forming on me too; and they congratulate me already on "looking quite different". As a matter of fact I can do nothing but eat: my brain refuses its accustomed work. The place smells as if someone had spilt a bottle of iodine over it. The sea is absolutely dirtier than the Thames under Blackfriars Bridge; and the cold is hideous. I have not come across a graveyard yet; and I have no doubt that sepulture is unnecessary, as the houses are perfect refrigerating chambers, capable of preserving a corpse to the remotest posterity.

'I am staying in Nuckell's Place; and they tell me that Miss Nuckell was the original of Betsy Trotwood in *David Copperfield,* and that the strip of green outside is that from which she used to chase the donkeys. A house down to the left is called Bleak House; and I can only say that if it is any bleaker than my bedroom, it must be a nonpareil freezer. But all this Dickens-mania is only hallucination induced by the ozone. This morning a resident said to me, "Do you see that weather-beaten old salt coming along?" "Yes," I replied; "and if you will excuse my anticipating your reply, I may say that I have no doubt that he is the original of Captain Cuttle. But, my dear madam, I myself am Corno di Bassetto; and in future Broadstairs anecdotage will begin to revolve round Me." Then, impelled to restless activity by the abominable ozone, I rushed off to the left; sped along the cliffs; passed a lighthouse, which looked as if it had been turned into a pillar of salt by the sea air; fell presently among stony ground; passed on into muddy ground; and finally reached Margate, a most dismal hole, where the iodine and ozone were flavored with lodgings.

'I made at once for the railway station, and demanded the next train. "Where to?" said the official. "Anywhere," I replied, "provided it be far inland." "Train to Ramsgit at two-fifteen,' he said: "nothing else till six." I could not conceive Ramsgit as being so depressing, even on Christmas Day, as Margit; so I got into that train; and, lo, the second station we came to was Broadstairs. This was the finger of Fate; for the ozone had made me so ragingly hungry that I burst from the train and ran all the way to Nuckell's Place, where, to my unspeakable horror and loathing, they triumphantly brought me up a turkey with sausages. "Surely, sir," they said, as if remonstrating with me for some exhibition of depravity, "*surely* you eat meat on *Christmas* day." "I tell you," I screamed, "that I never eat meat." "Not even a little gravy, sir? I think it would do you good." I put a fearful constraint on myself, and politely refused. Yet they came up again, as fresh as paint, with a discolored mess of suet scorched in flaming brandy; and when I conveyed to them, as considerately as I could, that I thought the distinction between suet and meat, burnt brandy and spirits, too fine to be worth insisting on, they evidently regarded me as hardly reasonable. There can be no doubt that the people here are mentally enfeebled. The keen air causes such rapid waste of tissue that they dare not add to it by thinking. They are always recuperating—that is to say eating—mostly cows.

'Nevertheless it was with some emotion that I trod sea sand for the first time for many years. When I was a boy I learnt to appreciate the sight and sound of the sea in a beautiful bay on the Irish coast. But they have no confounded ozone in Ireland, only ordinary wholesome sea air. You never see an Irishman swaggering and sniffing about with his chest expanded, mad with excessive oxygen, and assuring everybody that he feels—poor devil—like a new man.

'By the way, I did not escape the Waits by coming down here. I had not walked fifty yards from the railway station when I found them in full cry in a front garden. However, I am bound to confess that the seaside vocal Wait is enormously superior to the metropolitan instrumental one. They sang very well: were quite Waits off my mind, in fact. (This is my first pun: let who can beat it.) A couple of boys and the basso were conspicuous in the harmony. I suspect they were the church choir turning an honest penny.'

A week passed by, during which the readers of *The Star* must have been daily expecting to read the obituary notice of their musical critic. But on January 3rd, 1890, they were reassured:

'The other day, mad for want of something to do, I stood on the edge of the cliff and took a last look at sea and sky before plunging head-foremost to the rocks below. The preceding week had been a deadly one. I had been to Canterbury to see what the boy in Edwin Drood called the Kinfreederl; and my attempt to look right down the building from end to end had been baffled by a modern choir screen compared to which Costa's additional accompaniments to Mozart seemed pardonable and even meritorious. Why cant they let the unfortunate Kinfreederl alone? I rushed off angrily into the wilderness, and after wandering for eighteen miles or so found myself back here at Broadstairs again. I had also gone to Ramsgate to see a melodrama; but I had to leave the theatre at the eleventh murder, feeling that my moral sense was being blunted by familiarity with crime. As a last resource, I had been to the North Foreland Lighthouse to seek employment there; but the resident illuminating artist, whose intelligent and social conversation was an inexpressible relief to me, told me that the Trinity House catches its lighthousists young, as no man with an adequate knowledge of life would voluntarily embrace so monotonous a career. "I have come to such a state of mind in a rock house," he said, "that I believed at last that we two in it were the only people in the world" . . .

'When I had exhausted the Kinfreederl and the Lighthouse and the melodrama, suicide, as I have related, seemed the only thing left. But I was loth to cast myself off the cliff, for I had just read Mr Walter Besant's sequel to Ibsen's *Doll's House* in the *English Illustrated Magazine,* and I felt that my suicide would be at once held up as the natural end of a reprobate who greatly prefers Ibsenism to Walter Besantism. Besides, it seemed to be rather Walter's place than mine to commit suicide after such a performance. Still, I felt so deadly dull that I should hardly have survived to tell the tale had not a desperate expedient to wile away the time occurred to me. Why not telegraph to London, I thought, *for some music to review*? Reviewing has one advantage over suicide. In suicide you take it out of yourself: in reviewing you take it out of other people. In my seaside temper that decided me. I sent to London at once ; and the music came duly by parcels post.

'I have tried all the songs over carefully, and am under notice to leave when my week is up.'

Organized festivity never appealed to Shaw, who had an especial loathing for Christmas, even preferring the country to London during that festive season. One year he went to the Wye valley, 'a land of quietly beautiful hills, enchanting valleys, and an indescribable sober richness of winter coloring. This being so, need I add that the natives are flying from it as from the plague? Its lonely lanes, where, after your day's work, you can wander amid ghosts and shadows under the starry firmament, stopping often to hush your footsteps and listen to a wonderful still music of night and nature, are eagerly exchanged for sooty streets and gaslamps and mechanical pianos playing the last comic song but two.' Another Christmas he spent 'in an old-English manor-house,[1] where we all agreed to try and forget the festive season'. But they were not wholly successful because a troupe of local mummers came in one evening and gave an operatic entertainment that was the reverse of entertaining: 'We of the audience had to assume the character of good old English gentlemen and ladies keeping up a seasonable custom ; and it would be difficult to say whether we or the performers were the more out of countenance. I have seldom been so disconcerted ; and my host, though he kept it up amazingly, confessed to sharing my feelings ; whilst the eagerness of the artists to escape from our presence when their performance was concluded and suitably acknowledged, testified to the total failure of our efforts to make them feel at home. We were perfectly friendly at heart, and would have been de-

[1] Morris's at Kelmscott.

lighted to sit round the fire with them and talk; but the conventions of the season forbad it. Since we had to be mock-baronial, they had to be mock-servile; and so we made an uneasy company of Christmas humbugs, and had nothing to cheer us except the consciousness of heartily forgiving one another and being forgiven.'

Nothing but plenty of mental and manual labour could make idleness endurable to Shaw, whose happiest holidays occurred when a General Election forced him to rush about the country making speeches: 'It is a salutary thing after the worry and hurry of a London season to abandon one's typewriter, fly beyond the reach of the endless deliveries of the metropolitan postal service, and deliver one's soul face to face with one's fellow-man under the open sky.'

Perhaps Shaw's quietest holidays were spent with Sidney Webb, once in Holland and Belgium (Shaw's first foreign trip) and once at Ober Ammergau for the Passion Play. Webb, interested in everything, allowed Shaw to take him through all the picture galleries, into all the churches, and up all the church towers. They talked about everything on earth except socialism. At Ober Ammergau Shaw did his utmost to make his friend climb the mountains, but Webb settled himself in the heather at the base and promised to wait until Shaw came down again, which he did without tedium, as he was writing interminable love-letters to his future wife Beatrice Potter, with no facts or figures in them except his demonstration that one and one made, not two, but eleven. In Flanders Shaw was given a remarkable proof of Webb's memory. A parcel of official papers the size of an average pillow had to be despatched to the Colonial Office, and Webb, speaking fluent English-French and, with his Napoleonic imperial, looking exactly like a Frenchman, informed the clerk at the post office, who began to weigh it, that it could be sent for a sou. The clerk, aghast, expostulated. Webb cited the paragraph, page and volume of the code authorizing the rate he had quoted. The clerk wavered and went to consult his superior, who consulted the code, which justified Webb. 'After that,' said Shaw, 'he could have posted all his laundry home for a ha'penny.' But there was another side to the walking encyclopaedia-cum-calculating-machine known as Sidney Webb. On the journey from Haarlem to Ulm one day a policeman entered their steam tramcar. He was in charge of a young delinquent to whose wrists a long chain was fastened, and

154

who, under the severe stares of the company, appeared as wretched as a young man would be under such circumstances. It happened that Webb and Shaw had bought a packet of the famous local marzipan, ubiquitous on the Continent, and had been unable to eat it. At the next stop the police officer rose and beckoned his prisoner to follow. As the disgraced youth passed, Webb with miraculous adroitness transferred his marzipan from his pocket to that of the prisoner. The effect was magical. The youth, finding that what he had resented as reprobation was really sympathy, lifted his head, recovered his self-respect and, let us hope, lived blamelessly ever after.

Shaw told me that the gesture, in conception and execution, was entirely characteristic of the real Sidney Webb.

Shaw's physical recreations in the nineties were swimming and bicycling. He learnt to ride a bicycle in the spring of '95 while staying with the Webbs in the wooden hotel on Beachy Head: 'My efforts set the coastguards laughing as no audience had ever laughed at my plays. I made myself ridiculous with such success that I felt quite ready to laugh at somebody else.' So he laughed throughout a long essay at Dr Max Nordau. Apparently dancing was another physical recreation attended with ludicrous results. One February evening in 1890 he went to see the ballets at the Alhambra and the Empire, and was much struck by the dancing of a man named Vincenti at the former:

'When I arrived at my door after these dissipations I found Fitzroy Square, in which I live, deserted. It was a clear, dry, cold night; and the carriage-way round the circular railing presented such a magnificent hippodrome that I could not resist trying to go just once round in Vincenti's fashion. It proved frightfully difficult. After my fourteenth fall I was picked up by a policeman. "What are you doing here?" he said, keeping fast hold of me. "I bin watching you for the last five minutes." I explained, eloquently and enthusiastically. He hesitated a moment, and then said, "Would you mind holding my helmet while I have a try. It dont look so hard." Next moment his nose was buried in the macadam and his right knee was out through its torn garment. He got up bruised and bleeding, but resolute. "I never was beaten yet," he said, "and I wont be beaten now. It was my coat that tripped me." We both hung our coats on the railings, and went at it again. If each round of the square had been a round in a prize fight, we should have been less damaged and disfigured; but we persevered, and by four o'clock the policeman had just succeeded in getting round twice without a rest or a fall, when an inspector arrived and asked him bitterly whether this was his notion of fixed point duty. "I allow it aint fixed point," said the constable, emboldened by his new accomplishment; "but I'll lay half a sovereign *you* cant do it." The inspector could not resist the temptation to try (I was whirling round before his eyes in the most fascinating manner); and he made rapid progress after half an hour or so. We were subsequently joined by an early postman and by a milkman, who unfortunately broke his leg and had to be carried to hospital by the other three. By that time I was quite exhausted, and could barely crawl into bed. It was perhaps a foolish scene; but nobody who has witnessed Vincenti's performance will feel surprised at it.'

I quote this tissue of lies as an example of Shaw's method of telling the truth. It leaves one with a vivid notion of the effect produced by Vincenti's whirl round the stage. Shaw maintained, when I taxed him on the subject, that a literal account is neither true nor false: it tells just nothing. 'You may read the Annual Register from end to end and be no wiser. But read *Pilgrim's Progress* and *Gulliver's Travels* and you will know as much human history as you need, if not more.'

HENRY AND ELLEN

WHILE THE MUSICAL pedagogues were recovering their breath, the dramatists, actors and theatre-managers were holding theirs, for in the first week of January 1895 Shaw began to criticize the drama in *The Saturday Review* at a weekly salary of £6, continuing the treatment for three and a half years.

His new editor was Frank Harris, who believed in an absolute freedom of thought and a limitless licence of speech, though personally he was touchy enough. 'You sail the Spanish Main with the blackest of flags, the reddest of sashes, the hugest of cutlasses, and the thinnest of skins,' Shaw once wrote to him. Their first meeting was described by Shaw long afterwards: Harris had invited him to call and Shaw found the editor 'engaged with a visitor to whom he was speaking in resounding and perfectly fluent German. This impressed me, as I am the worst of linguists. I also appreciated his fine elocution, though, being a public speaker and a producer of my own plays, I was an expert at this game and proof against its theatrical illusion. I told myself that this was the man for me as an editor, but that he would bully me if I did not bully him first. All the editors who were any use to me were men of this sort. My bullying was very mild. He was telling me how he had upset himself by some athletic feat on the river. I immediately assumed the character of President of the Royal College of Physicians, and said severely, "Do you drink?" He was taken aback for a moment. Then he accepted the situation and gave me quite a long account of his symptoms and diet and so forth. After that we were on quite unreserved and intimate terms.'

Unreserved, perhaps, but scarcely intimate, since Shaw seldom came into close contact with him. To know a man intimately one must share some of his tastes and meet him constantly off duty. Harris was a big eater and drinker, a café-haunter, a city-gambler, a blackmailer, and, according to himself, a frequent fornicator; everything in fact that Shaw was not. When Harris asked him to the staff lunches at the Café Royal, he went once or twice merely to study the economics of the place, but disliked the meat-gorging and wine-swilling of his host and fellow-guests and objected on principle to the price of his own macaroni, a plateful of which only cost him tenpence elsewhere. His meetings with Harris were mostly confined to the office, which he occasionally visited when some legal action was pending in order to tell the editor that he had not a leg to stand on. Thus Shaw's knowledge of Harris was sketchy, his judgement of him insufficiently grounded.[1]

[1] Naturally Shaw does not accept this view. 'Harris was intensely disliked because he seemed a ferocious blackguard, and intimidated better men than himself,' wrote Shaw to me. 'His wonderful speaking voice and measured stylized delivery were tremendously imposing. But they did not impose on Julia Frankau (Frank Danby) nor on me. We knew poor Frank: the others didnt.'

Like Yates, Frank Harris possessed the main merit of a first-class editor: he chose his contributors with discrimination and gave them a free hand; so Shaw proceeded to make the theatrical world sit up.

The outstanding figure on the stage of that time was Sir Henry Irving, whose theatre, the Lyceum, was generally regarded as the chief temple of dramatic art in the kingdom. Shaw, as we know, had seen Irving in Dublin and had felt that he would be the leading exponent of modern drama. But Irving entertained other views for himself, and when not creating the bizarre characters in old-fashioned melodramas he hacked the plays of Shakespeare into shapes that set off his curious personality to advantage. This, from Shaw's point of view, was bad enough; but when in addition he engaged as principal lady the most enchanting actress who ever graced the stage, one who might have been born to play leading roles in the drama of her age, Shaw saw red. 'When questions of art are concerned I am really malicious,' he wrote. 'Retrogressive art and wasted or unworthily used talent . . . make me aware that I am capable of something as near to hatred as any emotion can be that has no taint of fear in it.' And he once told me that it made him quite savage to hear a work of art—a play, opera or symphony—murdered.

He first saw Ellen Terry shortly after he came to London. This was in Robertson's *Ours*, and she made little impression on him as an actress, having nothing to act. Then he saw her in *New Men and Old Acres*, which she made memorable just as Irving had made *Two Roses* memorable: 'I was completely conquered and convinced that here was the woman for the new drama which was still in the womb of Time, waiting for Ibsen to impregnate it. If ever there were two artists apparently marked out by Nature to make a clean break with an outworn past and create a new stage world they were Ellen Terry and Henry Irving.'

Throughout the eighties Shaw went regularly to the Lyceum Theatre, gnashing his teeth over the mangled Shakespeare and obsolete melodrama served up there and foaming at the mouth over the hideous waste of two wonderful talents. It is but fair to add that nearly everyone except Shaw was enchanted by the Shakespearean excerpts, impressed by *The Iron Chest* and *The Corsican Brothers*, and moved to ecstasy by the full flowering of two inimitable geniuses. But although Shaw felt the value of Ellen Terry's unique personality, and, full as he was of the school of superhuman acting which expired with Barry Sullivan (with Chaliapin in opera), found Irving's first attempts at it pitiable and ridiculous, he was quite capable of criticizing Ellen and praising Henry. In April '89, for instance, he went to *Macbeth* at the Lyceum 'and found Mr Irving playing very finely indeed, and quite irreproachable in my department. He and I are the only two men —not professional phonetic experts—in England who can distinguish a vowel from a diphthong. What a Lady Macbeth Miss Terry is! I would trust my life in her hands. It was a luxury to hear her speak of "the owl, the fatal bellman which gives the stern'st goodnight". I had not heard "goodnight" said in that exact tone since I saw her in the balcony scene in *Romeo and Juliet*.' At a Playgoers Club annual dinner he praised Irving to his face. Irving, in a speech, said that there ought to be a Conservatoire in England as in France for teaching elocution. Shaw, replying for the press, disagreed. There were already two magnificent schools of elocution in London, he asserted: one, he need hardly say, was the Lyceum. Irving, who had been expecting something nasty, sat bolt upright at this and looked extremely pleased with himself. The other, Shaw went on, was his own school in Hyde Park. Irving collapsed and looked extremely displeased with Shaw. Forty years after his visit to *Macbeth* Shaw wrote that Irving's 'peculiar nasal method of securing resonance obliged him to pronounce our English diphthongs as vowels', concerning which we may remark that if it contradicts what he had previously said, it contradicts it.

But Shaw would not have worried about Irving's pronunciation if only the man had produced the works of Ibsen, and in order to awake in him a consciousness of his own age, of the kind of drama he should have appeared in, Shaw frequently ridiculed the Lyceum plays, Irving's performances, and the parts on which Ellen Terry was wasting her exquisite personality. To understand Shaw's attitude towards Irving, and to appreciate Irving's feelings towards Shaw, we may take the latter's criticism (May 1895) of Irving's performance of Corporal Brewster in Conan Doyle's *A Story of Waterloo*, a performance that was hailed throughout the press as a masterpiece of moving and subtle acting which no other actor could have achieved.

There was absolutely no acting in the piece, wrote Shaw: 'There is a make-up in it, and a little cheap and simple mimicry which Mr Irving does indifferently because he is neither apt nor observant as a mimic of doddering old men.' When Irving enters 'he makes his way to his chair, and can only sit down, so stiff are his aged limbs, very slowly and creakily. This sitting down business is not acting: the callboy could do it ; but we . . . go off in enthusiastic whispers, "What superb acting! How wonderfully he does it!" The Corporal's grandniece prepares his tea : he sups it noisily and ineptly, like an infant. More whispers: "How masterly a touch of second childhood!" He gets a bronchial attack and gasps for paregoric, which his grandniece administers with a spoon, whilst our faces glisten with tearful smiles. "Is there another living actor who could take paregoric like that?" . . . He dodders across the stage . . . and sits down on another chair with his joints crying more loudly than ever for some of the oil of youth. We feel that we could watch him sitting down for ever. . . . Enter a haughty gentleman. It is the Colonel of the Royal Scots Guards, the Corporal's old regiment. According to the well-known custom of colonels, he has called on the old pensioner to give him a five-pound note. The old man, as if electrically shocked, staggers up and desperately tries to stand for a moment at "attention" and salute his officer. He collapses, almost slain by the effort, into his chair, mumbling pathetically that he "were a'most gone that time, Colonel". "A masterstroke! who but a great actor could have executed this heartsearching movement?" The veteran returns to the fireside: once more he depicts with convincing art the state of an old man's joints.'

With a hit at the critics for praising such a commonplace exhibition, Shaw asked: 'What, I wonder, must Mr Irving feel when he finds this pitiful little handful of hackneyed stage tricks received exactly as if it were a crowning instance of his most difficult and finest art?'

It is no good pretending that Irving laughed heartily over this or even that he appreciated the implied compliment that he and Shaw knew better than the critics. This sort of thing was always happening in *The Saturday Review*, and Irving could not even lecture at the Royal Institution without exposing himself to Shaw's awkwardly honest comments. In this lecture, delivered early in '95, Irving put forward 'a formal claim to have acting classified officially among the fine arts,' and remarked: 'Official recognition of anything worthy is a good, or at least a useful thing. It is a part, and an important part, of the economy of the State: if it is not, of what use are titles and distinctions, names, badges, offices, in fact all the titular and sumptuary ways of distinction?' Shaw promptly dotted the i's and crossed the t's of Irving's plea. If the composer, the poet, the painter, were given knighthoods, why not the actor? That, he said, was Irving's argument in a nutshell. Worthy and courageous fellow! As for the rest of the lecture, it was 'penny-a-liner's fustian' and Shaw declared that if Irving 'wrote it himself he wasted his time', but that if, as Shaw well knew, 'he got it written for him, he need not have paid the writer a farthing more than one-and-sixpence an hour'.

When it is added that Shaw had only recently attacked the whole policy of the Lyceum, with its obsolete tomfooleries, schoolgirl charades, blank verse and hashed Shakespeare, and had spoken of Ellen Terry as 'a born actress of real women's parts condemned to figure as a mere artist's model in costume plays', and had moreover summed up his emotions in the exclamation, 'What a theatre for a woman of genius to be attached to!' it will be understood why Irving did not receive a one-act play by Shaw with shouts of joyful enthusiasm.

The play was handed him by Ellen Terry. It was called *The Man of Destiny* and contained fat parts for himself (Napoleon) and Ellen (The Strange Lady), whose physical appearance was described in the stage directions.

The author and the actress had already commenced that lover-like correspondence which was to be published to the surprise and delight of everyone except Ellen Terry's son in 1931. It began badly. Ellen Terry wrote to Yates asking whether a young singer in whom she was interested had any chances of success. Yates gave the letter to his music critic Shaw, who made what Ellen called an 'exceedingly stiff and prim' reply. But he attended a concert at which Ellen recited and her friend sang, and wrote a long helpful letter in which he said that Ellen's recitation of Monk Lewis's silly poem *The Captive* had moved him but that her friend's singing had not: 'You brought tears to my eyes, not, you will understand, by the imaginary sorrows of the lunatic (sorrow does not make me cry, even when it is real) but by doing the thing beautifully. My whole claim to be a critic of art is that I can be touched in that way. Now your friend did not touch me in the least.'

After this the correspondence became triflingly gallant on

his part and teasingly indulgent on hers. The hobby of the male genius is to play at love-making, of the female genius to play at mothering; and these two played their parts for all they were worth. For years they did not meet, though Shaw told her of an occasion when she spoke to him without knowing who he was.

This paper-flirtation exactly suited Shaw's temperament; it exercised his imagination, soothed him, and enabled him to maintain an invigorating friendship without any of the drawbacks of personal contact. He loved Ellen Terry on the stage, and on paper, and had no wish to exchange an adorable dream for an incalculable reality. Ellen at a distance was enchanting: Ellen close at hand might have been disturbing. All the same he wanted her for his own plays as well as Ibsen's and did his utmost to make her break away from Irving, who was 'completely independent of the dramatist, and only approaches him in moments of aberration'.

Although Shaw warned her that *The Man of Destiny* was 'not one of my great plays . . . only a display of my knowledge of stage tricks—a commercial traveller's sample,' Ellen thought it 'delicious' and begged Irving to consider it for the Lyceum. Irving was cautious and crafty. He would not commit himself to an early production; on the other hand he did not wish to antagonize Shaw with a refusal. He had a 'princely manner of buying literary courtiers'; that is, of paying money for 'options' on plays by critics without the smallest intention of putting them on, and so purchasing praise for all his productions. Shaw was not amenable to such treatment, though Irving could scarcely be blamed for failing to realize it, most critics having discovered that his acting steadily improved on this basis.

Irving was a queer person: he was interested in nothing but his work and nobody but himself. Thus he was strangely ignorant about people and things, ignorant even about Irving, for he was too self-absorbed to objectify himself. The works of Shakespeare were merely the scenery in which his personality could move and express itself; if the words got in his way, he chopped them out, just as he would have changed a backcloth or toned down the lighting. He converted the characters of Shakespeare into so many projections of his stage-personality; whenever the words flatly contradicted his portrayal, they were removed. He scarcely concerned himself with the profession of acting; he cared solely for his own

162

performances. When Ben Webster, anxious to strike a responsive chord in 'the chief', asked whether he had seen in the papers that his son Harry was shortly to appear as Hamlet, Irving grunted: 'Harr-y? . . . Hm . . . Ham-let? . . . Hm . . . Sill-y . . .' His complete lack of interest in Shaw's play may therefore be assumed; nothing could have induced him to produce it; but he was cunning enough to appear keenly interested to Ellen and to talk of putting it on 'next year'.

Shaw saw through this manœuvre, and though he yielded to Ellen's entreaty that he should leave the play in Irving's hands, he told her that 'as long as I remain a dramatic critic I can neither sell plays nor take advances'. For some months he heard nothing further about it; so in July '96, he wrote to ask her why, and incidentally to make a suggestion: 'Come, I will teach you the part without your opening the book once. I will get a tandem bicycle; and we shall ride along over the celestial plains, I dinning the part into your head until you pick it up as one picks up a tune by ear. That is how all parts should be taught and learnt: in my ideal company there shall not be an actress who can read.' She at once spoke to Irving, who said he would do the play for a few nights next year and give it a run with another drama the following year. 'He wants the play very much,' Ellen assured the author, begging him a few days later to see or write to Irving 'about that confounded duck of a play'. Shaw wrote, and Irving proposed to give him £50 a year for the rights on the understanding that the play should be produced at the Lyceum when convenient. Shaw, as an honest critic, could only refuse, and offered to give Irving the play if he would produce some of Ibsen's works, or to give Ellen Terry the play without any conditions at all. Irving, unaccustomed to such generosity from author-critics, made no reply.

Meanwhile Irving had announced a production of Shakespeare's *Cymbeline* for the autumn of '96, and Shaw, having re-read the play and decided that Shakespeare was 'a damned fool', explained to Ellen at great length how she ought to treat the part of Imogen. Shaw's anti-Shakespeare campaign was part of his pro-Ibsen and anti-Irving campaign. If Ibsen was as wonderful as Shaw thought him, then Shakespeare was not as wonderful as other people thought him, and Irving, by neglecting Ibsen and producing episodes from Shakespeare's plays, was not only an enemy to the modern movement but a bardolater by false pretences. Shaw was fond, 'unaffectedly fond', of Shakespeare's plays, liking them chiefly for their poetry. Yet people did not remember his praise of Shakespeare ; they preferred such remarks as : 'I have long ceased to celebrate my own birthday ; and I do not see why I should celebrate Shakespear's . . . whoever expects me to put myself every 23 April in an attitude at all differing from my attitude on the 23 October is doomed to disappointment' ; or his criticism of Touchstone's humour, with which most intelligent folk would agree : 'Who would endure such humor from anyone but Shakespear?—an Eskimo would demand his money back if a modern author offered him such fare' ; or this peevish utterance : 'With the single exception of Homer, there is no eminent writer, not even Sir Walter Scott, whom I can despise so entirely as I despise Shakespear when I measure my mind against his. The intensity of my impatience with him occasionally reaches such a pitch, that it would positively be a relief to me to dig him up and throw stones at him, knowing as I do how incapable he and his worshippers are of understanding any less obvious form of indignity.'

Irving's production of *Cymbeline* was received by an outburst from Shaw which is partly explained by the story we have just followed. But it was also due to his dislike of *Cymbeline*, to the absurd enthusiasm displayed by people who pretended to like Shakespeare whenever Irving produced a version that the author himself would not have recognized, and to the abuse heaped upon Ibsen by critics who ought to have known better.

Henry Irving had a sardonic sense of humour, and, confident that Shaw's article would contain a phrase or two that would make the critic feel thoroughly uncomfortable in the presence of the actor, he asked Shaw to call at the Lyceum and discuss *The Man of Destiny* on the very morning when the criticism was due to appear. 'I shall see him with the Saturday article (which he will get up at five in the morning to read) up to the hilt in his heart,' Shaw wrote to Ellen Terry. Even so Irving was in a better position than his visitor, for the man who has driven in the sword must feel a trifle apologetic towards his opponent, and bits of Shaw's review probably recurred to him several times in the course of the interview : 'In a true republic of art Sir Henry Irving would ere this have expiated his acting versions on the scaffold. He does not merely cut plays : he disembowels them. . . . He has never in his life conceived or interpreted the characters of any author except himself.' Against this Shaw must have found comfort in his printed statement that Irving's Iachimo was in every respect better than Shakespeare's, which went far to neutralize the disadvantage at which Irving had him. The interview passed off without friction, and Ellen Terry thought that Shaw was a little awed by Irving. She got as far as the door of the office, intending to enter, but on hearing Shaw's voice within she 'skedaddled home again full tilt, and, oh I was laughing. I *couldn't* come in. All of a sudden it came to me that under the funny circumstances I should not be responsible for my impulses. When I saw you, I *might* have thrown my arms round your neck and hugged you! I *might* have been struck shy. The Lord knows what I might or might not have done, and I think H.I. might not have seen the joke!' Over a year later she recalled the episode: 'What is your voice like I wonder? You sang so *very* small that day I was eavesdropping at the Lyceum office door.' Shaw told her that he liked Irving but thought him without exception the stupidest man he had ever met: 'Simply no brains—nothing but character and temperament. Curious, how little use mere brains are! I have a very fine set ; and yet I learnt more from the first stupid woman who fell in love with me than ever they taught me.'

Not long after this Ellen peeped through a hole in the Lyceum Theatre curtain and saw Shaw for the first time: 'I've seen you at last! You *are* a boy! And a Duck! ... How deadly delicate you look.' Possibly the sight of him made her more than ever anxious that Irving should do his play ; at any rate she at last got Irving to the point of discussing the possibility of doing it with another play he wished to produce, and his manager, Bram Stoker, wrote to tell Shaw that while no date could yet be fixed he could draw on account of royalties whenever he wished. Shaw, more desirous to write with a free pen than to draw royalties, ignored this further attempt to buy him off, and at the close of '96 his pen took such liberties that Irving took offence. In criticizing the actor's performance of *Richard III*, Shaw said that Irving 'was not, as it seemed to me, answering his helm satisfactorily ; and he was occasionally a little out of temper with his own nervous condition. He made some odd slips in the text, notably by repeatedly substituting "you" for "I" . . . Once he inadvertently electrified the house by very unexpectedly asking Miss Milton to get further up the stage in the blank verse and penetrating

tones of Richard.' Shaw also accused Richard of playing the
love-scene with Anne 'as if he were a Houndsditch salesman
cheating a factory girl over a pair of second-hand stockings.'

This realistic description of a performance by a slightly
tipsy man annoyed Irving, who believed it to be an accusation
of drunkenness; and it was all the more annoying because
Irving actually had been drunk, though Shaw did not know it.
For a while Irving held his anger in check; but early in '97
Shaw went to see *Olivia* at the Lyceum, remarked that Henry
Irving's performance of the Vicar in that play was far surpassed by Hermann Vezin's and took occasion to add that
'my regard for Sir Henry Irving cannot blind me to the fact
that it would have been better for us twenty-five years ago to
have tied him up in a sack with every existing copy of the
works of Shakespear, and dropped him into the crater of the
nearest volcano'. Having absorbed this statement, Irving told
a friend that Shaw had a disagreeable lack of reverence for
persons in dignified positions, and in conversation with Ellen
Terry began to speak of him as 'Your friend Mr Pshaw.' He
also ordered his manager to return *The Man of Destiny* to its
author, signifying that he had changed his mind about producing it. Shaw was delighted: 'I am in ecstasies,' he wrote to
Ellen: 'I have been spoiling for a row.' Ellen was very much
upset and implored Shaw not to quarrel with Irving. Shaw
promised not to quarrel, kept his promise, and urged her to
take Irving's side in the dispute: 'It is when a man is too
much hurt to do the perfectly magnanimous thing that he
most needs standing by,' said Shaw, who further warned her
'Anything that you say in my favour, far from convincing
him, will only strike him as an act of treachery to himself.'
She still hoped that Irving would do the play, if given time;
but Shaw knew very well that he would not touch it and told
Ellen that her career had been 'sacrificed to the egotism of a
fool'. Shaw's considered opinion of the whole episode was
given me in a letter dated July 12th, 1939:

'In the nineties the bribery of critics had settled into a
routine so pleasant and friendly that actor managers did it as
a sort of ritual; and there was no feeling of anything improper about it.

'My own case illustrates the practice. George Alexander
wrote to me to say that he had bought the British rights of
Sudermann's play, *Sodom's Ende*, and would like me to advise

him about it. Sudermann was a playwright wildly unsuitable
to George and to the manners and tone of the St James's
Theatre under his management. Still, I politely took his copy
of the play, and, not knowing German (bar Wagner), read it
solemnly through and picked up what I could about it. I then
communicated the result to Alec, to the effect that Sudermann was just then a front line author, and the St James's a
front line theatre, and Alec a front line actor, and a play was
a play, and that was that. Alec then said that if I would
undertake the necessary translation and adaptation he was
prepared to buy a six months option on it for £50. My reply,
though very polite, grateful, and friendly in its terms, was
"Nothing doing."

'Next came Charles Wyndham with an old play by Scribe.[1]
This being in French gave me no trouble. I said, "Of course
this will succeed if you play the part of De Ryons." He then
asked what about the translation. "That," I said, "can be made
by Sydney Grundy." Wyndham grinned and could not resist
the temptation to give the show away. "Don Quixote!" he
said. So we parted good friends.

'Irving's case was different. This business of buying options
on translations that were never made, of plays which the
purchaser never meant to produce, had no other object in the
cases of Alexander and Wyndham than to tip the critic and
make him friendly. But Irving bought up plays, not to perform them, but to prevent any possible rival getting hold of
them. His direct bribery was frank and lordly: it was of the
kind known as Chicken and Champagne. His first nights ended
with a banquet on the stage to which it was a social distinction to be invited. On these occasions Bram Stoker, his
acting manager, invited me as I went in before the performance, as he did all the other presentable critics. I always
accepted the invitation as a princely favour; but I never went.

'Irving was not perspicacious enough to jump at *The Man
of Destiny* as a chance for him as an actor; but he was determined that Wilson Barrett (of whom he was ridiculously
afraid) or some other rival should not get it if he could help
it. His business clearly was to get the play safely on to his
shelves, which constituted a play cemetery, and at the same
time to attach to his literary retinue the rather dangerous
critic whom in conversation with Ellen Terry he spoke of

[1] To be precise, it was *L'Ami des Femmes* by Dumas *fils*.

as "your Mister Sháw". This I thoroughly understood when we met for the first and only time that morning at the Lyceum.

'I was quite friendly but also quite irreverent, as he was a baby in my hands. He, the greatest man in his own world, was a little bothered by this. He was prepared for hostility. He was prepared for veneration. He was not prepared for being treated like a baby, however kindly, and, being unable to conceive such a monstrosity, was puzzled. But he behaved very well under the circumstances. The conversation was in substance something like this:

"SHAW.—The question is how soon can you undertake to produce the play?"

"IRVING.—A date is not possible. I have many engagements. Perhaps, when I return from America, etc., etc. But if you should need an advance—"

"SHAW.—(Touched by the offer of £50). Thank you; but that is not my difficulty. I cannot have a play which I have just written produced twenty years hence as my latest work."

"IRVING.—(Acting a foxlike cunning). That can be arranged. I have means of explaining to the Press. There is a man named Bendall—"

"SHAW.—Bless you, I know all about Bendall; and I am on the Press myself. Let me put a question to you. I daresay when you were 23, you could have given—perhaps you did give—a very interesting performance of Hamlet. But would you like to give that performance now at the height of your powers as the best you could do to-day? Well, I hope to do better than *The Man of Destiny;* and I am not prepared to wait more than a season or two for its production."

'This virtually finished the conversation. Irving was fine enough to be incapable of saying "But damn it, man, I am offering you £50—a hundred if you like—for your rotten play, which nobody will ever produce." And he could not foresee *St Joan,* of which I was unconsciously prophetic. So we parted civilly without doing any business, though the play was still left under consideration, my attitude being that his position gave him a claim to it on his own terms (bar shelving) if he cared to produce it.

'Nothing more happened until the unlucky first and only night of his revival of *Richard III,* when he did one or two odd things on the stage and then fell downstairs and disabled himself by hurting his knee. I wrote a faithful but extremely stupid notice of the performance, in which I noted the oddities in the performance and said that he did not seem to be "answering his helm" as usual. I call this stupid because I ought to have seen that what was the matter was that he had drunk a little too much: an explanation which had not occurred to me.

'Irving, unfortunately, did not believe that I was so innocent, and regarded my criticism as a veiled and malicious accusation of drunkenness. He instantly repudiated *The Man of Destiny* and me for ever. Before I had received an official letter to this effect, I met Frederick Harrison (the Manager of the Haymarket Theatre, not the Positivist), who, to my astonishment, spoke of the appalling crime I had committed and the terrible commotion at the Lyceum about it. At first I was incredulous, and asked him who had told him all this. He said he had just had it from Harry Irving, whose characteristically Irvingesque comment was that it served the old man right and would teach him to keep sober next time.

'Irving himself must have thought me not only malicious but dishonest, as he evidently considered that it was part of our bargain that in future I should write him up. But since it had gone all over the press that he was to produce my play (this was not my doing ; for I knew he wasnt) I pressed him to make a presentable excuse for backing out. The only result was that his literary henchmen, L. F. Austin or Bram Stoker, began to write me elaborately sarcastic letters in his name. Thereupon I fired a thundering broadside into him, telling him that I knew quite well who were writing these letters, and asking him what he thought would happen to them if I took them on at that silly game. Immediately he disarmed me completely and for ever by writing me a genuine letter with his own hand, beginning with one of those harmless little illiteracies which abound in the letters of Queen Victoria. It was entirely sincere and unaffected, and, condensed into a single sentence, it amounted to "For God's sake let me alone." And that was the end of it, leaving me ashamed of having, however unintentionally, handled the baby as if it were a Japanese wrestler.

'There were incidents at his death which I have probably told you about. Anyhow, no more at present, from G.B.S.'

Although he let down Irving lightly on that occasion and even provided him with a dignified retreat, Shaw did not leave

169

him alone. In the course of an article on Forbes-Robertson's *Hamlet,* in October '97, he said that Shakespeare's works 'have been no more to him (Irving) than the word-quarry from which he has hewn and blasted the lines and titles of master-pieces which are really all his own'. In January '98 he informed his readers that Sir Henry Irving had not invited him to witness *Peter the Great*: 'Under the circumstances, this is something more than an omission: it is an appeal to me to stay away.' And when Irving died in October 1905, Shaw caused a sensation by writing in an Austrian paper that Irving had 'compelled the Court to knight him', and that he 'took no interest in anything except himself', that he was only interested in himself 'as an imaginary figure in an imaginary setting', and that he 'lived in a dream'. The last three statements, retranslated from the German, appeared in the English press as follows: 'He was a narrow-minded egotist, devoid of culture, and living on the dream of his own greatness.' Immediately all the people in England who, no doubt for sound personal reasons, disliked the truth in obituary notices, made public announcements that hanging, drawing and quartering was too good for Shaw. Laurence Irving wrote to say that all his relations thought Shaw the most appalling Yahoo and that his father had a most generous nature: indeed he was so truly kindhearted that he would have paid Shaw's funeral expenses willingly at any time. Shaw sent copies of his original article to all the leading newspapers in the country; but they showed their dislike not only of truth but of the true truth by refusing to print it.

Shaw however had not quite finished with Irving, though he kept his last action secret for over thirty years. Two eminent religious leaders, General Booth and Dr Clifford, urged the authorities to grant Irving a burial in Westminster Abbey. Unfortunately Irving's domestic life had not been all that the Free Churches could have approved; and as he had left his money in three equal parts to his two sons and a lady for whose friendly help and care in his declining years he was grateful, Lady Irving, who was ignored in the great actor's will, asked Shaw to assist her in preventing the Abbey burial. Shaw wrote her several pages of diplomatic sympathy, but added that if he were her solicitor as well as her friend he should feel bound to warn her that as the widow of a famous actor buried in Westminster Abbey she could obtain a civil pension by lifting her little finger, but that as the widow of an exposed adulterer no Prime Minister would dare to put her on the Civil List. Lady Irving pocketed her wrongs and her pension.

As a playwright of consequence Shaw received a ticket for the Abbey ceremony from George Alexander, who was greatly relieved when it came back with this note 'I return the ticket for the Irving funeral. Literature, alas, has no place at his death as it had no place in his life. Irving would turn in his coffin if I came, just as Shakespear will turn in his coffin when Irving comes.'

Many people thought that Shaw had been unfair to Irving and caustic as a critic, but when I produced a number of quips attributed to him by others he described them as 'unconsidered remnants of obsolete Green Room gossip, which was always full of the popular notion that wit is only a form of ill-natured rudeness. I assure you I was always, like Shakespeare, "a very civil gentleman". Even as a critic my attacks had something flattering implied which, as Laurence Irving spotted, took the malice out of them. Ellen Terry, when the Henry Irvingites attacked me furiously, said that I was the only critic who had really done him justice.'

THE DRAMA

SHAW HAD two very good reasons for attacking Shakespeare: firstly, he wished to draw attention to himself,[1] secondly, he wished to obtain a proper recognition of Ibsen's genius. He had been bowled over by Ibsen and had written a book, *The Quintessence of Ibsenism*, in order to bring Ibsen's philosophy

[1] This was not his view, for when I expressed it he gave me a volley: 'What a horrid libel! I never thought about drawing attention to myself, because I could not help doing it every time I put pen to paper. Besides, my own Shakespearean output was then unwritten. I had nothing (to speak of) to draw attention to.' 'Except, as I said, yourself,' was the reply.

into complete harmony with his own. Thus his reasons for smashing the idol Shakespeare were quite excusable because they were entirely personal. The enthusiastic and intelligent youths of every period like to discover their own gods and to kick the gods of their fathers, both discovery and kicking being healthy and enjoyable pursuits. Since Shaw fought for Ibsen, the younger generation has discovered Shaw and kicked Ibsen, or discovered Tchekov and kicked Shaw, or discovered someone and kicked someone else. It does not matter in the long run. The mental exercise of taking in and throwing out is thoroughly invigorating; youth grows up and achieves a more balanced view; while the immortals are all the better for the mud that has been thrown at them, because it has helped to protect them from the corrosion of time. No one today is so modern as Shakespeare, who owes a little of his freshness to Shaw's mud-slinging, which made it necessary for the succeeding age to clean him up and see what his features were really like.

Yet Shaw's line of attack on Shakespeare was as feeble as his reasons for it were sound. True he was not quite so stupid as Tolstoy, whose chief complaint was that Shakespeare had failed to face the question, 'What are we alive for?' which anyone but a fool would have to answer 'In order to live' or 'God alone knows!' But Shaw made the childish error, which a dramatist of all people should avoid, of confusing Shakespeare with his creations; and since his line of attack revealed his chief weakness as a man, and therefore as an artist, we must deal with it here.

One of Shakespeare's most famous characters is a witch-ridden, conscience-stricken, wife-chidden murderer, who wades through slaughter to a throne and shuts the gates of mercy on his friends, their wives and children, and who, following a course of ghostly apparitions and harrowing warnings from the infernal world, and surrounded on every side by conspiracy, rebellion and hatred, begins to be weary of life, takes refuge in self-pity, and regards the whole business of existence as a meaningless and sorry affair. 'Out, out, brief candle,' he says, reasonably enough under the circumstances. Shaw calmly took this as Shakespeare's considered attitude towards life, not as an expression of Macbeth's momentary emotion. 'I want to be thoroughly used up when I die,' he wrote, 'for the harder I work, the more I live. I rejoice in life for its own sake. Life is no "brief candle" for me. It is a sort of splendid

172

torch, which I have got hold of for the moment; and I want to make it burn as brightly as possible before handing it on to future generations.' Perhaps all that need be said about this impassioned outburst of rhetoric is that if Shakespeare had thought 'splendid torch' a truer symbol of life from Macbeth's point of view, or a more exact expression of a superstitious and disillusioned dictator's feelings than 'brief candle', he would no doubt have used it.

Shaw frequently made this error of condemning Shakespeare out of the mouths of his creations, and once he even did it when denying that the characters in a play of his own were so many projections of himself. 'Some of the critics imagine I am contradicting myself when my characters contradict one another,' he complained to an interviewer. 'According to these innocents all the persons in *John Bull's Other Island* are only mouthpieces of Shaw . . . and the difference between these characters are therefore, if you please, my inconsistencies, my insincerities, my levities!' Having poured scorn on the critics for being such chumps, he then went on to say: 'The business of a dramatist is to make experience intelligible. Shakespeare's notion that it was to hold the mirror up to nature was the blunder of a playwright who was a mere observer, not a thinker.' It was, however, Hamlet, not his creator, who talked about holding the mirror up to nature; so Shakespeare's characters could be used in evidence against him, but Shaw's characters could not be so used.

The assumption that Shakespeare was expressing his own opinions through his creations shows that Shaw, while refusing to admit that his own characters expressed himself, could not really understand a dramatist who was able to attain complete objectivity. Shaw's chief failing as a dramatist was his inability to portray types with whom he had no sympathy, all his men and women betraying their blood-relationship, just as his chief failing as a man was his inability to understand people with whom he did not agree.

One of Shaw's objections to Shakespeare was that he did not write like Bunyan; in other words, that he pictured life as it was and is, not as Bunyan or Shaw would have liked it to be. Later we shall have an opportunity of placing Shakespeare's portrait of a great man of action against Shaw's conception of the same man, comparing them with recent samples of the species in real life. For the moment we may

173

content ourselves with a typical specimen of Shavian absurdity on the theme of heroism.

The world was to Bunyan a more terrible place than it was to Shakespeare, said Shaw, 'but he saw through it a path at the end of which a man might look not only forward to the Celestial City, but back on his life and say: —"Though with great difficulty I am got hither, yet now I do not repent me of all the trouble I have been at to arrive where I am. My sword I give to him that shall succeed me in my pilgrimage, and my courage and skill to him that can get it." The heart vibrates like a bell to such an utterance as this: to turn from it to "Out, out, brief candle," and "The rest is silence," and "We are such stuff as dreams are made of; and our little life is rounded by a sleep" is to turn from life, strength, resolution, morning air and eternal youth, to the terrors of a drunken nightmare.'

Every single statement in this paragraph creates a totally false impression. The world could not have been a more terrible place to the author of *Pilgrim's Progress* than it was to the author of *King Lear*. The heart does not vibrate like a bell to the utterance of Bunyan's Mr Valiant-for-truth, unless with the object of drowning the smug sentiments of a boastful prig. Shakespeare did not mean to convey a sense of life, strength, resolution, morning air or eternal youth when Macbeth was on his last legs, Hamlet was dying, and Prospero was about to retire from the world and lead a meditative life. Nor has anyone except Shaw discovered the terrors of a drunken nightmare in the last words of those three characters. Nor is there the smallest evidence that those last words expressed Shakespeare's own feelings more accurately than the last words of Falstaff or any other of his great characters. Nor, for that matter, shall I be silly enough to call Bunyan a boastful prig solely on the strength of Mr Valiant-for-truth's high opinion of himself, which is precisely what one would expect from a man so named. When, by the way, Shakespeare wished to sound the heroic note, he did not resort to the moral babble and pietistic twaddle of Bunyan. He put into the mouth of an average man a simple remark which told ordinary people what they had to do and what made it worth doing:

Men must endure
Their going hence even as their coming hither:
Ripeness is all.

Apart from Ibsen, whose genius he praised on the slightest provocation, Shaw had not a very high opinion of contemporary dramatists. He championed Henry Arthur Jones, partly because he was a personal friend and partly because Jones was doing his best to criticize the morals of the age. He attacked Arthur Pinero, who was being praised by other critics for qualities his work did not possess, though Shaw was careful to add that he was in violent reaction against the Pinero school of playwrights and 'my criticism has not, I hope, any other fault than the inevitable one of extreme unfairness'. As a result the manager of the Court Theatre did not send tickets to *The Saturday Review* for the first-night of Pinero's *Trelawny of the Wells,* and Shaw told his readers exactly what happened: 'When a journal is thus slighted, it has no resource but to go to its telephone and frantically offer any terms to the box-office for a seat for the first night. . . . In response to a humble appeal, the instrument scornfully replied that "three lines of adverse criticism were of no use to it". Naturally my curiosity was excited to an extraordinary degree by the fact that the Court Theatre telephone, which knew all about Mr Pinero's comedy, should have such a low opinion of it as to be absolutely certain that it would deserve an unprecedentedly contemptuous treatment at my hands. I instantly purchased a place for the fourth performance . . . and I am now in a position to assure that telephone that its misgivings were strangely unwarranted, and that, if it will excuse my saying so, it does not know a good comedietta when it sees one.'

Sensitive dramatists did not enjoy Shaw's treatment of them, even though he openly confessed 'I do my best to be partial.' The actors and actresses of those days, being equally sensitive, disliked Shaw's suggestion that they behaved on the stage in a way that persuaded 'smart parties in the boxes that it would be quite safe to send them cards for an "At Home" in spite of their profession'; and none of them relished Shaw's description of their appearance in a typical modern play as 'a tailor's advertisement making sentimental remarks to a milliner's advertisement in the middle of an upholsterer's and decorator's advertisement'. They feared his praise as much as his blame, and when he offered to interview an American actress in order to help her in an Ibsen enterprise she exclaimed passionately that if he wrote a word about her she would shoot him. So the players had to comfort themselves with the reflection that G.B.S. was not a gentleman, a reflection with which he was in hearty agreement: 'I have never been able to see how the duties of a critic, which consist largely in making painful remarks in public about the most sensitive of his fellow-creatures, can be reconciled with the manners of a gentleman.'

Again he attacked a popular christian festival, beginning his notice of a Drury Lane pantomime: 'I am sorry to have to introduce the subject of Christmas in these articles. It is an indecent subject; a cruel, gluttonous subject; a drunken, disorderly subject; a wasteful, disastrous subject; a wicked, cadging, lying, filthy, blasphemous, and demoralizing subject. Christmas is forced on a reluctant and disgusted nation by the shopkeepers and the press: on its own merits it would wither and shrivel in the fiery breath of universal hatred; and any one who looked back to it would be turned into a pillar of greasy sausages. Yet, though it is over now for a year, and I can go out without positively elbowing my way through groves of carcases, I am dragged back to it, with my soul full of loathing, by the pantomime.' He described his notice as a gratuitous advertisement 'given as a Christmas-box by the newspaper to the manager who advertises all the year round'; but the manager of Drury Lane Theatre would willingly have dispensed with this Christmas-box, and must have felt gratified when the criticisms of G.B.S. received public recognition: 'I regret to say that the patrons of the gallery at the Princess's, being admitted at half the usual west-end price, devote the saving to the purchase of sausages to throw at the critics. I appeal to the gentleman or lady who successfully aimed one at me to throw a cabbage next time, as I am a vegetarian, and sausages are wasted on me.'

But what must have horrified the more respectable readers of *The Saturday Review* was his frequent reference to *Mr* Oscar Wilde when that dramatist was a convict in Reading Gaol and his name was neither mentioned in print nor whispered in public. This took some courage, the credit for which the critic must share with his editor, assuming the editor read the reviews and was conscious of the indiscretion.

Shaw's own works apart, Wilde was the author of the only English play written in the nineteenth century that has lasted to the present day, and this makes everything Shaw had to say about him interesting, especially as both of them were Irish and did not care for one another personally. Wilde said of

Shaw: 'An excellent man; he has not an enemy in the world, and none of his friends like him.' Shaw said of Wilde: 'He was my fellow-townsman, and a very prime specimen of the sort of fellow-townsman I most loathed: to wit, the Dublin snob. His Irish charm, potent with Englishmen, did not exist for me; and on the whole it may be claimed for him that he got no regard from me that he did not earn. What first established a friendly feeling in me was, unexpectedly enough, the affair of the Chicago anarchists . . . I tried to get some literary men in London, all heroic rebels and sceptics on paper, to sign a memorial asking for the reprieve of these unfortunate men. The only signature I got was Oscar's. It was a completely disinterested act on his part; and it secured my distinguished consideration for him for the rest of his life.'

The latter portion of the second article Shaw wrote for *The Saturday Review* dealt with Wilde's *An Ideal Husband,* which was produced in the first week of 1895. 'Mr Oscar Wilde's new play at the Haymarket is a dangerous subject,' began Shaw, 'because he has the property of making his critics dull. They laugh angrily at his epigrams, like a child who is coaxed into being amused in the very act of setting up a yell of rage and agony. They protest that the trick is obvious, and that such epigrams can be turned out by the score by anyone light-minded enough to condescend to such frivolity. As far as I can ascertain, I am the only person in London who cannot sit down and write an Oscar Wilde play at will. The fact that his plays, though apparently lucrative, remain unique under these circumstances, says much for the self-denial of our scribes. In a certain sense Mr Wilde is to me our only thorough playwright. He plays with everything: with wit, with philosophy, with drama, with actors and audience, with the whole theatre.'

About six weeks later, at the St James's Theatre, came *The Importance of Being Earnest,* Shaw's attitude to which may have been influenced by the fact that 'it missed fire all over the place on the second night' when he was present. He thought it immature, inhuman, mechanical, old-fashioned, funny but hateful. 'It amused me, of course; but unless comedy touches me as well as amuses me, it leaves me with a sense of having wasted my evening. I go to the theatre to be moved to laughter, not to be tickled or bustled into it; and that is why, though I laugh as much as anybody at a farcical comedy, I am out of spirits before the end of the second act, and out of temper before the end of the third, my miserable mechanical laughter intensifying these symptoms at every outburst. . . . On the whole I must decline to accept *The Importance of Being Earnest* as a day less than ten years old.' It is getting on for half a century old now, but the years do not seem to matter. Yet Shaw will not recant a word of his verdict. The play is to him that unpardonable thing 'a mechanical rabbit'. Even if that were so, Wilde was the only man who ever possessed the key to the mechanism.

Not long after the appearance of his review Shaw met Wilde at a lunch given by Frank Harris at the Café Royal and calmly asked him whether *The Importance of Being Earnest* had been written years before under the influence of Gilbert and furbished up for George Alexander as a potboiler. Although Wilde was then seriously concerned over his action against the Marquis of Queensberry, he was put out by this question and said in a lofty manner that he was disappointed in Shaw. After his trial and sentence and the newspaper scurrilities, Shaw felt a strong impulse to help him, and spent a railway journey to the north in drafting a petition for his release ; but apart from Stewart Headlam, the 'silenced' Christian Socialist parson, he could get no one to sign it, the only person who had signed a similar petition for the Chicago anarchists being in gaol. So he did the next-best thing: whenever possible he mentioned Wilde's work as an artist in his dramatic criticisms. In October '95, about four months after Wilde's conviction, he referred to a remarkable scene in 'Mr Oscar Wilde's *Ideal Husband*', comparing it with the crude handling of a like theme in a new play by Jerome K. Jerome. A year later he dealt with a comedy by Charles Hawtrey, in which Charles Brookfield acted a leading part. As both Hawtrey and Brookfield had done their utmost to ruin Wilde by procuring perjured evidence against him, they could not have read with much animation Shaw's judgement of their play: 'It cannot be compared to the comedies of Mr Oscar Wilde, because Mr Wilde has creative imagination, philosophic humor, and original wit, besides being a master of language ; while Mr Hawtrey . . .' —but we need not bother about Mr Hawtrey. In March '98, with Wilde out of prison though still unmentionable, Shaw referred to him four times in an article on 'The Theatrical World of 1897', while in April of the same year Shaw wrote of William Heinemann, who had just published a drama of his own, 'Will he ever handle a pen and play with an idea as Mr Max Beerbohm and Mr Oscar Wilde can?

Clearly never—not even if we were to wrap him in blotting paper and boil him in ink for a week to make his literary faculty supple and tender.' After his release from prison Wilde received inscribed copies of Shaw's books from the author and returned the compliment.

As a rule, of course, the plays and players G.B.S. was forced to notice were beneath serious consideration, but now and again the subject was worthy of him; and when Sarah Bernhardt and Eleanora Duse appeared in *La Dame aux Camélias* by Dumas and *Heimat* (known in English as *Magda*) by Sudermann during the same June week of 1895, he wrote one of the greatest critical essays in the language.[1] After reading it one is not surprised that such a critic should have drawn others in his wake. The articles signed 'G.B.S.' in *The Saturday Review,* said James Agate, 'made me determine that one day I would be a dramatic critic'; and Max Beerbohm admired Shaw 'beyond all other men' as a dramatic critic: 'I never tire of his two volumes. He was at the very top of his genius when he wrote them.' Above all, Shaw's appreciation of the Duse actually drew a tribute from the artist herself. Little, she said, as she deigned to notice the insects who infested the theatre on pretence of criticizing what they did not understand, she could condescend to acknowledge and encourage any symptom of real intelligence. She was particularly pleased with the recognition of the years of hard work behind her apparently spontaneous effects. In short, she was gratified and grateful. It is perhaps only fair to mention that Shaw confessed that his criticisms of the divine Sarah were worthless. 'I could never do her justice or believe in her impersonations because she was so like my aunt Georgina.' As with several of his funniest sallies, this was a simple statement of fact.

Towards the close of 1897 Shaw, having had more than enough of the drama and feeling that his brain was being affected by it, began to pine for something quite different from a theatrical performance. 'I felt that I must have a real experience of some kind, under conditions, especially as regards fresh air, as unlike those of the stalls as possible. After some

[1] But he greeted my statement that in this article he had been inspired to do his best with: 'Blast you! I *always* did my best. That was how the quality got into the criticisms. I am an artist, and cannot bear anything that I can better.' To which there was but one reply: 'Then you were inspired to do better than your best.'

consideration it occurred to me that if I went into the country, selected a dangerous hill, and rode down it on a bicycle at full speed in the darkest part of the night, some novel and convincing piece of realism might result. It did.' As a result of the accident his face was badly cut by a stone and sewn up by an Edgware doctor. 'Probably no man has ever misunderstood another so completely as the doctor misunderstood me when he apologized for the sensation produced by the point of his needle as he corrected the excessive openness of my countenance after the adventure. To him who has endured points made by actors for nearly three years, the point of a surgeon's darning needle comes as a delicious relief. I did not like to ask him to put in a few more stitches merely to amuse me, as I had already, through pure self-indulgence, cut into his Sunday rest to an extent of which his kindness made me ashamed; but I doubt if I shall ever see a play again without longing for the comparative luxury of that quiet country surgery, with the stillness without broken only by the distant song and throbbing drumbeat of some remote Salvation Army corps, and the needle, with its delicate realism, touching my sensibilities, stitch, stitch, stitch, with absolute sincerity in the hands of an artist who had actually learned his business and knew how to do it.' The doctor refused to take a fee because, as a fellow-Irishman, Shaw's Dublin accent aroused his sympathy. 'Here the West End manager will perhaps whisper reproachfully. 'Well, and do I ever make you pay for your stall?" To which I cannot but reply, "Is that also due to the sympathy my voice awakens in you when it is raised every Saturday?" . . . Besides, he said it was a mercy I was not killed. Would any manager have been of that opinion? . . . On the whole, the success of my experiment left nothing to be desired; and I recommend it confidently for imitation. My nerves completely recovered their tone and my temper its natural sweetness. I have been peaceful, happy, and affectionate ever since, to a degree which amazes my associates. It is true that my appearance leaves something to be desired; but I believe that when my eye becomes visible again, the softness of its expression will.more than compensate for the surrounding devastation.' However, he continued, 'a man is something more than an omelette', and he readdressed himself to his critical duties.

In April '98 something more serious happened to him: 'One of my feet, which had borne me without complaining for forty years, struck work. The spectacle of a dramatic critic hopping about the metropolis might have softened a heart of stone; but the managers, I regret to say, seized the opportunity to disable me by crowding a succession of first nights on me. After *The Medicine Man* at the Lyceum, the foot got into such a condition that it literally had to be looked into. I had no curiosity in the matter myself; but the administration of an anaesthetic made my views of no importance. . . . My doctor's investigation of my interior has disclosed the fact that for many years I have been converting the entire stock of energy extractable from my food (which I regret to say he disparages) into pure genius.' He had been overworking and heading for a breakdown. which started with a too tightly-laced shoe, which brought on an abscess, which resulted in necrosis of the bone, which involved two operations. We shall hear more of this shortly. Coming as it did with Frank Harris's sale of *The Saturday Review,* his own sickening of the theatre, and the fact that he was just beginning to make money as a dramatist, he decided to drop criticism. His post was filled by Max Beerbohm, and his 'Valedictory' appeared on May 21st:

'The English do not know what to think until they are coached, laboriously and insistently for years, in the proper and becoming opinion. For ten years past, with an unprecedented pertinacity and obstination, I have been dinning into the public head that I am an extraordinary witty, brilliant, and clever man. That is now part of the public opinion of England; and no power in heaven or on earth will ever change it. I may dodder and dote; I may potboil and platitudinize; I may become the butt and chopping-block of all the bright, original spirits of the rising generation; but my reputation shall not suffer: it is built up fast and solid, like Shakespear's, on an impregnable basis of dogmatic reiteration. . . .

'When a man of normal habits is ill, everyone hastens to assure him that he is going to recover. When a vegetarian is ill (which fortunately very seldom happens), everyone assures him that he is going to die, and that they told him so, and that it serves him right. They implore him to take at least a little gravy, so as to give himself a chance of lasting out the night. They tell him awful stories of cases just like his own which ended fatally after indescribable torments; and when he tremblingly inquires whether the victims were not hardened

181

meat-eaters, they tell him he must not talk, as it is not good for him. Ten times a day I am compelled to reflect on my past life, and on the limited prospect of three weeks or so of lingering moribundity which is held up to me as my probable future, with the intensity of a drowning man. And I can never justify to myself the spending of four years on dramatic criticism. I have sworn an oath to endure no more of it. Never again will I cross the threshold of a theatre. The subject is exhausted ; and so am I.'

A FABIAN VESTRYMAN

EIGHTEEN HUNDRED AND NINETY-TWO was an important date in the history of the Fabian Society and in the life of Shaw, for in July of that year Sidney Webb married Beatrice Potter and the combination was unique in the annals of Social Reform.

Beatrice Potter was the youngest but one of nine children, whose father had inherited a fortune, lost it and made another. He became a Director of the Great Western Railway, President of the Grand Trunk Railway in Canada, Director of the Hudson Bay Company and other remunerative concerns, living in a world where people talked in millions and dealt in nations. The Potters had houses in the Cotswolds, in Monmouthshire, Westmorland, London, and wherever it suited them to take a holiday. They knew everybody, leading politicians, scientists, economists, philosophers, theologians, and who-not: Cardinal Manning, Joseph Chamberlain, Herbert Spencer, Huxley, Tyndall, bishops, bankers, and innumerable barons. In such a varied society was Beatrice brought up, and between the ages of 18 and 24 she did all the usual things that were expected of her, enduring the deadly delights of 'the season' and visiting all the fashionable continental resorts. After her mother's death she ran her father's establishment, took part in his work, and before breakfast every morning studied logic, philosophy and economics. Herbert Spencer taught her much, Francis Galton impressed her deeply, Joseph Chamberlain argued with her, and, it was said, nearly married her. But she was drawn more towards statistics than to men and co-operation for her meant the Co-operative movement, on which she wrote a book after investigating the sweating system by the heroic method of disguising herself as a proletarian and working in a sweater's den, an experiment which —her brains being obviously superior to her needlework— usually ended in her being selected as an eligible bride for the sweater's son and heir.

She required historical background for the book; a friend told her who could supply it; and in 1890 she met Sidney Webb, who promptly wrote out a list of sources and handed it to her. A few days later he sent her a Fabian pamphlet on the Rate of Interest, and they began to correspond. His next packet of tracts included the poems of Rossetti. After that he dined with her in order to discuss social problems with the Charles Booths, and they went to Glasgow together for the Co-operative Congress. Their intimacy increased, their letters to one another became frequent and longer, they exchanged views on Trade Unionism. He wanted to marry her; she was less sure of what she wanted; her father, who would have objected to her marriage with a socialist, was ill, which added to her perplexity; but in the spring of '91 she sent Sidney a proof of her book on the Co-operative Movement, and in May they were privately engaged. Two months later Beatrice wrote in her diary: 'We are both of us second-rate minds, but we are curiously combined. I am the investigator and he the executant; between us we have a wide and varied experience of men and affairs. We have also an unearned income. These are unique circumstances. A considerable work should result if we use our combined talents with deliberate and persistent purpose.' Her father died in January '92, and they married in July, their honeymoon in Ireland being enlivened by an investigation into Trade Societies. Sidney left the Colonial Office and they settled down at No. 41 Grosvenor Road on £1000 a year.

This house soon became famous as the social centre of English socialism, where young men from the universities met rising politicians, where the ambitious poor mixed with the well-meaning rich, where the brilliant unknowns talked to the dull well known. People who were separated by class, profession or belief, met at 41 Grosvenor Road, where the leaders of the future Labour Party were mentally nurtured. The house and the entertainment expressed the personalities of the host and hostess. The drawing-room was furnished with extreme simplicity, the object being to get as many people into it as possible. The meals were severely plain: no choice of dish; just soup, fish, mutton, milk pudding; one took it or left it. Beer or whisky to drink; no wine.

The conversation at these parties, if brainy, was a little trying for those who just wanted to chat about one thing and another. Its note was high-pitched and informatory. Small talk was barred; the weather was ignored. Sidney Webb, short, dressed in blue serge, was a living encyclopaedia, unable to understand why other people did not know as much as he did. Beatrice Webb, tall, dark-haired, handsome, her eyes flashing, her slender body clothed in striking dresses, dictated programmes to cabinet ministers and lines of conduct to everyone else. Between them they knew everybody and every-thing and could out-argue anyone. Her hard clear mind, his supple quick brain, were more than a match for the keenest, cleverest antagonist, who was moreover handicapped by their serene self-assurance, their calm conviction that truth was on their side, error on the other; an attitude made less endurable by their large-minded tolerance of opposition.

Nothing is so irritating as omniscience, nothing so galling as moral superiority, and Mrs. Webb's controversial methods, her contempt of social foibles and disapproval of sexual lapses, sometimes made her disliked, especially by women, who were afraid of her; for she laid down rules of conduct with as much assurance as she gave forth advanced opinions, and her habit of ordering the general conversation was exasperating. Even when she indulged in gossip she seemed to be classifying scandals as she classified people, trades or emoluments. In her eyes human beings were types, not individuals, and she regarded them with cool detachment, mentally docketing them. 'She saw men as samples moving,' said H. G. Wells. What made her so very objectionable in the eyes of her detractors was that no chink could be spied in her armour. She had no weaknesses. She and her husband worked unceasingly, talked purposefully, lived virtuously, and took their innocent and hygienic pleasures vigorously.

Sydney Olivier, resident clerk at the Colonial Office jointly with Webb, became Governor of Jamaica; and after her marriage Mrs Webb took his place as one of the four leading Fabians. Shaw and Wallas were constant visitors at 41 Grosvenor Road and spent nearly all their holidays with the Webbs in Surrey, Suffolk, Monmouth, or wherever they took a house for the purpose. Holiday-taking did not, with these four, mean holiday-making. They worked in the mornings, studied or read in the evenings, and went for strenuous walks or bicycle rides in the afternoons. As Webb was incapable of looking after his own machine, Shaw attended to it when anything went wrong, becoming adroit in the craft of puncture-mending. One day he fished out an obsolete 'penny farthing' bicycle, terrifyingly tall, from the stable of the house where they were staying and tried to ride it, but found that it would only go downhill. As there were a number of sloping terraces in front of the house, the machine descended them with success, but the moment it reached flat ground it pulled up with a violent jerk, flinging Shaw to the earth. He repeated the performance several times, and each time he came a cropper Mrs Webb laughed heartily. Drawn by the sounds of mirth, Sidney appeared at the window and when he saw what was happening rushed out to try a fall. Upon which Beatrice flung her arms round him and forbade the experiment in such heart-rending tones that it had to be abandoned. Shaw might break his own neck if he pleased: it seemed natural that he should do such things, but not Sidney's.

The oddity in the Webbshavian combination was that Shaw had almost every characteristic that the Webbs disliked. It was impossible to index him: he would not fit into any of the Webb categories, and was finally classified by Beatrice as a Sprite. His education had been entirely artistic: he had never passed an examination, whereas Webb had lived on scholarships, which his swift reading and champion memory enabled him to pick up like daisies, until he walked easily into the upper division of the Civil Service. The Webbs, though they were socialists and did not go to church, were entirely English and respectable: Shaw was Irish, a vagabond, a bohemian, neither married nor celibate. He approached all the subjects they had in common in unexpected and incalculable ways. He had forced his acquaintance on Webb, having heard him speak for ten minutes at a meeting, and at once marked him as a leader. And this was what saved the situation when Beatrice, with equal perspicacity, picked him out years afterwards as the ablest of the Fabians and married him. She would as soon have married the devil as Shaw; and she would certainly have got rid of him as an undesirable but for a qualification, then unique, that made him indispensable: he knew Sidney's full value. So she took him on as an inevitable encumbrance, and soon found that he was a useful and unshakably loyal friend, very skilful with his pen, not too troublesome in the house, good company, and not without an amusing appeal to a certain gipsy strain in the Potter blood of which nobody suspected her, but which came out very strongly in the strange career of her artist sister. Shaw was soon allowed the privilege of his genius and became 'Franklyn our loyal friend' so completely that even his settling down as a prosperous moneymaker with a wife of unquestionable social position and a considerable property made little difference, and that little all for the better, in his standing with the Webbs.

The three arch-Fabians exercised one another's minds incessantly, often with such vigour that visitors who overheard could not believe that they were not witnessing a furious and irreconcilable quarrel. But it was all in the day's work; the calm was as perfect as the tempest had been noisy. 'We never really disagreed,' said Shaw to me, 'but an Irishman likes to know what he is doing; and there is nothing an Englishman hates more. My talent for lucid and realistic exposition without British moral titivation was such that whenever the Webbs devised a policy and I proceeded to make a definite statement of it they immediately protested before heaven and earth that such a thing had never entered their heads. When the surprise was over and the All Clear was sounded they concluded that I was right after all, without the least suspicion that it was they who were right, though they held it to be not honesty to have it so set down.'

No hole-and-corner meeting was too small, no market-square too large for Shaw to speak at. In the first twelve years of his apostolate he harangued a thousand public assemblies. The Webbs talked in drawing-rooms, club-rooms, working-men's institutes, wherever two or more were gathered together for the betterment of the human lot. Seven hundred lectures were delivered by leading members of the Fabian Society in a single year. We catch glimpses of Shaw doing all sorts of odd jobs: working on the committee of a Liberal Association and forcing on it the once famous Newcastle Programme, drafted by Webb; turning up at the first meeting of the Independent

Labour Party, where he planted the chief item of the party programme (taxation of unearned incomes) on Keir Hardie; being cheered to the echo by a poverty-stricken audience in Whitechapel for telling it that he hated the poor, who, like the House of Lords from Cromwell's point of view, were 'useless, dangerous, and ought to be abolished'; provoking an opposition to storm the platform of the old St James's Hall and substitute a meeting of its own, at which he spoke and carried the audience with him; and drafting letters to members of the Fabian Society asking why they had not paid their subscriptions—for example, this to Grant Allen:

'Do you mean us to strike you off the roll or do you not? I have stood between you and this doom until I am positively ashamed of you. Confound it, do you know what you cost us in postage and printing every year? Do you ever look at the tracts that are sent you or calculate how much time they cost literary men who are poorer than you are? Do you know how many hours a week the committee work of the Society costs? Do you know how many poor devils of workmen write to us when they can no longer spare us a few shillings to ask us to strike them off, so as to save our stamps? The executive committee burst into a downright fury today when your name was again brought up as a defaulter; and the secretary flatly refused to write to you again. Is this the new Hedonism? Have you any honor, any conscience, any survivals of shame left in you? I persuaded the committee to instruct the secretary to hold his hand until next Wednesday, and undertook in the meantime to write to you. This gives you at least time to resign. Do wake up.

> 'Yours out of all patience,
> 'G. BERNARD SHAW.'

Grant Allen sent his subscription and Shaw acknowledged it: 'The Fabian palm having been oiled, its indignation (simulated for the purpose of extracting money) will subside.'

Several years later Shaw complained when a Labour candidate named Joseph Burgess refused to compromise on some issue during a General Election, thereby losing a seat in parliament, and the complaint gives us a faint idea of the kind of work Shaw did in the cause of socialism throughout the eighties and nineties: 'When I think of my own unfortunate character, smirched with compromise, rotted with opportunism, mildewed by expediency, blackened by ink contributed to Tory and Liberal papers, dragged through the mud of Borough Councils and Battersea elections, stretched out of shape with wire-pulling, putrified by permeation, worn out by 25 years pushing to gain an inch here or straining to stem a back-rush there, I do think Joe might have put up with just a speck or two on those white robes of his for the sake of the millions of poor devils who cannot afford any character at all because they have no friends in parliament. Oh, these moral dandies! these spiritual toffs! these superior persons! Who is Joe anyhow that he should not risk his soul occasionally like the rest of us?'

Several times Shaw was asked to stand for parliament, but he knew he could do better work outside it. 'Better a leader of Fabianism than a chorus-man in parliament,' he once said to me. Besides, he was too outspoken ever to win votes. When Holbrook Jackson asked him to stand for a certain constituency, warning him at the same time that it would want a lot of nursing, Shaw replied that if he attempted to nurse a constituency he would make it howl. Thus, apart from his labours on the committee of the Fabian Society, his only official work for social welfare was done as a vestryman and borough councillor.

Before the old London vestries became borough councils the vestrymen got together and elected one another. They audited their own accounts and staffed the offices with the cadets of their own families. On the old St Pancras Vestry Shaw had two friends who came to an agreement with their anti-progressive opponents that certain of their nominees should be elected without a fight. Shaw was one of them, and a later event proved that he could never have won a contest. From May '97 he served as a vestryman, becoming a councillor in November 1900 when St Pancras was created a borough, and working from two to four hours on committee afternoons for over six years at the Town Hall.

To the amazement of his fellow-vestrymen Shaw displayed business ability, exceptional common sense (meaning uncommon sense), and such activity and regularity that despite his objection to being burdened with more than his fair share of work he was placed on the Health, Parliamentary, Electric Lighting, Housing and Drainage committees, such being the doom of the handful of members who really conducted the business. The borough of St Pancras then had a population of about 250,000, but it did not contain a single bookshop. It did contain three main railway centres, well surrounded with hotels which were really brothels. The ruthless clearances made by the railway yards and termini had overcrowded the inhabitants into single-room tenements which were in such an appalling condition that the sanitary inspectors had abandoned them in despair. Like most other districts, St Pancras was politically corrupt, a cheque for £1000, placed in the proper quarter, securing the donor a seat on the vestry or council. The object of the vestrymen was to keep the rates down, which meant that every suggested improvement or attempt at amelioration was instantly vetoed. Shaw and a young Methodist minister, named Ensor Walters, formed a party of two whose main object was to push the rates up and keep the death-rate down. The other vestrymen were so much astonished by this alliance between God and the Devil (since G.B.S. was a socialist, they felt sure he was an atheist) that many things were done under their very noses of which they were only partly aware.

On the whole Shaw enjoyed himself: 'It is good for me to be worked to the last inch whilst I last ; and I love the reality of the Vestry and its dustcarts and H'less orators after the silly visionary fashion-ridden theatres.' But it was a dreary uphill fight, and sometimes he had to do jobs he would willingly have left undone: for example, he had to hold inquests on tuberculosis cattle while serving on the Health committee, and he felt that a vegetarian was about the last person to attend to the condition of the meat in his parish. As a rule, of course, complaints were only made by people who were enlightened enough to be least in need of attention, which meant that nothing was ever done for the poorest classes unless some disinterested person brought a public scandal to the notice of the authorities. Shaw often found himself in a minority of one when a vitally necessary public service was being discussed, and once he was accused of indecency for saying that women ought to have the privileges of men and not pay for the use of public lavatories. 'An eminent member of the vestry immediately rose and expressed his horror at my venturing to speak in public on so disgusting a subject.' On that occasion the only female member of the vestry supported him ; she too was accused of impropriety ; they were squashed ; and women still have to pay for 'observing the common decencies of traffic in a city'.

Shop slavery, drainage, dust, lighting, disease, housing conditions ; the leading dramatist of the age devoted the whole of his mind and energy to the consideration of each subject as it arose, and tried hard to lighten the lot of the poor, a little here, a little there, as he went along ; which may explain why he once wrote of Shakespeare: 'If his class limitations and a profession that cut him off from actual participation in great affairs of State had not confined his opportunities of intellectual and political training to private conversation and to the Mermaid Tavern, he would probably have become one of the ablest men of his time instead of being merely its ablest playwright.' This is another way of saying that Shakespeare might have been Cecil if he had not been Shakespeare, which prompts the query: how many generations of Cecils would we give for one Shakespeare? But all men are liable to lapse into imbecility ; and since Homer sometimes nodded, Shaw must be excused for having occasionally drivelled.

His term of office expiring in October 1903, he stood as a Progressive candidate for the borough of St Pancras in the London County Council. '*Permanently* disinterested men of ability are very scarce,' he once informed an audience of Fabians: 'It is easier to find a thousand men who will sacrifice valuable chances in life once than to find a single man who will do it twice. . . . This is why I myself have so often urged working-class audiences to believe in themselves and not run after the tall hats and frock coats.' And he was willing to confess that 'the more my ability becomes known, the more do I find myself pressed to spend my time in shovelling guineas into my pocket instead of writing Fabian papers, attending to the Fabian Executive work,' and so on. Yet Shaw's public work proved that he was quite as disinterested as any man of ability in history, and a great deal more so than most. After six and a half years' drudgery at a thankless task, he faced the futilities and exasperations of an election with the possibility of another period of slavery, at a time too when his fame as a writer was growing, his future as a playwright assured.

As a start-off he antagonized all the Nonconformists, his natural supporters, by favouring improvements in Church schools. Anything that strengthened the Church of England in those days was attacked by Nonconformists with a most unchristian bitterness, and one of them told Shaw that he would not pay a farthing towards the schools of the Established

Church. 'Don't you know that you pay taxes now for the support of the Roman Catholic Church in the Island of Malta and for the prosecution of booksellers who expose the Bible for sale in British India and North Africa?' queried Shaw. The Nonconformist neither knew nor cared: he just hated the Church. Shaw insisted that half the nation's children had to choose between the Church school and no school at all; and he preferred a subsidized and government inspected Church school to one in which the teacher could be ordered to polish the parson's boots. He alienated another crowd of progressive supporters, the temperance societies, by advocating the municipalization of the drink traffic. They wanted to abolish it; he, though a teetotaller, wanted to nationalize it and get its profits and losses into the same ledger. Next, he flatly declined to pay the £1000 which would have got him the assistance of the people who mattered; and, worst of all, he informed all the Free Churches that his own religious opinions and theirs were identical with those held by Voltaire over a century before. He had recently published his confession of faith, which was reasonable enough to infuriate the sects, each of which voted against him to a man:

'My own faith is clear: I am a resolute Protestant; I believe in the Holy Catholic Church; in the Holy Trinity of Father, Son (or Mother, Daughter) and Spirit; in the Communion of Saints, the Life to come, the Immaculate Conception, and the everyday reality of Godhead and the Kingdom of Heaven. Also, I believe that salvation depends on redemption from belief in miracles; and I regard St Athanasius as an irreligious fool—that is, in the only serious sense of the word, a damned fool.[1] I pity the poor neurotic who can say, "Man that is born of a woman hath but a short time to live, and is full of misery," as I pity a maudlin drunkard; and I know that the real religion of today was made possible only by the materialist-physicists and atheist critics who performed for us the indispensable preliminary operation of purging us thoroughly of the ignorant and vicious superstitions which were thrust down our throats in our helpless childhood.'

A man who could write like that and talk like that must have known what to expect from his fellow-citizens: christians of every colour, agnostics of every hue, reactionaries of

[1] Later on we find G.B.S. defending the Athanasian Creed on the ground that it makes stupidity a damnable sin.

every complexion, progressives of every shade, honest fools and dishonest rascals, crowded the polling-stations on March 5th, 1904, in order to keep Shaw out and put a Jew in. Defeated by a large majority, Shaw made use of his past experience by writing *The Common Sense of Municipal Trading*, which shows what might have happened to 'one of the ablest men of his time' if he had not been primarily 'its ablest playwright'.

ART FOR THE ARTIST'S SAKE

ONE OF THE MYSTERIES of his age was that neither critics nor actors could perceive the born playwright in Bernard Shaw. 'I write plays because I like it, and because I cannot remember any period in my life when I could help inventing people and scenes. I am not primarily a story-teller: things occur to me first as scenes, with action and dialogue—as moments, developing themselves out of their own vitality.' In that respect he resembled Shakespeare, who was so bored by the prospect of having to invent stories for his characters that he lifted all his plots from writers who had enjoyed yarn-spinning.

Nearly every nineteenth-century critic in England believed in what was then called 'the well-made play': that is, a play that told a story in a particular way, leading the audience up to 'the situation' at the end of the second act and cleaning up the mess it had made in the third and last. Scribe, followed by Sardou, was the great master of this trick-drama in France ; Pinero in England. Shaw, claiming to be a classical dramatist, reverted to the naturalistic drama of Shakespeare: characters and situations 'developing themselves out of their own vitality'. But Shaw, like Ibsen and unlike Shakespeare, was intensely interested in the pressure of economic, political and religious institutions on his characters, finding it rich in dramatic situations and conflicts. His first play was denounced by the critics as a political pamphlet written by a Fabian crank utterly destitute of dramatic faculty. When this estimate became ridiculous, it was still contended passionately that his plays were 'not plays', a position which he sardonically encouraged by calling them discussions, conversations, and the like. This was how he produced an overwhelming impression of novelty, audacity, and rupture of all the rules, whilst in his methods, far from advancing on the well-made play, he was deliberately going back to primitive dramaturgy. 'Molière's technique and mine,' he said, 'is the technique of the circus, with its ring-master discussing all the topics of the day with the clown.' The effect on critics, many of whom had never seen a play in which the characters had any profession, any religion, any politics, or any interests except those of the police and the divorce courts, can only be faintly imagined nowadays.

In their British Museum days William Archer and Bernard Shaw used frequently to discuss the drama, and some time in 1885 Shaw confided to Archer that though he was no good at construction he was nothing less than a genius at writing dialogue, on which Archer confided to Shaw that though he was useless at dialogue there was very little he did not know about construction. This seemed an admirable basis for collaboration. A perfect plot by Archer, sustained by the brilliant dialogue of Shaw, would score a bull's eye. So thought Archer and so thought Shaw. With such a number of good plots crying aloud to be used, Archer was naturally not foolish enough to invent one himself ; he took what he required from an early play by Emile Augier, worked it up in the Parisian manner, provided it with a comic heroine, a serious heroine, and a noble-hearted hero, placed the scene of Act I in a hotel garden on the Rhine, and handed the scenario to Shaw.

Some weeks elapsed. Archer thought that Shaw had forgotten all about the play and did not remind him of it. Besides, Shaw was apparently composing an elaborate treatise, for Archer saw him every day at the Museum 'laboriously writing page after page of the most exquisitely neat shorthand at the rate of about three words a minute'. Some six weeks after the completion of the scenario Shaw staggered Archer by saying: 'Look here, I've knocked off the first act of that play of ours and haven't come to the plot yet. In fact, I've forgotten the plot. You might tell me the story again.' Archer stifled his annoyance and again carefully described the plot. Shaw thanked him warmly, left him, and three days later reported: 'I've written three pages of the second act and have used up all your plot. Can you let me have some more to go on with?' Archer sternly reminded him that the plot was an organic whole, and that to add to it was like giving a few additional arms and legs to a statue already provided with the necessary limbs. Shaw tried to reassure him and offered to read the first two acts when he had finished the second. Archer consented, and when the time came listened with a puzzled

194

frown to Act I and fell fast asleep during Act II. When he woke up he told Shaw exactly what he thought of him and declared the collaboration at an end. A fellow-dramatist, Henry Arthur Jones, to whom Shaw also read the unfinished play, reminded him that 'sleep is a criticism', but kept awake in the hope of being rewarded by a thrill, and at the conclusion of the performance asked, 'Where's your murder?' Shaw, concluding that play-writing was not his job, flung the unfinished work on his pile of discarded manuscripts and thought no more about it.

Seven years passed by. The Independent Theatre had been founded by a Dutchman named J. T. Grein, who had created a sensation with the production of Ibsen's *Ghosts,* fiercely denounced by most English critics as an obscene work. The object of the Independent Theatre was to encourage the New Drama, which Shaw declared was bursting to express itself, but after prolonged search Grein failed to discover any British specimens in the latest style. 'This was not to be endured,' wrote Shaw: 'I had rashly taken up the case; and rather than let it collapse I manufactured the evidence.' So he dug out the two acts written in '85, added a third, called the play *Widowers' Houses,* and sent it to Grein, who announced it for production on December 9th, 1892, at the Royalty Theatre. Archer's sentimental characters and machine-made plot had disappeared; all that remained of his scenario was the placing of the first scene on the Rhine; his serious and comic heroines had been turned into one character, quite unlike any he had envisaged; and the play had resolved itself into a tragi-comedy of slum-landlordism. The heroine, Blanche, was modelled on her amiable side on Florence Farr, who played the part, and on her less amiable side on a female Shaw had seen in the street: 'Once, when I was walking homewards at midnight through Wigmore Street, taking advantage of its stillness and loneliness at that hour to contemplate, like Kant, the starry heaven above me, the solitude was harshly broken by the voices of two young women who came out of Mandeville Place on the other side of the street a couple of hundred yards behind me. The dominant one of the pair was in a black rage: the other was feebly trying to quiet her. The strained strong voice and the whimpering remonstrant one went on for some time. Then came the explosion. The angry one fell on the other, buffeting her, tearing at her hair, grasping at her neck. The victim, evidently used to it, cowered against the railings, covering herself as best she could, and imploring and remonstrating in a carefully subdued tone, dreading a police rescue more than the other's violence. Presently, the fit passed, and the two came on their way, the lioness silent, and the lamb reproachful and rather emboldened by her sense of injury. The scene stuck in my memory, to be used in due time.'

The play was rehearsed at the 'Bedford Head' in Maiden Lane, and in the middle of one rehearsal a short young man, with an old-looking face and close-cut red hair, poked his head round the door. He was promptly seized by the producer and asked to read the part of Lickcheese, the rent-collector, which neither author nor producer had been able to cast. He read it so well that he was asked to play it. His performance was the hit of the piece, and made his reputation: his name was James Welch. The actors, and even Grein himself, were nervous of the play and not altogether at ease with the author, who was passing through his Jaeger clothing phase, turning up at rehearsals in a silvery creation which the inventor himself eventually abandoned because it squeaked when the sleeves rubbed on the body, and which Shaw discarded after a country-walk with Sydney Olivier, who objected to having his conversation interrupted by a noise like a cricket's.

Widowers' Houses had a mixed reception, the socialists in the audience applauding it loudly, their opponents hissing fiercely. At the final curtain yells of 'Author' mingled with shouts of disapproval, Shaw appeared and stood for a while 'drinking in the rapture' of an almighty hooting from the outraged conventional first-nighters. The storm abating, he said that the play's reception had been agreeable to him, for had it been received lightly he would have been disappointed. He assured the audience that what they had seen was a faithful picture of middle-class life and a truthful description of what was actually going on. He asked the critics to discriminate between the author and the actors who had so zealously striven to carry out his intentions, and having charmed everyone with his Irish accent he retired to the accompaniment of cheers. The critics did as he requested, and he awoke next morning to find himself infamous, the play being attacked so violently and creating so much discussion and dissension that (especially after the success he had planned for Welch) he felt convinced he was a born dramatist, more especially as William Archer advised him not to 'devote further time and energy to a form of production for which he has no special ability'.

Archer's criticism in *The World* drew a postcard from Shaw: 'Here am I, who have collected slum rents weekly with these hands, and for 4½ years been behind the scenes of the middle-class landowner—who have philandered with women of all sorts and sizes—and I am told gravely to go to nature and give up apriorizing about such matters by you, you sentimental Sweet Lavendery recluse.'

Shaw's next play, *The Philanderer* (1893), in part a satire on the Ibsenites, was regarded by Archer almost as a personal insult, and he felt like 'cutting' the author in the street for having committed an 'outrage upon art and decency'. Three years later Shaw rather sympathized with this view, for he read the play aloud to some friends and described it as 'a combination of mechanical farce with realistic filth which quite disgusted me'. It required better acting than a cast got together by the Independent Theatre could give it, and as Charles Wyndham, the only man who could play the leading part, turned it down, it was temporarily shelved.

Although Archer was completely converted by Shaw's third effort, *Mrs Warren's Profession* (1893), nearly everyone else was shocked by it. As in the case of his first play, the original idea was romantic, but there was not much romance left in the idea by the time Shaw had finished with it. Janet Achurch, the first actress to give a public performance in England of Nora in *A Doll's House*, spoke to him about a French novel which she thought would make a good play. On his assurance that he never read anything if he could help it, least of all a novel, let alone a French one, she told him the story, which was ultra-romantic. 'Oh, I will work out the real truth about that mother some day,' he said. Shortly afterwards Mrs Webb suggested that he should create for the stage a thoroughly modern emancipated woman. Result: the romantic heroine became Mrs Warren, the emancipated girl her daughter. As the play showed that female prostitution was the inevitable result of a capitalistic society, the managers who depended on capitalists to fill their stalls displayed no eagerness to put it on; and lest any public-spirited person should feel tempted to risk it, the Censor settled the matter by refusing it a licence. In May '97, nearly four years after writing it, Shaw thought it by far his best play, 'but it makes my blood run cold; I can hardly bear the most appalling bits of it. Ah, when I wrote that, I *had* some nerve.' When, at last, in 1924 the Censor lifted his ban, Shaw had grown tired of waiting and remarked, 'Better never than late.' Nowadays we may wonder what all the fuss was about, but we owe our present wonder largely to Shaw, who was the first to fight for the free discussion of serious social problems on the English stage, and whose own plays were the native pioneers of such work.

Mrs Warren's Profession was first performed by the Stage Society in January 1902, eight years after it was written. The Censor could not prevent private performances, like those given by the Stage Society to its members, but his refusal of a licence made managers so nervous that one after another broke their promises to let the play be performed in their theatres on a Sunday night. 'Over and over again the date and place were fixed and the tickets printed, only to be cancelled, until at last the desperate and overworked manager of the Stage Society could only laugh, as criminals broken on the wheel used to laugh at the second stroke.' It was difficult to get stages for rehearsals, which were usually held in corridors and saloon bars at all hours of the day and night. The play was produced on a Sunday evening at the New Lyric Club; the dramatic critics promptly went mad; and Shaw was delighted, for his sermon had gone home: 'No author who has ever known the exultation of sending the Press into an hysterical tumult of protest, of moral panic, of involuntary and frantic confession of sin, of a horror of conscience in which the power of distinguishing between the work of art on the stage and the real life of the spectator is confused and overwhelmed, will ever care for the stereotyped compliments which every successful farce or melodrama elicits from the newspapers.'

The action of the Censor branded Shaw 'as an unscrupulous and blackguardly author', though he had to admit that his career as a revolutionary critic 'kept me so continually in hot water that the addition of another jugful of boiling fluid by the Lord Chamberlain troubled me too little to entitle me to personal commiseration, especially as the play greatly strengthened my repute among serious readers'. The fact that the fluid scalded others was not his fault. In the autumn of 1905, against his advice, Arnold Daly produced the play in New York, and when in 1909 Shaw gave evidence on the censorship before a parliamentary committee he described what happened:

'*Mrs Warren's Profession* was proceeded against in New York, and it was proceeded against in a very summary manner. In consequence of the Lord Chamberlain having refused to license it here, an impression was created in America, naturally, that it was a hideously indecent and horrible play, because, as the American public were aware that many plays which are licensed here are exceedingly indecent, they naturally concluded that anything that the Censor refused to license must be of almost incredible indecency *a fortiori*. As a consequence of that, all the worst elements in the New York population came in enormous crowds. There were almost riots outside the theatre, and fabulous prices were paid for seats. The police then went in and arrested the entire company, and marched them off to the police court—actors, actresses, manager, and everybody else. The magistrate had to adjourn the case, because he said that he would have to read the play, and he publicly expressed his extreme loathing of the unpleasant task before him—that is exactly what occurred. He adjourned the case, intending to read the play in the meantime. At the next hearing he exhibited a certain amount of temper, which one would almost think suggested disappointment. He said that he had read the play and that there was not in it what he had expected it to contain from the accounts given of it.'

The defendants were acquitted on appeal to the Court of Special Sessions, and the play was praised as making vice less attractive than many plays that had escaped the attention of the police.

In the course of his evidence before the parliamentary committee Shaw said that immoral plays were the only plays worth writing, and that he was a conscientiously immoral writer. He used the word 'immoral' in the sense in which it was *not* used in the Bible: 'I would remind the committee that from one end of the Bible to the other the words "moral" and "immoral" are not used. They are not used in the plays of Shakespeare, and at the time that the 1843 Act was passed I believe that any person using the words "morality" and "immorality" as being synonymous with "righteousness" and "sin" was very strongly suspected of being a Rationalist, and probably an Atheist.' When he used the word 'immoral' he meant non-customary.

Having described what had happened to his play in New York, and having argued in favour of abolishing the censorship and substituting the annual licensing of theatres by the municipalities, a measure which had just cleaned up the old music halls with remarkable success, Shaw was asked by the chairman whether he thought an English court would prohibit the performance of *Mrs Warren's Profession*. 'I think it is possible,' he replied. 'It is a profoundly immoral play, exceedingly so ; more so than many of the people who have written about it really imagine.'

'Once more you use the word in your own special sense?'

'Not in my own special sense, but in which I say is the correct and classical use of the word in the English language.'

'And that is—?'

'As I have already explained to you, the play is a conscientiously immoral play.'

We should now call it an extremely moral play, meaning precisely what Shaw meant when he called it immoral, which, however, was not what the critics meant when they called it immoral, not being at all certain of what they meant.

Up to this point Shaw had written plays under external pressure from Archer and Grein, from the Independent Theatre and the Stage Society, from Janet Achurch and Beatrice Webb, all of them uncommercial. He had not made a penny out of them ; he had merely gained a new notoriety as a playwright. The public and critics thought them nasty ; and as their feelings on the subject were quite expected and intelligible to him, he labelled the plays Unpleasant. But now the external pressure changed : the next demand was for plays to be produced at commercial theatres for ordinary (if possible extraordinary) runs, which meant that he had to provide good parts for popular actors and actresses, and to please managers who were more anxious to attract society than to reform it. So he began to trade in comedy ; anti-romantic comedy, it is true ; but yet in laughter ; for 'by laughter only can you destroy evil without malice, and affirm goodfellowship without mawkishness'.

The first 'pleasant play' was *Arms and the Man* (1894), which he completed in a hurry. Miss A. E. F. Horniman, who later became famous for her work at the Gaiety Theatre in Manchester, had backed a season of plays at the Avenue Theatre, London, the ostensible manageress being Shaw's friend, Florence Farr. The first production failed, and Florence, left playless, proposed to revive *Widowers' Houses*. But Shaw had already started to write a play for her, and in the emergency finished it at top speed. The rehearsals were rushed, and on the first night, April 21st, 1894, the actors, who could make neither head nor tail of the business, played with anxious seriousness, and were rewarded with a crazy success. The audience laughed immoderately at nearly everything. Unfortunately, the actors, convinced by the laughs that this strange piece must be a farce, began to play for them on the conventional farcical comedy lines; and the first-night success was never repeated. Shaw had planned all the laughs unerringly, but only as responses to an earnestly sincere performance. When the performance became comic the play lost its hold. But the only hitch on the first night was when Bernard Gould, later famous as Bernard Partridge of *Punch*, had to make a remark about the Bulgarian army. By a slip of the tongue he applied it to the British army; and this was more than Golding Bright, then an unknown lad in the gallery, could bear. He hissed. When Shaw took his call as author at the end amid tremendous applause, young Bright heroically sent forth a solitary 'Boo.' Shaw, at the height of his practice as a mob orator, seized on the interruption to make a speech. 'I quite agree with you, my friend,' he said, 'but what can we two do against a whole houseful of the opposite opinion?'

This typical specimen of platform repartee (it was a flat and obvious lie) proved prophetic. In spite of the first-night furore the play did not catch on. It ran for eleven weeks at a heavy loss, and Shaw was forced to tell a German who wanted plays for some Berlin theatre that it 'has only twice drawn as much as half the cost of sending up the curtain, and has on two other less happy occasions in Whit week and the cab strike gone down to £14'. In fact the takings averaged £17 a night for the run. William Archer thought it quite as funny as *Charley's Aunt*. On the other hand Edward VII (then Prince of Wales) asked who the author was, and on hearing the name, which meant nothing to him, said quite seriously, 'Of course he's mad.' Shaw's own view of it underwent revisions. Re-reading it at the close of 1904 he was 'startled to find what flimsy, fantastic, unsafe stuff it is', and thought that 'it really would not stand comparison with my later plays unless the company was very fascinating'. But in 1927 he informed Alfred Sutro that *Arms and the Man* 'never had a really whole-hearted success until after the war, when soldiering had come home to the London playgoer's own door, and he saw that the play was a classic comedy and not an opera bouffe without the music'.

Unaffected by the financial failure and the inability of critics and audiences to see what he was driving at, Shaw settled down to his next play, *Candida*, and having finished it went early in December '94 to West Cliff Hotel, Folkestone, whence he opened his mind to brother-dramatist Henry Arthur Jones:

'For the general paying public there needs a long fight, during which my plays will have to be produced in spite of all economic considerations, sometimes because the parts are too fascinating to be resisted, sometimes because Pinero is not ready with his commissioned play, sometimes because I am willing to forgo an advance, sometimes because Nature will not submit wholly to the box office.

'Now here you will at once detect an enormous assumption on my part that I am a man of genius. But what can I do— on what other assumption am I to proceed if I am to write plays at all? You will detect the further assumption that the public, which will still be the public twenty years hence, will nevertheless see feeling and reality where they see nothing now but mere intellectual swordplay and satire. . . . Consequently, I am absolutely confident that *if my work is good* (the only assumption on which I can go on with it) all the miracles will happen, and it will be quite well worth my while to make £150 a play or even to make nothing and starve. . . .

'. . . . My passion, like that of all artists, is for efficiency, which means intensity of life and breadth and variety of experience ; and already I find, as a dramatist, that I can go at one stroke to the centre of matters that reduce the purely literary man to colourless platitudes. . . .

'Do you now begin to understand, O Henry Arthur Jones, that you have to deal with a man who habitually thinks of himself as one of the great geniuses of all time?—just as you necessarily do yourself. We may be deceiving ourselves ; but why add to the heavy chances of that the absolute certainty of such a deception as would be involved in the notion that we thought ourselves common fellows with a bit of talent.'

Many well-meaning people, perceiving that he had 'a bit of talent', were kind enough to explain how he could turn it to profit. To one of these, a literary agent, he wrote: 'What do you mean by giving me advice about writing a play with a view to the box-office receipts? I shall continue writing just as

I do now for the next ten years. After that we can wallow in the gold poured at our feet by a dramatically regenerated public.'

The difficulty was to reach the public at all, for the leading actors were quite satisfied with the unregenerated audiences which paid to see them in plays by Jones and Pinero. *Candida* was read to Charles Wyndham, who wept over the last scene and having dried his eyes assured the author that the play was 25 years before its time. George Alexander said that he would like to play the poet in it if he were made blind to gain sympathy. But after all one could not expect much from the actors when an exceptionally intelligent socialist like Edward Carpenter, after hearing the play read, remarked, 'No, Shaw ; it won't do.' Possibly the actors were a little discouraged by his method of writing his early plays, and by the peculiar way in which he submitted them for consideration. Clothed in a fashion of his own and looking rather like a Viking, he entered Wyndham's office one morning to read *Candida*. Sitting down at the table, he thrust one hand into a pocket of his trousers and produced a small note-book, thrust the other hand into a pocket of his coat and produced a second note-book, fished a third note-book from another pocket, a fourth from yet another, and so on until Wyndham wondered whether he was witnessing a conjuring trick. Then said Shaw:

'You appear surprised to see all these little pocketbooks. The fact is, I write my plays mostly on the tops of buses.'

He might have added that such parts of his plays as were not written on the roofs of buses were composed in the Underground Railway, which may account for the fact that all the characters in his early works seem to be talking at the tops of their voices.

Shaw's distinctive contribution to the theatre was first discernible in *Candida* ; he was, and remains, the only playwright who has successfully dramatized the religious temperament, which, being the only temperament he completely sympathized with and therefore understood,[1] was the source of all the

[1] I scarcely expected Shaw to see eye-to-eye with me on this point, and when I broached it he made a characteristic rejoinder: 'The dramatization of the religious character as such was child's play to me, as I was hand in glove with all the leading Christian Socialist parsons of that day, from Stopford Brooke on the extreme right to Stewart Headlam and Sarson on the left, whereas the fashionable playwrights did not know

emotion he was able to express on the stage. Shakespeare, one may add, completely understood every sort of character except the religious ; and this is the real difference between the two as dramatists. Shaw must have felt that he had at last struck the vein of his genius, for he would not trust *Candida* out of his hands: 'I never let people read that: I always read it to them. They can be heard sobbing three streets off,' he told Ellen Terry, to whom he also confided: 'Candida, between you and me, is the Virgin Mother and nobody else.' He would have liked Ellen to do it, for she was the only actress who had the secret of it in her nature, but she could not tear herself away from Irving, and Shaw had promised the part to Janet Achurch. At last he was prevailed upon to send the script to Ellen, who wrote to say that she had cried her eyes out over his *heavenly* play, and begged him to write a 'Mother' play for her. 'I *have* written THE Mother Play— *Candida*— and I cannot repeat a masterpiece,' he replied. Not all his friends agreed about Candida ; Mrs Webb, for instance, thought her 'a sentimental prostitute'; but most of them praised the play far above his previous works ; in fact, he got a little irritated by their continual harping on the subject, called them Candidamaniacs, and began to think it overrated, 'especially in comparison to the one I have just begun' —*The Devil's Disciple,* which turned out to be the nearest thing to a conventional melodrama he ever produced. Such is the nature of authors, who usually think their last work their best.

With Janet Achurch in the leading part, *Candida* was first done by the Independent Theatre during a provincial tour in the spring of '97, repeated during another provincial tour in '98, and produced in London by the Stage Society on Sunday, July 1st, 1900, at the Strand Theatre. In the two London performances Granville Barker made his first appearance in a Shaw play. 'I was at my wits' end for an actor who could do justice to the part of Marchbanks,' Shaw told me ;

---

of the existence of such strange animals, nor would have understood them if they had. I had all the temperaments at my fingers' ends: the religious, the poetic, the artistic, the scientific, and could make stage play with them as effectively as with mothers-in-law and greengrocers. In short, I lived in a world unknown to the actors, playwrights, and narrowly specialized playgoers of that day, and had to create my audiences as well as my plays.'

'when one day I dropped into a matinee of Hauptmann's *Friedenfest,* and instantly saw the very fellow for my poet. I wrote to announce my wonderful discovery to Janet and her husband, who replied that they had frequently mentioned Barker to me as the ideal man for the part.' The play was received by the London audience with so much pleasure that Shaw made a speech in which he congratulated them on being nineteen years in advance of their age, Charles Wyndham having informed him six years previously that *Candida* was twenty-five years before its time.

In the autumn of '95 Shaw wrote *The Man of Destiny.* Richard Mansfield, then strongly in the running in New York as its star actor, whom Shaw had seen as Richard II and had talked to for an hour, was his model for Napoleon, and, as we know, Ellen Terry was The Strange Lady. Mansfield, who rather fancied himself as the Napoleon of legend, did not see himself as the Napoleon of Shaw, and returned the play with a laconic note. Whereupon Shaw wrote to him: 'I was much hurt by your contemptuous refusal of *A Man of Destiny,* not because I think it one of my masterpieces, but because Napoleon is nobody else but Richard Mansfield himself. I studied the character from you, and then read up Napoleon and found that I had got him exactly right.' Richard however did not think that Shaw had got Mansfield exactly right, and nothing came of it. Following the breakdown of Ellen Terry's efforts to make Irving produce it, Murray Carson put it on at the Grand Theatre, Croydon, on July 1st, '97. Shaw attended the first-night, 'an agonizing experience for the author, but an intensely interesting one for the critic'. The performance was appalling, the applause at the end was like a groan, and the author 'was only seen to smile twice and that was when a rowdy little kitten, fluffy but disreputable, appeared in the vineyard and was chivied by the innkeeper, and when it subsequently revenged itself by unexpectedly walking on again at one of Napoleon's most Marengoesque moments and staring at him as if it could not understand how a man could go on in a way that no sane cat would dream of.'

A different sort of disaster attended Shaw's next play, *You Never Can Tell,* which he began in '95, and was still working at in April of the following year, for he wrote to Ellen Terry from Aldbury, Tring: 'My present play brings life and art together and strikes showers of sparks from them as if they were a knife and grindstone.' He must have finished it shortly after because George Alexander wrote to him in June: 'When I got to the end, I had no more idea what you meant by it than a tom cat.' Hearing from Cyril Maude, who was about to commence management of the Haymarket Theatre, that he would like to consider *Candida* for production there, Shaw replied that he would provide something more suitable for the Haymarket, and spent several weeks that summer, in Regent's Park and Suffolk, revising *You Never Can Tell,* and doing his best to make its meaning clear to a leading actor; apparently with some success, for on September 8th he reported that the new management seemed to be 'making up their minds to ruin themselves with it', though Mrs Cyril Maude (Winifred Emery) refused to appear as Gloria, the leading part, picking the part of Dolly for herself, 'her public reason being magnanimity,' thought the author, her private one that she doesnt understand the part and doesnt want to'. However, Shaw determined that she should change her mind, and when he read the play to the company on April 9th, '97 he contrived to make the silence of Gloria (objected to by Winifred) render her first speech so effective, that before the end of the first act she wrote 'I shall play Gloria' on a scrap of paper and passed it to her husband. Two other players were influenced by the reading. Jack Barnes, 'overpowered by fatigue and disgust', got up and walked off at the end of the second act, throwing up his part before the day was out; while Fanny Coleman abandoned hers with the remark that there were 'no laughs and no exits'. Sydney Valentine and Kate Bishop took their places. But not for long.

The reading lasted for two hours and forty minutes and Shaw decided, 'I shall have to spoil it to suit the fashionable dinner-hour.' He handed the script to Maude, telling him to cut it freely. Maude found himself unable to sacrifice a single syllable. Shaw then cut the last act ruthlessly, deaf to Maude's protests. The fact of the matter was that the greater part of the cast did not understand their parts or the play, and before the first rehearsal was over Shaw had given them up: 'We rehearsed the first act today,' he wrote on April 12th. 'Oh, if only they *wouldn't* act. They are tolerable until they begin that; but then—! Well, their sorrows have only begun, poor things! They think me a very harmless author so far. Wait until I begin silently and unobtrusively to get on their nerves a little.' Four days later the unobtrusive treatment was beginning to tell: 'The scenes at the Haymarket are not on the surface, but in the recesses of the hearts of the unhappy company. I sit there and stare at them. I get up and prowl. I sit somewhere else, but always with a dreadful patience and dreadful attention. It is useless to correct more than one speech per person per day ; for I find that the result of my interposition —consisting of saying the thing as it ought to be said (Heaven knows what my way of doing it may sound like to them!)— is invariably to paralyse them for five minutes, during which they are not only quite off their part, but utterly incapable of expressing any meaning whatever. So far we have only gone over the busy funny scenes repeatedly: all the big scenes for Gloria and so on are yet before us. Maude and Brandon Thomas will succeed no matter how they take their parts: that is all I can see at present.'

At one point in the rehearsals Shaw suggested that there should be a large table on the stage. Maude wanted to know why. Because, Shaw explained, the company would fall over it unless they behaved as if they were coming into a real room instead of rushing to the footlights to pick up the band at the beginning of a comic song. Maude had cast himself for the part of the Waiter, though Shaw advised him to play the young hero, warning him that if he insisted on playing elderly parts he would regret it when he was really elderly. Later on Maude at last ventured to take this advice, and immediately made a brilliant success as a *jeune premier* in Barrie's *Little Minister*.

According to Shaw, what put the finishing touch to the company's utter demoralization was his appearance one day in a new suit of clothes. He had previously attended rehearsals 'in a costume which the least self-respecting carpenter would have discarded months before', but 'in anticipation of the royalties on *You Never Can Tell*' he suddenly blossomed out into a suit, the mere sight of which would have made Talma himself break down. Having informed the management that their ruin and disgrace could only be averted by a heroic sacrifice on his part, he withdrew the play after a fortnight's rehearsals.

The relationship between Shaw and Maude was unaffected by this break and when the latter opened the Playhouse in 1907 Shaw wrote an Interlude for him and his wife. Maude's little boy was present when Shaw read it, and the more appreciative voice of the new generation was heard when the

207

lad asked his father: 'I say, why don't you get that man to write all your plays?'

Shaw quickly grew tired of *You Never Can Tell*. Even as early as September '97 his dissatisfaction with it was apparent: '*Could* anyone read it? It maddens me. I'll have my revenge in the preface by offering it as a frightful example of the result of trying to write for the *théâtre de nos jours*.' It was first produced by the Stage Society at the Royalty Theatre on November 24th, 1899, with James Welch as the Waiter. In May 1900 it ran for two weeks of matinees at the Strand Theatre, when the audience enjoyed it, William Archer called it 'a formless and empty farce', and Shaw wrote: 'I was ashamed of its tricks and laughs and popularities. It would make a great hit at the Lyceum with Irving as the Waiter.' Five years later it became the stock money-maker of the Vedrenne-Barker management and the Macdona Players in the provinces.

Within a week or two of finishing *You Never Can Tell* he was at work on a new and very different kind of play. William Terriss, the best actor of melodrama in the country, had asked him early in '96 to write something for the popular Adelphi Theatre audiences, which nightly cheered their pet hero Terriss, their pet heroine Jessie Millward, and their pet comedian Harry Nicholls. Terris 'wasted very little time indeed in flattering me,' Shaw wrote: 'instead, he showed me a bank-book containing a record of the author's fees on a very popular melodrama then running at the Adelphi. I believe he had no idea that he was an unrivalled executive instrument for my purposes as a dramatist, and that I accordingly had a strong artistic incentive to write for him; on the contrary, he had a confused idea that I was an extremely learned man, and that the only chance of inducing me to condescend to the Adelphi was by an appeal to my pocket, which he rightly regarded as a vital organ even in the most superior constitutions.'

Having, as he hoped, bribed Shaw with the promise of riches beyond the dreams of a socialist, Terriss, like Archer before him, produced a scenario. Shaw gave me a rough idea of it: 'Terriss wanted to tour the world as a star. He asked me to collaborate with him in a play, the plot to be supplied by him. It was more than a plot: it was all the plots of all the melodramas he had ever played in. At the end of every act he was dragged away to penal servitude through the treachery of the beautiful devil who was the villainess of the piece; and he turned up in the next as fresh as paint without an attempt to explain this happy change in his fortune. I told him that it would be splendid for the Adelphi, but that in foreign cities, where they would have their own particular native Terriss, they would not stand melodrama from him, but would expect something like Hamlet. He put his plot in the fire (having several typed copies in his desk) and said: "Mr Shaw, you are right."'

By the end of March Shaw was seriously thinking of doing something for Terriss. 'A good melodrama,' he reflected, 'is a more difficult thing to write than all this clever-clever comedy: one must go straight to the core of humanity to get it, and if it is only good enough, why, there you have Lear or Macbeth.' He began to write it in September '96. A young artist named Nellie Heath, who was 'tremendously attracted by Shaw's red ears and red hair, which grew on his forehead in two Satanic whirls', persuaded him to sit for a portrait which she hoped would be exhibited by the Royal Society of Portrait Painters. While he was being painted, he wrote most of *The Devil's Disciple*. 'The play progresses,' he reported on October 15th, '. . . such a melodrama! I sit in a little hole of a room off Euston Road on the corner of a table with an easel propped before me so that I can write and be painted at the same time. This keeps me at work; and the portrait, for which I have to pay the artist's top price for millionaires (£5), is to make her fortune when exhibited. I do not usually allow myself to be got round in this fashion; but this girl did it without an effort. I suppose I am a great fool; but I shall turn the sittings to account in getting on with the play. As for her, she is delighted, and thinks me a most interesting and celebrated old man to have for a sitter.' At first he thought the drama grim, gloomy, horrible and sordid, but later, though he had honestly tried for dramatic effect, he was afraid it might possibly be 'the most monstrous piece of farcical absurdity that ever made an audience shriek with laughter'. On November 30th he was able to announce: 'I finished my play today. . . . Three acts, six scenes, a masterpiece, all completed in a few weeks, with a trip to Paris[1] and those Ibsen articles thrown in.' He still had to revise it and work out all the stage business, and read up the history of the American

[1] To see Lugne Poe's production of *Peer Gynt* and write a criticism of it.

War of Independence to check his facts and put in a few dates; but he wrote at once to tell Terriss that he had kept his promise and had finished 'a strong drama', which included a fat part for the Adelphi favourite. Shaw described what followed in a letter to me:

'I read *The Devil's Disciple* to him in Jessie Millward's flat. He listened in deep perplexity until I had nearly finished the first act, when he said, "Excuse my interrupting you; but is this an interior?" (Melodramas usually begin on the village green.) I said it was. "Right," he said, "now I have it. Go on. You won't mind my interrupting you?"

'I went on. When I had read about two pages of the second act, he said, with despair in his face, "Sorry to interrupt you again; but is *this* an interior?" I said it was; and he assured me that I had now set his mind completely at rest, and would I excuse him for interrupting me, and fire away. I fired away. When the barrage had lasted two minutes longer he had fallen into a coma so profound that Jessie and I had to carry him into the next room and give him some strong tea before he was thoroughly awake and ashamed of the failure of his effort to live up to the higher drama.

'Nothing more passed between us until he heard that Richard Mansfield had at last conquered New York with a tremendously successful melodrama, and that this was *The Devil's Disciple*. He sent for me hastily to discuss business with him; but before the appointment came off he was stabbed by a lunatic at the stage-door of the Adelphi, which, in its old aspect as a temple of melodrama, may be said to have perished with him. . . .

'The play was written round the scene of Dick's arrest, which had always been floating in my head as a situation for a play. Mrs Dudgeon is a variation on Dickens's Mrs Clennam.'

Nellie Heath's portrait was rejected by the Royal Society of Portrait Painters, and Shaw's play was, as usual, misunderstood by nearly every actor who read it. The first English production was at the Princess of Wales's Theatre, Kennington, on September 26th, 1899, when the leading part was played by Murray Carson, who was influenced by a critic to introduce an outrageous piece of business which completely distorted the meaning of the play. 'As for me,' wrote the author, 'I was just then wandering about the streets of Constantinople, unaware of all these doings. When I returned all was over.

My personal relations with the critic and the actor forbade me to curse them. I had not even the chance of publicly forgiving them. They meant well by me; but if they ever write a play, may I be there to explain!'

Johnston Forbes-Robertson was attracted by the part of Dick Dudgeon, but wanted Shaw to write a nicer third act. About two years later he said he would produce it if the last act were altered into an English victory. 'I have cut him off without a shilling,' reported Shaw. Thus stimulated, Forbes-Robertson determined to put it on, and took the shilling out of Shaw by asking him to rehearse it: 'I am nearly dead with work because of the wiliness of Forbes-Robertson. I usually rely on my bad character to get me kept away from rehearsals; but Forbes politely begged me to *conduct* the first rehearsals and settle the business, besides reading the play. Of course the result is that everything goes on castors: at each rehearsal we take one act, and go through it twice. It goes without a hitch, and we are off in two hours to lunch, remarking, if you please, that the play is *quite easy*. And they think that since I only have to prepare an act at a time, it is holiday work for me, whereas with the Vestry, the Fabian, the printers (American and English) and a thousand other things, I am working like mad sixteen hours a day. Such is life—*my* life. The only dreadful thing is that as far as I can ascertain there are only two men in the company who can act. Of course, I have had to give them the two little parts (the sergeant and the silly brother) because these are comic and character parts; and you *must* have acting for comedy and character, whereas the big serious sympathetic parts take care of themselves with a little coaching. But imagine the feelings of a competent old professional, longing to play the big part and able to do it, when the author gives it to a good-hearted young duffer, and puts him (the c.o.p.) into a mere bit of clowning. I experience agonies of remorse every time I meet E. W. Garden's eye: I long to atone by writing him a curtain raiser all to himself.' The production was at the Coronet Theatre, Notting Hill, West London, in September 1900, and was followed by a moderately successful provincial tour.

But Shaw's financial independence was not won in England. It was Richard Mansfield's production of *The Devil's Disciple* in America that enabled him to throw up his job on *The Saturday Review*. Mansfield had already done *Arms and The*

Man in September '94, the first American production of a Shaw play, but without much success, for Shaw admitted in 1898 that he had only netted £800 from it on both sides of the Atlantic. After that Mansfield turned down *The Philanderer* and *The Man of Destiny.* He had hopes of *Candida,* saying he would produce it if on arrival it proved to be 'clean'. It proved to be not only 'clean' but 'sweet', and Mansfield started to rehearse it, abandoning the project the moment he realized that the part of the poet, 'a sickly youth', did not suit him, and that he was being acted off the stage by Janet Achurch, whom he had engaged to play Candida ; also, that there was 'no action' in the play, which consisted of preaching for two and a half hours. 'O ye Gods and little fishes!' exclaimed Mansfield. It was reserved for Arnold Daly to make *Candida* the hit of the New York season in 1904.

Mansfield produced *The Devil's Disciple* at Albany on October 1st, 1897, bringing it to the Fifth Avenue Theatre, New York, a few days later, where it enjoyed a long run. He then toured it with success. But something about Shaw's work, to say nothing of Shaw, irritated him, and when told by a senator that he ought to thank God nightly on his knees for such a play, he replied that he did, but that he could not help adding: 'Why, O God, did it have to be by Shaw?' They shouted insults at one another across the Atlantic. When Shaw sent *Caesar and Cleopatra* Mansfield called it an imbecile burlesque, upon which Shaw denounced him as an obsolete barnstormer, writing: 'I apologize to two continents for making people believe you a genius. . . . Farewell—*Pompey.*' Nevertheless, Mansfield's production of *The Devil's Disciple* made about £3000 for its author. This freed him from the drudgery of criticism, which, as practised by him, he declared to be much less easy, less illustrious and less re-munerative than the writing of plays.

It is worth noting that his first box-office success was the first play in which he portrayed the purely religious type—the militant saint—a type he excelled in portraying and would one day exploit in his greatest box-office success.

MARRIAGE AND A MASTERPIECE

IN THE LATE SUMMER OF 1896 there was a Fabian house-party at Stratford St Andrew Rectory, about three miles on the Ipswich side of Saxmundham in Suffolk. The Rectory had been taken for a few weeks by the Webbs, whose guests were Charles Trevelyan, Graham Wallas, Charlotte Perkins Stetson, Bernard Shaw and Charlotte Payne-Townshend. It was a fitting place for a party of world-reformers. Going towards Ipswich from Saxmundham, the traveller passes through the red-brick hamlet of Stratford St Andrew, turns up a drive to his right and walks about 150 yards between large trees with a rich meadow on his left. All is leafy and lush, excessively rural and reposeful. He expects to see a rambling Elizabethan mansion when he reaches the top of the drive, or at least an elegant Georgian building. He finds instead an efficient house of greyish brick, built in late Victorian style. He is chilled. If the day is drear, he moans. It was too much for Charlotte Stetson, who fled, leaving Mrs Webb and Miss Payne-Townshend to look after the males of the party. But it suited the Fabians, who worked for at least four hours every morning, bicycled for quite four hours every afternoon, discussed socialism over their meals and read books in the evenings. And it was the opening scene of a Fabian romance. Blind to the fact that a place called Stratford St Andrew might gravely affect the destiny of Shakespeare's successor and Macduff's descendant, Shaw fell in love while staying there with Charlotte Payne-Townshend.

She was Irish on her father's side, and she was wealthy, but she had been born with a social conscience, and having eluded a number of fashionable money-hunting suitors she flirted with socialism. Introduced to Mrs Webb, who quickly relieved her of £1000 to house the new London School of Economics, she became a Fabian. She went further; sick of

'society' life she expressed a desire to mingle with Fabians;
she asked Mrs Webb to share a country-house with her and
invite selected Fabians to stay with them. Mrs Webb replied
that she was in the habit of taking a place in the country
every summer, and that two leading Fabians, Bernard Shaw
and Graham Wallas, were in the habit of spending their
holidays with her: had Miss Payne-Townshend any objection
to such an arrangement? Miss Payne-Townshend had no
objection; she went to Stratford St Andrew, saw Bernard
Shaw, conquered him and was conquered by him. Shaw broke
the news to Ellen Terry on August 28th:

'We have been joined by an Irish millionairess who has had
cleverness and character enough to decline the station of life
—"great catch for somebody"—to which it pleased God to
call her, and whom we have incorporated into our Fabian
family with great success. I am going to refresh my heart by
falling in love with her. I love falling in love—but, mind, only
with her, not with the million; so somebody else must marry
her if she can stand him after me.'

Shaw spent most of his time finishing *You Never Can Tell*,
'mending punctures in female bicycle tyres', and reading his
own plays to the circle in the evenings; but he certainly found
time for talking privately to Miss Townshend on those long
afternoon bicycle rides to Ipswich and elsewhere, or on those
long walks, so popular with the Fabians, when the conversation often took such a serious turn that the walk became a
trot.

By the beginning of October, when he was back in London,
he had 'got to like so much that it would be superfluous to fall
in love with' his Irish lady with the light green eyes. Three
weeks later he asked Ellen Terry: 'Shall I marry my Irish
millionairess? She . . . believes in freedom, and not in marriage; but I think I could prevail on her; and then I should
have ever so many hundreds a month for nothing. Would you
ever in your secret soul forgive me, even though I am really
fond of her and she of me? No, you wouldnt.' The next day
he gave Ellen a few more details: 'She doesnt really *love*
me. The truth is, she is a clever woman. She knows the value
of her unencumbered independence, having suffered a good
deal from family bonds and conventionality before the death
of her mother and the marriage of her sister left her free. The
idea of tying herself up again by a marriage before she knows
anything—before she has exploited her freedom and money-

power to the utmost—seems to her intellect to be unbearably foolish. Her theory is that she wont do it. She picked up a broken heart somewhere a few years ago, and made the most of it (she is very sentimental) until she happened to read *The Quintessence of Ibsenism,* in which she found, as she thought, gospel, salvation, freedom, emancipation, self-respect and so on. Later on she met the author, who is, as you know, able to make himself tolerable as a correspondent. He is also a bearable companion on bicycle rides, especially in a country house where there is nobody else to pair with. She got fond of me and did not coquet or pretend that she wasnt. I got fond of her, because she was a comfort to me down there. You kept my heart so warm that I got fond of everybody ; and she was nearest and best. That's the situation. What does your loving wisdom say to it?'

Ellen replied: 'I'm not clever. I never was, and sometimes, looking at you all, I hope I never shall be!' But there was one thing she *knew*: 'You'd be all bad, and no good in you, if you marry anyone unless you know you love her. A woman may *not* love before marriage and really love afterwards (if she has never loved before).'

Still nothing decisive happened. Shaw recoiled, not from the lady, but from marriage, which to a bachelor in his forties did not seem to belong to his programme. Then there was the money difficulty: when Shaw faced the situation objectively he saw that an adventurer living from hand to mouth on a precarious £6 a week from the *Saturday* Review could not honestly advise a lady with at least a dozen times as much settled income to marry him. Even when the success of *The Devil's Disciple* removed that objection (as it happened it removed it for ever), he still had doubts and scruples, mostly on her account. 'She is a free woman,' he reported, 'and it has not cost her half a farthing, and she has fancied herself in love, and known secretly that she was only taking a prescription, and been relieved to find the lover at last laughing at her and reading her thoughts and confessing himself a mere bottle of nerve medicine, and riding gaily off.' But before November was out a letter from Ellen tells us what had happened: 'Oh I see you, you two, walking in the damp and lovely mist, a trail of light from your footsteps, and—I don't think it's envy, but I know my eyes are quite wet, and I long to be one of you, and I don't care which. The common usual things appearing so beautiful as you tell me. Yes, I know, It's a long time ago, but, praise be blessed, I'll never forget!'

Ellen suggested that Shaw should bring Miss Payne-Townshend round to her dressing-room after they had been to see *Cymbeline* together. He demurred: 'The difficulty is that you wont see Miss T. unless she shews herself to you. She is, normally, a ladylike person at whom nobody would ever look twice, so perfectly does she fit into her place. . . . Perfectly placid and proper and pleasant. Does not condescend to be anything more. And takes it all off like a mask when she selects you for intimacy. She is not cheap enough to be brought round to your room and *shewn* to you. She isn't an appendage, this green-eyed one, but an individual.' And again: 'She *shant* be brought round to your dressing-room as an appendage of mine, to be exhibited as my latest fancy. Will you never understand what I mean when I say that I can respect people's humanity as well as love their individuality.'

In the spring of '97 the Webbs were living at Lotus, Tower Hill, Dorking. Miss Payne-Townshend was with them; while Shaw, though a regular resident, was constantly on the move to London and back again, sometimes writing to Ellen Terry as the train 'joggle-joggled' its way through the night. 'Miss P.T. has found me out,' he admitted in one letter: 'she tells me that I am "the most self-centred man she ever met".' And he described the domestic scene at their inappropriately-named house: 'If only I could bring you down with me. There's nobody there but Mrs Webb, Miss P.T., Beatrice Creighton (Bishop of London's daughter), Webb and myself. Alas! *four* too many. I wonder what you would think of our life—our eternal political shop; our mornings of dogged writing, all in separate rooms; our ravenous plain meals; our bicycling; the Webbs' incorrigible spooning over their industrial and political science; Miss P.T., Irish, shrewd and green-eyed, finding everything "very interesting"; myself always tired and careworn, and always supposed to be "writing to Ellen". You'd die of it all in three hours, I'm afraid. Oh, I wish, I wish—'

The autumn of '97 found Shaw and Miss Payne-Townshend staying with the Webbs at The Argoed, Penallt, Monmouth. Spending his afternoons in a hammock 800 feet above the Wye, he was preparing his *Plays: Pleasant and Unpleasant* for publication. They were on familiar terms now, and she would say to him, 'What a curious person you are!' or 'What an utter brute you are!' just as the humour took her. At the close of '97 he again described her for Ellen's benefit: 'Miss P.T. is a restful person, plain, green-eyed, very ladylike, completely demoralized by contact with my ideas, independent and unencumbered, and not so plain either when you are in her confidence. So whenever you want to run away and hide, probably the last place you will be sought for in is the London School of Economics and Political Science. She will be pretty curious about you, not only on the usual grounds of your celebrity, but because she has discovered that "work" and "important business" on my part sometimes means writing long letters to you.'

By the beginning of '98 Miss Payne-Townshend had become his secretary; he dictated articles to her and she nursed him when he was tired out: 'I lay like a log whilst the faithful secretary petted me and rubbed the bicycle gash in my cheek with vaseline in the hope that diligent massage may rub it out and restore my ancient beauty.' The gash was caused by his bicycle accident at the close of the previous year. He was spending more and more of his spare time in her flat at 10 Adelphi Terrace, above the London School of Economics, and they did a lot of walking together: 'Miss P.T. used to have neuralgia a good deal; she now hasnt much of it. When she walked with me she used to stop in five minutes and get palpitations and say I must not walk like an express train. Now she hooks on and steeplechases with me without turning a hair.' In March she started off with the Webbs on a tour round the world, but she got no farther than Rome, where she was studying municipal administration, when Mrs Webb received a wire from Graham Wallas informing her that Shaw was seriously ill, and lying neglected in disagreeable surroundings at 29 Fitzroy Square. Mrs Webb strongly advised her companion to return home. Miss Payne-Townshend was in no need of advice: she took the first train back. Let us accompany her to the second floor of what Shaw described as 'a most repulsive house'.

He worked in a very small room which was in a perpetual state of dirt and disorder. He kept the window wide open, day and night, winter and summer, and the dust and smuts that entered thereby settled on books, furniture and papers, being scattered over a wider area whenever attempts were made to remove them. The mass of matter on the table was chaotic: heaps of letters, pages of manuscript, books, envelopes, writing-paper, pens, inkstands, journals, butter, sugar, apples,

217

knives, forks, spoons, sometimes a neglected cup of cocoa or a half-finished plate of porridge, a saucepan, and a dozen other things, were mixed up indiscriminately, and all undusted, as his papers must not be touched. The table, the typewriter, and the wooden-railed chair in which he sat almost filled the room, forcing anyone who entered it to move sideways like a crab. Occasionally he would have a general clean-up, a job that took two full days' hard work; he enjoyed doing this, as another man might enjoy two days' digging in a garden, because it rested his mind, tired his back and begrimed his face and hands. Besides there were always some forgotten cheques to repay such chores. Part of the awesome accumulation was due to his method of dealing with literature: 'Whilst I am dressing and undressing I do all my reading. The book lies open on the table. I never shut it, but put the next book on top of it long before it's finished. After some months there is a mountain of buried books, all wide open, so that all my library is distinguished by a page with the stain of a quarter's dust or soot on it.' But for many years he had practically accustomed himself to a condition that could only be cured by dynamite: 'I have long resigned myself to dust and dirt and squalor in external matters: if seven maids with seven mops swept my den for half a century they would make no impression on it.'

Into this room, at intervals, a maid would come, slap down a plate of lukewarm eggs on the nearest pile of papers and vanish, having long given up 'the study' as hopeless. Shaw's mother never came into this slovenly sanctum: they were on the best of terms but went their several ways, did not feed together, and neither of them was disturbed by the absence of the other, explained or unexplained. His sister Lucy, who had attached herself to her mother-in-law, lived elsewhere and never called to see them. A maternal uncle, a doctor, ruined by the development of a prosperous country practice into a wilderness of cheap suburban streets inhabited by clerks bringing up families on fifteen shillings a week, dressed in clothes of revolting shabbiness and dying slowly of diabetes, called at long intervals to borrow the interest due to his pawnbroker, and made jokes that only G.B.S. laughed at. All the rooms badly needed repapering and repainting.

Such were the surroundings in which Shaw was struggling against a general break-down in health. Already we know what started it: a tightly-laced shoe which produced an abscess. But this would not have occurred if his health had not been undermined by a long period of overwork, and the protracted breathing of bad atmospheres at political meetings, in concert-rooms, theatres and committee-rooms. During one fortnight just before his illness, for example, he went to three first-nights as a dramatic critic, spoke at two County Council election meetings, attended four Vestry committees and one Fabian committee, in addition to writing his weekly feuilleton, revising a Fabian pamphlet on some social question, and dealing with his everyday correspondence. 'If I dont write to you I shall die,' he started a letter to Ellen Terry at about this period: 'if I make another stroke with a pen I shall go mad. Oh Ellen, I am the world's pack-horse ; and it beats my lean ribs unmercifully.'

The abscess on his instep was opened ; necrosis of the bone was discovered ; and, in accordance with the prevailing fashion, Lister's antiseptic treatment being then part of the creed of the medical profession, iodoform gauze was left in the cavity after each dressing of the wound, which, naturally, refused to heal up. The invalid was moving, when at all, on crutches by the time Miss Payne-Townshend arrived at 29 Fitzroy Square. He was the centre of some excitement at the time, for he had 'just seriously distracted public attention from the American war by publishing' his *Plays: Pleasant and Unpleasant*. The general feeling with regard to them was admirably expressed by the dramatist whose pieces Shaw as a critic had persistently overpraised. 'Much of them is not dramatic and would never be interesting in any circumstances to any possible audience,' wrote Henry Arthur Jones, a prophecy that ranks high among the major fatuities of literature. Shaw tried Jones on a different matter: 'By the way, would you advise me to get married?' he asked. Jones favoured the step but suggested that he should consult Rabelais, reading the advice given to Panurge on the subject.

Marriage seemed the only solution. Miss Payne-Townshend, horrified at the second-floor ménage in Fitzroy Square, imagined that if he were left there he must almost certainly die of a deficiency of domestic servants. She promptly took a house near Haslemere, proposing to install him there and nurse him back to health. His mother raised no objection. If he was going to be looked after by someone else with ample means, so much the better for him. But Shaw saw that this did not exhaust the case. With Queen Victoria still on the throne a spinster living alone in a house with a bachelor, even though nurses were present to prove his invalidism, would gravely compromise herself. Familiar as he was with illicit unions he had never advised a woman to form one; and to allow his friend to lose her social status on his account was impossible to him. For one who felt as he did, it was therefore marriage and Haslemere or an illness at Fitzroy Square without Charlotte. He decided in favour of marriage, 'and that for a reason I never thought possible, namely, that I think more of somebody else than I do of myself'. They had, in fact, 'become indispensable to one another'. This was how he put it: 'When I married I was too experienced to make the frightful mistake of simply setting up a permanent mistress; nor was my wife making the complementary mistake. There was nothing whatever to prevent us from satisfying our sexual needs without paying that price for it; and it was for other considerations that we became man and wife. . . . Do not forget that all marriages are different, and that a marriage between two young people followed by parentage cannot be lumped in with a childless partnership between two middle-aged people who have passed the age at which it is safe to bear a first child.'

There was not much doubt as to the form of ceremony. 'If I were to get married myself,' he had written a few weeks before the arrival of Miss Payne-Townshend, 'I should resort to some country where the marriage law is somewhat less than five centuries out of date.' His main objection to a religious service had been stated in 1896: 'If, for example, I desire to follow a good old custom by pledging my love to my wife in the church of our parish, why should I be denied due record in the registers unless she submits to have a moment of deep feeling made ridiculous by the reading aloud of the naïve impertinences of St Peter, who, on the subject of Woman, was neither Catholic nor Christian, but a boorish Syrian fisherman.' Miss Payne-Townshend therefore bought a ring and a licence, and on June 1st, 1898, they were married en route for Haslemere at the West Strand Registry Office. Shaw wore an old jacket which had been reduced to rags by the crutches on which he hobbled about. His friends, Graham Wallas and Henry Salt, were present, both immaculately dressed. 'The registrar never imagined I could possibly be the bridegroom,' related Shaw; 'he took me for the inevitable beggar who completes all wedding processions. Wallas, over six feet tall, was so obviously the hero of the occasion that the registrar was on the point of marrying him to my betrothed. But Wallas, thinking the formula rather too strong for a mere witness, hesitated at the last moment, and left the prize to me.'

They went to Pitfold, Haslemere, where his wife commenced the difficult job of restoring his health. She was ably assisted by the nurses, who fell in love with him, and adroitly impeded by the patient, whose bursts of energy kept her on tenterhooks. 'My wife has been having *such* a delightful honeymoon,' he recorded on June 19th: 'First my foot had to be nursed and the day before yesterday, just as it was getting pretty well, I fell downstairs and broke my left arm close to the wrist.' This completely disabled him and temporarily held up a book on Wagner, which he had set himself to do as a honeymoon-task. But in less than three weeks he was at it again, finishing it on August 20th and writing to his publisher Grant Richards that 'it should be got up as a book of devotion for pocket use, and not bulked out as a treatise'. He was much concerned over the appearance of this work, giving advice on the margins, the type, the paper, etc., and suggesting that it should have gilt edges, clasps, a leather binding and a bookmarker of perforated card with a text worked in it in wool. He even favoured an *édition de luxe*, bound in mother-of-pearl and cased in Russian leather, at two guineas. As his object in writing the *Perfect Wagnerite* was to prove Wagner a sound Shavian, he naturally wished it to look as much like a book of devotion as possible.

The foot showing signs of healing, the doctor ordered his patient to the seaside for change of air, and on September 10th they went to the Freshwater Bay Hotel in the Isle of Wight, where Shaw forged ahead with his new play, *Caesar and Cleopatra*. After about a fortnight they returned to Haslemere, and Shaw celebrated the improvement in his health by trying to ride a bicycle with one foot. He fell and sprained his ankle, which gave him more pain than 'ten operations or two broken arms'. What with one thing and another he seemed a pretty hopeless case, and the doctors, unable to do anything for him, blamed his diet. 'My situation is a solemn one,' he noted. 'Life is offered to me on condition of eating beefsteaks. My weeping family crowd about me with Bovril and Brand's Essence. But death is better than cannibalism. My will contains directions for my funeral, which will be followed not by

221

mourning coaches, but by herds of oxen, sheep, swine, flocks of poultry, and a small travelling aquarium of live fish, all wearing white scarves in honour of the man who perished rather than eat his fellow-creatures. It will be, with the exception of the procession into Noah's Ark, the most remarkable thing of the kind ever seen.'

In November the Shaws took a house on Hindhead named Blen-Cathra, now a college, which was a great improvement: 'This place beats Pitfold all to fits,' wrote the invalid, 'I am a new man since I came here; the air would make a dramatist of—who shall I say?' Their gate was on the main London-Portsmouth road, about a hundred yards from the fortieth milestone from London. On December 2nd he wrote to Henry Arthur Jones: 'It now appears that the one all-important condition for the foot is disuse—rest brought to the verge of killing the patient with inaction. I went to my specialist last week, and demanded the immediate amputation of the bone and the attacked toe. He happens to understand the exact relation between science and good sense wonderfully well for a surgeon, and he observed that if it was his toe he would stick to it. He declares that my health is improving visibly; that I am pulling up from a breakdown; and that if I hold on a while, possessing my soul with patience, I shall either escape an operation and heal up by Christian Science, so to speak, or at least reduce the disease to a small and perfectly defined spot which can be removed without any great loss to my foot. So I am waiting; but I regret to say that I have used up my recuperative energies this week in a most tremendous fourth act of *Caesar and Cleopatra*.' On the 8th January '99 he announced that Cleopatra was 'nearly as good a part as Dolly in *You Never Can Tell*', that his foot was discharging again, and that he would get another bit of bone removed. Early that year he again sprained his bad foot, and in April he sprained it a third time while 'fooling with a bicycle'. The pain was frightful and the foot looked awful. All through his various incapacitations, which included two operations on his foot, a fall downstairs, a broken arm, a thrice-sprained ankle and innumerable contusions, he had been creating a masterpiece, concerning which he wrote to me in 1918:

'Why did it need a colossal war to make people read my books? The whole army seems to do nothing else, except when it lays down the book to fire a perfunctory shot at Jerry or to write me a letter asking me what I meant by it. . . .

222

'I wrote *Caesar and Cleopatra* for Forbes-Robertson and Mrs Patrick Campbell when they were playing together. But it was not played by him until they had gone their several professional ways; and Cleopatra was "created" by Gertrude Elliot, who had already played in *The Devil's Disciple* with Robertson, and is now Lady Forbes-Robertson. It is what Shakespeare called a history: that is, a chronicle play; and I took the chronicle without alteration from Mommsen. I read a lot of other stuff, from Plutarch, who hated Caesar, to Warde-Fowler; but I found that Mommsen had conceived Caesar as I wished to present him, and that he told the story of the visit to Egypt like a man who believed in it, which many historians dont. I stuck nearly as closely to him as Shakespeare did to Plutarch or Holinshed. I infer from Goethe's saying that the assassination of Caesar was the worst crime in history, that he also saw Caesar in the Mommsen-Shaw light. Although I was forty-four or thereabouts when I wrote the play, I now think I was a trifle too young for the job; but it was not bad for a juvenile effort.

'It may interest you, now that you are enduring the discomforts and terrors of active service, to know that when I wrote Caesar I was stumbling about on crutches with a necrosed bone in my foot that everybody believed would turn cancerous and finish me. It had been brought on by an accident occurring at the moment when I was plunging into one of those breakdowns in middle-life which killed Schiller and very nearly killed Goethe, and which have led to the saying that every busy man should go to bed for a year when he is forty. In trying to come downstairs on crutches before I was used to them I shot myself into empty space and fell right down through the house on to the flags, complicating the useless foot with a broken arm. It was in this condition that I wrote *Caesar and Cleopatra*; but I cannot see any mark of it on the play. I remember lying on the top of a cliff in the Isle of Wight with my crutches in the grass beside me, and writing the lines:

> *The white upon the blue above*
> *Is purple on the green below*

as a simple memorandum of what I saw as I looked from the cliff. The Sphinx scene was suggested by a French picture of the Flight into Egypt. I never can remember the painter's name ; but the engraving, which I saw in a shop window when I was a boy, of the Virgin and child asleep in the lap of a colossal Sphinx staring over a desert, so intensely still that the smoke of Joseph's fire close by went straight up like a stick, remained in the rummage basket of my memory for thirty years before I took it out and exploited it on the stage.'

Needless to say, Forbes-Robertson was not at first enthusiastic about the play, giving the excuse that he could not run the risk of such a heavy production ; but it gradually grew upon him and at last he produced it, as we shall see.

William Archer said of *Caesar and Cleopatra*: 'I think Shaw has invented a new genre in this sort of historic extravaganza, though fortunately no one but he is likely to practise it.' The description of the work as an extravaganza was of course inept, the prophecy that no one would be likely to copy it was quite absurd, and the statement that Shaw had invented a new genre was a rather foolish way of saying that Shaw had written a play that no one else could have written ; but every new play from Shaw was now a bitter disappointment to Archer because it was not another *Mrs Warren's Profession*.

Caesar and Cleopatra is the only play of Shaw's that has widely influenced the literature of his time, by initiating a natural and humorous treatment of historical subjects. In that respect it is his most notable achievement. For his biographer it has an interest quite unrelated to its literary significance. The portrait of Caesar is simply Mommsen's shavianized ; therefore, it is idolized ; it was heavily debunked by Ferrari, an Italiàn writing of an Italian. Shaw's is a fascinating and most endearing portrait ; and if only the Caesars of this world had distantly resembled Shaw's comedian, the history of humanity would have been happier. But Shaw could not find the real Caesar in himself and so could not draw him. Shakespeare understood the real article and could ; though naturally Shaw would not admit this, making excuses for what he considered his predecessor's failure. 'Caesar was not in Shakespear, nor in the epoch, now fast waning, which he inaugurated.' 'Shakespear, who knew human weakness so well, never knew human strength of the Caesarian type.' 'There is not a single sentence uttered by Shakespear's Julius Caesar that is, I will not say worthy of him, but even worthy of an average Tammany boss.'

Taking these remarks seriatim, we may say: (1) Shakespeare studied Caesar at first hand, his name in that epoch being

Queen Elizabeth. (2) Shakespeare pictured a Caesar who was living on his reputation, not winning it, whose weakness was therefore more in evidence than his strength. That Shakespeare could draw 'human strength of the Caesarian type' is proved by his Octavius in *Antony and Cleopatra*. (3) We have lived to see several Caesars bestriding Europe, not one of whom has ever written or uttered a sentence that an average Tammany boss would want to borrow. In short, Shakespeare knew the dictator type through and through, and did not have to resemble him in order to paint him to the life. His Caesar has recently reappeared on earth as Hitler and Mussolini, and will reappear whenever humanity responds to headlines like 'I came, I saw, I conquered', and gets hysterical over bombast. Shakespeare knew all the other types thrown up by revolutions too. 'What a Brutus!' exclaimed Shaw: 'A perfect Girondin, mirrored in Shakespear's art two hundred years before the real thing came to maturity. . . .!' But human nature scarcely varies from age to age. Well-meaning Girondins like Brutus, resentful Jacobins like Cassius, soulless political opportunists like Antony, flourished in Elizabethan England just as they did in revolutionary France under the names of Brissort, Marat and Bonaparte, just as they did in revolutionary Russia under the names of Kerensky, Lenin and Stalin, and just as they will do in any country at any future time under any other names. Shakespeare knew the lot (they showed their faces for an instant in the Essex rebellion) and has put them into print for all time.

Though Shaw could observe characteristics closely and reproduce them vividly, he could not penetrate to the emotions that lie at the root of character unless he shared them; he lacked Shakespeare's mediumistic faculty. Such knowledge as Shaw possessed of the man-of-action type came out, not in his full-length portrait of Caesar, but in his snapshot of Napoleon, who asks the landlord of an Italian inn: 'And you have no devouring devil inside you who must be fed with action and victory: gorged with them night and day; who makes you pay, with the sweat of your brain and body, weeks of Herculean toil for ten minutes of enjoyment: who is at once your slave and your tyrant, your genius and your doom: who brings you a crown in one hand and the oar of a galley slave in the other: who shews you all the kingdoms of the earth and offers to make you their master on condition that you become their servant! have you nothing of that in you?' Which, at least, is how the man-of-action idealizes himself.

Yet, though *Caesar and Cleopatra* is not ás Shaw thought it 'the first and only adequate dramatization of the greatest man that ever lived', which he now repudiates as 'a frightfully foolish remark if I ever made it', it is a unique and enchanting work, which contains incomparably the best of Shaw's self-portraits, some excellent scenes, many admirable strokes of character, and any number of fine phrases, such as Caesar's 'He who has never hoped can never despair,' and his 'One year of Rome is like another, except that I grow older, whilst the crowd in the Appian Way is always the same age.' The character of Caesar-Shaw is still the most satisfying male creation in English drama since Shakespeare, and Shaw was right when he asserted: 'Cleopatra is not a difficult part: Caesar *is*: whoever can play the fourth act of it can play anything. Whoever cant, can play nothing.' It goes without saying that Shaw's Caesar, like all his most vivid and deeply-felt creations, has a very unJulian affinity with Jesus Christ. But then he strangely maintained that Jesus's strength lay not in his unlikeness to everyone else, but in his likeness.

In the spring of '99 the antiseptic treatment of Shaw's foot was discarded for pipe water, and the wound at once began to heal. On May 3rd he started to write a play for Ellen Terry, sketching her character from her letters to him and her performances on the stage. Later experience might not have encouraged him to write a play in which brutality is tamed by sympathy: 'I lived for a time on the south slope of the Hog's Back ; and every Sunday morning rabbits were coursed within earshot of me. And I noticed that it was quite impossible to distinguish the cries of the excited terriers from the cries of the sportsmen, although ordinarily the voice of a man is no more like the voice of a dog than like the voice of a nightingale. Sport reduced them all, men and terriers alike, to a common denominator of bestiality. The sound did not make me more humane: on the contrary, I felt that if I were an irresponsible despot with a park of artillery at my disposal, I should (especially after seeing the sportsmen on their way to and from their sport) have said: "These people have become sub-human, and will be better dead. Be kind enough to mow them down for me." ' But such happenings did not affect his work, and many years afterwards he told me what follows:

226

'*Captain Brassbound's Conversion*, which, like my *Blanco Posnet*, is an excellent religious tract, was written for Ellen Terry. When her son Teddy (Gordon Craig) produced the first of his many children, Ellen said that nobody would ever write a play for her now she was a grandmother. I said I would; and *Brassbound* was the result. She was so disappointed with it that she made no attempt to conceal her opinion of it, telling me quite frankly that though no doubt it might be a clever book, I could not imagine that it was a play. I laughed and said it was my notion of a play, which passed as a very good joke. At that time Ellen used, like many actors and actresses, to go frankly to bed in the afternoon and have a good rest; and she always made her nurse read her to sleep with the dullest book in the house. *Brassbound* seemed an ideal book for the purpose, and was duly put into operation. But the nurse, just as Ellen was dropping off (like Terriss— though she was a hundred times as clever) the nurse suddenly stopped and exclaimed, "Why, Miss Terry, this is you to the life." Ellen's opinion of the play instantly bounded to the opposite extreme; and she tried to induce Irving to produce the play. But he put his finger on the scene where Brassbound comes in in a frock coat and top hat, and said, "Shaw put that in to get me laughed at." He was perfectly right; and the stroke was so successful that when Laurence Irving created the part the audience laughed for two solid minutes at him at this point. Years afterwards Ellen played it and made her farewell tour through the United States in it.

'I wanted Ada Rehan to play it in America; and an agent sent her the book. She was furious at being offered a thing that was not a play at all, and in which the man, she thought, had the best part. Years later, when I read it to her (not being supposed to know anything about this early miscarriage), it threw her into a condition of extraordinary excitement, in which she exclaimed incoherently that actresses of her generation had been taught to believe that they had nothing to do but be beautiful, and that here was something quite new, quite different. She declared that she must play it. But the illness which finally killed her intervened and ended her stage career. "I wish I dare play," she said, "but I cannot: I never know when I shall flop." "Flop away," I said: "we can drop the curtain till you get up again." "Oh, I wish I could," she said. But she never did.

'Now that even the old professionals who still find it difficult to admit that my plays are plays have adopted it as an article of faith that I write very good parts, it is hard to believe that so many actors and actresses to whom I offered parts that were first-rate chances for them, refused them as absurd and undramatic. Ada Rehan, Irving, Tree, Mansfield, Wyndham, Terriss, Alexander, Fanny Coleman, Mrs Campbell, Ellen Terry, Cyril Maude, Allan Aynesworth, Jack Barnes, all landed themselves in this way. They were like the old Italian singers confronted with Wagner.'

Shaw's memory of the incident between Ellen and her nurse was not quite accurate. What really happened was more interesting. The play, which he provisionally called *The Witch of Atlas*, was finished on July 7th. 'Now I have to go over it to get the business right, which will take many grievous brain-racking days. And then further delay whilst Charlotte deciphers my wretched notebooks and makes a typewritten draft, with such unprofessional speed as her housekeeping and wifely cares allow.' It was in Ellen's hands by the end of the month, and on August 1st he announced that he would give it 'the ugly but arresting name *Captain Brassbound's Conversion*'. He told her that it was her play, that it was the only thing on earth he had the power to do for her, adding 'And now no more plays—at least no more practical ones. None at all, indeed, for some time to come: it is time to do something more in Shaw-philosophy, in politics and sociology. Your author, dear Ellen, must be more than a common dramatist.'

On August 4th he received the last and most painful blow he ever got from an artist nurtured in the commercial theatre of his time. Ellen wrote to say that the play was not at all suitable for her, that it would never make a penny on the stage, and that the part of Lady Cicely ought to be played by Mrs Patrick Campbell. Shaw was really upset: 'Alas! dear Ellen, is it really so? Then I can do nothing for you. I honestly thought that Lady Cicely would fit you like a glove. . . . It is clear that I have nothing to do with the theatre of to-day: I must educate a new generation with my pen from childhood up—audience, actors and all, and leave them my plays to murder after I am cremated. . . . And so farewell our project—all fancy, like most projects. . . . Silly Ellen!' Her next letter contained the phrase, 'Of course you never *really* meant Lady Cicely for me,' which provoked him to a lengthy rejoinder: 'Oh you lie, Ellen, you lie: never was there a part so deeply written for a woman as this for you, silly, self-unconscious, will o' the wisp beglamoured child actress as you still are.' He told her to read two books of travel—Mary Kingsley's and H. M. Stanley's—and to 'compare the brave woman, with her common sense and good will, with the wild-beast man, with his elephant rifle, and his atmosphere of dread and murder, breaking his way by mad selfish assassination out of the difficulties created by his own cowardice. . . . Have you any real belief in the heroism of the filibuster? Have you had any sympathy with the punishments of the judge? Have you found in your own life and your own small affairs no better way, no more instructive heart wisdom, no warrant for trusting to the good side of people instead of terrorizing the bad side of them? . . . Here is a part which dominates a play because the character it represents dominates the world. . . . In every other play I have ever written—even in *Candida*—I have prostituted the actress more or less by making the interest in her partly a sexual interest. . . . In Lady Cicely I have done without this, and gained a greater fascination by it. And you are disappointed. . . . Oh Ellen, Ellen, Ellen, Ellen. This is the end of everything.'

His letter, which made her weep, must have inspired the bedside treatment already referred to. On August 20th she wrote from Wells House, Ilkley, Yorkshire, that she had been in bed for four days with 'flu and that her maid, who had read the play to her two or three times, had not thought Lady Cicely a bit like her, until one day they were visiting a poor district together and Ellen, who was surrounded by poor people, caught a peculiar expression on her maid's face. 'Much amused at something,' thought Ellen. A week later they were at Bolton Abbey amongst a crowd of smart people, and again Ellen saw that peculiar expression. When they were back at Ilkley she asked what had amused her companion. 'Oh, I'm very sorry,' the girl blurted out, suppressing her laughter with difficulty, 'but Lady Cicely is *so* like you! She gets her way in *everything—just like you!*' Ellen instantly asked Shaw if she might let Irving read the play.

Shaw was convalescing at Ruan Minor in Cornwall, where he bathed twice a day with good effect on his muscles: 'Swimming is the only exercise I have ever taken for its own sake. I swim now for the most part under water, as my wife learns the art by using me as a life-preserver.' He knew perfectly well that Irving would never do a play of his, but he indulged Ellen's whim so far as to write a long letter about royalties,

229

percentages and what-not, in case Irving went mad and decided to try it. Ellen did her best with Irving, for she loved the play more and more, and was 'transported' by the part of Lady Cicely, but he thought it 'like a comic opera', and her attempts came to nothing. She then hoped that she would be able to put it on herself.

In the autumn Shaw went with his wife on a cruise round the Mediterranean. Writing from 'somewhere between Villefranche and Syracuse', he called it 'a brute of a place, morally hideous, physically only pretty-pretty. Would it were Spitzbergen! I was born to bite the north wind, not to soak in this lukewarm Reckitt's blue purlieu of gamblers.' He got what he wanted ten days later in the Grecian Archipelago: 'Cold, storm, sleety grey, pitching and rolling, misery, headaches, horrors of universal belchings! . . . However, I am at least quit of Athens, with its stupid classic Acropolis and smashed pillars.' Constantinople looked rather well by moonlight, but stank: he spent a day there 'shuffling about the mosques in ridiculous overshoes'. The voyage got on his nerves; the enforced inaction did not suit him; and his wife described him as 'impatient of the confinement of the ship's life'.

Back in London early in 1900, his home at No. 10 Adelphi Terrace for the next twenty-eight years, he heard from Ellen, who was touring in the States, that she could do nothing about the play for nearly two years, as she had promised to stay on with Irving. 'Now for one of my celebrated *volte faces*,' answered Shaw. 'I hold on pretty hard until the stars declare themselves against me, and then I always give up and try something else with a promptitude which seems cynical and unfeeling to the slow-witted Englishman who only tells himself his misfortunes by degrees. . . . I have pitched so many dreams out of the window that one more or less makes little difference. In fact, by this time I take a certain Satanic delight in doing it and noting how little it hurts me. So out of the window you go, my dear Ellen; and off goes the play to my agents as in the market for the highest bidder.'

But apparently there were no bids, for in the autumn of 1900 Shaw asked Ellen Terry to play Lady Cicely in a performance to be given by the Stage Society. She was touring the provinces with Irving, and could not manage it, her part being taken by Janet Achurch when the play was performed for the first time by the Stage Society at the Strand Theatre on December 16th, 1900. Janet was not good in the part, and

230

the author told her why: 'I am like Molière in point of always consulting my cook about my plays. She is an excellent critic; goes to my lectures and plays; and esteems actors and actresses as filthy rags in comparison to the great author they interpret. Consulted as to Lady Cicely, she at once said: "No: she wasn't right: when she sat down she got her dress tucked in between her knees: no high lady would do that." Now that is an excellent criticism. You played the whole part, as far as comedy went, with your dress tucked between your knees.'

As the performance was on a Sunday evening, Ellen was able to be present, and she and Shaw met for the first time under the stage of the old Strand Theatre. She thought him 'a good kind gentle creature', not at all what she had expected from his letters and criticisms.

FIN DE SIÈCLE

ELLEN'S DESCRIPTION OF G.B.S. as 'a good kind gentle creature' would not have been endorsed by the average dramatist, composer, actor, singer, impresario or theatre-manager, who would have expressed themselves on the subject at greater length in stronger language. Yet he was a far more respectable member of the community than the majority of his famous literary contemporaries, many of whom closed their lives round about 1900 in the lunatic asylum, the opium den, the river Seine or the Roman Catholic Church. The trouble was that people did not know what to make of him. He seemed to be serious, yet he seemed to be playing the fool. The cause of the confusion was that he had an abundance of that wild gaiety of spirit which finds its safety-valve in play-acting. After a circus performance at Olympia he was introduced to Whimsical Walker. 'It is very nice of you to shake hands with an old clown,' said Whimsical. 'It's just one old clown shaking hands with another,' replied Shaw. His love of clowning, an effervescence of vitality, led many unimaginative people to believe that he was usually talking with his tongue in his cheek ; and even his unrehearsed effects had an irritant quality because his natural shyness made him appear extraordinarily cool. One day, at Westminster Bridge underground station, he slipped at the top of the stairs and shot down the whole flight on his back, while the onlookers held their breaths in horror. Then he rose to his feet without the least surprise and walked on as if that were his usual way of going downstairs. The shriek of laughter from the onlookers expressed relief, annoyance and mirth in about equal proportions.

But the impression of perversity he produced with the foolish that he was exploiting the mere trick of calling black white (to which his reply, 'Well: try it for yourselves,' was conclusive) was really a result of the time lag of the literary professions in England. A terrific reversal of social valuations had been produced by the publication of Marx's *Capital*. Nietzsche had, as he claimed, effected a 'transvaluation of values' in modern morals ; and this shift of scale had asserted itself in London in the conversations of Oscar Wilde, by far the greatest wit and raconteur of the *fin de siècle*. Ibsen's attack on conventional idolatry and domesticity had pilloried the Tennysonian heroes as pretentious cads. But in literary London, which had read no further than Macaulay and Anthony Trollope, and knew of Oscar Wilde only as a diner-out who paid for his invitations with a display of paradoxes, Shaw seemed a unique and scandalous phenomenon, whereas, having assimilated Marx and Henry George, anticipated Ibsen and Nietzsche, and taken his fellow-townsman Wilde seriously, he was simply in the forefront of a revolution in morals. This had not as yet seized political power in Germany, Italy, Russia and Turkey, nor incidentally stained its triumphs by shedding oceans of blood and by innumerable blunders and ineptitudes. Nowadays, up against Lenin and Stalin, Hitler and Mussolini, Ataturk and Rhiza Khan, Shaw seems a very harmless old gentleman ; but in the days when he made his reputation Europe was still Victorian: consequently his reputation was scandalous and mostly fabulous.

'It is interesting to compare the old morals of Shakespear with the new morals in Ibsen's plays and my own,' Shaw once wrote to me. 'Of course there is a considerable overlap, as human nature remains largely the same, and all dramatists are on common ground to that extent. But there is none the less a big difference. Shakespear had no creed and no programme: his plots were all reach-me-downs which he transfigured as best he might by his genius. In company with Shelley, Wagner and Ibsen, I was a social reformer and doctrinaire first, last, and all the time. My sensitiveness to social, political, and religious injustices and stupidities was certainly shared by Shakespear; but as he saw no way out it drove him to a Swiftian pessimism in which he saw Man in authority as an Angry Ape, and finally into a cynicism made bearable by the divine gaiety of genius. Mercutio and Benedick did not die: they aged into Gonzalo, with whose help, and that of Caliban and Autolycus, we hardly notice that the rest, except of course the young lovers, are Machiavellian scoundrels. Timon and Thersites remained unanswered; but they had said their say; and Shakespear was not the man to go on grousing uselessly. Not thus Shelley and Wagner, Ibsen and myself. We saw a way through the Valley of the Shadow and believed that when men understood their predicament they could and would escape from it.'

I lately reminded Shaw that his *Better than Shakespear?* was written forty years ago, and asked whether he had anything to add to it. He replied, 'Of course I have. But first get out of your head the superstition that I am a young man, and Shakespear an old one who has written himself out and retired to Stratford as William Shakespear, Gent. The truth is that Shakespear died prematurely: perhaps he drank too much, as Ibsen did. I know you are an old Bardolator and think the comparison with him is hard on me; but as a matter of fact it is grossly unfair to Shakespear. Do you realise that I have lived more than thirty years longer than he did, and that my biggest works were written at an age he never attained? All the great artists who have lived long enough have had a juvenile phase, a middle phase, and a Third Manner, as we say when we are talking of Beethoven. Well, Beethoven composed the Ninth Symphony and the Mass in D at the age at which Shakespear was dead. The enormous talent of Handel did not produce *Messiah*, which still enchants listeners who, like myself, do not believe a word of it, until Handel was six years older than Shakespear was at his death. Ibsen was sixteen years older than Shakespear ever was when he wrote *The Master Builder*. I was respectively thirteen and fifteen years older when I wrote *Methuselah* and *St Joan*. All these works are Third Manner works; and Shakespear had no Third Manner. I do not pretend that Shakespear at sixty would have written *Prometheus Unbound* or *Emperor or Galilean* or *The Niblung's Ring* or *Back to Methuselah*; but Gonzalo might

233

have gone further than stealing a few lines from Montaigne and Prospero done something better with his cloudcapt towers than knock them down. There was Saint Thomas More to be surpassed and John Bunyan to be anticipated. As it is he can claim that we are all standing on his shoulders. Whose shoulders had he to stand on? Marlow and Chapman, the best of his rivals, were mere blatherskites compared to him. And he was on the brink of the appalling *dégringolade* of the British drama which followed his death, and went on for three hundred years until my time. That is why I have to compare him with giants like Handel and Beethoven. There were no giants in the British theatre to compare with him. And his plays were so abominably murdered and mutilated until Harley Granville Barker, twenty years my junior, restored them to the stage, that it was shamefully evident that the clergymen who knelt down and kissed Ireland's forgeries and the critics who made him ridiculous by their senseless idolatries had never read a line of his works and never intended to.'

Perhaps it is hardly necessary for me to reply that Shakespeare dealt, not in morals, but in fundamentals. His theme was human nature, which never changes. The so-called 'new morals' of Ibsen, Shelley, Wagner, Shaw and Co., though dressed up to look attractive and novel in each age, are merely those of any gang of people who wish to attain power or clean up the mess made by previous gangs ; their new morality is as old as the Church Militant, as old as Mahomet, Attila and Darius, to say nothing of Moses and the hills. But by a sad dispensation of providence Shaw was fated to talk twaddle whenever he compared Shakespeare with himself and his favourite authors, and all I need add is that he had nothing to say against Shakespeare as a pessimist. What he offered us as his own optimism was nothing more cheerful than his conviction that if, as he thought probable, Man would have to be scrapped as a hopeless failure, the Life Force could be depended upon to fill his place with a better animal. When his friend, Henry Salt, wrote an autobiography, calling it *Seventy Years Among Savages*, Shaw chuckled appreciatively. He always regarded the world as a sort of zoo in which monkey houses and tiger cages filled the landscape. He pictured the man of genius, himself really, as condemned to a life among wild beasts. Naturally this did not please his contemporaries, who had a better opinion of themselves.

ROYALTIES AT THE COURT

IN THE SPRING AND SUMMER OF 1900 Shaw was at Blackdown Cottage, near Haslemere, writing a preface and notes to his *Three Plays for Puritans*, and preparing them for publication the following year. In February 1901 he was staying at Piccard's Cottage, St Catherine's, Guildford. These changes of address were due to the fact that it took him three hours to keep appointments in London from his Hindhead house, though the fortieth milestone was almost at his gate. Eventually he had to leave Surrey for Hertfordshire, taking The Old House, Harmer Green, Welwyn, in the spring of 1904, and leaving that a year or so later for Ayot St Lawrence, where he settled down permanently. In the churchyard at Ayot there is a tomb bearing the inscription: 'Jane Eversley. Born 1815. Died 1895. Her time was short.' Shaw felt that a place where the inhabitants who died at eighty were considered short-lived had the right climate for him.

He spent the first years of the century in the committee rooms of the old St Pancras Vestry and the new Borough Council, dealing with such matters as public health (including a smallpox epidemic), paving, lighting, drainage, rates, salaries; and in writing articles on Free Trade, the Boer War and other political questions of the hour. At the same time he was giving his mornings to the writing of *Man and Superman*, in which, as in all his plays, his economic studies 'played as important a part as a knowledge of anatomy does in the works of Michael Angelo'. Shaw never planned or plotted a play in advance. Having got the main idea, he sat down and trusted confidently to inspiration, never seeing a page ahead while writing and never knowing what was going to happen. 'What I say to-day, everybody will say to-morrow, though they will not remember who put it into their heads. Indeed, they will

235

be right; for I never remember who puts the things into my head: it is the Zeitgeist.' Thus he came to feel that the forms his plays took were inevitable, though he worked as carefully at the writing of them as the most industrious craftsman. 'I never let a play out of my hands until it is as good as I can make it, and until it is sufficiently light to be digested without difficulty. But the only thanks that people give me for not boring them is that they laugh delightedly for three hours at the play that has cost many months of hard labour, and then turn round and say that it is no play at all, and accuse me of talking with my tongue in my cheek.' On one point he was especially careful: 'Whenever I feel in writing a play that my great command of the sublime threatens to induce solemnity of mind in my audience, I at once introduce a joke and knock the solemn people from their perch.' But his love of anti-climax was not his sole reason for writing comedies. 'All genuinely intellectual work is humorous,' he declared. And: 'Why does the imaginative man always end by writing comedy if only he has also a sense of reality? Clearly because of the stupendous irony of the contrast between his imaginary adventures and his real circumstances and powers.' When he had completed and perfected a play to the utmost of his ability, he naturally would not allow less qualified hands to tinker with it. 'I wont have a line omitted or a comma altered,' he wrote in 1902 to the Austrian translator of his plays: 'I am quite familiar with the fact that every fool who is connected with a theatre, from the call boy to the manager, thinks he knows better than an author how to make a play popular and successful. Tell them . . . that I am a pigheaded, arrogant, obstinate, domineering man of genius, deaf to reason, and invincibly determined to have my own way about my own works.' Yet nobody could have been less respectful to his texts than he was himself. His cuts and changes appalled those who suggested them. Producers who wanted an extra line to help the stage business, and actors who found a climax coming too suddenly on them, instantly got what they wanted, and sometimes more than they bargained for. Shaw's contempt for authors who would not or could not do this was unbounded: he called them 'no tradesmen'. But the changes had to be made by himself, and not by the nearest amateur.

Man and Superman was the first play Shaw wrote that had no reference whatever to the conventional theatrical requirements of his age; and it contains, in the long third act known as *Don Juan in Hell*, 'a careful attempt to write a new Book of Genesis for the Bible of the Evolutionists'. The essence of Shaw's religious philosophy is given by Don Juan: 'I can tell you that as long as I can conceive something better than myself I cannot be easy unless I am striving to bring it into existence or clearing the way for it. That is the law of my life. That is the working within me of Life's incessant aspiration to higher organization, wider, deeper, intenser self-consciousness and clearer self-understanding. It was the supremacy of this purpose that reduced love for me to the mere pleasure of a moment, art for me to the mere schooling of my faculties, religion for me to a mere excuse for laziness, since it had set up a God who looked at the world and saw that it was good, against the instinct in me that looked through my eyes at the world and saw that it could be improved.'

Briefly, Shaw's belief was in a God who achieves his purpose by Trial and Error. God, as the Church of England puts it, has neither body, parts, nor passions. God is a Creative Purpose; and all living creatures are experiments in the production of instruments of that purpose, which is the attainment of power over matter and circumstance with the necessary accompanying knowledge and comprehension. The Purpose, *alias* the Life Force, *alias* the Evolutionary Appetite, *alias* God, may make frightful mistakes, which its creatures have to remedy. This constitutes the Problem of Evil, which the hypothesis of an Omnipotent God does not solve. The instrument may not function properly and destroy itself by cancer and epilepsy. The cobra and the tiger were designed for uses which they have survived; and they must now be examined. The Purpose has a sense of humour which it has gratified by the creation of grotesques which can be seen in every aquarium. It has a sense of beauty which can be studied in aviaries and in Greek sculpture. Creation never stops: therefore the current view of Causation which regards the present as an inevitable consequence of the past, and the future of the present, is a deadly error: the living cause is always in the future: hence there is always hope and always a sense of the miraculous.

To us the interesting thing about this belief is the light it casts on Shaw as the sort of man such beliefs (which we sum up as Creative Evolution) produce. It was as an instrument of the Life Force that he spent all his energy in preaching and fighting for his conception of social betterment. His belief in

237

a power working through man towards perfection is not only the explanation of his belief that his works are inspired, but a confession of his own deep dissatisfaction with human beings as they are.

The new gospel proved unacceptable to the late John Murray, publisher, who had apparently received a dissimilar revelation ; and thenceforth Shaw published his works on commission. Constable's brought out *Man and Superman* in 1903, and for the first time the critics took G.B.S. seriously as a social critic and philosopher. The change was reported, with several other matters, in a letter from the author to Forbes-Robertson, who was touring America and occasionally thinking of *Caesar and Cleopatra*:

21st & 22nd Dec. 1903.

'MY DEAR FORBES ROBERTSON,

'Your letter from Cincinnati finds me in a state of extreme prostration. I incautiously witnessed Tree's *Richard II* the night before last ; and the spectacle of our friend sitting on the ground telling sad stories of the death of kings, not to mention his subsequent appearance in Westminster Hall in the character of Doré's Christ leaving the Praetorium, has been almost too much for me.

'As to *Caesar,* it is to be produced with great splendour at the Neues Theater in Berlin in February, an event from which we may get some hints as to the Sphinx, which I have always conceived as something faked up with a clothes horse and a mangle. There is a Shaw boom on in Germany, because four of my plays have been produced in Vienna, Leipzig, Dresden and Frankfurt ; and they have all failed so violently, and been hounded from the stage with such furious execrations, that the advanced critics proclaim me the choice and master spirit of the age ; and no manager respects himself until he has lost at least 200 marks by me. My plays have become as Louis Parker's : they simply cannot be kept off the stage. The managers make me large advances on account of royalties : they think nothing of twelve-pound-ten apiece for myself and the translator ; and they never get it back, as two nights is the record run so far. Happily everyone here thinks these productions have been immense successes ; and for your sake and *Caesar's* I have said nothing to the contrary.

'But *Caesar* will cost a lot of money to dress, though the

cast will not cost much with the two title parts in the family. There are six scenes and a sphinx, even without the third act, which must, I fear, be clean cut out without benefit of clergy, for want of time. You could not play the first act alone except at the Stage Society or a charitable matinee: the literary scandal would be too great. Besides, it is in the other acts that Caesar is built up: in the first he might as well be Haroun al Raschid. You would not be taken with full seriousness in it. My last book has turned the tables on the people who will not admit that I am serious: they used to laugh when I was serious; but now the fashion has changed: they take off their hats when I joke, which is still more trying.

'But my position has become odder than ever; for I have been knocked out of time in a curious way by Barrie. His *Little Mary*, which is a vegetarian pamphlet—a didactic lark compared to which my most wayward exploits are conventional, stagey, and old-fashioned—is having as great a success as *Crichton*, to the intense astonishment of John Hare, who visibly wonders, as he brings the house down with line after line, what the devil they can see in such incomprehensible stuff; and Barrie is now first and the rest nowhere as a popular playwright. In fact, I have given the drama such a powerful impulse that it has jumped clean over my head. When you went away I had not yet arrived: when you come back you will find me obsolete; and if you play me at all, it must be as a classic, and not as a modern. I have actually taken to going to the theatre to see Barrie's plays; and I not only stand them without discomfort, but enjoy them.

'Have you ever thought of *Richard III* as a possible successor to your *Hamlet*? Nobody now alive has seen what can be done with Richard. The provinces have by this time forgotten Barry Sullivan; and Irving's Richard does not count. A really brilliant Nietzschean Richard would be fresh and delightful. I believe I could fill it with the most captivating business for you, and practically get rid of the old-fashioned fight at the end. No actor has ever done the curious recovery by Richard of his old gaiety of heart in the excitement of the battle. It whirls him up out of his vulgar ambition to be a king (which makes the middle acts rather tedious after the fantastic superhumanity of the first), and he is again the ecstatic prince of mischief of the "Shine out, fair sun, till I have bought a glass" phase which makes the first act so rapturous. All Nietzsche is in the lines:

Conscience is but a word that cowards use
Devised at first to keep the strong in awe.
Our strong arms be our conscience, swords our law!

And after all the pious twaddle of Richmond, his charging order is delicious:

Upon them! To't pell mell,
If not to heaven, then hand in hand to hell.

The offer of his kingdom for a horse is part of the same thing: any means of keeping up the ecstasy of the fight is worth a dozen kingdoms. In the last scene he should have a bucket of rose pink thrown in his face, and then reel on; all cut to pieces, killed already six times over, with a broken sword and his armour all in splinters, wrenching off the battered crown which is torturing his poor split head. Being hunted down just then by the Rev. Pecksniff Richmond and his choir, he is just able, after an impulse to hold on to the crown tooth and nail, to pitch it gaily to him and die like a gentleman. That would be real Shakespear too; for William's villains are all my eye: neither Iago, Edmund, Richard nor Macbeth have any real malice in them. When William did a really malicious creature, like Don John, he couldnt take any real interest in him. Now you would be a charming Richard; and though the production might or might not be a financial success in London, it would be a good investment, as it would last your life in the provinces as a repertory play. Mrs Robertson could play Edward V: she is not silly enough for Lady Ann. By all means keep up your banking account with *Lights that Succeed*,[1] but build up the big repertory all the same: it provides for old age, and is the only means of becoming the undisputed head of the profession.

'Caesar, of course, will be in the big repertory of the future; and you ought to create him. But you dont half believe in him; and the public might not believe in him at all. I never could get you quite up to the scratch with Richard IV:[2] you did the part; but you never did the play. Caesar would have a better chance with you because it is not only a much bigger part, but Mrs Roberston could make a hit with Cleopatra,

[1] Kipling's *The Light that Failed*: one of Robertson's greatest successes.
[2] Dick Dudgeon: Robertson's part in *The Devil's Disciple*.

240

whereas, she would have had to get her brains extracted and her face soft-boiled to play the poor pitiful creature Judith. Further, *The Devil's Disciple* requires three or four stars (Anderson and Burgoyne are more difficult to cast than Dick), whereas in *Caesar* the minor parts are within the scope of ordinary talent. *Caesar* is not a cheap venture. Even the Neues Theater has found it necessary to spend £1000 on the production (equal to, say, £6000 in London); and I have a certain cautious stinginess in me which makes me shrink from gambling with the bread of your infants. You could do *Richard III* for the same money; and Richard could not fail utterly, whereas the Lord only knows what might or might not happen with *Caesar*. I think you had better sample it at the Stage Society before committing yourself or me any further. I should give it without remorse to a better Caesar, either in England or America, if I could find one; but where is he? The only American star who would have the cheek to touch it is Mansfield; and he refused it long ago; whereupon I said "Adieu, Pompey," and disowned him. . . .

'By the way, if you want to benefit the charity, insist on a businesslike committee, *and charge full salary*, which you can then hand over as a subscription. Otherwise they will muddle all the money away in unnecessary expenses; and after a great success there will be either a deficit or a balance of fifteen shillings for the hospital, and your friend will be your enemy for the rest of his life. Whereas if you insist on the full value of your services and hand that over, the charity will secure it whether the committee is insolvent or not, and your friend will be so pleased that he will demand a repetition of the exploit every year until you are forced to cut him.

'I see that one Arnold Daly is playing *Candida* in New York. If he plays anywhere within your reach, ask Mrs Robertson to go and see it and tell me what it's like. There is a sort of snivelling success possible for *Candida* if the right cast could be got for it.

'You can read this letter as a serial, in instalments. I am so tired of writing about the Fiscal Question that I cannot help spreading myself on a genial human theme.

'Yours ever,
'G. BERNARD SHAW.'

Man and Superman was first produced by the Stage Society on May 21st, 1905, with Granville Barker, made up like a youthful edition of the author, in the part of Jack Tanner. Two days later it opened at the Court Theatre in Sloane Square, where Shaw was at last creating the plays, actors and audiences of his dreams.

In 1904 the Court Theatre, in the hands of J. H. Leigh, was giving a series of Shakespearean revivals. Early that year Leigh's manager, J. E. Vedrenne, asked Granville Barker, who had been producing for the Stage Society, to superintend a revival of *The Two Gentlemen of Verona*. Barker agreed on condition that Vedrenne would join him in giving half a dozen matinees of *Candida* at the same theatre. Vedrenne accepted the condition and the experiment was successful, the first matinee on April 26th being received with shouts of 'Author'. Vedrenne appeared on the stage and began a speech: 'Ladies and Gentlemen, I am not Shaw, who is probably on the platform of the station next door—' The audience heard no more, most of them jumping up and hurrying to Sloane Square underground station to catch a glimpse of Shaw, who, however, did not wait for them. Barker and the theatre made a modest profit out of the matinees, Shaw received about £30, and a partnership was formed between Vedrenne and Barker, who started a season at the Court Theatre in the autumn of 1904, on a guarantee from a few friends which was never called up, as the Shaw matinees paid their way, and the theatre was lettable to amateurs and others for casual night performances. The Vedrenne-Barker management of the Court Theatre, which lasted from October 18th, 1904 to June 29th, 1907, was without question the most noteworthy episode in English theatrical history since Shakespeare and Burbage ran the Globe on Bankside. Starting with matinees, they soon had to give evening performances as well, for success came quickly with the first performance of a new Shaw play, *John Bull's Other Island*, finished in a hurry and produced on the afternoon of November 1st, 1904.

The partners were as dissimilar in temperament as two men could be. Vedrenne having been a consul in Cardiff, passed in the theatre as a man of business. He was married and a father, desperately economical; otherwise he would have been ruined by Barker, who was solely interested in the art of producing plays, and ignored everything and everyone not directly concerned with it. He expected his actors to understand and to underplay their parts; he was at his best in producing the intimate type of drama written by himself and Galsworthy;

242

he could not do justice to Shaw, whose plays, with their carefully built-up speeches, required flamboyant acting. 'I truckle to Granville Barker in order to conciliate him when he is forty,' wrote Shaw in 1902. 'He regards me as a vulgar old buffer who did my best in my day to play up for better things—his things, for example. In revenge I call him "serious relief", etc. But he is always useful when a touch of poetry and refinement is needed: he lifts a whole cast when his part gives him a chance, even when he lets the part down and makes the author swear. He rebukes me feelingly for wanting my parts to be "caricatured".' Shaw considered him a genius, 'a cold-hearted Italian devil, but a noble soul all the same', which was another way of describing a very go-ahead young man who thought solely of himself and his work.

Shaw produced his own plays at the Court Theatre, Barker all the others; and although works by Euripides, Maeterlinck, Schnitzler, Hauptmann, Yeats, Hankin, Masefield, Galsworthy and Barker were seen there, the plays of Shaw gave the management its real distinction and incidentally its financial profit. Only once in his life had Shaw appeared as an actor: 'At the first performance of *A Doll's House* in England, on a first-floor Bloomsbury lodging-house, Karl Marx's youngest daughter played Norah Helmer; and I impersonated Krogstadt at her request with a very vague notion of what it was all about.' But that was back in the early eighties, and in the meantime he had learnt more about acting than any actor on the stage; among other things he had learnt that there were two types of actors: those who were only happy on the stage as themselves, and those who were solely at ease when disguised in character-parts utterly unlike themselves.

Having finished a play, the first thing he did was to read it to a selected group of personal friends. Next he read it to the company engaged to perform it. His readings were extraordinarily vivid. He had an unerring dramatic sense; each character was carefully differentiated, and he could maintain the voice peculiar to each right up to the end of the play without the least suggestion of strain; he was never monotonous; he used no gestures, getting his effects solely by the tempo and modulation of his voice; and he never seemed to strike a false note, his intonations exactly expressing the mood and meaning of the speaker. Such was the effect of his reading that it would have made a bad play appear good; but it disheartened the more modest actors, who knew that they could never play their parts as well as he had read them. However, he did his patient best with the actors, who thought him the most tactful and courteous of producers. 'You must pamper the company and not bully them,' he once advised Mansfield, and his own productions illustrated the value of his advice. After the reading, the actors received their parts and read them at their ease for about a week, with Shaw on the stage directing the stage business, planned thoroughly beforehand. When this was solidly established he left the stage and sat in the auditorium, note-book in hand, whilst the actors got to work without book. In this phase he never interrupted the dialogue nor allowed it to be interrupted until the play was completely learnt. But he was watching closely, usually from the front row of the dress circle, and making innumerable notes, which he ran over on the stage with the actors concerned at the close of each act, showing how the lines were to be spoken, giving the vocal inflections and the appropriate physical gestures and expressions, and always exaggerating his illustrations so as to prevent the actors from simply imitating him instead of grasping his meaning. His manner was genial and sympathetic, and he never uttered a harsh or hurtful word, laughing over his own lines, which he could never repeat accurately. His high spirits were as infectious as his Irish speech ; he was clown, conjurer, acrobat, actor, all in one ; and he got his own way in everything without the smallest friction.

He designed his scenery, chose his casts, managed his stage-manager, lectured his actors, wrote post-cards to them full of repetitions of the lines they could not get right, laughed at them, abused them humorously, and won their affection. He attended every rehearsal, and without appearing to interfere attended to pretty well everything else. When John Galsworthy sent his play, *The Silver Box*, to the Court Theatre management, Shaw read it at once and advised Barker to do it. 'I met Shaw who told me he'd read the play and thought it very fine. H'm!' noted Galsworthy, whose scepticism was ill-founded, for Shaw informed me that 'J.G. and I were always on cordial terms ; but there were no incidents. The elegance and economy of his style were pleasant to me—so unlike my own Italian-operatic manner.' He was enthusiastic over Barker's revivals of the plays of Euripides translated into English verse by Shaw's old friend Gilbert Murray, whom he portrayed vividly as Cusins in *Major Barbara*. Shaw ranked these translations as being in a class by themselves, and that the highest in twentieth century drama. Their production he considered the highest achievement of Granville Barker's management.

He tried hard to bring the novelists into the new movement, sometimes forcing the production of plays by other writers by threatening to withhold his own. 'Have you seen Kipling's story (*They*) in Scribner's, which I send you by this post?' he asked Ellen Terry. 'Wouldnt you like to play the blind woman? That is what I call genius: one forgives all the creature's schoolboy ruffianisms and vulgarities for his good things, of which this is one of the goodest. What a pity the thrilling turning-point of it—when he feels the child's kiss in his palm, and then, seeing that there is no child there, *realizes*—is impossible on the stage! I wonder could I get him to try his hand at the theatre in his fine style—not his Lights that Failed and Limmacons (*The Man Who Was*) and the like.' He tried to tempt Kipling but failed. He did the same with G. K. Chesterton, Maurice Hewlett, and H. G. Wells. None rose to the bait.

One of Shaw's most difficult jobs was to train a number of actors, who had been brought up in the anti-Shakespearean tradition and believed that speeches longer than ten words were fatal to popular success, to switch over to an author who specialized in long speeches and revived the classical rhetorical style in modern phraseology. He did not want 'modern' actors. He wanted 'classical' actors for his particular style of modern work. 'Do remember, ladies and gentlemen,' said Barker to a Shavian cast, 'that this is Italian opera.' The Shakespearean actors had the technique required by Shaw; but they had never associated it with modern realism, and felt like fish out of water in Ibsen or Shaw. To illustrate this point we may take the case of Louis Calvert, an admirable Shakespearean actor who, Shaw felt certain, would be exactly right as Broadbent in *John Bull's Other Island*. In '97 Calvert had played Antony to Janet Achurch's Cleopatra in Manchester, and Shaw had called him 'inexcusably fat', adding that he was 'borne off by four stalwart soldiers, whose sinews cracked audibly as they heaved him up from the floor'. He was therefore rotund enough for a British business man, though Shaw selected him because he had the requisite technique.

Yet when it came to rehearsal Calvert could make nothing of Broadbent's platform fustian. And he knew it. At last he came to Shaw and said, 'I know I am all wrong with these speeches ; and I hear that they are all right when you speak them. Well, I cannot get them right myself ; but if you will give them to me line by line I can reproduce you exactly.' So Shaw 'fed' him line by line as desired ; and the speeches came off to perfection. But Calvert was revolted. 'You are asking me,' he said, 'to turn my back on all my experience as an artist. If there is one thing that I think I know thoroughly it is that you must find the key words on which the whole speech depends. You drive these into the audience, and then they know what you are talking about, and you can get over the words they can guess—the prepositions and conjunctions and interjections—as fast as you like. But what is this that you are asking me to do? You want me to pick out all the insignificant words and hand them out syllable by syllable as if they were the last words of God's wisdom.'

'Exactly,' said G.B.S. 'That is the secret of British political oratory. Broadbent must be never so impressive as when he is talking nonsense and making the bloodiest fool of himself.'

Calvert, who was not lacking in intelligence, seized the idea ; and there was no more trouble: his Broadbent became perfect. But he was not so fortunate in his assumption of the part of Undershaft in *Major Barbara*. He delivered his lines with such a commanding eye and air that even Shaw was taken in until one day he happened to be behind the scenes, where Calvert was invisible, during the dialogue in the second act between the armament king and the translator of Euripides. When the commanding eye and air were shut off it became audible that Calvert did not understand a word he was saying, and that Granville Barker, playing Cusins, did.

Years later, when Calvert had been to America and played Undershaft there, he and Shaw met one day in the Haymarket. Shaw inquired about the American production. Said Calvert: 'I am going to tell you something that will astonish you.' Shaw looked becomingly grave and expectant. 'When I played that part in London I did not understand a word of it. But in New York I GOT it ; and you should have seen it.' Shaw acted incredulous amazement as well as he could. After that, whenever he was in any doubt as to whether an actor understood what he was saying, he shut his eyes and listened blindly.

John Bull's Other Island was written at the request of W. B. Yeats for the Irish Literary Theatre. Yeats appreciated it keenly, declaring it to be 'the first of Shaw's plays that had a geography'; but he saw that its expert stage trickeries were beyond the still brief and specialised experience of the Abbey Street players, wonderful as they were. Also, Shaw was wholly out of tune with the Celtic Movement. 'If I had gone to the hills nearby to look back upon Dublin and to ponder upon myself, I too might have become a poet like Yeats, Synge and the rest of them. But I prided myself on thinking clearly and therefore could not stay. Whenever I took a problem or a state of life of which my Irish contemporaries sang sad songs, I always pursued it to its logical conclusion, and then inevitably it resolved itself into comedy. That is why I did not become an Irish poet. . . . I could not stay there dreaming my life away on the Irish hills. England had conquered Ireland; so there was nothing for it but to come over and conquer England.' The success of *John Bull's Other Island* at the Court Theatre was largely due to the fact that in it the typical Englishman was sentimental and successful, which is how he likes to see himself, while the typical Irishman was clever and was assumed to be comparatively unsuccessful on no evidence whatever. The play also appealed to those in the audience who enjoyed a dash of mysticism with their flagon of fun, and Keegan's scene with the grasshopper was unexpected enough to be refreshing in a play by Shaw, though they probably missed the best thing in it: 'Ah, it's no use, me poor little friend. If you could jump as far as a kangaroo you couldnt jump away from your own heart an its punishment. You can only look at Heaven from here: you cant reach it.'

When Shaw followed up *John Bull* with *Major Barbara* he, to please Mrs Shaw, visited Ireland again after nearly thirty years, reaching Dublin from the south because the direct route was like 'going back' and his rule was 'Never go back.' 'It was not until I went to Ireland as a tourist that I perceived that the charm of my country was quite independent of the accident of my having been born in it, and that it could fascinate a Spaniard or an Englishman more powerfully than an Irishman, in whose feeling for it there must always be a strange anguish, because it is the country where he has been unhappy and where vulgarity is vulgar to him.' In the mouth of Keegan he expressed the feeling of a returned exile more poetically: 'When I went to those great cities I saw wonders I had never seen in Ireland. But when I came back to Ireland I found all the wonders there waiting for me. You see they had been there all the time; but my eyes had never been opened to them. I did not know what my own house was like, because I had never been outside it.'

What greatly helped *John Bull* as a box-office attraction was the example set by Arthur Balfour, the Prime Minister, who went to see it four times, taking Campbell-Bannerman and Asquith, the Opposition leaders, on two of his visits. And what finally established the Court Theatre as a money-making concern by sending fashionable society flocking to its doors was King Edward VII's Command Performance on March 11th, 1905. 'Short of organizing a revolution I have no remedy,' wrote Shaw to Vedrenne on hearing that the King was going to see his play. Vedrenne was not in search of a remedy; he rubbed his hands with glee, chuckled at Shaw's little joke, and hired a special suite of furniture for the Royal Box. King Edward, who had frowned his disapproval of *Arms and The Man,* laughed so heartily over *John Bull's Other Island* that he broke the chair on which he sat, the damage being debited to the management and paid for, if not with pleasure, at least without protest by Vedrenne. Indeed every performance aroused so much laughter that when the play was revived in 1913 Shaw remonstrated with the audiences in a leaflet:

'Do you not think that the naturalness of the representation must be destroyed, and therefore your own pleasure greatly diminished, when the audience insists on taking part in it by shouts of applause and laughter, and the actors have repeatedly to stop acting until the noise is over?

'Have you considered that in all good plays tears and laughter lie very close together, and that it must be very distressing to an actress who is trying to keep her imagination fixed on pathetic emotions to hear bursts of laughter breaking out at something she is supposed to be unconscious of?

'Do you know that even when there is no such conflict of comic and tragic on the stage, the strain of performing is greatly increased if the performers have to attend to the audience as well as to their parts at the same time?

'Can you imagine how a play which has been rehearsed to perfection in dead silence without an audience must be upset, disjointed, and spun out to a wearisome length by an audience which refuses to enjoy it silently?

'Have you noticed that if you laugh loudly and repeatedly for two hours, you get tired and cross, and are sorry next morning that you did not stay at home?

248

'Would you dream of stopping the performance of a piece of music to applaud every bar that happened to please you? and do you not know that an act of a play is intended, just like a piece of music, to be heard without interruption from beginning to end ?. . . .

'Can I persuade you to let the performance proceed in perfect silence just this once to see how you like it? The intervals will give you no less than five opportunities of expressing your approval or disapproval, as the case may be.'

As a result of this appeal the audiences refrained from laughter throughout the first act, making up for it by laughing immoderately during the rest of the play.

John Bull's Other Island was given 121 times during the Vedrenne-Barker management of the Court Theatre, its success being surpassed by *You Never Can Tell* (149 performances) and *Man and Superman* (176 performances). Each play was put on for a short run, taken off to make room for another, revived again if there was still a demand for it, and so on, this being the first successful attempt to establish a repertory theatre in England, Shaw describing the playgoers who came to the Court as 'not an audience but a congregation'.

With the production of *Man and Superman* Shaw became the idol of the rising generation of intellectuals, retaining that position for a decade. His influence over the more serious young men and women in the early years of the century, and indeed in the years following the war of 1914-18, was far greater than that exercised by Wells, Chesterton, Belloc, Galsworthy, Bennett, or any other writer. The qualities in him that specially appealed to youth were his irreverence for tradition and office, his indifference to vested interests and inflated reputations, his contempt for current morality, his championship of unpopular causes and persecuted people, his vitality and humour, and above all his inability to take solemn people seriously. There was always something of the rebellious schoolboy about him ; and when in *Man and Superman* Jack Tanner walked forward to congratulate Violet Robinson on her courage in becoming a mother before becoming a wife, Bernard Shaw walked straight into the hearts of the new generation ; one of whom, by the way, acted the part of Ann in *Man and Superman,* and at later dates several more of his leading female characters. This was Lillah McCarthy, whose performance in an amateur production of *Macbeth* in '95 had impelled him to write : 'As for Lady Macbeth, she, too, was bad; but it is clear to me that unless she at once resolutely marries some rich gentleman who disapproves of the theatre on principle, she will not be able to keep herself off the stage.' Lillah McCarthy thought him wonderful, and even tried to copy his diet when they lunched together at the Queen's Restaurant nearby during rehearsals of *Man and Superman*: apples, cheese, macaroni, salad, and a milk and soda. He seemed to know everything and always gave the right advice, even when the subject was one that most men leave to women. 'Don't have any light blue ribbon with the white muslin: use violet or purple,' he wrote to her concerning a dress she was wearing in *Man and Superman*: '. . . there should be a certain pomegranate splendour lurking somewhere in the effect.' She was surprised to learn that from the moment the curtain went up on the first performance of one of his plays, nothing could induce him to witness it again unless a change in the cast necessitated his presence.

As with *The Devil's Disciple,* Shaw made much more money out of *Man and Superman* in America than in England. Another youthful disciple of his named Robert Loraine, already known as a sound romantic actor with a wonderful voice, got the play the moment it was published and promptly went Shaw-mad. Bursting with excitement, he read it to Lee Schubert, who thought the chasing of a man by a woman 'indullicate'. Undaunted, Loraine went down to Welwyn one Sunday to discuss the American production with Shaw, and was a little put-out when the godlike author was hailed as 'ginger-whiskers' by a passing yokel. His energy and eagerness were at last rewarded. He produced it, with himself as Tanner, on September 5th, 1905, at the Hudson Theatre, New York, where it ran for nine months. Finishing up with a seven-months' tour, Loraine netted £40,000 from it. But his enthusiasm was not yet exhausted. On June 4th, 1907, the big Third Act was performed for the first time at the Court Theatre, London, Loraine playing the part of Don Juan. To gratify a whim of his sister-in-law, Shaw marked the occasion by making a balloon ascent with her, Barker and Loraine, a party of four. The start was from Wandsworth Gas Works; and to avoid being blown on to the spikes of the great gas holder the aeronaut snatched the balloon up with a swing that turned Shaw green. They rose 9000 feet, and, trying to descend on Cobham Common, were carried by a surface wind into a private park, where they crashed into a tree, and were fol-

George Bernard Shaw in 1892, aged thirty-six.

'Bernard Shaw having been set to music at The Lyric, may we not expect to find Hall Caine at Covent Garden?' The *Graphic* Vol. LXXXII No. 2118, September 24th, 1910.

Top Shaw with his wife in London, 1905.
Bottom Shaw at his London flat, 1935.

Above An involvement in advertising.

Left Topolski draws Bernard Shaw, 1944.

Top George Bernard Shaw broadcasting at the B.B.C. *Bottom* Shaw receives the deeds of the site of England's national theatre on the eve of Shakespeare's 374th anniversary. The twig and piece of earth are symbolical of the sale and purchase of land and maintain an old Shakespearian custom known as 'livery of seisin'.

Shaw and his wife photographed leaving Whitehall Court on their way to New Zealand, 1934.

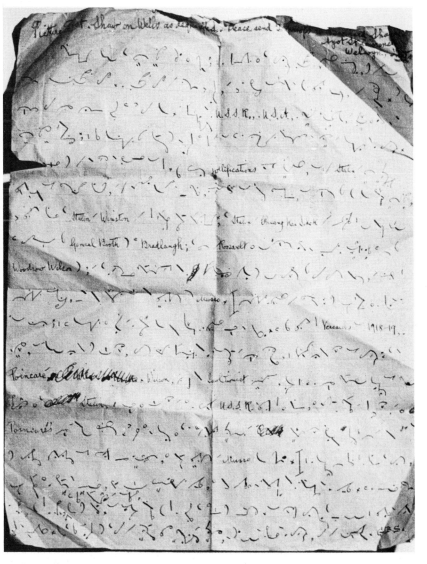

A copy of the shorthand note written by Shaw in 1944 as a comment on the article by H. G. Wells, 'Do We Want a Standing Anglo-U.S. Alliance?'.

George Bernard Shaw in 1946, aged ninety.

lowed by a crowd which ruined the unmown meadow. The aeronaut, who expected to be invited to tea on such occasions, was rescued from the infuriated owner by Shaw, who, gauging the situation better, disarmed him with suitable apologies, the affair ending handsomely and hospitably on the part of the outraged host.

Shaw's next play, *Major Barbara*, dealt with the Salvation Army and the crime of poverty. Two prominent characters were modelled on people he knew: Gilbert Murray and his imperious mother-in-law Lady Carlisle. His street-corner work at the east end, where he often shared the best pitches with the Salvation Army, drew his attention to the dramatic talent of some of the Salvation Lasses in their songs describing the trials of 'saved' women married to brutal husbands, culminating, when they were expecting a savage kicking, in their rapturous happiness as they saw in the tyrant's transfigured face that he, too, had found salvation. When some journalist described a horrible noise as 'worse than a Salvation Army band', Shaw wrote to the paper denouncing this ignorant libel, and vouching for the excellence of the bands on his authority as a famous musical critic. General Booth was delighted, and made the most of the very unexpected testimonial. Shaw was invited to the festival of the massed bands at Clapton Hall, and revelled in the sonorities of 43 trombones with the other instruments on the same scale. He wrote a technical criticism for the Army. He then suggested that the Lasses who were displaying such dramatic talent as singers could produce a greater effect if they got up little plays. He offered to write a simple playlet for them to show how it could be done. But though the Commissioners agreed, they said that the theatre was the gate of hell to many of their older soldiers, who would tolerate a play only if the author could pledge his word that the events in the play had really happened. Shaw, like John Bunyan when he was similarly challenged, cited the precedent of the parables. 'Do your people believe that the prodigal son was a real person?' The Commissioners replied that certainly they did. They would be horrified if it were suggested that Jesus could have uttered fictions. Shaw appealed to Mrs. Bramwell Booth as to whether she would have the sample playlet if he wrote it. She said she would rather have a cheque.

This did not end the incident. The notion of the playlet grew in Shaw's imagination into a big play: *Major Barbara*. In his evidence before the Censorship Committee, Granville Barker told how the Salvation Army lent their uniforms for the Court Theatre production and how the Censor, before licensing the play, had asked him whether the feelings of the Army would be outraged by its being put upon the stage: 'I was fortunately able to tell him that we had been in communication with the Salvation Army, and that so far from their feelings being outraged, they regarded it, I may say, as an excellent advertisement—to use the term "advertisement" in its very best sense. Had I not been able to assure Mr Redford of that, he might, I think, easily have been unwilling to license the play.' When I reminded Shaw of this his comment was: 'Redford did not care a rap about the feelings of the Salvation Army. It was "My God, why hast thou forsaken me?" that frightened him. He asked whether they were not the last words of Christ on the cross. Barker assured him that they were in the Psalms. He then gave in.'

The first performance of *Major Barbara* took place on November 28th, 1905, before an audience that included Arthur Balfour and 'all the intelligentsia of London', with a boxful of uniformed Salvation Army Commissioners who had never before crossed the threshold of a theatre. The first two acts were received with rapturous applause, and Shaw was congratulated by his fellow-dramatist Alfred Sutro, when they met in the lobby after Act 2, on having written his masterpiece. 'If the last act is as good as the other two—' Sutro continued. 'The last act plays for an hour,' interrupted Shaw, 'and it's all talk, nothing but talk.' Sutro's face fell. 'Don't you worry,' added Shaw, patting him encouragingly on the shoulder, 'you'll see—they'll eat it!' But even if they ate it they failed to digest it, and people left the theatre wondering whether the melodrama of the second act compensated for the prodigious length and depth of the last. According to Shaw, the last act 'almost drove the audience mad because Undershaft had not mastered his part sufficiently to make it interesting'. However, as Charles Frohman said, 'Shaw's very clever; he always lets the fellow get the girl in the end'; and *Major Barbara* went into the Court bill for six weeks, which was the longest run allowed for any play done there, though the more successful ones were constantly revived. Four weeks would have been better; for a General Election emptied all the theatres before the six weeks ended.

In the late summer of 1906 Shaw and his wife were staying

at Mevagissey in Cornwall when Granville Barker came down to press for a new play. Shaw, a keen swimmer, was spending his mornings in the sea, and had no idea ready for a new play. Mrs Shaw reminded him how, while chatting with Sir Almroth Wright, at St Mary's Hospital, they had been interrupted by an assistant who wanted to know whether the eminent physician could add another tuberculous patient to those he was already treating by his new opsonic method, the number he could so treat being necessarily limited. 'Is he worth it?' asked Sir Almroth. Shaw instantly saw that there was a play in the situation, and said so to Mrs Shaw, but thought no more of it until her reminder at Mevagissey. The subject also enabled him to take up a challenge issued by William Archer, who had stated in print that Shaw could not claim the highest rank as a dramatist until he had depicted death on the stage. He therefore determined to write a tragedy all about doctors and death, and to make it the most amusing play he had ever written.

His lifelong interest in the medical profession and their cures was part of his naturally inquisitive disposition, but a constantly recurring ailment had quickened his curiosity in medicine. About once a month, until the age of seventy, he suffered from devastating headaches which lasted for a day: they were due, he believed, to the fact that he could not let off sufficient steam in hard exercise and manual labour, so much of his work being of a sedentary nature. 'I endure, like many brain-workers, periodical headaches from which doctors of all sorts, registered and unregistered, have retired baffled; but a pleasant lady who volunteered to cure one of them by sitting near me and composing herself into a bland reverie unspeakably exasperating for a suffering man to contemplate, did actually take the headache away, or provoke it to take itself away, the very scepticism she inspired, or perhaps her good looks, acting as a sort of psychological stimulant to the phagocytes who eat the headache bacillus: a theory which I leave Sir Almroth Wright to elaborate.' But cures of this kind could not be depended upon, and Shaw was always on the look-out for a doctor who had meditated on headaches. One afternoon, just after recovering from an attack, he was introduced to Nansen and asked the famous Arctic explorer whether he had ever discovered a headache cure.

'No,' said Nansen, with a look of amazement.

'Have you ever tried to find a cure for headaches?'

'No.'

'Well, that is a most astonishing thing!' exclaimed Shaw. 'You have spent your life in trying to discover the North Pole, which nobody on earth cares tuppence about, and you have never attempted to discover a cure for the headache, which every living person is crying aloud for.'

Like Falstaff, Shaw turned his disease to commodity, using his headaches to learn all about doctors: 'I used to be a collector of uncanonical therapeutics. Whenever I heard of a new method of treating illness I presented myself for treatment when I had a spare hour. Though my celebrity made me an interesting patient I was medically a very disappointing one, as there was nothing more serious the matter with me than the occasional headaches which, like common colds, reduce Harley Street to impotence. The cure of a man who is obviously not ill cannot be claimed as a triumph by any physician, orthodox or unorthodox. Still, if I could not credit the practitioner with success, at least I could not reproach him with failure. And I gathered a good deal of first-hand information which I could not have obtained by any other means.'

Thus, when he wrote *The Doctor's Dilemma,* he was able to dramatize aspects of the leading physicians and surgeons of the day, and the result was extremely funny. Dubedat, the artist, was a composite portrait, owing his borrowing propensities largely to Edward Aveling. The artist's wife, Jennifer, was poorly realized, and we know from the author why: 'I am sorry to have to tell you that the artist's wife is the sort of woman I hate,' he wrote to Lillah McCarthy, 'and you will have your work cut out for you in making her fascinating.' The play was produced, with Barker as Dubedat, on November 20th, 1906, and was treated as a satire on the medical profession by the critics, who also accused Shaw of execrable taste for making the artist die after uttering what was to them a blasphemous creed: 'I believe in Michael Angelo, Velasquez, and Rembrandt.' Whereupon Shaw informed them that he had cribbed it from Wagner's story *An End in Paris,* in which the dying musician's creed begins, 'I believe in God, Mozart and Beethoven.' The critics were nonplussed, never having heard of Wagner's story; but one of them tried to get out of the difficulty by saying that Wagner's musician at least had the decency to mention God. 'Quite so,' said Shaw, 'but you see

Dubedat does not believe in God.' Archer, of course, complained that Shaw had not succeeded in treating the death-scene 'with a straight face'. Shaw agreed. The play ran its six weeks to good houses, and Shaw was now so generally regarded as a money-maker that the commercial managers, who were so uncommercial that they never produced anything that did not remind them of something else, began to appeal to him for plays. To one of them, Cyril Maude, he explained that the provision of plays for the Court Theatre was a whole-time job: 'This Doctor play was produced by a *tour de force*. Last summer not a line of it was on paper or in my head. By the time I get a moment to start again the Court will be howling for another play. This system of putting up plays for six weeks is certainly a wonderful success pecuniarily, for the plays dont die and the business doesnt slack; but it is the very devil in point of rehearsal. I spend months every year producing when I ought to be writing.'

At the end of June 1907 Vedrenne and Barker, exhausted by taking risks and incessant hard work on Barker's part in return for modest and precarious incomes, faced the fact that the Court Theatre was neither big enough nor central enough to hold the audiences and the money they needed. Towards the close of that year they moved to the Savoy Theatre, where they added to the Shavian repertory, besides taking the Hay-market Theatre for the production of a new Shaw play, *Getting Married*. A third theatre was taken for a new play by Laurence Housman. Three west end theatre rents broke the back of the enterprise, which had been pushed beyond its limits. 'Vedrenne got out with nothing but a reputation,' Shaw informed me: 'Barker had to pawn his clothes; and I disgorged most of my royalties; but the creditors were paid in full.' Honour was saved; and a great chapter in theatrical history was closed.

But if it had depended on the dramatic critics, that chapter would never have been written. Shaw explained the position to me:

'My first play to be done at the Court was *John Bull's Other Island*. The critics denounced it as no play at all and said that the actors did their best with impossible parts. Then came *Man and Superman*. This was voted dull and uninspired compared with its predecessor. *Major Barbara* followed, and the critics promptly burst into raptures over *Man and Superman*. But *Major Barbara* was duly described as a masterpiece when

255

its successor *The Doctor's Dilemma* was dismissed as a feeble joke in bad taste. So I seized the first opportunity to make a speech at a public dinner at which all the leading dramatic critics were present. "I want to make a suggestion to the press", I said. 'I don't ask you to stop abusing me. It gives you so much pleasure to say that my plays are no plays and that my characters are not human beings that I would not deprive you of it for worlds. But for the sake of the management, Vedrenne and Barker, not to mention the actors, may I beg you to reverse the order of your curses and caresses? Instead of saying that my latest play is piffle, the one before it brilliant, why not acclaim the latest as a masterpiece compared with the disgusting drivel I had the impertinence to serve up last time? That will satisfy you and assist us. In short, don't heave bricks at us while we are struggling in the water and then load us with lifebelts when we have reached dry land." '

I asked Shaw whether the critics had changed their tactics as a result of his suggestion. 'Yes,' he replied, 'but not quite on the lines I proposed. After we had finished at the Court in 1907, Vedrenne and Barker, flushed with success, took the Savoy Theatre and presented *Caesar and Cleopatra, The Devil's Disciple* and *Arms and The Man*. All three were treated by the press as if they were the libretti of light opera, and no reference whatever was made to the one-time brilliance of the Court Theatre propagandist. But the critics are incurable ; so let us leave them in the peace of their forgotten files.'

FABIUS *V.* SCIPIO

WHILE THE DRAMATIST was sailing to success before the breeze of popular applause, the propagandist was buffeting the squalls of criticism. The South African War broke out in the autumn of 1899 and nearly everybody in England thought the Boers would give in when they were faced with the might of a British army. But the Boers had powerful allies, chief among them being the British War Office, and the war dragged on for nearly three years. Shaw shared the general optimism in the early days. On December 24th, '99 he wrote from 30 Marine Terrace, Aberystwyth, whither he had gone to lecture after his Mediterranean trip and where he stayed over Xmas because the weather was fine: 'How I should like to do a pamphlet on the war! Only it will be over before I could find time.' British incompetence and Boer leadership between them gave him all the time he required, and on August 21st, 1900, he was able to announce the completion of his draft of *Fabianism and The Empire* in a letter, scribbled hurriedly on blue paper, to a fellow-Fabian, H. T. Muggeridge:

'You are in a devil of a hurry for an answer. I only got your letter six weeks ago, and now you set Pease on me like a bulldog. Six years is my usual time for answering letters—especially letters for lectures.

'I do not know where Wallington is ; and I despise its absurd Literary and Debating Society ; but for your personal sake I am willing to consider the matter. What day does it meet on, and at what hour? Perhaps you told me this in your letter ; but I am up in town just now, away from my papers. Drop me a line to Blackdown Cottage, near Haslemere, Surrey, and I will make a violent effort to answer promptly. You might mention your vacant dates, and the subjects you already have lectures secured for.

'I have just finished drafting an Election Manifesto for the Fabian. It is a masterpiece, enormously long (a regular volume), and so extra-ultra-hyper-imperialist that you will turn the colour of this paper and fall down in convulsions when you read it. Nevertheless I hope for your vote for it. I am convinced that the Liberal agitation against the Government is greatly strengthening it, because nobody will dare to vote for a merely negative and impossibilist policy in the middle of a war. The Labour Leader's "white list" is the final stroke —the white flag held up to Liberalism at the moment when we are on the verge of victory over it. And all over this Kruger case which is only a second edition of the Tichborne case—a poor man being done out of his rights. We have got to teach both Kruger and Chamberlain that countries are not bits of private property to be fought for by dynasties, or races, or nations. You must have some International Socialism hammered into that obstinate walnut head of yours: thats MY imperialism.'

Two months later, at a Borough Council election, Shaw

drew the Union Jack on a printed post-card which was being sent out from his committee room and wrote along the top VOTE FOR THE IMPERIALIST CANDIDATE. He had, in fact, surprised his admirers, and caused a split in the Fabian Society, by backing Kipling against Isaiah. 'I never got over Olive Schreiner's *Story of an African Farm*. Some few years before the war Cronwright Schreiner came to London. I asked him why he and Joubert and the rest put up with Kruger and his obsolete theocracy. He said they knew all about it and deplored it, but that the old man would die presently and then Krugerism would be quietly dropped and a liberal regime introduced. I suggested that it might be dangerous to wait; but it was evident that Oom Paul was too strong for them. During the war a curious thing happened in Norway. There, as in Germany, everyone took it for granted that the right side was the anti-English side. Suddenly Ibsen asked in his grim manner, "Are we really on the side of Kruger and his Old Testament?" The effect was electrical. Norway shut up. I felt like Ibsen. I was, of course, not in the least taken in by the *Times* campaign, though I defended the *Times* against the accusation of bribery on the ground that it was not necessary to pay the *Times* to do what it was only too ready to do for nothing. But I saw that Kruger meant the 17th century and the Scottish 17th at that; and so to my great embarrassment I found myself on the side of the mob. . . . It is astonishing what bad company advanced views may get one into.'

Thus, although he had no illusions concerning the gang who wanted the war because they wanted more money, he found himself on the side of the crooks in opposition to the christians. Being a natural-history student, he said, he felt no more indignation against Rockefeller or Rhodes than he did against a dog following a fox. 'If Rockefeller *deserves* hanging (an expression which belongs to your moral system),' he wrote to Hyndman, 'so does every man who would do the same as Rockefeller if he got the chance, say 99 per cent of his indignant fellow-men. You cannot hang everybody, including yourself; and yet moralism leads to that or nothing.' Such was his argument, which Hyndman might have answered with two simple statements: (1) Moral systems are the only safeguard against oppression and anarchy where there is no social conscience, as in any state of society known to men. (2) If most men were potential Rockefellers, there would be no Rockefellers who flourish because of certain qualities that

258

make them exceptional. Apparently his knowledge of natural history had not taught Shaw that the strong and pitiless prey upon the weak and merciful. On this and on several later occasions he should have remembered his own declaration: 'Progress depends on our refusal to use brutal means even when they are efficacious.' And he might have experienced an anxious moment during the 'Khaki' election of 1900 if he had been reminded of another of his sayings: 'Great communities are built by men who sign with a mark: they are wrecked by men who write Latin verses.'

The attitude of most social-democrats towards the Boer War differed from Shaw's; they felt that a small independent nation was being crushed in order to extend the domination of the very system they wished to destroy. True, it was a backward nation; but was modern capitalism a step forward? The official view of the Fabian Society, put forward by Shaw in his pamphlet, was that in the interests of civilization a great power must govern, and that though goldfields ought to be internationalized the British Empire was, at the time, the only available substitute for a World-Federation, the alternative being to leave the power of gold in the hands of a small irresponsible community. The fetish of gold has long been exploded and the Fabian argument strikes us now as very old-fashioned, for we have lived to suffer from the irresponsibilities of large communities; but backed by the dialectical skill of Shaw it impressed the members, only twenty of whom resigned.

All through the early years of the century he was a tireless speaker. Sometimes he was the conciliating influence, at other times the cause of turbulence. He once illustrated for me the kind of argument with which he had to deal in the former capacity, though the occasion was much earlier in his career. It happened just after the great dock strike of '89, when through the efforts of Cardinal Manning, John Burns and Tom Mann the dockers had won the day, or at least a penny an hour extra pay. Shaw was giving John Burns his due, when a man jumped up and not only denounced Burns but denounced Shaw for not denouncing him. 'What would you have done in John Burns's' place?' asked Shaw. 'Done!' shouted the man, who must have been a freethinker, 'I'd have taken the bloody cardinal by the scruff of his bloody neck and chucked him into the bloody river!' There were times when people felt like that towards Shaw. He lectured the Guild of St

Matthew, telling them that a religion which founded itself on certain tales in the Old Testament could have no modern man's respect, and many devout christians thought that drowning would be too pleasant for him. He spoke at the meetings of the Church and Stage Guild, where he noticed that one of the speakers, an old music hall star, from sheer force of habit winked at the audience every time he scored a point for Christ. Ethical Societies did not appeal to him in vain. On his way to one of their meetings he asked his companion, H. T. Muggeridge, 'Now tell me, what is an Ethical Society?' Muggeridge replied that it was a society devoted to ethics. Shaw pressed for further details. Muggeridge said that the service began with a song and continued with a reading from some classical work, say by Stanton Coit. 'Ah, I see,' said Shaw: 'It's atheism tempered by hymns.' He was never cornered by a question. For some curious reason, possibly the attraction of opposites, clergymen always flocked to hear him address the Fabian Society. Once he was lecturing on 'Flogging as a Punishment', and as usual questions were invited when he sat down. The last question was from a parson: 'In the army many men guilty of misdemeanours ask to be flogged. What has the lecturer to say to that?' Shaw had this to say: 'The subject of my lecture was "Flogging as a Punishment", not "Flogging as a Luxury".' His headaches never prevented him from speaking: he forgot them when he rose to speak. On one occasion he was reported to be ill, and a press agency wished to learn the nature of his illness. Shaw satisfied them: 'Kindly inform the public that I am dead. It will save me a great deal of trouble.'

Several people at various times tried to broaden the appeal of the Fabian Society. Two young enthusiastis from Leeds, Holbrook Jackson and A. R. Orage, founded an Arts Group, which received the encouragement of Shaw and Olivier, both of whom attended the meetings. But the Webbs were not interested in the arts, which they vaguely felt to be subversive of authority and inimical to economics, and Shaw at last advised Jackson to take the Group out of the Society and run it as a separate concern. When *The New Age* was for sale, Orage was anxious to buy it and edit it on socialistic lines. As he did not care for Shaw (possibly because Shaw used to pronounce his name French-fashion instead of 'Orrij') he got Jackson to ask Shaw if he would help to finance the venture. Shaw had just made £500 out of the London production of

Caesar and Cleopatra, and promised to let them have it if they could get a business man to put up an equivalent sum. 'I am not a financier,' he said; ' you must raid the city first.' A theosophist who was in sympathy with Orage's opinions came forward with the necessary backing; Shaw fulfilled his promise; and *The New Age* was soon devoted to criticisms of the Fabians by 'Orrij', who called Shaw Web-footed, and called Webb everything but Shaw-footed.

The most serious rift that ever occurred in the Fabian Society was caused by H. G. Wells, who, sponsored by Shaw and Graham Wallas, became a member in Febuary 1903, after which he practically ignored the existence of the Society for two and a half years. The Webbs took him up and made much of him. His scientific training appealed to them quite as much as his socialistic ardour and his reputation as a novelist. Shaw was also very friendly. They had met on January 5th, 1895 at the St James's Theatre after the first performance of *Guy Domville,* the author of which, Henry James, had been assailed with hisses by the audience. Wells was the dramatic critic of *The Pall Mall Gazette,* though not in the least interested in the drama. Desirous to join the staff of that paper, and the post of dramatic critic being vacant, he had been asked by Cust, the editor, what his qualifications were. Wells said that he had seen Henry Irving and Ellen Terry in *Romeo and Juliet* and Penley in *The Private Secretary.* 'Nothing else?' asked Cust. 'Nothing else,' replied Wells. 'Then you'll bring an entirely fresh mind to the theatre,' said Cust and engaged him on the spot. He accosted Shaw as a colleague and they walked homewards together after the play. Shaw talked of the noisy scene at the theatre and said that nobody in the audience, and hardly anybody on the stage, had appreciated the grace of James's dialogue. Wells noted Shaw's revolutionary first-night garb: a modest brown jacket suit: also his very white face and very red whiskers. 'He talked like an elder brother to me in that agreeable Dublin English of his. I liked him with a liking that has lasted a lifetime.' Leaving Shaw at his door in Fitzroy Square, Wells walked on to his lodgings near Primrose Hill, pondering their differences of taste and character, which were indeed considerable.

A first impression of the Fabians left Wells hostile. He went with a friend to a meeting in Clement's Inn 'and heard a discursive gritty paper on Trusts, and one of the most inconclusive discussions you can imagine. Three-quarters of the speakers seemed under some peculiar obsession which took the form of pretending to be conceited. It was a form of family joke; and as strangers to the family we did not like it.

The truth of the matter was that the Fabian Society was an utter misfit for Wells, who was just ten years too young for it. It was led and voiced, though never dominated, by 'the Old Gang', Webb, Shaw, Bland, Wallas and Olivier. Webb and Olivier were trained civil servants in the upper division. Wallas, a schoolmaster, also in the upper division of that profession, and a born teacher, was highly trained academically. These three had knocked Bland and Shaw, who as literary adventurers were as wild as Wells when they started, into shape as good committee men, knowing that they could not have their own way but must accept the greatest common measure of the group to go on with, and be able to manage committees and dictate their resolutions within this limit. They were keen on educating themselves and one another. They were so thoroughly in earnest, so hungry for facts, so intolerant of ignorant enthusiasm, however sympathetic, so contemptuous of the guff and bugaboo of popular revolutionary oratory, that though they as public speakers could hold audiences and were deadly debaters, their family joke, as Wells called it, was Shaw's precept that you must think your problem out until you have got to the bottom of it, and when you have reached a point at which your solution will seem so simple that it will sound like the first notion that would come into any fool's head, deliver it with the utmost levity. Thus, he argued, you entertain your audience and score irresistibly over the parliamentary humbugs whose art it is to cover up by the most impressive gravity the fact that they are saying nothing at the greatest endurable or unendurable length.

No doubt Shaw's example, if not his precept, created a certain Fabian mannerism in the rank and file of Fabian lectures which irritated Wells whilst it was still strange to him; but it never led to mere imitation among the leaders, who all had individualities quite as powerful as Shaw's.

What was to be done with Wells in this company? He was ten years younger. He was easily the worst committee man in the world, flying out at a word of contradiction into reckless rages in which he accused his opponents of every infamy, and put himself hopelessly in the wrong when, as often happened, he was entirely in the right. He was the most entertaining and friendly of talkers; but when it came to controversy Mrs Webb had to tell him that his bad manners would prevent him from ever attaining any presentability in public life. He had no ready-made physical advantages: beside six-footers like Olivier, Wallas and Shaw (Wallas was six foot two), and muscular giants like Olivier and Bland (Olivier could lift Wallas and throw him about; and Bland, whose shoulders were so big that Shaw always avoided sitting next him because he needed three chairs to accommodate them, was a skilled pugilist who had fought a gipsy at a race meeting for the fun of it), beside these Wells was a pigmy. Olivier was handsome and well-bred: Wallas was an upstanding specimen of the scholarly Englishman, and had no rival in London and America as a popular and instructive University Extension lecturer. Shaw, whose beginnings as a public speaker in 1879 had been pitiable until he learnt from an old opera singer, a pupil of the famous Delsarte, that for public purposes speech was a fine art that had to begin with learning the alphabet over again and learning it differently, had by street corner practice and phonetic study made himself a finished platform artist. He was not above practising his vowels and consonants as the opera singer practised his scales, and had declaimed Shakespeare in the hills above Loche Fyne for a fortnight before addressing a big meeting in Glasgow to answer Joseph Chamberlain's opening of the Tariff Reform campaign there. Alone of the five, Webb absolutely refused to improve his delivery. When he became a Cabinet Minister late in life he made, Shaw told me, the best speeches in the House without taking the smallest trouble to make them audible; but at the date of Wells's arrival in the Fabian Society he was an effective speaker and complete master of all his committees by his great ability and knowledge, which carried him through without any of Shaw's platform trickery. He easily led men with every advantage over him of voice, stature, style and bearing.

Up against such colleagues Wells would have had no chance at all but for the fact that they all read him and knew that he had much to say and could say it well and wittily. His voice, attractive in private, was a mere squeak in public halls; but he was listened to because he was Wells, and always worth listening to when he was keeping his temper. If only he could have kept it like Webb and been as adroit in handling other people he might have been as great a Fabian. But that, to the Society's great grief, was not to be. It must not be inferred, however, that Wells was conscious of being worse equipped for public life than the Fabian experts. He was far too irreverent a cockney for any such modesty, knowing well that he possessed mental powers and literary art compared to which plaform accomplishments were dust in the balance. He made game of Bland, the eagle-voiced domineering suburban Tory Social-Democrat, of the pedagogic Wallas with his donnish manner, of the tempestuous Olivier, the omniscient Webb, the hard, efficient Mrs Webb, and above all the elusive Shaw. 'I want to get hold of a fact,' wrote Wells, 'strip off her inessentials, and, if she behaves badly, put her in stays and irons; but Shaw dances round her and weaves a wilful veil of confident assurances about her as her true presentment.'

All this was good cockney fun; but there were some serious misunderstandings in it. Nobody was keener on facts than Shaw. He it was who insisted on throwing over the primitive Fabian tracts and inaugurating a new series with 'FACTS for Socialists', though Webb had to write it. He it was who tore Marx's value theory to pieces and warned the movement that the class war cut right through the working classes, and was a dangerous delusion if interpreted as a solid proletariat opposing a solid proletariat. He it was who rejected the Hegel-Marx dialectic as useless in England, and maintained that the epoch-making effect of *Das Kapital* on modern thought was due, not to its philosophy, but to its devastating bombardment of the very self-satisfied and self-righteous capitalist bourgeoisie with its terrific magazine of officially admitted facts. His insistence on concrete examples instead of abstract phrases was incessant.

Yet Shaw was a cast-iron theorist. He said that a fact could hit you in the face, but could not mean anything to you until it was fitted into a plan of thought. One of his reproaches to the universities was that they were full of learned fools with omnivorous memories who could remember any quantity of facts and could make no more use of their collections than of used postage stamps. He boasted of his bad memory which forced him to forget every fact except those of such importance that they could not be forgotten. He pooh-poohed the German historical school, which held that history was fact-collecting first and last, pointing out that it was no use in practical politics because nobody could possibly know all the contemporary facts: statesmen, he said, must have a political theory if they were to be anything more than blind drifters always turning their backs to the wind and following the jumping cat. He himself really could not think without a theory, or act without a hypothesis, without deduction as well as induction. Though he claimed flexibility of mind as a quality given him by the Irish climate, and said that every Englishman should be sent to Ireland for at least two years to acquire it, Gilbert Chesterton was right when he defended Shaw against the charge of paradoxical flightiness by hailing him as the one man of whom you could be sure that even in his extremest old age his views, and his readiness to strike you down if you questioned them, would be unshaken and unaltered. His Ricardian law of rent, his Jevonian theory of value, his theory of liberal education as æsthetic and not classical, his neo-vitalist theory of evolution as 'emergent', and his consequent denial that Darwinian Natural Selection was genuine evolution, his hypothesis of an 'evolutionary appetite' as the fundamental progressive force in life: these were his Mount Sinai and his Sermon on the Mount.

With such marble and granite as this in his mental make-up it is no wonder that in an English society, however much he might be petted and admired, he could never be quite trusted; for he held that a statesman should always know whither he is bound, and was always explaining to his colleagues whither he and they were marching; and this he found (or imagined) that Englishmen could not bear. One of his favourite quotations was Cromwell's 'No man goes further than the man who does not know whither he is going.' Shaw added, 'If he did he would perhaps think he oughtnt; and that would never do.'

To Wells nothing could be more foreign. He was very English without anything in his composition like the Huguenot strain that distinguished Olivier or the Scotch and perhaps French elements in Shaw's ancestry. He was not an economist nor an 'Ist' of any sort. He had a ravenous evolutionary appetite which was, in practice, a revolutionary one; but it was a simple direct passion and not the final term of a theoretic syllogism. That was why, when resisted, he did not argue: he raged and vituperated. He neither analysed nor criticized (Shaw was always doing both): he either reviled or recommended. He did not pick Marx to pieces and keep the good bits, admitting his revolutionary greatness: he savaged him, bludgeoned him, denounced him as a person of contemptible abilities and mean character. As to the Class

War, though his own books were full of it he flatly denied its existence, even when it was being fought out in Spain with fire and sword. In his novels his sense of character was wonderful as long as he was creating imaginary figures; but his sketches of real people whom he disliked were ferocious lampoons. If he had been capable of critical classification he would probably have described himself as an artist-biologist; but his biology was the biology he had learnt from Huxley in the days of his tutelage at South Kensington; and when Shaw, in the Fabian lecture in 1906 on Darwin, which subsequently became the preface to *Back to Methuselah,* threw over neo-Darwinism, ridiculed Weissmanism, and followed Samuel Butler into the neo-vitalist movement which is now leading Science back to metaphysics, Wells never stopped to examine the new position. He pooh-poohed Shaw as an ignorant sentimentalist who could not stand up to the cruelty of nature.

That cruelty had been for Huxley a potent weapon to slay the Evangelical God who was then the common enemy of Science. It became identified with Science quite thoughtlessly; and Wells had never reconsidered this nor detected its purely superstitious character. His dismissal of Shaw as a sentimental ignoramus in science, of Marx as a shallow imposter in sociology, of Napoleon as only a third-rate wicked cad, though they make amusing reading, with scraps of truth in them, have to be allowed for as 'H.G.'s way': a fact of which he was perfectly aware; for he warned his friends not to mind him when he went on like that; and they never did.

Thus we cannot say that Wells's Fabian failure was the result of a clash of personalities. The cheap platform victories of the Old Gang fell from him like water from a duck's back. When after a decent interval he quietly left the Society he did only what the stars of the Old Gang themselves did later on. The mistake he had made, naturally enough at his age, was in imagining that the Fabian Society needed only young blood and some courage and enterprise to become a big and powerful organization, able, finally, to control the government and feed the revolutionary appetite to repletion. The Old Gang, remembering their beginnings, knew better. They knew that the Society would never have more members than enough to keep a cheap office going and pay the secretary's modest grant-in-aid of his private income. Wells's forecast of magnificent offices, princely revenues, and millions of enrolled socialist converts, was a young man's dream; and the Old

Gang knew it. They did not even seek recruits: they were permeators to a man. Marx's First International in 1861 was an anticipation of Well's notion of a regenerated Fabian Society; and the Old Gang knew its history too well to have any, illusions as to its possibility. What the Society actually could do they were doing, and doing very well. They liked Wells, and wanted his fame as a feather in the Society's cap; but the coach did not need a sixth wheel; and all its most famous later recruits, especially women like Annie Besant and the American, Harriet Stanton Blatch, found that they were superfluous, and left it for other fields which were being less exhaustively cultivated.

The Old Gang itself eventually dissolved in the same way. Wallas was the first to go. When the Society had accomplished its academic task of discrediting *laisser-faire* and opening up the boundless prospect of state industry, its second task was the foundation of a parliamentary Labour Party; and Wallas, finding himself becoming associated with agitators who were very far from being scientific socialists, broke loose and took the University Extension platform, where he was freer than he could have been as a Labour Party electioneerer. When the Labour Party was established as the official Opposition in Parliament after 1906, the Fabian bolt was shot, and there was, for the moment, nothing more to be done. The Labour Party had all the money and all the opportunities and organization that Well's imagination had pictured for the Fabian Society; but it was Trade Union money and organization, not socialist, and even predominantly anti-socialist. Shaw was admitted *ex-officio* to the preliminary Labour Representation Committee as a Fabian; but he was middle class; and Keir Hardie, the first Labour leader, got rid of him immediately. The permeators were permeated with a vengeance; and the Fabian programme of state-managed industry, which the Labour Party proved incapable of handling, was appropriated by the capitalist employers in the form of state-financed private enterprise, and began its development into Fascism and Naziism. The Fabian Society, merged in the new Party and smothered by it, was dead, but could not at first realize this incredible catastrophe. Its office, still open, only kept its ghost walking.

The Old Gang held out until 1911, when Shaw resigned from the executive committee twenty-seven years after he had joined it. Ostensibly he was making way for young blood:

actually he was succeeded by members no younger than himself, and much 'safer'. By that time the work of keeping up the Fabian office routine was waste of time for the old leaders, who were full of work in other quarters. Bland was a popular weekly journalist with an assured pulpit in a widely circulated provincial paper. Olivier was governor of Jamaica, on his way to being Auditor-General (he found the national accounts kept still as in the days of King John, and introduced the startling novelty of book-keeping by double entry). Webb, Chairman of the Technical Education Board of the London County Council, had created the London School of Economics, founded *The New Statesman*, and was famous throughout Europe for the monumental series of works written by him and his wife on industrial democracy, Labour history, and British Local Government. Shaw was a leading playwright, publishing his plays with sociological prefaces whose scope would have been impossible in Fabian tracts. They all did what Wells had done, except that they retained their nominal membership of the poor old Society and paid their subscriptions.

When the Society revived under pressure of what Shaw called the second Punic War—not even the Four Years' War had roused it—the Old Gang was old indeed, Bland and Wallas dead, Shaw, Webb and Olivier octogenarians

So much for the history of the Fabian Society in its Shavian heyday, and the significance of the Wells episode as a prelude to its cataleptic decline and fall.

Yet the preliminary skirmishes and the final battle of the great Fabius-Scipio campaign call for a more detailed account.

Three years after he had joined the Fabian Society, Wells dropped a thunderbolt. In February 1906 he read a paper, *Faults of the Fabian*, in which he poked fun at the Old Gang, called it a 'drawing-room society', said that socialism was in the air and should be brought down to earth, told the Fabians to launch a vast propaganda, to support the Labour Party, to form hundreds of centres, to bring in thousands of members, to collect large sums of money, to distribute millions of leaflets and pamphlets, to send out scores of young men and women to spread the gospel, and, in fact, to make their appeal worldwide, or at any rate Wells-wide. The strategy of the Society should be modelled on that of Scipio the aggressor, not Fabius the retreater. His paper was hailed with delight by the younger members, and a special committee was formed to go into the whole question of Fabian policy. Wells was neither a committee-man nor a debater and was handicapped from the start; but all the enthusiasm in the Society was behind him, for his was the go-ahead method. The committee drew up a report, the Old Gang replied to it, and the issue was joined. Meanwhile, Wells visited America and wrote a book.

The report and the reply were discussed at seven sessions of the Society held at 3 Clements Inn between December 1906 and March 1907. The meetings were crowded and noisy; there was much dust and confusion; all the leaders took part in the debate: Webb, his head down, talking rapidly with a slight lisp, imparting volumes of information; Bland, wearing a frock-coat and black-ribboned monocle, laying down the law in parliamentary style; Wallas, speaking like a schoolmaster to refractory pupils; Haden Guest, red-haired, mercurial; Olivier, tall, brown-bearded, broad-shouldered, careless of routine, sometimes explosive; Mrs Webb, cold, commanding, too often right to be pleasant; Shaw, alert, exasperating, charming, infuriating, Puckish, debonair and Machiavellian. Against such a team Wells had not a chance, in spite of the roars of applause his hits elicited. He was a bad speaker, halting, often inaudible, and when audible squeaky. Pressing his knuckles hard on the table before him, addressing his tie, correcting himself frequently, losing the thread of his remarks, suddenly remembering a point, bursting into a long parenthesis and failing to get back to his main drift of thought, he droned and piped away in a wholly unimpressive manner. Conscious of his hopeless disadvantage, irritated with the Webbs ('Donna Quixote and Sancho Panza'), and jealous of Shaw (whom in moments of anger he called 'a sexless biped' and 'an intellectual eunuch'), he lost control of himself and made a personal matter of it, describing the Old Gang as liars, tricksters, intriguers, blackguards, reactionaries, enemies of human society, and all the other names invariably applied by one world-meliorist to other world-meliorists who have different plans for world-melioration. In his autobiography he recognized that he had not been at his best during the episode: 'On various occasions in my life it has been borne in on me, in spite of a stout internal defence, that I can be quite remarkably silly and inept; but no part of my career rankles so acutely in my memory with the conviction of bad judgment, gusty impulse and real inexcusable vanity, as that storm in the Fabian tea-cup.'

Bland and Webb were angry with Wells for calling them liars, tricksters and what-not; but Shaw did not suffer from righteous indignation; in fact he once confessed that, like everyone else, there were moments when he was every bit as bad as Wells painted him: 'It does not concern me that, according to certain ethical systems, all human beings fall into classes labelled liar, coward, thief, and so on. I am myself, according to these systems, a liar, a coward, a thief, and a sensualist; and it is my deliberate, cheerful and entirely self-respecting intention to continue to the end of my life deceiving people, avoiding danger, making my bargains with publishers and managers on principles of supply and demand instead of abstract justice, and indulging all my appetites, whenever circumstances commend such actions to my judgment. If any creed or system deduces from this that I am a rascal incapable on occasion of telling the truth, facing a risk, forgoing a commercial advantage, or resisting an intemperate impulse of any sort, then so much the worse for the creed or system, since I have done all these things, and will probably do them again.'

Shaw, therefore, was clearly the only member of the Old Gang who could be trusted to demolish Wells without losing his temper or splitting the Society. But he was under suspicion of being too friendly to Wells, and before being entrusted with the job of obliterating the rebel he had to promise that he would enforce Wells's unconditional surrender. The great day came, and Scipio stood up to fight Fabius. But this Fabius carried the war straight into the enemy's camp by accusing Wells of threatening to resign if defeated by a vote of the Society. Wells magnanimously pledged himself not to resign whatever happened. 'That is a great relief to my mind,' said Shaw; 'I can now pitch into Mr Wells without fear of consequences.' Having pitched in to his heart's content, he did a very crafty thing: he explained that Wells's onslaught was nothing more than an attack on the moral characters of the Old Gang, and that if the members supported it the Old Gang would be compelled to walk out and found a new Society. Thus, having spiked Wells's guns and loaded his own, he forced the Society to surrender without a shot. Finally, he eased the situation with the oil of comedy: 'Mr Wells in his speech complained of the long delay by the Old Gang in replying to his report. But the exact figures are: Wells ten months, the Old Gang six weeks. During his committee's deliberations he produced a book on America. And a very good book too.

But whilst I was drafting our reply I produced a play.' Shaw paused; for several moments his eyes glanced vacantly round the ceiling; he seemed to have lost his train of thought; members began to fidget uncomfortably; at last he went on: 'Ladies and gentlemen, I paused there to enable Mr Wells to say, "And a very good play too." ' The audience shouted with laughter, burst following burst, each louder than the last. Wells smiled self-consciously. Shaw sat down. Fabius had won.

After raising such questions as Women's Suffrage, the endowment of motherhood, the substitution of public for private authority in the education and support of the young, and getting very little encouragement, Wells resigned from the Society some two years after his defeat. In *The New Machiavelli* he pilloried his former colleagues, his portraits of them, as he assured me, being slightly caricatured so as to give the necessary bias to the writer's point of view. But his picture of a Webb-made world was fairly sound: 'If they had the universe in hand, I know they would take down all the trees and put up stamped tin green shades and sunlight accumulators.' Webb had, he told me, 'the sustained energy of an essentially second-rate mind', and a triumph for social democracy would, as they imagined it, be a triumph for functionaries—'Admirable Webblets, mysteriously honest, brightly efficient, bright with the shine of varnish rather than the gleam of steel. One sees these necessary unavoidable servants ōf the workers' commonwealth—trusted servants, indispensable servants, in fact, authoritative and ruling servants—bustling virtuously about their carefully involved duties and occasionally raising a neatly rolled umbrella to check the careless course of some irregular citizen who had forgotten to button up his imagination or shave his character.'

CONTROVERSY ON ALL FRONTS

THE FABIAN FRONT was by no means the only front on which Shaw was fighting. He took on the Vivisectionist Medical Researchers, the Compulsory Vaccinationists, the pessimist

271

physicists who taught that the sun was burning itself out and the human race doomed to be frozen to death presently, the corruptors of the General Medical Council into an ordinary professional association instead of a safeguard against professionalism, the Flagellomaniacs (as he dubbed the advocates of flogging in the criminal code, the fighting services, and the schools), and all sorts of abuses that came within the reach of his guns. Religion, which had to be strictly kept out of the Fabian programme, brought him into the field with such effect that in spite of his undisguised heterodoxy approving sermons were preached in cathedrals and free churches ; and he himself occupied the pulpit at the City Temple in London as guest preacher to congregations that were always crowded on such occasions, whilst the secularists and rationalists could not understand how a professed free-thinker could attack science and materialism like a bishop. 'Imposter for impostor,' he once asserted, 'I prefer the mystic to the scientist—the man who at least has the decency to call his nonsense a mystery, to him who pretends that it is ascertained, weighed, measured, analysed fact.' And in later years he was to write: 'There is nothing that people will not believe nowadays if only it be presented to them as science, and nothing they will not disbelieve if it be presented to them as religion. I myself began like that ; and I am ending by receiving every scientific statement with dour suspicion whilst giving very respectful consideration to the inspirations and revelations of the prophets and poets.'[1]

The truth was that the scientists were not scientific enough for Shaw. He attacked the vivisectionists not as monsters of cruelty but as intellectual imbeciles. He showed that their notions of evidence and of statistics were childish. He classed their experiments as crudities within the reach of any fool, and declared that all they claimed to have discovered by their most revolting experiments in the laboratory they could have found out with less trouble by asking the nearest policeman or dentist or anyone who had ever kept a pet dog. But he warned the anti-vivisectionists not to depend on their demonstrations that the discoveries were mares' nests. 'Beware,' he said. 'These duffers may blunder into some important discovery to-

[1] When asked by a Manchester paper, 'Have we lost faith?', Shaw replied, 'Certainly not; but we have transferred it from God to the General Medical Council.'

morrow; and then where will you be?' He pointed to the earthquake in San Francisco and the sinking of two battleships by a miscalculated fleet manoeuvre as examples of catastrophes which had established the very important facts that the new steel-framed skyscraper is far more stable than the old-fashioned bricks and mortar, and that the battleship which rams an adversary sinks itself. He demanded whether we were therefore to privilege builders and architects to produce artificial earthquakes with dynamite to test their materials, or admirals to sink the fleet and drown hundreds of sailors to find experimentally how to sink and drown our potential enemies. The point, he insisted, was not whether the vivisectioners had discovered anything or not, but whether professional physiologists were to be exempted from the moral laws on which human society depends. A Royal Commision was appointed; and the vivisectionists made great play with its report in favour of experiments. But Shaw was too old a hand at committee work to be taken in. Reading between the lines of the report, he saw that the Commission, carefully as it had been picked, had failed to obtain a verdict in favour of cruel experiments. 'Who,' he shouted, 'objects, ever has objected, or ever will object to experiments on animals or on human beings, or on anybody or anything? That was not the point. The Commission has not dared to say that a physiologist is to be allowed to do things in his laboratory for which a layman would be sent to prison. The report is not merely an evasion, it is a breakdown of the vivisectors' case.'

The climax of the campaign was reached when Pavlov, the Russian experimenter, published his famous treatise on Conditioned Reflexes, and H. G. Wells, in an impassioned eulogy of it, declared that if he stood on a pier in a storm, with Shaw and Pavlov struggling in the waves, and he, Wells, had only one lifebuoy to throw to them, he would throw it to Pavlov and not to Shaw.

Shaw, tickled by this very Wellsian extravagance, went for Pavlov full steam ahead with all his guns in action. He said he was concerned in this because Pavlov had taken the unpardonable liberty of presenting such an extraordinary personal resemblance to himself that their photographs were indistinguishable. He said that Wells could not have read the book through, first because nobody could read it through, and second because he had said that Pavlov's dogs loved him and were never hurt by him, whereas the book described how Pavlov had not only cut half their brains out, and pierced their cheeks and dragged their tongues through them to study their salivation, but by putting them into a 'little ease' had tormented and frustrated them until their discomfort and misery left them 'no use'. And from twenty-five years of this sort of thing all that the world learned was how a dog behaved with half its brains cut out, which nobody wanted to know, and, what was perhaps important, what sort of book a physiologist could write without having any brains at all. The press gravely applauded Pavlov's discovery that a dog's mouth watered when it heard the dinner bell. Shaw said, 'If the fellow had come to me I could have given him that information in less than twenty-five seconds without tormenting a single dog.'

It was always like that. Shaw's first appearance in the controversy was in the eighteen-eighties, when an eminent medical vivisectionist showed that a book by an anti-vivisectionist lady, Frances Power-Cobbe, contained several errors. Shaw dashed to the rescue of Miss Cobbe. 'The question,' he said, 'is not whether the book contains errors. If you knew anything about real science you would know that no book ever published, including the Bible and all the scientific treatises, is free from error, or ever will be. The question is whether or not you are a scoundrel: that is, a person who acts without regard to moral laws.' His highly indignant opponent stood on his dignity and refused to discuss on such terms. 'There you are!' said Shaw. 'Science, according to you gentlemen, knows nothing of your dignity or your wounded feelings; but the moment you are challenged on your own soulless terms you trot them out and hide behind them.' Thirty years later we find Shaw describing Pavlov quite logically and dispassionately as a scoundrel, and profoundly shocking Wells thereby.

Matters were not made more soothing for Wells by Shaw's disparagement of laboratory experiments as 'put up jobs', and by his declaring that his attention had been called to this by Wells's early novel, *Love and Mr Lewisham*. He claimed to be a genuinely scientific discoverer because his laboratory was the world, where he could not control the events nor manufacture the cases, whereas the laboratory researchers did nothing else except cook the results, or suppress them when they were not the intended ones. When they could not be suppressed they were not accepted, as 'he that's convinced against his will is of the same opinion still'. Even the physicists, whose work, unstained by cruelty and purely mental and mostly unremunerative, fascinated Shaw, amused him by their reception of the famous Michaelson-Morley experiment. The M-M instrument, a marvel of ingenuity, was designed to demonstrate the difference between the velocity of light when it was crossing the path of the earth's orbit round the sun and when it was travelling with the earth and sharing its velocity. The instrument proved that there was no difference; and so, said Shaw, bang goes Copernicus, and Young's hypothesis of an ether pervading space, and the velocity of light, and the whole fabric of astronomical physics. His own withers were unwrung, he said, because he had always denied that any mechanical experiment could make men believe what they did not want to believe, nor disbelieve what they wanted to believe. According to him the inspired guess comes first; and the mechanical experiment that is supposed to verify it is only a dodge to knock it into the thick heads of uninspired numskulls. Einstein presently explained the M-M experiment away; but, meanwhile, the laugh was with Shaw, as the physicists flatly refused to accept its apparent results.

Just as he fathered his views on laboratory experiments on H. G. Wells, he fathered his much wider views of hygiene on his friend Sir Almroth Wright, the leading bacteriologist of his day, and the hero of Shaw's play *The Doctor's Dilemma*. Shaw was lecturing at St Mary's Hospital when Wright, opposing Shaw's contention that the conquest of disease by inoculation (a hair of the dog that bit you) was really effected by sanitation, said quite casually that he believed the effect of sanitation to be purely aesthetic. Shaw instantly seized on this as an inspired guess and proclaimed Wright as the author of a discovery compared to which his bacteriological feats were child's play. Wright, puzzled by his mechanist education, protested his innocence of any such heresy; but Shaw persisted. 'Of course sanitation is aesthetic,' he said. 'Education is aesthetic. Why am I the best educated philosopher in England? Because, though I would not and could not learn anything from schoolbooks, I could sing, whistle, and hum all the masterpieces of modern music and recognize the work of all the old masters of painting when I was in my teens, while your academic scholars were translating dull filth like the epigrams of Martial and having the aesthetic pleasure of Virgil and Homer and the historical interest of Caesar spoiled for them by the drudgery of manufacturing sham Latin verses as school tasks, leaving them with the mentality of Ulysses, the points of honour of Ajax, and a hearsay impression of Beethoven and Mozart as boresome menial musicians good for amusing the ladies after dinner.'

All this was not conciliatory. Shaw's most sympathetic friends, Wells, Wright, J. B. S. Haldane and the rest, agreed that Shaw had a hopelessly unscientific mind, and that to discuss biology with him was impossible and ridiculous. When Haldane was explicit on this point Shaw immediately claimed that he was a disciple of Haldane's father, Scott Haldane, who had led the movement to restore psychology to its due predominance and elevated physiology into genuine psychological biology. 'I am only showing you fellows the value of your own discoveries,' he said. 'Why allow me all the credit for them?'

Even when 'you fellows', far from being his friends, detested him, they were disabled by the canniness with which he called them as witnesses on his side. They could not object to being ranked as important contributors to science, however exasperated they might be by the use he was making of their contributions. And all the time things were moving his way. Shaw will be remembered as a playwright and not as a man of science ; but a comparison of the scientific orthodoxy of 1877, when he came of age, with that of today, will show that official science was being dragged his way all the time, and that he was only quicker on the mark and could see a little farther ahead than the men who were actually doing the work.

What he learnt from his controversies was that his fiercest opponents were those whose views he was adopting and clarifying, and that the difficulty was not to induce men to accept new views, which they are always hungry for, but to clear out the old views which the new ones superseded. The counsel not to throw out dirty water until you got in fresh should, he said, be re-worded as 'When you arrive at the pump be careful to empty the dirty water from your bucket before you pour in the fresh.' All the newest faiths, he found, were muddled with the oldest superstitions.

One more of his controversies should be noted because it illustrated the qualities in him that provoked so much hostility. To say that he was continually in hot water throughout his career is merely to say that he took care never to open his mouth until he knew what he was talking about in a country where every man shouted at the top of his voice without dreaming of taking any such precaution. But there was an airy aloofness about him, a suggestion of alien superiority to the emotions that afflicted the majority of mankind, that gave a peculiarly irritating sting to his most direct statements of fact, which were always assumed to be satirical or derisive. And he was a professed socialist, which then meant something, though nobody knew exactly what. When Austin Harrison wanted to know why the reviews of Shaw's plays which he wrote for the *Daily Mail* were abbreviated or omitted, Lord Northcliffe thundered, 'I am not running my paper to advertise a damned socialist!' What he really meant was 'that devil Shaw', whose criticisms hit the bull's eye 'far too frequently to be ignored or to be dismissed as the 'gags' of an incorrigible comedian. 'The fact is', Shaw once wrote to Hyndman, 'when a man keeps up a joke for so long as you have known me, either he is mad or there is some kernel of earnestness in it. Your sense of humour may tempt you to embrace the former alternative: but I assure you I am only mad nor'-nor'-west: otherwise my views could not be so annoying as they sometimes are.'

His genius alone was sufficient to make him disliked, for people fear the truth and hatred is rooted in cowardice. 'A genius is a person who, seeing farther and probing deeper than other people, has a different set of ethical valuations from theirs, and has energy enough to give effect to this extra vision and its valuations in whatever manner best suits his or her specific talents.' Such was his definition of genius, and although it left out of account some of the highest manifestations it certainly defined about 75 per cent of his own exceptional gifts. The other quality in his writings which aggravated people as much as the truth in them provoked anger was explained in a remark he made to me: 'The English are all right, but they don't realize that I am a foreigner and have an inherited hate of what they call patriotism. I am intensely and quite unreasonably proud of being Irish.'

These two qualities, an inspired common sense and an alien detachment, were revealed more completely in his controversy with Sir Arthur Conan Doyle over the sinking of the *Titanic* than anywhere else in his writings until the war of 1914-18 gave him larger scope. Doyle represented the man in the street, Shaw the man in the moon, or some other planet.

The *Titanic*, a White Star liner of 46,328 tons, struck an iceberg just before midnight on Sunday, April 14th, 1912, and sank in less than three hours. Out of 2201 persons on board only 711 were saved. Instantly the newspapers were filled with romantic reports of the ·heroism displayed by the British officers and passengers. Shaw wrote to *The Daily News and Leader* pointing out that the Captain, who had been acclaimed in the press as a super-hero, had lost his ship 'by deliberately and knowingly steaming into an icefield at the highest speed he had coal for', that the officers had lost their heads, that general panic had prevailed, that everything had been thoroughly mismanaged from the start, that some boats had contained more men than women, and that the occupants of other boats had refused to save those who were struggling in the water. Sir Arthur Conan Doyle promptly rushed to the rescue of the British race, and said that he could not remember 'any production that contained so much that was false within the same compass' as Shaw's letter. Shaw replied, proving his case point by point, and expressed his amazement that Doyle should have accused him of lying. By this time several episodes unflattering to human nature had leaked out in the course of the Enquiry into the sinking of the *Titanic*, and Sir Arthur was unable to maintain the noble note he had struck in his first letter; so he decided to feel hurt. 'He says that I accused him of lying', wrote Doyle. 'I have been guilty of no such breach of the amenities of the discussion.'

Anxious to know whether their personal relationship had been affected by this interchange of views, I wrote to ask Shaw whether he and Doyle had met after the latter had accused him of falsehood without calling him a liar. He answered:

'When I lived on Hindhead for a time in 1898 I occasionally met or visited Conan Doyle and Grant Allen, who were within a few minutes walk. We were quite friendly. C.D. had not then taken to spiritualism. His explosion over the *Titanic* catastrophe did not lead to any personal contacts. Incidentally (in 1898) a speech which I made at a Peace meeting cured him rather too drastically of sentimental Pacifism and left him a raging Jingo.' ·

I may be reminded here that to Conan Doyle Shaw was not a foreigner. They were both Irishmen. But Doyle was the warm-hearted romantic Catholic Irishman who could see nothing in the *Titanic* disaster but the loss and pity and terror of it. Shaw was not that sort of Irishman. To him the loss of the ship was a statistical fact, a shipwreck like any other shipwreck. What threw him into a transport of merciless fury was the debasement of the moral currency by the venal mendacity and cheap melodrama of 'the new journalism' of which in his days on *The Star* he had been a pioneer. It was always a public question and not a private grief that brought Shaw into action.

Later on another liner went to the bottom and got him into trouble again. The Four Years' War began in 1914 with an appalling carnage. In Flanders the company officers put their expectation of life at six weeks. Our batteries, telephoning for more shells, were told that they had already had two, which was the utmost that could be spared for them. Excessive prices were charged for these few shells by the private firms who supplied them; and meanwhile men were standing idle in Woolwich Arsenal because the Liberal Prime Minister, Asquith, had been carefully taught that private industry must not be interfered with. Until Lord Northcliffe and Lloyd George grasped the situation and knocked out the doctrinaire liberals who were losing the war the position was ghastly, and Shaw knew it. But the journalists, the same who had dressed up the *Titanic* affair, kept writing up 'our gallant fellows in the trenches' and raising paeans of victory over every wave of British infantry flung uselessly on barbed wire entanglements and mowed down by machine-gun fire. And the British public found it as exciting as the cinema, and echoed the paeans.

Suddenly, off the Irish coast, a torpedo sank the *Lusitania*, a popular liner. Here at last was something small enough for the public mind to grasp. Everybody went war mad. Shaw went in the opposite direction, and immediately became Public Enemy No. 1, as we shall hear.

OVERFLOW

IN SOCIAL HABITS Shaw was impossible outside his own house, where he and his wife entertained most successful luncheon parties. Enticed by Maurice Baring to attend a typical bachelor's party, where men of all ages, from Lord Cromer to

H. G. Wells, were trying to behave like undergraduates, Shaw addressed them with deadly contempt for their efforts: 'Gentlemen, we shall enjoy ourselves very much if only you will not try to be convivial.' In the same manner Shaw refused an invitation to dine at a famous bohemian club, replying that nothing on earth would induce him to spend an evening with a number of gentlemen who had to get drunk in order to endure one another's company.

'A man's interest in the world is only the overflow from his interest in himself,' says Captain Shotover in *Heartbreak House*. Shaw's overflow was a cataract. He spent a normal man's lifetime on committees of this, that and the other thing: executive committees, general committees, special committees, sub-committees; political, theatrical, municipal, musical, literary, historical, archaeological, and heaven knows what committees. He was a first-rate committee-man, and constant training perfected his technique: 'I got the committee habit, the impersonality and imperturbability of the statesman, the constant and unceremonious criticism of men who were at many points much abler and better informed than myself.' Never frequenting the social world of art, he was seldom seen by his literary contemporaries. The committee room was his club and his pub, his drawing-room, study, salon and business office. One might almost say that he was truly 'at home' there ; he took his ease in a committee room as Falstaff took his ease in his inn, ceasing to be the irritating G.B.S. of the journals, the infuriating Shaw of the theatre and platform, and becoming tactful, modest, prudent, yielding, considerate ; in a word, safe. He was there to get a job done, and in a multitude of counsellors there was danger, which he circumvented by self-obliteration and a kind of crafty caution of which he was a master. In a sudden flare-up of passions he would soothe the disputants by taking the blame ; he could beat down any hostility by uniting all wrangling opponents in a common agreement that it was all his fault. They triumphed, and did not notice that his forgotten point was carried.

For twenty-seven years he kept the Fabian Society free from the quarrels that broke up all the other socialist organizations. He out-distanced everyone in thoroughness and application to work. 'I sometimes sat beside him,' wrote S. G. Hobson, 'watching his busy pen transferring, intercalating, deleting, all done with dainty neatness. Once we reached a blind end to some municipal problem. "Leave it to me," he said. Next week he brought replies from over sixty town clerks, all analysed and classified.' He hated waste of time and used his wits and knowledge of men to guard against it. Sitting next to Hobson one afternoon at the Fabian Executive, he genially observed: 'My dear Hobson, as a chairman you are brutal, domineering and scandalously unfair.' A quarter of an hour later he asked, 'By the way, are you going to the annual meeting of the Stage Society?' Hobson said he thought he would go. After a further interval Shaw added: 'Will you take the chair?' Hobson said he would. This was Shaw's way of speeding-up the meeting, as he was aware that Hobson would give all the speakers short shrift.

The Stage Society, as we know, produced several of Shaw's plays, and for many years he was on their committee. A hint of their difficulties and disagreements is given in a letter he wrote to W. Lee Mathews, dated 2nd October, 1905. I asked him in 1939 for one or two explanatory notes, which he provided: 'I havnt the faintest recollection of what this was about. I must have written a thousand letters like it. Hector Thomson was treasurer of the Stage Society. Lee Mathews a leading member. Peter was Lee Mathew's very sensible cat. Whelen also a leading member. L.M. is dead. So, I presume, is Peter.'

'DEAR LEE MATHEWS,

'I will see the Stage Society brimstoned first. Why should I? I asts you, Lee Mathews, as man to man, why should I? Why the devil should I? Why the —— —— —— —— should I?

'One thing is pretty clear. No matter what arrangements we make, from the moment it is made Whelen's craze for enterprise and Thomson's restless individualism will immediately set to work to upset it. Well, I dont care ; stagnation is death, and revolutions are amusing ; but the game is one at which I prefer to be a looker-on. There is no situation to be saved, no strong hand needed ; for nothing that we decide on is ever carried out except in the matter of the choice of plays, which requires only a discussion and a vote. The rest is all chance. We select a cast, not one member of which ever arrives at parturition. We select a theatre ; and the play is done somewhere else. We are so completely governed by circumstances that for want of anything real to do we keep altering our constitution and pulling up the plant to see how it is getting on. I am perfectly willing to have Peter in the chair, and spend the rest of the year conspiring to dethrone him and discussing whether a tortoiseshell or a tabby would be best for the realisation of our dreams.'

Shaw was on the Committee of Management and the Dramatic Sub-Committee of the Society of Authors, and in a long letter he wrote to Alfred Sutro in January 1909 he discussed their problems. 'The only way to do any good on a committee is to treat every meeting as a matter of life and death,' he said, urging Sutro not to serve because 'you are a man of unreasonable and violent character, who will do nothing but quarrel the whole time; and yet you are so amiable that everybody will believe that it is the other people who are ill-treating you.' After going into the pros and cons of the situation, Shaw gave Sutro a catalogue of the virtues required by those who aspire to govern in harmony with their fellow-men, a variation of Kipling's poem *If*:

'However, I am assuming in all this that you are not by nature and practice a committee man. If I am wrong: if you are invincibly patient; if you cannot lose your temper; if you can take Thring[1] to your bosom when he is thoughtlessly and quite unintentionally standing heavily on your corns; if you can spend precious working hours in drafting documents and then see your work wasted and spoiled without turning an outward hair; if you can use your wits to prevent the idle people from squabbling and then let all the bad blood pass off as being your fault; if all this makes your eyes glisten and your mouth water, then come on by all means and I will be your warmest supporter; but if not, then either withdraw or persuade somebody else to.'

Shaw was always in sympathy with the rising generation, taking their part in any dispute that arose between them and their elders and strongly advising them to assert themselves whenever they got the chance. 'I hold that an unknown author is either in a stronger position than a known one or else in no position at all,' he wrote to Lee Mathews. 'Suppose you are a known man. You try Barrie: he hasnt one written. You try manager, obliged to keep your theatre going or perish. You want a play badly. Naturally you dont want one by an un-

[1] G. Herbert Thring was secretary to the Society of Authors.

Pinero: he can let you have one in six months. You try Carton, Maugham, even Shaw. None of them have anything ready. You are forced back on an experiment with an unknown man. The unknown man looks darkly at you (if he is a good man of business), and says, "You must be in a devil of a hole if you come to me. I am nobody. I want the same terms as Barrie." "Monstrous," you reply: "You, an obscure scallywag, ask what Barrie would give me a play for!" "Well, my friend, go and ask him for one." Hankin acted on this principle when he was unacted; and Vedrenne and Barker never forgave him; but they had to pay. I think he got an advance of £200 on a first class contract. Moral: the beginner should be modest enough to know that his play will not be produced if anything better is on the market. And there his modesty should stop.'

There were noisy squabbles between the coming dramatists and those who had already arrived at the meetings of the Dramatists' Club, concerning which Shaw sent me a few details (1939): 'The Dramatists' Club, whatever it may be now (I dont even know whether it exists) began as a clique of old stagers who insisted on excluding everyone who was not "a dramatist of established reputation" which was their definition of one of themselves. They invited me to join in the sure and certain hope that I would refuse; but as I was for years trying to get them to organize the profession—any sort of organization being better than none—I joined and made a duty of attending their lunches for quite a long time. They hated me, and would have enjoyed nothing more than putting me and Ibsen into a fiery furnace heated seventy times seven. But all they could do was to blackball every candidate I proposed. I soon gave up my attempts to declique the place. They were on the point of blackballing Gilbert Murray when Pinero, of whom they were mortally afraid, appeared and sternly ordered them to elect him. Pinero's behaviour to me was irreproachable; but he concluded his letters to me "With admiration and detestation," which exactly expressed his feeling. He always assumed that I was friendly, though I carefully concealed the fact that I had procured his knighthood for him. Carton and I got on capitally, as the squirms of the clique delighted him.' In the early days of the Club a tragedy darkened its deliberations. St John Hankin was a promising young Edwardian dramatist, who, Shaw informed me, 'committed suicide because he thought that a disease which had wrecked his father's life was attacking *him*'. On the 23rd June, 1909, Shaw gave Sutro the benefit of his meditations:

'I feel pretty sure that Hankin knew nothing of what passed at the Club. There was nobody to tell him; and, anyhow, it would have been a breach of confidence and a damned ill-natured thing into the bargain. . . . I think, on turning it over in my mind, that we must amnesty all the young men who attack us, as otherwise we shall never get recruits worth having. Ever since I can remember, the younger generation's particular method of knocking at the door has been to denounce what they always call "the dramatic ring", meaning the older men who have fully arrived. I can remember Grundy's onslaught before the dramatic ring became Pinero, Jones, Carton and Grundy, perhaps the smallest and closest that has ever existed. You were really the man who broke that ring; and although I cannot bring any documents against you, I feel quite convinced that in the days when you translated Maeterlinck, and were a remarkably handsome young man with apparently a million in each pocket, you must have out-Hankined Hankin in contempt for the men in possession. The latest assailant is Arnold Bennett, who has published his *Cupid and Commonsense* with a preface which is a very capital preface in all respects except that it ends with a perfectly gratuitous insult to Pinero and to the older-than-Bennett school generally. Now Bennett is one of the men I want to get in, because, although he sedulously keeps up an air of being a fourth-rate clerk from the potteries, and out of a job at that, he has some knowledge of the world and of business, and is not afraid of the managers, as his preface very abundantly demonstrates.'

Shaw certainly helped to make the Club's sessions lively. During the 1914-18 war he described to me a meeting which he had attended a few years previously:

'My attitude to the war has made me very unpopular with the members of the Dramatists' Club; but they never liked me; I have been a constant thorn in their flesh. Some six years ago I caused an unholy rumpus at one of their luncheons. After they had drunk the health of the Club and were looking uncommonly pleased with themselves, I paralysed them by saying that, while I had never blackballed one of their candidates for admission, they had consistently blackballed mine. Following a long pause of shocked incredulity, each member trying his hardest to appear as if he had been mortally wounded in his most sensitive place, an absolute hurricane of recriminations swept the table. Challenged to name my candidates, I mentioned St John Hankin, Hall Caine and Gilbert Murray. A veritable tornado of protests then rent the air: Hankin had offended everyone, he was hostile and socially impossible; Hall Caine was a self-advertising monster who thought he was God; he would behave as if he had bought the Club; Conan Doyle and a dozen others wouldn't come to the lunches if Caine were present; Gilbert Murray was not a dramatist, he had never written anything of his own, he was a translator of other men's works; an excellent person, no doubt, but not "one of us". This went on for some time, and whenever the storm died down I raised it again to howling pitch with a few displeasing comparisons. Alfred Sutro made a brave attempt to reason with me, but the effort was too much for him and resulted in a frenzied declaration that in future he would blackball everyone proposed by any-one. I then remarked that members simply blackballed people they didn't like personally, and that henceforth, if they black-balled any one of my nominees, I should take it as a personal insult and blackball all of theirs. With a bark of rage Sydney Grundy accused me of placing my personal feelings above the interests of the Club. Then the shindy broke out afresh. When order was partially restored, I decided to teach them a lesson. I had noticed that Barrie was not present at the lunch, and as an example of how far blackballing should be determined by personal feelings I said that if Gilbert Cannan, who was living with Barrie's wife, were proposed as a member, I should cer-tainly blackball him unless he were nominated by Barrie himself. Sensation; during which I glanced round the room and caught sight of Barrie, who must have entered quietly while the tempest was at its height and heard every word I had just uttered. Of course he knew that I had been unaware of his presence, and it did not affect our friendly relations in the least, but it gave me a frightful shock at the time. Having presented my fellow-dramatists with something to bite on, I left them, and from the nature of the sounds that reached me beyond the door I fancied that they were discussing me.'

Many years later, although, as we shall find, he had been badly treated by the Dramatists' Club, Shaw agreed to go on slaving for his fellow-professionals, telling Sutro: 'As play-wrights are the most helpless parcel of silly sheep on God's earth in matters of business, I must do my best to shepherd the flock, though after ten years of it I am very tired of this most thankless of all public jobs.'

ADVANCING CONQUEST

THE MOMENT Vedrenne and Granville Barker, having done well with their matinees of *Candida* in the spring of 1904, decided to run the Court Theatre themselves, Shaw suggested that they should open the autumn season with Ellen Terry in *Captain Brassbound's Conversion*. They agreed, and he wrote to her explaining that they could only announce six matinees at first, that she would probably receive no more than £25, out of which she would have to 'find her own gowns', but that if she did not play the part at least once she would 'go down to all ages as the woman who made *il gran' rifiuto,* for there never was and never will be again such a part written for any mortal. I stooped for your sake to do what Shakespear did when he manufactured Rosalind. *He* gave her away by flinging her at the public with a shout of "as *you* like it" (Pilate washing his hands); but I will gravely offer this impossible quintessence of Ellen as a real woman; and everybody will be delighted. If you are too lazy to learn the part I will teach it to you speech by speech until you can repeat it in your sleep.'

An autumn tour prevented Ellen from accepting the offer, but a year later she agreed to play Lady Cicely in a production of the play arranged for the spring of 1906. 'I am looking forward with malicious glee to the rehearsals. I shall have my revenge then,' Shaw warned her. 'I will not leave a rag, not a wink, not a flippety-flop of that tiresome Ellen Terry who wouldn't do my play.' But when at last they met regularly at rehearsals, each was rather shy of the other, 'for talking, hampered by material circumstances, is awkward and unsatisfactory after the perfect freedom of writing between people

286

who *can* write', explained Shaw. The rehearsals went smoothly enough, and the author was delighted with the result: 'I never realized how well I did that job until I saw you rehearse,' he told her. The play was produced on March 20th, 1906, but although performed eighty-nine times it was not a box-office success. 'I seriously think the Court Theatre must be transferred to a tent on Putney Heath,' Shaw wrote to Lillah MCarthy in April. 'The returns for the week just to hand are disgraceful: only £67 17s. 5d. per performance. In short, *Brassbound* has been a failure.' Lillah McCarthy had just married Granville Barker, which was the last straw: 'I ask you, how is the thing to go on?' Ellen toured *Brassbound* in the provinces and in America, where it was more successful. She seldom met Shaw again; but once they ran across one another at Stratford-on-Avon, and another time on the roof of the Coliseum after a matinee, when a number of well-known people were being photographed. 'Why do I make you nervous?' he wanted to know. 'I know why *you* make *me* nervous. It is because people are looking on, and the way I want to and ought to behave would be ridiculous and indecorous.' A third chance meeting was on a summer day in the fields near Elstree, where she was at work on a film. She told him she no longer expected leading parts and was ready to play a charwoman if he would write a play with a charwoman in it for her. 'What would happen to my play if whenever the charwoman appeared the audience forgot the hero and heroine and could think of nothing but the wonderful things the charwoman was going to say and do?' His question was unanswerable, and Shaw said that they both felt rather inclined to cry.

Another discarded project seemed to be reviving when, in June 1905, Shaw received a letter from Forbes-Robertson, who, unable to find a better part than the one specially created for him in *Caesar and Cleopatra,* pressed for an immediate production. Shaw withstood the pressure:

'JOHNSTON FORBES ROBERTSON!

'*Patience!* thou young and rose-lipped cherubim! I have waited six years for you; and you ask me to be patient. No: the difficulty is all the other way: it is you who are impatient, with your six weeks holiday and your production in September. What you dont grasp is that unless I have a holiday I shall go raving mad and die. You think because I am going

287

away for three months, I am trifling with you. But in that three months I have to write a new play and to revise half a dozen French and German translations of my old ones. I have to see an old novel through the American press and write a preface for it. I have to prepare *John Bull's Other Island* for publication. I have to do half a dozen articles now months in arrear. The translators are howling, pressed by the Berlin and Viennese theatres for prompt copies. The publishers are howling, because the public are red hot for Shaw books. Everybody's fame and future is staked on my attending to him before the end of the week. How much holiday do you see for me in all this? You say I am to wait until the end of July to go, and to come back early in August. Well, I'm blowed if I will! The worm turns under the steamroller. And I wont risk *C & C* without rehearsing it myself. You are too deadly tired of the whole business to be trusted. You would go Phelpsing along, crushing poor Ian,[1] and taking no interest in the unfortunate crowd, who would be cast anyhow and snubbed into more than their natural dufferdom. That is all very well for a monologue like *Hamlet* ; but it will not do for *C & C*. I might be content with the first week and the last at a pinch ; but they must not come out of my three months. The idea of rehearsing now seems hopeless, because we havnt our cast. Rosina Filippi tells me that her husband insists on her leaving the stage at the end of her engagement to Gatti. Kerr has slipped through our fingers for the moment. The more I look into the play the more impressed I am with the importance of Rufio and Ftatateeta. And we have more than 20 other people to get into their places, not to mention crowds to be drilled. It looks to me much more like the 1st December than any earlier date. Can you not live on your fat until then? I quite agree that the Scala ought to open with *C & C* ; but it had better wait, since better, it appears, may not be.

'Remember, I have the strongest interest in getting *C & C* out of my way early ; for I am threatened with productions at the Court which will need rehearsing ; but there is no use heading straight for a breakdown by trying to put twelve months work into three.

'Anyhow, the difficulty is no more of my making than of yours. We are under the corner stone of Necessity, as cheer-

---

[1] Ian Robertson, Forbes' brother and stage-manager.

ful old Ibsen says. If you could start rehearsing on Saturday next, and produce on the 10th October, the thing might be done; but we have not the cast. McKinnel is absolutely no good for Rufio; and Calvert is wanted at the Court, like all the other people who are any good to me.

'Oh this cursed packing—fancy our having to change houses at this fatal moment!

'I am quite addled and barren of resource and suggestion.

'Why did I ever write the confounded play? I know I can get a magnificent performance out of it if only I can get a fair chance at it. Let's put it off to next year.—G.B.S.'

They did so. An offer from New York enabled Forbes-Robertson to produce the play at the New Amsterdam Theatre in the autumn of 1906. Shaw rehearsed the company in London. He had given many hints for Robertson's production of *Hamlet,* which had been found invaluable by the actor, who was only too glad to leave the whole production of *Caesar and Cleopatra* in the hands of such a master. But when Robertson begged him to cross the Atlantic in order to be present at the first performance, he drew the line: 'Were I to go with you to America I should become so popular that they'd want to make me President; and that would bore me to death.' Shaw was pleased with his play and pleased with Robertson's performance, writing on 13th July, 1906: 'The rehearsals have convinced me that I did this job extraordinarily well for you. If the dresses become you as well as the part, Simmons will be the King of costumiers. Caesar will place you absolutely *hors concours* on the English stage. When Hamlets are down to six a penny, there will still be only one Caesar. P.S.—Cleopatra will have a great success too.' Two days later he sent a parting word of advice: 'Many thanks for your very kind letter—all the more welcome as I was afraid I had been worrying too much at the rehearsals. . . . The bucina will require a little management and the help of the conductor of the band or whoever does the music for the piece. The one thing to put your foot on like iron is the use of the cornet. That easy and vulgar instrument is always at hand and always detestable except for sentimental melodies. If an ophicleide (which sounds like a bullock) can be got, it might be effective as the bucina. Or a tuba (bombardon) in E flat or B flat—the latter for preference. But probably the best thing is a tenor trombone, which is always easy to get. If only we could get some of the long trumpets

289

which came in a few years ago as Bach trumpets, and which are often now played by music hall virtuosos, they would be just the thing for a few high-ringing notes following the bellow of the bucina. Only, no cornets under any circumstances. . . .'

The play was well received by the New York critics, but in one respect not well enough for Shaw, who wrote to Robertson on March 21st, 1907:

'. . . I am not yet satisfied with the recognition of your Caesar. Some of the notices have been very gorgeous; but they have not taken it all in yet as a piece of acting. On the stage there is always somebody who is right in front of the main body simply because he can do things like your Caesar; and I want to get this well hammered in.

'My experience at the Court Theatre convinces me more and more that the system of producing plays for six weeks only, and then reviving them again and again later on, is in the long run the most economical one. Its enormous advantage is that you cannot have a failure, and you never kill a play. If only we could get hold of a suitable theatre, I should feel strongly disposed to suggest six weeks of *Caesar* in the West End at the height of the summer season, and then a descent on the provinces with it to pick up gold and silver; then return to London and give another six weeks of it, followed by six weeks of *Hamlet* or anything else in your repertory. In the meantime you could feel the pulse of the public in any new part that you were doubtful about by means of matinees. I forewarn you that, if you ever try this system, it will require a fearsome strength of mind to take off a play at the end of six weeks when it is filling the house every night, and let down the business with a newer play or an older one; but anything is better than killing a good play under you. It is like galloping a good horse until he drops dead. . . .

'At all events dont assume that I want you to produce *Caesar* for the run of the piece. I had far rather you played it a fortnight every year for the next ten years, than ran it to death for a year straight on end. And I should like it to be seen in the first instance not as a big commercial speculation, but as a piece of the finest acting coming for a moment to London because all the best things are supposed to come there.

'I hope you are not getting very tired of the part or over-

290

worked at it. Tell Mrs Robertson that I am greatly shocked at the photographs I see of Cleopatra. She gets fatter and fatter in every successive one. If this goes on, the scenery will all have to be redesigned for London with wider doors, and the pedestal of the Sphinx will have to be strengthened . . .'

That autumn Robertson was back in England giving *Caesar and Cleopatra* at various provincial centres, and so keen to produce it before Christmas in London that he was considering the possibility of renting the Savoy Theatre from Vedrenne and Granville Barker, who were having an anxious time there. On November 1st Shaw advised caution:

'I understand that there was some question about your taking the Savoy either wholly or partly off Vedrenne and Barker's hands after the appointed four weeks of *Caesar and Cleopatra*. As Vedrenne's friend, I urge you strongly to do this, and impress on you the advantages of this splendid west-end theatre with its unbroken tradition of success. As *your* friend, I am bound in honor to advise you not to touch it with a pair of tongs. Thus I have a divided duty in the matter; and my heart is torn accordingly. But as it must be plain to you that if the Savoy were a silver mine, Vedrenne would be grappling it to him with hooks of steel instead of hawking it up and down the Strand, and dashing out frantically after reading every return to sack the second trombone and another couple of stage-hands, I may leave you to the guidance of your excellent judgment in the matter. Fortunately matters are not quite so bad as Vedrenne thinks them. He has suffered so much from iritis and from want of a holiday that his nerves have gone to pot; and he was so terrified by Barker's expenditure on scenery that he funked the advertising, and the *The Devil's Disciple* was kept more or less of a family secret. Now, however, London is contemplating a poster with an encouraging picture of Matheson Lang being hanged; and there is a sandwich man at the corner of Adam Street for my especial benefit. Further, the King has deigned to patronize the entertainment with his family and certain wandering Royalties from the continent of Europe. Also, the pit, gallery, upper circle, and half the balcony, are sticking to us nobly: the deficiency is in the stalls; and the moral of that is that Vedrenne and Barker should perform only when parliament is sitting. That will be all right when you come; but even admitting that your arrival will complete the improvement that is going on, and fill us up to our capacity, I still think that you will do better with one meteoric month in London, and then another trip round the Provinces to reap the harvest of its glory, than you would be holding on in London to either risk new plays or exploit old ones that you have already worked pretty hard there. In fact, if it were not for the fatigue and worry of the nomadic life, I should say without hesitation that your most profitable policy is to take to the Provinces and die a millionaire like Barry Sullivan.

'Charlotte saw your *Caesar* in Dublin and came back in a state of insanity about you.[1] It is flatly impossible that any human actor could be so out-of-the-way splendid as she reports you to have been; so I put the impression down, more or less, to personal infatuation. Still, I have no doubt that your Caesar will be a stroke of work of the kind that this generation of Londoners has seen nothing of. Indeed the whole difficulty is that the grand school has gone under so completely that the public has got rusty in its perception of it; and Caesar will begin by puzzling them. But after a little that will wear off; and the play will steadily improve as a property. The only thing that I am afraid of is that it will get hold of you so completely that you will be unable to do anything else. This terror was suggested to me on a recent visit to the Grand at Fulham, where I saw Ellen Terry in *Captain Brassbound's Conversion*. Her whole company was blind and mad with nightly repetition of their wretched parts. Her blushing young husband, looking like a Cherokee Chieftain made up pink as a juvenile lead, visibly restrained himself with the greatest difficulty from uttering savage yells and scalping everybody within his reach; but Ellen herself was magnificent. She has actually become Lady Cicely. She no

[1] Mrs Shaw saw the play and wrote to Robertson, 13th October, 1907: 'I am so sorry I could not see you last night to tell you how profoundly I was affected by Caesar. I think your performance is one of the finest things I ever have seen upon the stage! I was more moved and stirred than I could have thought it possible to be by words I know so well. I thank you from my heart for what you have done for my favourite among all my husband's character studies: for, easy as it seems to you to do when one watches the finished creation, I know how much thought and study must have gone to make this really noble impersonation.'

longer hampers herself as she did at the Court by trying to remember my lines: she simply lives through Lady Cicely's adventures and says whatever comes into her head, which by the way is now much better than what I wrote. I immediately said to myself, "Good God! Suppose this happens to Forbes Robertson, and he becomes incapable of playing Hamlet!" So be warned if it is not already too late.

'I explained why I cannot go to Birmingham; but I am not quite sure that I should have gone anyhow. I have a sort of fancy for seeing you for the first time at the first performance in London. There was some question of my going down to see you with Barker, the idea being to make quite sure that you are a sufficiently presentable actor to be allowed to appear without some supervision in a theatre made classical by the illustrious traditions of Vedrenne, Barker, and Bernard Shaw. But I thought on the whole I would chance it. In fact I was conscious of a certain internal revolt against this aspect of the matter; and I finally told Barker that I'd be damned if I'd go. It then turned out that even so superior a youth as Barker shared my sentiments, though he pleaded that it would be very hard on them if they had a lot of first-rate Court Theatre actors hanging about doing nothing on full salary when they might be replacing the weaker members of your crowd to advantage. However, even if Vedrenne does not sack them all in the meantime, I see no reason to suppose that your Company will not be a good deal better after all the practice they have had than the Court people would be after a few rehearsals. . . .'

Caesar and Cleopatra appeared at the Savoy on November 25th, and on December 12th Shaw scribbled a line to Robertson saying that he had 'made a rush round last night and saw most of *Caesar*', advising Robertson to abolish his free list because deadheads disliked good plays and good acting, criticizing the performances of the rest of the cast as being in places too sing-songy, regretting that business was not better, adding that 'the public may hold back for a while, but it cannot get away from *Caesar*: there is nothing within two hundred miles of it on the stage at present', and wishing he could snatch a clear six weeks in order to 'write another solo for the same instrument'. The play, rather provincially cast and produced, was not a gold mine; and on January 31st, 1908, Shaw condoled with Julius:

'I am ashamed to have been so much more a gainer than

you over *Caesar*; but I suppose there is nothing to be done but shove the old Sphinx into a railway arch and wait till the clouds roll by. If it were a reasonably cheap play, I should say go on with it, as it will grow steadily if it is rubbed in; but as it is, there are limits to what one can be expected to spend on educating the provinces. So away with it, and forgive the author. He meant well.

'The annoying thing is that the very people who could not take *Caesar* in at once, and bleated worst about it, now calmly say what a splendid thing it was, as if they had been the first to recognise its merits. Well, let them do without it for a year or two whilst you make money out of them, and be d——d to them!

'The Press, headed by Walkley, said of *Caesar* exactly what they said of *Arms and The Man* in 1894—Offenbach and Meilhac and Halévy—opera bouffe. Now, *Arms and The Man* is a masterpiece. In 1920 *Caesar* will be a masterpiece. Cheerful for both of us, eh?

'Still, it was worth doing. It put everybody else behind you—restored the perspective of the stage, with the character actor in his place in the middle distance, and the classic actor sunlike above the horizon.

'Business was not very heroic, certainly—*but*—do you know what the other theatres were doing, with the bank-rate at 7? You were a most envied man. . . .

'If only I had time to write a play for you—you *two*; for the lady is a regular ace of spades to a dramatist who knew how to play her.'

Shaw's prophecy was fulfilled. The play steadily grew in favour the more it was seen, each visit to a provincial town resulting in larger audiences, and when in 1913 Forbes-Robertson gave a Farewell Season at Drury Lane Theatre *Caesar and Cleopatra* packed the house. For these Farewell performances the first scenes of the first and fourth acts were omitted, the third act was restored, and a prologue spoken by the god Ra was specially written, concerning which Shaw wrote to Robertson (29th August, 1913):

'Ever since your letter of the 30th July reached me, I have been in a condition of distracted imbecility which has prevented me from giving my mind to answering it, though not from worrying about it. I feel that that prologue must be adapted to the history of the country it is spoken in. I confess I also feel that it ought to be spoken by you, even at the cost of leaving Caesar to the call boy. When Androcles is produced on Monday, I will have another look at it and see what can be done . . .

'I should rather like to do a fifty minutes sketch about Mahomet, with you as the Prophet. There is nothing like announcing a farewell for bringing down a deluge of new plays upon you. My terror is, that when you insist on retiring, Gertrude will keep going round doing the old repertory with some quite inconceivable duffer in your parts. Could you not bind her over to be of good behaviour or something of that sort?'

Following Robertson's season at the Savoy business went from bad to worse. 'What with Barker gradually losing all desire to act, and Vedrenne gradually losing all desire to do anything else but act, the position had been becoming more and more impossible,' complained Shaw to Lee Mathews. 'If I could only get V on the stage and B off it, I should amaze the world. As it is, after forcing Arms and The Man on by sheer despotic violence and thereby staving off actual entry of brokers, I have been forced to let my over-strained and entangled cables go and make fast to Miss Horniman, if only to keep a stage for Barker if America fails him.' Miss Horniman was about to send Candida on tour. In November 1908 Granville Barker had a serious illness, and we get a snapshot of his partner in a note from Shaw to Lee Mathews: 'Barker must already be nearly cured of homeopathy by that amazing diagnosis of typhoid as influenza. Anything more ghastly-absurd than Vedrenne in his favourite part of The Voice of Conscience, hurling the news at Lillah at 2 in the morning, and returning at intervals to the telephone to wake her up and tell her that her place was by the bedside of her dying husband, I defy any satirist to imagine. I am in a muddle of work, and am wrecking Europe and America by helplessly throwing the most urgent letters about and forgetting them. I hardly felt the news about Barker—shant believe he's dead until I see it. I did not even weep for the Emperor of China.'

Having discovered that deadheads, however intellectual, did not keep the drama alive, the Vedrenne-Barker management dissolved. Shaw always hated the practice of giving free seats to people who were supposed to be walking advertisements for plays, and a chance visit to the Coronet Theatre, where a touring company was playing *You Never Can Tell*, drew a protest from him to the business manager: 'From my box it seemed that the house was full, but from the returns I find that it was only a third full. I imagine from this that the house was what is technically known as "papered". Will you please let it be understood that no person shall see a play of mine unless he pays the full price of admission. If then the house is only a third full, slips may be put on the posters stating that for a single seat the patron may obtain the use of three, on which he may place his stick, his umbrella, his overcoat, or even his feet if he feels like it.'

Whether his plays were doing well or ill, Shaw was always in the wildest high spirits. We catch sight of him staying for week-ends at The Beetle and Wedge, Moulsford, where he rowed on the river, making rapid strokes without troubling to feather his oars, and where he bathed, the water soothing him and giving him the sensation of being in another world. Sometimes he went abroad. In July 1908 he wrote to Forbes-Robertson from Bayreuth: 'I regret to inform you that this is my 52nd birthday, and that I hope you will have the gentlemanly feeling NOT to congratulate me on that melancholy fact. An American (young—too young to understand) has sent me a pearl scarf-pin in honor of the date. I never wear scarf-pins. Should you at any time require a pearl scarf-pin, second-hand, at a reasonable price, you may depend on my best attention. It is a sort of thing Macbeth would have worn. . . . The mob here is insufferable, and the whole thing, from the Wagnerian point of view, a huge irony. My wife desires to be remembered to you; and I desire to be remembered to your wife.'

Two summers running the Shaws spent at Mevagissey. Robert Loraine stayed there with them in 1907. They drove about in his little Maxwell car, Shaw taking innumerable snapshots, and behaving like a light-hearted schoolboy. The following summer Loraine put in a week or two with them at Llanbedr in Wales. There were long tramps in the hills, Shaw talking nineteen to the dozen. They rose early, Shaw going for a walk before breakfast, and retired early, seldom later than 10 p.m. After 7 o'clock dinner they went to the sitting-room, where Mrs Shaw read philosophy, Shaw sat in

296

a corner reading or writing, and Loraine occupied himself with a book. They bathed regularly at 10.30 a.m. Shaw told me what happened to them one rough morning: 'I was bathing with Robert Loraine at Llanbedr in north Wales when the flood tide turned and we were swept out to sea and had five or ten minutes of certainty that we were for it. I swam until I was exhausted. My last kick struck a stone. Instead of saying Thank God I said Damn! Then we found ourselves standing up to our knees in water on solid ground. I concluded that it was a sandbank; but the natives told me that it was an old abandoned causeway. To America probably. I knew it was no use swimming against the current and so had my mind quite free for the appropriate reflections. After dismissing the possibility of a rescue from the shore (a quite cool calculation) I thought of two things only. (1) That in my will I had made no provision for agreements with my translators. (2) That my wife would wonder why I was not back for lunch.' When they were safely on land Shaw remarked 'That was a near thing,' and went off to fetch his sandshoes.

The plays he wrote in the years 1907-11 were not of much account. *Getting Married,* produced at the Haymarket Theatre in 1908, and *Misalliance,* at the Duke of York's Theatre in 1910, were daring experiments in the Aristotelian unities, which Shaw always defended as of cardinal importance. Both were exceptionally long plays—an hour over the usual three-act length; and both were in a single act with unity of time and place unbroken. The curtain had to descend twice for the convenience of the audience; but when it rose again the characters were just where they were when it fell, and their discourse continued as if there had been no interruption. Neither play had anything even remotely resembling a plot: they simply showed a day in a bishop's palace and a day at a Surrey villa. The saving in scenery and dresses pleased the management; but the critics complained that the plays were not plays but long talks, upon which Shaw challenged them to name any play that was not a long talk, and asked whether they had expected a ballet. He provoked them by such booby traps as announcing them as discussions, conversations and the like, instead of as classical comedies depending on contrasts and conflicts of character and brainy dialogue.

Getting Married was a success on the modest high-brow

297

scale at the Haymarket Theatre, where it ousted an old-fashioned play by Sydney Grundy. The critics mostly fell into the booby trap; but the unities triumphed. There can be no doubt that in his return to them Shaw was influenced by .Gilbert Murray's translations of the plays of Euripides, which had been a feature—the noblest feature, said Shaw—at the Court Theatre under the Vedrenne-Barker management.

Misalliance was not so fortunate. Charles Frohman, an American manager who ran the Duke of York's Theatre in London, was tempted by Barrie and Barker to turn it into a large-scale Repertory Theatre. He fell, and witnessed with growing amazement such plays as Barker's *The Madras House,* Galsworthy's *Justice,* Shaw's *Misalliance,* and a triple bill comprising playlets by Barrie, Pinero and Shaw, whose contribution was *Overruled.* The stupefaction with which Frohman sat through these plays, the like of which he had neither seen nor dreamt of, was surpassed by his horror when he studied the box-office returns; and although he was assured that houses averaging £120 were unbelievably good for high-brow drama, he preferred the class of business in which he could believe, bade Barker a firm farewell, and did his best to erase the word 'Repertory' from his memory. *Misalliance* vanished after a few performances; and the audiences seemed to think that *Overruled* should never have appeared, for when I asked Shaw whether he had ever been hissed or hooted since the memorable Sunday performance of *Widowers' Houses,* he replied: 'I once experienced something far worse than a hissing or a hooting, and that was polite indifference expressed by half-hearted applause from a few well-wishers and dead silence from the large majority. But I had a companion in my misfortune, no other than Sir Arthur Pinero. It was during Charles Frohman's attempt to establish a repertory at the Duke of York's Theatre a year or two before the first World War. Everyone thought it would be a wonderful thing if the playbill could announce three one-act plays by the three leading dramatists of the hour: Pinero, Barrie and myself. Accordingly we set to work. Pinero did a neat bit of craftsmanship called *The Widow of Wasdale Heath.* I did what I thought an entertaining thing called *Overruled.* Barrie did a charming piece of barriefication called *Rosalind.* Pinero's playlet fell flat, mine fell flatter, and by contrast Barrie's magic worked as it never had before and never has done since. The relief to the audience after the Pinero-Shaw mystifications was stupendous. They simply howled for Barrie, whose pleasant little comedy made them realize how much they had hated us. If we had dared to take a call after the show, one author would have been carried shoulder-high round Trafalgar Square, the other two would have been torn limb from limb. Next morning Frohman's producer, Dion Boucicault, rang me up to suggest a few cuts. I replied that there were only two possible cuts—Pinero's piece and my own—and I advised him to advertise a WARN-ING in capital letters in the press and over the box-office window, with the following simple statement beneath: "Mr Barrie's piece commences at 10, before which the theatre bars are open." '

Shaw then relapsed into crude melodrama with *The Shew-ing-Up of Blanco Posnet,* which, completed in March 1909 for a projected benefit' performance in aid of a Children's charity at His Majesty's Theatre, terrified Beerbohm Tree even more than *Missalliance* had terrified Frohman, though the part of Blanco, written for Tree, would have fitted him like a glove. He was rescued by the Lord Chamberlain, who refused to license it, taking it to be blasphemous. Really it was, as Shaw claimed, a religious tract. It was produced by Lady Gregory at the Abbey Theatre, Dublin, in the teeth of official opposition, during Horse Show Week, August 1909. Shaw sent Tolstoy a copy of the play with a letter in which he said that 'To me God does not yet exist; but there is a creative force constantly struggling to evolve an executive organ of godlike knowledge and power: that is, to achieve omnipotence and omniscience; and every man and woman born is a fresh attempt to achieve this object. . . . We are here to help God, to do his work, to remedy his old errors, to strive towards Godhead ourselves.' Tolstoy had complained that in *Man and Superman* Shaw had not been serious enough, that he had made people laugh in his most earnest moments. 'But why should I not?' Shaw rejoined innocently. 'Why should humor and laughter be excommunicated? Suppose the world were only one of God's jokes, would you work any the less to make it a good joke instead of a bad one?' Tolstoy received 'a painful impression' from this. Apparently he could not see himself as part of a joke, either good or bad, which was a pity.

Just after finishing *Blanco Posnet* Shaw and his wife went

motoring through Algeria, and while there he wrote a topical skit called *Press Cuttings*. This too was censored; but the suffragettes achieved a production by the trick of forming a club and giving 'private' performances, membership carrying tickets with it.

That same year the Lord Chamberlain prevented the public performance of Maeterlinck's *Monna Vanna*, because the leading lady repeatedly threatened to undress on the stage. Immediately such a clamour rose from the nudists that parliament appointed a committee to go into the question of the censorship. Shaw prepared a long pamphlet, which paralysed the committee, and gave evidence, which floored them. For us the interesting thing in his evidence is the revelation of his legal frame of mind. A single instance will suffice. Having asserted that 'a very large percentage of the performances which take place at present on the English stage under the censorship licence have for their object the stimulation of sexual desire', and having corrected the chairman's phrase 'sexual immorality' to 'sexual vice', he was asked by the chairman:

'I gather that while you think that the theatre should be uncontrolled in relation to religious representations and political representations, there should be power of prosecution if incitements to sexual vice take place on the stage. . . ?'

'No,' he answered, 'I could not admit that, because if you prosecute for incentives to sexual vice you immediately make it possible to prosecute a manager because the principal actress has put on a pretty hat or is a pretty woman. I strongly protest against anything that is not quite definite. You may make any law you like defining what is an incentive to sexual vice, but to lay down a general law of that kind with regard to unspecified incentives to sexual vice is going too far, when the mere fact of a woman washing her face and putting on decent clothes, or anything of the kind, may possibly cause somebody in the street who passes to admire her and to say, "I have been incited to sexual vice." These generalizations are too dangerous. I do not think that any lawyer should tolerate them.'

He summed up his personal grievances in the statement that the censor had 'absolutely at his disposal my livelihood and my good name without any law to administer behind him. That, it appears to me, is a control past the very last pitch of despotism.' But other despots afforded him some consolation: 'In Germany and Austria I had no difficulty: the system of publicly aided theatres there, Court and Municipal, kept drama of the kind I dealt in alive ; so that I was indebted to the Emperor of Austria for magnificent productions of my works at a time when the sole official attention paid me by the British Court was the announcement to the English-speaking world that certain plays of mine were unfit for public performance, a substantial set-off against this being that the British Court, in the course of its private play-going, paid no regard to the bad character given me by the chief officer of its household.'

Shaw wrote a number of one-act plays in addition to those already mentioned during the period under review. Mostly written for some occasion or some actor, they display his generosity, not his genius, and are hardly worth mentioning, *Great Catherine* and *The Dark Lady of the Sonnets* being the pick of the bunch. The latter was written in response to an appeal for a national theatre by a committee of wealthy and eminent people, inspired thereto by the forthcoming ter-centenary of Shakespeare's death. 'After some years of effort,' reported Shaw, 'the result was a single handsome sub-scription from a German gentleman. Like the celebrated swearer in the anecdote when the cart containing all his household goods lost its tailboard at the top of the hill and let its contents roll in ruin to the bottom, I can only say, "I cannot do justice to this situation," and let it pass without another word.'

In *Fanny's First Play* (1911) he ridiculed the dramatic critics who had steadily refused to accept his plays as 'plays' in their sense of the word, an attitude he should have regarded as a compliment. 'I have not put my name to it,' he said when handing it to Lillah McCarthy, and he urged her to 'do every-thing to suggest the play is by Barrie. . . . You can say with a good conscience that the author's name begins with a capital B.' It was a potboiler, and it kept the pot boiling, hav-ing a record run (for Shaw) of over 600 consecutive per-formances. It was not a big money-maker, its long run being due to a reasonably low-salaried cast and a small low-rented theatre. He did not like to be told that it was beneath his genius. The first letter I ever received from him was in answer to a string of questions, one of which implied that *Fanny's First Play* was not up to scratch:

'If you wont read my works by degrees, you must at least

301

ask questions about them by degrees. How can I answer for my whole life to you between one bit of crowded work and another? You are worse than the Recording Angel.

'Hastily, I have said a good deal about judges and the criminal law in the course of my writings; and I do not know that I have anything to add. I wish I had taken làw up as a profession, as it is a subject that interests me very strongly; but it is too late now, and I have said my say as to the general human aspect of it.

'I do not waste my time writing pot-boilers: the pot must be boiled, and even my *pot au feu* has some chunks of fresh meat in it.

'The Golden Treasury is no doubt needed, but I have to take my work as it comes. Other people must do the same. There is no royal road to Shavianism. My wife has made a book of "selected passages"—but it is no use. The mess of plays, prefaces, tracts and articles from which my philosophy has to be extracted is not only the form imposed by circumstances, but the only form in which it can be properly assimilated. I have no time to boil myself down; and anyhow I could not do so and preserve all the necessary nutriment and the flavoring on which the digestibility depends.'

Shaw soon made up for all his polemics, pot-boilers and *pièces d'occasion* with a masterpiece, *Androcles and The Lion*, produced by Granville Barker and financially backed by Lord Howard de Walden, at the St James's Theatre on September 1st, 1913. Agreeing with Max Beerbohm's view that *Peter Pan* was an artificial freak which missed its mark completely, and was foisted on children by the grown-ups, Shaw confessed, 'I wrote *Androcles and The Lion* partly to show Barrie how a play for children should be handled.' Doubtless the children would have thoroughly enjoyed it, but unfortunately the grown-ups, never having given Christianity a thought, considered the play blasphemous, and instead of foisting it on their offspring forbade them to see it.

In many of his dramatic discussions I had received the impression that Shaw wrote the dialogue without worrying about who would speak it and then fitted it to the characters, so I asked him if this were the case. 'Certainly not,' he replied: 'My dialogue and characters are absolutely inextricable, each being of the essence of the other. I write the dialogue first, leaving the mechanical business of the stage for the revision ; but I usually find that I have sub-consciously seen everything theatrically from the start.' With *Androcles* there could never have been much doubt ; the characters, being religious types, are more clearly differentiated and more vividly conceived than in any other of his plays. The Emperor, too, is perfectly done, the reason being that he is rightly drawn as a self-conscious type. All Shaw's best characters, as I have said, express religious emotion in one form or another ; his other characters are self-conscious, or at least Shaw-conscious : that is, they say the sort of thing and strike the sort of attitude expected of them, conscious that it is funny, or profound, or stupid, or what-not. Thus, apart from the religious, the only kind of character of which he can give a convincing portrayal is the purely self-conscious type, the polished, urbane, witty, intelligent, master-of-himself, Shavian aristocrat, such as the Emperor in *Androcles,* General Burgoyne in *The Devil's Disciple,* and Charles II, all of whom are the creatures of Shaw's intellect, just as his religious characters are the creatures of his soul.

I first set eyes on Shaw at a rehearsal of *Androcles and The Lion.* Having gone on the stage in 1911 and spent a year or so with Tree at His Majesty's Theatre, my next engagement was with Granville Barker, who cast me for the part of Metellus in *Androcles,* probably the only character in all Shaw's plays who could truthfully be described by the author as 'not a talker'. Barker drilled us through August and Shaw entered like an avalanche when we were all standing about in our costumes and make-up before the curtain went up on the final dress-rehearsal. At its conclusion he reappeared and began to go through the notes he had made, upsetting Barker's instructions in a manner that can only be described as outrageously light-hearted. To give an example from my own part : at one point in the last act I had to check Lavinia, who was addressing the Emperor in a presumptuous manner. Barker had told me to do it with a kind of scandalized dignity. But Shaw said, 'Good gracious! you mustn't behave like an offended patrician. You must treat her as one who has committed sacrilege. Jump at her! Fling yourself between them! Shut her mouth! Assault her!' In the course of four hours Shaw transformed the play from a comedy into an extravaganza. He danced about the stage, spouting bits from all parts with folded arms, turned our serious remarks into amusing quips and our funniments into tragedies, always exaggerating so as to prevent our imitating him, and making us all feel we were acting in a charade. Meanwhile, Barker had retired from the contest and was looking on at the destruction of his month's work with a face that registered amusement and annoyance in about equal degree. Yet, though Shaw got every ounce of fun out of the acting, he did it with the sound Shakespearean object of putting every ounce of emotion into the play: by contrast with the comedy, the tragedy was all the more grim. 'Be very careful not to start public opinion on the notion that Androcles is one of my larks,' he warned Percy Burton, who was arranging for the American production: 'It will fail unless it is presented as a great religious drama—with leonine relief.' Incidentally he visited the London Zoo with the actor who played the lion and wanted to study the movements of lions before getting to work on his very unleonine part. There was no lion in the least like the friend of Androcles; but Shaw was delighted to be allowed to handle a magnificent maneless lion and to pet a cheetah.

The generation that had been nurtured on *The Sign of the Cross* and other pseudo-religious dramas could see nothing but irreligious tomfoolery in *Androcles*, and the imbecility of the pre-Shaw dramatic critics almost made the author lose his temper. 'Have you seen tonight's *Pall Mall Gazette*?' he asked Lillah McCarthy. 'I see no prospect of anyone (except myself) kicking the British Public into good manners. I shall peg away until the theatre is as silent as the grave.' The programme (two plays) did not draw its excessive expenses long; and after eight weeks of the overloaded double bill Barker revived in rapid succession plays by Molière, Ibsen, Maeterlinck, Galsworthy, Masefield and Shaw, whose *Doctor's Dilemma* was the success of the repertory and encouraged Barker to transfer the company to the Savoy when his tenancy of the St James's ran out. Shaw shared the rehearsing of his own work with Barker; but from a card to Sutro on December 3rd we may guess that this method of throwing on plays at a moment's notice did not appeal to him: 'I shall have to dash in and out again, as *The Doctor's Dilemma*, down for production on Saturday, is not within three weeks of being decently ready; but I will appear: Have some cheese sandwiches and a lettuce for me. That, and a bottle of ginger beer, is all I need. I am getting too old for hot lunches: they dissolve the soul within me.'

From highbrow drama drawing £800 a week at best Shaw now suddenly jumped to a huge box-office success at the largest fashionable theatre in the west end with the arch enchantress Mrs Patrick Campbell in the leading part. *Pygmalion* was produced at His Majesty's on April 11th, 1914. Back in the early nineties she had captivated him by her piano-playing in *The Second Mrs Tanqueray*, and when she became Forbes-Robertson's leading lady he began to rave about her physical dexterity, declaring, to her great indignation, not that she was a great actress, but that she could thread a needle with her toes. In February '97 we find Ellen Terry reproving him: 'So now you love Mrs Pat Cat?' And in September of the same year, after seeing Robertson's Hamlet and Mrs Campbell's Ophelia, he got the first idea for *Pygmalion,* some fifteen years before he wrote it: '*Caesar and Cleopatra* has been driven clean out of my head by a play I want to write for them, in which he shall be a west-end gentleman and she an east-end dona in an apron and three orange and red ostrich feathers.' Already he was thinking of her as 'that rapscallionly flower girl'. The years went by and one evening he dropped in to see *Bella Donna* at the St James's Theatre. George Alexander sent for him between the acts. 'Why don't you write a play for us?' asked the actor-manager. Shaw went away and wrote *Pygmalion*. Having finished it, he read it to Alexander, who said 'That play is a cert, a dead cert. Now listen to me. I will get you any actress you like to name for the flower girl. I will pay any salary she asks. You can settle your own terms. But go on for another play with Mrs Campbell I will *not*. I'd rather die.' But Shaw had already promised the part to that lady, for whom he had written it.

'It is almost as wonderful a fit as Brassbound; for I am a good ladies' tailor, whatever my shortcomings may be,' he informed Ellen Terry.

But there was danger ahead. No leading lady, least of all such a splendid person as Mrs Campbell, would 'see herself' as a vulgar dirty flower girl, using awful language, wearing an apron and three ostrich feathers, having her hat put in the oven to kill the livestock, and being removed from the stage for a good scrubbing. Shaw funked the ordeal: he simply dared not offer it to her as a part that would fit her like a glove. So he asked his friend Edith Lyttelton if he might come and read the play to her, and if she would arrange for Mrs

Campbell to drop in for tea the same day. Accordingly Mrs Campbell dropped in 'reeking from *Bella Donna*', quite innocent of the plot, and keen to enjoy her favourite sport of disconcerting and humiliating authors and actors and conceited persons generally. Tea over, the reading began. Shaw described to me what followed. All went well until he came to the first 'Ah-ah-ah-oh-oh-oh-oo!' of the Flower Girl. Mrs Campbell, not yet dreaming that the guttersnipe girl was the leading part, saw her chance and took it. 'Oh, please, Mr Shaw, please! Not that unpleasant noise: it's not nice.' Unmoved, Shaw continued reading, and presently he repeated the cry more cacophonously. Again she broke in, 'No, no, no, really, Mr Shaw, you mustn't make that horrible sound. It's vulgar.' Again Shaw took no notice. Again he repeated the 'Aaaaaaaaaaaah-oh-ooh!!!' worse than ever. A frightful suspicion darted into her quick mind. Could this possibly be *her* part? She knew she could do it. Shaw was capable of anything. She dropped her fooling at once, and began to listen attentively. The reading went on in dead silence; after which she was no longer the suburban persifleuse, but the noble and beautiful Italian patrician (she was a hybrid of the two) thanking him with incomparable dignity for the honour he had done her in reading his wonderful play to her and selecting her for the leading part.

It was agreed that he should call on her to talk things over. Before entering the room in which she received him he felt calm, businesslike, hard as nails, insolently confident of his superiority 'to a dozen such Delilahs'. But nobody could resist Mrs Campbell when she went all out for capture. To his astonishment he presently found himself head over ears in love with her, 'and dreamed and dreamed and walked on air for all that afternoon and the next day as if my next birthday were my twentieth'. Business was banished from his mind: 'I could think of nothing but a thousand scenes of which she was the heroine and I the hero. And I am on the verge of 56. There never has been anything so ridiculous, or so delightful, in the history of the world. On Friday we were together for an hour; we visited a lord; we drove in a taxi; we sat on a sofa in Kensington Square; and my years fell from me like a garment. I was in love for nearly 35 hours; and for that be all her sins forgiven her!'

In a few days business reasserted itself. She wanted to do the play under her own management and collar the proceeds.

Who was to play the leading male part? 'She proposed all sorts of impossible people. I proposed Loraine. She would not hear of him. I pressed my choice. She said awful things about him. I repeated them to him. He said unpardonable things about her. I repeated them to her. This sort of Shavian horse-play startled her: she said I was a mischief-maker. I made some more; and finally they had to assure one another of their undying esteem and admiration, which was what I wanted.' But Loraine had to fulfil a contract in America first, and the business-talks ended in rows. 'She said that she would never, never, never play Liza,' and dashed off to Aix-les-Bains for a holiday. All this was in July-August 1912, while arrangements were being made for the play to be done in Berlin and Vienna, in both of which it was seen in the autumn of 1913, before the London production.

Shaw could lose his heart easily enough: after all it was in him only a rudimentary survival from earlier stages of evolution; but he could not lose his head. He knew quite well that domestic life with Mrs Campbell would be impossible. Also it was understood between them that she had made up her mind to marry a friend of his who was equally enslaved, and whose name would give her an unchallengeable standing in London society. Here is his own account of their relations: 'For some years before the war I was on much the same intimate terms with Mrs Campbell as King Magnus with Orinthia in *The Apple Cart*. Yet I was as faithful a husband as King Magnus; and his phrase, "our strangely innocent relations" is true.' As Gregory says in *Overruled*: 'We court the danger; but the real delight is in escaping, after all.' There is a curious prevision of Shaw's relationship with Mrs Campbell in *Misalliance*, when Tarleton says to Lina, 'You touch chords. You appeal to the poetry in a man. You inspire him. . . . I want to make a fool of myself. About you. Will you let me?' Lina asks: 'The lady here is your wife, isnt she? Dont you care for her?' Tarleton replies: 'Yes. And mind! she comes first always. I reserve her dignity even when I sacrifice my own. Youll respect that point of honor, wont you?' Lina wonders: 'Only a point of honor?' Tarleton impulsively rejoins: 'No, by God! a point of affection as well.' We may therefore read without surprise Mrs Campbell's statement that Shaw's 'very well-regulated house came before everything. Whatever might betide Charlotte (Mrs Shaw) must not be kept waiting ten minutes.' No doubt, too, Mrs Campbell, like

Orinthia in the play, sometimes lost patience with what she called his 'inflexible domesticity', and did her best to make him late for his lunch of apples with Charlotte.

'Unlike the general reader,' Shaw had written years before, when he was criticizing music, 'I have been in love, like Beethoven, and have written idiotic love letters, many of which, I regret to say, have *not* been returned ; so that instead of turning up among my papers after my death, they will probably be published by inconsiderate admirers during my lifetime, to my utter confusion. My one comfort is, that whatever they may contain—and no man is more oblivious of their contents than I am—they cannot be more fatuous than Beethoven's.' His prophecy was in due time fulfilled, but the suspicion that it might be did not deter him from plying his new and 'glorious white marble lady' with idiotic love letters.

Years later, when his correspondence with Ellen Terry had an enormous success, Mrs Campbell wanted to repeat and eclipse it with a publication of his letters to her ; but he was adamant in his refusal to allow this. It would be time enough, he said, when the copyright would expire fifty years after his death. Then Mrs Shaw could no longer be annoyed by misunderstandings.

When Mrs Campbell was duly married again, she wrote her own memoirs, and promised the publisher such an incomparable collection of love letters—from a well-known duke, from a famous painter with illustrations, from James Barrie, from Shaw and hosts of others whom she had enchanted—that he advanced £2000 on it. But she had reckoned without the Copyright Act. The executors of the letter-writers absolutely refused to authorize such an exhibition of infatuation ; and Mrs Campbell was left in debt to the publisher with nobody to extricate her but Shaw and Barrie. They had to allow her a few edited samples and thus save the situation for her.

She would not let Shaw see the book in manuscript lest it should be said that he had helped her to write it ; and she did not send him a copy. Long after it was forgotten he came across a copy in New Zealand, and read it there for the first time. Without the lady herself it was nothing, said he.

She called him Joey, the name of the pantomime clown ; and he clowned away to his soul's content, revealing his nature as he turned intellectual somersaults. He told her that his shyness, his cowardice, his lack of self-respect, had been beyond belief ; and he explained why Englishwomen were terrors to young Irishmen: 'If you pay an Irishwoman a gallant compliment, she grins and says, "Arra, g' long with you." An Englishwoman turns deadly pale and says in a strangled voice, "I hope you meant what you have just said." And it is devilish difficult to explain that you didnt.' Lest she should mistake his own feelings, he explained them carefully: 'There are such wonderful sorts of relations, and close togetherness, and babes-in-the-woodinesses, besides being in love, which, as you point out, my diet and feeble nature forbid. I may have moments of being in love, but you must overlook them.'

Meanwhile, *Pygmalion* was being held up by Mrs Campbell's Orinthian moods. Tree came after the play, possibly having heard something of it from Alexander; but .Mrs Campbell at once gave Shaw to understand that Tree had treated her so unpardonably during her last engagement at his theatre that his name must never be mentioned in her presence. Curzon, of the Prince of Wales's, came forward with a most courteous and generous offer of his theatre, which he placed entirely at their disposal for the run of the piece. Mrs Campbell thereupon held Curzon on the telephone for twenty minutes explaining to him that he was not a gentleman, and had interfered impertinently with her private business. Shaw, always too busy to have time for producing a play, and interested in his next play but never in his last one, took no further trouble; and the play might have remained on the shelf but for Mrs Campbell's creditors, who finally became so pressing that she had to come to Shaw and ask 'What about Tree?'

Shaw then inquired about the unpardonable quarrel and found that it was a storm in a teacup; and the play was announced for production at His Majesty's. For years Shaw and Tree had been pleasantly acquainted [1] Like all the theatrical celebrities of that generation, Tree could not accept Shaw as a normal and proper playwright, but had been slowly and reluctantly forced by the facts to admit that he could some-

[1] Shaw had been present as a dramatic critic at the opening of Tree's new theatre, Her Majesty's, in Jubilee Year, 1897, and had described Tree's speech on that occasion: 'Mr Tree told us that he would never disgrace the name the theatre bore; and his air as he spoke was that of a man who, on the brink of forgery, arson, and bigamy, was saved by the feeling that the owner of Her Majesty's Theatre must not do such things.'

how deliver the goods, if only as a sort of Punch and Judy operator, and could write devilishly effective actor's parts.

The rehearsals were terrible. A set of photographs of Shaw, taken immediately after, were suppressed by him because he 'looked like an old dog who had been in a fight and got the worst of it'. Tree, scatter brained and with no rehearsal method and consequently no rehearsal etiquette, was repeatedly guilty of quite unintended but very trying breaches of it. In the middle of a scene somebody would tell him that a visitor had called, whereupon he would walk off and leave the company to await his return for minutes or hours, as the case might be. When on his return he found that Shaw had proceeded with his understudy, he was deeply hurt, and insisted on going back to where he had left off. Shaw did not contest the point, but made it clear by his manner that the incident was not correct; and Tree at last took some pains not to offend again. But what could not be cured was that neither Tree nor Mrs Campbell had the stage technique that Shaw had learnt from Barry Sullivan, Salvini, Coquelin and Ristori. Both had extraordinary personalities which they had learnt how to exploit effectively; but they did not know the A.B.C. of their profession: they only knew the X.Y.Z. Mrs Campbell did not know how to use the front of the stage, at which Shaw was an adept. She wanted too much limelight on her face, not knowing that she was making it look, as Shaw said, like a dinner plate with two prunes on it instead of the beautifully modelled head it actually was. Both of them regarded Shaw as an eccentric outsider who knew nothing about the stage. One day, when the three were lunching together at the Automobile Club, Shaw asked them whether they had noticed that though they had all three risen to the top of the tree in their professions they were all treating one another as beginners who had to be taught everything.

The worst of it was that Tree was entirely sincere in his efforts to do the very best for the play, conceiving it to be his business to turn it into an effective entertainment. The notion that the author had done this beforehand, and that all that remained for him to do was to embody his part exactly as he found it, never entered his head; and it puzzled him that he could think of nothing better than he found cut and dried for him in *Pygmalion*, and that Shaw, with his platform technique, could build up speeches by tricks that were beyond the compass of his voice. Shaw said to him at last, 'We have mistaken our professions. You should have been an author and I an actor.' Tree, who could write quite cleverly, was flattered.

Some of Tree's defects were useful on the stage. He was so completely preoccupied with himself that he was always surprised when anyone else spoke; and this delighted Shaw, one of whose hardest tasks as a producer was to induce his actors to speak as if they had never heard their cues before instead of betraying the fact that they knew all about it beforehand.

Of this peculiarity of Tree's, and of the conditions that usually prevailed during rehearsals at His Majesty's Theatre, Shaw wrote:

'Tree always seemed to have heard the lines of the other performers for the first time, and even to be a little taken aback by them. Let me give an extreme instance of this. In *Pygmalion* the heroine, in a rage, throws the hero's slippers in his face. When we rehearsed this for the first time, I had taken care to have a very soft pair of velvet slippers provided; for I knew that Mrs Patrick Campbell was very dexterous, very strong, and a dead shot. And, sure enough, when we reached this passage, Tree got the slippers well and truly delivered with unerring aim bang in his face. The effect was appalling. He had totally forgotten that there was any such incident in the play; and it seemed to him that Mrs Campbell, suddenly giving way to an impulse of diabolical wrath and hatred, had committed an unprovoked and brutal assault on him. The physical impact was nothing; but the wound to his feelings was terrible. He collapsed in tears on the nearest chair, and left me staring in amazement, whilst the entire personnel of the theatre crowded solicitously round him, explaining that the incident was part of the play, and even exhibiting the prompt-book to prove their words. But his *moral* was so shattered that it took quite a long time, and a good deal of rallying and coaxing from Mrs Campbell, before he was in a condition to resume the rehearsal. The worst of it was that as it was quite evident that he would be just as surprised and wounded every time, Mrs Campbell took care that the slippers should never hit him again, and the incident was consequently one of the least convincing in the performance. . . .

'Tree was always attended in the theatre by a retinue of persons with no defined business there, who were yet on the salary list. There was one capable gentleman who could get things done; and I decided to treat him as the stage-manager;

311

but until I saw his name in the bill under that heading I never felt sure that he was not some casual acquaintance whom Tree had met in the club or in the street and invited to come in and make himself at home. Tree did not know what a stage manager was, just as he did not know what an author was. He had not even made up his mind any too definitely what an actor was. One moment he would surprise and delight his courtiers (for that is the nearest word I can find for his staff and entourage) by some stroke of kindness and friendliness. The next he would commit some appalling breach of etiquette by utterly ignoring their functions and privileges, when they had any. It was amiable and modest in him not to know his own place, since it was the highest in the theatre ; but it was exasperating in him not to know anyone else's. I very soon gave up all expectation of being treated otherwise than as a friend who had dropped in ; so, finding myself as free to interfere in the proceedings as anyone else who dropped in would apparently have been, I interfered not only in my proper department but in every other as well ; and nobody gainsaid me. One day I interfered to such an extent that Tree was moved to a mildly sarcastic remonstrance. "I seem to have heard or read somewhere," he said, "that plays have actually been produced, and performances given, in this theatre, under its present management, before you came. According to you, that couldnt have happened. How do you account for it?" "I cant account for it," I replied with the blunt good faith of a desperate man. "I suppose you put a notice in the papers that a performance will take place at half-past eight, and take the money at the doors. Then you *have* to do the play somehow. There is no other way of accounting for it." On two such occasions it seemed so brutal to worry him, and so hopeless to advance matters beyond the preliminary arrangement of the stage business (which I had already done), that I told him quite cordially to put the play through in his own way, and shook the dust of the theatre from my feet. On both occasions I had to yield to urgent appeals from other members of the cast to return and extricate them from a hopeless mess ; and on both occasions Tree took leave of me as if it had been very kind of me to look in as I was passing to see his rehearsals, and received me on my return as if it were still more friendly of me to come back and see how he was getting on. I tried once or twice to be-lieve that he was only pulling my leg ; but that was incredible :, his sincerity and insensibility were only too obvious. Finally, I had to fight my way through to a sort of production in the face of an unresisting, amusing, friendly, but heart-breakingly obstructive principal.'

From time to time the confusion was relieved by bouts of repartee between three people. 'Shall we give Shaw a beef-steak and put some red blood into him?' asked Tree one day. 'For heaven's sake don't,' Mrs Campbell chipped in, 'he's bad enough as it is: but if you give him meat no woman in London will be safe.'

Tree wanted to play the dustman, but yielded to Shaw's reminder that he must not play a secondary part in his own theatre. He had never met or heard of such a person as a professor of phonetics (his own diction was, as Shaw put it, 'the same as all the rest of him, like nothing on earth') and could not conceive a hero who was not a Romeo. He set to work to make the brusque professor sympathetic in the character of a lover; but Shaw had given him no opportunities for that; and he was quite baffled until he lit on the unhappy thought of throwing flowers to Eliza in the very brief interval between the end of the play and the fall of the curtain.

Mrs Campbell, preoccupied just then with her matrimonial scheme, would not get to work. She came to the theatre and repeated her lines listlessly and only half-audibly. When Shaw sent her a note she returned it unopened, and reduced him to enclosing a further communication in a typewritten trades-man's envelope. When the rest of the play was ready, and the date of production threateningly close at hand, she had hardly given it a day's serious attention. She demurred to Shaw's arrangement of the furniture, and lost no chance of furtively pushing it up stage. Shaw finally told the stage manager to screw it down, but gave her leave to push the grand piano where she pleased. There were moments when Tree rushed about the theatre with his hands raised to heaven, screaming in his rage and despair. But Stella had her part up her sleeve all the time, and did not make a single mistake 'on the night'.

The play had an enormous success everywhere, no matter who played it. It was Shaw's *As You Like It*. On the London run Tree netted £13,000. In the highest spirits he discussed a revival with Shaw one morning as they walked home together from the Council of the Academy of Dramatic Art. A few days later Tree suddenly and astonishingly died.

An attempt by Mrs Campbell to revive *Pygmalion* in London in her own fashion, with the professor transformed into a courteous and adoring worshipper, came to nothing. Shaw attended one performance, laughed, and went to sleep. Before that Barrie had fallen under the spell and had written a new play for her. Had she been twenty years younger it might conceivably have succeeded as a *jeu d'esprit*. It presented her as a murderess whose charm was so irresistible that she was forgiven by everyone, including the judge and jury who tried her. But the waning charm failed; the audience, feeling that its intelligence was being insulted, refused to condone the murder; and the result was the instant and catastrophic withdrawal of the play. It was actually hissed. It was her only failure, and Barrie's only mistake. After the *Pygmalion* revival she appeared in London in elderly parts in two very successful plays; but Shaw and Pinero, for whom she had earned fortunes, though they wrote new plays with parts she could once have played to perfection (Iris, Hesione, Orinthia, Prola), did not cast her for them; and the older managers mostly felt as Alexander had felt.

Her second marriage was a failure. To love Stella was inevitable, to live with her impossible. She went to America, to find herself unwanted there. Later on she found herself in Paris, unable to come to England because it would have involved six months separation from her pet dog. As her means were becoming exhausted, she moved to Pau in the Pyrenees, where living was cheaper. There she had an attack of pneumonia, 'not necessarily fatal, but,' said her doctor, 'I cannot save the life of a patient who has no intention of living.' And so she died. Her last intelligible words were about 'Joey'. Her old adorers were free at last to remember only that side of her which was noble, generous, and honourably proud.

EN PANTOUFLES

WHEN I FIRST SAW HIM in 1913 Shaw's hair was white; yet only nine years before someone had described his beard as red; the transformation had therefore taken place between the ages of 48 and 57, and during the same period he had become world-famous. His mother lived to see him grow white with notoriety. He was able to keep her in comfort for the last ten years or so of her life, but he told me that she took no interest in his activities.

'Surely she was interested in your music criticism?' I said.

'I dont suppose she ever read a word of it.'

'But your plays: did she never see them?'

'Good gracious, no! Wait a moment though. She must have read *Misalliance* because I remember she called Tarleton's daughter "a horrid girl!" So she is, by the way.'

In 1912 he refused an invitation in these words: 'My own mother (82) has just had a stroke; Charlotte is blue and gasping for life in paroxysms of asthma and bronchitis; and I am rehearsing no less than three plays: therefore my reply to your letter is a hollow laugh.' The following year his mother died. He had never been on bad terms with her. 'We lived together until I was forty-two years old, absolutely without the smallest friction of any kind; yet when her death set me thinking curiously about our relations, I realized that I knew very little about her.' He chose Granville Barker to accompany him as sole other mourner at the cremation. He had a horror of earth burial, knowing too much of it from behind the scenes of Mount Jerome, Dublin's great extramural Protestant cemetery, of which his uncle-in-law was resident secretary and manager. The service was Church of England, not because his mother had ever had any relations with that institution but for two reasons: (1) Shaw felt that as between one professional man and another he could not decently do the chaplain out of his fee. (2) He wanted to test the service by its effect on himself. Accordingly he and Granville Barker sat it out, they two and the chaplain being the only persons present.

The effect was not satisfactory. When later on the Reverend Dick Sheppard, who ranked Shaw as a considerable religious influence, asked him to revise the Prayer Book, he condemned the burial service very strongly as morbid and macabre. But when he went behind the scenes and saw the coffin pushed into what seemed a chamber radiant with sunshine, and bursting into twirling ribbons of soaring garnet-coloured flame, he was transported by the wonderful aesthetic effect, and became more ardent then ever in his advocacy of cremation, which

315

he carried to the length of declaring that earth burial should be made a criminal offence.

When the furnace closed he went for a walk with Granville Barker. Before they returned the cremation was finished. They found the calcined remains of Mrs Carr Shaw strewn on a stone table at which two men in white caps and overalls, looking exactly like cooks, were busily picking out and separating the scraps of molten metal and wood ash, so as to leave nothing on the table but the authentic relics of the deceased lady. Shaw's sense of humour at once extinguished his sense of propriety. He felt that his mother was looking over his shoulder and sharing his amusement. He was recalled to the decencies of the occasion by Granville Barker's amazed comment: 'You certainly are a merry soul, Shaw.'

At the funeral service of Mrs H. G. Wells many years later he advised Wells, who was greatly distressed, to enter the furnace-room. 'Take the boys and go behind: they should see it. It's beautiful. I saw my mother burnt there. You'll be glad if you go.' Wells went, and was glad he went. 'It was indeed very beautiful,' he agreed.

At the cremation of Shaw's sister after the Four Years' War the scene was very different. The will of the deceased absolutely forbade any religious service. Yet Shaw found himself confronted, not with a solitary friend, but with a crowd that filled the chapel, all strangers to him, and all devoted to 'darling Lucy'. They expected a ceremony, and he told me how he met the difficulty. 'I could not let her be thrown on the fire without a word, like a scuttleful of coals. So I had to mount the pulpit and deliver a full dress elegy, concluding with the dirge from *Cymbeline*. Coal was very scarce then; and Lucy burnt with a steady white light like that of a wax candle.'

After hearing him describe these experiences I was not surprised to learn that he had shares in several of the new crematoria.

Shaw had a Kiplingesque love of knowing how things were done; technicalities delighted him; and he liked visiting laboratories and peeping at bacteria through the microscope. Machine tools of all kinds interested him; and so did pianolas, gramophones, wireless, and calculators; but for old-fashioned factory machinery his contempt was boundless: he said a louse could have invented it all if it had been keen enough on profits. He experimented for hours with his cameras, and

316

never tired of talking about photography to people who were equally enthusiastic. When nearly sixty he bought a motor-bicycle, rode it away from the factory for 77 miles, took a corner near his house too sharply; and contemplated the machine from a different angle. Until he was past eighty his favourite exercises were motoring and swimming. When at Ayot he dashed through the country lanes on a bicycle or in a car. When in London he swam every morning before break-fast, winter and summer, in the bathing-pool at the Royal Automobile Club. 'As an Irishman I dislike washing myself,' he said, 'but I cannot do without the stimulus of a plunge into cold water.' Such were his hobbies. He never played games, explaining that no one liked playing with him because he did not care whether he won or lost, and flatly declined to bother his head with counting scores when he was amusing himself.

But in other respects his activity was amazing, and when exhausted by overwork he had to go into a dark room and lie for hours flat on the floor on his back with all his muscles relaxed. Except on such occasions, of which only his wife was aware, he was incurably restless. Even when conversing he could not keep still: jumping up and sitting down, crossing and uncrossing his legs, shoving his hands in his pockets or pulling them out, sitting straight up or lying right back in his chair, bending forward, stretching backward, never remaining in one position for two minutes together.

His clothes were perhaps symbolic of his soul: at least they differed from everyone else's. His collars were always soft and he did not wear a shirt, believing that it was wrong to swaddle one's middle with a double thickness of material. Instead, he wore some head-to-foot undergarment known only to its maker. He made a suit of clothes last him from six years to sixteen: 'The result is that my clothes acquire in-dividuality, and become characteristic of me. The sleeves and legs cease to be mere tailor-made tubes; they take human shape with knees and elbows recognizably mine.' His reputa-tion for sartorial eccentricity once put him in an awkward position. R. B. Haldane, the liberal politician, gave a dinner-party to a number of social nobs—Balfour, the Asquiths, and so on—and having heard of Shaw's refusal to wear evening clothes as a dramatic critic, asked him to come in morning dress. Assuming he was going to meet a few Labour M.P.s, and, excepting his evening dress, having nothing but his everyday clothes to appear in, Shaw bought a respectable black suit with his hard-earned savings, and walked right into a party of white shirt-fronts and low necks, the only person not dressed for the occasion. 'It was a social galaxy which I could depict only by quoting Byron's description of the Waterloo ball at Brussels in 1815. I felt, as to my double-breasted tailless jacket, like a ship's purser at a wedding, and, as to my trousers, like a city missionary. But I did my best to make them all feel that they had committed a painful solecism in dressing for dinner. I took Margot Asquith in to dinner with unshattered *aplomb* and carried it off as best I could. But the surest way of making me swear is to revive the legend of my objection to wearing evening dress.'

Although it seemed almost impossible for Shaw to sit still doing nothing, Mrs Shaw's determination to have a worthy memorial of him in his prime forced him to begin his remarkable series of experiences as an artist's model which at last drove H. G. Wells to complain that it was difficult to move about Europe without knocking against some effigy of his eminent contemporary. Fortunately for us he wrote an account of his sittings to Jacob Epstein, the last great sculptor to tackle him, which is available to me for quotation. Here are the relevant passages:

'I have just finished reading your [Epstein's] book, from which I have learnt a good deal, learning being one of the privileges of old age. To repay you I will tell you some things you dont know. Being a creator you have not had to learn them; but I, being a critic, had to. I stood one day in the Paris Salon with Paul Troubetskoy, in a wilderness of statues: acres and acres of them, it seemed. Paul looked glumly over the wilderness and said with complete conviction, "There is no sculpture here. These men are not sculptors." I quite understood what he meant; but when I was earning my bread and butter by criticism such a *dictum* would have led to my being immediately sacked. What he said was in its entirety neither true nor untrue; and it was my business to find out how much of it was true and how much untrue. These poor fellows who were "not sculptors" had as much right to live as Paul: they could all model or carve images of a sort; and some of them were getting well paid for them whilst Paul's bill for his daily dinners at a leading hotel was eighteen months in arrear.

'Since then I have sat to so many well-known sculptors and painters that H. G. Wells complains that he cannot move about Europe without knocking against some image of me. That gives me an experience that you lack; so I will tell you all about it. I began with Rodin, who, never having heard of me, made every possible excuse to avoid a job that had no interest for him. But my wife would not be put off. She ascertained from the poet Rilke, then acting as Rodin's secretary, what his terms were. Rilke named £1000 for a marble, or £800 for a bronze. She then wrote to Rodin explaining that her husband was a famous writer with a great knowledge of art; that she wanted a memorial of him; and that he had refused to sit to anyone but Rodin, declaring that he would go down to posterity as a fool if, being within reach of Rodin, he selected any lesser genius. She also lodged £1000 in his bank on the understanding that it was a contribution to the general expenses of his activities, and that it placed him under no obligation to do a bust of me, or, if he began such a work, to continue it or finish it, or postpone any more important work for it.

'Rodin could not resist such treatment. He asked would it be possible for me to come to Paris and sit to him there in the studio provided by the French Government for the completion of his *Gate to Hell* (which he accordingly took care not to complete). We were there next morning. I suppose he rather liked us; for after a little talk he asked, with some hesitation and an evident fear that he might be going too far, whether it would be at all possible for me to make daily journeys to Meudon and sit to him in his home studio. We said that I would sit to him wherever and whenever would be most convenient to him, and that I should be at Meudon next day at ten. This made him perfectly happy; and for the next month I spent my days at Meudon and became quite at home there. It was a curious experience, for the bust, which began at the end of fifteen minutes work like a brilliant sketch by Sarah Bernhardt, went through the whole history of sculpture since the Middle Ages. When it reached the twelfth century it was such a jewel that I begged him to let me take it away; but he said he could "carry it further"; and to my horror it became successively a Bernini, a Canova or Thorwaldsen, a Gibson or Foley, before it finally became a Rodin. Nothing like this has occurred again in my experience as a sitter. Another point in which he was unique was that he worked like

319

a draughtsman rather than a sculptor, turning the bust and making me turn almost inch by inch and modelling profile by profile, testing every dimension by his callipers. At the end of a month he said he would carry it no further at present, but whenever I came to Paris we could go on with it. Of course we never did ; but it was clear that he never regarded a portrait bust as finished as long as the sitter was alive ; for he complained that his sitters got tired of sitting and sent forged telegrams to themselves calling them away on pressing business to escape. He had never, he said, had a sitter who stuck to it as I did, and he would carry the bust further than he had ever been able to carry one before.

'Now for the merits and failures of the bust. When my wife said something to him about the way in which artists persisted in drawing my reputation instead of drawing myself, he said, "I know nothing of Monsieur Shaw's reputation ; but what there is there I will give you." He should have said, "What I can see in him I will give you." This should interest you ; for Rodin with his callipers was extremely conscientious in getting the visible physical facts right, whereas you disregard them to the point of flat mendacity. That is why your sitters' wives cannot endure your busts. You have not learnt the first lesson of a fashionable sculptor, which is : that no woman will look twice at a bust of her husband if its hair is not properly brushed.

'Well, what were the visible physical facts that Rodin had to suggest in clay? I am a civilized Irishman with a thin skin and hair of exceptionally fine texture, always well-brushed. Though six feet high, I weighed only ten stone eight instead of twelve stone ten or thereabouts. I am obviously a brain worker, not a manual laborer. All this Rodin conveyed perfectly. As we talked and talked, in that lingua franca of philosophy and art which is common to all languages, I made myself known to Rodin as an intellectual and not as a savage, nor a pugilist, nor a gladiator. He gave that in the bust unmistakeably. But I am a comedian as well as a philosopher ; and Rodin had no sense of humor. I think I saw him laugh once, when I took a specially sweet tit-bit from Madame Rodin, and gave half of it to his dog Kap. I am not quite sure that he went as far as to laugh even then. Accordingly, the bust has no sense of humor ; and Shaw without a sense of humor is not quite Shaw, except perhaps to himself. Here the barrier of language was unsurmountable. I am hopeless as a linguist and cannot joke in French. When a lady asked Rodin whether I spoke French well, he replied with his characteristic serious veracity, "Mr Shaw does not speak French well; but he expresses himself with such violence that he imposes himself."

'When Troubetskoy saw the Rodin bust he said, "This face has no eyes. All Rodin's busts are blind." He swooped down on me and demanded one sitting of half an hour. He was not a man to be refused: at all events I could not refuse him. The half-hour of course meant three hours, and involved two sittings in Sargent's studio, where Troubetskoy flung clay about so recklessly that he covered not only himself but Sargent's pictures and carpets with it. At the second sitting everything was covered with canvas. Troubetskoy, maternally American, paternally Russian, had for his native language a barbarous Milanese dialect, and spoke all the other languages at least better than I spoke French. My humor was as lost on him as on Rodin; but the bust was a marvel as the result of three hours work; and as it made me flatteringly like a Russian nobleman I rather liked it. It is not to be compared to the bust in the Tate Gallery, the life-size statue, and the statuette, all of which he made of me years later from unlimited sittings in his own studio at the Villa Cabianca on Lago Maggiore.

'My next famous sculptor was an American, who knew enough English to regard me as a humorous subject: the very view that was missing in the Rodin and Troubetskoy busts. He was the genial Jo Davidson; and his facial resemblance to Karl Marx was almost perfect. But he had only a few days left before leaving London; and a wrong dimension which I pointed out and which the callipers verified, obliged him to make a change at the last moment which he had not time to incorporate completely. Still, he turned out a lively presentation of me as a jolly old wisecracker.

'Next came a sculptor of whom I had never heard: Sigmund Strobl: a Hungarian. He got all that the others had got and all that they had missed. He was as right as Rodin as to my physical type. In my right and left profiles he shewed the philosopher in the one, and the comedian in the other. My wife made him carve it in marble for her, which he did in an intensely hard block (not Carrara) with apparent ease. Everyone who comes to our house has to look at that bust.

'Finally you, Jacob Epstein, come along, waving your hand over Rodin, Troubetskoy, Davidson and Strobl, and saying in effect, "These men are not sculptors." There is something that you want to get out of me that they have not got. Though I have had more than enough of being a sculptors' model when I should have been writing plays I cannot refuse to sit: you are great enough to claim that a bust by you is a more valuable contribution to the world's art than a play by me. So I sit patiently and you do exactly what you want to do, which is, to strip from me the mask of my civilization, to abolish the artificial refinements copied by Strobl and Rodin, to shew me in my crude humanity as you learnt it in Brooklyn. Your first sketch, copied from the facts before you, is a brilliant thumb-nail version of me as I am. Then you went on to perform marvels of modelling on lips and cheeks and mouth with all the mastery that makes your busts precious. But you had also to introduce the theories with which you are obsessed; and here you were recklessly mendacious. I became a Brooklyn navvy in your hands. My skin thickened, my hair coarsened, I put on five stone in weight, my physical strength trebled. The brilliant sketch became a thundering lie. When the bust went to the Leicester Galleries, a workman, who was evidently a profound critic, completed the effect by putting his hat on it; and a press photographer snapped it in that condition. My wife saw the picture, and immediately said that if that bust came into our house she would walk out of it. She was far more outraged than Mrs Conrad had been; for your Conrad, though a bit unbrushed, is not a savage. There is no question of art here: it is a question of fact. Theoretically I may be only a sickly veneer over a Brooklyn navvy; but without my veneer I am not Bernard Shaw: and without the peculiar critical lift at the outer ends of my eyebrows I am only a barbarous joker and not a high comedian. The bust is a masterpiece; but it is not a portrait. If you desire to leave your wife a bust of yourself as a memorial dont make it yourself: get Strobl to make it. God knows what sort of Brooklyn larrikin you would make of yourself; for not even your self-respect could get the better of your incorrigible atavistic theorizing and your love of Pacific Ocean and Central American stylyzation.

'Talking of that, by the way, what was wrong with the Strand statues (I passed them every day when I lived in Adelphi Terrace) was not the statues but the Strand. And what was wrong with Rima was not Rima but Hyde Park. Nobody ever objected to the statues round the plinth of the

Albert Memorial. They are in their right surroundings there. Nobody would object to Rima in Luxor.

'That is enough for to-day. What it all comes to is that sculptors are set working by two impulses (among others). (1) Some deficiency in the treatment of an interesting stock subject which they believe they can make good. (2) Temptation by the sight of materials. Your Consummatum Est was promoted by a block of alabaster, as Michael Angelo's David was by a giant block of marble.

'Your book was very well written to get all this out of me.'

The Rodin episode produced one of Shaw's rare excursions into rhyme. Rodin's collection was rich in sculpture, though it consisted largely of heaps of broken stones with spots on their surfaces, no larger than postage stamps, on which some sculptor had worked. But of artistic printing and book-making he knew nothing, and was treasuring commonplace presentation volumes of no aesthetic importance. To begin his education in this department Shaw, who was lucky enough to pick up a Kelmscott Chaucer for £50, gave it to Rodin with the inscription:

> I have seen two masters at work, Morris who made this
>   book,
> The other Rodin the Great, who fashioned my head in clay:
> I give the book to Rodin, scrawling my name in a nook
> Of the shrine their works shall hallow when mine are dust
>   by the way.

Shaw had a deep respect for Rodin's truthfulness. When people said that the bust was not like him he always declared, 'This is the thing I am: the others are parts that I play.'

The Chaucer is in the Rodin Museum in Paris. The marble is in the Dublin Municipal Gallery. The bronze is at home with Shaw, as also is the Strobl marble and the Troubetskoy statuette. The early bust by Troubetskoy is in the foyer of the Theatre Guild in New York, the later in the Tate Gallery. The life-size statue, representing Shaw in his pose as an orator, has for the moment disappeared: neither I nor Shaw can trace its whereabouts.

Rodin was not the only Frenchman who had never heard of Shaw, the truth of whose assertion that, artistically, France was half-a-century out of date being confirmed by the tardy recognition of his own works there. One day he found himself with Anatole France in the Sistine Chapel. They climbed a scaffold resembling the old pictures of the Tower of Babel that had been erected to pin up some loosening parts of Michael Angelo's ceiling, and found that at close quarters the frescoes were as finely finished as alabaster reliefs. Anatole France mounted the workman's table and delivered a set speech, dutifully firing off all the conventional phrases—Angelo's wrist of steel and heart of fire and so on—and concluding with a quotation from Théophile Gautier. Shaw wondered how on earth, or even on a rocking Tower of Babel, a man could think of Gautier with the Delphic Sybil staring him in the face. After a perilous descent, France turned to Shaw, known to him only as 'un Monsieur', and, apologizing for not having caught his name, asked who he was. 'Like yourself, a man of genius,' answered Shaw. Staggered by this (to a Frenchman) almost incredible exhibition of bad taste, Anatole could only shrug his shoulders and reply, 'Quand on est courtisane on a le droit de s'appeler marchande de plaisir.' Some years later the Fabian Society gave a grand soirée to Anatole France ; and Shaw, in the chair, eulogized him in a speech the climax of which so moved him that he sprang up, threw his arms round Shaw, and kissed him repeatedly. The ecstatic amusement of the Fabians may be imagined. If France had been staggered in the Sistine Chapel, he certainly got a bit of his own back on this occasion.

Like Shakespeare, Shaw knew little Latin and less Greek, having been at a school where they taught little else. He spoke no language at all fluently except his own, but could make himself understood in French, which he read with ease. In Italy and Spain he could gather the news from the local newspapers, and he had a smattering of German. Occasionally his familiarity with operatic libretti was helpful. He was lunching on one of his tours with the Art Workers' Guild at a café in Milan when the members wanted to have their bills separately. This being too complicated for their scanty Italian they appealed to Shaw to explain. He racked his brains and suddenly remembered a line from the Italian version of Meyerbeer's *Les Huguenots: Ciascun per se ; per tutti il ciel.* (Each for himself ; and heaven for us all.) He said casually, '*Ciascun per se*' ; the waiter said, '*Si, si, signore*' ; and his credit as a master of Italian was firmly founded. Of the Scandinavian and Slavonic tongues he knew no word. Taking advantage of a visit to Stockholm, he called on Strindberg to advise him to appoint William Archer as his English translator. 'Archer is not in sympathy with me,' objected Strindberg. 'Archer wasnt in sympathy with Ibsen either,' returned Shaw, 'but he couldnt help translating him all the same, being accessible to poetry, though otherwise totally impenetrable.' Having reported this conversation verbatim to Archer on a postcard, Shaw continued: 'After some further conversation, consisting mainly of embarrassed silences and a pale smile or two by A.S., and floods of energetic eloquence in a fearful lingo, half-French, half-German, by G.B.S., Strindberg took out his watch and said in German, "At two o'clock I am going to be sick." The visitors accepted this delicate intimation and withdrew.'

Though an erratic improvisor in French and German, Shaw talked English as wittily and well as he wrote it; indeed after 1879, when he began speaking in public, his writings read as if they were verbal discourses; one can catch the tone of the talker in them. An entry in Arnold Bennett's *Journals,* referring to a dinner with H. G. Wells, runs: 'Shaw talked practically the whole time, which is the same thing as saying he talked a damned sight too much.' Bennett thought Shaw self-conscious and egotistic, and felt 'constrained as always in the society of G.B.S.' I asked Shaw whether he had noticed Bennett's constraint. 'Confound him,' cried Shaw, 'I did my utmost to make him talk, but he wouldnt. I had to entertain my guests, and if they wouldnt talk I had to. My wife, who knows all my old stories and conversational stunts by heart, having heard them hundreds of times, often begs me to give other people a chance; and so I do; but they wont take it. They come to hear me talk—to be entertained by me, not to entertain me. When people go to a recital by Paderewski they do not complain that he plays the piano too much. No wonder he often played it as if he hated it. Well, often enough when I speak my piece I have to conceal the fact that I have said it all a hundred times already and am grinding it out again because I have to keep things going. Wells or Belloc or Olivier or Barrie or Nansen, who could and did take the job off my hands and let me eat my lunch in blessed peace, were my most welcome visitors. Even bores were a relief to me.'

Like all accomplished talkers, Shaw talked because he was expected to talk, even when he was tired and would rather have held his tongue. He could switch over to any subject at a moment's notice and talk on it like a book (by himself). His Irish speech, his hearty and frequent laugh, his habit of rubbing his hands vigorously while talking, his lively grey-blue eyes, and the way he flung his arms out to emphasize a point, all gave vitality and charm to his monologues. One of his most lovable social characteristics was his consideration for younger men who felt shy and out of it. Frank Swinnerton never forgot how as a youngster of no account he arrived late, hot and dishevelled for a luncheon party given by H. G. Wells, and how everyone bowed distantly to him except Shaw, who walked right across the room, shook hands and went in to lunch with him.

Another of his characteristics, admirable if not lovable, was the unexpectedness of his repartees. Lady Astor gave me an instance. Over breakfast at Cliveden she remarked, 'I hate killing for pleasure,' a sentiment with which she knew Shaw was in hearty agreement. 'Do you hate killing for pleasure?' one of her children asked Shaw. 'It depends upon who you kill,' he replied. Another example. A strange lady giving an address in Zürich wrote him a proposal, thus: 'You have the greatest brain in the world, and I have the most beautiful body; so we ought to produce the most perfect child.' Shaw asked: 'What if the child inherits my body and your brains?' This story has been foisted on to Isadora Duncan, who was not the lady.

Shaw illustrated for me the difficulty of giving pleasure without pain: 'I was staying with Lady Chudleigh, a devout Roman Catholic, when a Prussianized foreign visitor made the appalling *gaffe* of describing how his brother had been imprisoned for saying that the doctrine of the Immaculate Conception was all rot. Lady Chudleigh, a saintly Catholic, did not know what to say. I at once flung myself into the breach by remarking in my most matter-of-fact manner that all conceptions are immaculate. The Bismarckian collapsed, as this was a leaf out of his own book; and Lady Chudleigh looked gratefully at me. Then her look changed to one of doubt as to whether I had not hit him below the belt; but by that time the social crisis had passed.'

In the same way the people who asked him to lecture frequently got more than they had bargained for, or something they had never bargained for. 'I remember causing an awful rumpus,' he told me, 'when the National Secular Society, looking round just then for a successor to Bradlaugh, sampled me among other possibilities. I lectured them on Progress in Freethought, and proved that all the beliefs they condemned as base superstitions were simple statements of fact: the Trinity, the Immaculate Conception, and so forth. Needless to add, I was not chosen. The old materialist Bible-smashing freethinkers never quite forgave me.'

While exercising all the art of the orator, Shaw (like Lenin) carefully avoided its airs, and talked on the platform always as man to man. He was one of the best public speakers and debaters of his age—to my taste, easily the best. Every word he uttered was heard, as he said, with 'exasperating distinctness'. Standing with military erectness, hands up and active, head tilted back, his beard seeming to bristle, he could hold his audience, when in form, for ninety minutes and leave them wanting more.

Debates between himself and Hilaire Belloc or G. K. Chesterton were sometimes staged, and they were among the most entertaining events in the London of that period. Shaw's description of his two antagonists shows the difference between them. 'Belloc combines the intense individualism and land hunger of a French farmer with the selfless Catholicism and scholarship of an Aristotelian cardinal. He keeps his property in his own hand, and his soul in a safe bank. He passed through the Oxford rowdyism of Balliol and the military rowdyism of the gunner; and this gave him the super-rowdyism of the literary genius who has lived adventurously in the world and not in the Savile Club. A proletariat of Bellocs would fight: possibly on the wrong side, like the peasants of La Vendée; but the Government they set up would have to respect them, though it would also have to govern them by martial law.' For Chesterton, however, 'neither society nor authority nor property nor status are necessary to his happiness: he . . . might be trusted anywhere without a policeman. He might knock at a door and run away—perhaps even lie down across the threshold to trip up the emergent householder; but his crimes would be hyperbolic crimes of imagination and humor, not of malice. He is friendly, easy-going, unaffected, gentle, magnanimous, and genuinely democratic. He can sacrifice a debating point easily: Belloc cannot.' Shaw's remark on another occasion that Belloc believed whatever he did believe 'in a Pickwickian sense', and that Chesterton was a real Peter Pan, a boy who never grew up, merely qualifies without contradicting his

327

previous estimate. He was fond of Chesterton, who wrote in his autobiography: 'I have never read a reply by Bernard Shaw that did not leave me in a better and not a worse temper or frame of mind; which did not seem to come out of inexhaustible fountains of fairmindedness and intellectual geniality . . . I have learned to have a warmer admiration and affection out of all that argument than most people get out of agreement.'

Their argument was carried on in the press as well as on platforms, and at last Chesterton delivered himself of a book on Shaw, who told me what he thought of it: 'Chesterton's book is a very good one in itself. It has little to do with me, as G.K.C. has never made any study of my works, and in one place actually illustrates my limitations by telling the world something I should have made one of the characters say in *Major Barbara* if I could have transcended those limitations: the joke being that it is exactly what I did make the character say, as Chesterton might have found had he taken the trouble to open the book (probably he never possessed a copy) and refer to the passage. But if you leave me out of account, you will find, I think, that the book is full of good things, and very generous into the bargain.'

Neither was biographical accuracy among G.K.C.'s virtues. In his autobiography he stated that Shaw was present at a male party held in a vast tent in a Westminster garden, where the proceedings included the boiling of eggs in Beerbohm Tree's top hat, specially selected because it shone more brightly than the others. Shaw alone remained sober, and at one point got up, sternly protested, and stalked out.

'Chesterton's memory played him a trick,' was Shaw's comment to me. 'I usually avoided all social gatherings for men only, as men would not enjoy themselves decently in the absence of women. All that about a tent in Westminster, and boiling eggs in a top hat, if it really took place, is quite new to me. I wasn't there. But there was a male party in the house of a friend in Westminster at which I sat next Chesterton. After dinner, they began throwing bread at one another; and one of them began making smutty speeches. They were actually drunk enough to expect a contribution from me. I got up and went home. You must remember that I am a civilized Irishman, and you cannot civilize an Englishman, nor an Englishwoman either, except superficially. When I first saw an assembly of respectable and sober English ladies and gentlemen going Fantee, and behaving like pirates debauching after a capture, I was astounded. I am used to it now; but it is not possible for me to take part in such orgies.'

Chesterton professed to believe in fairies, an attitude which Shaw found excusable because he never dragged children into it; but when J. M. Barrie played the trick in *Peter Pan* of making the children in the audience 'scream out the unanimous lie that they believed in fairies', he was shocked by its unscrupulousness. It happened that just after Barrie's death I was asked by a publisher to write his life. I knew very little about him and liked none of his plays except *The Admirable Crichton*; but I sat down to read his works carefully, applying to Shaw and one or two others for any personal reminiscences they cared to pass on. Just after I had decided not to write his life I heard from Shaw:

'I was always on affectionate terms with Barrie, like everyone else who knew him; but though I lived for many years opposite him in the Adelphi and should, one would suppose, have met him nearly every day, we met not oftener than three times in five years in the street. It was impossible to make him happy on a visit unless he could smoke like a chimney (mere cigarettes left him quite unsatisfied)); and as this made our flat uninhabitable for weeks all the visiting was on our side, and was very infrequent.

'I fancy Barrie was rather conscious of the fact that writers have no history and consequently no biography, not being men of action.[1]

'His wife's elopement, and the deaths of some of his adopted children in the war, were the only events in his life I knew of. Though he seemed the most taciturn of men he could talk like Niagara when he let himself go, as he did once with Granville Barker and myself on a day which we spent walking in Wiltshire when he told us about his boyhood. He said that he had bacon twice a year, and beyond this treat had to content himself with porridge. He left me under the impression that his father was a minister; but this was probably a flight of my own imagination. Actually, I believe he was a weaver.

'He had a frightfully gloomy mind, which he unfortunately

---

[1] In that case he must have been unconscious of Plato's *Socrates*, Boswell's *Johnson*, Lockhart's *Scott*, and nearly every great biography in this or any other language.

329

could not afford to express in his plays. Only in child's play could he make other people happy.

'You will have a bit of a job to make a full-sized biography for him; but I daresay you will manage it if anybody can. I really knew very little about him; and yet I suspect that I knew all that there was to be known about him from the official point of view. Anyhow I liked him.'

Barrie knew so little about Shaw that he tried to enlist him in the scratch cricket elevens he loved to get up. A more desperate enterprise can hardly be imagined. Once, however, Shaw allowed himself to take part in a public tomfoolery. In 1913 it seems to have struck a lugubrious member of the Dickens Fellowship that something ought to be done for Dickens or the Fellowship. Accordingly it was decided to hold a public 'Trial of John Jasper for the Murder of Edwin Drood', to be conducted by a number of eminent Dickensians. G. K. Chesterton agreed to act as Judge, Cecil Chesterton as Counsel for the Defence, J. Cuming Walters and B. W. Matz as Counsel for the Prosecution, and Bernard Shaw as Foreman of a Jury wholly composed of prominent authors. The 'Trial' was to be held on January 7th, 1914, in the King's Hall at the National Sporting Club, Covent Garden. The Dickens Fellowship hoped it would bring them much kudos. To them the question of whether John Jasper had murdered Edwin Drood was a weighty one: it had been discussed at many of their meetings. Dickens had taken the secret with him to the grave, and it remained a 'Mystery', worthy to be unravelled by the best brains of the day. They foresaw a great display of forensic ability, a big splash in the papers, a triumph for the Dickens Fellowship. Humour of course was to be expected and even encouraged. An occasional witty fling from G.K.C., a quip or two from G.B.S., a little smart back-chat from Counsel, a ripple of amusement from the audience: such things would help, for after all Dickens had been a bit of a humorist himself. Nevertheless the event was to be solemn and judicial: gravity seasoned with pleasantry was to be the note.

But it was not to be. J. W. T. Ley, writing in *The Dickensian*, explained why. 'This trial was taken seriously, not only by members of the Dickens Fellowship, but by the public at large, by every newspaper of any importance at all, and by almost every critic and author of distinction.' It was, he said, 'regarded by all concerned as a serious effort to find a logical solution of the mystery. Cuming Walters and Cecil Chesterton had gone to very great pains to prepare their cases. Nearly a score of brilliant men had agreed to attend, listen carefully . . . and a true verdict give in accordance with the evidence. In that spirit the whole of the proceedings was conducted, and then right at the very end everything was spoiled by the impishness of Mr G. Bernard Shaw. . . . He wouldn't agree, but most people would, that a very high compliment had been paid him when he was asked to be Foreman of a Jury of such distinction.' According to J. W. T. Ley, Shaw was the only man in the building who treated the thing as a joke ; but when we learn that the case lasted for nearly five hours, we may safely assume that he was the only man in the building who thought the thing past a joke. Anyhow, he did his best to liven it up from the start. Before any evidence had been called, he 'popped up in the box':

Foreman: My lord, one word. Did I understand the learned gentleman to say that he was going to call evidence?
Mr Matz: Certainly.
Foreman: Well then, all I can say is that if the learned gentleman thinks the convictions of a British jury are going to be influenced by evidence, he little knows his fellow-countrymen.
Judge: At the same time, in spite of this somewhat intemperate observation—

The rest of the Judge's remarks were inaudible, the audience having seen the Foreman's point. Later, when Canon Crisparkle was giving evidence, Shaw popped up again:

Foreman: May I ask one question, my lord?
Judge: Certainly.
Foreman: Do I understand the witness to say that the prisoner was a musician?
Witness: He was, my lord.
Foreman: His case looks black indeed.

At the conclusion of his summing-up, G.K.C. said, 'Gentlemen of the Jury, you will retire and consider your verdict.' But the Foreman had not finished popping, and now gave that exhibition of impishness which the Dickensians thought out of place: 'My lord,' said he: 'I am happy to be able to announce to your lordship that we, following the tradition

331

and practice of British juries, have arranged our verdict in the luncheon interval. I should explain, my lord, that it undoubtedly presented itself to us as a point of extraordinary difficulty in this case that a man should disappear absolutely and completely, having cut off all communication with his friends in Cloisterham. But having seen and heard the society and conversation of Cloisterham here in court to-day, we no longer feel the slightest surprise at that. Now, under the influence of that observation, my lord, the more extreme characters, if they will allow me to say so, in this Jury were at first inclined to find a verdict of Not Guilty, because there was no evidence of a murder having been committed ; but, on the other hand, the calmer and more judicious spirits among us felt that to allow a man who had committed a cold-blooded murder, of which his own nephew was the victim, to leave the dock absolutely unpunished, was a proceeding which would probably lead to our all being murdered in our beds. And so you will be glad to learn that the spirit of compromise and moderation prevailed, and we find the prisoner guilty of manslaughter. We recommend him most earnestly to your lordship's mercy, whilst at the same time begging your lordship to remember that the protection of the lives of the community is in your hands, and begging you not to allow any sentimental consideration to deter you from applying the law in its utmost rigour.'

The audience, which had been wonderfully patient for five hours, expressed their appreciation of this speech in a manner that would have forced any English judge to clear the court if the explosion had not followed one of his own jokes. But the Dickensians had a champion in Cuming Walters, who rose and addressed the Judge: 'I should like to urge that the Jury be discharged for not having performed their duties in the proper spirit of the law. We have heard from the Foreman that the verdict was arranged in advance, and I decline to accept that verdict, and ask for your lordship's ruling.' This necessitated a further pop. 'The Jury,' said the Foreman, 'like all British juries, will be only too delighted to be discharged at the earliest moment—the sooner the better.' By this time the Judge, feeling an urgent call to the bar, had had enough of it. 'My decision as Judge,' said G.K.C., 'is that everybody here except myself be committed for contempt of court. Off you all go to prison without any trial whatever.'

Such were the amusements of literary folk in those days,

though Shaw very seldom allowed himself to be drawn into them. When not working, or relaxing himself with work, he preferred the peace of his home to the pastimes of his contemporaries. His outburst, 'Holidays! I never took one in my life!' was broadly true; but his week-ends at Ayot St. Lawrence were restful and recuperative. He sometimes spent whole mornings developing photographs in the dark room, emerging therefrom at intervals to play his Bechstein with a pianola. Music always meant more to him than literature, and, if superficial on Shakespeare, he was sound enough on Beethoven, who, he asserted, was no reserved gentleman but a man proclaiming the realities of life: 'Beethoven was the first man who used music with absolute integrity as the expression of his own emotional life instead of as material for pleasing sound patterns. Others had shown how it could be done—had done it themselves as a curiosity of their art in rare, self-indulgent, *unprofessional* moments—but Beethoven made this, and nothing else, his business. . . . In thus fearlessly expressing himself, he has, by his common humanity, expressed us as well, and shewn us how beautifully, how strongly, how trustworthily we can build with our own real selves. This is what is proved by the immense superiority of the Beethoven symphony to any oratorio or opera.'

Like all vegetarians, human and animal, Shaw could not endure a completely sedentary life. But neither could he endure physical exercises. Eugen Sandow tried to entice him as a pupil and develop him physically. Shaw said, 'You misunderstand my case. I have seen you supporting on your magnificent chest twenty men, two grand pianos, and a couple of elephants; and I have no doubt you could train me to do the same. But my object as to pianos and elephants and crowds is to keep them off my chest, not to heap them on to it.' Sandow gave him up as hopeless and presently died prematurely, thus confirming Shaw's mistrust of exercises and his resolution not to burden himself with superfluous muscle. He had quite as much muscular strength as he needed, had sound capacious lungs and good digestion, and could not discover any advantage to Hubert Bland in his exceptional physique. He walked, he swam, he bicycled, he drove his car for forty years over Alps, Pyrenees, Atlas, and English roads when they were in a state that drivers cannot now imagine; and this was enough for him. Above all, he had a secret activity. He sang. Nobody except his mother and his

wife and his domestic staff ever heard him sing, or suspected
him of doing anything so apparently unShavian; but he sang
on Lee's method, imparted by his mother, every night before
he went to bed: opera, oratorio, cantatas, ballads, everything
singable, soprano, contralto, tenor or bass, transposing an
octave up or down, as Astriffiamante soared above his baritone range, or Sarastro dived beneath it. And though he
looked on all medical treatments with the greatest suspicion,
if he heard of a singer, or pianist, or elocutionist, who had
been disabled by wrong methods and who had cured himself
by perfecting better ones and was now teaching it, he was on
the track immediately in quest of a new discovery in aesthodic
technique. Aesthodic was a word invented by Sir Almroth
Wright, a great inventor of needed new words, when Shaw
called his classification of sanitation as aesthetic a revolutionary inspiration.

Shaw, by the way, had a particular objection to his first
christian name. 'Jawj,' he once said, 'is so horribly ugly and
difficult that all attempts to call me by it are foredoomed to
failure,' and he warned an acquaintance that 'nothing exas-
perates me more than to be Georged in print'.

His domestic life was well arranged, his habits and hobbies
were carefully organized, his meal-times were punctual:
efficiency and equabilty reigned in his home, as might be
expected from one who said, 'The people who talk and write
as if the highest attainable state is that of a family stewing in
love continuously from the cradle to the grave, can hardly
have given five minutes serious consideration to so outrageous
a proposition.' Perhaps it was as well that he had no children:
they would have upset the even tenor of his ways. Moreover,
though children were fond of him, because he never patronized
them and treated them as adult equals, he was not fond of
children: 'Affection between adults (if they are really adult
in mind and not merely grown-up children) and creatures so
relatively selfish and cruel as children necessarily are without
knowing it or meaning it, cannot be called natural.' Still it
would have been interesting to watch the growth of a child
whose father maintained, 'I never observe rules of conduct,
and therefore have given up making them.'

His private life was not wholly without incident; indeed
he had to barricade his flat in Adelphi Terrace in order to
secure privacy:

'A man stole £500 from me by a trick. He speculated in

my character with subtlety and success; and yet he ran risks of detection which no quite sensible man would have ventured on. It was assumed that I would resort to the police. I asked why. The answer was that he should be punished to deter others from similar crimes. I naturally said, "You have been punishing people cruelly for more than a century for this kind of fraud; and the result is that I am robbed of £500. Evidently your deterrence does not deter. What it does do is to torment the swindler for years, and then throw him back upon society, a worse man in every respect, with no other employment open to him except that of fresh swindling. Besides, your elaborate arrangements to deter me from prosecuting are convincing and effective. I could earn £500 by useful work in the time it would take to prosecute this man vindictively and worse than uselessly. So I wish him joy of his booty, and invite him to swindle me again if he can. . . ." I must however warn our thieves that I can promise them no immunity from police pursuit if they rob me. Some time after the operation just recorded, an uninvited guest came to a luncheon party in my house. He (or she) got away with an overcoat and a pocketful of my wife's best table silver. But instead of selecting my overcoat, he took the best overcoat, which was that of one of my guests. My guest was insured against theft; the insurance company had to buy him a new overcoat; and the matter thus passed out of my hands into those of the police. But the result, as far as the thief was concerned, was the same. He was not captured; and he had the social satisfaction of providing employment for others in converting into a strongly fortified obstacle the flimsy gate through which he had effected an entrance, thereby giving my flat the appearance of a private madhouse.'

Whether it was his abstemious diet, his singing, his wife's care, or all three, Shaw avoided serious illness; though in early life he had suffered from smallpox in the 1881 epidemic, a very light touch of scarlet fever, caught from his sister shortly afterwards, and a general breakdown in 1898. His headaches came and went, but otherwise he was immune from the complaints that attacked winebibbers and animal-eaters. I once asked whether his diet had been good for his health. 'How do I know?' he rejoined. 'How do I know what health I might have enjoyed if I had been carnivorous? But I remember one occasion very vividly when I suffered all the tortures that should have been reserved for corpse-

335

devourers and whisky-swillers. It was about thirty years ago, and I was in the middle of a rehearsal when I became acutely conscious that all was not well in my interior. I handed over the production to someone else and managed to get out of the stalls without giving the game away. But I collapsed with pain in the corridor, where one of the theatre-staff, assuming I was dead drunk, passed me without a word. Somehow I got into a taxi, becoming delirious after giving my address. The taxi-driver was most solicitous, and helped me indoors with sooth-ing words—"There, there! Go to bed. You'll soon be better," and so on. A doctor was summoned and stone in the kidney was diagnosed. I couldn't believe it. Stone in the kidney after a manhood nourished on the diet of Pythagoras! Out of the question! Preposterous! Another doctor was sent for, and he agreed with the first. For hours I lay in bed writhing in agony and being hideously sick at regular intervals. The stone eventually left my kidney for my bladder, after which the pain changed in kind but not intensity. Three hours of my raving and groaning and cursing and bawling got on the doctor's nerves and he administered morphia. When I re-turned to consciousness the pain of the stone's unhurrying journey racked me again, and the damned thing didn't emerge until about 8 in the morning, after I had sped its departure with a series of unparalleled paroxysms that broke the bed-springs. Having been X-rayed I dashed up to Southsea for a Labour Conference, where I made the speech of a man who has fought with wild beasts and then fed on them. However the reading public won't be interested in my inside, so you'd better content yourself with the announcement that I am an unrepentant vegetarian on health grounds. The stone in my kidney was probably inherited from a long line of alcoholic ancestors.'

On another occasion it seemed as if he might be seriously incapacitated, and then he was treated by a well-known un-registered doctor and ex-pianist, Raphael Roche, to whom he sent me when I returned home from Mesopotamia in 1919, and who cured me of dysentery and malaria inside six months. Shaw developed what was known to the medical profession as a hydrocele, an extremely inconvenient and unpleasant sort of localized dropsy: 'It did not hurt; but it was an unseemly nuisance. My medical friends assured me that it could be dealt with by a very simple operation, and that it was positively indecent of me to go about with such a disfigurement when its removal was so easy.

'But on reading up the subject I found that the operation was one of the mechanical kind practised by Mrs Squeers. It consisted of just boring a hole in me over the dropsical region. Its ease and simplicity for the surgeon was beyond question; and it was perhaps natural for him to conclude that it was equally easy and simple for me. But it seemed to me that the same might be said of a bayonet thrust. According to the books there was much more diversity of opinion as to the operation than my medical friends had been taught in the course of their training. It was suggested that as the operation did not cure, and had to be repeated over and over again as the dropsical condition recurred, a speculative antiseptic injection of iodine might follow the tapping. Also that the only radical operation was excision of the sac of the gland. As it happened, I had an opportunity of observing the case of a sufferer,[1] who obeyed his doctor and underwent the recommended simpler operation. It was much more distressing and disabling than the doctors thought; and the condition recurred.

'On this evidence it did not seem to me that I could, as a sane man, allow myself to be coopered in the proposed manner, especially as I was aware that Nature has a therapy of her own for which there is at least more to be said than for Mrs Squeers. However, I exhibited my misfortune to an osteopath. He noted that the gland most nearly concerned was not quite normal, and warned me, with a somewhat grave expression, that if it became painful I should have to do something about it. And indeed it presently began to blacken rather ominously, and to protest uncomfortably against being disturbed in any way.

'Here was a rare opportunity for one of my therapeutic experiments. I knew that Mr Raphael Roche claimed that chronic malignant conditions are amenable to treatment by drugs in infinitesimal doses. I challenged him to try his hand on my hydrocele. He accepted the challenge without hesitation; and for some weeks or perhaps less I every day solemnly put on the tip of my tongue a grain or two of some powdered sugar which he gave me.

'Mr Roche won the game: whether by luck or cunning I

[1] A neighbour at Ayot St. Lawrence had the same complaint at about the same time.

know not. All I can say is that the appearance of the gland became less threatening, and that the hydrocele suddenly discharged itself without notice. Fortunately I was in bed at the time.[1] Twice afterwards it discharged a blob of transparent lymph. And that was the last of it. My return to healthy normality was complete ; and though many years have elapsed there has never been the slightest recurrence.

'Now Harley Street would certainly have claimed this as a cure if it had treated a case with a similar result. As Mr Roche, who denounces Harleian practice as lethal, treated it, the Street will no doubt contend that the relation of his treatment to my cure was one of pure coincidence. . . . I can only state the facts as they occurred, and confess that I prefer Mr Roche's pleasant coincidences to distressing operations that do not cure. I did not ask Mr Roche what drug he used, as he strenuously denies that he has any specific drugs for specific diseases. I cannot prove that he used any drug at all, as he defied me to discover it by any known process of analysing the sugar. I had, he held, cured myself by the operation of my own vital forces, roused from their previous neglect by the attack made on them by an infinitesimal quantity of a drug which in larger quantity would have aggravated or even produced not merely the symptoms and sensations attendant on the hydrocele, but those of the entire Shavian diathesis, physical and mental, representing the vulnerable idiosyncrasies of my vital force—what he calls the directions in which I have a tendency to be wounded. This is much more than the serum therapists claim for their inoculations. And who would not prefer the taste of Mr Roche's sugar to the *malaise* and risks of inoculation with preparations which disgust healthy-minded people and involve ill-usage of animals?

'It also, by the way, is much subtler than ordinary homeopathy, which, though it prescribes infinitesimal doses, is still obsessed by lists of specific diseases curable by specific drugs, and to that extent can be practised by anyone with intelligence enough to look up a number in a telephone directory.'

A good example of Shaw's limitless curiosity and openness of mind was given me by Raphael Roche, who, in a conversation with Shaw and Sir Almroth Wright, mentioned that he

[1] 'One night I woke up and thought my water-bottle had burst,' was how Shaw described it to me.

had cured certain diseases which every orthodox specialist considered incurable. Wright expressed complete incredulity. Roche offered to produce the evidence and suggested that Wright should personally examine the cases. Wright pooh-poohed the offer. Shaw remonstrated with him.

'Look here!' exclaimed Wright, 'the thing's absurd and impossible. Let me put it this way: would you, Shaw, trouble to get out of your chair if I called from the next room, "Do come in here and see what I've just done—I've turned a pint of tea-leaves into pure gold"?'

'Certainly I would,' replied Shaw.

THE WAR TO END SHAW

HIS TIME being fully occupied with 'working out the practicalities of English socialism', Shaw did not pay much attention to foreign policy until an attempt was made by Count Harry Kessler to bring England and Germany together on the somewhat insecure ground that, having produced Shakespeare and Goethe, Newton and Leibniz, they had much in common with one another. This resulted in an exchange of manifestoes between the cultural descendants of Shakespeare, Goethe, Newton and Leibniz, and Shaw was asked to draft the English one. He did so ; but feeling that a common admiration of Shakespeare and company would not necessarily prevent a war between the two countries, especially as the Germans thought that Shakespeare was a German, and the English did not think of him at all, he inserted a sentence which was more to the point. Far from being jealous of the German fleet, proclaimed the Shavian manifesto, England regarded it as an additional guarantee of civilization. The cultural descendants of Shakespeare and Newton flatly declined to sign the manifesto until that sentence was expunged. Everyone except the author signed it when the sentence was expunged. Shaw drew the conclusion that

Shakespeare's countrymen would not be happy until the German fleet was reposing at the bottom of the North Sea, and he decided to make them conscious of their responsibilities, writing two articles, the first appearing in *The Daily Chronicle* on 18th March, 1913, the second in *The Daily News* on 1st January, 1914.

Like all sensible men he hated war, knowing it to be as imbecile as it was criminal, but, recognizing its inevitability while the world was governed by imbeciles and criminals, he made two practical proposals which could at least be understood by those who wished to prevent it. The first was that England should 'propose to France and Germany a triple alliance, the terms being that if France attack Germany we combine with Germany to crush France, and if Germany attack France, we combine with France to crush Germany . . . further, that if any other Power were to attack either France or Germany, the three would line up together against that Power.' The next proposal followed as a natural consequence. If England's guarantee were not to be worthless she had to be strong enough to attack ; she had to have ready a powerful expeditionary force. He therefore urged compulsory military service, mitigated by full civil rights and proper pay for the soldiers, together with a considerable increase in the national armaments. These perfectly reasonable proposals were, of course, ignored, because the people who were steadily preparing for a war with Germany were afraid to show their hand, and the people who lived in a coma of kindly thoughts would not face the realities of the situation. Among the former were the diplomatists, one of whom declared that if Shaw were in the Foreign Office there would be a European war in a fortnight ; to which Shaw later retorted that as he had not been in the Foreign Office there was a European war in eighteen months. Among the latter was John Galsworthy, who in 1911 launched a public appeal against the use of aircraft in war. All the cultural descendants of Shakespeare and Newton signed this appeal except Shaw, who wrote:

'I cant sign that absurdity. I might as well revive Fielding's suggestion that armies should fight with their fists. All this about "the burden of armaments" is rubbish: the cost of the biggest armies at present is not worth counting beside the cost of our idle property holding. We know perfectly well that aerial warfare will not be ruled out, any more than (virtually) explosive bullets have been ruled out, no matter what pious hope we express. It may be horrible; but horror is the whole point of war: the newspapers will be really jolly when the showers of shells alternate with showers of mangled aeronauts on crowded cities. The really interesting question is how far the new development will make an international combination against war irresistible. Nations will not stop fighting until the police make them: the difficulty is to organize and effectively arm your European-North American police, if you get it. Meanwhile, "burdens of armaments", etc., etc., is all pious piffle.'

Apparently the war that began in August 1914 took everyone in England by surprise except the War Office, the Foreign Office and Bernard Shaw. But as the nation as a whole believed that the War Office and the Foreign Office were as innocent of the outbreak as the press said they were, and as all the other leading writers were lying as heartily as the press, it became the duty of Bernard Shaw to set down the facts in their proper perspective. Collecting all the documents he could obtain, he went off to Torquay, where for two months he sunned himself on the roof of the Hydro Hotel, writing a manifesto on the causes of the war and cognate themes. 'I felt as if I were witnessing an engagement between two pirate fleets, with, however, the very important qualification that as I and my family and friends were on board British ships I did not intend the British section to be defeated if I could help it. All the ensigns were Jolly Rogers; but mine was clearly the one with the Union Jack in the corner.' Sometimes he descended from the roof of the Hydro Hotel to listen to Basil Cameron's symphony concerts at the Pavilion, with rows of convalescent wounded Belgians in the front. 'The band played Tipperary for these warriors, who, instead of rising on their crutches and bursting into enthusiastic cheers, made it only too clear by their dazed demeanour that they were listening to this tune for the first time in their lives.' One day, when Basil Cameron was lunching with the Shaws, someone announced that the Anti-German League had brought about the closing of a church at Forest Hill because the service was conducted in German by an old gentleman who had worshipped God in that language all his life. 'It's like passing a vote of censure on God for creating Germans!' remarked Shaw.

The writing and publication of the manifesto, which he called *Common Sense About the War,* now seems the most courageous act in Shaw's career. But the fact that *The New Statesman* did not hesitate to publish it as a War Supplement which immediately reached a circulation of 75,000 copies, and that it was at first quite favourably received, indicates that Shaw, as usual, was a better judge of what could safely be said than his critics, hostile or friendly. It was not until its contents were forgotten or absorbed by the militant press that it began to be denounced by journalists who had never read it. Shaw knew that it had to be swallowed, and suffered not a day's uneasiness on its account. But in any case he accepted a professional obligation to face personal risks in moral causes exactly as a soldier accepts that obligation in physical warfare. 'You may demand moral courage from me to any extent,' he was fond of saying, 'but when you start shooting and knocking one another about, I claim the coward's privilege and take refuge under the bed. My life is far too valuable to be machine-gunned.' No doubt he knew that brave men can face the truth and flourish on it, that cowards hide beneath lies and are crushed by them; but he must also have known that there are more cowards than brave men in any given community, and that in a crisis the teller of truth runs a grave risk of being lynched. In his own case there was a special danger, because past experience had taught him that numbers of people who had never betrayed the slightest hostility would, the moment they thought they had him at a disadvantage, vent the bitterness and envy that had been rankling within them for years. His manner no less than his matter had always infuriated humourless folk. 'When a thing is funny, search it for a hidden truth,' says the He-Ancient in *Back to Methuselah*. Unfortunately the people who take themselves seriously always search for a hidden bludgeon, and the publication of the first half of *Common Sense* in the monthly supplement of the New York *Times* provoked a torrent of invective from a rival playwright, Henry Arthur Jones. Shaw's levity was bad enough, but this combination of rectitude with levity was unendurable. A good example of these displeasing ingredients must be quoted. Referring to his pre-war articles, in which he had made a vain attempt to avert the catastrophe, he wrote: 'Nobody took the smallest public notice of me; so I made a lady in a play say "Not bloody likely," and instantly became famous beyond the Kaiser, beyond the Tsar, beyond Sir Edward Grey, beyond Shakespear and Homer and President Wilson, the papers occupying themselves with me for a whole week just as they are now occupying themselves with the war, and one paper actually devoting a special edition to a single word in my play, which is more than it has done for the Treaty of London (1839). I concluded then that this was a country which really could not be taken seriously. But the habits of a lifetime are not so easily broken; and I am not afraid to produce another dead silence by renewing my good advice, as I can easily recover my popularity by putting still more shocking expressions into my next play, especially now that events have shewn that I was right on the point of foreign policy.'

Dead silence, however, was about the only condition not produced by *Common Sense*. No really intelligent person could possibly have taken exception to a syllable in it; which must be why nearly everyone took violent exception to every syllable of it. The author simply pointed out that the violation of Belgian neutrality was a trumped-up excuse for British intervention, and a poor one; that if the soldiers of every army engaged were wise they would shoot their officers and return home; that if the citizens of every belligerent country were wise they would refuse to pay for diplomatic wars; that there were Junkers (i.e. country squires) and militarists in England as well as in Germany; that the English had a reputation abroad for hypocrisy; that self-glorification and abuse of one's enemy were not the best ways of winning a war; that the war might have been averted if Sir Edward Grey, the British Foreign Secretary, had made England's attitude clear before it began; that the real case against Germany was much stronger than the lying official case; and so forth. In fact a most patriotic pamphlet, in which the true stand of democracy was clarified and the fictitious stand demolished.

Yet no work since *The Rights of Man* by Tom Paine, who wrote 'Common Sense' about another crisis, has gained for its author such a generous measure of hatred and vituperation. Robert Lynd summed up the situation by saying that, while nobody could take any reasonable exception to the pamphlet, yet from the moment it appeared the war was spoken of and written about as a struggle between Great Britain, France, Russia and Belgium on the one hand, and Germany, Austria, Turkey and Bernard Shaw on the other. The press suggested that his plays should be boycotted. Old friends kept clear of him. Acquaintances cut him. People left the room when he entered it. Herbert Asquith expressed the view of many brother-officers when he said one evening in the Royal Naval Division mess, 'The man ought to be shot!' Even his friendliest critics were heard to murmur, 'Why can't the blighter play the game?' People who had not read *Common Sense* were particularly vitriolic. The author's letter-box was crammed with filthy abuse by every post. At a Charity Matinee many of the 'stars' who had taken part flatly refused to be photographed in his company. The feeling he had aroused crossed the Atlantic. When G. S. Viereck was thrown out of some author's league, Shaw declared that any literary society which expelled a member because of his political opinions was not a literary society but a political party. Whereupon a member of the league wrote to tell Shaw that an Anglo-Irishman had no right to intrude his counsel and command in the affairs of an American society. Shaw replied: 'Your letter . . . fills me with a wild hope that you may be able to recover for me the considerable sums I have paid into the United States Treasury since 1913 as income tax. As the United States were founded on the principle of No Taxation without Representation, it seems to me that if you can succeed in establishing your contention that I have no rights in America, I shall get my money back. Until I do, you may depend on it I shall take advantage of the position its payment confers on me to express my opinion, and to issue what you call my "counsel and command", in American affairs with the utmost freedom.' In December 1914 Shaw was able to assert with absolute truth, 'I have been giving exhibitions of moral courage far surpassing anything achieved in the field; but so far I have not received the V.C.; in fact sarcastic suggestions that I should receive the iron one have not been lacking.'

One notable figure in the political world, and only one, expressed what the tiny gagged minority felt. 'May I now say that which I failed to muster enough courage to say when first I felt the thrill of your article,' wrote Keir Hardie to Shaw, 'that its inspiration is worth more to England than this war has yet cost her—in money I mean. When it gets circulated in popular form and is read as it will be by hundreds of thousands of our best people of all classes, it will produce an elevation of tone in the national life which will be felt for generations to come. In Scottish ploughman phrase, "God bless ye and send ye speed." I prohibit any reply to this, or even acknowledgement. It is the expression of a heart which now throbs towards you with almost feelings of devotion. . . .

P.S. Only a Celt could have done it.' Shaw agreed with the postscript, for about twenty-five years after he had provoked that outburst of delirious raving and hysterical gibbering he gave me the explanation of it: 'If you read *Common Sense About the War* now in cold blood you may be puzzled to find out why it infuriated some people—especially those who had not read it, but had learnt that I had warned them not to use the word Junker as a term of abuse, as the most typical Junker in Europe was Sir Edward Grey. The secret was that as my patriotism was Irish, and therefore anti-English, there was something unbearable in the complete objectivity of my presentation of the British case.'

The national lunacy took a sharp upward curve when the *Lusitania* was sunk by a German submarine: 'Immediately an amazing frenzy swept through the country. Men who up to that time had kept their heads now lost them utterly. "Killing saloon passengers! What next?" was the essence of the whole agitation; but it is far too trivial a phrase to convey the faintest notion of the rage which possessed us. To me, with my mind full of the hideous cost of Neuve Chapelle, Ypres, and the Gallipoli landing, the fuss about the *Lusitania* seemed almost a heartless impertinence, though I was well acquainted personally with the three best-known victims. . . . I even found a grim satisfaction, very·intelligible to all soldiers, in the fact that the civilians who found the war such splendid British sport should get a sharp taste of what it was to the actual combatants. I expressed my impatience very freely, and found that my very straightforward and natural feeling in the matter was received as a monstrous and heartless paradox. When I asked those who gaped at me whether they had anything to say about the holocaust of Festubert, they gaped wider than before, having totally forgotten it, or rather having never realized it. They were not heartless any more than I was; but the big catastrophe was too big for them to grasp, and the little one had been just the right size for them.'

Shaw's outspokenness over the *Lusitania* frightened the late Clifford Sharp, then editor of *The New Statesman*, which had been founded by the Webbs in 1913 with the financial assistance of Shaw. Sharp refused to publish the comments of Shaw on the sinking of the *Lusitania*. Shaw bore no malice, for when misfortune overcame Sharp he did everything in his power to help. But he wrote no more on such topics for *The New Statesman* until 1939 brought a renewal of the war. Meanwhile, H. W. Massingham, editor of *The Nation*, published the more important of Shaw's later utterances on the war.

The sanity of Shaw grated harshly on the nerves of his fellow-scribes. Even before the *Lusitania* episode, one of them, W. J. Locke, a gentle, mild-mannered man with whom a fly could have taken its chance, was thirsting for his blood. At one of the lunches of the Dramatists' Club, Shaw reported to Sutro, 'I said that when the Germans fired on Rheims Cathedral my first reaction was a lively impulse to hurl the artillerist on his head from the summit of the tower. Locke, sitting opposite, expressed his warm approval and his surprise and pleasure at my rightmindedness. I had to explain that nothing could be more unreasonable, as any British artillery officer would blow all the cathedrals in Europe to smithereens without a moment's hesitation if they served as actual or even potential observation posts to the enemy. That was my first discovery of the fact that the war was getting on Locke's West Indian nerves.' After the torpedoing of the *Lusitania* Shaw's views were discussed at another lunch of the Dramatists' Club by Locke, Henry Arthur Jones, Justin Huntly McCarthy, and a number of the lesser fry. Shaw related the sequel in a letter to me:

'They thereupon, without notice, solemnly expelled me. I pointed out that this proceeding was null and void, and that I was still a member of the club, but that to please them I would resign. A few members resigned as a protest, including Granville Barker, who had a sovereign contempt for them and never attended the lunches. Zangwill would have resigned ; but I persuaded him to stay and carry on his campaign for the admission of women to the club. The others were as bored as I was and as out of place there, and jumped at the excuse for escaping.

'It was then or thereabouts that I was at a committee meeting of the Society of Authors, with W. J. Locke, a West Indian by birth and temper. Suddenly, apropos of nothing, he rose screaming, "I will not sit in the room with Mr Bernard Shaw," and dashed out, banging the door violently. Jack Squire demanded in print that I should be tarred and feathered.

'But this phase of war delirium soon passed off. Locke and Squire came to me and mutely invited me to shake hands, which of course I did. To me war fever is like any other epidemic, and what the patients say or do in their delirium is no more to be counted against them than if they were all in bed with brain fever.

'My public meetings were crowded and successful. The *Daily Mail* sent a reporter to see me mobbed. He found me being bombarded with questions about the soldiers' allowance by a friendly audience. One meeting, just before the Dramatists Club incident, had an enormous crowd at the Press tables: I never saw the like before or since. But the government forbade any reports; and both I and Lord Willoughby de Broke, who orated in the same week, were extinguished, and the poor reporters left penniless. The *Manchester Guardian* alone defied the interdict.

'Later on, the Dramatists' Club, now open to women, and probably enormously improved thereby, invited me to dinner as guest of honor; but though I bore no malice I had had enough of them and made some excuse. Anyone who is a pioneer in art is hated by the old gang and should not join their clubs, as it enables them to expel him, and to that extent places him in their power. It is the novices and amateurs who carry the day for him. Wagner suffered all his life from this sort of professional hatred.

'The clique that abhorred me is long since dead; and as I cannot find the name of the club in any of the lists I presume it no longer exists. Henry Arthur Jones, a personal friend of mine, held out to the end with magnificent rhetorical denunciations of me and of H. G. Wells; but his case was pathological. I have somewhere a pathetic little scrap of paper on which he tried to scrawl when he was dying that he had no personal feeling against me.'

The case of Jones was a sad one. 'I do not think I can meet him in the future,' he said when Shaw expressed indignation over the fuss that followed the loss of the saloon passengers in the *Lusitania*. Having heard from the secretary that several members of the Dramatists' Club had expressed a desire that he should not be present at their lunches, Shaw wrote to Jones: 'I hope you are not one of the "several members", though in these raving mad times it is hard to know. Cheerful sort of club, isnt it?' Jones answered that he had been in favour of the secretary's letter and proceeded to attack Shaw for his attitude to the war. Shaw rejoined: 'Henry Arthur, Henry Arthur; what is your opinion of the war? If you think you are going to put ME off with a sheet of notepaper containing extracts from the *Daily Express* copied with your own fair hand, you have mistaken your man. Come! give me a solid Buckinghamshire opinion. . . .' Asking whether Jones would rather lunch with Horatio Bottomley than with himself, Shaw then dealt with certain points in the attack, sending up his blood-pressure to such a degree that Jones launched a sort of crusade against Shaw, keeping it up until death intervened. The fact that Shaw could not take him seriously almost drove him out of his mind, and would have driven him into the law courts if Shaw had not maintained the friendliness that made him so frantic. In 1921 Jones withdrew his name from the committee of a Testimonial Matinee to J. H. Barnes when he discovered that Shaw's name was on the list of members. He attacked Shaw in England and America, describing him as 'a freakish homunculus germinated outside lawful procreation'. In his reply Shaw explained that he was 'unmistakeably the son of my reputed father', and 'the unquestioned lawful heir of my mother's property and my father's debts', and concluded a long article with: 'I flatter myself that his publishers would never have ventured on such a roaring libel if he had not given them his guarantee that my friendship could be depended on. And he was quite right.'

In April 1925 Shaw was asked to propose the toast to the Immortal Memory at the Stratford-on-Avon Shakespeare Festival. This inspired Jones to write a book, *Mr Mayor of Shakespeare's Town*, which was so abusive that Shaw was asked if, in the event of publication, he would give an undertaking not to bring an action against the publisher and printer. He declined on the ground that he would do everything in his power to prevent Jones from wasting his talent on futile invective and to make him return to his natural business of play-writing. In 1926 Shaw made a last attempt to re-establish the old relationship, writing to Jones from the Regina Palace Hotel at Stresa: 'I meant to congratulate you on my seventieth birthday, but was afraid of sending your temperature up 10 degrees at a critical moment. I am assured now by Max Beerbohm that you are well enough to stand anything; so I insist on affirming that the news of your illness gave me as much concern, and of your safe deliverance as much relief, as if we were still the best of friends. Our quarrel has always been a hopelessly one-sided affair; and I have rejoiced in your vigorous invective far too much to feel any malice at the back of it. Some of it, by the way, was very sound Shavian economics. . . . At present I feel that my bolt will be shot when I have got through the final struggle to finish my book on socialism, with every word of which you will agree. The truth is, I am for the moment so completely done-up by work on top of illness (the result of an accident) that the writing of this letter would tire me for the rest of the day if the feeling it expresses were not so nourishing. So you really are doing me good. Do not bother to reply—though I warn you I shall put the friendliest interpretation on silence.' Jones did not answer this letter, feeling that if he resumed friendly relations with Shaw he would be weakening his position and betraying the admirers he had gained in the course of his crusade. Max Beerbohm asked him to 'shake hands with the demon', telling him that Shaw was free from malice and, in his way, the most gifted man since Voltaire. But Jones stuck to his colours till the moment came when approaching death made him try to scrawl on that 'little scrap of paper' what he had forgotten when his feelings as a human being had been perverted by political frenzy.

Shaw's other famous contemporaries disapproved of his *Common Sense* without becoming so violent as Jones. H. G. Wells described his behaviour as that of 'an idiot child laughing in a hospital'. Arnold Bennett thought the pamphlet inopportune and himself made the best of the opportunity. John Galsworthy entertained scruples on the question of taste. Joseph Conrad felt that, in a matter of life and death, some dignity should be observed: in any case he disliked socialists on principle, feeling, no doubt, that people who had panaceas for human perfection would be wasting their time on him. G. K. Chesterton and Hilaire Belloc would, of course, have attacked Shaw if he had echoed their own views. Pretty well every one had a nasty word to say ; which only goes to prove that political and religious fervour curdles the milk of human kindness.

Alfred Sutro had not been present at the Dramatists' Club luncheon when Shaw was 'warned off', but he wrote to say that *Common Sense* was ill-timed and received a full Shavian blast in return:

October 30, 1915.

'MY DEAR ALFRED,

'Whats this you tell me? *You* working in a Government office! You! You! Of all the damned ridiculous pro-German follies ever committed by a British patriot, this is quite the
349

damnedest. Dont you know that with the exchange at its present rate and ammunition pouring in from America every day, the man who can transfer a hundred pounds from America to England without exporting anything but a scrap of paper helps us more than six dozen thoroughly inefficient amateur clerks? Come out of it this instant. Write me a handful of film scenarios and sell them to the Los Angeles people for £500 apiece. Write me a comedy for the American market, also a drama, *The Walls of Chicago*,[1] and a melodrama, *The Orphan of Louvain*, the *Spectre Nurse* and *The Tyrant's Deathbed*, or what you will ; only write it, and set up a stream of royalties every week from New York to London. Confound you, dont you *know*—you an old City man— that this is the way to fight Germany, and that the one man in ten thousand who can do it and doesnt ought to be shot? What are you dreaming of? Dont you care? Is it all nothing but a romance to you? And if the plays are done here too, will they be of no use? Are the clerks who can do nothing better than clerking to have no recreation? Are the young soldiers in training to have nothing to lift them above cowboy films and whoring? Alfred, you are a criminal, a traitor, a waster of the sacred fire on kitchen grates, a spiller of the seed on the ground. Go up, thou baldhead, and do what the God of your fathers meant you to do. *Auf! Ans werk!* And this— THIS is the man who lectures ME on what I have been doing with my time. You tell me that "it was not the moment". I was offered £300 to postpone for six weeks ; and I went ahead because in another month it might have been too late. We were driving Sweden into the arms of Germany. We were heading straight for a war with America, and would have reached it if Wilson had been Roosevelt.[2] We were robbing right and left on the high seas as if it were still the nineteenth century ; and we were sickening and infuriating the world by praising ourselves, adoring ourselves, calling our retreats glorious victories, exulting in those death traps, Brussels, Antwerp and Warsaw, into which our consummate strategists, our Caesars and Napoleons, were luring the doomed Germans, enshrining Asquith above Cavour and Grey above Marcus Aurelius, and reviling the Germans as cowards and imbeciles like bargees and prostitutes. Our men were being

[1] A reference to Sutro's most popular play, *The Walls of Jericho*.
[2] Theodore Roosevelt.

350

slaughtered in heaps for want of munitions because the firms we had grossly jobbed into the work had all been depending on the same small shops to farm it out to. We were lying like Trojans about everything. Our bellies were full of the East wind ; and though all this has come out since, and *The Times*, the *Morning Post* and the rest are now screaming to the seven heavens in the most mischievous way everything that I said carefully and politely, you have the *toupet* to tell me that it was not the right moment! You are right ; it was too late ; I held back too long. But there were difficulties. I did not dare to write red hot. I had to slave for months getting the evidence ; and I had to revise and revise, and give the stuff to people to read, and ask them was it unfair, was I hitting below the belt, was I off the evidence and so forth. As it was I had to anticipate it by my appeal on behalf of Belgium to President Wilson. It makes me sick to recollect the drudgery of it all! But, at least, I broke the spell of silent cowardice ; and I stated a case against Germany that was not a tissue of ridiculous and hypocritical lies. The Germans were cleverer about it than we were. After the first outburst of rage, in which I was a *Vaterlandslose geselle* and deuce knows what else, they began to cite me as an authority and to start the legend that I am a pro-German. And our press, instead of exposing the move, confirmed them, caring for nothing but the wound to their vanity made by my demonstration that they had all been talking the rottenest cinematographic balderdash. This has gone on ever since, even now that they are all yelling what they never dared to say until I gave them a lead ; and I dare say many of my disciples (I have a few thousand) have decided that Germany is in the right, and refused to enlist or help because they are told every day that the prophet Shaw said so.

'Only yesterday I had to write for A. E. W. Mason a long oriental letter to show to the Sheikhs of Morocco, whom the Germans have been trying to urge into rebellion by (with incredible tactlessness) saying that *I*—as if the Moors knew or cared anything about me or about Belgium—did not believe in the Treaty of 1839. The Belgians were the most sensible. When King Albert's Gift-Book appeared without my promised contribution, which the *Daily Telegraph* was scared out of inserting at the last moment, the Belgian Government came to me and asked me to write them an appeal to the world at large. They politely said that they did this because I was the only man whose voice would be listened to ; but what they meant was that I was the only one who would state the real nature of our obligations to them and not use them merely as a stick to beat the Germans with. And all this time you have been fooling away your time in a Government office, preventing everybody from working by the charm of your conversation, and eating up the provisions of England instead of bringing argosies across the sea to her, and telling people that I ought to be shot. Well, I forgive you, but only on condition that you go back to your proper work at once, and that you go to that silly Club and tell its idiot members to go and do likewise. Not that I suppose they are doing anything but superfluously making fools of themselves about me; but still, you might just save a soul or two. In great haste, dear Alfred,

'ever, G.B.S.'

King Albert's Gift-Book was a book of contributions by leading authors, sold for the benefit of the Belgians. Sir Hall Caine was asked to edit it by *The Daily Telegraph*, and Shaw was one of the authors to whom he applied. But the *Telegraph*, terrified by *Common Sense*, would not let Shaw's contribution appear; and Hall Caine, for whose novel *The White Prophet* Shaw had written a preface in 1909, said he would resign. Shaw dissuaded him from such a course, assuring him that nothing mattered but raising the money for the Belgians; in which respect the omitted contribution was not entirely fruitless, for Shaw told Archibald Henderson, 'I wrote such a moving appeal for the Belgians that when I read it over in proof I found that consistency obliged me to send in a substantial subscription myself.' Immediately after this the Belgians insisted that Shaw should draft an appeal on their behalf to America, which much surprised *The Daily Telegraph*.

As for Shaw's letter to the sheikhs of Morocco, the full story has been narrated by him: 'Early in the war the German Government, wishing to stir up a rebellion against the French in Morocco and Algeria, circulated a document written in very choice Arabic to the effect that I am a great prophet, and that I once told an American senator that the violation of Belgian neutrality was an incident of the war and not the cause of it. I am quite unable to follow that operation of the German mind which led to the conclusion that any Moorish sheikh could be induced to rush to arms because some dog of an unbeliever had made a statement that was neither interesting nor even intelligible in Morocco to some other dog of an unbeliever; but the Germans formed that conclusion and spent money on it. Thereupon a distinguished literary colleague of mine, A. E. W. Mason, who had plunged into active service in the war, and was busy circumventing the Germans round the Mediterranean and thereabouts, came to me and asked me for "a concise and straightforward denial" of the implication that the great prophet Shaw was a pro-German. Having been among the Moors and spoken to sheikhs and marabouts myself, I had no difficulty in convincing Mason that conciseness is not a virtue in Barbary. Also, I am not the man to lose an opportunity of preaching at the utmost admissible length when I find myself installed as a great prophet. Mason and I were not men of letters for nothing. We combined the style of our Bible with that of Burton's *Arabian Nights* in a prophetic message, which will, I hope, find a permanent place in Arab literature as an additional surah of the Koran. It was, I assume, duly translated and circulated; anyhow the Moors lay low and did nothing. It had every quality except that of conciseness.'

In January 1915 Shaw wrote to Robert Loraine, who was in the air force: 'Everybody wants to know whether we shall have in future to live under bomb-proof shelters by electric light and never see the sun, or else give up war.' Since then the world has suffered from firmament-phobia; but when, after the first Zeppelin raids on London, Shaw wrote to *The Times* urging the authorities to provide bombproof shelters for the defenceless citizens, especially in the school playgrounds, the editor 'indignantly refused to publish a communication countenancing the monstrous doctrine that civilians are not sacred, and that the soldier who would raise his hand to a fellow creature in mufti, save in the way of kindness, is not unworthy the name of Briton'. So he sent his letter to the leading liberal daily, the editor of which declared that he had never expected to agree with *The Times* editor, but that it could not be published in any civilized country. (It was, however, published by Massingham in *The Nation*.) A little later these editors were rudely awakened from their dreams of civilization by a shower of bombs, and no doubt agreed with Shaw that 'in the next war the only safe people would be the soldiers in their dug-outs'.

While he was putting forth all his efforts in the cause of the Allies, the English newspapers were doing their best to discredit Shaw. They reported that he was a prisoner in his flat, unable to go out for fear of being mobbed, that his career was over, his reputation gone, that he was repudiated by his partisans, in disgrace with his disciples, exploded, annihilated, finished and done for. These reports were given currency, with embellishments, in the Berlin and Vienna papers. In actual fact he was addressing large open meetings in London every week to huge applause. Reporters sent to see him hounded off the platform witnessed ovations instead. Resolutions of thanks for his *Common Sense* poured in daily from labour gatherings all over the country, and at length his correspondence became so large that he had to have cards of acknowledgment printed, containing the statement that he would either have to give up writing letters or have to give up writing anything else.

Before leaving for Mesopotamia I went to see him several times in 1916. On my first visit I was astonished by the formidable spikes that topped the wicket-gate leading up to his flat and wondered whether they were a war-time measure. He explained their presence, as already recorded. On the mantelpiece in his sitting-room were carved the words, 'They have said. What say they? Let them say.' He told me that some other philosopher had lived there before him and had recorded that simple memorandum of his feelings. 'I should have spoilt the thought by expanding it into a preface,' said he, 'so I left it there.' Most of our discussions were about Frank Harris, who will reappear later on, but I made notes of a few of his remarks on other subjects ; these were scattered over our talks, but must appear together here.

'How d'you like the army?' he asked me.

'I don't ; but I haven't the courage to be a Conscientious Objector.'

'They certainly have all the discipline on their side, but it's the wrong side for all that. They can't understand that a war is being fought. A man can take precautions against a fire, but when his house is alight he doesn't worry about the precautions he has failed to take. He tries to put it out. And this war can't be stopped by arguing about who started it or by saying that it's wrong. We all know it's wrong, but none the less we must drill ourselves to finish it by fighting the flames ; though I admit we could finish it far more quickly if we killed off a few politicians.'

'What are you writing now?' I asked.

'In my spare moments I've been working on a play in the Tchekov manner.' (This was *Heartbreak House*.) 'It's one of the best things I've done. Do you know Tchekov's plays? There's a dramatist for you!—a man who had a sense of the theatre in the finest perfection. He makes me feel like a beginner. I now want to tackle a big religious subject. I read the Bible when I have time to read anything.'

'I had enough of that in my childhood to last me a lifetime.

'It's not a child's book. You can't begin to appreciate it until you are sick of the novels and plays and other trash our grown-up babies feed on.'

'Then it's not a great book,' I tried to hit back. 'All the greatest literature is simple enough for the nursery.'

'In that case the alphabet is the greatest work in English literature.'

I subsided ; though on later reflection I regretted that I had not replied : 'A couple of eggs, a pat of butter and a pennorth of gas are not the same as a simple omelette made by a *cordon bleu.*'

How the subject cropped up I cannot recall, but he confessed to 'a bog-trotting hatred of agriculture', and shuddered as he spoke of 'weasels, stoats, rabbits, worms, and all the other subterraneous horrors'.

He told me that for some weeks after the publication of *Common Sense* his letter-box could not hold the mail, which was delivered by the sack. Most of the letters were from lunatics and the language in them was quite unprintable. 'As I employ a lady-secretary I published a request that my correspondents should write the word "Obscene" on the top left-hand corners of their envelopes.'

'I suppose,' he said, 'that I escape lynching solely because people treat everything I say as a huge joke ; the point being that if a solitary word I uttered were taken seriously the social order would be endangered. Well, there's something in that. If people didn't laugh at me they couldn't endure me. As an ordinary human being I am frankly impossible ; even as a Variety "turn" I am only just bearable. My mental and moral superiority are insufferable. No chink can be observed by the naked eye in my armour. Such a preposterous personification of repulsive virtues is intolerable. So my fellow-citizens stuff their fingers in their ears and drown my words in senseless cackle.'

I was about to leave England, had said good-bye to him after our last meeting, and was half-way down the stairs to the wicket-gate, when he leant over the balustrade and called out:

'The war will last another thirty years.'

With these words of comfort he waved a cheery farewell and vanished.

Although Shaw did not agree with the attitude of the Conscientious Objectors he wrote several letters to the press pleading that they should receive humane treatment and common justice. But in war-time people are deaf to such remarks as 'Physical torture is the one means by which the lowest humanity can degrade and destroy the highest,' and his appeals merely added to his unpopularity with the oligarchy and their hangers-on, who were out to torture anyone who did not agree with them. Another black mark was scored against him when it leaked out that he had drawn up one of six petitions on behalf of Sir Roger Casement, who had been captured in Ireland and was being tried for high treason. Curiously enough, Conan Doyle was responsible for one of the other five. Shaw did not sign his petition, because his name might have frightened off certain people whose signatures carried more weight; but he expressed his views in a letter which was turned down by *The Times*, *The Daily News* and *The Nation*, and published by *The Manchester Guardian*. He then drafted a speech for Casement to deliver at the trial before the verdict. The line he took was that Casement, being an Irishman, was no traitor and should be treated as a prisoner of war. He realized that if Casement left himself in the hands of his lawyers, and put up the fallacious defence of denial, he would be lost. Describing his interview with Casement to an officer on the western front who had given him a ride in a tank, Shaw said: 'I told Casement that he was as good as dead already. "Roger," I said, "they mean to hang you. They'll dig up some statute dating from the time of William the Conqueror, if necessary; but hang you they will. Now, look here, don't go wasting your money on expensive lawyers. The result is a foregone conclusion. Plead guilty, and then, when you are asked to say what you have to urge in mitigation of punishment, read out this speech, which I have specially written for you on the subject of Ireland and her wrongs. It is the best thing ever written and would cause a tremendous sensation." Would you believe it? Casement flatly refused, and lost the greatest chance in history. They hanged him, as I told him they would, in spite of all his costly lawyers.'

In February 1917 Shaw toured the Flanders front at the invitation of Sir Douglas Haig, the British Commander-in-Chief, and for a week enjoyed himself 'enormously and continuously'. At Ypres he begged the Town Major to let him drive the car across the square alone. 'It's rotten that serving soldiers like you and the chauffeur should run any risk in taking joy-riders about,' he said. The Town Major, a tall Irishman from Youghal, gasped, though his contempt for the official driver's risk was unbounded. No other civilian visitor had ever made such a suggestion, though he had conducted many noisy patriots and martial orators over the same scene. C. E. Montague, who was in charge of Shaw throughout the visit, was one of the party, and made the episode known. The square was crossed at full speed in safety, and Shaw was taken up to a pinnacle, whence a bird's-eye view of Ypres could be obtained. 'Go flat on your face if anything comes over,' said the Town Major. Shaw would have been delighted to do so: 'In my youth I had learnt, by sedulously imitating the pantaloons in the harlequinades, to drop flat on my face instantly and then produce the illusion of being picked up neatly by the slack of my trousers and set on my feet again. I had a wild hope that Brer Boche would send over something that would give me an excuse for exhibiting this accomplishment to my new friend. But nothing came over just then; and I left Ypres with my dignity unimpaired.'

He did all the sights—Arras, the Somme front, the Vimy ridge. He visited Sir Almroth Wright at Wimereux and stayed with Robert Loraine at Trezennes, where he roared with laughter during a dress rehearsal of his war-time playlets, *The Inca of Perusalem* and *O'Flaherty, V.C.* 'I'm glad you appreciate our poor efforts at your play, sir,' said an officer. 'If I had thought the stuff would prove to be as poor as this,' returned Shaw between convulsions, 'I'd never have written it.'

Back in England he heard that Loraine had been seriously wounded and was in danger of losing a leg. Shaw tried to comfort him with the reflection 'After all, having two available legs, I have never groused because I have not three; so why should a man with one be wretched because he has not two?' Probably because he has been used to two, Loraine might have replied: instead he asked whether he ought to take the doctor's advice and have his leg amputated, his knee-cap

357

having been shattered. Shaw was dubious: 'I dont know what to say about the leg. If you lose it, an artificial leg of the best sort will carry you to victory as Henry V. If you dont and are lame, it means a lifetime of Richard III, unless I write a play entitled Byron. Then there is the pension. How much for a leg? How much for a limb? One must look at these things from a business point of view.' But, thought Shaw, 'there is no reason why an actor should, like a Roman Catholic priest, be perfect in all his members to discharge his function'. He made the best of his own ailments as well as other people's, writing to Charles Ricketts in February 1918: 'I have been knocked out for a week by ptomaine poisoning and a fall on my precious head down a flight of steps—a form of exercise which I have somewhat outgrown. Therefore, now that I have got over it, I find that it has bucked me up remarkably; and the bumps on my head are taken for intellect.' He had, however, 'quite lost the iron nerve with which I faced the bombs of Ypres and Arras; the raids now terrify me into heartrending palpitations; and I am too lazy to go down into the excellent Adelphi cellars.'

After the war he gave some hints to the politicians and diplomats who were going to make the world safe for democracy at the Versailles Peace Conference; but he knew quite well that he might have saved himself the trouble. His remarks 'had about as much effect on the proceedings at Versailles as the buzzing of a London fly has on the meditations of a whale in Baffin's Bay'. While the fighting was still in progress he had written that 'a victory for anybody is a victory for war'; so, naturally, the Peace Conference made the world safe for the warmongers.

He refused to attend a Conference to limit armaments at Washington, U.S.A. 'The notion that disarmament can put a stop to war is contradicted by the nearest dog-fight,' said he; and with regard to security he professed to have done without it all his life, never having had less of it than when all the cowards in Europe were fighting for it. 'I know that security is impossible, and that nobody but a hopeless idiot or a person condemned to Parliament for the term of his natural life (much the same thing) could for one moment believe it to be possible, its first condition being that one Power shall exterminate all the other Powers, and its final condition that one man in that Power (which one, by the way?) shall exterminate all his fellow-men, and thus enjoy the security of Robinson

358

Crusoe until he slips on a piece of orange peel and breaks his leg, without having left anyone alive to set it.'

Although he had never in his life listened to a debate in the British House of Commons, Shaw attended the annual assembly of the League of Nations in 1928. He found the whole business unspeakably dull and stupid, though the meetings were occasionally enlivened by the sudden and spectacular appearances of the young ladies of the Secretariat. In spite of all this, or possibly because of it, Shaw felt that the League was justified as a school for international statesmanship, opposed to the old Foreign Office diplomacy: 'In the atmosphere of Geneva patriotism perishes: a patriot there is simply a spy who cannot be shot.' In fact the atmosphere of Geneva was of such a rarefied nature that, following the demise of patriotism, everything else perished.

But while peace and war came and went, while Conferences assembled and dispersed, while monarchies collapsed, democracies crumbled and dictatorships crashed, the Theatre stood, firmly founded on the rock of genius: 'Prime Ministers and Commanders-in-Chief have passed from a brief glory as Solons and Caesars into failure and obscurity as closely on one another's heels as the descendants of Banquo; but Euripides and Aristophanes, Shakespear and Molière, Goethe and Ibsen remain fixed in their everlasting seats.' With, we may add, Bernard Shaw.

THE STRANGE CASE OF
FRANK HARRIS

So MUCH LIGHT was thrown on Shaw's character in the course of his dealings with Frank Harris that no biography of him would be complete without the story now to be related.

We already know that Harris, as editor of *The Saturday Review*, engaged Shaw to write the dramatic criticisms. The initials 'G.B.S.' became known to a large public between '95 and '97, and in that sense Harris helped to seal the critic's reputation; but as Shaw's articles were the most widely-read feature of the paper, it may fairly be claimed that the genius he put into them far outweighed the cash he got out of them. Yet his gratitude to Harris was such that many years later he told his former employer, 'As long as you edit a magazine anywhere on earth, you can expect contributions from me.' No other member of Harris's staff shared these sentiments or behaved with such generosity. The explanation of Shaw's persistent affection and loyalty is: firstly, that certain of Harris's qualities appealed so strongly to him that he could not be antagonized by the qualities which repelled other men; and secondly, that as he was never really intimate with Harris he found it difficult to understand why those who knew him well turned against him at last. Harris's character has been drawn with skill, humour and insight by Hugh Kingsmill, whose book should be read by everyone who is interested in the complexities of human nature. Here we must concentrate mainly on what attracted Shaw to Harris.

'All the literary blokes loathe me, and I should spoil the dinner,' wrote Shaw to Sutro in 1924. 'Many thanks, all the same, for rashly including me.' This was roughly true. The literary blokes did not like Shaw, and Shaw did not like the literary blokes. Harris was not a literary bloke; in fact he raged against the majority of writers, especially the professorial crew. He belonged to no clique, though he had no objection to being the centre of one. He was acquainted with a world outside literature, a world of gamblers, financiers and other crooks. A large portion of his life was devoted to the arts of feeding, drinking, swindling and seduction. He had taken part in amazing adventures, which he narrated in an artistically metrical bass voice that would have made his reputation as the Statue in *Don Juan*. He claimed to have met everyone of note in the world of his time, and retailed stories of them, with salacious details, in a diapason that could tell above an orchestra. He tromboned his way through the worlds of Fleet Street, the Stock Exchange, Mayfair and Monte Carlo, bragging, bullying, blustering and brawling, never unimpressive but always unprintable. In addition to which he read, intoned, and raved about poetry, loved Shakespeare and Jesus Christ, and proclaimed his adoration of the highest whenever it suited his purpose to see it. All this was very refreshing to young men who were in rebellion against the conventions and welcomed anything that did not remind them of school or university or home life; and as none of them could ever have had a master, a professor or a parent who remotely resembled Harris, he did not want for disciples, nearly all of whom earned the title of 'Judas' as the years went by and they grew out of their Harris phase. But Shaw, unconventionally educated, was never a disciple, and so his emotions were disengaged from the start. 'Why do you describe me as a buccaneer?' complained Harris, who regarded himself as a modern gentle Jesus, and was ridiculously unconscious of the fact that his appalling language was not the current vernacular of polite society, male and female. Shaw really classed him as a monster (which he was), and delighted in imitating his *basso profondo*; he loved the incredible adventures, the shocking stories, the blasphemies and obscenities to which his own maternal uncle had hardened him in his boyhood. Harris was a holiday for him; an hour of his company was more invigorating than a day in the country. But an hour was quite enough of it.

H. G. Wells assured me that Shaw disliked 'intellectuals', preferring people who could deliver a good round oath on occasion. This is hardly consistent with Shaw's liking for Wells, the truth being that Irishmen are much more profane in conversation, and Shaw blasted and damned everything to hell, invoking Christ and all the saints on provocation that would not have elicited a tinker's oath from his English friends. Harris did not shock him; and he maintained that Harris's blackguardism was pure innocence. Consequently he never ceased to save his old friend's face, eventually at the expense of his own. He regretted that so many of Harris's criticisms were unprintable. One day, meeting Harris outside a theatre, he asked him what he was doing there.

'I am going to read a play to that son of a bitch, Charles Wyndham,' Harris intoned in the rhythm of Chopin's funeral march.

'Ah, well! you might do worse. Wyndham's ideas are old-fashioned; but he has a kind of flair for a good play,' said Shaw encouragingly.

'The pump will give water if you pee in it!' Harris replied in the tones of a Russian choir.

This is a very mild specimen of the estimates of his contemporaries which Harris could put into a sentence. Shaw, however, credited him with one virtue: he knew good work from bad in literature; liked the good and scorned the bad; and for this Shaw forgave him everything.

After selling *The Saturday Review* Harris gambled for a while in hotels and other less reputable property, lost his money, and successively edited *The Candid Friend* and *Vanity Fair*, in the last of which several articles appeared attacking Shaw, who read them with amusement because, though signed 'F.H.', they were 'obviously written by the office boy, Frank's activities in those days being confined to drawing his salary'. He next edited *Hearth and Home* and *Modern Society*, a libel in the latter landing him in gaol. Shortly after the commencement of the war he went to America, becoming editor of *Pearson's Magazine*, and writing for it a 'Contemporary Portrait' of Shaw which was as much like Shaw as a crocodile is like a kangaroo. At that time I was trying to enlist the interest of England's leading writers in Harris's *Life and Confessions of Oscar Wilde*, copies of which the author had sent me for that purpose. As a young disciple it never dawned on me that Kipling, Conrad, Barrie, Wells, Bennett and others might deny the master, and their curt or pungent replies saddened me. What they called his pro-German attitude in the war riled them, and they had never cared for his pro-Harris attitude before the war. Shaw was not in tune with this chorus of condemnation. He sent me a long letter addressed to Harris, in which he described his own meetings with Wilde and declared that Wilde's memory would have to stand or fall by Frank's book, which had wiped out every previous work on the subject. Shaw suggested that his letter might help to sell a cheap edition, which meant a small fortune for the biographer. He gave me his actual opinion of the book at the time. 'Boswell invented Johnson, just as Shakespear invented Falstaff. Frank has not invented Oscar, nor made him more interesting than he actually was; therefore I dont think the book will be read for its own sake by people who are not curious about Wilde. All the same I would read it more often on a desert island than Dorian Gray.'

After the rebuffs I had experienced, Shaw's magnanimity amazed me, especially as I had sent him a copy of *Pearson's* containing Harris's inept and hostile 'Portrait' of himself, receiving this acknowledgment: 'You will see by the enclosed that MacCarthy is a man after your own heart. I have told him to keep the book, also that I have sent his letter to you. Thank you for *Pearson's*, which I will return when I have read it more completely. Frank is really a frightful liar, writing imaginary conversations in an imaginary character, with odd little scraps of actual reminiscence in them; and most of his victims will be furious; but it cant be helped: he must live for the present by apocryphal memoirs.' Desmond MacCarthy was also in those days one of Harris's admirers, though not so warm as I.

Shaw did his best to explain why I could not expect enthusiastic replies from the other authors to whom I had written. The following extracts from his letters to me tell their own story:

'Wells may not have returned from Italy. He is not ungenerous, though his sudden transports of fury carry him beyond all bounds for an hour at a time. But Frank is going to be very irritating for a while. He has become editor of the American *Pearson's Magazine*; and he has already started personal reminiscences in it, which he will keep up for three numbers at least—the usual period of his attention to any rag he professes to edit. It is even possible that he may be kept to his work by his circumstances and by American slave-driving. I have read the first instalment; and it is clear that he is going to tell how he discovered and rescued from poverty and obscurity not only Wells, Kipling and myself, but probably Henry James, Thackeray, Dickens, Goldsmith, Shakespear and Chaucer. He is quite welcome as far as I am concerned; but the others may be more touchy. On the other hand they may not; but anyhow it is not good policy to set them going on the subject until the book is formally published in England.'

'Frank's present tack of describing to the Americans how he discovered Wells, Kipling, Conrad, myself, and other neglected geniuses, and rescued them from obscurity, is no doubt quite sincere; for he probably believes that America was discovered at the moment when he first landed there; but if these writers refuse to take it good-humoredly as I do, you cannot reasonably quarrel with them on that account.'

'Do not send your letter to Conrad. You are not his tutor. Write simply, "Dear Mr Conrad, I have done my best with you for Frank Harris. You will not, I hope, bear 'malice against *me* for that. Thank you for returning the book. I, of course, did not know that it would be unwelcome." That will not sow a dragon's tooth, and it will probably make him feel doubtful whether it was kind to write in the third person.'

'As to Wells's attitude towards Frank, you must be prepared for that. Frank is a sort of monster: a man with a range which extends from the most delicate susceptibility to the most callous blackguardism; and no man is bound to put up with his extravagances in one direction for the sake of his achievements in the other. When Wells says, "I *know* Harris," it is quite possible that Harris has outrageously offended him or some of his friends; and Wells is highly susceptible of offence. You have already remarked that Harris believes that my own behaviour towards him was mean (his own expression) although I treated him as well as any reasonable man can expect to be treated in this world. The fact that he regards himself as Well's benefactor does not give you the least guarantee that he may not have treated Wells in an infuriating manner.'

'MacCarthy was delighted when I told him that you were furious with the papers because they dismissed Frank's book in a brief paragraph while devoting whole pages to Mr Britling and an insignificant little item like the war. He said you were quite right. . . . The notice in *The Manchester Guardian* is very generous for an old man of 70. Did you expect him to write three columns proclaiming Frank as the Messiah?' (At the author's request I had sent his *Wilde* to several leading papers.)

Later I called on Shaw and he amplified the sketch of Harris which he had already given me in these letters, repeating in much the same words some of the foregoing passages.

After the war I wrote a 'portrait' of Harris for my first book, sending the proofs to Shaw for permission to publish some of his letters. He asked me to reconsider my essay, as in his opinion it made Harris out to be 'an odious character . . . repudiated by authors of such high standing as Conrad and Wells. . . . Why rake up his tantrums and follies, which are only too well known, in an article which does not say a word about the qualities that induce some of us to put up with them? . . . If you call witnesses to Harris's character, why call hostile ones unless you want to discredit him? Do you want to quarrel with Frank? If so, is it not easy to do it without quarrelling with Conrad and Wells also? . . . Nothing is easier than to tell the story without a word against Harris's standing or character. You need not dramatize my magnanimity by alleging that he treated me badly: I can spare that brick from my pyramid.' Shaw's advice was sound and I ought to have taken it. Harris was not pleased with my well-meaning attempt to re-establish him in England, although I had called him the most dynamic writer alive, the author of the greatest novel in English, the greatest biography in English, and heaven knows what else in English.

It was also just after the war that Harris had an offer from a film company, which promised to pay him a substantial sum if he could get Shaw's co-operation in a screen version of his book on Oscar Wilde. Harris wrote asking me to help his wife, who had crossed the Atlantic in order to persuade Shaw to allow parts of his letter about Wilde to be flashed on the screen while the film was being shown; at least that was how Harris explained the object of her mission to me. Shaw, I felt sure, would not hesitate for a moment: nor did he. Mrs Harris called upon him; and after expressing his amazement that she had not divorced Frank years before and married a millionaire, he pointed out that the story could not be screened, as too many of the characters were still alive and powerful, notably Edward Carson. Mrs Harris, unconvinced, appealed to me, and I went to see Shaw.

'Why won't you do this for Frank?' I asked.

'Frank's a baby, Mrs Frank's a baby, and you're the biggest baby of the three,' he answered.

'Then give me my comforter. In a word, do as I ask.'

'Are you really such a thundering lunatic as you make yourself out to be? Do you honestly believe that the only thing these American people want is my permission to flash passages of my letter on the screen? They could do that without my permission. What's to prevent them? They could, if they wished, reproduce passages from the *Times* criticism of Frank's book, but they couldn't advertise that the scenario was by the *Times* as well as Frank. Can't you see that what they want to do is to advertise the fact that the scenario is by Bernard Shaw (in capital letters) and Frank Harris (in small letters)?'

'Oh, but Frank told me—'

'Humbug! Frank knows nothing about these film people. I do. They have approached me hundreds of times. They have offered me a quarter of a million pounds to release half a dozen of my plays for the screen. I have refused, and I shall continue to refuse. Shavian plots are as silly as Shakespearean plots, and, like Shakespeare's, they are all stolen from other writers. Until my words can be heard as well, they can whistle for my stories.'

'So you think that's what they are after—'

'Think, my uncle! I *know*. They are trying to bamboozle Frank—and me. Well, let them try! If my name is even breathed as having written a syllable of their wretched scenario, I'll have the law on them!'

'I see your point.'

'Loud cheers!'

'But why won't you help Frank with his scenario?'

'Well, of all the—! Hesketh, I'm surprised at you. Why has it never occurred to you to ask me to sign one of your own works? I could make £20,000 for you by putting my name to a book by you. Why not ask me to do so?'

'Well, I—'

'I'll tell you why. Because it would be forgery, and, though a fool, you're not a scoundrel.'

'Still, I might easily ask you to write a preface to a book by me.'

'Then you'll ask in vain. If your work isn't worth reading for its own sake, put it in the fire and sweep a crossing. You shall not become a Best Seller by scrambling on to my back.'

'So the situation is this: you refuse to be connected in any way with the scenario of this Wilde film—'

'Or any other film—'

'But you raise no objection to their using passages from your letter about Wilde published in Frank's book.'

'If you care to waste your time writing such nonsense, by all means do so. But they know perfectly well what they can do and what they cannot do. As to the scenario—NO! And that's final. I hope Mrs Frank didn't cross the Atlantic for an answer that could have been given by cable.'

'I'm afraid my intervention has been useless.'

'Not at all! It has taught you a much-needed lesson: to leave Frank to stew in his own juice. Now go and sin no more.'

As I wanted to show Harris that I had done all I could for him, I wrote to Shaw and he summarized in a letter the objections he had raised during our conversation.

In the summer of 1928 Shaw was staying at Antibes and several times went over to Nice to see Harris, who in his retirement there had published an autobiography of such a nature that Mrs Shaw, not considering it the sort of reading to place within reach of her maids, burned it, to the intense indignation of Harris, who regarded it as pre-eminently a book for ladies and even nuns. He was then meditating a book on Christ; but the publishers demanded a book on Shaw instead. By that time Harris was at the end of his tether, bankrupt in money and health, and, as to Shaw, hopelessly out-of-date. He made a desperate effort to produce the desired book. He invented a wildly fictitious story of Shaw's boyhood, making him the son of a bog-trotting beery peasant, persecuted as a Methodist. A eulogy of *Candida,* with quotations (it was the only Shaw play he knew), followed. Then came what he called a Sex Credo, with a few of Shaw's letters, and another fiction concerning Shaw's marriage. Harris, exhausted, then threw in his hand and left the rest to a stray American journalist who knew less of the subject than Harris. On this he got what advances he could from his American publishers until they submitted the book to Shaw for his approval, as it was highly libellous. Shaw had to veto it ; and presently Harris died, leaving his widow destitute ; whereupon Shaw spent many weeks eliminating the fictions and filling up the hiatuses and rewriting the work, which, when published, he described to me as 'my autobiography by Frank Harris' He had conscientiously preserved all Harris's disparagements of himself whilst correcting the facts.

Unfortunately the advances made to Harris by the publishers had left the book a squeezed lemon for the moment ; and the only other lucrative asset was Harris's *Life and Confessions of Oscar Wilde,* published in the United States in several editions, but stopped in the British Empire by Lord Alfred Douglas, whom it left under the intolerable imputation, started by his own father, that he was not only Wilde's friend but his accomplice in the events that led to Wilde's disgrace and ruin.

Shaw set to work to produce an inoffensive edition of the *Life and Confessions,* and to do justice at long last to Lord Alfred. This, as to the latter, he accomplished by his favourite weapon, a preface. The task of editing was greatly facilitated by the existence of a revision made by Lord Alfred himself on which he found it unnecessary and impossible to improve. This very competent revision had come into existence in the following circumstances.

In order to get his biography of Wilde published in England, Harris had offered to remove all the libels on Lord

367

Alfred Douglas, and to write a new preface explaining how he had been deceived by Robert Ross into making Douglas the villain of the piece. Douglas was quite willing to let the book be issued in England on these terms, and Harris wrote the preface. But he refused to alter the original text on the ground that he possessed plates of it and could not afford to have it set up afresh. Douglas naturally insisted, and even made the revision afterwards adopted by Shaw. But Harris in a rage broke off the negotiations, writing a further preface in which he implied that he had been deceived by 'Douglas into making Ross the villain of the piece and that the original work was after all 'the true truth'.

It seemed to me that such proceedings were not those of a scrupulously honest biographer. Further, I had discovered for myself or learnt from others that very few of Harris's *Contemporary Portraits* (five volumes of them) were even partly reliable, whilst the majority were obviously fictional. Next, I read an unpublished letter of Wilde's which made it perfectly clear that he had not travelled to the Riviera in Harris's company, a journey which had resulted in one of the most important "confessions" in the book. I decided that a man whose indifference to facts was so complete, however entertaining he might be as a character or a Casanova (and I still thoroughly enjoyed him as an unconscious comedian), should have stuck to fiction and left biography severely alone. I was further impressed by an attack on Frank's veracity by Robert Harborough Sherard, a rival biographer. I wrote to Sherard; and he sent a copy of my note to Shaw, whose statement that Wilde's memory would have to stand or fall by Harris's portrait had done so much to sell the book and establish it as an authority. Shaw forwarded the copy on to me, with this letter:

'R.M.S. *Rangitane,*
outward bound London to New Zealand.
'Mid-Pacific,
28*th Feb.,* 1934.

'DEAR HESKETH PEARSON,

'Now that I have a moment's leisure—the first for many months—and am reminded of you by your monument to that old joker Sydney Smith among my stock of books to read, I must drop you a line about the enclosed fragment of shrapnel from the Sherard bombardment.

'You need not recant your opinion of F.H.'s life of Wilde. It is still, as far as I know, by far the best literary portrait of Oscar in existence, simply because Frank was the best writer who tackled the job, and because he knew Wilde well personally. Sherard's idolatrous picture of Wilde is obviously false; you can say of it what William Morris said of the Droeshout portrait of Shakespear: "We know it's not like Shakespear because it's not like a man."

'Sherard makes the mistake of thinking that by convincing Frank of inventions and inaccuracies he invalidates the portrait, much as if Millais had painted Oscar in a red tie with a green umbrella. Wilde was never seen with either; but the portrait would be far more truthful than one by a common painter perfectly accurate in every detail. As I am myself the victim of a biography by Harris which did not contain a single objective statement that was even approximately true (though it conveyed quite truthfully what he thought and felt about me) I have no illusions about Frank's style of painting; but I do not think that there is anything essentially false about his presentment of Wilde from Harris's point of view.

'Harris did not intend to tell lies about Wilde or to represent him as other than he appeared to him. Sherard is setting up an idol which is like nothing on earth, and vilifying every one who does not worship it. He will drive himself crazy if he is encouraged to go on with it.

'As when you were younger you had a generous admiration for Frank there is nothing that we can tell one another about him that we dont already know; and all Sherard's wonderful detective feats do not amount to a row of beans for us; but do not let yourself be seduced by them into a recantation of a verdict of yours which was quite sound.

'I shall not be back in London until the middle of May. Anyhow this needs no answer: I know what a bother letter writing is.

'G. BERNARD SHAW.'

My answer was that though Harris may not have intended to tell lies about Wilde, he had never been able to discriminate between what was true and what was false; that though a fancy might be more vivid than a fact, the value of a biography lay in its accuracy; that no one would have raised any objection if Harris had called his book on Wilde 'a romance'; and that if Shaw studied Sherard's criticisms with an open mind he would be the first to recognize that the biography was worthless.

But I could not move Shaw, who held that if a biography showed what manner of man its subject was it did not matter a straw if every line of it was inaccurate.[1]

Sherard's full exposure of Harris's inventions, entitled *Bernard Shaw, Frank Harris and Oscar Wilde,* came out in 1937. I rashly assumed that after reading it Shaw would recant. But he only made fun of Sherard's simultaneous statements that: (a) Harris's book was a tissue of lies from beginning to end, and (b) that it was all plagiarized from Sherard's own biography. Shaw also thought that Sherard's explanation of Wilde's perversion—an adulterous intrigue causing syphilis and madness—was a tactless fiction which left Harris's imaginative flights nowhere.

Harris's *Life of Wilde,* with Shaw's preface, was duly published. Desmond MacCarthy in *The Sunday Times,* Harold Nicolson in *The Daily Telegraph* and myself in *The Observer* promptly denounced the book as utterly unreliable and wondered why Shaw had done this thing. Shaw gave the reason in a letter to *The Sunday Times,* wherein he expressed a wish that Desmond MacCarthy should 'feel a little for Mrs Harris, left with no property except Harris's copyrights. I suggest that Messrs Desmond, Sherard, Pearson and Co. subscribe to purchase the copyright of this book from her. They can then withdraw it at their own expense.' Thus Shaw was again being loyal to Frank Harris by helping his widow. Hugh Kingsmill's comment was: 'There is an obvious difference between helping Mrs Harris at his own expense and at Wilde's.'

Since Shaw knew that Harris was 'a frightful liar' and completely irresponsible, that Harris's book on himself 'did not contain a single objective statement that was even approximately true', and that Sherard had convicted Harris of numerous errors, his persistence in maintaining that Harris's biography of Wilde was the only true one calls for some explanation. The main elements in his character explain his attitude. The rebellious and adventurous schoolboy in him was attracted to Harris from the start, and the first impres-

[1] I have not noticed that his attitude is quite the same to a biography of himself.

sion never wore off. His generosity responded to what was generous in Harris, whose recklessness and fire complemented his cautiousness and timidity. Never having been swindled by Harris, he had not suffered personal disillusion, and having no malice in his nature, he felt no annoyance when Harris tried to belittle him. He never ceased to be grateful to Harris for having given him a free hand as a dramatic critic and standing by him when litigation seemed imminent. He overvalued the work of Harris because he retained an adolescent love of force and rhetoric in literature. Outside his own provinces of music and the drama he did not exercise his critical ability because his interests were not aroused. 'These novelists *will* persist in inventing strings of fiction and calling them plays instead of seizing a theme and developing it,' he complained to Sutro of Zangwill's and Bennett's dramatic efforts. But as these two were novelists, they were chiefly interested in strings of fiction. The same with biography. 'It is the doctrine and not the man that matters,' said Shaw of Jesus Christ. But the man alone interests his biographer, to whom the doctrine is merely valuable for the light it casts on the man. Here is a case in point: Shaw's doctrine that the man does not matter illuminates himself, for it explains why he so carelessly accepted Harris's picture of Wilde as fundamentally authentic. If he had taken an objective interest in Wilde for his own sake, instead of as a theme for Harris to develop or as a text for Harris to moralize upon, Shaw would have perceived the falsity of the portrait. Whether, perceiving it, he would have withdrawn his recommendation, I cannot say; for through his nature ran that strain of vanity and wilfulness which characterized another historical personage, who, equally vague about the value of truth, insisted that what he had written he had written.

RETREAT TO MOSCOW

As a man of business Shaw was so much better informed in law and economics than the publishers and managers with whom he had to deal—'all romantic dreamers' he called them

—that he had to take care of their interests as well as his own in his contracts, which were always drafted by himself. He once presented a contract for signature to Forbes-Robertson with the words, 'Will you sign or will you argue?' 'I will sign,' said the great actor, and did so without reading a word, knowing that Shaw would take better care of his interests than he could himself, and that, anyhow, Shaw could argue the hind leg off a donkey. Shaw was consistent and calculable in business for anyone who understood business. He knew that a good contract is one which is good enough for both parties, and that the money value of a work of art is what it will fetch and has nothing to do with its merits as such. His *esprit de corps* was inflexible: to exact less than the market price of his work or to obtain a production by underselling his competitors was to him the crime of a blackleg. He never sold his rights. After his first commercial production in the theatre a speculator bid £150 for the continental rights in *Arms and The Man*. In those days British playwrights jumped at such offers. Shaw said, 'How are foreign authors to live if the managers are able to pick up British plays for next to nothing?' When his plays were demanded abroad later on, he ascertained the highest fees paid to native authors, and insisted on these for himself, or, if they were inadequate, on his full British (London) terms. In certain countries these, though moderate enough, were protested against as unheard-of and impossible. Shaw was adamant ; and when he had his way the astonished and impoverished native authors demanded the same and succeeded. This was the sort of trade-union triumph which he thoroughly enjoyed.

In dealing with local theatrical ventures, 'Little' theatres, repertory theatres, and similar dramatic struggles for life in places outside the commercial grooves, it was usual for playwrights, or rather their agents, to class these adventurers as amateurs, and make them pay fixed fees—usually five guineas —for each performance. Such fees were prohibitive for any but rich people indulging the vanity of imitating fashionable players in fashionable plays, and giving the profits (if any) to charities. And the authors felt that, as ladies and gentlemen, they could not accept less in fees than guineas. Shaw broke with this system ruthlessly by granting professional terms in every instance in which the profits went into the theatre or were appropriated by the performers. When the performance was in a village schoolroom, and the gross receipts were fifteen shillings, the author's fee being ninepence, Shaw pocketed the pennies and touched his hat, trusting for a continuance of the little Society's custom. The ninepence did not pay for the postage and the overhead; but it made possible a dramatic activity all over the country which yielded Shaw an income on which many a clerk or small shopkeeper could have lived and brought up a family.

All this may suggest a keen and able man of business prospering accordingly; but Shaw protested that he had lost oceans of money by being so preoccupied with writing and public work that he seldom attended to his business until he was forced to do so. 'I should have taken a business partner with a flair for advertisement,' he said. 'People say that I am always advertising myself. What they mean is that hundreds of fools keep writing foolish lies about me that simply damage me. The result is that everybody talks about me; but nobody reads my books.'

In fact, Shaw's settled income, though sufficient to keep him comfortably in the surtaxed section of the professional class, and reinforced by his wife's resources, which were substantial, did not justify the common descriptions of him as a millionaire. I once asked him about such windfalls as the extraordinary success of the *Pygmalion* film, estimated by the press at £55,000. He said: 'Divide by four to get rid of exaggeration. Deduct British and American taxation. Invest the balance at two and a half per cent if you can get it. Deduct from the interest taxation at about twelve shillings in the pound. That will give you the gingerbread with the gilt off. Nine tenths of our people know nothing about money when it runs into two figures, never having had any. You can imagine what their guesses are worth when it runs into four or five.'[1]

He admitted that a reputation for colossal wealth was sometimes useful. But it had to be accompanied by a defensive reputation for rapacity and meanness. This he deliberately cultivated. Having answered a reply-paid wire by post-card, he was asked to return the pre-paid telegram form. 'I return the form under protest,' he complained. 'Reply-paids are my perquisite. I always answer by post, and get my telegraphing free in consequence.' When he was asked why he had

[1] In January 1942, he wrote to me: 'The *Pygmalion* film has brought me in £29,000 in royalties and cost me £50,000 in war taxation. Heaven defend you from such successes. Another will ruin me.'

lent the Durham coalminers £30,000 for the construction of cheap dwelling-houses, he replied, 'Six per cent.'

Had he been as avaricious as he wished to appear, he would not have neglected the theatre for three years after his biggest box-office success in order to write *The Intelligent Woman's Guide to Socialism* (1928), which contains everything that he had thought and felt on the subject for over forty years, expressed with a clarity and cogency never before or since achieved by any writer on a technical theme. He defined the purpose of the work in the course of a talk with me:

'Early in the present century I threw a bombshell. I said that the man in the street was right. This was considered revolutionary. The man in the street had always said that socialism meant equal incomes for all, and I staggered every one by saying that I entirely agreed with him. That, I think, is my sole original contribution to socialist thought. I spent four years studying economics, only to find that no one knew anything about it; and having discovered that the whole capitalist system was just one of plunder, I said that the citizen had to decide on what provocation he would cut his neighbour's throat, my rough and ready judgment being that if A had 3/6 and B 2/6, B should cut A's throat, and of course vice versa. I defy any one to estimate the merits of individuals in terms of money; and as no one can say in what proportions wealth should be distributed, equal incomes for all is the only possible alternative to the present distribution by robbery. I have two friends: Dean Inge and Gene Tunney. What auctioneer is going to value their relative worth in pounds or dollars? At present Gene can buy Dr Inge up ten times over without overdrawing his bank account. Is that distribution an ideal one?'

As one who enjoys neither preaching nor punching, I agreed that a decision in the case he mentioned would be difficult.

Shaw did not believe, as so many socialist do, that the possession of money would solve all the problems that perplex humanity: 'All the thoughtful ones will assure you that happiness and unhappiness are constitutional, and have nothing to do with money. Money can cure hunger: it cannot cure unhappiness. Food can satisfy the appetite, but not the soul.' Not being a materialist he drew his morality from a deeper source than that of most utopians: 'Good conduct is a respect which you owe to yourself in some mystical way; and people are manageable in proportion to their possession

374

of this self-respect. . . . There is a mysterious something in us called a soul, which deliberate wickedness kills, and without which no material gain can make life bearable. . . Good conduct is not dictated by reason but by a divine instinct that is beyond reason. Reason only discovers the shortest way: it does not discover the destination.' His belief that people are consciously or unconsciously stumbling upwards to the throne of God made him light of heart and bred in him such a large toleration for the shortcomings of human nature that he could picture a saintlike Inquisitioner in *Saint Joan*, which is much the same as portraying a voluntary hangman as a gentle soul or a born garrotter with a heart of gold or for that matter any judge that ever lived with a Christlike disposition. His religion also inclined him to blame external conditions for the wickedness of man: 'Street arabs are produced by slums not by original sin . . . he who would reform himself must first reform society.' This seemed like putting the cart before the horse, for what were slums produced by? 'The Ricardian law of rent which nobody understands,' was his reply. One might have asked how the Ricardian law of rent had been conceived and exploited, but life is short. Shaw, however, insisted that not evil but ignorance was the matter. 'The malignant demon,' he assured me, 'is not Shakespear's angry ape dressed in a little brief authority, but the impersonal Ricardian law of rent, which remains the *pons asinorum* of political science. If only it could be knocked into people's heads as effectively as the Apostles' Creed, they would react to it as Henry George did, or Karl Marx, or Sidney Webb, or myself.' A man's nature is revealed in his hopes for the world, and Shaw's belief in the possibility of an international brotherhood through communism is creditable to his heart if not to his head.

It is possible that Shaw himself would have been content in a state of society where equal incomes prevailed. For him money meant nothing more than security and exemption from petty tyrannies. Otherwise he found it troublesome, for it attracted parasites and hatred, and he loathed charity and patronizing: 'When I have to relieve people financially I hate them as heartily as they hate me.' People who had a vague notion that socialism is a state of society in which everyone gives away his possessions to everyone else sometimes reproached him for not beggaring himself. He retorted that only a madman behaved as if he were living in his own particular utopia. If the rich unloaded their riches, it would not be the poor who would pick them up. When I reminded him that Jesus advised the rich man to sell all that he had and give it to the poor, Shaw replied: 'As Jesus never had any property and left all the business of his ministry to Judas, he simply did not know what he was talking about. He should have advised the opulent young man that under Roman rule he could do no better than invest his money in gilt-edged or in land and drop what he could spare into Judas's bag. Taking an interest in Christianity would make him much happier and better than spending what it cost him on chariot racing or on harlotry.' Shaw's advice might have pleased the rich man; but Jesus was concerned with individual salvation, not general prosperity.

The manuscript of the *Guide* was sent to six of Shaw's expert friends, including of course the Webbs, for criticism and correction. The result was the elimination of sundry slips and clerical errors, and the publication of the book with thirty blunders described by the author as 'howlers which blazed to the heavens'. These got corrected one by one in letters from total strangers all over the country. Which explains why Shaw hated first editions. They are always the worst, he declared.

Passing from socialism in theory to socialism in action, it is difficult to reconcile many of Shaw's pronounced opinions with his support of the Bolshevik régime in Russia. For example: 'Progress depends on our refusal to use brutal means even when they are efficacious.' 'A civilization cannot progress without criticism, and must therefore, to save itself from stagnation and putrefaction, declare impunity for criticism.' 'Civic education does not mean education in blind obedience to authority, but education in controversy and liberty . . . in scepticism, in discontent and betterment . . .' 'No single criminal can be as powerful for evil, or as unrestrained in its exercise, as an organized nation . . . it legalizes its crimes, and forges certificates of righteousness for them, besides torturing any one who dares expose their true character.' None of these remarks would at any time have been read sympathetically at the Kremlin. 'Had we not better teach our children to be better citizens than ourselves?' demanded Shaw. 'We are not doing that at present. The Russians *are*.' He had already been answered by the author of *Man and Superman*: 'The vilest abortionist is he who attempts to mould a child's character.'

But a human being who has spoken as many words as Shaw would be a miracle, not a man, if his opinions had not occasionally clashed; and in any case Shaw's hatred of stagnation was enough to make him see pink when Russia went red. I once happened to say that, though revolutions seldom do much good, they sometimes do a lot of very refreshing harm; a remark that pleased him so much that I felt it partly explained his attitude towards the Russian affair. But we must make an effort to see what happened from his own angle.

When the Russian revolution of 1917 put modern Marxist Communism—Shaw's professed political creed—to its first serious practical test, the Bolshevists were, if possible, more venomously execrated by the British socialists and labour leaders than by the capitalist parties. This lasted until, at a public meeting of the Fabian Society, Shaw rose and said, 'We are socialists. The Russian side is our side.' A stunned silence followed; but when the debate was resumed there were no more disparagements of the Soviet. Shaw sent one of his books to Lenin with a highly complimentary inscription of which a lithographed facsimile was made and circulated in Russia. When he visited Russia in 1931 he was made as much of as if he had been Karl Marx in person.

Nevertheless he was under no illusions as to the first effects of the attempt to govern 160 millions of people on Marxist principles by a handful of ex-underground conspirators with no experience of practical administration. They called Shaw 'a good man fallen among Fabians': Fabians being to them an utterly contemptible little gang of *petit bourgeois* triflers. And they began, on principle, by destroying their capitalist institutions before they had provided communist organizations to carry on, the very error against which Shaw in his Fabian preaching had warned them. His pet lesson was that a government must not take a penny from the private capitalist until it was ready to perform the social function he was performing, however anti-social his incentives might be. It took three years of indescribable ruin, starvation and civil war to convince Lenin that he must adopt what he called the New Economic Policy, which was, in fact, nothing but the toleration of the old economic policy of private trade, until the Soviet organization was ready to take its place. Shaw, commissioned handsomely by the Hearst Press of America to

377

visit Russia as H. G. Wells had done, and to tell the world what was going on there, refused, knowing only too well what he would see. He was not surprised when Tolstoy's daughter called on him, disillusioned and almost broken-hearted, to describe how the prosperous well-farmed countryside round the Tolstoy family seat at Yásnaya Poliana was now a wilderness of weeds and waste where no man could make a living. He could only have said, 'I told you so' if he had been unkind enough. The Soviet had thrown out the prosperous farmers as kulaks on principle, because they were exploiters of labourers and horses; but it had not provided for the cultivation of their farms; and the time was to come when it would be glad to throw them in again pending the arrival of the collective farmers and the organizing commissars to carry on the national agriculture. The streets and shops of Leningrad and Moscow told the same tale; and Shaw had no intention of telling it over again for the capitalists of London and Chicago to exult in. He knew that it was a passing phase, and that bitter experience would compel the remedy, which was not more destruction but, in his opinion, more communism.

Meanwhile, however, he stuck to the Fabian Society and would have nothing to do with the so-called communist parties who regarded their countries, on internationalist principles, as local branches of the World Revolution of Trotsky and the doctrinaire Marxists, and accepted not only guidance but money from Moscow. When he was outvoted in a Research Committee on which he sat as a Fabian delegate by a majority of wild young communists on the money point, he resigned at once, in spite of his usual advice to novices never to resign. It was characteristic of him to resign on a point of diplomatic etiquette; for another of his favourite counsels to revolutionists was, 'Be as correct as possible in your general conduct; for your socialism will set up quite as much friction as you will have time for in your private affairs.' Also he insisted on the socialist movement in England being characteristically British. When imitation Fascists and Bolsheviks began to sport black shirts and red ties, he warned them that such fashions would make them outsiders in England. He maintained that the Fabians alone had studied socialism scientifically and carried it farther than Marx, who, like the first Bolsheviks, had no practical experience of public administration, and wrote about capitalists, employers and proletarians like a man who had never talked to one of them

378

in his life. All Shaw's Fabian facts and authorities were British facts and authorities, mostly gathered by the omniscient Sidney Webb ; and this goes far to explain how Shaw, an artist-philosopher and an Irishman, kept his hold on the intensely philistine middle-class English Fabians, who regarded metaphysics as cloudy nonsense, and artists as disreputable bohemians. Shaw as the perfect Fabian was also the perfect philistine ; for no mistake could be more complete than to suppose that the Fabians were in the very least Shavians. Like all leaders Shaw had his handful of idolators ; and there were, of course, individual exceptions to the philistine rule. But the bond between him and the Fabians as a whole was one of reciprocal usefulness in the pursuit of their common political aim. He valued the Fabian atmosphere highly because it forced him 'to keep his feet on the ground' (another pet prescription of his) and taught him to handle all sorts of antipathetic people, making it impossible for those who disliked him intensely to quarrel with him ; but it was no more native to him than to William Morris, who could not breathe in it.

When Stalin split with Trotsky on the question of the possibility of establishing socialism in a single country without waiting for a revolution of the proletariat all over the world, Shaw, believing that not only would socialism begin, as it had already begun in single countries, but could not possibly begin in any other way, took Stalin's view as a matter of course as part of the inevitable Fabianising of Bolshevism. Accordingly, when he at last visited Russia in 1931, by which time the Bolshevist régime had become presentable and in fact imposing, he was in complete sympathy with Stalin's policy and better able to understand and judge what he was to see than ninety-nine per cent of the inhabitants, in spite of the desperate efforts of the Soviet to inculcate the Marxian dialectic and the early chapters of *Das Kapital* (erroneous and unreadable, according to Shaw) on all its infants.

Nevertheless, the visit was quite unintended by Shaw, who was by his own confession curiously dependent on external pressures for any activity outside his daily routine. 'If I had been let alone,' he said, 'I should have died in the house I was born in.' And again, 'My nature is arboreal. Why does an oak grow taller and live longer than a man? Because it does not waste its energy moving about from one spot to another that is no better.' Mrs Phillimore, authoress of works on St

379

Paul, called him an old tramcar, always on the same set of rails.

It was, however, easy enough to derail him if others did the job. One day the Marquess of Lothian called on him to say that Lady Astor badly needed a holiday, and that he and Lord Astor proposed a trip to Russia and would like Shaw to join them. Shaw desired no better company, and packed his bag at once.

The legends that have grown up about that visit are, Shaw declared, all lies. The popular one about his taking with him a stock of provisions, and having to throw them out of the railway-carriage window when he found that Russia was a land of plenty, was invented by a journalist who knew much less about Russia than Shaw; but Lady Astor, deluded by the tales in *The Times,* did actually take sufficient tinned food for five people (her son David was of the company) for a fortnight. This was not thrown out of the window: there was a grand distribution of it to the hotel staff the day before their departure for home, making a noble addition to the tips which hotel servants accepted without scruple, though in other directions Shaw's experiments in tipping were all refused.

The Russian food suited Shaw. He found Kasha 'the best porridge in the world'. Black bread and cabbage soup were for him an ideal diet. The dozens of cucumbers which were served at every Russian meal did not dismay him; and he soon got used to the soup appearing at the end of his dinner instead of at the beginning. His companions, not being vegetarians, were perhaps less appreciative; but they had nothing to complain of. The hotel, which they had expected to find full of police spies, was full of Americans, with the management doing its best to feed and entertain them in the fashionable western manner, and the guests talked treason (in English) much more freely than they would have done in London at the Ritz. There was only one breakdown, and that was in the lift, which stuck between floors and caged Lady Astor and G.B.S., who were hauled out ignominiously by the ears with so little space to spare that they took care not to trust themselves in it again.

The impression made by Moscow on Shaw and Lady Astor was naturally very different. To her, prosperity meant beautifully dressed ladies and gentlemen in Rolls-Royces against a background of Bond Street and the Rue de la Paix where the shop-windows were ablaze with goods costing pounds and even thousands of pounds. What she actually saw were cheaply-dressed people, all with business or labour of one kind or another on hand, against a background that can be seen any day in Lambeth and Southwark, where the great main streets put the west-end ones to shame by their spaciousness, but where the shops deal in half-pence and invite poor customers instead of frightening them away. Only, most of the Moscow shops were closed; and those that dealt in objects of art exhibited them with cloak-room number tickets attached and without the least attempt at window-dressing, evidently with no knowledge of their values. 'If you spotted a treasure you went in and said you wanted its number,' Shaw informed me. 'The shop assistant, very unpretentiously attired, accepted your entrance as a friendly social call; consulted a list as to the price of your number; and concluded the transaction without taking the smallest commercial interest in it.' Needless to add, all the good bargains, ridiculously underpriced, had been snapped up by connoisseurs long before Shaw's arrival. To a western millionaire nothing could be more depressing. To Shaw it was better than he expected, and full of novelty and promise. The absence of ladies and gentlemen was such a relief to him that when, on leaving Russia, he went into the Polish first-class waiting-room and saw two young ladies there, his first impulse was to call the police and have them removed and set to hard labour. He noted with hopeful satisfaction the faces free from those marks of continual money troubles and, among the manual workers, of disillusion too resigned and hopeless to be called cynical, which he considered the stigmata of capitalist civilization. The lack of luxury shops did not trouble him: he was fond of saying that he had walked through Bond Street and Regent Street with empty pockets and with full ones, and the result was the same in both cases: he bought nothing. The Goldsmiths' Alliance once tried to tempt him with a blue diamond ring for £4000: he found Woolworth jewellery at fourpence prettier, and did not buy either. The rate at which the Soviet was clearing up its messes from day to day exhilarated him; and the public factories, the collective farms, the palaces and great shooting-lodges full of workers and artists putting in their week-ends there, the magnificent public art collections, the pleasant police courts where the magistrates were sensible women and there were no police, no docks, no apparent

381

coercion, the prisons which were threatened with overcrowd-
ing because the prisoners would not leave when their sentences expired, all pleased and interested Shaw immensely.

On the other hand, he roundly denounced the revolutionary museums, which glorified the old rebels of the Tsarist
régime, many of whom he had met. To the astonished cura-
tors, eagerly expecting his approval, he said, 'Are you mad,
to glorify rebellion now that the Revolution is the Government? Do you want to have the Soviet overthrown? Is it wise
to teach the young that it would be an act of immortal
heroism to assassinate Stalin? Clear out all this dangerous
rubbish, and turn the place into a Law and Order Museum.'
Through the great cathedral, which contained a historical
collection illustrating the atrocities of priestly rule and was
labelled anti-religious, he was piloted by a nun-like girl, who
bore the badge of the League of the Godless, and who had
not the least suspicion that she was a congenital devotee. He
pointed to an exhibit of two mummified bodies and asked
what they were doing there. 'These are the bodies of two
peasants which we found undecayed,' she replied. 'The priests
pretend that this is a miracle that happens only to the bodies
of saints ; but this shows that it may happen quite naturally.'
'How do you know that these two were not saints?' asked
Shaw. This possibility had not occurred either to the Soviet
Government or to the League of the Godless ; and the little
novice was struck dumb. She, by the way, was one of the
subjects on whom Shaw tried his tipping experiments. She
proved incorruptible. Shaw's verdict on the show was that it
was an excellent if somewhat one-sided illustration of the
dangers of ecclesiasticism, and that the municipalities of
Geneva or Belfast would endow it enthusiastically. It had
practically no native visitors, and was being converted into
an advertisement of the first Five Year Plan then in operation.

Shaw was already on the track of saint-worship under the
Soviet. On his arrival in Moscow he and his companions had
gone straight to the Red Square to see the embalmed Lenin
lying in state, and had been surprised to find that the dark
and burly dictator was in fact a slight blond, with aristocratic
hands that had never known manual labour. Later in the evenings they saw queues of many hundreds of workers, their
day's work done, waiting their turns to visit the shrine, which
was to most of them not a mere curiosity but the tomb of

a saint. A commissar, to whom Shaw mentioned his visit, was shocked, and on being asked whether he himself had not made the pilgrimage, indignantly denied that he had been guilty of such an act of superstition. Yet Shaw puzzled them by calling the Comintern a State Church, and prophesying that Church and State would have to fight it out for supreme authority as they had had to in the old Christian States.

To please the English visitors they were conducted to a race-meeting, where Shaw had to hand the prize to the winning jockey. Shaw said that as the Soviet had discarded competition he had presumed that there would be only one horse in each race. The winning jockey did not look like a Russian. He was in fact an Irishman.

In the social way all that Shaw wanted was to see Krupskaya, the widow of Lenin. The rest of the party were determined to have a talk with Stalin. No objection was made as to the widow; but the visit got postponed from day to day on one pretext or another until it became clear that it was not intended to take place at all. Krupskaya, it was said, was in bed with a cold. She was old and of a solitary disposition, and must not be disturbed at the moment. She was living, not in Moscow, but in a log hut in the woods in the country. When a drive thither was suggested, she was living in Moscow. At last Shaw put his foot down. He had been entrusted with a book to deliver to her. He did not wish to intrude on her; but he was determined to leave the book and his visiting-card at her door, wherever that door might be. Lady Astor, hearing that Krupskaya had fallen out with Stalin on the subject of education to such an extent that he had threatened to appoint another lady as Lenin's official widow, emphatically declared that she would not leave Russia until they had set eyes on her. At last the excuses suddenly collapsed; and a visit was arranged to the log hut in the woods. It turned out to be a princely shooting-lodge. Krupskaya, who was perfectly well, gave them such an enthusiastic welcome that they could scarcely believe in her reported passion for solitude, the place being full of her courtiers. She was visibly relieved and delighted to find the terrible Shaw quite charming. Not a word was said about Stalin. The truth was that all the evasions had been made up by Krupskaya herself, who had imagined Shaw to be personally an unbearably disagreeable fellow.

Shaw was even more surprised and delighted than his hostess. She shared with Mrs William Booth of the Salvation

Army the distinction of being photographically the ugliest woman in Europe. And just as General Booth spoke of Mrs William passionately as 'my beautiful wife', and their daughter Evangeline also described her mother as extraordinarily beautiful, Shaw found Krupskaya irresistibly lovable. He declared that if she were sent into a roomful of children they would be 'all over her' in a second. He raved about her strangely set Mongolian eyes. The tea at the shooting-lodge was an immense success.

In spite of the fact that no visitor had been granted an interview with Stalin, who had not been seen even by the British and American Ambassadors, an exception was made in the case of Lord Astor and his friends. Though the request was greeted with a splutter of appalled amazement, a meeting was fixed, the Astors, who arranged it, being pledged to secrecy. Shaw never heard of the pledge ; and I am therefore able to relate what happened at a meeting which, though unsought by Shaw, who had no mission to Stalin and did not want to waste his time to gratify mere curiosity, was secured by Lord Astor. Let it therefore be recorded with Voltaire's meeting with Frederick the Great and Goethe's with Napoleon.

'Unlike the other dictators, Stalin has an irrepressible sense of humour,' summarized Shaw. 'He is not a Russian: he is a handsome Georgian› with the attractive dark eyes of his race. There is an odd mixture of the Pope and the field-marshal in him: you might guess him to be the illegitimate soldier-son of a cardinal. I should call his manners perfect if only he had been able to conceal the fact that we amused him enormously. First of all he let us talk ourselves empty. Then he asked if he might say a few words. We couldn't understand a syllable he uttered: the only word I caught was "Wrangel", the name of one of the generals England had backed against the Bolsheviks. He was soon brimming with amusement ; but as the utterly incompetent interpreter's teeth were chattering with fright, the point of his pleasantries escaped us. But for Litvinoff, who was present, we should have left without a translation.'

'Stalin is a quiet, dark-eyed person, well-behaved and very grim. He did not smile once while we were with him,' Lady Astor informed me.

These flatly contradictory accounts of eye-witnesses of the same scene, a constant occurrence which makes life so difficult for the biographer, explain the mental states of the reporters.

On one point, at least, there is no doubt. It was Lady Astor, and she alone, who got the better of Stalin. She told him that the Soviet did not know how to treat children. Stalin, confident that everything in Russia was sacrificed to the nurture and education of the young, suddenly became stern, and without dissembling his astonishment and indignation made a gesture like the slash of a whip, exclaiming with real feeling, 'In England you BEAT children.'

'All Russia would have been abashed and silenced had all Russia been present,' said Shaw, in describing the scene to me. 'The attempt to abash and silence Lady Astor was about as successful as an effort by a fly to make head against a whirlwind. Her fearless impetuosity rocked the Kremlin to its foundations. He (Stalin) did not know what he was talking about. She (Nancy Astor) did. She had not fostered and financed the sisters Macmillan in their Child Welfare experiment in Deptford for nothing. Those prettily-dressed little girls in their dainty nursery at the collective farm, with their unbroken new toys: why were they not out of doors? The nurse had said that it had rained that morning. Rubbish! A child should not know nor care whether it was rain or shine. And the spotless dresses and the clean faces and hands! A child should be grubby, dirty, clayey, except at meals. It should not have a dress from the wardrobe of the Russian ballet: it should have a tough linen frock that could be washed in half an hour. "Send a good sensible woman to me in London," she ordered, "and I will take care of her and show her how children of five should be handled."

'Stalin, overwhelmed, soon guessed that this feminine tornado had perhaps something to teach him. He took an envelope and asked her to write her address on it. This was nice of him; but we took it as a polite attention and expected to hear no more of it. But that is not what happens in Russia. Lady Astor had bargained for one sensible woman. She was hardly safe at home when he sent her a dozen, whom she had to entertain and instruct and take to Deptford. It was a comfort to know that her eloquence had not been wasted; but she must have felt that Uncle Joe had got a bit of his own back.'

Lord Lothian took the floor next. He explained the plight of the liberal intelligentsia in England, where the remnant of the party had divided, its right wing joining the conservatives

385

and its left wandering in the wilderness, because it could not join the labour opposition, which was not up to its level in statesmanship. It was the only body capable of establishing a really scientific communism in the west; and this aim must carry it to the left of the labour party as a new factor in British politics. So far so good; but when Lord Lothian suggested that the Politbureau should invite Mr Lloyd George, as the official leader of this section, to Russia to see the progress made there, Stalin smiled, and evidently thought the proposal too good a joke to be officially possible. He explained, with more humour than was quite reassuring, that the part taken by Mr Lloyd George in the civil war as lately as ten years ago, when General Wrangel was leading the Whites against the Reds, made an official invitation impossible. However, if Mr Lloyd George would come as a private tourist, he would be shown everything and have nothing to complain of. Shaw interposed for the first time to ask whether Mr Winston Churchill would be equally welcome. Stalin replied enigmatically that he would be delighted to see Mr Churchill in Moscow, as they had every reason to be grateful to him. (Shaw explained the joke to me: 'Churchill equipped the Red Army with boots, uniforms and guns. When he was Secretary for War he handed over a hundred millions, which parliament had voted for the war against Germany, to help the royalist counter-revolution in Russia. The Bolsheviks won and managed to clothe and arm themselves with the material so generously provided by Great Britain.')

Lord Astor, as the principal on whose account the interview had been accorded, then very wisely did his best to let Stalin know that in spite of the violent anti-Sovietism of the British newspapers there was in England plenty of friendly feeling towards Russia, and interest in her great social experiment. In his characteristic desire to undo mischief and create good feeling, he went so far that Shaw finished the interview by asking Stalin whether he had ever heard of a person named Oliver Cromwell. After a brief consultation with Litvinoff the two recalled their history lessons and grasped the new subject. 'But what is the point?' said Litvinoff. 'Only this,' replied Shaw. 'In an old ballad, well known in Ireland, Cromwell's word to his soldiers is to "Put your trust in God, my boys, and keep your powder dry." All that Lord Astor has told you about your having friends in England is true. But keep your powder dry.'

Stalin said nothing about putting his trust in God, but intimated that Russia would keep its powder very dry.

And so, with a gracious compliment from Stalin to the venerable Fabian, and cordial farewells all round, the interview ended. The visitors thought they had been considerate enough to detain Stalin for only half an hour. On looking at their watches they found that it was past midnight, and that the actual time had been two hours and thirty-five minutes.

The British and American newspapers were more interested in gossip than in economics, and for them the outstanding episode of the trip was that Lady Astor had been seen washing Shaw's beard, at the request, it was rumoured, of Mrs Shaw. But 'the mob of newspaper men who pursue celebrities in the west do not exist in Russia—or didnt in 1931', Shaw told me: 'Their persecutions and molestations are most blessedly unknown there.' The beard-washing incident was therefore founded on hearsay, and Shaw explained its origin to me: 'All of us needed to have our heads washed after three days and nights in the train. Lady Astor had the necessary sort of soap. When I complained that she was splashing my shirt she said, "Take it off"; so I stripped to the waist. Between talking and scrubbing we forgot our surroundings. When some noise made us look round, there were no reporters and no cameras, but the entire staff of the hotel and as much of the population of Moscow as could squeeze in behind them were enjoying the spectacle. No charge was made for admission as far as we knew.'

APOTHEOSIS

SHORTLY AFTER THE WAR there was a Shaw boom among the repertory theatres scattered about the country, and Charles Macdona toured the plays throughout the provinces with success. The Everyman Theatre at Hampstead throve on his works and sometimes he made an appearance at the final rehearsals. Scores of stories have been invented about him on these occasions, but I have had to exclude every anecdote not authenticated by himself. One story has been told by so many actors that its origin must here be given in Shaw's words to me: 'In the garden scene in *John Bull's Other Island* John Shine, playing Larry Doyle, asked me whether one of his exits did not convey the impression that he had gone off merely to relieve himself. I said, "Of course it does. That is why he retires." Shine made a convulsive effort to keep his face straight. Then he fled to tell the story, which by this time has been told of all my plays, I suppose.'

One of his early plays was also seen in the west end within a year of the war when Robert Loraine revived *Arms and The Man* at the Duke of York's Theatre. Shaw could not attend the first performance because he had to lecture that evening, and Loraine was rather hurt that he did not put off the lecture. But he went on the second or third night, 'and was horrified to find that the experience of 1894 was repeating itself. On that occasion there was a wildly successful first night, on which the company was anxiously doing its best with the play, and wondering what would happen. What happened was that they were overwhelmed with laughter and applause. This set their puzzled minds completely at ease; they concluded that the piece was a farcical comedy. At the subsequent performances they played for the laughs and didnt get them. This was the beginning of that detestable effect as of all the characters being so many Shaws spouting Shavianisms, and provoking first a lot of shallow but willing laughter, and then producing disappointment and irritation.' Shaw told Loraine that his own performance was infamous; that he was simply collecting laughs, asking for them, waiting for them; and then followed this bit of advice which ought to be branded on the memory of every actor: 'The only way to compel the audience to take matters into their own hands is to ignore the laughs and go steadily through them, actually trying to make the audience lose as much as possible of the play through their own noisiness. Remember that the lines one does not hear are always imagined to be the best in the play. And though the words may be lost, the play can at least be seen without any interruption or disillusion. . . . *I* should give orders that the audience was to be absolutely ignored and that the company must play deftly and blindly in the play and for the play, no matter whether they were heard or not. But you like the audience to join in the representation. The result will be a failure. In spite of the first night notices, the public will soon find that the play is an irritating Shavian bore, with no characters in it and no emotion ; and they will stay away. Your eight weeks will become six. Never mind: I shall be blamed.' A month later Shaw paid another visit and was so much struck with something in Loraine's performance that he wrote to ask whether the actor was taking morphia, adding: 'By the way, what is so very exasperating about me in spite of my amiable qualities is not that I am an egotistical and ridiculous author. Consider it a moment, and you will admit that an author's vanity would make you laugh quite good-humoredly. What infuriates people is my incorrigible habit of constituting myself, uninvited, their solicitor, their doctor, and their spiritual director without the smallest delicacy. I have no right whatever to concern myself with your personal habits or your private welfare ; but you see I do. I treat every one sympathetically as an invalid, injudicious in diet, politically foolish, probably intemperate, more or less mendacious and dishonest ; and, however friendly my disposition and cheerful my way of putting it, they dont like it. I cant help it. After all, you cannot reasonably expect a playwright to mind his own business. Other people are his business. And his infernal meddlesomeness is sometimes useful. So be as charitable as you can.' Loraine was naturally furious, and vented his feelings in an explosive letter which did not produce the smallest ill-feeling on the part of Shaw, who expected it as a doctor expects a reaction to his prescription. Loraine, having blown off steam, soon forgot it.

But it so happened that Loraine never acted for Shaw again, though the friendliness of their relations was quite undisturbed. The reason was purely economical. Loraine, not from cupidity but for glory, demanded impossible salaries. His artistic triumph as Cyrano de Bergerac was a huge popular success ; but the play was an enormously expensive one ; and the management, finding that even full houses could not cover the cost, handed over the enterprise to Loraine, who accepted it without a suspicion that he was bleeding it to death instead of, as he imagined, making his own and everybody else's fortune by it. He seemed always able to dazzle managers into allowing him to name his own terms, however extravagant ; but Shaw was too keen an economist to be dazzled, and wrote off Loraine as a luxury that his plays could not afford. The

London managers were at last forced by ruthless experience to the same conclusion; and Loraine, driven into management, had no luck, and had to leave for America in serious financial straits. When he became economically possible there, Shaw did his best to bring about a production of *On the Rocks*, with Loraine in the leading part; but Loraine either did not 'see himself' in the role or believe in the play, which was left to become one of the successes of the short-lived Federal Theatre, to which Shaw allowed the run of all his plays on condition that no seat in the theatre was to cost more than fifty cents. Loraine's death ended the saga.

In the tussle between artist and prophet which has occurred during the mental development of many famous men, the artist has usually been ousted by the prophet, because detachment is a much rarer human attribute than self-assertion. Somehow Shaw managed to maintain a balance. With him, as with Voltaire, his nearest parallel, the artist and the prophet lived in harmony. While the 1914-18 war was calling forth all his powers as a preacher, he was quietly putting the finishing touches to *Heartbreak House*, begun in 1913, and conceiving that cycle of dramas which became known as *Back to Methuselah*.

Among the plays of Shaw *Heartbreak House* occupies a unique place. As with Dickens's *A Tale of Two Cities*, his disciples place it either first or nowhere. Shaw himself had a curious feeling about it. 'There is something about the play that makes me extraordinarily reluctant to let it go out of my hands,' he wrote after completing it. At first he would not allow anyone to read it; he did not offer to read it to his friends; and a suggestion by Lee Mathews in December 1916 that he should give a public reading of it to the Stage Society drew from him the following:

'MY DEAR LEE MATHEWS,

'This is really not a possible thing. If the Stage Society, having had a specially successful season, were to give an at-home to the members to celebrate it, then undoubtedly a reading of an unperformed and unpublished play by an author of eminence might be swallowed as a delightful *bonne bouche*. But to collect subscriptions for complete theatrical performances, and then try to put the subscribers off with a reading, is to invite putrid eggs and dead cats, with the unfortunate author as target. I can, as you know, face unpopularity when the destiny of civilization is at stake; but the role of chairman at a meeting of shareholders who have to be informed that their money has been embezzled is far more trying; and in this case I should have actually to do the embezzlement to their faces.

'It is clear to me that if any change is to be made in the nature of the entertainment to be given, it can be done only by summoning a general meeting and obtaining the consent of the members to the change, the dissentients to have their money back if they demand it.

'There is another difficulty. I can read a play to you *in camera*, or to a few indulgent personal friends, with tolerable effectiveness on the string quartet scale. But our membership is so large that we should have to take a theatre and do it on the symphony scale. I once saw that tried at the Haymarket Theatre by an American lady who read Ibsen's plays quite as well as I read mine. It was rescued from frightful failure only by Gladstone, who had been induced by private influence to attend. After twenty minutes of it he toppled forward with a loud choking snore over the front of the balcony tier stage box, and was saved from a horrible death by his party seizing the old man's heels and dragging him back into the box, whereupon he left the theatre in a rage, gratitude being unknown to politicians.

'I do not propose to share the fate of that American lady now that Gladstone is dead.'

Shaw was not even anxious to have the play produced, making excuses that it could not run more than a fortnight in war-time, because lights had to be out by 10.30 and the curtain would have to rise at 7.15. 'We must be content to dream about it. Let it lie there to show that the old dog can still bark a bit,' he advised Lillah McCarthy; and when in 1919 Lee Mathews asked if it might be produced by the Stage Society, he wrote: 'I must hurry on with such work as I can hope to have time on earth to finish unless I can get a regular production with a magnificent cast and a guarantee of at least six weeks run.' His admiration of Tchekov had moved him to write it; he talked of it as his favourite play, saying that Captain Shotover was a modernized King Lear; and when someone asked him to explain its meaning, he made his stock reply: 'How should *I* know? I am only the author.'

Eventually it was done by J. B. Fagan at the Court Theatre

in the autumn of 1921. At the opening performance the last change of scene, timed to occupy four minutes, took twenty-five through an electrical breakdown. The delay at a moment when the audience was exhausted by the length of the play was disastrous. 'Last night I had to go to Shaw's *Heartbreak House*,' wrote Arnold Bennett on October 19th: '3 hours 50 minutes of the most intense tedium. I went to sleep twice, fortunately.' The play drew only £500 a week; and Fagan, discouraged, took it off and substituted *She Stoops to Conquer*, which drew nothing and closed the theatre.

When the Birmingham Repertory Theatre, under Barry Jackson, did *Heartbreak House* Shaw travelled up to see a matinée. 'He was obviously impressed,' Sir Barry Jackson informed me, 'and noticing this I asked him whilst waiting for his train if he would allow us to tackle *Back to Methuselah*, hitherto only given in New York by The Theatre Guild. "Is your family provided for?" he asked. I was able to reassure him on this point, and he said, "Yes." So we went ahead. He attended the last rehearsals although he must have been in considerable pain, having suffered a fall just previously in Ireland.' The fall had been a serious one. Staying at Parknasilla in County Kerry while writing *Saint Joan*, he was scrambling over some rocks one day when he slipped and fell flat on his back, the camera which was slung across his body being driven so deeply into his flesh by the impact that Mrs Shaw said she could post a letter in the hole it made. The Irish doctors failed to get his cracked ribs back into shape; and he arrived almost a cripple in Birmingham, where Elmer Pheils, a famous local osteopath, set him on his feet after a wrestle which lasted 72 minutes, and left the oeteopath breathless but triumphant.

It took the producer nearly two months to prepare *Back to Methuselah* for the stage, and Shaw turned up for the final week of dress rehearsals, frequently reviving himself in a cinema nearby, where the boy actor, Jackie Coogan, must have helped him to forget the He-Ancients in his play. The five plays were given from October 9th to 12th, 1923, and when the curtain came down at the conclusion of the cycle there was a deeply impressive silence, followed by applause which gradually increased in volume. 'When Mr Shaw appeared,' wrote the critic of *The Times*, 'he was met by a shout very different from the ordinary gallery cheer—a short, sudden, involuntary outbreak of long-held emotion, such as we have never before heard in a theatre.' Shaw seldom took a call, but this time he even made a speech:

'I know my place as an author, and the place of the author is not on the stage. That belongs really to the artists who give life to the creations of the author and are the real life of the play. I have had the luxury of seeing my own play, which only existed until they took it and made it live.

'I should like to ask one question: and that is, whether, apart from a few personal friends of mine, there are any inhabitants of Birmingham in this house? This has been the most extraordinary experience of my life. I have had five magnificent performances in four days and, what is more extraordinary, this has been done in Birmingham. I remember Birmingham when it was, dramatically and theatrically, the most impossible place in the world for work of this description. That is why I ask: Are you all pilgrims or strangers, or are there one or two genuine inhabitants of Birmingham here?

'It is astonishing to me that this, perhaps the crown and climax of my career as a dramatic author, has happened in Birmingham. I suppose Mr Barry Jackson must be a changeling, or is it that there is occurring in Birmingham some change such as that in this play? The first two of the people who live 300 years are people who never imagined it would be possible, and people whose friends never imagined it would happen to them. Their surprise can be compared to my experience; for Birmingham, the last place in the world one would imagine to become the centre of dramatic art, has produced a play of an intensity I think unparalleled. Without the co-operation of the audience such a feat would have been impossible.'

The moment the curtain came down the assembled cast witnessed with amazement the sixty-seven-years-old author, but recently prostrated by an accident, gleefully executing a *pas seul* on the stage.

As with many of his plays *Back to Methuselah* underwent changes during conception. On July 25th, 1918, he reported: 'I have written a play with intervals of thousands of years (in the future) between the acts; but now I find I must make each act into a full-length play.' The change was noted in the Lord Chamberlain's office, for when the work was submitted as 'a play in eight acts' the official reader decided that it consisted of one three-act play, one two-act play, and three one-act plays, and demanded fees accordingly. The idea behind

393

the work had long been in the air, but Shaw gave it an original turn. Back in the eighteenth century Erasmus Darwin had written: 'The thinking few in all ages have complained of the brevity of life, lamenting that mankind are not allowed time sufficient to cultivate science, or to improve their intellect,' and one of his ingenious prescriptions for prolonging human life was a warm bath to be taken twice weekly. Shaw also thought that life was too short, but not because people would profit by a longer experience. He believed that men and women made no serious attempt to better the world or their own condition simply because they only had 30 or 40 years of maturity to enjoy: their conduct and character were determined, not by their experience of life, but by their expectation of it. The proof of the pudding will be in the digestion of it, and until we have produced long-livers we cannot say what they will make of life; but if they make nothing more exhilarating of it than Shaw's Ancients, there will still be a strong argument in favour of pole-axing everybody at the age of fifty.

That is the real weakness of the work, which begins with a couple of superb scenes, continues with a rattling good farce, featuring Asquith and Lloyd George as knock-out comedians, gets a little heavy when 'the thing happens', becomes almost boring over the Tragedy of an Elderly Gentleman, and closes flatly as if the effort to go 'as far as thought can reach' had exhausted the thinker. 'It is not in man's nature to be grateful for negative mercies,' Shaw wrote in the 'nineties. 'When you have the toothache, the one happiness you desire is not to have it: when it is gone, you never dream of including its absence in your assets.' This seems to be the trouble with the Ancients. Their mercies are negative: 'they have taken the agony from birth', and with it the joy from life; they have nothing to be grateful for. The only object of their existence is to prove that life is not worth living.[1] Still, from first to last,

---

[1] When I suggested this to Shaw I failed to carry him with me. 'Are you so lazy-headed or self-unobservant or (which seems improbable) devoid of intellect that you cannot conceive the activity of the mind being a pleasure or intellect being a passion?' he asked. 'Can you really not imagine a stage of development at which a young human female, after four years dancing and dressing-up and fine art, should wander in the woods solving mathematical problems instead of sleeping, and an old man, accused by a gay young Hesketh P. of being incapable of enjoyment, could reply that a moment of such ecstasy as his intellect gave him continually would strike Hes-

Back to Methuselah is studded with fine passages, and few people who witnessed its London production at the Court Theatre would have agreed with Arnold Bennett: 'I went to the 1st of the Shaw plays in the 1st cycle, but had to sleep,' he noted on 25th February 1924. 'It was terrible. I think this is the general opinion. I wouldn't go to any more.' As Bennett was shortly to write the most tedious novel in the English language, his criticism was a well-merited tribute to the excellence of the opening scenes in the play.

For many years Shaw had been meditating a play on a prophet. The militant saint was a type more congenial to his nature than any other, a type he thoroughly sympathized with and could therefore portray with unfailing insight. In all history the one person who exactly answered his requirements, who would have made the perfect Shavian hero, was Mahomet. In 1913 he wanted to write a play on the subject for Forbes-Robertson. Four years earlier he had informed the parliamentary committee on the censorship that he had 'long desired to dramatize the life of Mahomet. But the possibility of a protest from the Turkish Ambassador—or the fear of it —causing the Lord Chamberlain to refuse to license such a play' had prevented him from doing it. Nevertheless his fancy continued to play around the prophet, who is described by the Elderly Gentleman in *Back to Methuselah* as 'a truly wise man, for he founded a religion without a Church'. He makes a personal appearance in *The Adventures of the Black Girl*, and is discussed by Cauchon in *Saint Joan*. But as the Censor's objection to the exhibition of Christ on the stage applied in the east to the exhibition of Mahomet, and as the production of a play on the Prophet would probably have resulted in the assassination of the author by a fanatical Moslem, Shaw wrote *Saint Joan* instead.

---

keth dead? Unless you grasp this your opinion of *Methuselah*, favourable or unfavourable, will be like a blind man's opinion of the Sistine Chapel.'. I replied that I was incapable of imagining a stage of development at which any human being, young or old, male or female, could find pleasure in solving mathematical problems, because in creating me God had left out an appreciation of mathematics; but that I could easily conceive the activity of mind being a pleasure and intellect being a passion; and my criticism of *Methuselah* was simply that the Ancients did not appear to extract half the pleasure from mental activity that I could derive from mental vacuity.

Although the subject was ideally suited to his genius, I wanted to know what had first put it into his head. 'I am the creature of circumstances,' he explained. 'If I am asked to write a play, and I happen to have an idea for one, I write it, usually to find that it is not the sort of play I have been asked for. But sometimes the urge to write a play comes over me and I cannot think what to write about. That happened before I started *Saint Joan*. I wanted to get to work on something, but I hadnt a subject. "Why not write a play on Joan of Arc?" said my wife. So I did. I had already read the reports of the trial and the rehabilitation, and found that they contained a drama that needed only arrangement for the stage—child's play to me—and that all the old Joan plays and histories are romantic poppycock. I stuck to the contemporary reports and did not read a word of the critics and biographers until I had finished the play. I was interested in Joan as the first Protestant, quite insufferable as all great beginners are. My Epilogue was a device to include what happened after Joan's death; the rest is a pure chronicle of events. Of course the play was much too long at first, and I had to cut it down to the bone. Even then some people seemed to think that three and a half hours of it made a fairly substantial bone.'

Wishing to glean every detail I could about the creation of this masterpiece, I asked him in August 1939 where he had written it. He replied: 'I distinctly remember writing *Saint Joan*, or working on it, at Parknasilla on the Kenmare Estuary in Co. Kerry, where two friendly priests discussed the trial scene with me. But it is amazing how completely I forget where my plays were written. The exceptions are *The Philanderer* (Monmouth), *You Never Can Tell* (Regent's Park and Suffolk), *Caesar* (Isle of Wight), and *St Joan* (Kerry).'

While busy on it in 1923 he was being pestered to do this, that and the other thing by people who imagined that after *Back to Methuselah* he had nothing more to tell the world and had retired from business. The Stage Society was on the alert, and three times that year Shaw had to remind Lee Mathews that life was real, life was earnest:

'Jan. 18. I cannot write prefaces for any books but my own. The reason is that the Shaw preface is now a standard commercial article, which takes some months to write and revise, it being really a treatise on its subject, running to perhaps 100

pages. If a single preface not up to this mark were put on the
market, the reputation of the article would be gone for ever.
... I had ten days at Bournemouth to recuperate ; and yesterday, the day after my return, I nearly died of the worst headache I have had for years. Nothing so deadly as a holiday.'

'June 6. No—hang it all! Would *you*—would *anybody*
write to the papers asking people as a personal favor to see
Volpone? ... Anyhow Ben Johnson must draw his own crowd
and not mine.'

'Nov. 5. Bulletin be blowed! 3000 words are impossible just
now. I must get my Joan of Arc play through the press and
on to the stage. I must, after years of delay and locked-up
capital at the printers, get the Collected Edition of my works
together. If I stop to write articles to help the deserving this
work will never get done. So, for the moment, spare me. I
will make good later.'

A sidelight on friendship was provided by A. B. Walkley,
the dramatic critic of *The Times*, to whom Shaw had dedicated
Man and Superman. When *Saint Joan* was announced Walkley
heralded it in *The Times* by a long article against a work he
had neither seen nor read, protesting that the subject was far
too solemn and serious to be dealt with by a playwright of
Shaw's description. It was a step unprecedented in criticism ;
but *The Times* incautiously published it. Poor A.B.W. was
soon sorry he spoke.

Shaw had decided on the actress for the leading part before
starting on the play. Many years earlier he had advised Sybil
Thorndike, who wanted to play Candida, to 'go home and
learn housekeeping and have four children, or six if you'd
rather, and then come back and show me Candida'. She had
taken his advice, and in due course had played Candida. After
the war she and her husband, Lewis Casson, did a season of
popular plays. 'I wasn't contented,' she told me : 'I wanted to
do one really great play, and Lewis and I decided to put on
The Cenci for a few matinées. Every one was against it. Lady
Wyndham said it would be an utter failure. All our friends
said we should be ruined. But for us it was sink or swim : we
just didn't care ; we wanted to justify our existence ; and for
once the ideal triumphed. *The Cenci* was so successful that it
covered the loss on the popular plays. And it got me the
greatest part of my career. It was after the trial scene, I think,
that Mr Shaw said he had found the actress for Joan.' Sybil

Thorndike and Lewis Casson went down to Ayot St Lawrence, where Shaw read *Saint Joan* to them. It was a wonderful day for Sybil. 'His reading was marvellous. It was like listening to a great executant who knows intuitively how every note should be played. The lines came like music; each character was a different instrument in the orchestra, and he could play them all. Listening to that symphony was the greatest experience of my life.' She heard him read the play three times and caught every inflection in her part from him. None of the other famous actresses who played it had this advantage, and none, in his opinion, gave such a fine, intelligent and satisfying performance as she.

Meeting her before rehearsals started, he asked:

'Have you read any books about Joan?'

'Yes, as many as I have been able to get.'

'Then forget them. I have dramatized the original documents. Everyone has romanced about Joan. I have told the story exactly as it happened. It is the easiest play I have ever had to write. All I've done is to put down the facts, to arrange Joan for the stage. The trial scene is merely a report of the actual trial. I have used Joan's very words: thus she spoke, thus she behaved.'

Joan's outburst at the end, however, when she realizes that her recantation means imprisonment, was taken from no contemporary report, and the chronicler became a poet:

'Bread has no sorrow for me, and water no affliction. But to shut me from the light of the sky and the sight of the fields and flowers; to chain my feet so that I can never again ride with the soldiers nor climb the hills; to make me breathe foul damp darkness, and keep from me everything that brings me back to the love of God when your wickedness and foolishness tempt me to hate Him: all this is worse than the furnace in the Bible that was heated seven times. I could do without my warhorse; I could drag about in a skirt; I could let the banners and the trumpets and the knights and soldiers pass me and leave me behind as they leave the other women, if only I could still hear the wind in the trees, the larks in the sunshine, the young lambs crying through the healthy frost, and the blessed, blessed church bells that send my angel voices floating to me on the wind. But without these things I cannot live; and by your wanting to take them away from me, or from any human creature, I know that your counsel is of the devil, and that mine is of God.'

Saint Joan was produced at the New Theatre, London, on March 26th, 1924, and a little later in New York by The Theatre Guild, which did some remarkably fine productions of Shaw's plays. When the author's permission to cut *Joan* was solicited by The Theatre Guild, because the performance lasted till midnight, he advised them either to begin earlier or to arrange later train services. In spite of its length *Saint Joan* was deservedly successful wherever it was performed, its author's biggest box-office success. Roman Catholics liked it as much as Protestants ; indeed, the fairness with which Shaw had put the case for Mother Church prompted someone to ask him whether he was turning Catholic. 'There's no room for two Popes in the Roman Catholic Church,' he said. I, on the other hand, was more impressed by the Protestant emotion in the play and suggested that he should make William the Silent the hero of his next historical drama. His reply was on a post-card which I no longer have, but it ran to this effect : 'William being Silent at the top of his voice for three and a half hours in a Shaw play may appeal to you ; but the modern world does not see itself in the story of the Dutch Republic.'

Naturally he had to keep up his quarrel with Shakespeare in the preface. Shakespeare, said he, could not understand the Middle Ages, because he believed that if a man were true to himself he could not be false to anyone else, 'a precept which represents the reaction against medievalism at its intensest'. That may be so ; but it happens also to represent the insight of a great man against the distortions of institutionalism, whether of Rome, Moscow or anywhere else. Joan of Arc was great because she was true to herself, and Shaw's play is great, not because he 'let the medieval atmosphere blow through' it freely, which any third-rate historian could have done, but because it reveals the spirit of the individual uncrushed by the machinery of authority, the light of God undimmed by all the powers of darkness embodied in Churches and States.

The production of *Saint Joan* crowned Shaw's career. It gave him an extraordinary prestige. Henceforth, whatever he said or did was treated with respect, tinged with awe. When he clowned people laughed dutifully, when he cut a caper they applauded reverentially. Every word he uttered was cabled across several continents. Every nonsensical joke he made, and many more that were ineptly invented for him, were gratefully accepted as the garnered wisdom of a profound thinker. If the author of his next play had been announced as Saint Shaw, no one would have been surprised. He did not encourage this adulation, telling the students at the Royal Academy of Dramatic Art in 1928 that he would never be a really great author because, just when he was about to achieve tragic heights, some absurd joke occurred to him and he could not resist the anti-climax: 'I have got the tragedian and I have got the clown in me, and the clown trips me up in the most dreadful way.' All the same a note to Ernest Rhys proved that canonization had not tempered his style: 'The more I learn about other men's methods the more I perceive that nobody except myself ever dreams of taking the trouble to attain really exhaustive literary expression. In fact I am quite the most extraordinary man in London; and you are quite welcome to give this fact on my authority.'

Joan also made good the financial losses he had sustained as a result of the war. The royalties due to him from Germany, Austria and Russia would have kept him in comfort for the rest of his life; but the first two countries had been ordered to pay for the war, which they did by the simple process of printing millions of notes; and as Shaw had no use for a supply of waste paper, its value as money being nil, he took no interest in its arrival. On the other hand, he was able to make a little money for Siegfried Trebitsch, the Austrian translator of his works, by turning one of that author's plays, *Jitta's Atonement*, into English. It achieved a suburban production in London, and had a run in the United States. Trebitsch wrote: 'It is a marvellous translation; but you have changed my tragedy into a comedy.' Shaw pleaded in excuse his ignorance of German. He had, in fact, converted the jealous husband of Spanish tragedy into a first-rate comedy part for a British Coquelin; but Jitta was still recognizably Jitta, which in his view was all that mattered.

Any other author known to fame would have rested for a while after such a resounding success as *Joan*. Not so Shaw, who took on the appalling job of explaining socialism to the Intelligent Woman. And he did not spare himself: 'In spite of the most fervent resolutions to order my work more sensibly, and of the fact that an author's work can as a rule quite well be divided into limited daily periods, I am usually obliged to work myself to the verge of a complete standstill and then go away for many weeks to recuperate.' In July 1924 he recuperated in Scotland, writing to Lee Mathews from The Grant Arms Hotel, Grantown-on-Spey: 'We are motor-mountaineering here, and my handwriting betrays driver's cramp: I can hardly make a legible sign.' He went north again in the summer of 1925, reporting to Forbes-Robertson: 'We *did* take warm clothes with us, only to find, to our amazement, that Caledonia stern and wild stops being stern north of Inverness, and that the extreme north of Scotland has the climate of the extreme south of Ireland, fuchsia trees, Gulf Stream, and all. Torquay is arctic compared to Shetland. The air here in Tongue is like the air on the coast of Kerry. Thurso is milder than Queenstown. The people here would die of cold in Edinburgh. We have been all over Orkney and Shetland and Caithness and Sutherland; and it holds good all through. Nobody seems to know it. Come and see.'

Forbes-Robertson had retired from the stage during the war, and had begun to compile his memoirs in 1918. 'You have only to let yourself go, and then leave the country by the next boat,' wrote Shaw, who advised him to start a chapter on *The Stage in My Time* in the following manner: 'I have met and played with all the men and women who figured prominently on the London stage during the last quarter of the nineteenth century, including a few actors.' Robertson's book shows that he was not in sympathy with Shaw's suggestions: it was published in 1925 and Shaw gave his opinion of it in a letter to his favourite actor dated 17th July:

'MY DEAR FORBES-ROBERTSON,

'When I rose to leave the platform after your speech at King's College on the 13th May, I found myself thunderstruck with some appalling illness which had turned my spine into a bar of rusty iron grating horribly on the base of my skull. I managed to walk home because I was afraid to get into a cab. Thirty days later at the same hour I found myself miraculously well again at a moment's notice.

'I could do nothing all that time but doze and read; and the first book I finished was yours. I even began a letter to you about it; but it was delirious, and I had to discard it. I was struggling mostly with the resemblance of your case to that of Macready and Shakespear, in whom to the end something rebelled against their profession. I, being an accomplice and an accessory before the act, am concerned in this too, and share the feeling; and if I could escape from imposture and make-believe by abandoning the theatre, I would perhaps do so, like Sheridan Knowles and Racine. But it is my considered opinion that there is far less imposture and make-believe in the fine arts than in the so-called serious professions. Reading this life of yours I perceive that as compared with our Lord Chief Justices, our front bench politicians, our medical baronets, our archbishops, you, the actor, stand out with extraordinary distinction and loveableness because you are not a humbug. Instead of being the man who pretended to be Hamlet, you are precisely the man who never pretended to be anybody but Forbes-Robertson playing Hamlet. Beside the judge in his ermine and scarlet pretending to be justice, and the fashionable doctor pretending to be the Omniscient master of life and death, and the priest with his apostolic succession and his bunch of the keys of heaven and hell, you, whether as actor or painter, have the advantage of a celebrity that is not idolatry and a regard that is untainted by a secret abhorrence of the angry ape posing as a god. When Shakespear wrote, "All the world's a stage," he should have gone on like this:

> *All the world's a stage: trust not the man*
> *That swears he's more than actor; for that lie*
> *Waves like the devil's banner over murder,*
> *Theft, rapine, etc., etc., etc.*

'I hope you have given a copy of the book to the library of the R.A.D.A.; for now that you have left the stage there is only the printed word to show the students that to reach the highest rank it is not necessary to be an egotist or a monster, and that though good-looking spooks can do very well on the stage as long as there are authors and producers to fit their poor hollow bodies with souls, still, the man with positive character and artistic culture, difficult as it is at first for him to surrender himself to a fictitious personality, is the only man who can become finally a classic actor.

'Also, you support my old contention that the stagestruck actor is a bad actor. . . .

'I like the story about the man at The Profligate who suddenly said, "My God! I have seen this play before." My mother found a bookshop in the Euston Road where she could take any of the books to read for twopence. She forgot them immediately after reading them; so the stock never failed her: she read the same books over and over again without recognizing them. But if by any chance some chord of memory was struck, she instantly flung the volume away, exclaiming, just like the man at The Profligate, "Bother! (or Damn!) I have read that before." And nothing would induce her to read another line of it. . . .'

Shaw's next holiday was taken abroad. For nearly thirty years he had enjoyed good health, but a breakdown, following overwork and an accident, occurred when he was nearly seventy. On May 20th, 1926, he wrote: 'My health has given way at last; I have been ill for two months, and have only half-recovered, the pre-seventy part of me being as dead as a doornail. I am a ruin.' From Stresa he acknowledged Sutro's letter of congratulation on his 70th birthday: 'Never mind; I forgive you; you meant well. When the entire population of the civilized world congratulates a man on his misfortune, in messages which vary from telegrams to canons by famous composers in albums, not to mention suggestions that the most acceptable acknowledgment would be a loan of £500, he feels as if he were being stoned, and finally relapses into cynical insensibility. Skip your 70th birthday, Alfred, if you wish to have a 71st. Shun notoriety; and live happily ever after. Your message shortened my life less than most of them: for that, accept the blessing of the wretched moribund G. Bernard Shaw.'

Another congratulatory message was sent through the German Embassy in London by Dr Gustav Stresemann, German Minister of Foreign Affairs. 'It is the sort of thing that would never occur to a British Foreign Secretary,' commented Shaw in the course of his reply to the Ambassador, 'because, as you well know, we are a barbarous nation in matters of culture. We have a genuine dread of intellect in any form and a conviction that art, though highly enjoyable clandestinely, is essentially immoral. Therefore, the sole notice taken on my seventieth birthday by the British Government was its deliberate official prohibition of the broadcasting of any words spoken by me on that occasion.'

Honours of various sorts, however, came thick upon him after the success of *Joan*. 'In my native Ireland, now nominally a Free State, one of my books is on the index; and I have no doubt all the rest will follow as soon as the clerical censorship discovers their existence.' When the Labour Party took office, he suggested certain additions to the honours list to Ramsay MacDonald, having already succeeded in obtaining a knighthood for (among others) Arthur Wing Pinero. MacDonald noted the names and said, 'What about yourself?' 'Not on your life,' was the reply. 'How would you like to be Sir Ramsay MacDonald?' When it was suggested that he might be useful to the Party in the House of Lords, he pleaded that he could not afford to be a duke, and nothing less could decently be offered to him. Many friends pointed out that the Order of Merit was not open to his objections. 'I have already conferred it on myself,' he replied. 'Besides, it has come to mean simply Old Man ; and I have only one toe in the grave as yet.' Like Dickens, Carlyle, and August Manns (the famous conductor of the Crystal Palace classical concerts) he knew that his name was title enough, and that no one had ever heard of Sir Bernard Shaw, or Baron Ayot St Lawrence. He held that titles were for persons whose public services, however valuable, were unknown to the nation. He held a similar view with regard to ceremonial dinners. When the Critics' Circle gave a dinner to J. T. Grein, whose pioneering in the theatre had not been recognized, Shaw attended it. The postprandial speakers said so much about Shaw and so little about Grein that Shaw rose and began: 'I came here to-night in all humility to do honour to my old friend Jack Grein, but I find that the dinner is in honour of me. Nevertheless, you'll excuse my dragging him in for a moment, won't you?' The critics, as hosts, being present in force, he took the opportunity of thanking them 'for the very generous way in which they always receive my last play but one'.

When, however, he was asked by T. P. O'Connor to attend a dinner in honour of Ramsay MacDonald, he wrote: 'Absence from town and a strong sense of humour will prevent me from accepting your invitation to dine in acknowledgment of the political eminence of Ramsay MacDonald. Considering that the man has been Prime Minister of England, I should have thought his eminence had been noticed. If the dinner is a success, I suggest that it be followed by another to acknowledge the piety of the Pope, yet another to emphasize the mathematical talent of Einstein, and a final one to call attention to the existence of milestones on the Dover road. If you could throw in a lunch to remind people that I am rather good at writing plays, all the better. These meals would have come in more handily 50 years ago. Still, they are well meant, and I hope you will all enjoy yourselves very much.'

I wanted to know whether Shaw had liked MacDonald. 'He was not the sort of man one could like,' he replied. 'Many years ago he belonged to the Fabian Society; but as he was also a leading member of the Independent Labour Party, all the Fabians thought him an I.L.P. spy and all the I.L.P. folk thought him a Fabian spy. It struck me that he was doing himself no good, so I wrote to tell him quite frankly what the situation was. Now I think you'll agree that most people would have received my letter with a scream of indignation, and I certainly expected MacDonald to sever our relationship and thenceforth to cut me dead. But not a bit of it! He took no offence at being called a spy. His reply was shrewd, tactful, conciliatory and diplomatic. So I knew that he would make a first-rate politician.'

In 1925 the Nobel Prize for literature was awarded to Shaw, who assumed it to be 'a token of gratitude for a sense of world relief' that he had published nothing that year. He refused the prize, writing to the Permanent Secretary of the Royal Swedish Academy that 'the money is a lifebelt thrown to a swimmer who has already reached the shore in safety'; which reminds one of a passage in Dr Johnson's letter to Chesterfield: 'Is not a Patron, my Lord, one who looks with unconcern on a man struggling for life in the water, and, when he has reached ground, encumbers him with help?' The money, hinted Shaw, could 'be used to encourage intercourse and understanding in literature and art between Sweden and the British Isles'. When it became known that he had refused the prize, hundreds of people, especially Americans, wrote to suggest that as he was so wealthy he might lend them something. This added to the burden of life: 'I am now practising a complicated facial expression which combines universal benevolence with a savage determination not to save any American from ruin by a remittance of five hundred dollars. . . . I can forgive Alfred Nobel for having invented dynamite. But only a fiend in human form could have invented the Nobel Prize!' Finally, as his refusal created an unforeseen and insoluble problem by leaving £7000 in the air, he accepted it for the fraction of a second which elapsed between his signatures of the receipt for it and the trust deed passing it on to the Anglo-Swedish Literary Alliance devised by Baron Palmstierna to meet the emergency.

Such was his reputation that he could not even escape joining the P.E.N. Club, which had been promoted for the general getting-together of authors of all nations. He struggled against it at first, but when John Galsworthy insisted he capitulated: 'Whitemailer! Very well, I will go quietly. It's your doing though. But I will not face the recurrent irritation of a guinea a year. Here is twenty guineas for a life subscription. (I am 68.) If they wont accept that, they can make me an honorary member and be damned to them! . . . My objection to the Club . . . has always been that literary men should never associate with one another, not only because of their cliques and hatreds and envies, but because their minds inbreed and produce abortions. . . . I shall not change my habits. It is on the international basis, not the prandial one, that I succumb to your decree of Compulsory Service.'

It had by this time begun to dawn on various municipal bodies that Shaw was a playwright of distinction, and he visited Bath to unveil a memorial to Sheridan and Stratford to toast the Immortal Memory of Shakespeare. When the Stratford theatre was burnt down, he sent a wire congratulating everybody concerned on the destruction of a detestable building; and when he attended the annual junketing he annoyed several of the governors present by condemning every aspect of the old structure, capping his behaviour by drinking to the I.M. in water. Thirteen years later, in 1938, he was asked to receive the deeds of the London National Theatre site, which had been excavated in South Kensington, opposite the Victoria and Albert Museum. In handing the deeds on to the trustees, he expressed his pleasure that the National Theatre had at last got a piece of land to stand on. 'The English people do not want a National Theatre,' said he, 'any more than they ever wanted a British Museum or a National Gallery. But once those institutions were built the British people accepted them as natural phenomena without which the Empire would be incomplete. In the same way, if we make a beginning with the National Theatre, it will become an institution, and the Government will have to recognize it as something which for some inscrutable reason it must keep going.' He then solemnly received 'the sod and twig' as the material token of the transaction. This was a superstition from his boyhood as clerk in an Irish land agency. No Englishman had ever heard of the sod and twig; but the press agents

406

of the National Theatre saw its value in the headlines, and jumped at the almost Druidical ceremony.

In 1930 the standard edition of Shaw's collected works, delayed for years by his dislike to the drudgery of what he called 'picking up his droppings', began to appear. For this purpose he had to read his hitherto unpublished first novel *Immaturity,* to which he supplied an autobiographical preface. 'The novel is very funny—unintentionally,' he wrote to his old friend, Steward Headlam: 'I have shrunk from looking at it since it was written, but now it amuses me more than *The Young Visiters*[1] did; and I find it quite readable and classically Victorian in style. There are scraps of my latest play in it. When they talked to Goethe about experience, he said, "I knew it all along.' Apparently I did, too, although Henry George followed by Karl Marx made a complete change in my view of our civilization. Are you ever tempted to autobiography? I have had to make some prefatory notes about myself for this Collected Edition; and I dont like it. But then my record is as plain as the trail of a paper chase.'

Fame takes men to strange places and forces them to do unaccustomed things. Though Shaw was an inveterate haunter of old churches he wanted to be alone in them. The last spot on earth where one would have expected to see him was Westminster Abbey fashionably crowded on a great occasion. Yet he was a pall-bearer at the funeral of Thomas Hardy in the Abbey, along with John Galsworthy, James Barrie, Rudyard Kipling, A. E. Housman and Edmund Gosse; and the occasion was made memorable by the introduction of the prophet of imperialism to the prophet of socialism, the two leading literary representatives of the two leading forces in the political history of their time. They had never met, and as far as Kipling was concerned did not desire a meeting. Edmund Gosse, however, took no account of this. He seized Kipling and by main force introduced him to Shaw. 'Kipling was nervous and fidgety,' Shaw informed me. 'He made a little dive at me, thrust out a hand quickly, said "Howdyedo," withdrew the hand instantly as if he hardly dared to trust me with it, and bolted like a rabbit into a corner where Housman was there to protect him.'

After the ceremony Shaw and Gosse left the Abbey together. Shaw described how he had just slept in a house where

[1] Written by a Child.

Gosse's *Father and Son* was on the shelf by the bedside. He had read it from end to end. Gosse asked rather forlornly whether Shaw had not read it before. 'Of course I have,' was the reply: 'that is why I read it again. The point is that I read it right through at one go. I tell you that the description of your baptism in it is one of the immortal pages in English literature.' Gosse swung round with open arms. 'My dear Shaw,' he exclaimed, 'you are the only one who ever encourages me.' Now Gosse had begun by loathing Shaw as heartily as Kipling did. But nobody could resist Shaw's flair for what was best in his or her achievements. He would certainly have conquered Kipling had Kipling lived long enough. But the Westminster Abbey encounter was their only meeting; and Kipling died unreconciled.

Describing the ceremony to me, Shaw said: 'We must have made a curious procession up the aisle. Galsworthy and I, as six-footers, were the most imposing figures. I had just been posing to Troubetskoy for a full length statue, and could hold an attitude without flinching for half an hour. Galsworthy was always imposing. Barrie, realizing that he could not stand up to us, made his effect by miraculously managing to look exactly three inches high. As we marched, pretending to carry the ashes of whatever part of Hardy was buried in the Abbey, Kipling, who fidgeted continually and was next in front of me, kept changing his step. Every time he did so I nearly fell over him.'

The demands on Shaw's time, increased enormously by a reputation that made him the most widely-quoted man alive, did not break his habit of writing to the press whenever some monstrosity or absurdity came to his notice. When a convict escaped from Parkhurst Prison, and on being captured was put in chains for six months, that being the prison routine, Shaw pointed out in *The Daily News* that the authorities were taking a savage revenge on the convict for their own carelessness: 'The man was sentenced to be imprisoned, not to imprison himself. The commonest instinct of decent sportsmanship, to put it no higher, insists on the sacred right of the prisoner to escape if he can. The odds on the side of the prison authorities are overwhelming: all that public money, bolts and bars, sentinels and rifles, walls and spikes, and the unmistakeable brand of the prison dress can do to baffle a single destitute and unaided man are leagued against him. Were he the worst of criminals, public opinion must applaud the feat when he wins even for a few days.' This outburst was successful, and chains for escape were abolished.

In May 1928 Dr Serge Voronoff visited London and a famous bacteriologist, Dr Edward Bach, wrote to *The Daily News* saying that the monkey-gland treatment to rejuvenate people was dangerous because it would reproduce the worst characteristics of the ape either in the persons operated upon or in their progeny: he added that the characteristics possessed in a high degree by the ape were cruelty and sensuality. That was enough for Shaw, who put the case for the apes over the signature of 'Consul Junior' (Consul was a famous performing chimpanzee), addressing his letter from The Monkey House, Regent's Park. 'Has any ape,' he asked, 'ever torn the glands from a living man to graft them upon another ape for the sake of a brief and unnatural extension of that ape's life? Was Torquemada an ape? Were the Inquisition and the Star Chamber monkey-houses? Were "Luke's iron crown and Damien's bed of steel" the work of apes? Has it been necessary to found a Society for the Protection of Ape Children, as it has been for the protection of human children? Was the late war a war of apes or of men? Was poison gas a simian or a human invention? How can Dr Bach mention the word cruelty in the presence of an ape without blushing? We, who have our brains burnt out ruthlessly in human scientists' laboratories, are reproached for cruelty by a human scientist!' After asserting that 'vaccination and anti-toxin inoculation have given to men neither the virtues of the cow nor the qualities of the horse', Consul Junior concluded: 'Man remains what he has always been: the cruellest of all the animals, and the most elaborately and fiendishly sensual. Let him presume no further on this grotesque resemblance to us ; he will remain what he is in spite of all Dr Voronoff's efforts to make a respectable ape of him.' Shaw would not even have admitted that the habits of human beings were more hygienic than those of apes, for about three years later he complained to the St Albans Rural Council that the Islington Borough Council dumped its refuse at Wheathampstead, a mile from his house, and 'when the wind is in that quarter I am not reminded of Shakespear's "Sweet south that breathes upon a bank of violets" ; I am reminded of Stromboli, of Etna, of Vesuvius, and of hell.'

All through these years Shaw was too busy to think of death. He told George Bishop that between the ages of 50 and

60 life is at its worst, and he had to reflect on his mortality and arrange for his decease, but that afterwards he scarcely gave it a thought, except when he had to alter his will, and even then put it off far too long. The subject seldom cropped up in his conversation, though he once declared that he would 'prefer to die in a reasonably dry ditch under the stars', and early in 1935, after an illness, he observed that he had 'missed the psychological moment for dying'. Meanwhile, his friends were following one another 'from sunshine to the sunless land', his strongest feeling on such occasions having been expressed in his article on the death of William Morris: 'You can lose a man like that by your own death, but not by his.' Perhaps the passing of William Archer in 1924 gave him a deeper pang of grief: 'When I returned to an Archerless London it seemed to me that the place had entered on a new age in which I was lagging superfluous. I still feel that when he went he took a piece of me with him.' Just before undergoing the operation that killed him, Archer had written to Shaw: 'Accidents will happen, and this episode gives me an excuse for saying, what I hope you don't doubt—namely, that though I may sometimes have played the part of all-too-candid mentor, I have never wavered in my admiration and affection for you, or ceased to feel that the Fates had treated me kindly in making me your contemporary and friend. I thank you from my heart for forty years of good comradeship.' In 1920 Shaw's sister Lucy died. She had been married and separated from her husband: 'She had not seen him for years when she discovered that at the date of their marriage there had been another lady in the case. This so enraged her that she insisted on divorcing him at my expense. Then, being free of him, and he very lonely, she entertained him daily until his death, when his bachelor brother succeeded him at her fireside until he, too, died. Years after these events, when she and I were in our sixties, I called on her one sunny afternoon and found her in bed alone. She told me she was dying, and presently did actually die whilst she held my hand.' The brother and sister had lived for many years in different circles and had seldom met. 'Her heart, if she had one, was quite unbreakable,' Shaw summed up; 'and the hearts she broke, not at all lethally by the way, were innumerable.'

The fame of the dramatist was fitly sealed by Sir Barry Jackson's inauguration of the Malvern Festival in August 1929, when *Back to Methuselah, Heartbreak House, Caesar and Cleopatra* and *The Apple Cart* were given. The last named had first appeared at the Polsky Theatre, Warsaw, in June. Its later success in London was due to its topical theme: the futility of capitalist democracy, shown up and outwitted by a clever constitutional monarch.[1] Shaw wrote it in six weeks, and such was the importance attached to everything he did that the London critics travelled by train to Malvern on Sunday, August 18th, to witness the dress rehearsal. It was a sweltering hot day, but Shaw spent the morning tramping the Malvern Hills. He had worked as hard as usual over the production, and a long screed he handed to Cedric Hardwicke, who played the King, showed how thoroughly he had attended to details. From a letter of Shaw's to Sutro in October of the same year we learn that *The Apple Cart,* like many of his plays, transformed itself during composition: 'Sempronius *père* was a false start. I began with a notion of two great parties: the Ritualists and the Quakers, with the King balancing them one against the other and finally defeating a combination of them. But I discarded this, as there wasnt room for it. However, I thought the opening would make a very good Mozartian overture to get the audience settled down and in the right attentive mood before the real fun began: hence its retention. But the whole affair is a frightful bag of stage tricks, as old as Sophocles. I blushed when I saw it.'

At an accidental meeting during the London run of the piece I asked G.B.S. whether there was any truth in the general belief that King Magnus in his comedy was a veiled portrait of the then reigning monarch, George V. He replied cautiously that if people liked to think so, he had no objection. I pressed him to be more precise. 'Well, there is a King on the throne, and there is a King in my play, and if the King on the throne happened to behave like the King in my play you could say they resembled one another.' I remarked that there was not the slightest resemblance between them. 'The real King Magnus is sitting within a few feet of you', he announced. 'Never having been offered a throne, I have had to seize one

---

[1] Shaw's attitude to the dictators who were springing up like toadstools all over Europe became more and more friendly as the years went by. In October 1933 he wrote to Lady Astor: 'As to the man with "a profoundly liberal mind; an English mind," he must be as great a curiosity as a man with a profoundly peaceful mind: a tiger's mind. All these anti-Mussolinians are idiots.'

and crown myself. But I have a lot in common with the present monarch: we are both human beings and we were both christened George, and I dare say he dislikes the name as much as I do.'

On the same occasion Shaw assured me that the part of Orinthia in the play was a lifelike portrait of Stella Patrick Campbell, and that the wrestling-match between Orinthia and Magnus had actually occurred between himself and Stella. 'Sometimes, when I got up to leave her, she would pin me down and do her utmost to make me late for meals at home. It used to be a real tussle between us until I learnt how to grip her wrists: then I became master of the situation. One of our bouts did actually end with both of us on the floor fighting like mad.' Stella got to hear that Shaw had portrayed her in *The Apple Cart*, and insisted that he should read the play to her before it was produced. He was nervous and did his best to get out of it. But after several excuses and evasions he surrendered, called at her house in Kensington Square, and went through the performance, which he described to me:

'The first act nearly sent her to sleep. She yawned through it. "Now for us!" I said when we arrived at the Interlude. She instantly became attentive, and I was keenly conscious of her interest throughout the scene. The atmosphere was like that of a law-court just before the jury's verdict is pronounced. I expected a few laughs, but she didn't oblige me with so much as a chuckle. It would have been heart-rendering if my heart had been rendable. At its conclusion there was a long pause. I was determined not to speak first. Then she said: "The whole thing is invented; it's not a bit like you or me." I jumped into the opening she gave me: "Of course it's invented. This is fiction not history." She couldn't think of an immediate reply, and to gain time told me to go on. I read the last act, but she wasn't listening: she was thinking of what to say about the Interlude. The job finished, she asked to look at the play. I handed it over, saying "Chuck it in the fire if that will relieve your feelings; I have plenty of copies." She went through the Interlude, objected to several passages, which I promised to alter, and told me that, if true, the scene was libellous; if invented, it was rubbish; and in both cases it was vulgar. Having expressed my disagreement at some length, and said that, whether fact or fiction, the scene would immortalize her, I made a dignified exit just before, as I fancied, she was about to hurl a cushion at my head.'

The Malvern Festival was an annual institution until 1939, when it was interrupted by 'the second Punic War'. Though established to the glory of Shaw it soon began to produce the works of other playwrights, past and present.[1] Until 1937 Shaw always stayed at Malvern for the Festival and was, of course, the lion of every occasion, the centre of pushing persistent crowds of autograph-hunters and hero-worshippers. He tired of this in time, and in 1938 stayed at Droitwich, motoring over for any play he wanted to see. But in the first years a great attraction for him was the presence of Sir Edward Elgar at Malvern. They became close friends and were seen together on all sorts of occasions. They had long talks on music. The subject was a dangerous one ; for Elgar's musical temper was volcanic ; but Shaw knew his man and shared his tastes and technical interests, and they never quarrelled. At a public meeting in the Malvern Library Elgar declared that Shaw knew more about music than he ; but Shaw, who when asked to lecture on drama always excused himself on the ground that he was 'a practitioner, not a professor', and would have paid the same compliment to Gosse, knew its value too well to have his head swelled by it. He described Elgar on that occasion as a greater man than himself, which naturally pleased the composer, who called Shaw 'the best friend to any artist, the kindest and possibly the dearest fellow on earth', and dedicated the Severn Suite to him. In 1922, seven years before they began to see so much of one another at Malvern, Shaw had complained in the press of the scanty audience and absence of official patronage for Elgar's *The Apostles* at Queen's Hall :

'I distinctly saw six people in the stalls, probably with complimentary tickets. . . .

'The occasion was infinitely more important that the Derby, than Goodwood, than the Cup Finals, than the Carpentier fights, than any of the occasions on which the

[1] Shaw was constantly advancing the interests of young dramatists, and he had the uncommon virtue of praising people behind their backs. Here is an extract from a letter to Lady Astor, dated 9th February, 1934 : 'Sean O'Casey is all right now that his shift from Dublin slums to Hyde Park has shewn that his genius is not limited by frontiers. His plays are wonderfully impressive and *reproachful* without being irritating like mine. People fall crying into one another's arms saying God forgive us all! instead of refusing to speak and going to their solicitors for a divorce.

official leaders of society are photographed and cinematographed laboriously shaking hands with persons on whom Molière's patron, Louis XIV, and Bach's patron, Frederick the Great, would not have condescended to wipe their boots. . . .

'I apologize to posterity for living in a country where the capacity and tastes of schoolboys and sporting costermongers are the measure of metropolitan culture. Disgustedly yours . . .'

I wanted to know how Shaw had first met Elgar. He satisfied my curiosity:

'I first met Elgar at lunch at the house of Madame. Vandervelde, the wife of the Belgian socialist statesman. No sooner had we been introduced than we plunged into a long talk on music. He had devoured and chuckled over my articles signed Corno di Bassetto when they came out in *The Star* in the eighteen-eighties, and could still quote some of the jokes in them which I had long forgotten. We did not stop talking until our hostess reminded us that our food was getting cold on the table before us, and a silence fell, broken only by the noise of our knives and forks. Roger Fry was there, so far completely out of it while Elgar and I were going deeper and deeper into our subject. At any rate, when silence fell between us, Fry decided to pontificate, and after a short pause declared in his beautiful voice like the *chalumeau* register of a clarinet, "After all there is only one art: the art of design." A threatening growl from the other side of the table stopped him. I looked at Elgar. His hackles were all out, and we had not long to wait for the explosion. "Music is written in the skies: that's where it comes from," he spluttered furiously. "And you compare it to a damned imitation!" Every one waited breathlessly for Fry's reply. But his only alternative to flinging the decanter at Elgar's head was to smile and shut up ; and he shut up.'

I asked Shaw whether Elgar had been a very devout Roman Catholic.

'Good heavens, no! He avoided the subject with a deliberate reticence which convinced me that he was a nineteenth century unbeliever, though he wouldn't have admitted it and wouldn't have liked to be told so. As he was the musical hero of the three great Protestant cathedrals of Worcester, Gloucester and Hereford, and really belonged to Worcester in his soul, the world did not think of him as an R.C.

All his emotion went into his music. One of his very finest works was his setting of O'Shaughnessy's *Music-Makers.'*

Shaw's next play, *Too True To Be Good*, was produced at the Malvern Festival in 1932. The character of Private Meek in it is an obvious portrait of T. E. Lawrence ('Colonel Lawrence'), the hero of the Arabian campaign. Lawrence thought the play 'magnificent. Tempestlike, almost, as a valediction.' The two met first when Sir Sydney Cockerell, then curator of the Fitzwilliam Museum in Cambridge, brought Lawrence to the Adelphi, and incidentally carried off one of Augustus John's portraits of Shaw for the Museum. Lawrence and the Shaws made friends at once; and thenceforth 'the Prince of Damascus' came and went at their house when he pleased, and when he was away wrote many letters, now in the British Museum, to Mrs Shaw.[1] He perhaps felt all the more at home with them because his incurable playacting could not impose on stage-hardened Shaw, who made fun of it and of his extravagant literary idolatries, in which, said Shaw, he uniquely combined the credulity, preciosity, and futility of the amateur and dilettante with first-rate professional mastery of the pen. Shaw greatly enjoyed his penetrating intelligence, his practical inventiveness, his utter irreverence for bigwigs, and his extraordinary talent for literary description; but he maintained that the arrest in Lawrence's physical development produced by an accident in his teens had arrested his mental development also; for he had none of the specifically adult interests in politics and religion.[2] He was more a boy of genius who never really grew up than even Gilbert Chesterton, another marvellous Peter Pan, who was not, however, a man of action. Neither was Shaw for that matter; and in estimating the value of his verdict on Lawrence it must be remembered that more than once he classed the entire English nation as non-adult.

Shaw at first denounced Lawrence's enlistment as a private soldier as 'a shocking tomfoolery' and pressed Baldwin to

[1] On June 30th, 1929, we find Lawrence writing to Lady Astor: 'Mrs. Shaw sees only my virtues, I fear. So I think her a very understanding soul. She and G.B.S. mix like bacon and eggs into a quintessential dream. I would rather visit them than read any book or hear any music on earth.'

[2] Shaw's view seems to be that unless one takes an interest in the two chief means whereby mankind has been doped throughout the ages, one has not an adult mind. He may be right; but the point is arguable.

grant him a decent pension, without success. The shocking tomfoolery went on; and Shaw gave Lawrence a bit of his mind: 'Nelson, cracked after his whack on the head at the battle of the Nile, coming home and insisting on being placed at the tiller of a canal barge and on being treated as nobody in particular, would have embarrassed the Navy far less. A callow and terrified Marbot, placed in command of a sardonic Napoleon at Austerlitz and Jena, would have felt much as your superior officers must in command of Lawrence the great, the mysterious, save in whom there is no majesty and no might. . . . You talk about leave as if it were a difficulty. Ask for three months leave and they will exclaim, with a sob of relief, "For God's sake, take twelve, take a life-time, take anything rather than keep up this maddening masquerade that makes us all ridiculous." I sympathize with them.'

But it is clear from the Private Meek version of Lawrence that Shaw changed his mind on this point, and that Lawrence as a private and as an aircraftman of the lowest grade actually had not only more freedom but more command than if he had had his hands tied by a commission.

With the exception of *On the Rocks* (1933), *The Six of Calais* (1934) and *The Millionairess* (1937), Shaw's later plays were first seen at Malvern: *The Simpleton of the Unexpected Isles* (1935), *Geneva* (1938) and *In Good King Charles's Golden Days* (1939). Sometimes an idea for a play had been floating in his head for years before it took shape: for example, *The Six of Calais*, which had come to him during a motor trip not long before the 1914 war, when he had visited Domrémy for the sake of Joan of Arc, and had reached Boulogne by way of Ypres, Furnes, Dunkirk and Calais, where the memory of Rodin's Burgesses had stimulated him to invent a play on that theme as the evening shadows lengthened.

None of these later plays, except *Good King Charles*, can bear comparison with his best. The increasingly chaotic state of the world seems to be reflected in his work. But in historical plays he escaped from the chaos; and in this respect Charles II was the most satisfying thing he had done since *Saint Joan*. He told me that he had really wanted to write a play on George Fox, religion again being the main theme. Then he had thought: why not introduce Isaac Newton?—an astonishing creature with a terrific memory, the most prodigious feat of which, a chronology of the world, was reduced to absurdity by his assumption that the world was created in 4004 B.C. Then Shaw's mind had played about Charles II, the cleverest monarch who had ever sat on the English throne. Finally, he had decided to introduce all three, with a few of Charles's mistresses thrown in 'to relieve the intellectual tension'. The result is entertaining.

One feels, indeed, that Shaw was always at his happiest when he left his own period and lived for a while with the people of another age; that although *Heartbreak House, John Bull's Other Island* and *The Doctor's Dilemma* may be revived as 'period pieces' quite as often as *The School for Scandal, She Stoops to Conquer* and *The Importance of Being Earnest*, yet the most natural, most convincing, most imaginative, least self-conscious of his works are *Caesar and Cleopatra, Androcles and The Lion* and *Saint Joan*. These will live as long as there is an English stage devoted to anything better than the sort of play from which he redeemed it. For reasons we have seen, most of his characters do not get far enough away from himself to attain a life of their own, and the really vital ones, the religious and self-conscious types, come straight from their creator. But in the three plays just mentioned the subsidiary characters catch some of the radiance spread by the protagonists and the strings of the puppet-master are fainter. Shaw must have felt where his real weakness lay as a dramatist of contemporary life; for he confessed that he had always been a sojourner on this planet rather than a native of it; that his kingdom was not of this world; that he was at home only in the realm of his imagination, and at ease only with the mighty dead: with Bunyan, with Blake and with Shelley; with Beethoven, Bach and Mozart.

GRAND OLD BOY

'I AM JUST OFF to circumnavigate the globe,' wrote Shaw to Sutro on December 9th, 1932. 'Shant be back until April—if ever.'

Apart from a certain amount of sight-seeing in the Mediterranean and in Germany on the way to Bayreuth, Shaw did no globe-trotting until he was about 75 years old. He knew that the greatest men scarcely ever travelled outside the countries in which they lived—Shakespeare, Beethoven, Rembrandt, Christ, Buddha, Mahomet. He declared that, left to himself, he would never have moved a mile from the spot on which he was born. He was free from the illusion common to so many modern writers that travel broadens the mind or adds to one's knowledge of life. He was perfectly well aware that Shakespeare could deal with the universe between Stratford and London, that Beethoven might have composed his symphonies in a Viennese café, and that Rembrandt did not have to leave Leyden for Amsterdam in order to portray human nature. But Mrs Shaw was nomadic, and needed holidays from her double housekeeping in London and Hertfordshire. And Shaw, though not self-mobile, was curiously ready to go wherever anyone else would take the trouble to push him. Besides, he liked motor driving when he was at the wheel, finding that it satiated his need for work while giving his pen a rest. On board ship he could work on a crowded promenade deck as easily as in noiseless solitude, and he had a way of securing freedom from interruption: 'I have an unerring eye for the unprotected lady who is ripe for a friendship with a celebrity,' G.B.S. said to William Rothenstein. 'Having made my choice I plant my deck chair beside hers and ask her whether she minds my working at a new play instead of talking. She is so delighted at being given the role of protector of G.B.S. that whenever anyone comes near she makes agitated signs to warn him off, whispering that *Mr Shaw is at work on a new play.* So I make a new friend and get perfect peace during the entire voyage.' His playlet entitled *Village Wooing* turns on an acquaintance made in this way. Mrs Shaw, therefore, had her way, and, as he said, 'dragged me all over the globe'.

'Tell me: were you deeply impressed by anything you saw in the course of your travels?' I asked him.

'No. One place is very much like another.'

'By anybody?'

'No. They're all human beings.'

'Did you see the Taj Mahal at Agra?'

'No. The rest of the party tried to see all India in a week.

I stayed in Bombay, where I found that my religion was called Jainism.'

'Did you see the Great Wall in China?'

'I flew over it in an aeroplane.'

'Interesting?'

'As interesting as a wall can be.'

'Surely you were impressed by the Rocky Mountains?'

'I didn't see them. The Three Rock Mountain near Dublin was enough for me.'

To a journalist who asked whether he had anything to say about the countries he had visited, he replied:

'Siam is worth a visit because there the young generation respects the wisdom of the very old. They even seek the advice of their more experienced elders. Now here in England I have to give my advice unsought, and no one pays the smallest attention to it.'

'Do the young take the advice of the old in Siam?'

'Of course not! As there is no Siamese Shaw they would be very stupid if they did. But at least they have the grace to ask for it.'

At the beginning of 1932 he was in South Africa with his wife. Travelling eastwards by motor-car from Cape Town, they met with an accident. Shaw was driving the car, in which were Mrs Shaw, a naval officer who was showing them round, and a great deal of luggage. Shaw was not at his best when faced with a bit of mechanism to which he was unaccustomed: 'The first time I was ever in one of those electric lifts which the passengers work for themselves instead of being taken up and down by a conductor pulling at a rope, I almost cried, and was immensely relieved when I stepped out alive.' But when he was in control of the mechanism he could face anything without blenching. The story he unfolded to me ran as follows:

'In moments of crisis my nerves act in the most extraordinary way. When utter disaster seems imminent my whole being is instantaneously braced to avoid it: I size up the situation in a flash, set my teeth, contract my muscles, take a firm grip of myself, and, without a tremor, always do the wrong thing. That happened once in Pall Mall. I was bicycling past the National Gallery when a Great Western Railway van emerged from the Haymarket making for Cockspur Street. A lady put up her parasol; the horse shied, turned

419

left, and bolted straight for me on its wrong side. However, I was ready for it. Instead of getting off my bicycle and on to the pavement, as any ordinary human being would have done, I pulled myself together with a supreme effort, went full tilt at that horse, hit it square on the chest, was flung to the ground, and only escaped death by springing up from my ankles and landing an inch or two outside the cart wheels as they passed. The bicycle screamed as it was run over like a spider being torn to pieces.

'There arose the question of compensation. I would have lazily let the matter drop; but every time I saw Mrs Sidney Webb she asked, "Have you made the railway company pay for your bicycle?"; and at last, not wishing to look a fool whenever I met her, I made the application. A man from the railway company called on me in Fitzroy Square. "We are not responsible," he said. "Then you need not pay," I replied. "How much do you want?" he asked. "Well, if I had been selling that machine the morning before the accident, I should have been content with fifteen guineas for it,' said I. "Too much! Far too much! Quite out of the question!" he exclaimed. I beamed at him and wished him good-morning. "We are not responsible," he repeated. I knew better, but did not contradict him. He took ten golden sovereigns out of his pocket and placed them on the table before me, knowing that few people can resist precious metal when it is placed within their reach. "We do not wish to treat you unkindly," he said, "but that's the utmost we can go to. It's extremely generous." "Let us leave it to the lawyers," I suggested. "After all, the accident may have consequences we cannot foresee. I may get all sorts of diseases and disablements from the shock. I may have to take a dozen actions against you.' Then he played his last card. Pocketing his money, he walked slowly to the door, opened it slowly, passed through it, and had almost closed it very slowly behind him, when he surrendered. With a melancholy resignation which touched me, he returned, and patiently handed over the fifteen guineas and the receipt for my signature. The truth is I did not care twopence about the guineas; but I wanted to see how this sort of thing was done.

'But all that is by the way. My accident in South Africa was more serious. I learnt to drive in 1908 on a car that had its accelerator pedal between the clutch and the brake. That arrangement became automatic for me; and when I changed to cars with the accelerator to the right of the brake I became a deadly dangerous driver in an emergency when I had not my trusty chauffeur next to me to turn off the spark when I mistook the pedals. He was unfortunately not with me in South Africa. Well, we were on our way to Port Elizabeth from a pleasant seaside place called Wilderness. I was at the wheel and had done a long drive over mountain passes, negotiating tracks and gorges in a masterly manner, when we came upon what looked like a half a mile of straight safe smooth road; and I let the car rip. Suddenly she twisted violently to the left over a bump and made for the edge of the road. I was more than equal to the occasion: not for an instant did I lose my head: my body was rigid: my nerves were of steel. I turned the car's head the other way, and pressed down the wrong pedal as far as it would go. The car responded nobly: she dashed across the road, charged and cleared a bank, taking a barbed wire fence with her, and started off across the veldt. On we went, gathering speed, my foot hard on the accelerator, jerking and crashing over the uneven ground, plunging down a ravine and up the other side, and I should have been bumping over the veldt to this day if Commander Newton, who was in charge of me, hadnt said sternly, "Will you take your foot off the accelerator and put it on the brake." Well, I am always open to reason. I did as he suggested and brought the car to a standstill, the last strand of barbed wire still holding, though drawn out for miles. I was unhurt; but my wife had been rolled about with the luggage in the back seat and was seriously wounded. The Commander rendered first aid; and we finished the journey at Knysna, where she developed a temperature of 108 and was laid up for a month. I bathed every day and wrote *The Adventures of The Black Girl in Her Search for God.*'

In a letter to Lady Astor, written in pencil from The Royal Hotel, Knysna, C.P., on 18th February, 1932, he described the accident, and its effect on Mrs Shaw:

'Except for a few negligible knocks I was not hurt, nor the man beside me, nor even the car. But oh! poor Charlotte! When we extricated her crumpled remains from the pile of luggage which had avalanched her I feared I was a widower until she asked: were we hurt? Her head was broken; her spectacle rims were driven into her blackened eyes; her left wrist was agonizingly sprained; her back was fearfully bruised ; and she had a hole in her right shin which something had pierced to the bone. And there was fifteen miles to go to reach this hotel.

'That was eight days ago. The bruises and sprains do not worry now ; but she is still flat on her back with the shin hole giving no end of trouble. She put up a temperature of 103 yesterday (my heart jumped into my mouth) but today the wound took a favorable turn, and the temperature is down to 100. She is very miserable. By the time this reaches you I hope to have her at Wilderness recuperating ; and you may assume that all is well again unless I have cabled in the meantime.

'I have cancelled all my arrangements so as to leave her mind quite easy as to having to travel and shall keep her in this climatic paradise (in which she blossomed like the rose until the mishap occurred) until she is well enough to propose the return journey herself. . . . Last night I woke up and found myself happy and perfectly callous. I concluded that the danger was over ; but Charlotte was extremely indignant. She does not know how serious the thing *might* prove ; but I do.

'By a miracle the accident has not got into the papers. It would bring a deluge of inquiries, and for other reasons should be kept as secret as possible. So keep it within our more intimate circle.

'Up to the moment of the catastrophe the trip was a great success. For sunshine, scenery, bathing, and motoring, the place is unbeatable. In Cape Town I did a stupendous lecture on Russia, speaking for an hour and three-quarters without turning a hair, at the City Hall, and enriching the local Fabian Society beyond the dreams of avarice. I also made the first broadcast to be relayed all over the Union of S.A.

'The two political parties, Nationalist (in office) and South African (Opposition), keep going with a sham fight about the Gold Standard, which neither of them understands. The real difference is a racial feud between Dutch and English which we know nothing of in England ; but which is quite venomous here. . . .'

Whether or not the bumps and gullies on the veldt reminded him forcefully of the religious obstacles that had so violently jolted mankind through the ages, he did not know. At any rate the fable of *The Black Girl* ejected every idea for a play with

422

which to wile away his time, and it expressed his general attitude to religions, as well as his own faith, more clearly and simply than any of his plays had done. He reviewed the various beliefs of men, showed what was divine and what idolatrous in them, and closed on a note of rational mysticism in which he combined the teaching of Voltaire with his own. The Old Philosopher is Voltaire, the Irishman is G.B.S.:

'And shall we never be able to bear His full presence?' said the black girl.

'I trust not,' said the old philosopher. 'For we shall never be able to bear His full presence until we have fulfilled all His purposes and become gods ourselves. But as His purposes are infinite, and we are most briefly finite, we shall never, thank God, be able to catch up with His purposes. So much the better for us. If our work were done we should be of no further use: that would be the end of us; for He would hardly keep us alive for the pleasure of looking at us, ugly and ephemeral insects as we are. Therefore come in and help to cultivate this garden to His glory. The rest you had better leave to him.'

'Then you did not come in to search for God?' said the black girl.

'Divvle a search,' said the Irishman. 'Sure God can search for me if he wants me. My own belief is that he's not all that he sets up to be. He's not properly made and finished yet. There's somethin in us that's dhrivin at him, and somethin out of us that's dhrivin at him: that's certain; and the only other thing that's certain is that the somethin makes plenty of mistakes in thryin to get there. We've got to find out its way for it as best we can, you and I; for there's a hell of a lot of other people thinkin of nothin but their own bellies,' And he spat on his hands and went on digging.

While the Black Girl was searching for God several white boys were looking for fun. One day, while Shaw was bathing in the sea, he observed a youngster swimming purposefully towards him. At a few yards' distance the lad's heart seemed to fail within him, for he turned and was about to make off when Shaw asked him what he wanted.

'They bet me a shilling I wouldn't duck you,' spluttered the youth.

'Well?'

'I took it on.'

'Well?'

'It's off,' said the youth, beginning to retreat.

'Nonsense,' returned Shaw: 'it's easy money. If you wait a moment while I get my breath, I'll let you push my head under water.'

The boy returned in triumph to his friends and collected his shilling.

With the help of his letters to Lady Astor we can see Shaw here and there on his travels. From Bombay, on 13th January, 1933, he wrote: 'We are alive; but that is all. We started tired to death, hoping for rest; but this ship keeps stopping in ports where the water is too filthy to bathe in and shooting us ashore for impossible excursions to see the insides of railway carriages, and to be let out, like little dogs, for a few minutes exercise and a glimpse of a temple or a hotel meal or a cobra-mongoose fight. We absolutely refused, and were roasted for a week at Luxor and are now roasting at Bombay for another week.' A certain Begum, he reported, 'concentrated all the native nobility on me at a grand reception full of Nizamesses and Indian highnesses; and oh my! cant they dress, these native plutocrats. The place blazed with beauty. The British are right to boycott them (there was only one white real lady, spouse of a Chief Justice); for the dusky damsels would not leave their daughters an earthly. I have been hung with flowers in the temples and drenched with rosewater and dabbed with vermilion in the houses; and the ship is infested with pilgrims to my shrine. Charlotte and I curse the day of our birth and the hour of our sailing incessantly. Our sole comfort is to think of THEE and wish we were within reach of you.'

On April 28th, 1934, he wrote from the R.M.S. *Rangitane*, Wellington to London, describing his visit to New Zealand:

'If the engines dont break down again (the ship is too full) we should be in the Thames on the 17th. But I am not sure. We lost a day in starting to take a lot of what are called naval ratings. They turned out to be human beings. Perhaps we shall dump them at Plymouth, though we do not stop there officially. . . .

'Although New Zealand actually has a law prohibiting the

landing of any person who has recently visited Russia I had the same Royal Progress as we had in the U.S.S.R. After a week at Auckland I positively refused to visit any other city except Wellington, from which I had to sail. Nevertheless at the last moment I made a dash south for Christchurch. The Mayor waylaid us 30 miles out; and after a civic reception (broadcast) I returned to Wellington a pitiable old wreck, and only escaped a second one by inviting the Mayor to lunch and pleading extreme exhaustion.

'I wish you and Waldorf had been with us. There is a municipal milk supply in Wellington, and an amazing maternity welfare institution centering on a strange old genius, Sir Truby King, with the result that the infant mortality rate in N.Z. is *less than half* the English rate. I wished extremely you had been with me there. And the agricultural problems would have filled all Waldorf's time. You both ought to have a look at this queer Empire at close quarters. Tramping the deck for exercise and playing childish deck games is not worse than the division lobbies. The En-zeds are intensely imperial-patriotic, and call England HOME. Their devotion takes the form of expecting us to exclude all butter and wool except theirs; to wage tariff wars against all Powers refusing to do likewise; to fight all Asiatic States who demand access to the island which its piously Victorian but resolutely birth-controlling British inhabitants resolutely refuse to populate; and to allow all their exports freely into England whilst they pile up protective duties against us and buy freely from Czechoslovakia, China, and anywhere else where we are undersold. . . .

'I am flying this letter from Panama to New York; but it wont reach you more than a few days ahead of ourselves. Charlotte is longing to see you. I am moderately eager myself.'

Lastly, on April 8th, 1935, Shaw wrote to Lady Astor from somewhere 'In the Red Sea approaching Bab of Mendeb':

'Charlotte is flourishing extremely in this hellish heat. I am a mere spectre of myself. My clothes are dropping off my attenuated body. The frightful cold I caught in the freezing Mediterranean has been nearly baked out of me at last; but I am the wretchedest of men, working furiously to distract my attention from myself.

'I am finishing—practically rewriting—my play called *The*

425

Millionairess. People will say you are the millionairess. An awful, impossible woman. . . .

'I can no more. They are making up the mail for Aden, which we expect to reach to-morrow morning. Not the dim and distant Aidenn where a rare and radiant maiden whom the angels name Lenore—no such luck, but at least a place where one can post a letter to you.'

Shaw's only visit to the United States took place in 1933.[1] He landed at San Francisco, went by aeroplane to stay with William Randolph Hearst, one of whose newspapers was advertised in huge letters on the machine, re-embarked at Los Angeles, sailed down the Pacific coast to Panama and up the Atlantic coast to New York, where he spent a single day and addressed a large audience at the Metropolitan Opera House in the evening before returning to the ship. His references to the Americans had never been flattering: 'To rouse their eager interest, their distinguished consideration and their undying devotion, all that is necessary is to hold them up to the ridicule of the rest of the universe. Dickens won them to him forever by merciless projections of typical Americans as windbags, swindlers and assassins. . . . I myself have been particularly careful never to say a civil word to the United States. I have scoffed at their inhabitants as a nation of villagers. I have defined the 100 per cent American as 99 per cent idiot. And they just adore me.' He had described their homage to Purity as 'a quaint conspiracy to convict creation of indecency', had remarked that 'Idiocy and nothing else is what is the matter with America to-day,' and had asked, 'Why

[1] When Anthony Hope, on behalf of Major Pond (who ran lecturers in America), asked Shaw early in the century, whether he would undertake a tour of the United States, G.B.S. replied: 'I cant face America: I should be mobbed to death. For some years past I have received proposal after proposal for a lecturing tour. Every conceivable kind of pressure has been brought to bear, the highest point being £300 per lecture, a private fee of £500 from a leader of New York Society on condition that the first words that I breathed with American air should be uttered in her drawing-room, and a liner or an American battleship all to myself for the journey out. As I have resisted all this there is really no use in wasting Pond's time by extracting proposals from him which I dont really mean to accept, though I generally let people make them because I like to know my market value as a matter of business and personal vanity.'

should any one who is in London want to go to America? ...
I do not want to see the Statue of Liberty. . . . I am a master
of comic irony. But even my appetite for irony does not go
as far as that!' Exception having been taken to such statements, he said that his descriptions of Americans applied to
every other race on earth, and that in taking them as personal
insults the Americans were conceited enough to think themselves the only fools in the world.

Before his arrival in New York the story had got about
that he had been rude to Helen Keller, the blind, deaf and
dumb lady whose intelligence had made her famous throughout the States. It was reported that on being introduced to her
Shaw had said, 'All Americans are blind, deaf and dumb.' I
asked him whether there was a word of truth in the story.
'Not a syllable!' he declared. 'I met her at Cliveden when
she was staying with Lady Astor. What I may have said, and
probably did say after meeting her, was, "I wish all Americans
were blind, deaf and dumb." We got on famously together.
She didnt actually kiss me ; but she smiled all over.' What
with one thing and another there may have been some hostility in the audience when Shaw rose to his feet ; but it was
quickly dissipated by the charm of his voice and the brilliance
of his discourse. 'I ruthlessly attacked the financial magnates
and the whole financial system,' he told me, 'and was afterwards informed that the imposing array of gentlemen sitting
on the platform behind me consisted exclusively of financial
magnates.'

In 1928 Shaw and his wife left Adelphi Terrace, where
they had lived for nearly thirty years, because it was shortly
to be demolished. They moved to 4 Whitehall Court (130),
which was more convenient in every way, if less picturesque.
Except for their travels to New Zealand, to South Africa, to
Madeira, and round the world, their habits did not vary. They
entertained people ; they were entertained ; they were social ;
they were domestic : like the majority of their fellow-citizens.
They also admired one another, Mrs Shaw thinking there was
no one like her husband, Shaw thinking there was no one
like his wife, for was she not the only woman in the world
who knew that a man's right and left feet required different
sizes in stockings? Like most people, Shaw had his private
rituals. Maurice Colbourne noticed him performing one of
them very early in the morning at the swimming-bath of the
Royal Automobile Club. Having emerged from the bath,

Shaw stood 'towel-less, brushing and flicking the water from his limbs methodically, symmetrically, and even artistically, first from his ankles, bending down to reach them, then from his calves, and so upwards, from thighs, body, arms, beard, ending, if I remember rightly, with a final flick to his eyebrows. Then he retired from view.' But unlike most people he objected to public rituals, refusing to attend a friend's wedding because he had not a proper suit for the occasion and sending a cheque for fourteen guineas, the price he would have had to pay for a suit in order to attend. He also drew the line at dining with monarchs, writing to Lady Astor on October 3rd, 1934: 'It's not possible: I'm working against time, Sundays and weekdays. As to your list of guests, you want to frighten me away. Marie doesnt want to meet that old lot. Cant you collect a few young artistic disreputables for her? Why not bring her to see me? I'm not proud; and I can put the shyest of queens at her ease in two minutes. But when I am counting the remaining hours of my life to clear up my work I cant give queens three days in a country house and never catch a glimpse of you except at mealtimes. Last time I came across Marie Carmen Sylva was at the Gare de Lyon, where up to the final moment I thought the grand reception was all for ME.'

Between the ages of 50 and 60 Shaw not only pondered on death but dreaded the possibility of declining into doddering idiocy. After 60. he reached what he called his second childhood, got his 'seventh wind', attained a delightful sense of freedom, became adventurous and irresponsible. There is certainly not a trace of old age in his later Prefaces. Some people, especially those who cannot perceive that apart from Shakespeare he is the only considerable dramatist in the English language, regard his Prefaces as his best and most characteristic productions; and it is certain that without them his plays would never have obtained a wide reading public. 'I always considered that books should be sold by weight, like Government blue books, at so much the ounce,' he said to me, 'and as I wanted my books to take a long time in going round the family, I determined to give full value for money. I remember trying to interest Heinemann in the volume containing *Man and Superman*. He showed me the sales returns for Pinero's plays, which proved that except for an occasional dozen copies sold to an amateur society that had performed one of them there was no demand for them. The fact that I had provided a Dedicatory Epistle, a Handbook for Revolutionists and a bunch of Maxims, did not impress him. There was absolutely no sale for plays or books on political economy, he assured me. John Murray was actually shocked by the volume ; he wrote me quite a touching letter, confessing that he was perhaps old-fashioned, but that the book seemed to him wrong-headed and hurtful, and his conscience would not let him publish it. That settled it. I began to publish my works on commission, and the prefaces made their publication as much of a literary event as the production of the plays was a theatrical one.'

Shaw's Prefaces cost him far more labour than his plays, and as they expressed his personal views he thought them more important. They are invaluable to the biographer because they directly reveal his character. But we cannot say whether they have helped to enlighten the unenlightened. When they were issued in one volume Shaw sorrowfully confessed that 'people get nothing out of books except what they bring to them. . . . You may well ask me why . . . I took the trouble to write them. I can only reply that I do not know. There was no why about it : I had to : that was all.'

Many people were vexed by the exigence of his nature : they saw no reason at all why he 'had to' explode periodically ; and they were incoherently furious whenever he treated a disturbing public matter with what they considered heartless levity. None of the squibs he kept for moments of national gravity made so many worthy folk jump as the one he let off early in December 1936. There was a constitutional crisis. King Edward VIII had fallen in love with an American lady who had been twice married, and England promptly went mad. Archbishops, bishops, peers, cabinet ministers, debated the matter behind closed doors. Could an English king contract a morganatic marriage ? Could British peeresses and royal highnesses walk behind an American commoner ? Why could not this English king do as so many previous English kings had done ? The questions were endless. Nothing else was discussed for weeks. Nearly everyone treated it as a matter of life and death. Nearly everyone suddenly became conscious of the Church of England, the British Constitution, Duty, Virtue, and the Ten Commandments. Even football was temporarily forgotten. A little common sense was highly desirable, and Shaw supplied it ; but as the vast majority of his readers were suffering from what may euphemistically be termed 'temporary insanity', he merely helped to intensify their craziness. Under the heading of *The King, the Constitution and the Lady* he published a 'fictitious dialogue' in *The Evening Standard,* prefacing it with a brief summary of the situation in England, or, as he called it, 'The Kingdom of the Half-Mad':

'The new King, though just turned 40, was unmarried; and now that he was a king he wanted to settle down and set a good example to his people by becoming a family man. He needed a gentle soothing sort of wife, because his nerves were very sensitive, and the conversation of his ministers was often very irritating. As it happened he knew a lady who had just those qualities. Her name, as well as I can remember it, was Mrs Daisy Bell; and as she was an American she had been married twice before and was therefore likely to make an excellent wife for a king who had never been married at all. All this seemed natural and proper; but in the country of the Half-Mad you never could count on anything going off quietly. The Government, for instance, would let whole districts fall into ruin and destitution without turning a hair, and then declare that the end of the world was at hand because some foreign dictator had said bluntly that there are milestones on the Dover road. And so the King was not surprised when he was suddenly told one day at noon or thereabouts that the Archbishop and the Prime Minister had called and insisted on seeing him at once. The King, having spent the morning with Mrs Bell, was in a good humor, so he had them up and offered them cocktails and cigars. But they not only refused this refreshment quite sternly but exhibited such signs of acute mental disturbance that the King had to ask them, with some concern, what was the matter.'

The rest may be given in dialogue form:

PRIME MINISTER: How can you ask, sir? The newspapers are full of it. There are photographs. We are not spared even the lady's little dog. What is your Majesty going to do about it?

KING: Nothing out of the regular course. I shall be crowned in May; and in April I shall marry Daisy.

PRIME MINISTER (*almost shrieking*): Impossible! Madness!

ARCHBISHOP (*whose pulpit voice is a triumph of clerical art*): Out of the question. You cannot marry this woman.

KING: I had rather you called her Mrs Bell. Or Daisy, if you prefer it.

ARCHBISHOP: If I were to officiate at your proposed marriage, I should have to speak of her as 'this woman'. What is good enough for her in the House of God is good enough for her here. But I shall refuse to officiate.

PRIME MINISTER (*shouting*): And I shall resign.

KING: How awful! Would it be too brutal to remind you that there are others? Sandy McLossie will form a King's Party for me in no time. The people are behind me. You may have to resign in any case long before the Coronation.

ARCHBISHOP: Your taunt does not apply to me. The Church will not solemnize an unconstitutional marriage.

KING: That will get me out of a very grave difficulty. Religious matters are not so simple for me as they were for William the Conqueror, of whose death some of you don't seem to have yet heard. William had only a handful of adventurers to consider, all christians, and christians of one sort. I have to consider 495 millions—call it 500—of my subjects. Only eleven per cent of them are christians ; and even that tiny minority is so divided into sects that I cannot say a word about religion without hurting somebody's feelings. As it is, my Protestant Succession is an insult to the Pope and his Church. If I get married in a church, especially one with a steeple on it, I shall offend the Quakers. If I profess the Thirty-Nine Articles of the Church of England, I shall bind myself to hold most of my loving subjects as accursed, and oblige hundreds of millions of them to regard me as an enemy of their God. Now, though all the religious stuff in the Coronation business is out of date, I cannot alter it: that is your affair. But I can get legally married without offending the religious feelings of a single soul in my Empire. I shall be married civilly by the district registrar. What have you to say to that?

ARCHBISHOP: It is unheard of and outrageous. But it would certainly get me out of a very difficult situation.

PRIME MINISTER: Archbishop, are you deserting me?

ARCHBISHOP: I cannot on the spur of the moment find the reply to his Majesty's very unexpected move. You had better take up the constitutional point while I consider it.

PRIME MINISTER: It is impossible for your Majesty to defy the Constitution. Parliament is all-powerful.

431

KING: It has that reputation as long as it does nothing. However, I am as devoted to the Constitution as you are. Only understand that if you push me to a General Election to ascertain the wishes of my people on this question, I am quite ready to face that extremity. You will get a glorious licking. Your very mistaken ballyhoo in the press does not impose on me.

PRIME MINISTER: But there is no question of a General Election. Are you prepared to act by the advice of your ministers or are you not? That is the simple issue between us.

KING: Well, what is your advice? Whom do you advise me to marry? I have made my choice. Now make yours. You cannot talk about marriage in the air—in the abstract. Come down to tin tacks. Name your lady.

PRIME MINISTER: But the Cabinet has not considered that. You are not playing the game, sir.

KING: You mean that I am beating you at it. I mean to. I thought I should.

PRIME MINISTER: Not at all, sir. But I cannot choose a wife for you, can I?

KING: Then you cannot advise me on the subject. And if you cannot advise me, I cannot act by your advice.

PRIME MINISTER: This seems to me to be a quibble. I should never have expected it from your Majesty. You know very well what I mean. Somebody of Royal stock. Not American.

KING: At last we have something definite. The Prime Minister of England publicly classes Americans as untouchables. You insult the nation on whose friendship and kinship the existence of my Empire in the East finally depends. All my wisest political friends regard a marriage between a British king and an American lady as a masterstroke of policy.

PRIME MINISTER: I should not have said that. It was a slip of the tongue.

KING: Very well, we will wash that out. But you still want a bride of Royal stock. You are dreaming of a seventeenth-century dynastic marriage. I, the King of England and Emperor of Britain, am to go a-begging through Europe for some cousin, five or six times removed, of a dethroned down-and-out Bourbon or Hapsburg or Hohenzollern or Romanoff, about whom nobody in this country or anywhere else cares one single dump. I shall do nothing so

432

unpopular and so silly. If you are still living in the seventeenth century, I am living in the twentieth. I am living in a world of republics, of mighty Powers governed by ex-house-painters, stonemasons, promoted ranker soldiers, sons of operators in boot factories. Am I to marry one of their daughters? Choose my father-in-law for yourself. There is the Shah of Persia. There is Effendi Whataturk. There is Signor Bombardone. There is Herr Battler. There is the steel king of Russia. That is the Royal stock of today. I wonder would any of these great rulers allow a relative of his to marry an old-fashioned king! I doubt it. I tell you there is not a Royal House left in Europe today into which I could marry without weakening England's position ; and if you don't know that you don't know anything.

PRIME MINISTER : You seem to me to be entirely mad.

KING : To a little London clique some two or three centuries behind the times I no doubt seem so. The modern world knows better. However, we need not argue about that. Name your lady.

PRIME MINISTER : I cannot think of anybody at the moment, though there must be lots available. Can you suggest any one, Archbishop?

ARCHBISHOP : No ; the unexpectedness of the demand leaves my mind a blank. I think we had better discuss the possibility of an abdication.

PRIME MINISTER : Yes, yes. Your Majesty must abdicate. That will settle the whole question and get us out of all our difficulties.

KING : My sense of public duty, to which your friends appeal so movingly, will hardly allow me to desert my post without the smallest excuse for such an act.

ARCHBISHOP : Your throne will be shaken to its foundations.

KING : That is my look-out, as I happen to be sitting on it. But what will happen to the foundations of the Church if it tries to force me to contract a loveless marriage and to live in adultery with the woman I really love?

ARCHBISHOP : You need not do that.

KING : You know that I will if I listen to your counsel. Dare you persist in it?

ARCHBISHOP : I really think, P.M., that we had better go. If I were superstitious I should be tempted to believe that the devil was putting all these arguments into his Majesty's head. They are unanswerable; and yet they are so entirely off the track of English educated thought that they do not really belong to your world and mine.

KING (*rising as his visitors rise*): Besides, my brother, who would succeed me, might strongly object. And he is married to a homegrown lady, who is more popular than any foreign ex-princess could be. And he would never be the real thing as long as I was in the offing. You would have to cut my head off. You can't tomfool with the throne: you must either abolish it or respect it.

PRIME MINISTER: You have said enough, sir. Spare me any more.

KING: Stay for lunch, both of you. Daisy will be there. Or must I make it a command?

ARCHBISHOP: It is past my lunch hour; I am very hungry. If it is a command, I shall not demur.

KING (*whispering to the stricken Prime Minister as they go downstairs*): I warn you, my dear Goldwyn, that if you take up my challenge and name your lady, her photograph shall appear in all the papers next day with Daisy's beside it. Daisy and her little dog.

'The Prime Minister shook his head sadly; and so they went in to lunch together. The Prime Minister ate hardly anything; but the Archbishop left nothing on his plate.'

Shaw could tell every actor how to play his part, but not every actor could learn the lesson. Edward had all the trumps in his hand; but he could not or would not play them, and let himself and his lady be 'squeezed out' without any resistance from Premier or Archbishop.

The author of this was eighty, but he might easily have been eighteen, and it was useless to call him, as someone did, the Grand Old Man of English letters. The title of Grand Old Boy would have been far more fitting, for no one knew what he would be up to next. His youthful high spirits and constitutional vitality were amazing. In the spring of 1938 he was stricken with an illness that would have killed anyone twenty years younger. 'I had pernicious anaemia and was treated by inoculations of liver extract,' he confessed to me in November 1939: 'Then one day at Londonderry House I fell down dead, so the inoculations had to be discontinued, but I still take spoonfuls of horrid extracts, of which they

434

have about 60 or 70 varieties.' His vegetarian diet, which had never excluded animal products like eggs, butter, cheese and honey, remained unaltered. It was one of his sayings that 'you must let people eat what agrees with them, even if it seems to you to be garbage', or, as in this case, gland. No doubt the careful nursing of his wife contributed to his recovery. He never trusted himself to hospitals or nursing-homes: 'In a hospital they throw you out into the street before you are half-cured, but in a nursing-home they dont let you out till you're dead.' On July 4th, 1938, he announced his convalescence in a letter to me: 'I have been a complete invalid, forbidden to touch a pen, for a month past, passing the time in reading *Thinking It Over* and other masterpieces.' In October of that year I decided to write his biography. 'If you want to be debunked with a loving hand, I'm your man,' I said. 'I need inbunking, not debunking, having debunked myself like a born clown,' he replied. I found him as healthy and juvenile as ever.

On his 83rd birthday *The Daily Express* published an interview with him. The world was on the brink of war, but he could not believe it would be mad enough to topple over: 'The peace at present is maintained by funk; anything that intensifies funk makes for peace. The polite name for funk is common sense. . . . A lasting peace is a dream. But any statesman who is not desperately afraid of starting a cannonade should be sent to a mental hospital.' He also said that 'we made a wicked treaty in 1918 and covered Central Europe with military frontiers instead of ethnographic ones. Thereby we put ourselves in the wrong and put mutilated Germany in the right'; but he prophesied that in the long run the Jews would be the ruin of Hitler, who 'is terribly handicapped by his anti-Semitism, which is a crazy fad and not a political system'.

Within a month Hitler accepted Russia's general offer of non-aggression commercial treaties to all countries willing to be friends and keep the European peace. This was mistaken for an aggressive military alliance. Shaw dashed off a letter to *The Times*: 'A week ago Dean Inge, writing in *The Evening Standard*, guessed that Herr Hitler had gone to Canossa. A few days later the joyful news came that the Dean was right and that Herr Hitler is under the powerful thumb of Stalin, whose interest in peace is overwhelming. And every one except myself is frightened out of his or her wits! Why?

435

Am I mad? If not, why? why? why?' Having bought off Russia, Hitler attacked Poland, smashed her and then divided the spoils with Stalin, England and France meanwhile having declared war on Germany for invading Poland.

At the end of August Shaw went to Frinton, whence he again wrote to *The Times,* pointing out that England ought to be grateful to Stalin for checking Hitler. He also wrote to Lady Astor:

'*28th September* 1939.

'I think it is time for you, as a sensible woman trying to keep your political household of dunderheads and lunatics out of mischief, to get up in the House and point out the cruelty of keeping up the pretence of a three years war when every one who can see three moves in front of his or her nose knows that the war is over. The pretence is ruining people in all directions at home and slaughtering them abroad.

'The thoughtlessness of our guarantee to Poland has left us without a leg to stand on. Most unfortunately we pledged ourselves to go to her aid WITH ALL OUR RESOURCES; and when it came to the point we dared not use the only resource that could help her (our air bombers); for we had not a soldier within hundreds of miles of her frontiers nor a sailor in the Baltic; and a single bomb from us on the Rhine cities or Berlin would have started a retaliation match which would have left all the cities of the west in the same condition as Madrid and Warsaw. We should have warned the Poles that we could do nothing to stop the German steam-roller, and that they must take it lying down as Czechoslovakia had to, until we had brought Hitler to his senses.

'Fortunately our old pal Stalin stepped in at the right moment and took Hitler by the scruff of the neck; a master-stroke of foreign policy with six million red soldiers at its back.

'What we have to do now is at once to give the order Cease firing, and light up the streets: in short, call off the war and urge on Hitler that Poland will be a greater trouble to him than half a dozen Irelands if he oppresses it unbearably. But we must remember that as far as Poland's business is anybody's business but Poland's, it is more Russia's business and Germany's than ours. Also that we cannot fight Germany *à l'outrance* without ruining both ourselves and Germany, and that we cannot fight Russia at all (neither can Hitler).

The diehards who are still dreaming of a restoration of the Romanoffs and Bourbons and even the Stuarts, to say nothing of the Hapsburgs, must be booted out of politics.

'We should, I think, at once announce our intention of lodging a complaint with the International Court against Hitler as being unfitted for State control, as he is obsessed by a Jewish complex: that of the Chosen Race, which has led him into wholesale persecution and robbery. Nothing should be said about concentration camps, because it was we who invented them.

'I write this at Frinton in Essex; but we return to Ayot tomorrow and shall perhaps see you soon. Charlotte has had a terrible time here, but is much better this last week.

'Waldorf might wave the red flag a bit in the House of Lords. Chamberlainism is no use on earth to him; and he might incidentally give America a lead. Geoffrey Dawson has heroically inserted two letters of mine in *The Times,* and has a third in his locker. I am deeply obliged to him.

'Proletarians of all lands, unite!

'The Labor Party is making the damndest fool of itself.

'Our best love to you both.

> 'In haste—packing,
>
> > 'G.B.S.'

Exactly one week later he addressed another letter to Lady Astor:

'Send out instantly for this week's *New Statesman.* There you will find full instructions as to your line about the war. Everybody wants to have these instructions issued; but nobody but myself can afford to—or dare—issue them.

'The worst is over with Charlotte. She bore the journey here last Friday without turning a hair; and though she still will not venture beyond the gate on foot for fear of bringing back the lumbago, she is quite herself again.

'Waldorf has been letting the Government have it for taking a month to do a day's work. I have seen Governments take thirty years to do a week's work, and then have it settled over their heads by fire and sword, including the burning of several of Charlotte's birthplaces. That is how people who want things done prefer even Hitler and Musso and Ataturk to Westminster. It is a pity you did not spend a few years on a municipal corporation to learn the difference between real government and the party game. You should write up in your study my old warning IF YOU TAKE THIRTY YEARS TO DO HALF AN HOUR'S WORK, YOU WILL PRESENTLY HAVE TO DO THIRTY YEARS' WORK IN HALF AN HOUR, WHICH WILL BE A VERY BLOODY BUSINESS.

'As you are the only living person known to have bullied Stalin with complete success; and as he is by countless chalks the greatest statesman you ever met, and the pleasantest man except myself, you must stop blackguarding him like an *Evening Standard* article writer. To our shame we have betrayed and ruined Poland out of sheer thoughtlessness; but it is to our credit, and to that of France and Germany, that when it came to the point of starting a European bombing match we funked it and left Poland to her fate.

'Stalin rescued her. Do you remember that journey through Poland with the harvest still standing and the long wheel spokes of golden strip cultivation turning round us? It looked lovely; but did you know, as I knew, that strip cultivation means poverty and ignorance, savagery, dirt, and vermin? Not to mention landlordism. Well, Stalin will turn that into collective farming; and the Pole will no longer be a savage. The Pole will keep his language, his laws, his character as a citizen of a Federation of Republics like the United States, only much more highly civilized. And with such an object lesson staring his part of the booty in the face, Hitler will have to make his National Socialism emulate Russian Communism or else find Poland worse for him than ten Irelands. So be comforted; and join me in three cheers for the Red Flag (*young* Glory), the Hammer and the Sickle.

'We two are both absentee landlords; yet Stalin was civil to us.

'Forgive these politics; but you cannot get away from them, and I may as well give you some with hope and comfort in them to enable you to bear all the murderous cant and folly with which you are deluged.

'So Proletarians of All Lands, Unite; and to hell with the Pope by all means;[1] and may whiskey be ever thirteen and ninepence a bottle![2]

'Take care of yourself, dear Nancy: we love you.'

---

[1] Lady Astor being a staunch Protestant and teetotaller.
[2] So that none but capitalists may drink it presumably.

438

In his *New Statesman* article, which he wisely called *Uncommon Sense About The War*, Shaw again praised Stalin, gave a summary of the chaotic bungling of the British authorities under the first impact of war, and stated that but for the Versailles Treaty Hitler 'would have now been a struggling artist of no political account. He actually owes his eminence to us; so let us cease railing at our own creation and recognize the ability with which he has undone our wicked work, and the debt the German nation owes him for it. Our business now is to make peace with him and with all the world instead of making more mischief and ruining our people in the process.' In conclusion he referred to 'the primitive instinct that is at the bottom of all this mischief and that we never mention: to wit pugnacity, sheer pugnacity for its own sake.' A sage observation. Pugnacity won the day, and in November he threw in his hand: 'There are now no war aims, and can be none, except the aim of winning the fight. . . . The prospect is not tempting; for if we lose we shall be bled white by the victors, and if we win we shall have to bleed ourselves white. . . . When the war is over we shall have to settle up exactly as if there had been no war at all. If I were a gambler I should back the neutrals for the real win, with Russia and the United States neck and neck. . . . We are in it for all we are worth. . . . Only I wish we could adopt Henry Fielding's suggestion that we should fight it out with our fists. All this hiding in the dark is humiliating; and a hit with a high-explosive shell cannot be reckoned as a fair knock-out.'[1]

While he and the rest of the world were busy fighting about what they were fighting about, I was struggling with his biography. Just after his first letter appeared in *The Times* I

[1] When Hitler attacked Russia in June 1941, even the shrewdest observers thought Russia would rapidly fold up, and the most optimistic among them gave her six weeks before she sued for peace. Several newspapers implied, rather desperately, that if Russia could only hold out for three months it would give us all the time we needed to prepare for an attack on Germany. G.B.S. was the only man in England who at once proclaimed his belief in a Russian victory. 'The news is too good to be true,' he said. 'It is beyond anything we could have hoped for. Only yesterday we and America were faced with the tremendous job of smashing Hitler—with Russia looking on smiling. To-day, owing to the inconceivable folly of Hitler, we have nothing to do but sit and smile while Stalin smashes Hitler. Germany has not got a dog's chance.' (*News Chronicle*, 23-6-41.)

wrote to ask whether he had any favourites among his plays, and incidentally to express my surprise that he should have praised Dean Inge for 'guessing' at the eleventh hour what some of us had been prophesying as a certainty for several years. Back came his answer on a post-card: 'I praise Dean Inge because to disparage him is to brand oneself as a sixteenth-rate intellect. He is 700 years out of date with his terrible bringing-up and schooling; and yet he lives. So, on your life, good words. I have no favorite plays. I am not a schoolmaster giving examination marks. Why insult me?' My reply was as curt. I said that as Beethoven had informed the world which were his best and favourite works, there was no reason why Shaw should be so sniffy when asked which were his. This brought the following:

'HOTEL ESPLANADE,
'FRINTON, ESSEX,
'4th Sept. 1939.

'DEAR H.P.,

'Have I hurt your feelings? It was unintentional; but I meant to convey that you must produce a biography, not a birthday book.

'When an old colonel (British) called on Beethoven in his latter days and offered him a commission to compose something like his *Septet* (an infantile work) Beethoven dismissed him with imprecations. But if the colonel had asked him to name his favorite symphony the result would have been the same.[1] Favorite is the wrong word. The births of *Fanny's First Play* and *Back to Methuselah* were things that happened. Fanny was a potboiler; and Methuselah was an important work, for the moment impracticable commercially. I know that as well as you do. But I have no birthday book feeling about it.

'Dickens had a birthday book preference for *David Copperfield* because he had put certain experiences of his own into it; but he knew quite well that *Great Expectations* was a better book and *Little Dorrit* a bigger one.

---

[1] Shaw is wrong. Christian Kuffner, a poet, asked Beethoven in 1817 which was his *favourite* among his symphonies. 'The "Eroica",' replied Beethoven with the utmost good humour. 'I should have guessed the C minor,' said Kuffner. 'No, the "Eroica",' repeated Beethoven, who had already written his first eight symphonies.

'Plays which I wrote completely in the air (*Heartbreak House* was one of them) interest me more than the potboilers written for immediate production like *You Never Can Tell*; but I really have no sentimental preferences.

'As to Inge, read his *Outspoken Essays* and my review of it headed *Our Great Dean*. And never mind his pre-Marxian political economy. Labor politics are not his job. When he is on his job he is easily one of the first minds in England. Remember: you have to account for my admiration of him.'

His next letter, dated 13th September, began with a quotation from my answer to the above:

'DEAR HESKETH PEARSON,

' "Into which of your works had you felt you had poured most of your inmost self, your spiritual passion? That was what I meant. But as you seem unwilling to answer, I do not press it."

'This, honest Injun! does not describe any process of which I have been conscious. I hammer away as a smith makes horseshoes. When I write *As Far As Thought Can Reach* I argue out the statements until I reach a verdict—often comic in its simplicity—and then I give the verdict. The fact that I desire to get at a right verdict and that the search for it is a pleasurable activity and its achievement a satisfaction convinces me that intellect is as much a passion as sex, with less intensity but lifelong permanency, and that in the course of evolution it may become so intense that life will be much happier and free from the revulsions of sex, which will become less tyrannous and finally have its reproduction function fulfilled in a less unpresentable way.

'There is a passage at the end of *Too True To Be Good* which caused the then Dean of Worcester (Moore Ede) to preach an impassioned sermon on it. I scribbled it down at rehearsal because we could not get the curtain down at the right instant to choke off Cedric Hardwicke's oration; and I had to provide some lines for him to go on with in case of need. Lilith's "great" speech at the end of *Methuselah* was ground out as pure argument, as Lilith wasnt anybody, and there was no character to express. You may take it that Shakespear wrote "The cloud capt towers" and "There's a divinity" just as he wrote "Now is the bawdy hand of the dial upon the prick of noon," all in the day's work.

441

'As to Inge, I withdraw apologetically. I thought you didnt know him and were merely expressing Trade Union resentment and current ribaldry. But allow for his frightful clerical bringing-up; and dont forget his *jeux d'esprit,* which are of the best.

'We are in the thick of this evacuation idiocy. Indescribable. Our first terrified attempts at Military Communism are beyond words.

'What a comfort to know that if we kill 20 millions or so of one another, we'll none of us be missed!'

The last sentence reveals Shaw in his totalitarian vein. On the reasonable assumption that every living human being has three people who would regret his or her demise, twenty millions would be missed by sixty millions.

It is not necessary for me to account for Shaw's admiration of Dean Inge; he might just as well have insisted that I should account for his dislike of whisky: there is no accounting for taste. But a passage in his criticism of *Outspoken Essays* is worth quoting. After describing Dean Inge as a great Protestant, he goes on: 'I am so thorough an Irish Protestant myself that I have all my life scandalized the Irish Protestant clergy, and made the Irish priests chuckle, by declaring that a Protestant Church is a contradiction in terms. The true Protestant is a mystic, not an Institutionalist. Those who do not understand this must read the Dean's superb essay on Institutionalism and Mysticism, which contains an inpired page (232) which ought to be included in the canon.'

Shaw managed somehow to be a mystic in spiritual matters and an institutionalist in temporal matters, presumably on the principle that one cannot serve God without Mammon. For us, for his biographer at any rate, Shaw's greatness lay not in his beliefs but in his humour, not in his preaching but in his personality. Humour is the poetry of life, its justification and reward, and Shaw distributed a great deal of that element, not always of the richest quality but of an unequalled quantity. Humour is also the flower on the stem of character.

'Is there a conscious portrait of yourself in any of your plays?' I once asked him.

'No,' he replied, 'except the character of "G.B.S." in all of them.'

Which explains why he never created a great character that

was not an essential part of himself. But himself was that rarest of creations: a great character, whose humorous sanity irradiated an epoch which will probably be known to history as the Shavian Age.

The original Life, which was published in 1942, ended at this point. What follows was issued as a Postscript in 1951.

SHAW CRITICIZES HIS BIOGRAPHER

ALL THINGS CONSIDERED Shaw bore up pretty well when he read the final proofs of my Life of him. But he had several comments to make.

'You are still a bit in the 19th century in respect of arranging religion, politics, science and art in braintight compartments, mostly incompatible and exclusive,' he said. 'They don't exist that way at all. There is no such thing as the religious man, the political man, the scientific man, the artistic man: in human nature they are all mixed up in different proportions, and that is how they are mixed in my plays. In *St Joan* the Bishop, the Inquisitor and the feudal baron are as religious as Joan without her peculiar delusions ; and I have brought out the fact that she was a very dangerous woman as well as a saint. Your preference for Caesar, Joan and Charles II is due, not to their being better plays, but to their having a political and religious framework with which you are familiar and which gives you no trouble, whereas my post-Marx, post-Bergson, ultra-Shavian plays bother you ; and you turn them down as inferior when what is wrong is that they are less easy to take in.'

To this I answered:

'I'm afraid you're wrong in saying that there are no such things as the religious man, the political man, the scientific

443

man, the artistic man, and so forth, because I happen to know there are. Not only is the world dotted with doctors who are solely interested in medicine, lawyers who can talk of nothing but their cases, politicians who spend their lives lobbying and wire-pulling, business men who can think of nothing but money-making, sportsmen who do little but dream of "winners", clergymen who cannot be dragged from theology, and engineers who are lost when they have nothing to tinker with, but I myself am absolutely and exclusively artistic: that is, I am interested in human beings, not in doctrines and theories, in the substance, not the shadow. Shakespeare, too, was solely interested in human nature, the material for his art, and did not care a rap for religion, politics, science, philosophy, and all the rest of the rot wherewith mankind is perpetually doped. That is why I can understand Shakespeare, and you cannot. I love your religious creations because they are primarily human beings and express emotions, not creeds. In *Androcles* you really get away from polemics and write poetry ; and all great art deals with the nature of man, not the dogma of man, though of course humbug (another word for dogma) is the comic framework within which human nature reveals itself.'

He let this pass, and launched another attack:

'Your contention that Shakespeare's "brief candle" passages are all strokes of idiosyncratic character and do not indicate a phase of acute pessimism through which he passed is in flat contradiction to your book on the Bard. Why attack me for something you have said yourself?'

'I do not think, nor have I said, that Shakespeare was passing through a phase of acute pessimism when he wrote the later version of *Hamlet*, and *Macbeth* and *Lear* and *The Tempest*, though he was obviously tired out when he wrote the last. His phase of depression and pessimism is expressed in *Troilus*, *All's Well* and *Measure for Measure*, which in consequence are very inferior works. He had come through his period of bitterness and disillusion when he reached the great tragedies ; but he was taking life more seriously than when he wrote the earlier comedies, just as you were taking it more seriously in *Man and Superman* than in *You Never Can Tell*. Compare *Lear* with *Timon*: the former is far more tragic than the latter ; but my God! the artistic detachment in *Lear* is superhuman, whereas the vituperative qualities of *Timon* are all-too-human, and because he was allowing his feelings to run away with him during a mental breakdown his art suffered proportionately. I repeat, therefore, that the "brief candle" passages are every bit as much in character as Mistress Quickly's account of Falstaff's death, and what I have written in my Life of Shakespeare explains this and bears it out. Please be good enough to read my book ; then you will be kind enough not to misinterpret me.'

He now asked me, 'Is it worth while compiling an itinerary? I have been something of a globe trotter since I married a nomadic wife ; but I don't think it has left much mark on any of my plays except *The Simpleton of the Unexpected Isles*, which you don't appreciate. I could not have written it exactly as it is if I had not been in India and the Far East, though almost all my life as a playwright I have hankered after a dramatization of the Last Judgment.'

I adumbrated that an itinerary might be interesting. He went on:

'It would be wiser to say of *As Far As Thought Can Reach* that as you are neither a biologist nor a philosopher your thought does not reach so far, and that you are too old a dog to learn new tricks, or more exactly that you cannot afford to spend a couple of years reading my prefaces and digesting them. But of course I don't advise you to say this ; for between ourselves your practically complete ignoring of the prefaces makes the book more readable and not intolerably long ; and for my part I want people to read my prefaces and not read about them. But your enemies on the press (if you have any) will say that it is pretty evident that you never read my preface On Bosses (to *The Millionairess*) or you would not have repeated the silly complaint that I have collapsed into dictator-worship in my old age because I have pointed out that Peter the Great, Napoleon III and Mussolini could and did build or rebuild Petrograd, Paris and modern Rome, while our Party Parliament cannot even build a bridge across the Severn, much less harness the terrible tides of the Pentland Firth and enable us to live without going underground for our horse power. They will say, if they are intelligent enough, "This is not classical biography : it is gossip." To this you can reply "That is exactly what classical biography is : if you want Shavian philosophy instead, read Shaw's works." This will be perfectly sound in principle and effective as repartee ; but you must be prepared with it, otherwise I should not bother you about it.'

'I do not say that you have collapsed into dictator-worship,' I replied. 'I merely say that you have been imposed upon by the dictators, that you prefer the gangsters who get things done to the imbeciles who don't. I, on the other hand, knew all along that war and slavery resulted from dictatorship, and so I hated these criminal lunatics whom you and so many others admired or half-admired.'

Towards the end of the book I had written that Communism and Fascism were interchangeable terms. He took me up on this:

'As to Communism and Fascism being interchangeable terms, anyone who thinks so understands neither the one nor the other. Formerly the capitalists were all for *laisser-faire ;* the State must not touch industry: it must just police the conflict between capital and labour. Then came the Fabians, who showed that enormous economies could be effected, and privately impossible but very lucrative enterprises achieved, by State aid. The Fabian moral was that the State should own the industries. But the capitalists seized the idea and realized that if they could use the powers and money of the State without giving up their ownership of industry they could become richer than ever. And this they proceeded to do. This new policy of State-aided capitalism is Fascism. It is social organization without Socialism, public enterprise without Communism, Hamlet without the part of Hamlet. Big British and American capitalists are now Fascist and as anti-Communist as ever ; and the defeat of Germany and her relapse into Fascism of the British-American type will throw her into the arms of the victorious Allies in a new world war to suppress Communism in Russia, unless Labour is prepared to face civil war rather than fight Russia. Fascism and Communism will then be seen plainly to be deadly rivals for the mastery of the world.'

To which I returned:

'When I say that Fascism and Communism are interchangeable terms, what I mean—obviously—is that to the man in the street it doesn't matter a damn whether the State is the capitalist or the Individual backed by the State. Whatever happens he is enslaved ; and the mental slavery of Moscow and Berlin is just as intolerable to free men like myself as the spiritual slavery of Rome. Fascists, Communists and Nazis submit their minds to an Institution, and whether it is called the State or the Church matters nothing: they have committed the unforgivable sin, the sin against the light within them, the sin against the Holy Ghost. From which it follows that the struggle of the future will be a repetition of the struggle of the past. Just as our predecessors had to fight for their spiritual freedom, for the right to worship God in their own way, so our successors will have to fight for their temporal (as well as spiritual) freedom, for the right to live their own lives and speak their own thoughts; and so the opposing creeds will not be Communism and Fascism, but Individualism and Collectivism, Independence and Subservience, Freedom and Slavery. The State was made for man, not man for the State; but unless human beings make the State their servant, it soon becomes their master, as we have seen in the last few years. However, as some readers may not understand that in calling Fascism and Communism interchangeable terms I am speaking in terms of common sense instead of political ideology, I'll take your tip and accept your correction.'

My Life of Shaw was widely and favourably reviewed and Shaw reported to me: 'It has been a good selling press.' A little later he wrote: 'The book has created a sort of Shavian furore, and brought me a heap of letters from old people whom it has reminded of old contacts with me.' Among the letters I received was one from a schoolmaster who had been annoyed by Shaw's answer to the request that a scene from *St Joan* should be published in a schoolbook: 'NO. I lay my eternal curse on whomsoever shall now or at any time hereafter make schoolbooks of my works and make me hated as Shakespeare is hated.' My correspondent pointed out that an educational publisher had actually included a scene from *St Joan* in a schoolbook with Shaw's permission. I asked Shaw for an explanation. He admitted that the schoolmaster 'is no doubt right about that particular scene. I seem to remember that lately there was an appeal from India for an authorization to print some passage of mine for the use of students who could not get at my plays in my own editions. I refused at first; but the Press convinced me that if I persisted the demand would be met by piracy which I could not afford to fight. So I had to give in. But my rule is not relaxed: school editions are still proposed both here and in America; but they are all ruthlessly turned down.'

As a consequence of the book's success I had offers for its film rights. One firm approached Shaw and me simultaneously.

Shaw promptly gave them to understand that he would do everything in his power to prevent a screen version of his Life. I went down to Ayot St Lawrence in the hope of talking him over. But he had made up his mind that no one on earth could play the part of G.B.S. except himself, that none of his living contemporaries would endure being impersonated, that there was no story to tell, and in fact that his life would be burlesqued and his teaching parodied. I intimated that his decision meant a serious loss to me.

'Your financial situation was the first thing I thought of,' he replied; 'and my reason for squashing the project so promptly and violently was that I know how films always sing of Africa and golden joys to begin with, and end in leaving all the singers disappointed at best and destitute at worst. Forget the Oscar Wilde biography' (this refers to a projected film of Frank Harris's Life of Wilde, in which I had once tried to interest Shaw): 'It was absurd under any circumstances to make a film hero of Oscar. Take the much more apposite case of the film they wanted to make of *The Seven Pillars* with Lawrence of Arabia as its hero. It seemed to have everything in its favour, and everybody except Lawrence. A good deal of money may have been spent on it. Lawrence's death seemed to remove the last obstacle. But nothing came of it; and Lawrence lives in fiction only as the hero of the second act of *Too True To Be Good,* which delighted him. The interlude in *The Apple Cart* does all that can be done on the stage with myself and Stella Pat Campbell: the rest is leather and prunella. All the other attempts to put Stella on the stage have been ghastly failures. Then there are all the difficulties which I have already explained.

'Now as to the money. Suppose you have a film success and receive £20,000 for the first time in your life! That is what happens at best. Immediately you are taxed 19s. 6d. in the pound not only on the £20,000 but on your ordinary earnings as well. That is, you collect money for the war and get a commission of sixpence in the pound, which does not pay for the overhead. In short, you are a ruined man, as I am at this moment, thanks to the colossal success of *Pygmalion*. To avoid this you would have to stipulate that you should be paid nothing until you asked for it, and to run a considerable risk of its not being there when you did ask for it.

'Still, as you could draw a thousand or two every year at

first, that would be a good deal better than nothing. Its possibility, though a delusion, may tempt the film speculators to
buy your film rights for a lump sum too small to be taxed
to extinction but quite big enough to be very useful to you.
You might get several thousands; for there is no limit to the
folly of film speculators. Consequently there is nothing to
prevent you getting what you can out of these people, provided you tell them that you have nothing to sell but your
rights and cannot guarantee my consent or anybody else's:
they must take all the risks of the project proving impracticable, as you will not return the money in any case. I don't
advise you to do this: I only point out its possibility. They
cannot complain if they lose their money, as they have been
very fully and pointedly warned by me that I will do what
I can to stop them.'

Next came a request from Shaw's American publishers,
Dodd Mead and Company, that I should edit one or two
volumes of Shaw's letters. 'The success of your book has
driven the whole trade mad,' said Shaw when I told him of
this offer. 'They all want a book about me, a film about me,
anything about me. This will soon evaporate; but my correspondence is a serious problem. I have written an enormous
number of letters in my long lifetime, none of them unnecessary (there has never been time for that) and therefore never
absolutely vapid and unreadable. That, I suppose, is why so
many of them were preserved even before they had any
value as autographs. But as I have never kept copies they are
scattered over the earth like wrapping paper over the Malvern
Beacon after a bank holiday. However, one serious attempt
was made to collect them. An American named Gabriel Wells,
a famous dealer in rare books to whom thousands of pounds
were as sixpences, began offering fancy prices for Shaw letters,
and accumulated bushels of them before he got tired of trying
to persuade me to edit collectors' editions of them. He asked
Ashley Dukes to make a selection; but Ashley selected
theatrical ones with Janet Achurch as the leading lady; and I
did not want to repeat the Ellen Terry success and figure as a
theatrical celebrity instead of as an artist philosopher. Gabriel
Wells still presumably has his mountain of letters which will
be scattered again at his death, which cannot be very much
more distant than my own. The copyright in them remains a
part of my estate which will some day be valuable.

'But I strongly advise you to fight shy of the job, though
449

it will be done some day by somebody. It would take as long as half a dozen biographies; and overloaded as it would be with Wells's profits and my royalties there would not be enough money in it. I could not possibly co-operate even if I were alive: it would take all my time; and I shall never again have any to spare for picking up my old droppings.

'I suggest that you write to Dodd Mead to say that you see no prospect of being able to undertake the work on any terms that any publisher could afford to offer you, and must leave it to some enthusiast with private means enough to do it as a labour of love.'

I did as he suggested.

'And now, to change the subject,' continued he, 'as you have done Shakespeare and Shaw, are you not bound to do Dickens? All the recent lives of him have been malignant utterances by devil's advocates. All his contemporary celebrities have been dead long enough. Some of them, like Queen Victoria and Disraeli, have been screened already. Anybody but Dickens will be a come down after Shakespeare and G.B.S.'

I replied that I had several times meditated on Dickens as a subject. On different occasions Shaw had tried to dissuade me from writing biographies of (1) Gilbert and Sullivan, (2) himself, (3) Conan, Doyle, and (4) Oscar Wilde. He now produced a positive plan of action:

'When you are through with Dickens you might consider Walter Savage Landor, whose Imaginary Conversations will show you how boring characters are which are not idiosyncratically differentiated like those of Shakespeare, Shaw, Scott and Dumas. And Leigh Hunt might be worth thinking of. They are in *Bleak House* as Boythorn and Skimpole.'

Feeling that, if I welcomed these proposals, Shaw would go on to suggest that I might re-write the Dictionary of National Biography, I said no more.

DEATH OF CHARLOTTE SHAW

THE GREATER PART OF Shaw's last years was spent at Ayot St
Lawrence. Occasionally he visited London in order to give
the servants at Ayot a holiday and to see the many people
who wished to see him. On these visits the mornings were
taken up with a stream of friends and acquaintances, and he
scarcely had time to attend to his more urgent correspondence.
The servant problem in wartime was a constant source of
anxiety to his wife, who was also fighting a disease. At the
end of 1942 he informed Raphael Roche that 'my poor wife,
bowed with *Osteitis deformans,* and suffering much pain for
three years past, is *pronounced* incurable. Both of us deafish,
and rather dotty!' Fortunately his own health throughout the
war caused him no uneasiness. 'My doctor has just overhauled
me and passed me A1,' he told me in '42 ; and age did not
seem to lessen his activity. After a heavy snowfall in January
that year, his secretary, Blanche Patch, found him in the
garden at 5 p.m. shovelling the snow from the steps and
wearing neither hat nor overcoat ; and again, early in 45, she
arrived from London to find him on a ladder pruning a fruit-
tree. Although the gardener said that it would bear no fruit
the following season, Shaw was satisfied with his efforts, telling me 'I prune my trees aesthetically and have discovered
that it is the correct way of pruning them horticulturally.'

There was a danger that his housemaid would be called
up for national service towards the close of '42, so he prepared 'a battery of figures' for the authorities to prove that
he was doing work of national importance. 'I have brought
over a million and a half dollars to London for nothing but

my signature to an agreement,' he said, adding that he was losing money and working overtime to make more dollars to pay our debt to America. But his main care in the years '41-43 was the health of his wife. 'I cannot stop Charlotte from worrying,' he confided to me. 'My skill in Christian Science is not sufficient. It would be brutal to tell her that it doesn't matter tuppence what happens to us in the few months of life that are left to us. What if we freeze or starve to death? We have had our day, and should scorn to lag superfluous. This seems to me a cheerful way of looking at things, but she would merely think I was making light of her sufferings.'

In his last years Shaw developed a trick of repeating in conversation to one person the passages he had written in letters to others. In a communication of this period to Lady Astor, which she showed to me, there appears something very much like the above scrap of talk.

In the last year of her life Charlotte became very exacting, and his day's routine was largely determined by her condition. Usually he rose at eight, and having dressed went into her bedroom for a talk. After breakfast he worked until lunch, at which she joined him. Then he lay down for a nap: 'She always fixes my pillows for me, or thinks she does,' he told me. They had tea together, following which he went out for a walk, but 'I always have to present myself a little before dinner to show her that nothing has happened to me.' Over dinner, and in the drawing-room afterwards, they talked ; but her memory and hearing towards the end were so bad that he had to repeat many things several times in a loud voice and tell her one day what he had told her the day before. When she had gone to bed he listened to the wireless or read until his own bedtime between ten-thirty and eleven. They were staying in their London flat during the summer of '43, and towards the end of August she began to suffer from hallucinations, saying that there were people in her bedroom and that the management should be asked to expel them. For what follows I am deeply indebted to Miss Eleanor O'Connell, who had been a close friend of Shaw's for some years and had received many of his confidences. Everything he said was deeply impressed upon her mind, and on that of Mr John Wardrop, who was also present, and she wrote it all out for me the same day.

G.B.S. looked his normal cheerful self, and for some time

after his arrival he discussed questions of copyright with Wardrop. Breaking off suddenly, he said:

'Do you or Eleanor notice anything different about me today?'

'You have new shoes on,' guessed Wardrop.

'Oh, no! they are at least ten years old. I have not a garment that is not quite that. . . . But I thought you might see something different about me today because I became a widower at 2.30 this morning.' His listeners feeling too confused to speak, he continued: 'On Friday I noticed a change in Charlotte; she seemed so much happier, the wrinkles went out of her forehead, and she was not complaining. After dinner I took her, as I always do, into the drawing-room, and she suddenly said "Where have you been? I haven't seen you for two days." I replied that I had been with her, as usual, and she smiled, just as she did when she was young; and, looking at her, I saw her once more as she was when I first knew her, and I told her that she was beautiful again and that her illness was leaving her. We talked together for a little while, but most of what she said was incoherent and only here and there could I make any sense of it. She then said, thinking we were at our Ayot house, that she must go upstairs and that I must take her. There are of course no stairs in our flat, but I said nothing and took her along to her room, leaving her rather earlier than usual, at which she made no protest. I was aroused early yesterday morning by the maid, who had found Charlotte lying on the floor of her bedroom with blood on her forehead. We got her back into bed. I don't think she had been long out of it, and the cut was only a slight one. I at once arranged for her to have a night nurse. All yesterday she was happy and uncomplaining, but because of her bent shoulders her lungs were compressed and her breathing was difficult, though this had been so for months. I was again struck by her returning beauty; she was as I had never seen her before, smiling so easily, and happy because I told her she was looking young again. I talked to her for a long time, and all her little worries seemed to have gone. I don't think she knew that she was near her end; in fact I am sure that she thought she was much better and was happy because of it. At eight o'clock this morning the nurse woke me and said, "Your wife is dead: she died at two-thirty a.m." I went in and looked at her lying there. Her face was just like a young girl's. You know we have a portrait of her painted when she was about twenty-two, long before I knew her, and people are always asking who it is: they can't believe it was Charlotte. But now she is just like that. I was amazed. I have never seen anything so beautiful, and I could not keep myself from going into her room again and again and talking to her. Once I thought that her eyes opened slightly while I was talking to her, and she seemed so alive that I took my microscope glass and held it to her lips: I could not believe she was dead.'

He had been strangely moved by the alteration in his wife's appearance and the urge he had felt all that morning to go into her bedroom and see and speak to her; and a little later, while still on the subject, he paused and said with a smile: 'Could the world imagine the stage Shaw thinking and feeling and behaving like this?' He stayed on for some time, and as he was on the point of leaving Eleanor O'Connell asked him whether he was not sorry now that he had no children. 'Charlotte always set her face against that,' he replied. 'She had a feeling against children, but sometimes I have been sorry that I was not more insistent on the point. . . . I don't think I ought ever to have been married: I am not the marrying kind; but Charlotte was interested in intellectual things, although unable to do anything herself, and in that way she helped me, and I could not have been married to any other type of woman. . . . She asked me some time ago, if she died before me, to take her ashes to Ireland and scatter them on the Three Rock Mountain; but when the war came, and it was difficult to get to Ireland, I told her that I should keep her ashes myself and leave instructions that when I died my own were to be mingled with hers; and now the undertaker will keep hers in a bronze urn until mine are added.'

As they were walking across Regent's Park Shaw recalled that when he was married 'a friend said that my wife had a face like a muffin, and you know that is really what she was like. She would never be photographed, and I used to tell her "Avoid photographers if you can, but if you can't for heaven's sake smile!"' The beauty of Charlotte's face just before and after death, which had fascinated him, disappeared in twenty-four hours, and she became again as he had known her in the last years.

He had been looking forward to the cremation of his wife, having been interested in the process when his mother and sister were incinerated. 'But cremation is not what it was,' he reported: 'you can't see the body burned: it's a very unsatisfactory ceremony these days.' His secretary, Blanche Patch, and Lady Astor, were with him. First Handel's Largo was played on the organ; then the anthem, 'I Know That My Redeemer Liveth', towards the close of which Shaw stretched out his arms and sang the words quietly. In the car, on their way back to Whitehall Court, Lady Astor suggested that he should accompany her to Cliveden. He replied: 'You ask me to come for a quiet time, and you know you will have at least thirty people there, most of them women—and after all I am now the most eligible man in England. It can't be done.' The day after the cremation John Wardrop rang him up on some business and began with an apology for disturbing him. 'Tut-tut!' said G.B.S., 'there is no need to prolong this state. The guns have been fired, and now it's time to strike up the music.'

The following paragraph appeared in the personal column of *The Times* on September 20th: 'Mr Bernard Shaw has received such a prodigious mass of letters on the occasion of his wife's death that, though he has read and values them all, any attempt to acknowledge them individually is beyond his powers. He therefore begs his friends and hers to be content with this omnibus reply, and to assure them that a very happy ending to a very long life has left him awaiting his own turn in perfect serenity.'

For about a year after his wife's death he spoke of her at intervals, and whenever he did so Eleanor O'Connell gave me the benefit of his memories:

Sep. 26, 1943. 'I told Charlotte when we married that she must keep her own solicitor and bank account separately, but that I must have a marriage settlement. You see I was only earning £6 a week at that time, and I told her that if anything should happen to me I did not like to think of my mother having to beg from her. . . . Of course she did this, but very soon I was earning more than her income, so it didn't matter, and I think the marriage settlement was dissolved some time later.'

Oct. 16, 1943. 'Everybody tells me that I am looking well, and I can't very well say it's relief at my wife's death, but it is you know.'

April 20, 1944. (At Ayot St Lawrence.) 'If you had had forty odd years of love and devotion such as I have had, you would know what freedom meant, and I am enjoying this here for the first time.' 'You should never have been married,' said Eleanor O'Connell. 'No, that's perfectly true,' he replied emphatically slapping his knee.

May 18, 1944. (At Ayot.) 'When one has been married for over forty years there is something quite indestructible that grows up between people which has nothing to do with emotions in any way.'

'Lady Astor remarked how well both Miss Patch and I were looking since Charlotte's death; but, you know, if she had lived much longer we should have predeceased her: she completely wore us out.'

Questioned whether he thought Charlotte had been happy, he answered: 'No, she was always discontented, with everything in the world to make her happy, but she had the idea that happiness was always in the place she wished to be or had just left. One year we had a very lovely house at Woking. I thought it excellent from every point of view, but I knew she did not like it, and then I discovered that she could not stand it a moment longer because the front door opened almost on to the street, with no drive and only a very small pathway leading to it.'

'Just before we married she had a serious love affair with Axel Munthe in Italy, and she told me her heart was broken. I answered, "Rubbish! your heart is certainly not broken." And from then on she seemed to attach herself to me. At first she was inclined to belittle what I said, thinking her own views best and wisest, but in the end she nearly always had to admit that I was right. . . . It takes a long time for two people to get to know each other; and from a diary I discovered lately, and some letters which she wrote to T. E. Lawrence, I realize that there were many parts of her character that even I did not know, for she poured out her soul to Lawrence.

'If we had had children, Charlotte would certainly have quarrelled with me over them, and would have been jealous. Besides, she would never allow anything like that.'

Nov. 1944. On being asked what his wife had looked like in their early days together, he said: 'I remember when we went to the first Fabian Summer School she was dressed in a very masculine costume, tailor-made, with a stiff white collar; and I said, not to her but to the assembled gathering, how much

I disliked the way women had of dressing like men: it detracted from their charm and made them look ridiculous. That evening she appeared in a lovely dress with a low cut chiffon bodice, through which her skin showed very attractively, and she never reverted to the masculine garb again.'

STELLA AND ISADORA

Shortly after the publication of my book on Shaw I was at Ayot St Lawrence and had a fairly long talk with his wife. She was moving about with the help of two sticks and was obviously suffering much pain. I strongly advised her to consult Raphael Roche, who was I believed the only person who could cure her if she was curable, and when later I told Shaw what I had done he thanked me for having backed his own advice. 'I want to have a long talk with you about your book,' were her opening words to me. 'Do you like it?' I asked. 'Yes and no,' she said. 'Let's take the "no" first,' I suggested. It then appeared that she liked everything in the book except the chapter entitled 'women', which she thought far too outspoken, excusing herself with the confession 'I am very Victorian in such matters.' Beyond the statement that I was post-Victorian, I had no adequate explanation to offer, for one cannot expect a man's wife to take the same attitude as his biographer. When Shaw came in, she went out, and I gave him a brief account of what had passed. He laughed and said:

'When Stella Campbell's book was published, with quotations from my love-letters to her, I had to work overtime. Charlotte and I were staying at Stratford-on-Avon, and every post brought great bulging packets of press cuttings, most of which quoted the less restrained passages from my letters in extenso. As a rule, to save me labour, Charlotte used to go through the press-cuttings, putting aside only those that would interest me, such as the notices of the provincial performances of my plays. But I knew she would feel thoroughly uncomfortable if she realized that the main topic of conversation throughout Great Britain and America was my correspondence with Stella; so when the huge bundles began to arrive, I made a point of getting hold of them first, and extracting all the pertinent comments and reviews. As the only paper she ever read was *The Times,* she remained in complete ignorance of what the whole world was discussing.'

While on the subject I asked whether Mrs Campbell had sometimes tried, like Orinthia in *The Apple Cart,* to prevent him from going home to his wife.

'Oh, yes!'

'And did she ever succeed?'

'The scene in *The Apple Cart* where Orinthia and Magnus roll on the floor is taken from life. Sometimes, when I got up to leave her, Stella would pin me down and do her utmost to make me late for meals. It used to be a real tussle between us until I learnt how to grip her wrists: then I became master of the situation. One of our bouts did actually end with both of us on the floor fighting like mad. . . . That woman could be an unholy terror. Once when she was fooling about during rehearsals for the *Pygmalion* revival, and trying hard to annoy me by doing the very opposite of what I asked her to do, I told her that she was like a Belsize Park amateur actress; at which she collapsed, to the great delight of Marion Terry, who had heard that I was a preposterous person and was on her guard against me, and I completed my conquest of her when I said that her version of one of my speeches in the play was better than the original, and that if she could remember it I'd substitute it for mine. But her memory was bad and she couldn't. . . . Stella was a monster. I remember her saying to the fellow who was playing the Colonel—what was his name? anyhow he was a most distinguished-looking man with perfect manners, and an admirable actor—she actually said to him during a rehearsal "Put that chair there, please, and do it as much like a gentleman as you can." I wonder why he did not throw the chair at her head. He would have got three cheers from me if he had.'

Though I felt that Mrs Shaw would scarcely approve, I could not help making the most of the occasion by asking whether Annie Besant had attracted him physically. 'She had absolutely no sex appeal,' he answered. 'Did I ever tell you that she is Raina in *Arms and The Man?*'

'What about Isadora Duncan? People still insist that she was the woman who said to you, "As you have the greatest brain in the world and I have the most beautiful body, we ought to produce the most perfect child," although I have contradicted it on your authority.'

'There's no smoke without a fire; and I dare say the incident was fathered (or mothered) on to her after a scene between us. One day I went to a party given by Lady Kennet of the Dene. Sitting alone on a sofa, clothed in draperies and appearing rather damaged, was a woman whose face looked as if it had been made of sugar and someone had licked it. This was Isadora. We were introduced. She rose, held out her arms, and cried "I have loved you all my life. Come!" Well, I went. We sat down together on the sofa; the entire party gathered round us as if they were witnesssing a play; and for an hour we performed an act of *Tristan and Isolda* for their benefit. After it was over, she begged me to call on her, when she declared that she would dance for me undraped. I gravely made a note of the appointment, but forgot to keep it.'

PERAMBULATING LONDON

I MET SHAW several times during his visit to London in the summer and autumn of 1943: at Whitehall Court, at Eleanor O'Connell's house, and twice out of doors. 'During the three years or more that I have spent at Ayot I have almost forgotten how to walk,' he said when we met one afternoon near Fitzroy Square. 'Now, back in London, I am learning to walk again.' Pointing to the church on the other side of the road, he remarked, 'That is where my sister Lucy was married. I remember the occasion well: the place was filled with young men, all of whom thought they were engaged to her.' He told me that he was revisiting many of the spots he had known in the years before his marriage. He had just been to look at the house in which he had once lived in Osnaburg Street, and found that it was now a factory. He had also spent some minutes gazing at his old home, No. 29 Fitzroy Square. I asked him what rooms he had occupied there. 'My bedroom overlooking the Square took up the whole front of the top floor. Immediately beneath it were the drawing-room and a little room at the side, also overlooking the Square, which was my study. My mother and I lived in the two top floors, but when I began to make money (about £2500 a year) I bought the whole house for my mother. Later I took No. 8 Park Village West for her, and there she died.'

'Where else have you been to?'

'Oh, all over the place! I have been to see Victoria Park, where Candida lived, and to get to it I had to take a train to Shoreditch and then wait in two bus queues. The other day I walked to Wandsworth, and I have visited my old pitches at the Docks and Lambeth and Bermondsey and Clapham, and I have walked all down the Fulham Road to Putney, and had a look at Brompton Square on the way.'

'Why Brompton Square?'

'Jenny Patterson lived there. I have never forgotten how an old woman next door put her head out of the window at 3 o'clock one morning as Jenny was seeing me off, and made some most objectionable comments at the top of her voice. Neither of us enjoyed the experience, and thereafter I came and went in a less conspicuous manner.'

We arrived in Oxford Street, and he asked me to accompany him to Hyde Park. 'I usually prefer to make these jaunts alone,' he explained, 'but I find your company both restful and invigorating. Why is that?' 'Possibly because I am interested in human beings instead of humanity,' was the only explanation that occurred to me. We bused to Marble Arch, entered the Park, walked in a westerly direction for a while, and then turned south. I noticed that at moments he was a little shaky on his legs, but the walking did not seem to tire him. We sat down by the Serpentine, and he talked about Hitler, whose *Mein Kampf* he had been reading with close attention:

'His book stands with Calvin's *Institutes,* Marx's *Capital,* and Adam Smith's *Wealth of Nations*: it is epoch-making. Of course he's mad on some points, but who isn't? The one chance for the Tory Party in this country is to adopt him as their leader. Of course we must thrash him, because of his phobias and his ruffianism; but we mustn't hang him. He can teach us a lot.'

'I am sick to death of his very name,' said I, 'and I long for the day when I can pick up a paper and not see it. What *bores* the Germans are! And what bloody fools! I've been reading Eckermann's *Conversations with Goethe,* and if, as I am told, Goethe is the greatest thing the Germans have produced, then all I can say is that anyone who thinks the idiots could ever win a war, or do anything else except bore

461

mankind to death, had better make a careful study of Eckermann.'

Shaw laughed heartily, and remarked that praise of Hitler and dispraise of Goethe was 'something novel in the England of today'.

'Do you think,' I asked, 'that there has been any real progress in the world during the last thousand years or so?'

'Who knows? *I* don't. Perhaps we are aware of a little more than our remote ancestors, but whether that knowledge denotes true progress is debatable. One might have said a few years ago that we were more comfortable than the aborigines of these islands, but the war makes one doubt even that. Man may have to give way to a better animal, who will do the job he has bungled. But there's no need to despair on that account. We can put our trust in God or the Life Force or the Creative Purpose or whatever else you like to call It.'

'Have you the slightest belief in a hereafter, or wish for it?'

'In the sense you mean, neither belief nor wish. When I die, I die. I have never believed in personal survival. An eternity of G.B.S. or anyone else is unthinkable. Individuals perish, but creation goes on. I believe in Life Everlasting, not in Smith, Brown, Jones and Robinson everlasting. People who imagine that they will continue for ever also imagine that they will be transformed in the next world. As this means that they will be totally unrecognized by their worldly selves, their friends and relations, they might just as well admit bravely that they die before becoming someone else.'

Some weeks or months previously it had been announced that Russia had decided on a new national anthem. Shaw now told me that many years ago he had suggested that the second verse of the British national anthem should be scrapped, and at Elgar's request had written a verse to take its place. He gave a comical recitation of the verse which in his opinion ought to be expunged:

> *O Lord our God arise!*
> *Scatter his enemies,*
> *And make them fall!*
> *Confound their politics,*
> *Frustrate their knavish tricks;*
> *On Thee our hopes we fix,*
> *God save us all!*

And he followed this with a rhetorical recitation of his own emendation:

> *O Lord our God arise!*
> *All our salvation lies*
> *In Thy great hands.*
> *Centre his thoughts on Thee,*
> *Let him God's captain be,*
> *Thine to eternity,*
> *God save the King.*

After discussing certain people we both knew, he folded his arms and for perhaps half a minute seemed lost in thought. Suddenly he spoke: 'I have been too busy all my life to sit back and have a real look at myself; but since I have had time to do so, I have come to the conclusion that I am a great man.' This was said quite naturally and unassumingly, and I did not feel that it called for affirmation or otherwise. It was, for him, a patent fact, and I would not have expressed disagreement even if I had felt it.

We walked back through Green Park, and when close to my club I invited him in.

'What is your club?'

I named it.

'You are asking me to enter the gates of hell.'

'Am I? Then it is your duty to come in and purify us.'

'You are too far gone for anything short of dynamite,' he replied with a chuckle, and would not be tempted.

One August day in '43 John Wardrop and I emerged from the London Library and met G.B.S. on the pavement a few yards south of it. He asked us what we were doing, and we told him we had just left the London Library. 'Where is it? My wife is a Life Member, but I have never seen it.' So we asked him in and took him upstairs to the reading-room, where he sat for a while in one of the comfortable chairs. Then we showed him the list of his works in the catalogue. 'I should like to scrap all those old editions,' he said. We noticed that his presence caused something of a sensation among the library members and assistants, and one of the latter nearly dropped an armful of books on catching sight of him. We accompanied him down the Duke of York's Steps as far as the Admiralty Arch. On the way I pointed out the house that Charles II had built for Nell Gwynn, which interested him, and he retailed his experiences with Rodin, a description of

463

which had already appeared in my book. In his last years he often repeated stories that he had told me in a crisper style when I was writing his biography. Many people recognized him as we strolled along; and one man stopped John Wardrop with the request that he should give Mr Bernard Shaw the compliments of the Free French.

He went on tramping the streets of London until the late autumn of '43, wearing a white overcoat in the black-out. At the end of October my friend Colin Hurry ran across him in Great Queen Street, and after the usual salutations said 'What brings you into these parts?'

'Necessity. I prefer Lambeth where there are no ladies and gentlemen.'

'There are none here.'

'I know, but they have to pretend to be.'

Shaw had been busy on a summary of his life's teaching from 1939 onwards, and it appeared in 1944 under the title of *Everybody's Political What's What*. Much of it had to be re-written and written again, and in the proof which I read there were many repetitions, not only of ideas but of whole passages in almost the same words. He was helped greatly by John Wardrop, who went through the proofs repeatedly, correcting and re-correcting, until his brain reeled. Sometimes, when Wardrop deleted a passage because it appeared in another section of the book, Shaw replaced it in a different section. This game lasted for the better part of a year, and it says much for Wardrop's patience and zeal that the book managed to survive its author's failing memory. Though it shows a marked declension of vigour and humour, it was an astonishing effort for a man of his years.

A NEW ALPHABET

IN THE SPRING OF '44 I heard from a friend that the repertory company at Tunbridge Wells were going to put on *Arms and The Man* in Basic English, and afterwards I learnt that it had been a dismal business; so when next I saw the author I spoke angrily about it, assuming that he had encouraged the vandals.

'Keep calm, dear Hesketh,' was his reply: 'a flop in Tunbridge Wells will not draw the attention of the universe, and does not worry me nor matter a tuppenny damn. A flop of the original version would have been less negligible. Assuming that the acting was presentable the experiment goes to show that the story does not live in Basic but does in Bernard. I quite agree. In any case I did not encourage the vandals. But for you, I should never have known of their folly. Miss Patch licenses these performances by the dozen without letting me be bothered about them. If I *had* known I should have told them they were damned fools; but I should have let them try. Why not? You don't suppose the play is a penny the worse, do you? I wish I'd been there. It would have been interesting to see how a play of mine would fare as pure story without any of my tricks of dialogue. Anyhow, if Basic can kill *Arms* let it die. I have read Basic versions of pages from my works, and not noticed any of the changes!'

Later that year I read in *The Author* that Shaw was making his will, and intended to leave his property to the nation for the purpose of establishing 'a fit British alphabet containing at least 42 letters, and thereby capable of noting with sufficient accuracy for recognition all the sounds of spoken English without having to use more than one letter for each sound, which is impossible with the ancient 26-letter Phoenician alphabet at present in use.' He declared that, if adopted, this would mean an unimaginable saving of time, labour and expense, and he invited various Government departments, colleges, trusts, societies and public organizations to undertake the job of inventing and propagating a new alphabet. The scheme, he said, was of enormous economic importance, and only economists should deal with it. I promptly wrote to him:

'What is happening to you? Is reason tottering on her throne, or has the heart ceased to function? I gather that it is your intention to leave your estate to be whittled away in the course of the next two or three hundred years by countless committees of spelling-reform cranks or economists. The big idea seems to be that you wish to save posterity's time. But saving time is of no significance: it is what one does with one's time that matters; and as there is no earthly reason to assume that posterity will make a better use of its leisure than we, why fuss about it?

'I strongly advise you to let the future deal with its own problems and put your money to immediate and urgent use. W. S. Gilbert left his property in such a way that it would eventually benefit the profession which helped him to make it. He set a good example. I know that you hate charities; but remember your own wise remark that no one should behave as if he lived in his own private utopia. Charities are essential in this wretched civilization, and none more so than those which the State would not dream of supporting: literary and theatrical ones. After this war the literary profession will probably suffer more than any other; and it is your duty to help those members of it who have not been as lucky as yourself. Leave the major part of your property to the Royal Literary Fund, which helps struggling authors, and distribute the remainder among theatrical charities. Such an action on your part would be a blessing to many a fellow of whom you might have said: "There, but for the grace of God, go I." Recall your own poverty-stricken days: help needy human beings who are alive *now*: forget fads and abstractions: and let posterity look after itself.'

About a month later I had to see him on a business matter, and he at once discharged the following:

'Hesketh, you are a born anti-Shavian: I shall never convert you. You think I should join the camp-followers and salvation-mongers of Capitalism, who try to sweep up its messes with their charities and indulgences. Well, I won't. I am neither a philanthropist nor a cadger by temperament. I don't want to be kind to the poor: I hate the poor, and am doing all I can to exterminate them. If ever you have a lump of money large enough to be of any use, and can spare it, don't give it away: find some needed job that nobody is doing and get it done. If you cannot find one, invest in the loan stock of the newest garden city, and get something for your money. Throw it into the sea rather than feed parasites and make enemies with it. Of course you cannot be a complete Gradgrind. Hard-up people who can't help themselves must have a lift occasionally. But it is better not to meet or know the lifted. If you knew them and had to deal with them personally, you would curse them and they would curse you. So give a cheque occasionally to the Royal Literary Fund, which will administer it for you without any shaming or patronizing or cursing.'

'I hate poverty as much as you do,' I rejoined, 'as much as anyone can who has been revoltingly poor; but I am convinced that, the greater power the State gets, the more necessary will it be to help artists. All writers worth their salt are born rebels and individualists—you, my dear communist, being one of them—and they'd see any State or institution damned in hell before they'd lift a pen to write its lying propaganda. The worst thing Dr Johnson ever did was to write Taxation no Tyranny, and he knew it. No artist worth bothering about will ever be looked after by the State or get a cushy job, and therefore it is the sacred duty of anyone who cares for the Holy Spirit of man to see that such people don't starve. That's why I said that you ought to leave most of your money to the R.L.F. The lives of good writers are more important than a new alphabet for bad ones. What does it matter if those you help curse you? You aren't giving money for love, are you? You are giving it so that men may lead their own lives and speak their own thoughts and enrich the community by being themselves. You are giving it to save them from selling their souls. But it's no use preaching to the unconvertible.'

'My dear Hesketh,' returned Shaw, with the patient air of one who indulges a half-wit: 'our instruction in citizenship as children was that if we did not do as we were told and obey rules made by our tyrants we should be maliciously hurt in some manner. Consequently it was our point of honour and the object of our conspiracies with other children to break the rules and do just the opposite of what we were told whenever we could without being found out. If they had only told us how and why our meals and clothes and houses and our personal safety would be impossible unless we all agreed to do certain things in the same way at the same hours, and not to do other things however tempting, we should have understood, and become intelligent Conservatives instead of romantic rebels with highwaymen for our heroes. I have had to find all that out for myself: you haven't thought about it, and are still dreaming of a rebellious, anarchic, and utterly impossible liberty and individuality. The only hope for the artist is in a society so thoroughly organized and regimented that he can always find a job by which he can feed and dress and lodge himself for, say, three hours of brainless robot

467

labour like machine minding or driving, leaving him twice as long to write books or paint pictures or compose symphonies until he finds a market for them. Until Socialism has achieved this for him, he will remain the begging, borrowing, stealing, self-pitying parasite he is at present when he has no private means. So you just shut up, and keep your eye on me as the Always Right.'

I shut up, not because he was always right, but because he was eighty-eight.

He then began talking about my Life of Conan Doyle, which had been published the previous autumn. In January '42 he had done his best to put me off it. 'I doubt whether C D. will bear a book,' he had said, 'in view of his appalling lapse into the crudest sort of Spiritualism, in which any mischievous little girl could impose on him. (It is usually a little girl. Frank Podmore, a skilled investigator of ghost stories, told me he could spot the imp before he had been ten minutes in the house.) Now the hero of a book must have either a successful end or an impressively tragic one. A ridiculous one like Doyle's is impossible.' He now ate his words, a most unusual operation with him: 'I've just been having another look at your Life of Doyle. In spite of your material you've managed to write a first-rate book on him. I didn't think you'd got much to build on, but you've produced an interesting human being, and you've given a convincing explanation of his Spiritualism without making him look absurd, for which his fans, if they have any sense, ought to be eternally grateful.'

'Sense is not a characteristic of fans,' I remarked. 'They are never satisfied unless one paints their pet as a god; and even if one were to produce a statue instead of a man, they would still want one to daub it all over, so that not a single feature remained recognizably human. By the way, I am told I am wrong in identifying Doyle with his creation of Dr Watson. Some seem to think he was Sherlock Holmes to the life.'

'What a libel!' Shaw exclaimed. 'Sherlock was a drug addict without a single amiable trait, and Watson was a decent fellow.'

I asked how he was occupying his time, and he told me that he had been studying the newest books on Pitman's Shorthand: 'I wished to refresh myself by learning the latest changes. Some days I find it difficult to write—my right hand wobbles—and I want to send my articles to the papers in shorthand.' His speed of authorship, he said, still averaged about fifteen hundred words a day, and he continued to give interviews, write articles, review books, and send letters to *The Times,* on military, religious, political, medical and economic subjects. 'Do you know anything about these infernal Shaw societies?' he asked. 'They are digging up all sorts of information about me and discovering documents which I supposed safely burnt or torn up years ago.' I replied that I was a biographer, not a mole, and that I could not endure societies, organizations, institutions of any kind, for the boosting of creeds or people. Apparently he turned on the wireless nearly every evening, and even listened to the speeches: 'Most of the politicians are awful. Lloyd George was bad enough, and Churchill is no better. Someone ought to tell them that their House of Commons style, with long pauses between every word to think out what they are going to say next, is pitiful through the mike, especially when they pronounce their prepositions and conjunctions as if they were speaking oracles.'

His daily round had slightly altered since the death of his wife: he got up at eight, washed, looked through his letters, read the papers over breakfast at nine, spent the morning replying to letters and seeing callers, lunched at one-fifteen, had a nap from two to three, lay on the sofa reading anything of interest in the magazines till three-thirty, went for a walk between three-thirty and five-thirty, worked from five-thirty till near seven, washed and changed into a black coat for dinner at seven-fifteen, and from eight till ten or eleven he either read or listened to the radio or did a little more work. Sometimes he could not be bothered with his letters in the morning and dealt with them over lunch, when Miss Patch would vary a rather monotonous meal, her attempts at conversation being received with grunts from G.B.S., by discussing his correspondence and getting his answers. Now and again he would take a quite disproportionate interest in letters from peculiar people, who wrote to him at great length about their domestic affairs. And, though a routineer, his habits could not always be relied on, for at least once at Ayot he started banging on his piano and singing away at the top of his voice at ten-thirty p.m., and as the piano was in the hall everybody in the house was either awakened or kept awake.

In the autumn of '44 he announced that the appeal to the

Government departments, colleges, trusts, societies and what-not concerning his New Alphabet had been a complete failure, and that he had decided to empower his executors 'to accumulate a fund from which they may finance any promising scheme for providing a new phonetic alphabet capable of expressing the forty-two sounds listed by the late Henry Sweet, Oxford Reader of Phonetics, and then publishing and depositing in the leading libraries certain English classics transliterated into the said alphabet. Failing the achievement of these objects within twenty years from my death (the legal limit of accumulation) the money will go to other public purposes.' So that was that, and I could no longer hope to live on grants from the Royal Literary Fund in my declining years.

PLAYWRIGHT OR PROPAGANDIST?

SHAW WAS IN London again for a few weeks in the summer of '45, and I saw him several times. On Sunday, July 22nd, and the following Sunday, he came to tea at 10 Park Village West, and on both occasions took photos of those present: Eleanor O'Connell, my wife, John Wardrop and myself. He told us that he had once been awed by a Jewish rabbi, and had felt discouraged, which had surprised him. I remarked that the experience had illustrated his conceit: he was surprised that anyone could awe such a phenomenon as G.B.S., whereas the average man constantly felt awed, whenever for instance he prostrated himself before God, and the experience encouraged him because he recognized that there was something greater and mightier than himself. Shaw agreed, and added that, on looking back, it seemed to him that in his youth he had quite unconsciously frightened people. A little later he pointed to the house next door and mentioned that his mother had died there.

'Would you call your mother a good mother?' my wife asked him.

'The worst in the world.'

'Would you have changed her for a better mother?'

'I would not have changed her for any other mother in existence.'

'She does not seem to have been very human.'

'She was fond of animals and flowers, not of human beings. If she had any bowels of affection at all, she had them for my sister Agnes, who died young and whom she called "a Gurley" after her own family. A cat was once run over in Fitzroy Square, and a small crowd collected round it. My mother saw what had happened through the window and emerged from Number 29 with shattering dignity, took the cat in her arms and carried it into the house, while the spectators gaped. . . . When I began to make money I allowed her £400 a year to live on and told her to have a car or a box at Covent Garden or any other luxury she liked, which I would pay for. But she refused the car and the box. . . . She became interested in Spiritualism, because she wanted to get into touch with her daughter, Agnes. Tiring of Agnes, she tried her husband, which was not successful ; then Vandaleur Lee, who was really her man, with little more success. Finally she got into touch with Father John, and he lasted until she died. Talking in the garden shortly before her death, I asked her whether Father John was a definite person or some undefined spirit of her own. She replied that he was a very definite person, a Cistercian monk, who had lived 6000 years before Christ.'

Shaw seemed rather concerned because a doctor had just informed him that there were brown spots on his wrists, which denoted old age. 'I had not noticed them,' he remarked. Like Sophocles he wanted to write a play in his ninetieth year, but he did not know what subject to choose. I suggested that, as music had been the real love of his life, he should dramatize Beethoven. 'I have already dealt with him in *Love Among the Artists*,' he said. 'Very badly,' was my comment. 'Very,' he agreed. 'Why not make a play out of your own life? After all, you are far more interesting than any of the historical subjects you have chosen.' He smiled: 'All my plays are about myself . . . and my friends.'

'Were you ever particularly fond of any of your friends?'

'Fondness is not the word. I liked them when I was with them, but when we separated I did not miss them.'

'Then I will put it in another way: Whose company did you most enjoy?'

'My own.'

I persisted, asking him which friend's company he had especially liked. He mentioned Granville Barker, and then, on being prompted by me, added William Archer and Sidney Webb. From this I inferred that perhaps his happiest days were those when, with Granville Barker acting the leading parts in his plays, he had first conquered the London stage at the Court Theatre between 1904 and 1907.

My wife and I had a standing disagreement on the question of Shaw's most valuable work, she regarding his speaking and writing for socialism as his main achievement, I considering that he should have applied the whole of his genius to the theatre. She now asked him whether he thought his propaganda or his plays were his more important gift to humanity.

'Anyone could have done the propaganda,' he replied. 'No one else could have written my plays. I had to write them: they were a part of me.'

My wife wanted a different answer and pressed him further on the point, but received no comfort from his admission that the time he had spent on *The Intelligent Woman's Guide* might have been more profitably employed in play-writing.

'But when you get to heaven,' she persevered, 'which of your activities do you think God will give you most marks for?'

'If God starts giving me examination marks for any of my activities, there will be serious trouble between us,' he said.

SHAW DICTATES HIS OBITUARY

I HAD BEEN ASKED by the B.B.C. to record an obituary of Shaw for use when the time came, and one day I called at Whitehall Court to see him on the subject. 'But, damn it, I'm not dead yet!' he exclaimed. However, he soon warmed to the theme when I showed him what I had written, and made several suggestions, one of which was 'You must say that I have provided for the greatest players a modern grand repertory comparable only to that left by Shakespeare.' But his only real complaint was that I had made little of his contributions to science and sociology, and at my request he dictated to me that part of his own obituary which he felt that I had neglected. On consideration I did not include it in my final draft, and so I give it here, written in the third person exactly as he imparted it to me:

'When questioned about his reputation Shaw amused himself by interjecting, "Which reputation? I have made fifteen." He quite seriously and emphatically claimed to be a pioneer in science, though he had never worked in a laboratory, and contemptuously dismissed laboratory experiments as "put-up jobs". His laboratory, he said, was "the wide world, in which I can control nothing except to a very limited extent my own mind". He classed politics as a science, and denounced popular democracy as the government of everybody by anybody, the government of the ignorant by vulgarly ambitious adventurers foolish enough to imagine that government is a voluptuously omnipotent sinecure, civilization having always to be rescued from the messes they make by military geniuses. Genuine practicable democracy, he contended, meant government in the general interest by rulers chosen from panels of the five per cent or so of tested qualified rulers. The assumption underlying Adult Suffrage that at the age of twenty-one everybody becomes infinitely wise politically, and that the voice of the people is the voice of God, he regarded exactly as Coriolanus does in Shakespeare's most mature chronicle play. What democracy needs, he declared, is a scientific anthropometrical test. Finally, to secure genuine democracy by proportional representation of men and women, he invented and advocated the Coupled Vote, obliging the elector to vote, not for a single representative but for a woman as well as a man, thus securing the presence of men and women in equal numbers on all elected authorities. But he would not admit that any electoral reform could secure good government unless and until the span of human life was extended sufficiently to make political maturity possible, and this he estimated at three hundred years, allowing a century for non-adult scholarship, another for practical administration, and a third for oracular voteless senatorship. In *Back to Methuselah* he placed no limit to human life except the statistically certain fatal accident which must occur to everyone sooner or later.

'In this apparent extravagance he claimed to be a scientific biologist, or, as he sometimes called himself, a metabiologist. Official biology in his day was completely dominated by the Mechanists and neo-Darwinists; and he fought them tooth and nail as a creative neovitalist evolutionist, taunting them with their failure to account for the difference between a live body and a dead one, and postulating a creative Life Force or Evolutionary Appetite, proceeding experimentally by trial and error, with mankind as its most elaborate instrument. There is consequently no problem of evil: the evils we suffer are the mistakes of the experimenting Life Force, which aims always at increased power and deeper knowledge. He did not disparage the Baconian observation of facts, but insisted that anyone (any fool, as he put it) can observe, but only the gifted few can rationalize their observations, a criticism which culminated in his attack on Pavlov, then at the height of his reputation, dismissing him as an intellectual blunderer and moral imbecile. He steadily denounced the claims of the laboratory researchers to be exempt from moral law in their pursuit of scientific knowledge. As he put it, "to boil your mother merely to find out at what temperature she would die would be an addition to knowledge; but people who forget that there are things that no man ought to know are better dead." Inhuman experiments by inhuman persons moved him to abhorrence. He maintained that human experiments could always be devised by scientific workers who were not too lazy, callous, or stupid for high science. Popular and official Darwinism he discounted as nine-tenths nothing but anti-clerical reaction against the Bible.

'It is not possible to summarize the controversy in an obituary notice, nor is it now necessary, as it has on the whole gone Shaw's way, and metabiology has come to its own again. The Russian political experiment begun in 1917 has tried crude catastrophic Socialism only to be forced back by inexorable facts into the Fabian methods prescribed by Shaw and Webb. Many of his Shavian suggestions that seemed subversively revolutionary or fantastic when he first put them forward are now commonplaces, though the old view of their author still persists long after its basis has dissolved. In any case they interest and are understood by few, whereas there is a relatively enormous publicity for his exploits as a playwright. How he will stand in future centuries cannot be foreseen. He himself was fond of saying that reputations that are

474

not for an age but for all time mean world stagnation, and that the sooner he is forgotten the better. It remains to be seen whether the memory of the man who survived five reigns will survive fifty.'

Having completed the obituary I forwarded it to G.B.S., then at Ayot St Lawrence. He kept it for several weeks, and when I demanded its return he sent it back with so many corrections and additions that I rebelled, and recorded my own version.

PILGRIMS AT AYOT

IN THE AUTUMN OF 1945 I was writing a book with my friend Hugh Kingsmill, and it occurred to us that we might include in it an account of a visit to Shaw; so I wrote to say we would like to see him. One of his little peculiarities was a pretence that he could only spare time to see people on business; but I knew that was nonsense, and when he did not reply within three or four days I sent him a wire which ran: 'What the hell! Unless you forward doctor's certificate, expect us on Monday.' Immediately on receipt of this he rang me up to say he was expecting us, and on November 5th we motored down to Ayot. On the way I recalled that the last time I was there Shaw told me that he had once made a speech in his native town of Dublin. 'I addressed the Gaelic League,' he said, 'and annoyed them very much by claiming that I wrote in a language understood by at least three hundred million people in preference to one that could be read by at most three million. I was subjected to a good deal of heckling, and there were attempts to shout me down. I stood it for a time, but at last determined that either I or the noise must stop. So I warned them: "If you won't listen to me quietly, I'll make the rest of my speech in Gaelic, and not one of you will understand a syllable of it." They were not so foolish as they behaved. At once the calm of death descended upon them, and I finished the speech, not in their mother-tongue, but in the tongue of their mothers.'

Hugh Kingsmill was impressed by the rustic seclusion of Ayot, saying that Gray's Country Churchyard was Piccadilly Circus compared with Shaw's retreat. On our arrival we were shown into the drawing-room, from the window of which we could see G.B.S. nodding drowsily in a chair in the dining-room. He joined us after a minute or two, and to my conventional 'How are you?' said 'Ninety.' 'Yes, but how are you feeling?' 'Well, how does anyone feel at ninety? You'll know when you get there. I'm all right here at home, but it's troublesome in London; and if I fell down there, I might be picked up by a policeman and run in for being drunk.'

In the course of our conversation, which was faithfully recorded by Kingsmill and myself in *Talking of Dick Whittington* (1947), Shaw spoke of Dickens, Edmund Yates and H. G. Wells:

(Of Dickens.) 'The truth is, he'd a very large and stupid family, and he had to earn all that money for them, and kept himself going with brandy and other poisons. He was really dead before *Edwin Drood*. Sapsea and Grewgious repeat all the old tricks, but the fire has gone out of them. That reminds me of a farce of mine. I had to secure the copyright of *Cashel Byron's Profession,* and wrote *The Admirable Bashville* for the purpose, and the Stage Society produced it. I wanted a burlesque actor, and at last I found the man. His name was Wyse. He seemed to have all the tricks at his finger-tips, but at the very first rehearsal I discovered that the lines which I had thought so funny weren't funny at all. I asked Ben Webster what was the matter with Wyse, and he replied "Oh, he'll be all right on the night." But he was *not* all right on the night. All the tricks were there, but they weren't amusing. The audience laughed at the lines, because they could hear them, but not at the way they were said. The next day Wyse lay down on a sofa and died, and I realized that he had been dead before the rehearsal. Well, the point of all this rigmarole is that people die before they're ready for burial, and Dickens was dead before *Edwin Drood*.'

(Of Edmund Yates.) 'No one liked him. He was a bully. I had to write for him on fiction at fivepence a line, and I got very tired of it, and of having to sign myself F. B.—you know, Fred Bayham, a character in Thackeray's *Newcomes*. I aired my grievances, and received a letter from his secretary beginning "Mr Yates requests me to inform you that . . ." Well, there's only one possible answer to an opening like that, and

I began my letter "I have yet to learn . . ." Things got better after that, and when Yates was dying I used to write to him to cheer him up. But I found out later that his family hadn't dared to read him my letters, for it seems he was frightened of me.'

(Of H. G. Wells.) 'No one could be angry with Wells for long. He frankly admits that his temper is hysterical. I remember meeting him the day after the appearance of an outrageous article which he had written on me. Really, I'd have been entitled to punch his head. But he was looking small and uneasy, and I just shook hands with him. Another time, when he was very angry with me, he wrote to me that everyone believed me to be homosexual, and that he, Wells, had always denied it, but that in future he wouldn't. Incidentally, I have just written an obituary of him for *The New Statesman*; but please keep that to yourselves.'

Wells did not die till the following August, when Shaw's nine-months old tribute duly appeared.

Two hours were passed in pleasant talk, during which we had tea, and when we got up to go we both said that it had been delightful to see him. 'And why wouldn't it be?' he replied.

THREE SCORE YEARS AND THIRTY

THE YEAR 1946 saw Shaw's ninetieth birthday, but the Labour Government made no gesture of recognition. As the Webbs and he had done more than anyone to found the parliamentary Labour Party, its quiescence on this occasion may seem curious. But against the fact that a British Government is perhaps the only government in the world that would have passed such an event unnoticed, we must remember that no other government in the world would have had the chance to celebrate it. Long before his seventieth year his fate in other countries would have been decided. In France he would almost certainly have been assassinated; in the United States, if the treatment of Eugene Debs is anything to go by, he would have been gaoled for life ; in Russia, Germany, Italy, Spain, Turkey and Japan he would have been 'liquidated'. That he was tolerated and unmolested in England proves, what in his better moments he used to admit, that we are the only civilized, or rather semi-civilized, great power in the world.

But the year did not pass by without some public acknowledgment of his eminence. The leading newspapers of every country published tributes. The National Book League held an exhibition at 7 Albemarle Street of Shavian first editions, manuscripts, photos, etc., and Shaw motored up from the country to see it on the first day, July 19th. He arrived some time after the opening speech by Dr Inge, glanced at the exhibits, said 'Well, ladies and gentlemen, you have seen the animal: good-bye,' and motored back to Ayot. He accepted the invitation to become an Honorary Freeman of Dublin, stating that he had hitherto evaded credentials from foreign sources, and 'Dublin alone has the right to affirm that in spite of my incessantly controversial past and present I have not disgraced her.' Delegates from the Corporation went to Ayot, and he signed the roll of Honorary Freemen on August 28th. He also accepted the offer of St Pancras, on the vestry and council of which he had served nearly fifty years before, to become its first Honorary Freeman. The cistern at his country house had to be renewed, so he came up to his London flat for a week, intending to be present at the ceremony in St Pancras Town Hall on October 9th. But the day before it took place he fell from his chair, hurt his hip, and had to lie on the floor for a while to recover from the shock. His doctor, his osteopath and X-rays discovered no harm, but he was compelled to rest, as it hurt him to put any weight on his left leg. Unable to go to St Pancras he recorded a speech, which was broadcast in the council chamber. 'I tumble down about three times a week quite regularly,' he confessed, but he did not add that his present tumble was rather more painful than his usual ones.

On the evening of October 10th my wife and I called to see him. Whitehall Court had been buzzing with reporters, two of whom had taken a flashlight photo of him, but the excitement was now subsiding, and we enjoyed a tranquil talk. He was lying in bed, looking better than I had seen him for years ; his complexion was rosy, like that of a child ; he seemed to be thoroughly enjoying the effects of his accident ; and he talked with vigour, though the lower set of his den-tures was on the table beside him. The crutches with which he had hobbled about during his breakdown in 1898 had been discovered, and were propped against the wall by his bed. The object of my visit was to find out all he could tell me about Keir Hardie, a film of whose life I had been asked to write ; but before we left we had heard his views, not only on Hardie, but on Sir Edward Grey, Ramsay MacDonald, Napoleon, Wellington, Field-Marshal Montgomery, T. E. Lawrence and Tom Paine. The English, he said, were a nation of amateurs, not professionals: their generals, like their authors, were amateurs. 'Which explains why we have always won our wars and have produced the greatest literature in the world,' I remarked. Giving him no time to reply, I asked him what Montgomery had talked about when they met. 'I did all the talking,' Shaw said. 'He wanted to know what I thought of English generalship. I answered that there was no such thing as English generalship. There was Haig, and there was Montgomery. Then I told him that there were two kinds of general: those who followed the rules, and those who broke them, the professional and the amateur, Napoleon and Wellington. Montgomery hinted that he, like Wellington, made his own rules as he went along. He said that he wanted to see war abolished.'

'Rather ungrateful of him,' I commented. 'Like a writer who, having made his reputation as an author, wants to see writing abolished. Is Montgomery at all like T. E. Lawrence?'

'Not in the least. Lawrence was a pure undiluted actor. A few weeks before his death I asked my wife, who was an intimate friend of his, why we had not seen him for some time. "Oh," said she, "he's such an infernal liar!"'

I was amused by Shaw's complete silence on the subject of my Life of Oscar Wilde, which had been published the previous June. He had shown much interest in my biographies in the past, writing or talking to me at some length about them ; but on at least three occasions he had done his utmost to dissuade me from tackling Wilde, partly because he had committed himself to an approval of Frank Harris's entirely untrustworthy record, and partly because he really disliked Wilde ; of whom, I believe, he was also jealous, because the only time I noticed real hostility towards a fellow-being in Shaw's manner and speech was when we were discussing his famous fellow-countryman. I sent him a copy of my book, but I doubt whether he did more than peck at it. His silence therefore did not surprise me, for he had said so much in praise of Harris's book that he would have had to eat more words than any mortal could be expected to digest, and he never had a good appetite in that respect.

His dislike of Wilde made him absent-minded. He left it on record that they were uncomfortable in their personal relationship, though they had taken one another seriously as writers ; that when Wilde was sentenced to prison he had drafted a petition for his release ; and that during Wilde's last phase each of them had sent inscribed copies of his books to the other. But Shaw never confessed that when he was a relative nobody he had sent Wilde, then famous, his *Quintessence of Ibsenism* and *Widowers' Houses*, and that Wilde had written him most appreciative and encouraging letters about both, acknowledging the play on May 9th, 1893, in these terms: 'I must thank you very sincerely for Op. 2 of the great Celtic School. . . . I look forward to your Op. 4 —as for Op. 5 I am lazy, but am rather itching to be at it.' Op. 1 was obviously *Lady Windermere's Fan ;* Op 2 *Widowers' Houses* ; Op. 3 *A Woman of No Importance,* then running at the Haymarket Theatre ; Op. 4, Shaw's next play, *The Philanderer* ; Op. 5, Wilde's next play, *An Ideal Husband.* And so on. Wilde thus paid Shaw the compliment of ranking their works together in the dramatic literature of the age, though he had just scored his second huge success with *A Woman of No Importance,* while Shaw's *Widowers' Houses* had practically been hooted from the stage the previous December.

It is worth mentioning that I noticed a rather glassy look in Shaw's eye when next we met, which I attributed to his disapproval of my having ignored his advice and done my best to rescue Wilde from Harris and recreate him as the fascinating fellow he undoubtedly was. But Shaw was not the man to maintain an attitude from which he could derive no credit, and the enormous revival of interest in Wilde's work and personality produced one of those quick-changes which surprised so many of the sage's more slow-witted admirers. In February 1948 the *News Chronicle* asked Shaw what famous man of the past he would like to meet, and he replied: 'If I craved for entertaining conversation by a first-class raconteur I should choose Oscar Wilde.'

In spite of occasional tumbles, Shaw maintained his usual good health all through 1946, though on Sunday, August 25th, be described a strange physical sensation to Eleanor O'Connell, who had gone down to see him at Ayot. The moment he entered the drawing-room, he asked: 'How do I look?'

'Very well.'

'No, seriously, how do I look?'

'Why?'

'Because I am going to die.'

'Don't be absurd! You look as well as ever.'

'Well, when I got up this morning I felt extremely queer. I've never felt quite like that before, and I'm sure I'm going to die.'

'How do you feel now?'

'Not so bad, but still rather queer.'

'Then you're all right. On the day you're going to die you'll get up feeling like a boy of ten.'

A few days later his one-time friend and associate, Harley Granville Barker, died in Paris. 'The shock the news gave me,' he wrote to *The Times Literary Supplement,* 'made me realize how I had still cherished a hope that our old intimate relation might revive. But

> *Marriage and death and division*
> *Make barren our lives . . .'*

A BARDIC BATTLE

As LIVELY AS USUAL, and as totalitarian in temperament as he had ever been, G.B.S. had a final skirmish with me. Inevitably the subject of our disagreement was Shakespeare; and as so much of Shaw's character was revealed in the course of the argument, I cannot do better than record our exchanges.

In the spring of '42 I had sent him a copy of my Life of Shakespeare, published by Penguin Books, and though he had expressed his general approval of it he had raised several interesting queries which I had promptly answered. At the end of '46 I wanted to get the book published in a more durable form, and it struck me that our argument was interesting enough to be printed as an appendix to the new edition. So I showed him an exact record of our debate, which he now read (November 1946) some four and a half years afer it had taken place:

G.B.S. Well, you have made a good job of it, which is more than I can say for the older biographies. I am specially pleased with your disposal of the horse-holding tradition, which in its old form was incredible by anyone who got Shakespeare's class exactly. But that he got a foothold in the theatre by organizing the horse boys and making money out of it is just what would have happened to a man who had picked up some business experience with his father whilst the other dramatic poets were disqualifying themselves as scholars at the universities. Actors are so unbusinesslike that if one of them can keep a cash book he gets shoved into management willy nilly. For instance, C. B. Cochran and Barry Jackson, both of whom wanted to act, not to manage.

H.P. All the same the greatest actor since Burbage was a firstrate man of business: David Garrick.

G.B.S. A descendant of French Huguenots ought to know his way about a ledger. Besides, he started life in the wine trade, didn't he? He probably held a monopoly of the drinks sold in Drury Lane Theatre, just as Shakespeare kept up his horse-holding business after becoming an actor.

H.P. If I write a Life of David Garrick I'll let you know.

G.B.S. If you revise your work there are one or two points which you should reconsider. Marlowe was not Shakespeare's rival: he was established before Shakespeare arrived, and was the champion whom Shakespeare challenged. Thus Shakespeare was Marlowe's rival, and could sling 'mighty lines' about so easily that in *Richard III*, for instance, it is impossible to say which of them wrote 'So now prosperity begins to mellow, and drop into the rotten jaws of death.' Marlowe might have written that, though Shakespeare could never have written such nonsense as 'the

gaudy blabbing and remorseful day'. The proud-sailing rival
was Chapman, who flaunted his scholarship very proudly—
stage directions all in Latin: not merely *exit* and *exeunt
omnes,* which anybody could pick up. Tyler made this
identification ; and I see no reason to question it. Chapman
was the only genius thundering enough to alarm Shakespeare as a new business rival.

H.P. I cannot believe that Shakespeare ever regarded Chapman as a serious rival. Chapman is dull and pedantic, the
very opposite of Shakespeare, whose enormous success in
his prime must have put him beyond fear of any rival.
Marlowe, on the other hand, overshadowed Shakespeare's
youth ; they were born in the same year, and Marlowe's
unique position and resounding success must have had a
permanent effect on an ambitious and supersensitive fellow
like Shakespeare. I am sure that, until he had written his
great tragedies, Shakespeare always felt conscious of Marlowe's potential superiority. Don't forget that Marlowe, cut
off in his prime, left a memory of greatness which his
actual performance did not justify. I think Shakespeare
had Marlowe on his mind until he got *Hamlet* off his chest.

G.B.S. Talking of that, the context in which you quote
Polonius's blessing shows that you don't know that it, like
Gonzalo's Utopia, is a straight lift out of Montaigne.

H.P. On the contrary, I mention that *Hamlet* shows how
Shakespeare had profited from Montaigne's outlook on
life. An author often quotes another's words when they
express what he feels, but you can hardly expect a character
in a play to preface his remarks with 'As Montaigne
observes . . .'

G.B.S. That raises another point. No doubt Shakespeare was
a snapper-up of unconsidered trifles from real life ; but, like
Frank Harris, you make far too much of this and far too
little of his susceptibility to literary suggestion, never even
mentioning the astonishing fact that the only play he did
not get out of a book was *The Merry Wives.*

H.P. That certainly is an omission. It is one more proof, and
a conclusive one, that the play had to be written in haste

at the command of the Queen. But I think I have said quite a lot about Shakespeare's book-learning, though I have not bothered the reader with the origins of all his plots, my work being primarily a biography, not a critical study.

G.B.S. Then you have outharrised Harris in suggesting that Anne was a guilty Hermione, and that Ajax is a lampoon on Ben Jonson. About *Troilus and Cressida* you go quite mad, finding nearly all the main characters autobiographical. Why did you miss your chance of identifying Mrs John Shakespeare with the queen in *Hamlet*?

H.P. You must re-read my book more carefully. I make it clear that if Anne were guilty she was only so in Shakespeare's imagination. Further, I do not say that Hermione was Anne: I merely pose the possibility that one aspect of her behaviour is glanced at in the character. There is no doubt whatever in my mind that the Leontes-Hermione relationship is taken from life: it is altogether too vivid to be the effect of fancy. Later reflection however has led me to believe that the whole situation centres on Shakespeare's position in the Davenant household. He was Mrs Davenant's lover, and the father of one of her children. I now think that Hermione is a portrait of her, and that Leontes is partly Shakespeare and partly Davenant.

G.B.S. And what about Ajax?

H.P. A caricature, not a portrait, of Ben Jonson.

G.B.S. At that rate you can turn anything into anybody to suit your own convenience.

H.P. I have no convenience to be suited, not being any kind of fanatic. I am simply and solely interested in Shakespeare as a man: I therefore have no belief to buttress, no institution to support, no pet theories to propagate. Anyone can see that Shakespeare was in a state of mental and physical disturbance when he wrote *Troilus and Cressida,* and when a dramatist is not in command of himself he is not in command of his characters. He reveals himself in the most unexpected places, and he cannot attain coherence of portraiture. That is why, biographically speaking, an inferior work like *Timon of Athens* is far more interesting than a masterpiece like *Macbeth*.

G.B.S. You say nothing about the queer difference of *All's Well* and *Measure for Measure* from the Shakespeare canon generally ; also to some extent *Troilus*. Robertson, who was a Chapmaniac, gave them to Chapman. There is no mistaking Shakespeare's hand in them, but there seems to be another mind at work in them as well as his, whereas in the other plays the original author counts for nothing.

H.P. Again I ask you to re-read my book, where you will find the explanation of the seeming difference of those plays set forth quite clearly. Shakespeare was not only ill (I should say with venereal disease) when he wrote *Troilus and Cressida,* but he had just passed through a crisis in his affairs: the Essex business, which involved the fate of his patron Southampton. He had not recovered when he wrote *All's Well,* and was only convalescent when he reached *Measure for Measure*. The same lack of balance reappears in his last plays, and for the same reason. I myself am certain, and I have more than hinted it in my book, that his death was hastened by what Pistol calls 'malady of France'.

G.B.S. I doubt if such a view would be popular in England.

H.P. No: the only views that are received with credulity in England are wholly imbecile: (1) that he did not write his plays, and (2) that he was a pederast. Your friend Robertson dealt with the first, which of course could only be held by an ass who is also a snob. The people who disagree as to who wrote the plays, he said, all agree that they could only have been written by a peer of the realm. The second view, naturally, is mostly held by pederasts, who like to mistake sycophancy for homosexuality.

G.B.S. All the same the hackneyed plea that Shakespeare's sonnets are only a fashionable convention won't do. Mr W. H. was evidently one of those rare persons whose personal beauty enchanted lovers of their own sex, *not* sexually. The only living W. H. as far as I know is Lord Alfred Douglas (now in his seventies), and his edition of the

Sonnets is the only book about them worth your reading. He was an amazingly pretty youth, not a pederast.

H.P. I stand by every word I have written in my book. I am as certain that Shakespeare was addressing his patron Southampton as I am certain that I am addressing you at this moment. I know all about Douglas ; and having spent about thirty-six years in the constant company of Shakespeare, through the medium of his plays, I think I may claim that I know a good deal about *him*.

G.B.S. I won't gainsay it, for your book proves it. You have come out of it very successfully because you are a genuine soaker in Shakespeare, and have not read him as a task. You have him by heart ; and your quotations leave all the other biographers nowhere. I had no idea of this : it throws a new spotlight on you.

H.P. On Shakespeare, too, I hope.

On reading this Shaw became more irritable than I had ever known him to be. Apart from his natural dislike of having his attitude to anything controverted, I fancy that the favourable reception by press and public of my Life of Wilde had annoyed him a good deal.

'Burn all this rubbish!' were his opening words. 'It lets the book down and lets us both down.' He then proceeded to lecture me, his opinions being those of a respectable don delivered in the style of a ruthless dictator :

'You must revise and correct the book. The passage about Jonson is such a howler that anyone with the most elementary Elizabethan competence would shut the book and throw it into the dustbin after a glance at it. You think of Jonson as a coarse old curmudgeon, and Shakespeare as a young aspiring poet. Shakespeare was ten years older than Jonson, fully established in the theatre when Jonson came to it as an unknown beginner. Shakespeare, the elder and admittedly greater playwright, spotted his talent and helped him into notice. This relation between them never changed : to the end Jonson venerated Shakespeare "this side idolatry". His tribute to him after his death is one of the noblest and most obviously sincere in literature. Your suggestion that Ajax was a caricature of Jonson is an outrage. It is utterly stupid. That Shakespeare should have described his young friend who wrote not only biting comedies but exquisite lyrics, toasts and epitaphs, and who loved him "this side idolatry", as a beef-witted mongrel, is going beyond all toleration. Ajax is clearly not a caricature of anyone. He is simply a stage blockhead.'

This outburst took me by surprise; but I pulled myself together and gave him shell for shot:

'What you have just said merely proves your complete ignorance of the Elizabethan stage. Apparently you have never heard of the famous War of the Theatres, when Jonson and Shakespeare were in opposite camps spitting rage at one another. Let me remind you of what Jonson had to say when in a mood of disgust with the theatre and with Shakespeare's continued popularity long after his death:

> *No doubt some mouldy tale*
> *Like Pericles, and stale*
> *As the shrieve's crusts, and nasty as his fish—*
> *Scraps out of every dish*
> *Thrown forth, and raked into the common tub,*
> *May keep up the Play-club:*
> *There, sweepings do as well*
> *As the best-order'd meal;*
> *For who the relish of these guests will fit,*
> *Needs set them but the alms-basket of wit . . .'*

'*Pericles* must have been a disappointment to Jonson from the author of *Lear, Macbeth* and *Hamlet*,' Shaw replied, 'and he ridiculed it accordingly. When the play I have just finished is published it will most pitiably disappoint people who are expecting another *St Joan* or *Heartbreak House;* but that will not establish a lifelong feud between us.'

Feeble, but I let it go, and continued:

'In *Every Man out of His Humour* Jonson poked fun at Shakespeare's gentility and at his coat of arms, and again in *The Poetaster* he scoffed not only at Shakespeare's social pretensions but at his high-faluting style of writing. Shakespeare replied in *Troilus and Cressida,* concerning which a contemporary wrote that "our fellow Shakespeare hath given him (Jonson) a purge that made him bewray his credit". The purge is obviously Ajax, who is partly, as you say, a stage blockhead, but definitely Jonson, as Shakespeare felt about him during their quarrel, in this passage: "He is as valiant as the lion, churlish as the bear, slow as the elephant: a man

487

into whom nature hath so crowded humours that his valour is crushed into folly, his folly sauced with discretion: there is no man hath a virtue that he hath not a glimpse of, nor any man an attaint but he carries some stain of it. He is melancholy without cause, and merry against the hair; he hath the joints of everything, but everything is so out of joint that he is a gouty Briareus, many hands and no use; or purblind Argus, all eyes and no sight." No stage blockhead or beef-witted mongrel about that! but the most brilliant thumbnail sketch of a perverse genius in all literature, and exactly fitted to everything we know about Jonson.'

'The great passage about Ajax which you quote, and which I had forgotten, is not a caricature, but a gorgeous tribute from a friend,' said Shaw.

I waited for more, but waited in vain. He felt that he had settled the question conclusively, and I was accustomed to his method of never admitting an error, a trait common to all totalitarians, and getting out of a difficult situation by making his opponent's thunder appear to be his own lightning. While I was still musing on this he launched another attack:

'Chapman was Shakespeare's contemporary and his rival. He was famous as a scholar and the translator of Homer. The "proud sail" of his blank verse very exactly describes it. To call a man who wrote the Bussey d'Amboise plays dull and pedantic, and negligible as a rival, is to put yourself out of court as a critic. The death of Chapman in poverty is so pitiable that it is not only stupid but ungenerous to disparage him. He was really a great literary figure.'

I took a deep breath, and then let fly:

'Your ignorance extends from the Elizabethan stage to your own works. You seem to be unaware of the fact that, in the preface to a play called *The Admirable Bashville,* a writer named Bernard Shaw referred to Chapman as "a blathering unreadable pedant, like Landor". Elsewhere you speak of his balderdash and his bullying heroes, you describe Jonson as a brutish pedant, and you sum up the Elizabethan dramatists as braggarts, liars, humbugs, cut-throats, penny-a-liners, and so on. Yet you have the calm effrontery to tell me now that Chapman was a really great literary figure, and that it is not only stupid but ungenerous to disaparage him because his death in poverty was so pitiable. This from the man who wrote of Fielding's and Smollett's small and smutty literary property, from one who wished to dig up Shakespeare and

488

throw stones at him, who expressed his contempt for the mental equipment of Homer, Shakespeare and Walter Scott, who spoke of Thackeray's clumsy hand and enslaved mind, of Dr Johnson wasting his time talking with literary fools in a tavern, and of the resemblance between Wordsworth, the greatest poet since Shakespeare, and George III! Did Oscar Wilde's pitiable and poverty-stricken death prevent you from saying (on the sole evidence of Frank Harris, the biggest liar in literature) that he ended as an unproductive drunkard and swindler?'

My feat of memory shook him, and for a moment I expected something in the nature of a climb-down. But he had not been a platform performer for nothing, and he recovered his poise before I recovered my breath.

'When I had to smash Bardolatry in the lump,' he said, 'I had to fight so foully that any critic can disqualify me by a few quotations; but I did the trick and shattered the idol set up by Coleridge, Lamb and Swinburne. That does not prove that Jonson was the rival mentioned in the *Sonnets*.'

I had never in my life so much as hinted that Jonson was the rival in Shakespeare's *Sonnets*; but as he had accused me of saying so on several previous occasions, and as I had continually denied it in vain, I let it pass. It was clearly useless to prolong the controversy. After all, he was ninety years old, and it flashed upon me that if I lived to the age of seventy I should long have lost the power and the inclination to argue about anything.

AN IRVING STORY

I NEXT SAW G.B.S. on Saturday, 18th January, 1947. Mr Sebastian Shaw, the actor, was keen to build up a repertory of Shavian works and asked me to take him down and introduce him to the sage of Ayot St Lawrence. I did so. It was a fine day, and when we arrived G.B.S. was strolling round his garden with the aid of a stick. We stayed to tea and enjoyed two hours of his conversation. One of the first things he asked was whether my companion knew who had produced *The Adventures of the Black Girl in her Search for God* on the wireless recently. 'No.' 'Then I wish you'd find out who he is,' said G.B.S., 'and tell him I am annoyed that the commencement of the story has been dragged in at the end of it.'

When the subject of the repertory came up, he said that the Macdona Players had been 'awful' and that it was high time a permanent Shavian repertory was in being: 'It is needed as much as a Shakespearean or a Gilbert and Sullivan repertory.' He told us very emphatically what he thought of the film that had been made of *Caesar and Cleopatra*, and said that he would like to see me in the part of Caesar on the stage. I appreciated the compliment but felt that it would have been more serviceable some fifteen years earlier when I was still an actor. He talked of Barry Sullivan, whose methods he described, giving us certain lines in *Hamlet, Macbeth* and *Richard III* as he had heard Sullivan render them. He assured us that Sullivan was the last of the school of superhuman actors: he had the grand manner: he was a being from another sphere: no one to compare with him had appeared on the stage since his day.

After some business chit-chat between Shaw the author and Shaw the actor, I mentioned that I had at last decided to write a Life of Dickens. This appeared to please G.B.S. greatly, and he said that I must concentrate on the Ellen Ternan affair. 'My job is to concentrate on Charles Dickens,' I replied, 'though Ellen Ternan will have to be dealt with as an important influence on his life and art.' I inquired whether he had kept any of the letters which he had received from Kate Perugini, Dickens's daughter.

'No. She requested me to send back all her letters shortly before her death; and when I asked her why, she replied that she did not like to think that they would be read by other people after my death. In particular she did not wish her description of Sir Henry Irving's behaviour at her own table to become known.'

'I'm sure you don't share her secretiveness. How did Irving behave? I promise not to report it except in print.'

'One evening Irving and Ellen Terry dined with the Peruginis. From the moment of his arrival until dinner was half over Irving behaved exactly like an archbishop, very grave, very stately, scarcely opening his mouth except to put

490

something into it, occasionally agreeing with what was said with a faint inclination of the head, now and then intimating his disagreement with a slight lifting of the nostril. Ellen tried hard to draw him out, but her failure to make him look less like a Chinese mandarin posing for a statue was as complete as that of their host and hostess. At last someone mentioned a press notice of one of his performances. Instantly his face flashed into life, and he burst into speech: in fact he talked so fluently that no one else could slip in a syllable. He went on and on and on, all about the press notice, until Ellen had to stop him with "Really, Henry, I think the subject is exhausted. Let's discuss something else." '

When G.B.S. was seeing us off in the hall I asked whether he had finished his new play. He replied that he had a lot of revision to do, that the writing of it had nearly killed him, and that he doubted if it would ever be done to his satisfaction. While he was speaking the telephone bell rang, and he was informed that *The News of the World* wanted a word with him. He took the receiver, and we heard him say that his new play would first appear at Malvern, if at all, but that it would probably never be fit for production. He added: 'I am an old man, and I write drivel.' With these words he closed the conversation, though the sounds that came from the receiver as he put it back suggested to us that the fellow at the other end was in a communicative mood.

WAITING TO DIE

LORD PASSFIELD died in the autumn of 1947, and Shaw wrote to *The Times*: 'May I claim Westminster Abbey for the ashes of Sidney Webb, even should St Paul's demand him as our greatest Cockney?' Accordingly the urns containing the ashes of Sidney and Beatrice Webb were placed in the Abbey; and everyone, except perhaps a few Anglican zealots, felt that these were the right relics in the right place.

On March 14th, '48, Eleanor O'Connell visited Shaw at

Ayot, and on the same day sent me one of her excellent boswellian reports:

'Why are you going to America?' was his greeting.

'Because I want more freedom than I can get at present in England.'

'The only country in the world where you can get real freedom is Russia,' lectured Shaw, who, like a good totalitarian, had all his words by heart. 'The greatest man alive is Stalin; another, nearly as great, Masaryk, has just been driven to suicide: I knew him personally, and he was a very fine man. You know, Russia does not want another war; you must not believe what you read in the newspapers. Stalin realizes that a war would kill Russia, and he will not make any great mistakes, because if he did he would be shot.'

'If you had lived in Russia instead of England during the greater part of your life, you would certainly have been shot,' she countered.

'Stalin is a good Fabian, and that's the best that can be said about anyone,' replied Shaw.

They then discussed Freedom, Shaw advancing all the hoary arguments in favour of control ('Where would we be without policemen?'), she making all the obvious replies, until he got tired of it and said: 'I cannot try in the space of a short visit to teach you the elements of socialism.'

Their conversation became personal; but as it partly dealt with me, mock-modesty prevents me from recording it. It was interrupted by the announcement that two people had called and wished to see him. 'They must wait,' he said in tones that were audible to the callers. She discovered that all through the winter he had refused to have fires, carrying an electric stove with him from room to room, in lifting which he had one day ricked his back and sent for an osteopath to put it right. She was delighted to find that he had become much attached to a large ginger Persian cat, which followed him about, sat on his knees, and was the recipient of his confidences in appropriate language. She noticed that he was deafer and more frail than when she had last seen him, that he never moved without a stick, and was reluctant to leave his chair. 'I am waiting to die,' he said. 'I have nothing more to do. And I am very tired.' He kissed her good-bye with the words, 'Old men's kisses are like dust.'

He was however in fairly good form when I spent a couple

of hours with him some weeks later, and he even remembered that I had asked him for details of Keir Hardie about eighteen months before:

'Did you do that film?' he asked.

'No. I didn't find him interesting enough.'

'He was a simple fellow. He couldn't understand how an English gentleman like Sir Edward Grey could tell the most appalling lies without a flicker of shame and then leave the House of Commons with the impression that his opponent was the liar. I remember Hardie saying that he had once spoken on socialism to the dockers for an hour in the pelting rain, most of his audience cowering under a wall to keep dry. When he had finished a man asked "Why has the speaker not uttered one word about politics? What is his opinion on Welsh Disestablishment?" At an I.L.P. meeting in Bradford Hardie was in a quandary as to his policy over the landlords. He mentioned his difficulty to me on our way in. I briefly outlined a policy for him, and said "Tell them that all unearned income must be taxed." He promptly made that the main item in his programme. He was not adroit; he couldn't handle people, hadn't the smallest notion of how to deal with politicians or parliament. He was just a plain honest man, the very opposite of Ramsay MacDonald, who understood the whole game at once.'

It occurred to me that I had never asked Shaw whether he had met or tried to meet or correspond with the god of his early idolatry, Henrik Ibsen, so I put the question to him now. 'No contacts whatever,' he replied. 'But I was intimate with William Archer who had Norwegian cousins and spoke the language. He was more than a bit of a poet, and was deeply affected by the poetic side of Ibsen. He communicated this influence to me, and translated passages to me viva voce before Ibsen was generally known in England. Archer had visited Ibsen, in whose study was a striking portrait. He asked whose portrait it was. Ibsen replied with a chuckle "Strindberg. Isn't he MAD!" Much later I asked Nansen what Ibsen was like personally. All I got from him was that Ibsen drank enormously.'

I remarked that Ibsen had longed for power; and if he had got it, he would have played merry hell with humanity like all the other power-maniacs, whom I mentioned.

'When you start slanging Caesar, Cromwell, Napoleon, Mussolini, Hitler and the rest, don't forget that they all tried democracy and found it couldn't even keep them out of prison,' said Shaw.

He had written this in an article some years before, and I had made the same comment on it as now:

'Precisely the same thing may be urged in favour of Charles Peace, Crippen, Landru, Jack the Ripper, Burke, Hare, and all the totalitarians who are now doing seven-year sentences on Dartmoor. But none of the loonies you name tried democracy when they were in a position to do the job properly, any more than Stalin tries it now.'

'You are quite hopeless on the subject.'

'I hope so.'

Without wishing to waste more time on this tedious and unprofitable theme, I handed him a typed report of what he had told me on two previous occasions about his final relationship with Granville Barker, assuring him that I had no intention of publishing it until all the people concerned were dead. He read it through carefully, said it was absolutely correct, and at my request agreed to send me his confirmation of it in writing—which he did a few days later.

'When Granville Barker first met his second wife Helen, she was married to Archie Huntington. But Barker and Helen quickly fell in love with one another and he asked me to persuade his then wife, Lillah MacCarthy, to divorce him and to offer her £500 a year if she agreed. She indignantly refused to do anything of the kind, was tempestuously furious with him and extremely angry with me for my lack of decency in proposing such a thing. Barker went completely mad when I passed this on to him and said that if ever he met Lillah in the street he'd strike her. He was infatuated to the point of silliness by Helen, his present wife; he was no longer a rational individual, but behaved like a raving lunatic. In a state of frantic desperation he implored me to do everything I could to move Lillah; so I went to see her again, pressed his proposal on her, and said that if she agreed to divorce him she'd get £500 a year for life, but that if she refused she'd get nothing, as Barker was a poor man. This of course was pure blackmail. Her outraged vanity made her very crafty, and she remarked that Barker and her rival must be together. "No," said I easily, "he is in Paris, but she is in New York with her husband." "In that case," she pounced, "how has he been able to make these arrangements at such short notice?" I was completely cornered, but sneaked out by saying that they probably corresponded by cable in cipher. I then left her to consider the question. But consideration like a devil came; and she promptly wrote to Helen's husband telling him that Barker was sending cables in cipher to his wife. There was an almighty explosion at the other end, and Helen never forgave me for being, as she thought, solely responsible for Lillah's letter. In addition she hated the Shavian influence on Barker. Never having got beyond 1865, with a political outlook which was that of Henry James and George Meredith and entirely pre-Marx and Bergson, everything that has happened in literature since then is anathema to her, especially the works of Shaw.

'Anyhow the divorce went through, and Lillah got her £500 a year. Later she was told by an American lawyer that she could sue the other lady in the American courts for seducing her husband, and as Barker's second wife was very rich the lawyer suggested action. Lillah sent this information on to me, but I strongly advised her not to rake up all the mud that was then settling and to possess herself in patience for a while. I wrote to tell Barker of the latest development, with the result that Lillah got another £500 a year to keep quiet.

'Meanwhile Barker was being completely dominated by his new wife: he ceased to be the independent human being we had all known. She made him throw over Socialism as well as Shaw; she made him do translations of Spanish plays, or put his name to her translations; she cut him off from all commerce with the theatre; she tried to turn him into a country gentleman, but as he could neither hunt, shoot, nor fish, it was a hopeless proposition. She was incensed by Lillah's marriage to Sir Frederick Keeble, and spent a day with Mrs Thomas Hardy, my informant, storming about "Lady Keeble" and complaining bitterly that Barker had not been knighted. When the Labour Party came to power Ramsay MacDonald and the rest tried hard to find some supporters who would not disgrace them in the Upper House, and Barker would certainly have been given a peerage if his wife had not forced him to abandon Socialism, a reflection that must have been gall and wormwood to her.

'Her hatred of me manifested itself in a most uncomfortable manner. In May 1925 there was a meeting at King's College in the Strand to hear Barker give an address on the theatre. A. J. Balfour was in the chair; I was down to second the vote of thanks, Forbes-Robertson to propose it. When I arrived I was shown into the Green Room and found Balfour there alone. We chatted together for several minutes when in walked Mrs Barker, with chains of pearls decorating her neck and bosom. She is one of those people whose face I can never remember, her appearance being entirely negative, so that each time I see her I seem to see her for the first time; but I recognized her pearls, so all was well. Naturally I expected her to be distant, if not openly hostile; but to my surprise she came straight up to me and spoke in a most friendly manner. Then I recalled that Balfour had recently been made an Earl, and all became clear. She could swallow me with Balfour, but she could not take me neat.

'After Barker had delivered his address, and Forbes-Robertson had proposed the vote of thanks, I rose to second it. The devil entered into me and I was at the top of my form. I praised Barker's speech to the skies and said that his retirement from the stage to become a professor was inexcusable. Barker as a professor! I exclaimed—it was preposterous. Why, the speech he had just given contained enough matter to make twenty professors! I then delivered a sustained eulogy of his work for the stage, repeated my assertion that his retirement from active work in the theatre was a public scandal, brought down the house, and resumed my seat. Barker was now placed in a very ticklish position, and I was not wholly unconscious of what his wife would be thinking of me. But Balfour saved Barker's face by cleverly bringing the meeting to a close.

'What happened then was most extraordinary. The moment I got up to leave the platform I felt that my spine had been converted into a bar of rusty iron which grated on the base of my skull. The pain at the top and bottom of my spine was so frightful that I could not even bend down to get into a taxi. Somehow I reached home on foot, and when my wife arrived I was lying flat and helpless on my bed. The doctors could make nothing of it, and I really thought I was done for. I was brought down here to Ayot and after a while began to hobble about a bit; but I daren't go further than the garden gate; until, one day, with a great effort of the will, I decided to walk down the road, come what may. Instantly and miraculously the pain left me, and I recovered completely. I noticed that it was exactly one month to the hour since I had been stricken down by this inexplicable and horrible disablement.

'Some time later I met Lady Colefax, who had been present at the King's College meeting, and I told her what had happened to me. That, she said, was easily explained. She had watched Mrs Barker, who was sitting exactly behind me, and who had been leaning forward in her seat while I was speaking, every muscle in her face and body rigid with hate. There was not the slightest doubt that she had bewitched me. And after hearing this I could conceive of no other explanation.

'All communication between Barker and myself ceased until Lillah wrote her memoirs and asked me to do a preface. Naturally I had to send the preface to Barker, who suddenly blew in here one day as if he had only been away a few hours. The Webbs were with us, and Barker looked rather uncomfortable. He asked if he could speak to me for a few minutes in private. "I never thought I would come here again," he said when we were alone, and he went on to assure me that if Lillah's book were published he would take proceedings. I replied that he couldn't, as there was not a detrimental word about him in it ; I warned him that any action on his part would result in a lot of mud-stirring and I absolutely declined to advise Lillah's husband to withdraw the book. At last I got a smile out of him ; he saw that he hadn't a leg to stand on, and left me with some approach to friendliness. About twenty minutes later (he must have gone some distance in his car) he returned to take an effusive farewell of my wife. As a result of Barker's attitude Keeble decided to take out all the references to him in Lillah's book, much to the annoyance of both the Barkers when they read it.

'When Barker died I handed over to the British Museum all the papers and unpublished plays of his that were left in my hands. The separation between us which followed his marriage was not an estrangement. I communicated the death of my wife in 1943 to him—they had been attached friends—and his reply was on our old terms. Gabriel Pascal had pressed him to return to the stage and play the Inquisitor in a projected filming of *Saint Joan ;* and he had entertained the suggestion until his wife's disapproval put a summary end to his relations with Pascal. He knew the story of my bewitchment at King's College. I told him. I always respected strictly Mrs Granville Barker's right to a share in his circle of friends; and, much as I regretted her antipathy to me, never acted against her in any way. As far as I know, her complete ascendancy over him remained unshaken until the end.'

Having read my report of what he had told me, Shaw put it aside and said 'I give you full marks as a Boswell. By the way, it may interest you to know that Archibald Henderson has just written to say he is thinking of bringing out a new edition of his monumental work on me. I have advised him not to be in a hurry with it, as your biography is still selling enormously and is practically up to date; and I have told him that though he may be able to improve on your work critically, as biography NO.'

'Thank you. But what's wrong with my book critically?'

'Good God!' he cried: 'are you claiming infallibility? Whaur's your Julius-Boney-Adolf noo?'

'A hit, a very palpable hit,' I quoted. 'I had forgotten your admirable example.'

'What admirable example?'

'When it suits your purpose, you act on the principle that there is no recommendation like self-dispraise.'

'A touch, a touch, I do confess,' he laughed, adding: 'We are both well up in *Hamlet,* it seems.'

He next spoke of someone who was 'so determined to be my oldest and dearest friend' that he was extremely useful; and when I asked him whether he ever felt lonely, he said 'Lonely? No such luck! I could do with a little solitude. This place is like the editorial office of a big newspaper on the eve of a great war. What with the telephone bell ringing, the door bell buzzing, the door knocker banging, and the number of people who try to force their way in or climb trees to take snapshots of me as I totter about the garden, I believe life in Piccadilly Circus would be relatively monastic.' I laughed and he continued: 'But even if I cannot enjoy solitude, since the death of my wife I have been my own master, which I find very restful. She was so careful of my privacy that I hardly had a moment to myself. That of course is an exaggeration; but it will give you some idea of her attentiveness when I say that during one of my illnesses she got up from her sick bed and sat outside my bedroom door waiting for the doctor, as she wanted the very latest news from an authoritative source. In the last few years of her life she made me sing to her every night, and I had to be in bed by eleven.

Since her death I haven't touched the piano and am never in bed before twelve. She made me drive her all over Great Britain and the Continent, and travel all over the world. But my real nature is to remain rooted to one spot, like a tree, and since her death my longest journeys have been from Ayot to London and back. Funny how she hated caricatures of me—I don't much care for them myself—and wouldn't have one in the house. Max Beerbohm once did a clever thing of me in which I look slightly tipsy. She bought it at the exhibition and tore it up in front of his face. She was rather given to tears, and would cry all over me, but I got used to it and realized that one of my marital duties was to represent a sort of wailing-body.'

Admittedly this must have been a little trying, but Shaw sometimes got his own back by leaving the wireless on until his wife, who loathed it, left the room, when he switched it off and settled down to read. Blanche Patch told me that in August '47, when she was spending a week-end at Ayot, the wireless, just behind her chair, was kept going during dinner, making conversation impossible. After about twenty minutes of it Shaw said 'D'you think anyone takes any interest in this?' The cricket results were being broadcast. But as the Week in Parliament followed, which at least interested *him*, the noise continued for the rest of the meal. On a later visit she learnt that, though it was quite unnecessary in his case, he paid the weekly insurance required by the new medical service, because he was 'a socialist on principle'.

Shaw began a new play a day or two before his ninety-second birthday, and told me on a post-card replying to something I had asked him that he had got into 'the second wind of his second childhood'. His card was dated July 26th, and he wished me many happy returns of his birthday, which made me wonder whether a second wind was good for him. The Arts Theatre Club gave a special performance of *Too True To Be Good* that evening, and Esmé Percy, whose production of it was well-nigh perfect, had asked me to contribute a few words on the play for the programme. For the sake of what followed the appearance of my Note, I print it:

'The main theme of *Too True To Be Good* is the wretchedness of the rich, and the play is therefore a variation or development of *Heartbreak House*. It was written in 1931; but to say that it is dated because it is seventeen years old is like saying that the Russian menace is dated because it is seventy years old. As most of Shaw's plays were antedated when written by about half a century, this one has the peculiarly Shavian quality of being more up to date now than when it was first produced, more modern than any play by someone young enough to be the author's great-grand-child; and though Private Meek is a portrait of Lawrence of Arabia, the type is perennial. But the play's chief quality, as always with Shaw, is the gaiety with which a serious subject is treated. An amusing sidelight on the famous closing speech was given me by the writer: "There is a passage at the end of *Too True To Be Good* which caused the then Dean of Worcester (Moore Ede) to preach an impassioned sermon on it. I scribbled it down at rehearsal because we could not get the curtain down at the right instant to choke off Cedric Hardwicke's oration; and I had to provide some lines for him to go on with in case of need." '

The programme containing this must have been sent to Shaw, because I received a card from him on which the single word was written: 'Why?' The question being obscure, I replied: 'What?' He returned: 'The Note.' I parried, 'Oh, that!' He answered: 'Yes.' I gave in: 'God knows!' Back came the assertion: 'He doesn't.' There was but one retort: 'Nor do I.' This interchange was more like the cross-talk of two Music Hall comedians than the correspondence of a philosopher with his biographer; but it explains why this philosopher appealed to this biographer.

Nothing short of death could stop Shaw's pen or shut his mouth. In the autumn of '48 he told a newspaper reporter that he always would be a foreigner in England 'because I am one of the few people here who think objectively', and that he would be quite willing to write an article for £1000 in which the whole relationship between England and Ireland would be shown in its proper light. He sent a long letter to *The Times* advocating the production of a political dictionary, as people were hopelessly fogged over the meaning of such terms as communism, and the present misunderstandings would lead to a war that nobody wanted. Another long letter appeared in *The New Statesman*, the subject being Napoleon; while in *The Daily Worker* the most widely publicized man in the world, complaining that his public utterances had been boycotted by the British press for many years, took the opportunity of praising Russian communism
500

and dispraising everything and everyone antagonistic to Stalin's conception of democracy. His new play *Buoyant Billions,* which closes with a paean to the glory of mathematical passion ('Our pleasure in it promises a development in which life will be an intellectual ecstasy surpassing the ecstasies of saints'), was produced at Zurich in October '48 before a respectful if uncomprehending audience. The original title of this 'comedy of no manners' was *O Bee! Beezy Bee,* but on reflection the author thought worse of it.

In the first week of March '49 Shaw issued *Sixteen Self Sketches,* perhaps the only example in history of a readable book by a nonagenarian. Some of it had appeared elsewhere ; much was repetitive ; but there were two biographical novelties. Shaw had come across some letters which his father had written to his mother, who was on a visit to her relations, in July 1857, G.B.S. being then one year old. From these we learn that the baby caused as much uneasiness in the domestic circle as the man was later to arouse in theatrical and political circles. Unruly and outrageous, he howled the place down when he could not get what he wanted, pulled his hat to pieces, signified an early contempt for journalism by tearing the newspaper to bits, and was the despair of his nurse. Once he fell out of bed on to his head ; but most babies seem to be made of indiarubber, and he took it in his bounce. Another time he fell backwards off the kitchen table, his head going clean through a window-pane and hitting the iron bar outside. The household was in a panic ; but he remained calm. If his experiences in the next ten years at all resembled those at the age of one, he was fated to become a dramatist.

But the only novelty of importance in the book is what Shaw called a shameful secret, which he had kept all his life, not even confiding it to his wife. In the nineteenth century the religion of the ruling classes in Ireland was Protestant, and their children were brought up to regard Roman Catholics as untouchable. As Shaw learnt nothing at the Wesleyan school he attended, he was removed from it at the age of twelve and sent to a school where the pupils were the children of lower middle-class Catholic shopkeepers, whom he had always been taught to despise. He instantly lost caste, and was cut dead by the friends he had made at the Protestant school, who treated him as a social leper. After seven months of it he struck, and was sent to another Protestant school, where he continued to learn nothing but recovered his self-respect. For eighty years he was unable to mention this incident in his life, he wrote, 'yet now that I have broken through the habit of ashamed silence, and made not only a clean breast of it but a clear brain, I am completely cured'.

Psycho-analysts will reap a rich harvest from this Shavian revelation ; but my own feeling is that Shaw was making the best (i.e. the worst) of something he had just remembered. By this means he was able to add another touch of drama to his self-portrait, hardly to be expected from a man of ninety-two. He was able to get abreast of Dickens, whose experience in a blacking warehouse, of which he made full use in his work, was a 'shameful secret'. I recall that Shaw became quite peevish over the comparison between Shakespeare and Barker at the close of my essay on the first production of *Androcles,* which I showed him before broadcasting a part of it in February '49. He did not like to think that Shakespeare had been through more soul-searching experiences than himself. 'There is no evidence that Shakespeare was ever hungry or ill-clad,' he said. 'I was worse off, as my father was never successful in business. Shakespeare never had to fight his way: he rose soon by sheer gravitation and never looked back, any more than Wells and Kipling and Dickens. Think of *my* nine years of utter failure!' I did not wish to start a debate, so I thought of *King Lear* and held my peace.

Shaw liked to see himself as a missionary, not as a man ; as a prophet, not as a person ; and in one of these Sketches he explained why he had never written an autobiography, his two reasons merely proving that his sense of reality was intermittent. (1) Ninety-nine-point-nine per cent of him, he asserted, was the same as everyone else, and he could not pick out and describe the point-one per cent that differed from other human beings. Though it may not appear so on the surface, this was part of his propaganda as a social reformer. In a socialist state all have to be treated alike : therefore socialists have to assume that everyone requires a like treatment ; in other words, that people are all the same, Jesus Christ being another name for Julius Caesar, Stalin for St Francis, and Bill Smith for Bernard Shaw. Such is the cant of our time ; whereas the truth is that people are as dissimilar as their tastes, their beliefs, their reactions, their faces and their finger-prints. (2) He further declared that he was not interesting biographically because he had never killed anyone and had experienced no physical adventures. This

502

notion that a melodramatic career provides material for a good book is contradicted by every first-class biography in literature. I once discussed the point with Shaw, but apparently my words fell on deaf ears. 'What goes on in the mind is far more adventurous and exciting than what happens to the body,' I said.

'That may be,' he replied: 'and as all my mental adventures will be found in my works, there's no need for a biography.'

'But there's a great deal you've had to leave out of your works, and a great deal in your works that can only be explained by a knowledge of your life and character. And the fact remains that the really great biographies are about thinkers, not doers.'

Challenged to name them, I mentioned Plato's Socrates.

'Plato invented Socrates,' said he.

'Did Xenophon invent him too?' I asked. 'He gives a more vivid portrait than Plato.'

'It's the Socrates of Plato that everyone knows.'

'Well, what about Dr Johnson?'

'A creation of Boswell's.'

'Then there must have been a crowd of great creators busy on him,' I retorted, 'because many people reproduced his conversation quite as well as Boswell.'

'But it is Boswell's picture that survives.'

It was useless to prolong the discussion, because Shaw always acted on the principle: Never argue, repeat your assertion. Which, of course, is the favourite stand-by of prophets and utopians. But Plato and Boswell proved my point. Even on the fantastic assumption that they had created Socrates and Johnson, at least it did not occur to them to create men of action, though physical adventures are far more easily imagined than spiritual ones.

Before leaving the autobiographical notes he issued in 1949, I must mention that a very significant phrase, omitted from the letter he wrote to Frank Harris about his sex life as published in Harris's book on Shaw, was slipped into the same letter as printed in *Sixteen Self Sketches*. It deals with himself and his wife, and finally disposes of all conjecture on the nature of their marriage: 'As man and wife we found a new relation in which sex had no part.' It was characteristic of Shaw to interpolate this passage, leaving it to be understood that it was in the original letter. He had a habit of altering or adding to his private letters and even his essays when his permission was sought for quoting them in other people's books. It was part of his policy of bringing facts up to date, as he once put it, which perfectly describes the tricky methods of totalitarians in all ages.

In May 1949 G.B.S. determined to get rid of all his possessions in his Whitehall Court flat. As he had no intention of visiting London again, 'except in a hearse to Golder's Green', he had made up his mind some months previously to abandon his London flat and take a small one in the same building merely as an office for his secretary. But Blanche Patch was informed at the end of May that everything, furniture, books, pictures, even carpets, had to be cleared out of the flat in two days. This sudden move was not only unnecessary but impossible, and she protested. But he was adamant. The job was done, not in two days, but within a week ; and except for the furniture of his office, the rest was removed for an auction sale. He wished to keep nothing, not even the many copies of books presented to him by famous contemporaries like Wells, nor the bust of Lady Astor, which was duly catalogued as 'the bust of Mrs Sidney Webb'. Two carpets were sent down to Ayot because they would be useful there ; but he ordered them to be returned, as he wanted cash not carpets. Innumerable papers had to be destroyed and everything turned into money, said the man who was quite unable to deal with the huge sums he received regularly from film, play and book royalties. It was a form of mania, induced no doubt by a life-long preoccupation with economics, just as the decision to move his belongings at a moment's notice was the insane whim of a man who had never ceased to admire dictators.

His genial ferocity, adopted as a mask in earlier days, had become second nature ; and his comments on the wireless performances of his plays were of a nature to make the officials of the B.B.C. nervous of approaching him for permission to broadcast his works. His humour, seldom of a rich nature, had become inhuman. He was still pleasant and amusing in personal converse ; but with a pen in his hand or speaking from the other end of a telephone, he was frequently abrupt. He had not mellowed with age. A good deal of this may have been due to the irritating feeling that, while persisting in his praise of Russian communism, he had backed the wrong horse. His persistence was due to something in his nature which forbade him to admit that he could ever be wrong. He could not go back on his life's work, the issue of which, though resulting in tyranny, mendacity, iron curtains, slavery, and every known form of cruelty, he had hailed as the coming of a new world, *his* world, the civilization for which he had fought. Perhaps it was too much to expect that a nonagenarian should perceive the dawn of his dreams to be the night of his endeavours. Anyhow, this one stuck to his guns, and banged away at everyone who questioned the infallibility of his judgement. He considered himself the Pope of his faith and the Stalin of his creed. His word was law, to himself no less than to others, and in killing his social conscience he passed on some of his internal discomfort to his fellow-creatures.

His play *Buoyant Billions* was admirably produced by Esmé Percy at the Malvern Festival, the first for ten years, in August '49, and was favourably received, though it only ran for five weeks when put on in London at the beginning of October. Towards the close of the year I showed him an article I had written on Granville Barker for my book *The Last Actor-Managers*. He made a few corrections, and while on the subject told me that no one within his experience had made such a habit of falling in love and getting engaged to be married as Barker, whose infatuation with Helen Huntington, his second wife, and utter subjection to her for the rest of his life, Shaw described as a tragedy.

We discussed one or two other matters, and then I asked him how he had first got to know Lady Astor. 'I have always refused to play the society clown and declined all the invitations she sent me,' he replied. 'Then I met her at someone else's house, liked her at once, and began to accept her invitations.' She had been extremely useful to him, because she had influenced *The Times* to publish his letters, which was the only sort of official recognition he cared about, and meant far more to him than a dukedom or the Order of Merit.

I wished to know whether he ever missed any of his old friends, H. G. Wells for example. 'I don't miss anyone except myself.' 'Yourself?' 'The man I used to be.' 'Oh!' He again told me, what I could not publish while Wells was alive, that the big dust-up in the Fabian Society had been due to the fact that the Webbs had warned Bland and Olivier to advise their daughters to keep clear of Wells, who would try to seduce them. When Bland spoke to his daughter about it, she calmly informed him that Wells had described him as a fearful roué and had mentioned some of the women who had surrendered to him. As a result Bland was furious with Wells, who was equally furious with the Webbs. This private vendetta was carefully camouflaged by the pretended disagreement over policy and explains Shaw's ruthless debating methods in disposing of Wells.

Before I left, Shaw said 'I am not *persona grata* with the Cabinet just now,' which, considering that he more than anyone else had been responsible for a Socialist Government, amused me. He also complained that he was being robbed by the Revenue. Further inquiry elicited the fact that he had asked the film companies to withhold his royalties until he applied for them, that the Income Tax authorities had declined to let him use the film people as his bankers, and that as a consequence he would have to pay £140,000 to the Revenue during the year 1950.

THE MODERN METHUSELAH

I LAST SPOKE TO Shaw at the end of June 1950. We had a pleasant talk, but little worth recording. Two queries had recently been sent me by correspondents, and I put them to him:

'There seems to be a tradition in the theatre that in the original production of *Androcles* the Blue Danube waltz was played when the Lion and Androcles dance off together. I can't remember. Can you?'

'It was not the Blue Danube but the Turkey Trot, then very popular,' and he whistled it.

'As William Morris died in 1896 when Oscar Wilde was in Reading Gaol, what is your authority, quoted by me, for saying that Wilde was the only person Morris could bear to see on his deathbed?'

'Morris took a terrible time to die: nearly two years. Wilde paid his visit in the early stages before Reading Gaol was thought of. Morris said he was never so entertained in his life.'

He asked what I was then writing, and I told him a Life of Disraeli.

'I could not read his novels because they are all about upper ten ladies and gentlemen, whom I cannot abide,' said Shaw. 'The same applies to Meredith. Disraeli is historically important as the founder of Tory Democracy.'

'I find him interesting as a man; otherwise I wouldn't be writing about him. By the way a great admirer of yours wants to shake you by the hand. May I bring him down?'

'I don't want to see ANYBODY, and I don't want anybody to see me. You don't know what it is to be as old as I am. Do you suppose I want the great G.B.S. to be remembered as a doddering old skeleton?'

His ninety-fourth birthday was celebrated by the Arts Theatre, which put on *Heartbreak House*; and at the request of Mr Alec Clunes I again wrote a Note for the programme, but this time the author did not ask 'Why?' His *Far-Fetched Fables* was produced at the Watergate Theatre on September 5th, but they were too far-fetched for the critics. Shaw had once described them to me as 'the noddings of a nonagenarian'.

On Sunday evening, September 10th, he was trying to lop a branch from a tree in his garden; being a dead one, it came away too suddenly, and he lost his balance, falling and fracturing his thigh. He was taken in an ambulance to the Luton and Dunstable Hospital, and an operation was performed on Monday night. He made good progress, was visited regularly by his housekeeper Mrs Alice Laden, and was bright enough to tell the surgeon, 'It will do you no good if I get over this. A doctor's reputation is made by the number of eminent men who die under his care.' The Radio Review of Dublin telegraphed to ask if he would like any particular tune to be played. He replied: 'Play the tune the old cow died of.' A few days later it was discovered that his prostate gland had failed, and a minor operation was performed, as he was too old to bear the major one.

On Monday, October 2nd, Eleanor O'Connell called to see him at the hospital where everything possible was being done for him. She asked how he was.

'Everyone asks me that; it's so silly when all I want is to die, but this damned vitality of mine won't let me.'

'Are you looking forward to dying?'

'Oh, so much, so much,' he said tremulously. 'If only I

could die! This is all such a waste of time, a waste of food, a waste of attention. But they won't leave me alone.' Then, speaking loudly: 'I'm in HELL here. They wash me all the time; they massage me; when I'm asleep they wake me; when I'm awake they ask me why I'm not asleep—routine, routine, I'm sick of it. Each time they pounce on me they tell me it will be just the same as last time, and then I find they've added a new torture!'

'Never mind; you are going home on Wednesday; your room is all ready and looks most comfortable; then you'll feel happier.'

'Happier? No. But at least I shall be able to die in peace. . . . Yes, I shall be glad to go home and get out of hell. Ah, if only I could walk! I would get up and go home at once. I tell you I am in hell. I want to die and I can't, I can't.' There was almost a sob in his voice, and the pleading tone of a prayer.

The nurse returned and Eleanor had to leave. She kissed him, saying, 'I shall never see you again, but for me you will never die.' He kissed her, saying 'Be off with you,' and she thought his eyes were moist.

He was taken home on October 4th, and spent the final month of his life in comfort, displaying little interest in anything; though when his secretary Blanche Patch read him a letter from Dr Inge, he smiled and said 'I must write to him.'

Just before becoming unconscious on Tuesday, October 31st, he spoke his last words with all the emphasis of one who intended to do what he said: 'I am going to die.' In the last days of his life he slept a great deal, and one minute before five o'clock on the morning of November 2nd, 1950, he fell asleep for ever.

INDEX

509

Shaw, G. B.—*continued*

289; further advice to F-R, 291-3; holidays, 296-7; writes *Getting Married* and *Misalliance*, 297; writes *Blanco Posnet*, 299; writes *Press Cuttings*, 200; on censorship, 300-1; some one-act plays, 301; writes *Fanny's First Play*, 301; writes *Androcles and the Lion*, 302; on characters and dialogue, 302-3; rehearses *Androcles*, 303-4; writes *Pygmalion*, 305; persuading Mrs Patrick Campbell to play Eliza, 305-6; relations with Mrs Campbell, 308; rehearsing *Pygmalion*, 310-13; at mother's and sister's funerals, 315-16; delight in technicalities, 316-17; clothes, 317-18; sits for Epstein, 318, 321-2; sits for Rodin, 319-21; sits for Troubetskoy, 321; sits for Jo Davidson, 321; sits for Sigmund Strobl, 321; on Epstein's work, 322-3; presents a *Chaucer* to Rodin, 323; whereabouts of his busts, 323; encounter with Anatole France, 324; his smattering of languages, 324-5; as a talker, 325-6; repartee, 326; as lecturer and debater, 326-7; on Chesterton and Belloc, 327-8; on Barrie, 329-30; takes part in 'trial' for Dickens Fellowship, 330-2; on Beethoven, 333; as a singer, 333-4; well ordered domestic life, 334; swindled of £500, 334-5; his health, 335; stone in kidney, 336; cured of form of dropsy, 336-7; proposals to prevent the Great War, 340; writes *Common Sense About the War*, 341; shunned and attacked for his views on the war, 343-4, 345, 346; resigns from Dramatists' Club, 346; public meetings during war, 347; loss of H. A. Jones's friendship, 347-8; tries to restore friendship with Jones, 348-9; answers Sutro's criticism of his *Common Sense*, 349-52; contribution dropped from King Albert's Gift-Book, 351, 352; letter to sheikhs of Morocco, 352-3; on air-raid shelters, 353; efforts for the Allies, 352-3; on Tchekhov, 355; appeals on behalf of conscientious objectors, 356; appeals on behalf of Sir Roger Casement, 356-7; tours Western Front, 357-8; attends League of Nations assembly, 359; relations with Frank Harris, 359-71 *passim*; on Harris's *Life of Wilde*, 362-3, 369; revises Harris's biography of him, 367; as a businessman, 371-3; income, 373; writes *The Intelligent Woman's Guide*, 374; on equality of income,

374, 375-6; his religious philosophy, 374-6; views on Soviet Russia, 376-8; visits Russia, 377, 379-87; enjoys Russian food, 380; sees the embalmed Lenin, 382; visits Krupskaya, 383-4; meets Stalin, 384-7; chides Loraine for performance in *Arms and the Man*, 388-9; on *Heartbreak House*, 390-1; at opening night of *Back to Methusaleh*, 392-3; the writing of *B to M*, 393; contemplates play on Mahomet, 395; the writing of *Saint Joan*, 396; chooses Sybil Thorndike for Joan, 397-8; accepted as an oracle, 399-400; on Forbes-Robertson's memoirs, 410-3; breakdown in health, 403; refuses honours and titles, 404; on Ramsay MacDonald, 405; refuses Nobel Prize, 405; joins P.E.N. Club, 406; honoured by municipal bodies, 406; on the National Theatre, 406; prepares standard edition of works, 407; pall-bearer at Thomas Hardy's funeral, 407, 408; introduced to Kipling, 407; protests at chaining of prisoners, 408-9; puts the case for apes, 409; on rubbish dumping, 409; on death, 409-10; praises Sean O'Casey, 413n; meets Elgar, 413, 414; meets T. E. Lawrence, 415; opinion of Lawrence, 415-16; happiest writing historical plays, 416-17; makes world tour, 417-27; views on his travels, 418-19; on his bicycling accident, 419-20; car accident in South Africa, 420-21, 422; writes *Adventures of the Black Girl*, 421; on Luxor and Bombay, 424; on New Zealand, 424-5; in the U.S.A., 426-7; on the Americans, 426-7; on dining with monarchs, 428; his prefaces, 428-9; on the abdication crisis, 429-34; suffers from pernicious anaemia, 434-5; views on possible World War II, 435-6; views at start of WW II, 436-9; belief in Russian victory over Germany, 439n; opinions about his plays, 440-1; review *Our Great Dean*, 441, 442; his greatness, 442-3; opinion of Pearson's biography, 443-5; on dictators, 445; on Communism and Fascism, 446; on use of scenes from his plays in textbooks, 447; opposed to film of biography, 448-9; opposed to published collection of letters, 449-50; a fit octogenerian, 451; concern at his wife's health, 452; daily routine, 452; tells of the deaty of his wife, 453-4; at his wife's cremation, 454-5; on marriage and children, 454, 455-6; on